STRE...S

Leicestershire

and Rutland

Hinckley, Leicester, Loughborough, Market Harborough, Melton Mowbray

www.philips-maps.co.uk

First published in 2000 by

Philip's, a division of
Octopus Publishing Group Ltd
www.octopusbooks.co.uk
2-4 Heron Quays, London E14 4JP
An Hachette Livre UK Company

Third edition 2007
First impression 2007
LEICA

ISBN-10   0-540-09174-X (pocket)
ISBN-13   978-0-540-09174-4 (pocket)

© Philip's 2007

Ordnance Survey®

This product includes mapping data licensed from
Ordnance Survey® with the permission of the
Controller of Her Majesty's Stationery Office.
© Crown copyright 2007. All rights reserved.
Licence number 100011710.

Data for the speed cameras provided by
PocketGPSWorld.com Ltd.

Ordnance Survey and the OS Symbol are
registered trademarks of Ordnance Survey, the
national mapping agency of Great Britain

Printed by Toppan, China

Contents

II **List of mobile speed cameras**

III **Key to map symbols**

IV **Key to map pages**

VI **Route planning**

X **Administrative and Postcode boundaries**

1 **Street maps** at 2⅔ inches to 1 mile

259 **Street map of Leicester city centre** at 5⅓ inches to 1 mile

260 **Index** of towns, villages, streets, hospitals, industrial estates, railway stations, schools, shopping centres, universities and places of interest

Digital Data

The exceptionally high-quality mapping found in this atlas is available as digital data in TIFF format, which is easily convertible to other bitmapped (raster) image formats.

The index is also available in digital form as a standard database table. It contains all the details found in the printed index together with the National Grid reference for the map square in which each entry is named.

For further information and to discuss your requirements, please contact james.mann@philips-maps.co.uk

Mobile speed cameras

Adrian Sherratt / Alamy

The vast majority of speed cameras used on Britain's roads are operated by safety camera partnerships. These comprise local authorities, the police, Her Majesty's Court Service (HMCS) and the Highways Agency.

This table lists the sites where each safety camera partnership may enforce speed limits through the use of mobile cameras or detectors. These are usually set up on the roadside or a bridge spanning the road and operated by a police or civilian enforcement officer. The speed limit at each site (if available) is shown in red type, followed by the approximate location in black type.

Leicestershire and Rutland

A1
70 Empingham, Great North Rd

70 Stretton, Great North Rd

A5
60 Churchover, Watling Street (Clifton Fisheries)

60 Hinckley, Watling St (B578 to M69)

50 Hinckley, Watling St (M69 to A47)

70 Sharnford, Watling St (Highcross to B4114)

A6
40 Birstall, Loughborough Rd

40 Leicester, Abbey Lane

30 Leicester, London Rd (Knighton Drive)

30 Loughborough, Derby Rd

40 Oadby, Glen Rd/ Harborough Rd

A47
60 Barrowden, Peterborough Rd

60 Bisbrooke, Uppingham Rd

30 Earl Shilton, Hinckley Rd

40 Houghton on the Hill, Uppingham Rd

30 Leicester, Hinckley Rd

30 Leicester, Humberstone Rd

50 Morcott, Glaston Rd

50 Skeffington, Uppingham Rd

50 Tugby, Uppingham Rd

A50
40 Leicester/Glenfield, Groby Rd/Leicester Rd

30 Woodgate

A426
50 Dunton Bassett, Lutterworth Rd

40 Glen Parva, Leicester Rd

60 Lutterworth, Leicester Rd

60 Whetstone, Lutterworth Rd

A444
50 Fenny Drayton, Atherstone Rd

30 Twycross Village, Main St

50 Twycross, Norton Juxta

A447
60 Cadeby, Hinckley Rd

40 Ravenstone, Wash Lane

A512
30 Loughborough, Ashby Rd

40 Shepshed, Ashby Rd Central

A514
30 Hartshorne, Main St

40 Swadlincote to Hartshorne

A563
30 Leicester, Asquith Way

30 Leicester, Attlee Way

30 Leicester, Colchester Rd/Hungarton Boulevard

30 Leicester, Glenhills Way

40 Leicester, Krefield Way

30 Leicester, New Parks Way

A594
30 Leicester, St Georges Way

A606
60 Barnsdale, Stamford Rd

60 Leicester, Broughton/Old Dalby

60 Tinwell, Stamford Rd

A607
30 Leicester, Melton Rd

50 Thurmaston, Newark Rd

60 Waltham on the Wolds, Melton Rd

60 Waltham/Croxton Kerrial, Melton Rd

A4304
40 Market Harborough, Lubbenham Hill

A5199
30 Leicester, Welford Rd

30 Wigston, Bull Head St

30 Wigston, Leicester Rd

A5460
40 Leicester, Narborough Rd

A6004
30 Loughborough, Alan Moss Rd

A6005
40 Breaston to Long Eaton

A6030
30 Leicester, Wakerley Rd/Broad Avenue

A6121
30 Ketton, Stamford Rd

B568

30 Leicester, Victoria Park Rd

B581
30 Broughton Astley, Broughton Way

B582
30 Blaby, Little Glen Rd

B590
30 Hinckley, Rugby Rd

B591
60 Charley, Loughborough Rd

B4114
40 Enderby/ Narborough, Leicester Rd/King Edward Avenue

30 Leicester, Sharnford

B4616
30 Leicester, East Park Rd

B4666
30 Hinckley, Coventry Rd

B5003
40 Norris Hill, Ashby Rd

B5350
30 Loughborough, Foreset Rd

30 Loughborough, Nanpantan Rd

B5366
30 Leicester, Saffron Lane

UNCLASSIFIED
30 Barrow upon Soar, Sileby Rd

30 Blaby, Lutterworth Rd

30 Glenfield, Sation Rd

30 Ibstock, Leicester Rd

30 Leicester, Beaumont Leys Lane

30 Leicester, Fosse Rd South

30 Monks Kirby, Coalpit Lane

40 Norris Hill, Ashby Road

30 Shardlow, London Road

30 Shepshed, Leicester Rd

III

Symbol	Description
Motorway with junction number	
Primary route – dual/single carriageway	
A road – dual/single carriageway	
B road – dual/single carriageway	
Minor road – dual/single carriageway	
Other minor road – dual/single carriageway	
Road under construction	
Tunnel, covered road	
Speed cameras - single, multiple	
Rural track, private road or narrow road in urban area	
Gate or obstruction to traffic (restrictions may not apply at all times or to all vehicles)	
Path, bridleway, byway open to all traffic, road used as a public path	
Pedestrianised area	
Postcode boundaries	
County and unitary authority boundaries	
Railway, tunnel, railway under construction	
Tramway, tramway under construction	
Miniature railway	
Railway station	
Private railway station	
Metro station	
Tram stop, tram stop under construction	
Bus, coach station	

Ambulance station

Coastguard station

Fire station

Police station

Accident and Emergency entrance to hospital

Hospital

Place of worship

Information Centre (open all year)

Shopping Centre

Parking, Park and Ride

Post Office

Camping site, caravan site

Golf course, picnic site

Important buildings, schools, colleges, universities and hospitals

Built up area

Woods

Water name

River, weir, stream

Canal, lock, tunnel

Water

Tidal water

Non-Roman antiquity

Roman antiquity

Adjoining page indicators and overlap bands
The colour of the arrow and the band indicates the scale of the adjoining or overlapping page (see scales below)

Enlarged mapping only

Railway or bus station building

Place of interest

Parkland

Acad	Academy
Allot Gdns	Allotments
Cemy	Cemetery
C Ctr	Civic Centre
CH	Club House
Coll	College
Crem	Crematorium
Ent	Enterprise
Ex H	Exhibition Hall
Ind Est	Industrial Estate
IRB Sta	Inshore Rescue Boat Station

Inst	Institute
Ct	Law Court
L Ctr	Leisure Centre
LC	Level Crossing
Liby	Library
Mkt	Market
Meml	Memorial
Mon	Monument
Mus	Museum
Obsy	Observatory
Pal	Royal Palace
PH	Public House

Recn Gd	Recreation Ground
Resr	Reservoir
Ret Pk	Retail Park
Sch	School
Sh Ctr	Shopping Centre
TH	Town Hall/House
Trad Est	Trading Estate
Univ	University
W Twr	Water Tower
Wks	Works
YH	Youth Hostel

■ The small numbers around the edges of the maps identify the 1 kilometre National Grid lines

■ The dark grey border on the inside edge of some pages indicates that the mapping does not continue onto the adjacent page

The scale of the maps on the pages numbered in blue is 4.2 cm to 1 km • 2⅔ inches to 1 mile • 1: 23810

0	¼	½	¾	1 mile
0	250 m	500 m	750 m 1 kilometre	

The scale of the maps on pages numbered in red is 8.4 cm to 1 km • 5⅓ inches to 1 mile • 1: 11900

0	220 yards	440 yards	660 yards	½ mile
0	125 m	250 m	375 m ½ kilometre	

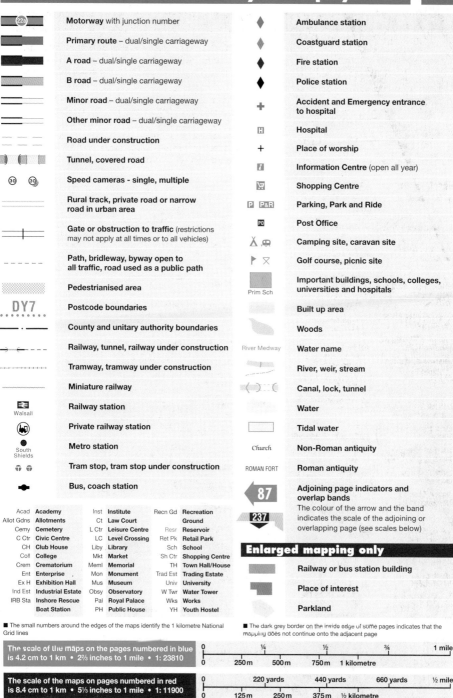

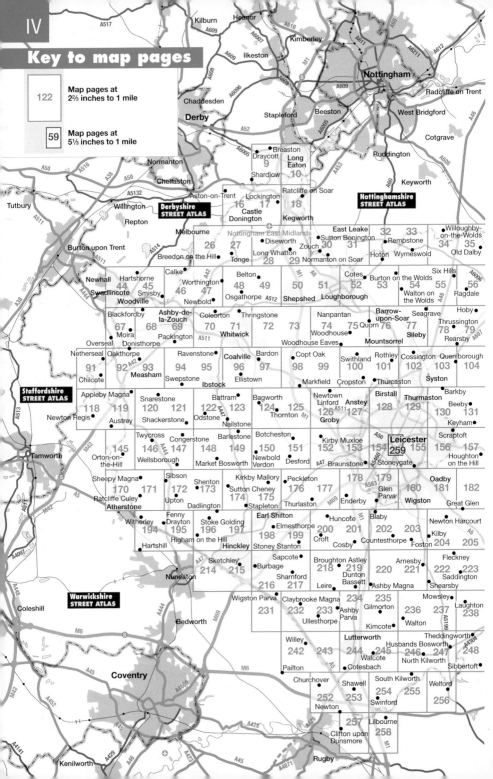

IV

Key to map pages

122 — Map pages at 2⅔ inches to 1 mile

59 — Map pages at 5⅓ inches to 1 mile

Kilburn
Heanor
Kimberley
Ilkeston
Nottingham
Radcliffe on Trent
Chaddesden
Stapleford
Beeston
Derby
West Bridgford
Cotgrave
Normanton
Breaston
Long Eaton
Draycott 9
Ruddington
Keyworth
Chellaston
Shardlow 10
Aston-on-Trent
Ratcliffe on Soar
Willington
Lockington 16 17 18
Nottinghamshire STREET ATLAS
Tutbury
Repton
Castle Donington
Kegworth
Melbourne
Nottingham East Midlands
East Leake
Willoughby-on-the-Wolds
Derbyshire STREET ATLAS
Diseworth
Sutton Bonington
32 33
Burton upon Trent
26 27
Zouch 30 31
Rempstone
34 35
Breedon on the Hill
Long Whatton
Hoton
Wymeswold
Old Dalby
Calke
Tonge
28 29
Normanton on Soar
Newhall
Hartshorne
Worthington
Belton
Cotes
Burton on the Wolds
Six Hills
56
Swadlincote
Smisby
46 47
48 49
50 51
52 53
54 55
Ragdale
Woodville
Newbold
Osgathorpe
A512
Shepshed
Loughborough
Walton on the Wolds
Hoby
Blackfordby
Ashby-de-la-Zouch
Coleorton
Thringstone
Nanpantan
Barrow-upon-Soar
Seagrave
Thrussington
67
68 69
70 71
72 73
74 75
Quorn 76
77
78 79
Moira
Packington
Whitwick
Woodhouse
Sileby
Rearsby
Overseal
Donisthorpe
A511
Woodhouse Eaves
Mountsorrel
Netherseal
Oakthorpe
Ravenstone
Coalville
Bardon
Copt Oak
Swithland
Rothley
Cossington
Queniborough
91
92 93
94 95
96 97
98 99
100
101
102 103 104
Chilcote
Measham
Swepstone
Ellistown
Markfield
Cropston
Thurcaston
Syston
Ibstock
Appleby Magna
Snarestone
Battram
Bagworth
Newtown Linford
Birstall
Barkby
118 119
120 121
122 123
124 125
Anstey
128 129
130 131
Newton Regis
Shackerstone
Odstone
Thornton
126 127
Beeby
Austrey
Nailstone
Groby
Keyham
Twycross
Congerstone
Barlestone
Botcheston
Kirby Muxloe
Leicester
Scraptoft
145
146 147
148 149
150 151
152 153
154 259 155
156 157
Orton-on-the-Hill
Wellsborough
Market Bosworth
Newbold Verdon
Desford
Braunstone
Stoneygate
Houghton on the Hill
Sheepy Magna
Sibson
Shenton
Kirkby Mallory
Peckleton
178 179
Oadby
170 171
172 173
176 177
180 181 182
Ratcliffe Culey
Upton
Sutton Cheney
174 175
Glen Parva
Wigston
Atherstone
Dadlington
Stapleton
Thurlaston
Enderby
Great Glen
Witherley
Fenny Drayton
Stoke Golding
Earl Shilton
Huncote
Blaby
Newton Harcourt
194 195
196 197
198 199
200 201
202 203
Kilby
204 205
Hartshill
Higham on the Hill
Hinckley
Stoney Stanton
Elmesthorpe
Croft
Cosby
Countesthorpe
Foston
Sketchley
Sapcote
Broughton Astley
Arnesby
Fleckney
214 215
Burbage
216 217
218 219
220 221
222 223
Nuneaton
Sharnford
Leire
Dunton Bassett
Ashby Magna
Saddington
Shearsby
Warwickshire STREET ATLAS
Wigston Parva
Claybrooke Magna
234 235
Mowsley
Coleshill
231
232 233
Ashby Parva
Gilmorton
236 237
Laughton
238
Ullesthorpe
Kimcote
Walton
A5199
Bedworth
Willey
Lutterworth
Husbands Bosworth
Theddingworth
242 243
244 245
246 247 248
Walcote
North Kilworth
Sibbertoft
Coventry
Pailton
Cotesbach
Churchover
Shawell
South Kilworth
Welford
252 253
254 255
256
Newton
Swinford
Lilbourne
257 258
Clifton upon Dunsmore
Kenilworth
Rugby

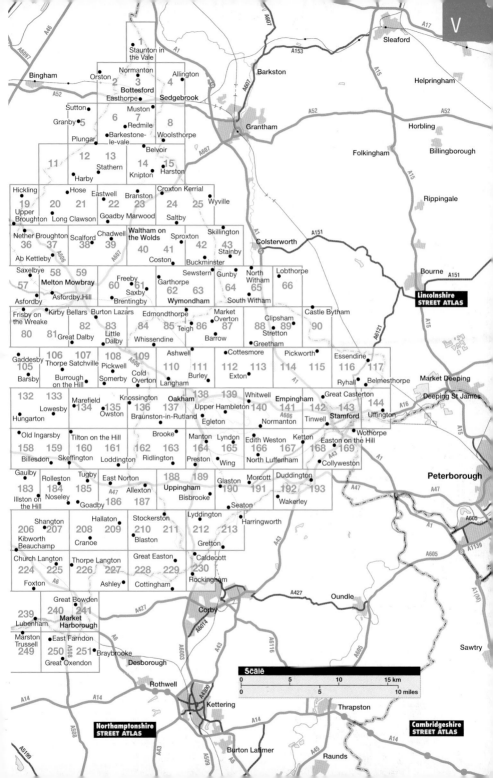

V

Sleaford

Helpringham

Bingham

Barkston

Orston

Normanton

Allington

Staunton in the Vale

Bottesford

Easthorpe

Sedgebrook

Grantham

Horbling

Billingborough

Sutton

Muston

Granby

Redmile

Woolsthorpe

Folkingham

Plungar

Barkestone-le-vale

Belvoir

Rippingale

Harby

Stathern

Knipton

Harston

Hickling

Hose

Eastwell

Branston

Croxton Kerrial

Wyville

Colsterworth

Upper Broughton

Long Clawson

Goadby Marwood

Saltby

Bourne

Nether Broughton

Scalford

Chadwell

Waltham on the Wolds

Sproxton

Skillington

Ab Kettleby

Coston

Buckminster

Stainby

Lincolnshire STREET ATLAS

Saxelbye

Melton Mowbray

Freeby

Sewstern

Gunby

North Witham

Lobthorpe

Asfordby

Asfordby Hill

Saxby

Garthorpe

South Witham

Brentingby

Wymondham

Frisby on the Wreake

Kirby Bellars

Burton Lazars

Edmondthorpe

Market Overton

Clipsham

Castle Bytham

Great Dalby

Little Dalby

Teigh

Stretton

Whissendine

Barrow

Greetham

Gaddesby

Thorpe Satchville

Pickwell

Ashwell

Cottesmore

Pickworth

Essendine

Barsby

Burrough on the Hill

Somerby

Cold Overton

Burley

Exton

Ryhall

Belmesthorpe

Langham

Market Deeping

Lowesby

Marefield

Knossington

Oakham

Whitwell

Empingham

Great Casterton

Deeping St James

Hungarton

Owston

Braunston-in-Rutland

Egleton

Normanton

Tinwell

Stamford

Uffington

Old Ingarsby

Tilton on the Hill

Brooke

Manton

Lyndon

Edith Weston

Ketton

Easton on the Hill

Billesdon

Skeffington

Loddington

Ridlington

Preston

Wing

North Luffenham

Collyweston

Peterborough

Gaulby

Rolleston

Tugby

East Norton

Glaston

Morcott

Duddington

Illston on the Hill

Noseley

Goadby

Allexton

Uppingham

Bisbrooke

Wakerley

Shangton

Hallaton

Stockerston

Lyddington

Seaton

Harringworth

Kibworth Beauchamp

Cranoe

Blaston

Gretton

Church Langton

Thorpe Langton

Great Easton

Caldecott

Foxton

Ashley

Cottingham

Rockingham

Great Bowden

Oundle

Lubenham

Market Harborough

Corby

Marston Trussell

East Farndon

Braybrooke

Desborough

Sawtry

Great Oxendon

Rothwell

Kettering

Thrapston

Northamptonshire STREET ATLAS

Cambridgeshire STREET ATLAS

Burton Latimer

Raunds

Scale

| 0 | | 5 | | 10 | | 15 km |
| 0 | | | 5 | | | 10 miles |

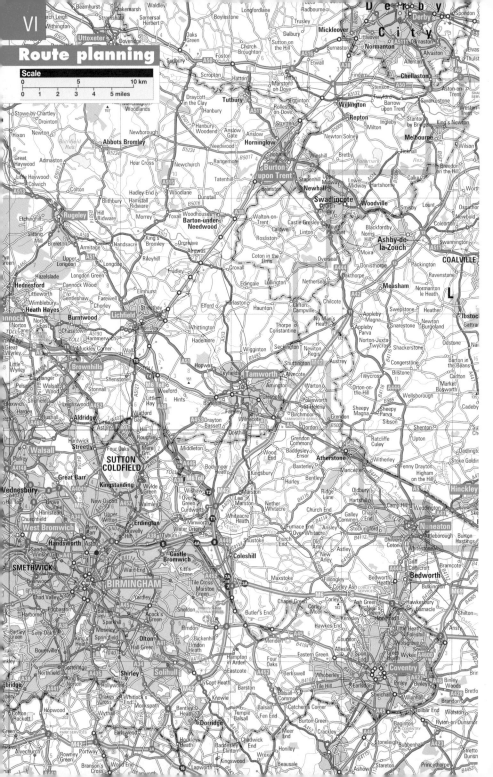

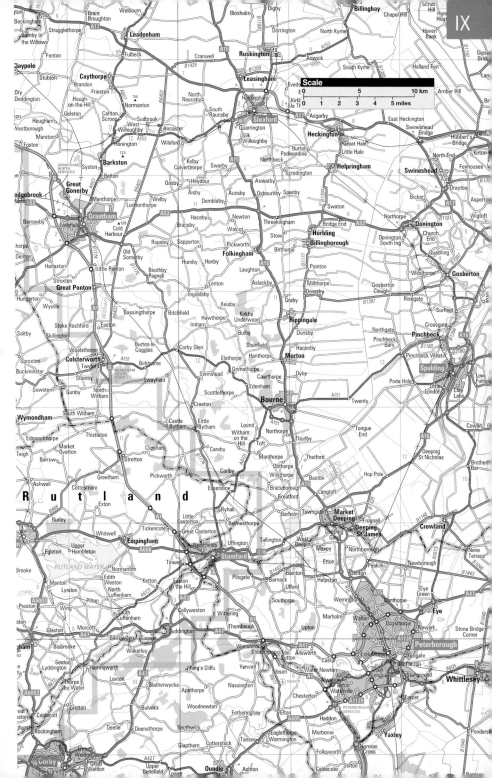

Major administrative and Postcode boundaries

Scale

0   5   10   15 km
0   5   10 miles

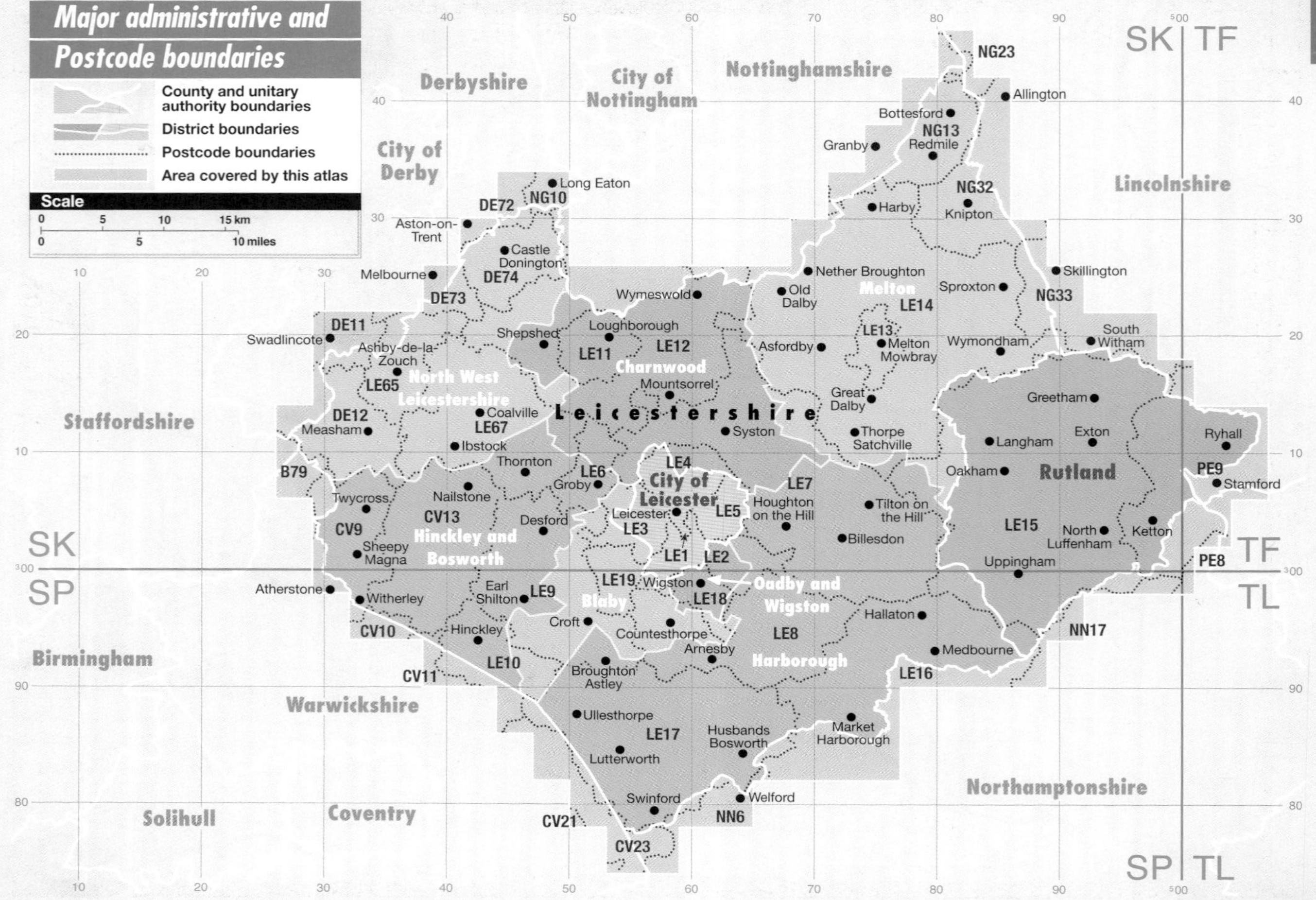

— County and unitary authority boundaries
— District boundaries
— Postcode boundaries
— Area covered by this atlas

Lincolnshire

Nottinghamshire

City of Nottingham

Derbyshire

City of Derby

Staffordshire

Birmingham

Solihull

Coventry

Warwickshire

Northamptonshire

Leicestershire

Rutland

City of Leicester

Charnwood

Melton

North West Leicestershire

Hinckley and Bosworth

Blaby

Oadby and Wigston

Harborough

SK | TF
SP | TL
TF | TL
SP | TL
SK | SP

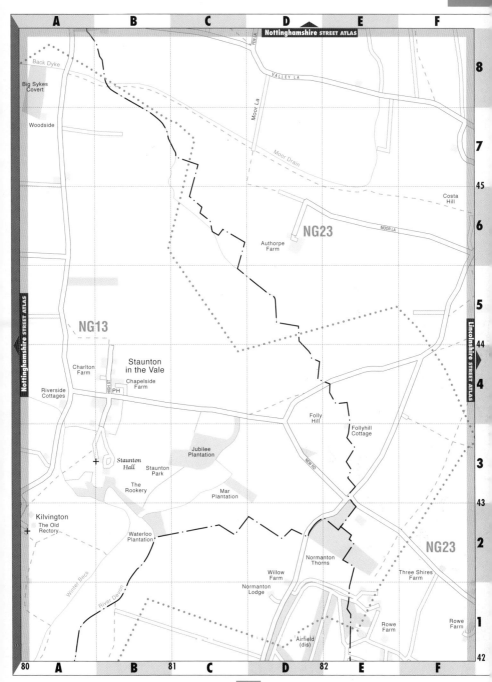

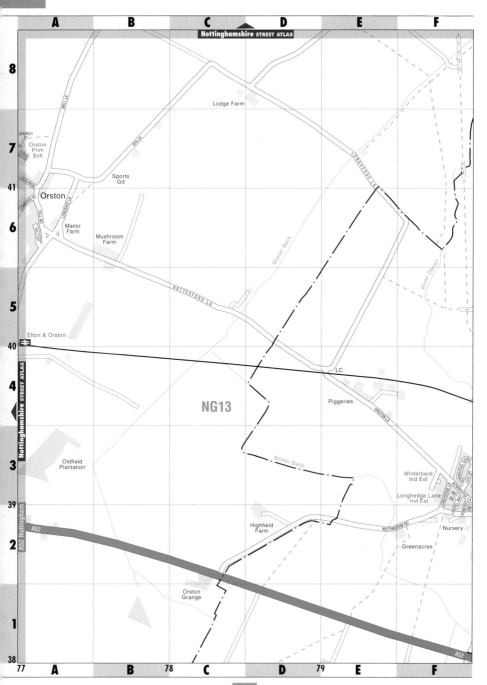

Lodge Farm

MILL LA

SPA LA

CHURCH
ST

Orston
Prim
Sch

LOUGHTON

Sports
Gd

Orston

LONGSIDE LA

LOMBARD ST

HILL RD

HILLTOP

Manor
Farm

Mushroom
Farm

LONGHEDGE LA

Winter Beck

River Devon

BOTTESFORD LA

Elton & Orston

LC

Piggeries

ORSTON LA

NG13

Oldfield
Plantation

Winter Beck

Winterbeck
Ind Est

Longhedge Lane
Ind Est

A52 Nottingham

A52

Highfield
Farm

NOTTINGHAM RD

Nursery

Greenacres

Orston
Grange

A52

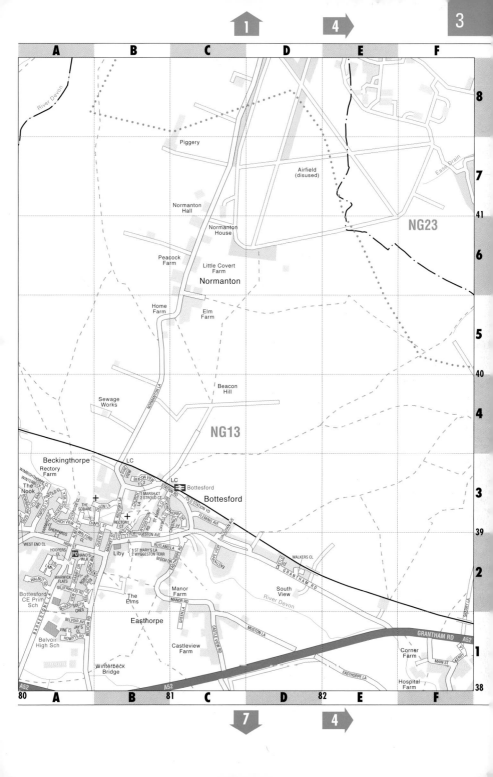

The Ashes

Camp (dis)

Thackson's Well Farm

Moss' Plantation

NG23

Ease Drain

The Spinney

Lowfield Farm

The Bungalow

LOWFIELDS LA

Stonepit Plantation

RED HOUSE GDNS 1
BURTON S LA 2
MARSTON LA 3
GONERBY LA 4

PARK RD

Allington with Sedgebrook CE Prim Sch

Hillside Plantation

Allington Hall

SIDE ST

Allington

PH

West Wong Plantation

WEST MDWS

PO

Manor House

DALESTORTH CT

Old Rectory

MANOR PADDOCK

LAMBERT RD

Endcliffe Farm

BOTTESFORD RD

Glebe Farm

NG32

Salt Well (Chalybeate)

ALLINGTON GDNS

WEST WAY

Debdale Barn

SEWSTERN LA

Viking Way

The Debdale

Keeper's Plantation

Manor Farm

ALLINGTON RD

NG13

Barra-Don

SEWSTERN LA

Cox's Walk Farm

Station Farm

A52

GRANTHAM RD

PH

CHURCH LA

LC

A52

Manor House

CHURCH LA

Lincolnshire STREET ATLAS

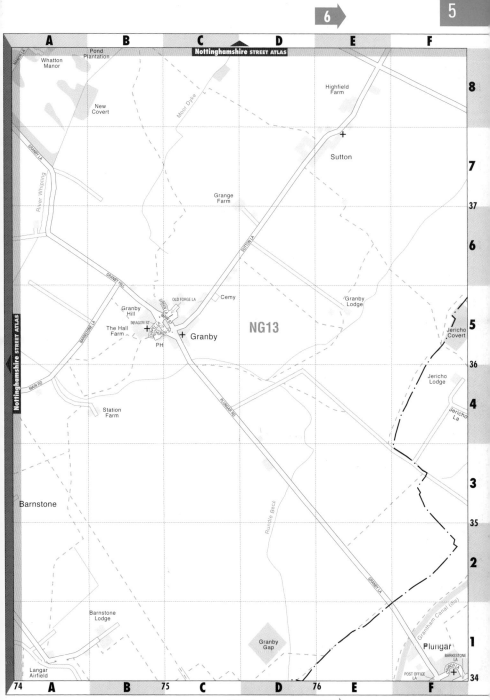

Nottinghamshire STREET ATLAS

Nottinghamshire STREET ATLAS

8

7

37

6

5

36

4

3

35

2

1

34

Whatton Manor

Pond Plantation

New Covert

Moor Dyke

Highfield Farm

+

Sutton

Grange Farm

River Whiping

GRANBY LA

SUTTON LA

Granby Hill

GRANBY HILL

BARNSTONE LA

OLD FORGE LA

Cemy

Granby Lodge

NG13

DRAGON ST

MAIN ST

The Hall Farm

CHURCH ST

PH

+ Granby

Jericho Covert

Jericho Lodge

Jericho La

MAIN RD

Station Farm

PLUNGAR RD

Rundle Beck

Barnstone

GRANBY LA

Barnstone Lodge

Granby Gap

Grantham Canal (dis)

Plungar

BARKESTONE LA

CHURCH LA

POST OFFICE LA

Langar Airfield

74
A
B
75
C
D
76
E
F

A   B   C   D   E   F

8

The Becks
Plantation

New Vale
Farm

7

Eady's
Farm

37

The Grimmer

6

Old Hill
Farm

Lodge
Farm

BARKESTONE LA

Glebe
Farm

5

Jericho
Covert

36

Grantham Canal (dis)

NG13

4

The
Lodge

MAIN RD

MAIN ST

CHURCH LA

PH

LASTHORPE
LA

DRIFT HILL

BELVOIR RD

PO

Jericho La

REDMILE LA

VERNON
ROW

3

Sewage
Works

Redmile
CE Prim
Sch

Redmile

35

Ivy House
Farm

THE GREEN

MARSHALL FARM CL

JERICHO LA

NEW CAUSEWAY

FRIARDALE CL

MILL ST

Barkestone-le-Vale

2

ORCHARD LA

THE OLD LA

PH

MAIN ST

RUTLAND RD

TOWN END

PLUNGAR LA

WOOD LA

LONG LA

1

34

Vale
House

CHERRY TREE
DR

77   A   B   78   C   D   79   E   F

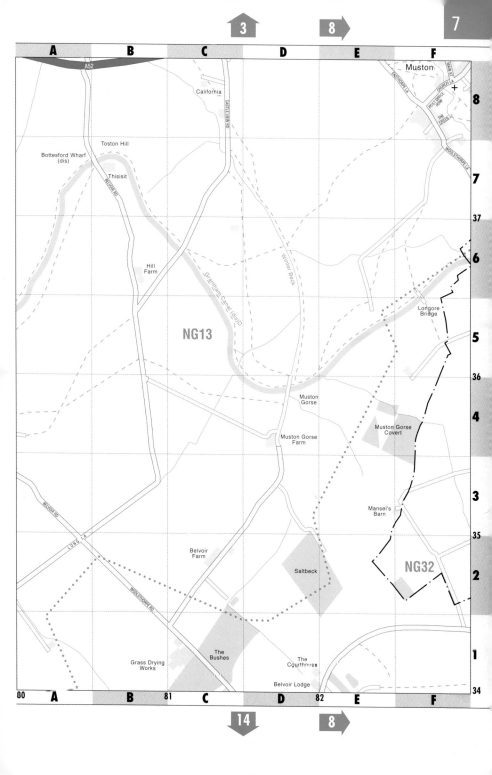

A B C D E F

3 8

Muston

MAIN ST

EASTHORPE LA

CHURCH LA

POST OFFICE ROW

California

THE CREDIT

+

8

WOOLSTHORPE LA

Toston Hill

7

Bottesford Wharf (dis)

BELVOIR RD

Thisisit

37

Hill Farm

Winter Beck

Grantham Canal (dis'd)

CASTLE VIEW RD

6

NG13

Longore Bridge

5

36

Muston Gorse

4

Muston Gorse Farm

Muston Gorse Covert

3

Mansel's Barn

BELVOIR RD

LONG LA

Belvoir Farm

35

NG32

WOOLSTHORPE RD

Saltbeck

2

The Bushes

1

Grass Drying Works

The Courthouse

Belvoir Lodge

34

00 A B 81 C D 82 E F

14 8

A52

Sedgebrook

White House Farm

VILLAGE
THE PADDOCKS
CHURCH LA
ABBEY LA
SCHOOL
KING'S WAY

A52 Grantham

NG13

Mill Farm Cottages

SEDGE LA

Willow Bridge

Mill Farm

Mill Farm

8

7

Shipman's Plantation

DENTON LA

37

6

Muston Bridge

Breeder Hills Farm

New Cottages

Casthorpe Farm

Coe Farm

Lock House

WOOLSTHORPE LA

Lincolnshire STREET ATLAS

5

Stenwith

Stenwith Bridge

36

Viking Way

NG32

4

Barlow's Farm

River Devon

Grantham Canal (dis)

Grange Farm

3

PEDGEBROOK RD

PH Woolsthorpe Wharf (dis)

Woolsthorpe Bridge

Longmoor Bridge

35

2

HUNT COTTS

Cliff Wood

Glebe Farm

Sewage Works

HILLSIDE RD

Belvoir Hunt Stables

NEW ROW

Mickledales

Lanes Plantation

1

WORTHINGTON LA

CHAPEL ST

ELM RD

BELVOIR LA

PH

Woolsthorpe by Belvoir

34

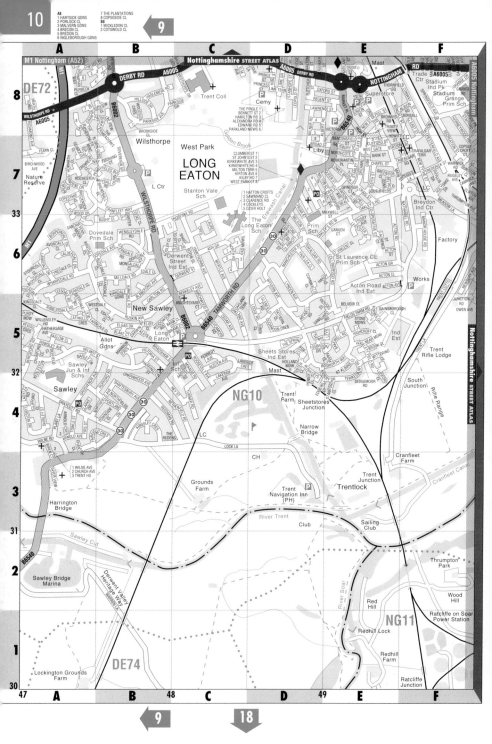

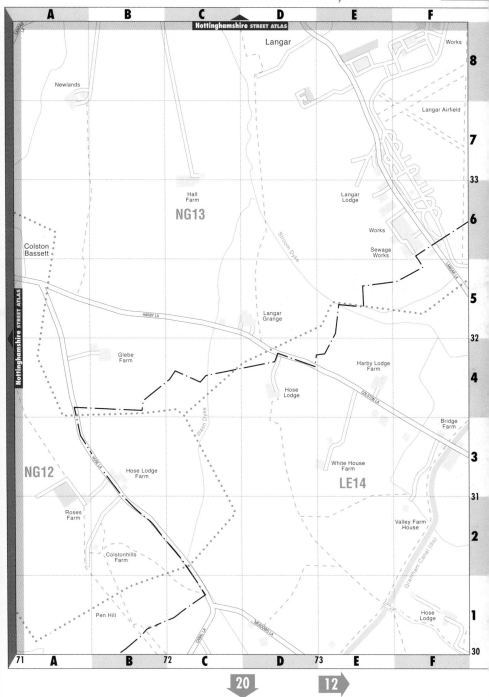

Nottinghamshire **STREET ATLAS**

Langar

Newlands

Langar Airfield

Hall
Farm

NG13

Langar
Lodge

Stroom Dyke

Works

Colston
Bassett

Sewage
Works

HARBY LA

Langar
Grange

Glebe
Farm

Harby Lodge
Farm

Wash Dyke

Hose
Lodge

COLSTON LA

Bridge
Farm

NG12

HOSE LA

Hose Lodge
Farm

White House
Farm

LE14

Roses
Farm

Valley Farm
House

Colstonhills
Farm

Grantham Canal (dis)

Pen Hill

CANAL LA

MEADOWS LA

Hose
Lodge

Nottinghamshire STREET ATLAS

8

7

33

6

5

32

4

3

31

2

1

30

11
5

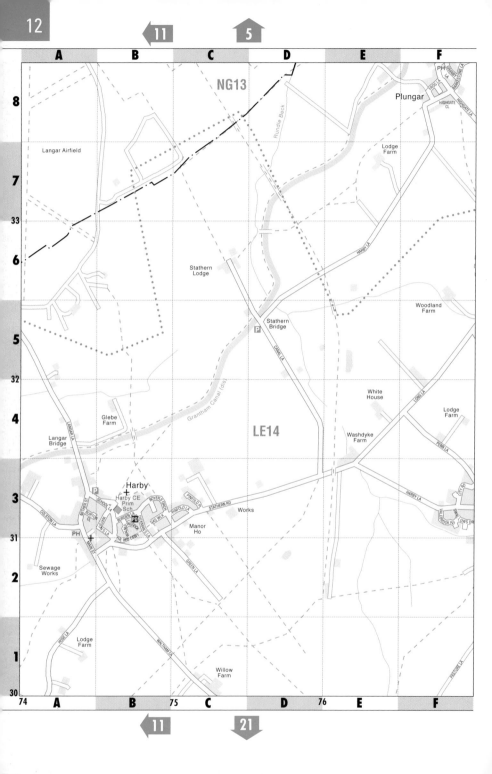

11
21

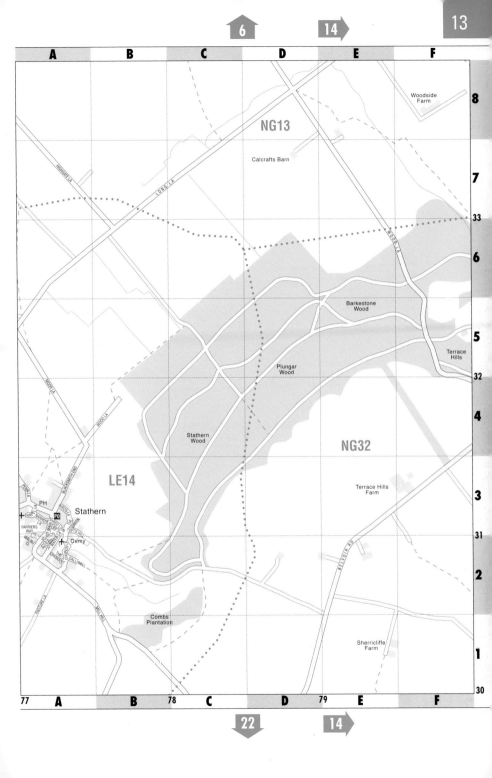

13
7

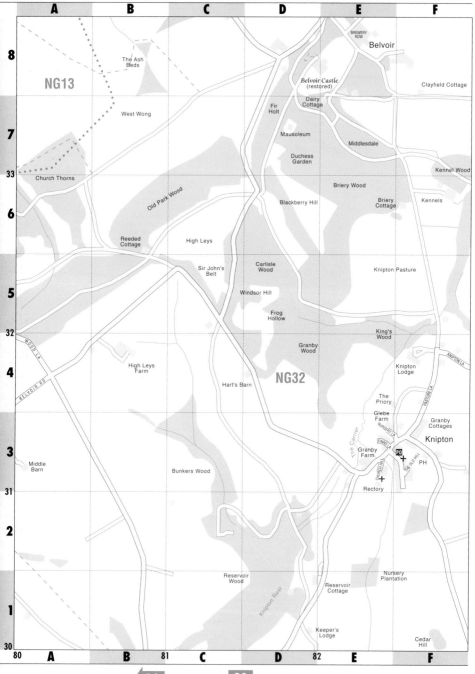

13
23

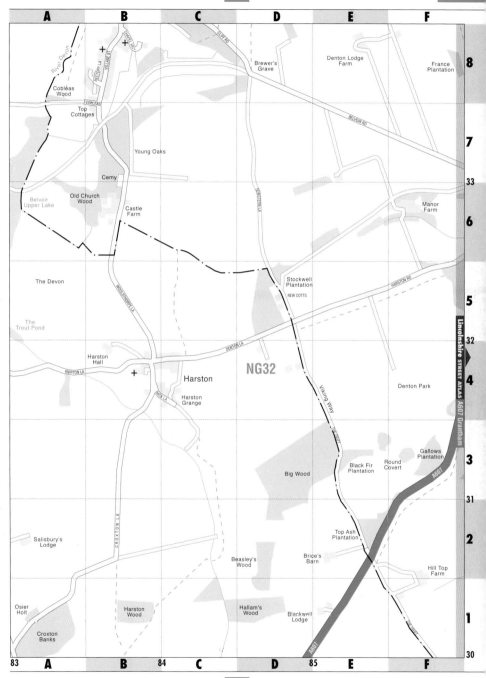

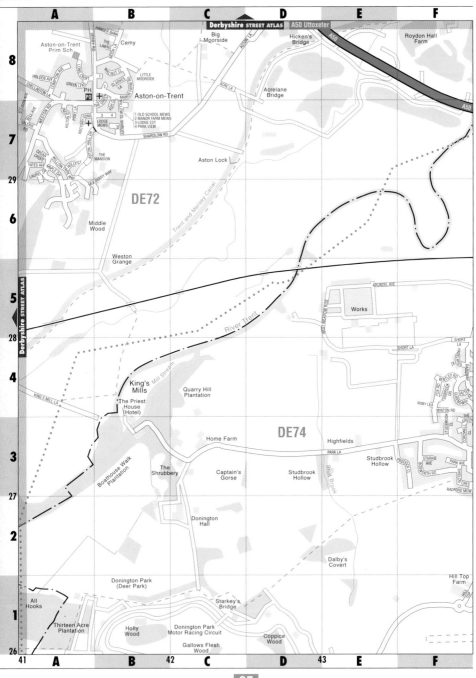

A   B   C   D   E   F

Aston-on-Trent
Prim Sch

HANGER BANK

THE LAWNS

Cemy

Big
Moorside

Hicken's
Bridge

Roydon Hall
Farm

8

LITTLE
MOORSIDE

Acrelane
Bridge

ACRE LA

GREEN LEYS

PH
PO

Aston-on-Trent

1 OLD SCHOOL MEWS
2 MANOR FARM MEWS
3 LODGE EST
4 PARK VIEW

LODGE
MEWS

RECTORY LA

SHARDLOW RD

7

THE
MANSION

Aston Lock

29

DE72

MULBERRY WAY

Middle
Wood

Trent and Mersey Canal

6

Weston
Grange

ARUNDEL AVE

5

Works

River Trent

SHORT LA

SHORT
LA

28

King's
Mills

Mill Stream

Quarry Hill
Plantation

KING'S MILL LA

The Priest
House
(Hotel)

4

ROBY LEA

MINTON RD

THE
GREEN

BENTLEY RD

SALTER
CL

Home Farm

Highfields

DE74

PARK LA

3

Boathouse Walk
Plantation

The
Shrubbery

Captain's
Gorse

Studbrook
Hollow

Studbrook
Hollow

STARKIE
AVE

PARK AVE

Stud Brook

RADFORD MDW

27

Donington
Hall

Dalby's
Covert

2

Donington Park
(Deer Park)

Starkey's
Bridge

Hill Top
Farm

1

All
Hooks

Thirteen Acre
Plantation

Holly
Wood

Donington Park
Motor Racing Circuit

Coppice
Wood

26

Gallows Flesh
Wood

41   A   B   42   C   D   43   E   F

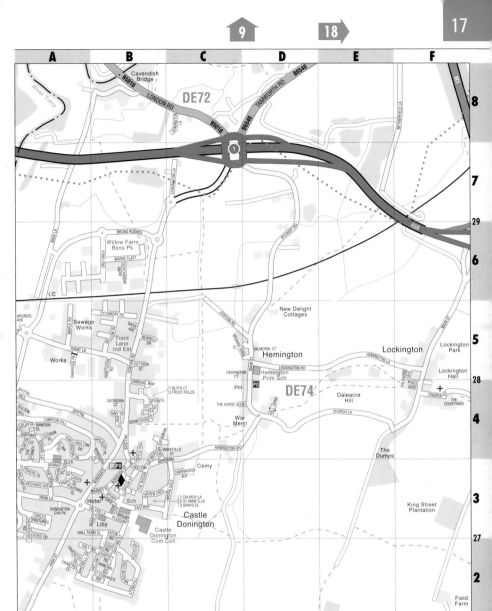

River Trent

Cavendish
Bridge

B5010

LONDON RD

DE72

TAMWORTH RD

B5540

B5010

DONINGTON LA

B5540

NETHERFIELD LA

M1

A50

BACK LA

LC

BROAD RUSHES

Willow Farm
Bsns Pk

PONDHEAD

WARKE FLATT

BAPP

COCKCHARME

DONINGTON LA

New Delight
Cottages

Lockington

Lockington
Park

MAIN ST

ARUNDEL
AVE

MAPLE RD

SYCAMORE RD

GAGNY
AVE

Sewage
Works

NEWBOLD
DR

Trent
Lane
Ind Est

STYLES RD

GRANGE FARM

MAIN ST

HEMINGTON LA

Lockington
Hall

TRENT LA

VICTORIA ST

DALEACRE
AVE

KINGS
GATE

CHURCH

DERBY RD

HAWTHORN RD

OAKRIDGE

Works

BALMORAL CT

Hemington

LOCKINGTON RD

DALE CL

CARNIVAL WAY

HEMINGTON
CT

Hemington
Prim Sch

DE74

Daleacre
Hill

THE
COURTYARD

SPITTAL
HILL

HOLTON
HILL

SPITTAL

GEORGINA CT

TANY

UPTON CL

1 BLYTH CT
2 FROST FIELDS

PH

PO

CLOVER CL

THE HORSE SHOES

CAMPION HILL

BORLEY CL

DARSWAY

HARLEY CL

DUDGON

RAWDON
CL

HAZELTON
DR

HENRY ST

MINTON DR

SCHOOL LA

DERBYSHIRE

WAR
Meml

HALL CHURCH
LANE

War
Meml

CHURCH LA

The
Dumps

Sch

GRANGE DR

P PO

HARCOURT PL

WELDON

CARBIS

CARPSON

CASTLE

WAKEFIELD
CT

MOIRA DALE

HEMINGTON HILL

Cemy

King Street
Plantation

KILBURN CL

ORCHARD AVE

CARRS

PEARTREE

MARKET ST

AIRPORT

THE BIGGIN

CHARNWOOD
AVE

EDEN CRES

1 CHURCH LA
2 ST ANNE'S LA
3 GRAYS CL

PARK LA

Hotel

Liby

Sch

EASTWAY

Castle
Donington

DONINGTON
CVN PK

DELVEN LA

MOUNT
PLEASANT

Castle
Donington
Com Coll

TOWLES
PASTURES

COOKS DR

HALL FARM CL

EATON CL

ORY AVE

BONDGATE

CRABTREE

BASFORD

GAWENDISH

BAKEWELL

ST EDWARD'S
RD

WINDMILL

STONEHILL

HILLTOP

OSWORTH RD

The
Aeropark

Nottingham
East Midlands
Int Airport

Mast

Field
Farm

44 A 45 C D 46 E F

8
7
29
6
5
28
4
3
27
2
1
26

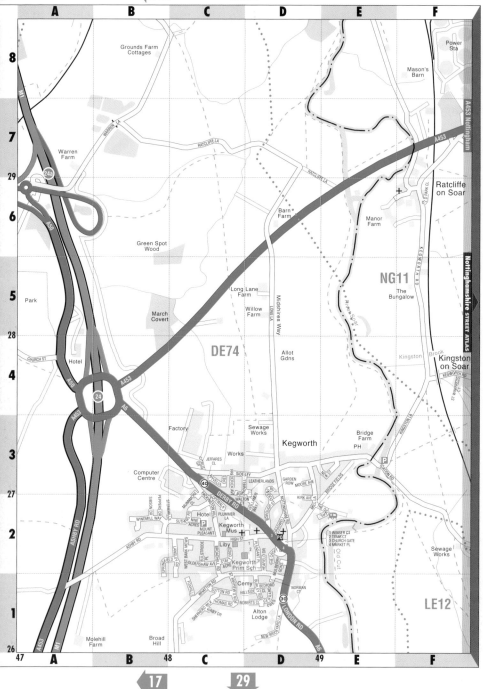

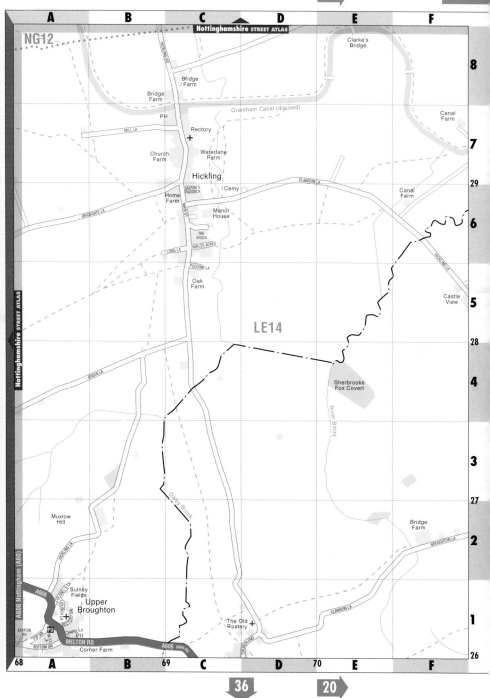

Nottinghamshire STREET ATLAS

NG12

Nottinghamshire Street Atlas
A606 Nottingham (A60)

Hickling

Grantham Canal (disused)

Clarke's Bridge

Canal Farm

Canal Farm

Castle View

Bridge Farm

Bridge Farm

PH

Rectory

Church Farm

Waterlane Farm

Marsh's Paddock

Cemy

Home Farm

Manor House

THE GREEN

HARLES ACRES

LONG LA

PUDDING LA

Oak Farm

LE14

Sherbrooke Fox Covert

River Smite

Dalby Brook

Muxlow Hill

Bridge Farm

Sulney Fields

Upper Broughton

The Old Rectory

Corner Farm

STATION RD

BOTTOM GN

MELTON RD

A606 MAIN RD

HICKLING RD

MILL LA

BRIDGEGATE LA

MAIN ST

GREEN LA

HICKLING LA

CLAWSON LA

CLAWSON LA

BROUGHTON LA

A606

CHURCH END

CHAPEL LA

PO

PH

8

7

29

6

5

28

4

3

27

2

1

26

A   B   C   D   E   F

68   69   70

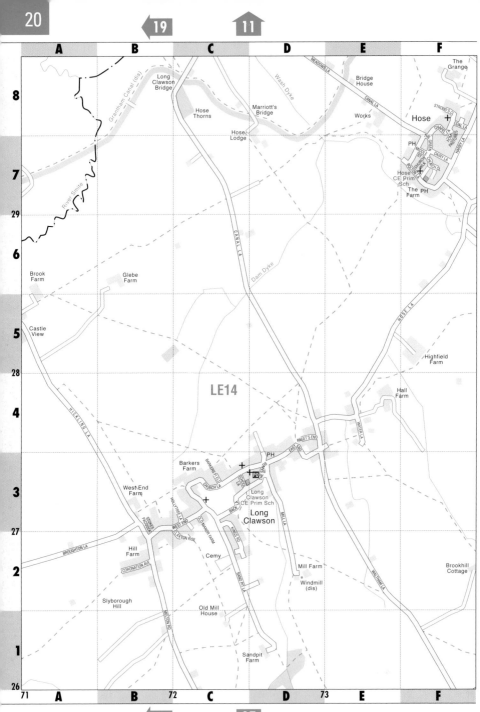

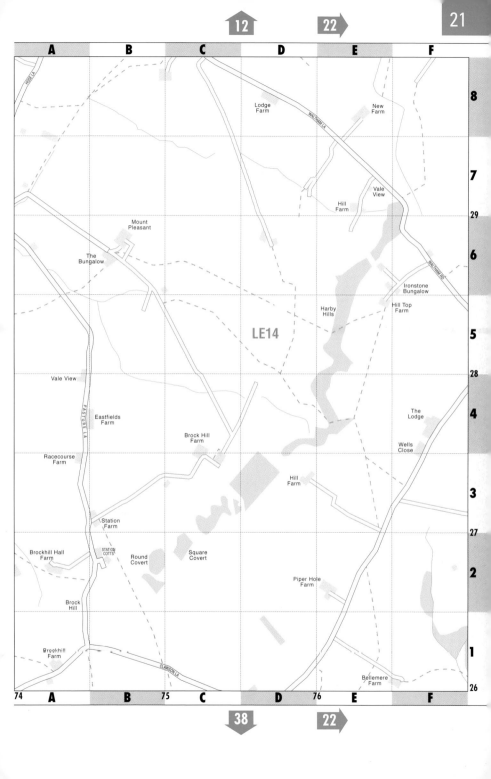

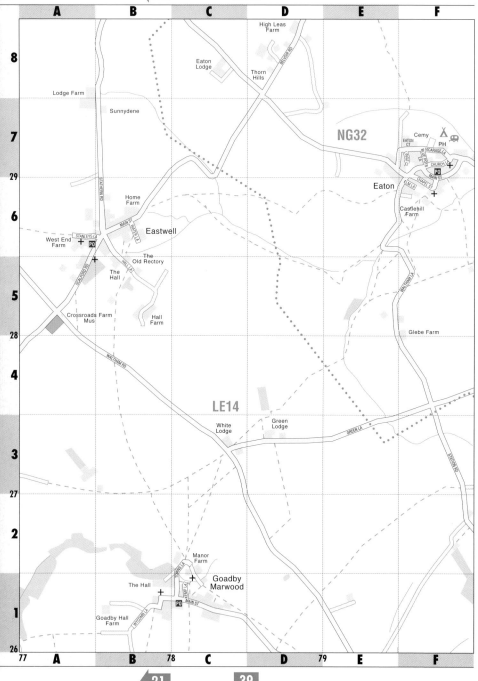

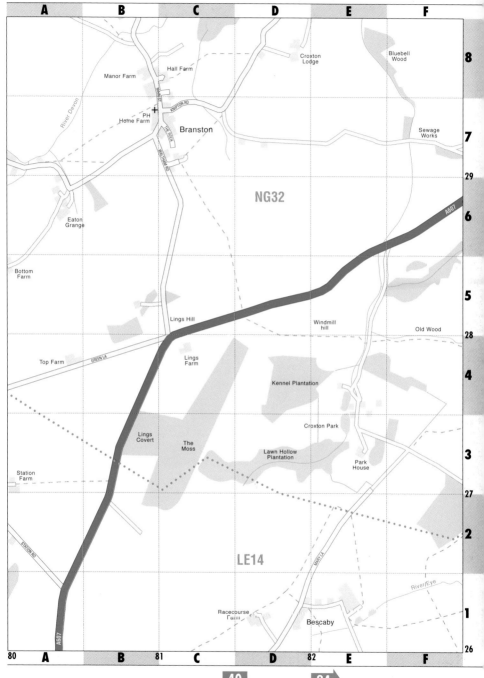

A B C D E F

8
7
29
6
5
28
4
3
27
2
1
26

NG32

LE14

River Devon

Manor Farm
Hall Farm
Croxton Lodge
Bluebell Wood

MALT ST
KNIPTON RD
PH
Home Farm
THE ROCK
Branston
WALTHAM RD

Sewage Works

Eaton Grange

Bottom Farm

Lings Hill

Windmill hill
Old Wood

GREEN LA
Top Farm

Lings Farm

Kennel Plantation

Lings Covert
The Moss

Croxton Park

Lawn Hollow Plantation

Park House

Station Farm

STATION RD

A607

MARY LA

River Eye

Racecourse Farm
Bescaby

80 A B 81 C D 82 E F

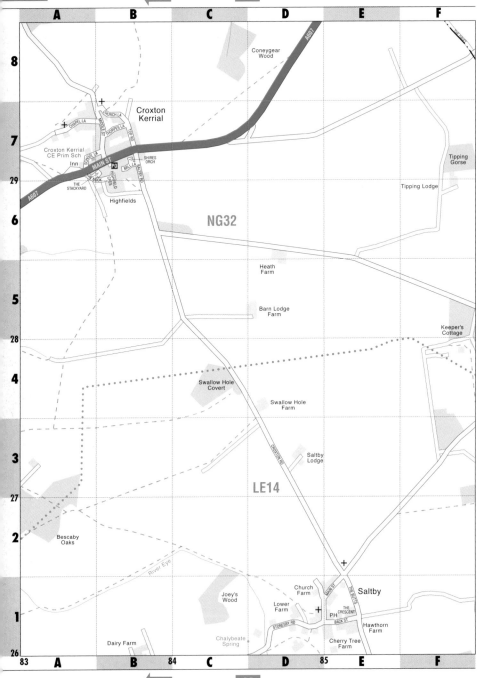

A　**B**　**C**　**D**　**E**　**F**

8

Coneygear
Wood

A607

7

Croxton
Kerrial

CHURCH LA
CHAPEL LA
MIDDLE ST
THORPES LA
TOP RD

Tipping
Gorse

Croxton Kerrial
CE Prim Sch
Inn

29

SCHOOL LA
MAIN ST
PO
HIGHFIELD
CRES
MILL LA
SALTBY RD
SHIRES
ORCH

Tipping Lodge

THE
STACKYARD
A607

Highfields

6

NG32

Heath
Farm

5

Barn Lodge
Farm

Keeper's
Cottage

28

4

Swallow Hole
Covert

Swallow Hole
Farm

3

CROXTON RD

Saltby
Lodge

LE14

27

2

Bescaby
Oaks

River Eye

Joey's
Wood

Church
Farm

MAIN ST
THE BUTTS

Saltby

Lower
Farm

THE
CRESCENT
PH

BACK ST

1

STONESBY RD

Hawthorn
Farm

26

Dairy Farm

Chalybeate
Spring

Cherry Tree
Farm

83　**A**　**B**　84　**C**　**D**　85　**E**　**F**

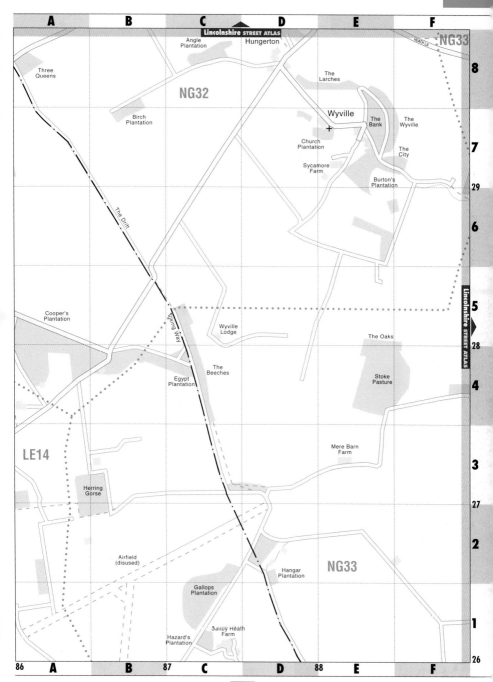

NG33

8

Three
Queens

Angle
Plantation

Hungerton

The
Larches

NG32

Wyville

The
Bank

The
Wyville

7

Birch
Plantation

Church
Plantation

The
City

Sycamore
Farm

Burton's
Plantation

29

The Drift

6

Cooper's
Plantation

Viking Way

Wyville
Lodge

The Oaks

5

28

The
Beeches

Egypt
Plantation

Stoke
Pasture

4

LE14

Mere Barn
Farm

3

27

Herring
Gorse

2

Airfield
(disused)

Hangar
Plantation

NG33

Gallops
Plantation

Hazard's
Plantation

Saltby Heath
Farm

1

26

86

87

88

A8
1 LOAKE CT
2 THE CROFT
3 REDWAY CROFT
4 LAMPAD CL

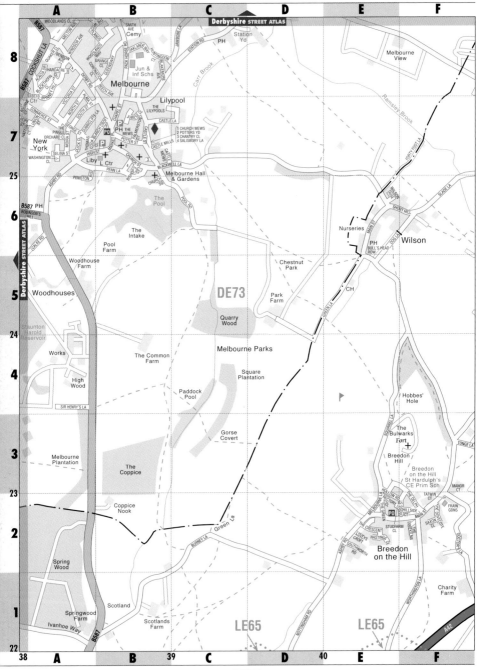

Derbyshire Street Atlas

Derbyshire STREET ATLAS

Melbourne

Lilypool

New York

Melbourne View

Melbourne Hall & Gardens

The Pool

The Intake

Pool Farm

Woodhouse Farm

Woodhouses

Staunton Harold Reservoir

Works

High Wood

Nurseries

Wilson

Chestnut Park

DE73

Park Farm

Quarry Wood

Melbourne Parks

The Common Farm

Square Plantation

Paddock Pool

Hobbes' Hole

The Bulwarks Fort

Breedon Hill

Breedon on the Hill St Hardulph's CE Prim Sch

MANOR CT

Gorse Covert

Melbourne Plantation

The Coppice

Breedon on the Hill

TATWIN CT

Coppice Nook

Green La

Spring Wood

Charity Farm

Scotland

Springwood Farm

Ivanhoe Way

Scotlands Farm

LE65

LE65

A42

1 CHURCH MEWS
2 POTTERS YD
3 CHANTRY CL
4 SALISBURY LA

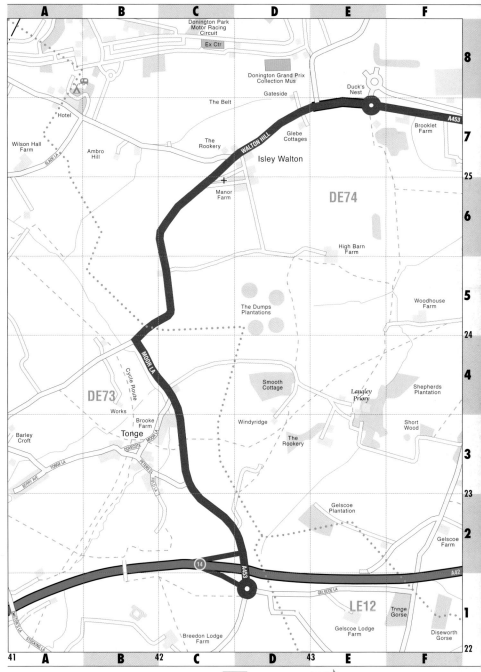

A   B   C   D   E   F

8

Nottingham
East Midlands
Int Airport

Finger
Farm

LANCER DR
ANSON RD
VANGUARD DR
DAKOTA RD

Passenger
Terminal

BEVERLEY RD
ARGOSY RD

P

DOVE RD

VISCOUNT RD

P

Hotel

P

P

A453

A453

AMBASSADOR RD

ASHBY RD

A453

7

Charnock
Hill

Bleak
House

Donington Park
Services

M1

25

Green La

GRIMES GATE

HYAM'S LA

6

Wartoft
Grange

Diseworth
CE Prim
Sch

PH

23a

THE BINDLEY

SHAKESPEARE DR

HALL GATE

PH

CLEMENTS GATE

LONG HOLDEN

TOFTHEFIELD

LINTHWAITE
CT

THE GREEN

ORCHARD

BROOKSIDE

Diseworth

A42

PINGLE LA

HALL GATE CRFT

LADY GATE

THE GREEN

THE GREEN

5

The Green

Town
End

Diseworth Brook

DE74

24

Wood Nook
Farm

WEST END

4

WESTMEADOW LA

M1

LONG MERE LA

3

New Wood

Little Rise
Farm

23

LE12

2

Scaffacre
Farm

Westmeadow Brook

Riste
Farm

DRY POT LA

Glebe
Farm

A42

David's
Hill

1

Long Mere
Farm

WV8

22

44 A   B   45 C   D   46 E   F

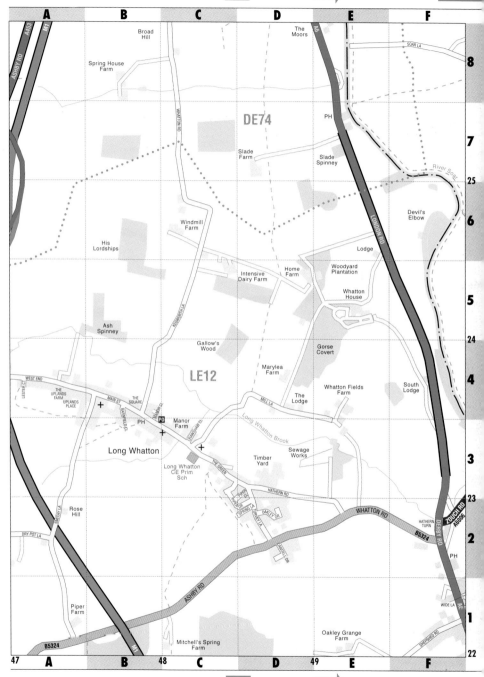

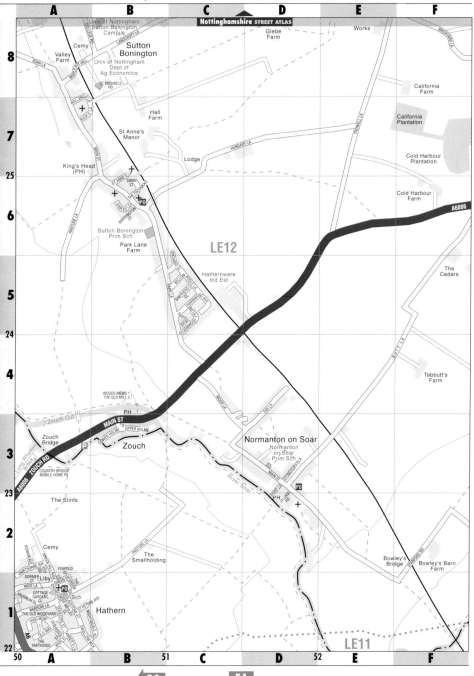

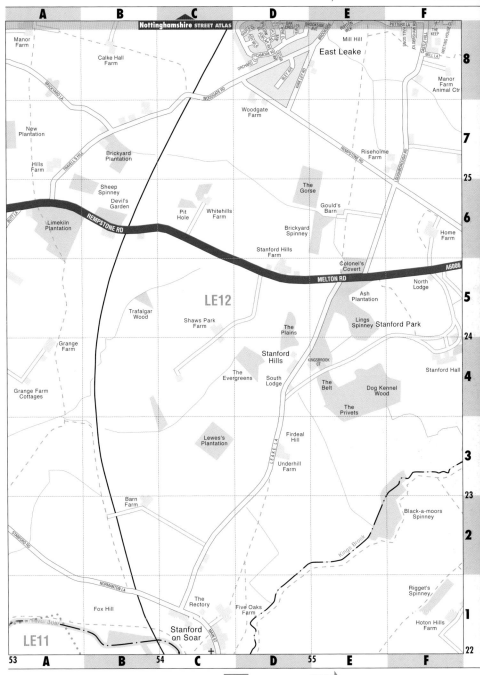

Manor Farm

Calke Hall Farm

BRICKYARD LA

WOODGATE RD

East Leake

Mill Hill

POTTERS LA

CASTLE HILL

THE KEEP

MILL LA

Manor Farm Animal Ctr

8

New Plantation

Hills Farm

TRAVELL'S HILL

Brickyard Plantation

Woodgate Farm

REMPSTONE RD

Riseholme Farm

LOUGHBOROUGH RD

7

25

Sheep Spinney

Devil's Garden

The Gorse

Gould's Barn

6

REMPSTONE RD

BUTT LA

Limekiln Plantation

Pit Hole

Whitehills Farm

Brickyard Spinney

Home Farm

Stanford Hills Farm

Colonel's Covert

MELTON RD

A6006

North Lodge

5

LE12

Trafalgar Wood

Shaws Park Farm

The Plains

Ash Plantation

Lings Spinney

Stanford Park

24

Grange Farm

Stanford Hills

The Evergreens

South Lodge

KINGSBROOK CT

The Belt

Dog Kennel Wood

Stanford Hall

4

Grange Farm Cottages

Lewes's Plantation

LEAKE LA

Firdeal Hill

The Privets

3

Underhill Farm

23

Barn Farm

Black-a-moors Spinney

2

STANFORD RD

Kings Brook

NORMANTON LA

The Rectory

Fox Hill

Five Oaks Farm

MAIN ST

Rigget's Spinney

1

LE11

River Soar

Stanford on Soar

Hoton Hills Farm

22

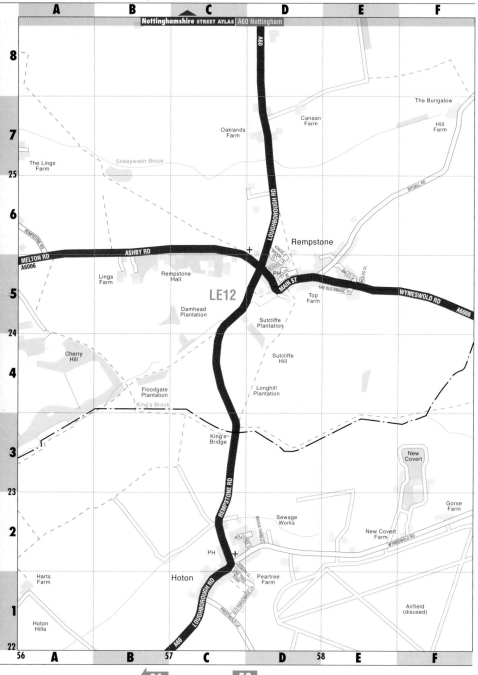

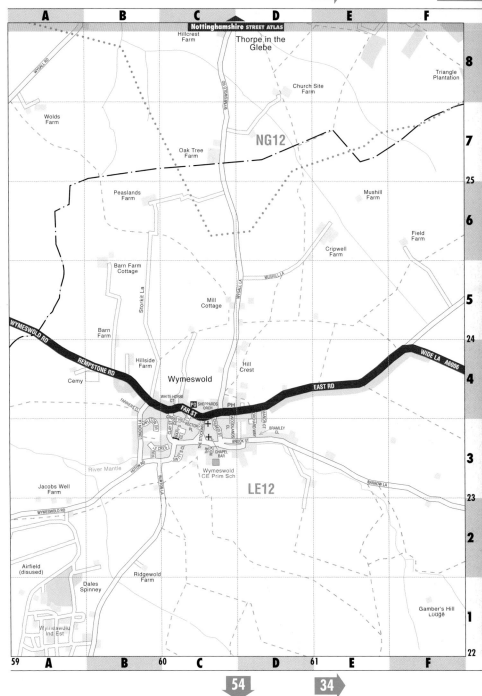

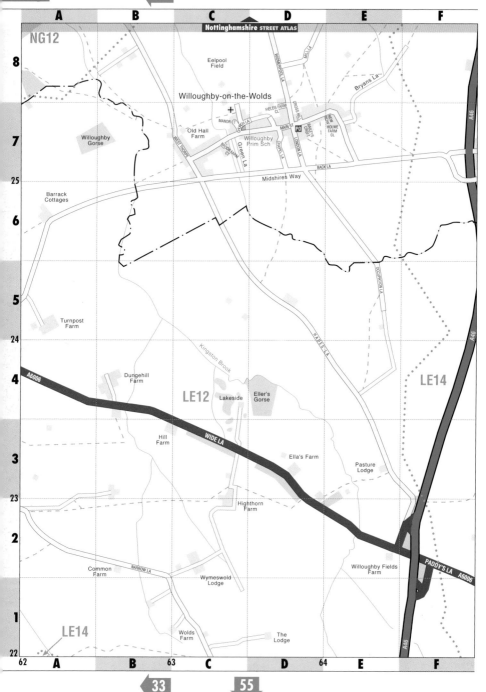

NG12

8

Eelpool
Field

Willoughby-on-the-Wolds

WIDMERPOOL LA

MILL LA

Bryans La

FIELDS FARM CL

CROSS HILL

7

Willoughby
Gorse

Old Hall
Farm

MANOR CT

WEST THORPE

Green La

BROOK FARM CT

Willoughby
Prim Sch

MAIN ST

CHURCH LA

LONDON LA

PO

PAKE'S CROFT

NEW ROW

HOLME FARM CL

BACK LA

25

Midshires Way

6

Barrack
Cottages

OCCUPATION LA

5

Turnpost
Farm

A46

24

Kingston Brook

4

A6006

Dungehill
Farm

LE12

Lakeside

Eller's
Gorse

FLAX FIELD LA

LE14

A46

Hill
Farm

WIDE LA

3

Ella's
Farm

Pasture
Lodge

23

Highthorn
Farm

2

Common
Farm

NARROW LA

Wymeswold
Lodge

Willoughby Fields
Farm

PADDY'S LA

A6006

A46

1

LE14

Wolds
Farm

The
Lodge

22

Manor Barn Farm

Manor Farm

STATION RD

Brookeside Cottage

Top Cottage

Depot

Hotel

Fairham Brook

Dalby Brook

Longridge

Wad House Farm

NOTTINGHAM LA

Spruce Haven

Longcliff Hill

Beazley's Farm

Midshires Way

North Lodge Farm

North Lodge

Old Dalby CE Prim Sch

LONGCLIFF HILL

Dalby Lodges

LE14

HAWTHORN CL

LONGCLIFF CL

Cemy

STATION RD

DEADALE HILL

CROFT CL

PH

CHAPEL LA

MAIN RD

PARADISE LA

PO

Vale View Farm

THE GREEN

QUEBEC LA

Old Dalby

Wood's Hill

WOOD HILL

Hall

Fishpond Plantation

Woodhill Farm
Woodhill Ind Est

Lawn Farm

Hall Plantation

Hill Top Farm

Upper Grange Farm

Yard Farm

Old Dalby Wood

Old Dalby Lodge

GIBSON'S LA

Grange Cottages

Wavendon Grange

LANE LA

PADDY'S LA

Lower Grange Farm

A6006

Old Dalby Grange

Bridgets Covert

SIX HILLS LA

Lodge Farm

Dalby Wolds

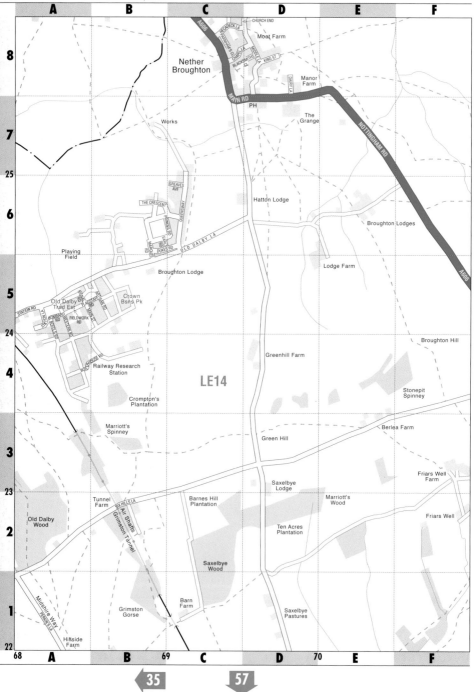

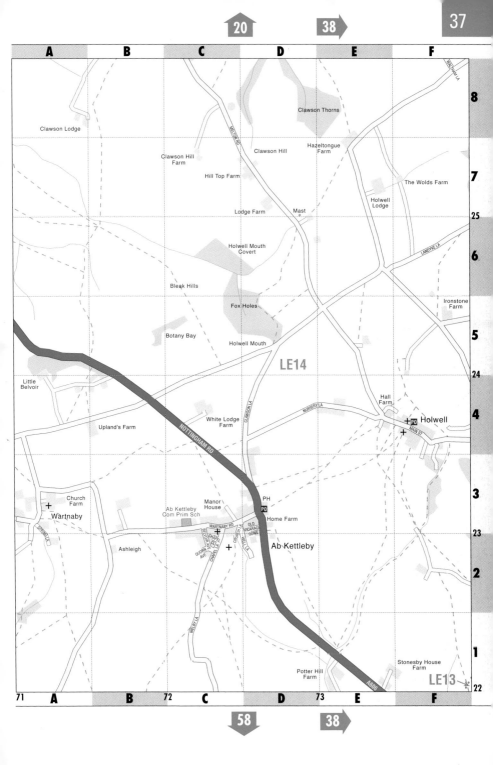

A B C D E F

8
7
25
6
5
24
4
3
23
2
1
22

Clawson Lodge

Clawson Thorns

Clawson Hill Farm

Clawson Hill

Hazeltongue Farm

Hill Top Farm

The Wolds Farm

Lodge Farm

Mast

Holwell Lodge

MELTON RD

LANDYKE LA

Holwell Mouth Covert

Ironstone Farm

Bleak Hills

Fox Holes

Botany Bay

Holwell Mouth

LE14

Little Belvoir

Hall Farm

NURSERY LA

White Lodge Farm

CLAWSON LA

Holwell

PO
MAIN ST

Upland's Farm

NOTTINGHAM RD

Church Farm

Manor House

PH
PO

Wartnaby

Ab Kettleby Com Prim Sch

WARTNABY RD

Home Farm

OLD VICARAGE GDNS

Ashleigh

BELVOIR PL
CHURCH ST
BEVERAGE LA
AVE
CHAPEL LA
WELL LA

Ab Kettleby

SCHOOL CL

WELL LA

Potter Hill Farm

Stonesby House Farm

A606

LE13

37
21

A B C D E F

8
7
25
6
5
24
4
3
23
2
1
22

CLAWSON LA

Cranyke
Farm

Wolds
Farm

LIONVILLE
COTTS

Deben
Farm

Red House
Farm

LANDYKE LA

The
Cottage

Mawbrook
Lodge

Old Brickyard
Cottages

Landyke Lane
Farm

Mawbrook
Farm

Manor
House

The
Willows

Scalford

Grange
Farm

The
Elms

PH

Cemy

PH
SOUTH
CL

Netherhall
Barn

Scalford
CE Prim
Sch

STONESTYLE
GDNS

SANDY LA

KING ST

QUEEN'S

SCHOOL LA

SOUTH ST

NEW ST

MELTON RD

LE14

THORPE RISE

Mill Top
Farm

Scalford
Lodge

Clayfield
Farm

Brown's
Hill

Scalford Brook

Scalford
Hall

Sans
Souci

Cumberland
Lodge

Old Hills
Wood

Long-gate
Lodge

Old
Hills

MELTON SPINNEY RD

Glebe
Farm

SCALFORD RD

LE13

Melton
Spinney

Scalford
Gorse

LE13

Melton
Spinney
Farm

74 A B 75 C D 76 E F

37
59

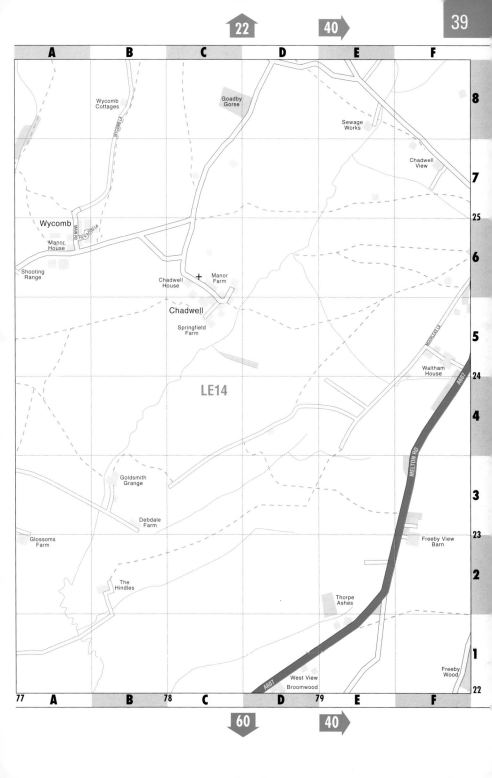

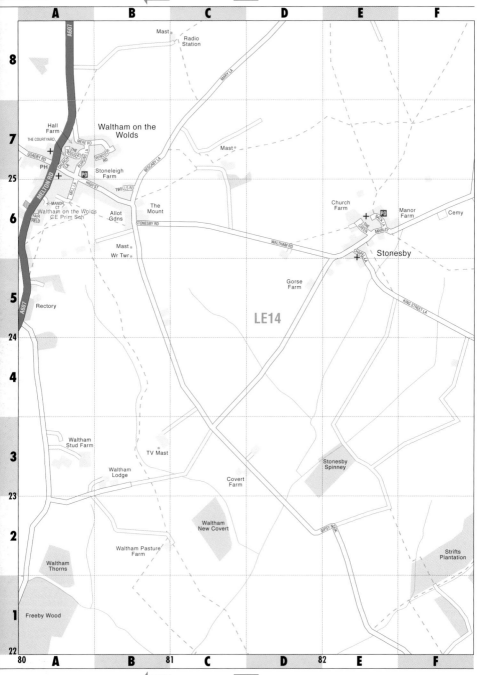

| | A | B | C | D | E | F |

8

Mast
Radio
Station

MARY LA

7

Hall
Farm
THE COURTYARD
GOADBY RD
PH

Waltham on the
Wolds

MERE RD

WINDSOR RD

BESGABY LA

Mast

25

Stoneleigh
Farm
PO

MILL LA

HIGH ST

TWELLS RD

Church
Farm
PO

Manor
Farm

Cemy

6

MANOR
CT
Waltham on the Wolds
CE Prim Sch
FAIR
FIELD

Allot
Gdns

The
Mount

STONESBY RD

WALTHAM RD

THE
GREEN
MAIN ST

BACK LA

Stonesby

Mast
Wr Twr

CHAPEL LA

5

A607

Rectory

Gorse
Farm

LE14

KING STREET LA

24

4

3

Waltham
Stud Farm

TV Mast

Waltham
Lodge

Covert
Farm

Stonesby
Spinney

23

2

Waltham Pasture
Farm

Waltham
New Covert

GIPSY LA

Strifts
Plantation

Waltham
Thorns

1

Freeby Wood

22

| 80 | A | B | 81 | C | D | 82 | E | F |

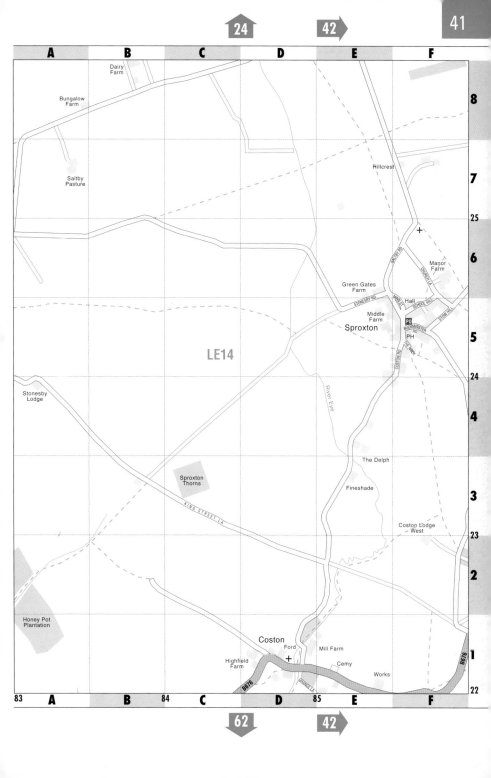

8

41

25

7

25

6

NG33

LE14

5

24

4

3

23

2

1

22

Annises Plantation

Sproxton Lodge

Cringle Brook

Jackson's Plantation

Gorse Plantation

Bottom Plantation

Cams Hill

The Ashes (Wr Twr)

New Rookery

Park Oaks

Buckminster Park

Parkside Wood

The Roundle

Buckminster Hall

Hanby House

Manor House Farm

Buckminster

Viking Way

Viking Way

THE GRIFT

STAINBY RD

Manor Farm

PH

Grange Farm

B676

COW ROW

MAIN ST

BACK ST

SPROXTON RD

PO

COSTON RD

Brick Yard Wood

Gorse Close Plantation

East Plantation

Royce's Plantation

B676

B676

B676

SCHOOL LA

Old School House

Buckminster Prim Sch

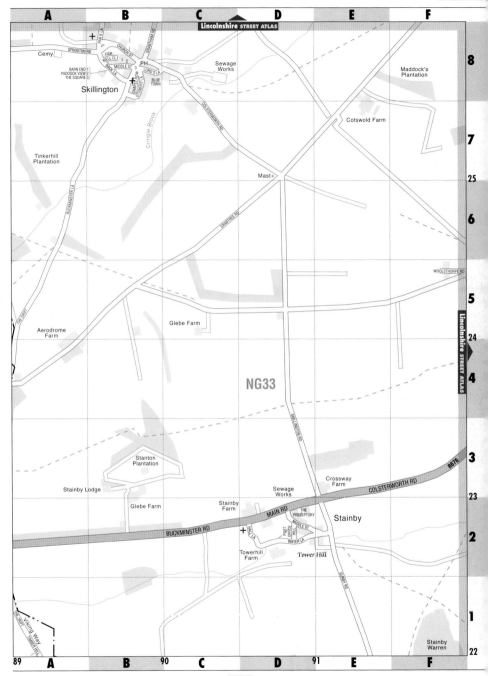

Lincolnshire STREET ATLAS

A · **B** · **C** · **D** · **E** · **F**

SPROXTON RD
Cemy
PARK LA
CHURCH ST
GRANTHAM RD

FISH WELL CL
BARN END/1
PADDOCK VIEW/2
THE SQUARE/3
MIDDLE ST
BACK LA
PH
LORD'S LA
STONEPIT LA
BLUE TOWN

Skillington

Sewage Works

Maddock's Plantation

Cringle Brook

Cotswold Farm

COLSTERWORTH RD

Tinkerhill Plantation

BUCKMINSTER LA

Mast

CRABTREE RD

25

7

6

WOOLSTHORPE RD

THE DRIFT

Aerodrome Farm

Glebe Farm

5

24

NG33

SKILLINGTON RD

4

Stanton Plantation

B676

Stainby Lodge

Crossway Farm

COLSTERWORTH RD

3

23

Glebe Farm

Stainby Farm

Sewage Works

MAIN RD

THE PRECEPTORY

Stainby

BUCKMINSTER RD

HILL LA

POST OFFICE HILL
MIDDLE ST
WATER LA

2

Towerhill Farm

Tower Hill

ILSEY RD

THE DRIFT
VIKING Way
TIMBER HILL

Stainby Warren

1

22

89 **A** 90 **B** **C** 91 **D** **E** **F**

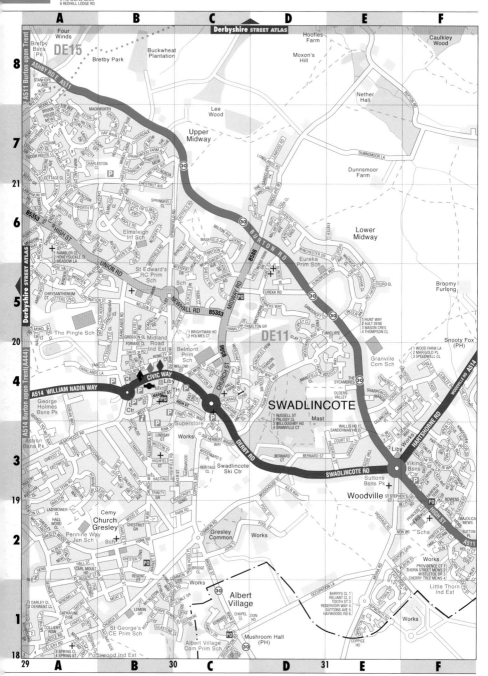

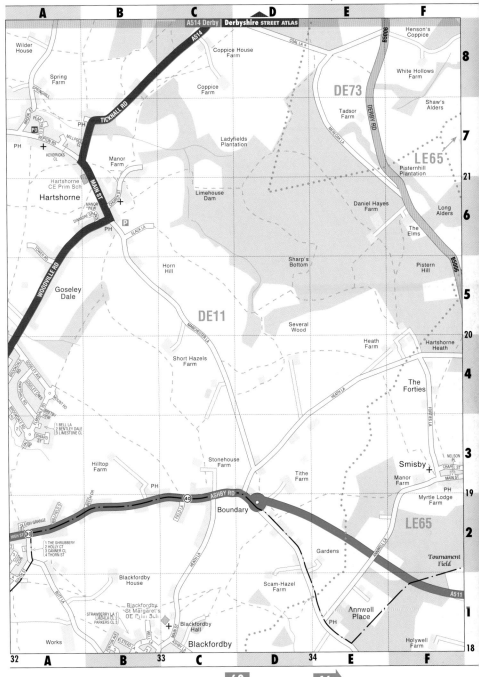

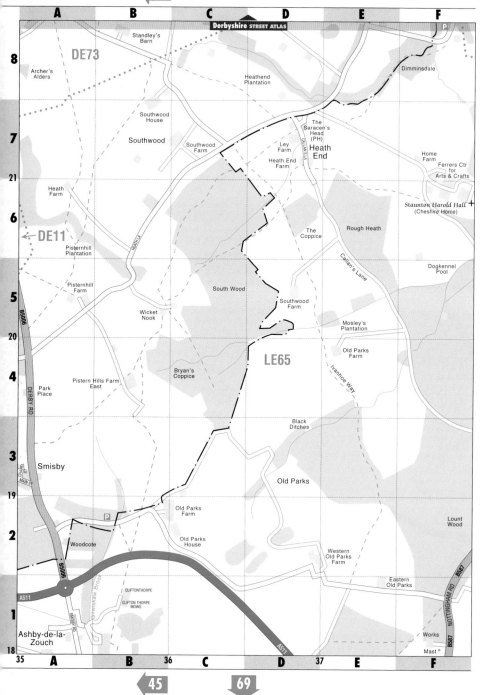

Derbyshire STREET ATLAS

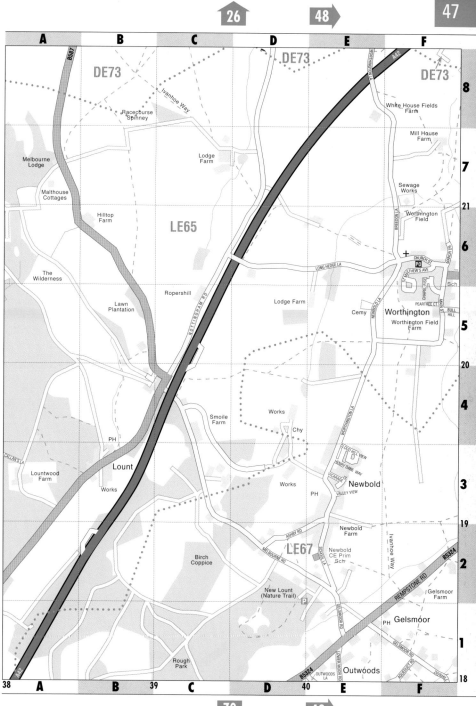

DE73

DE73

DE73

8

Ivanhoe Way

White House Fields Farm

Racecourse Spinney

Mill House Farm

Melbourne Lodge

Lodge Farm

7

Malthouse Cottages

Sewage Works

21

Hilltop Farm

LE65

Worthington Field

6

Church St
PO
St Matthew's Ave

The Wilderness

Long Hedge La

Ropershill

Chapel Rise

Sch

Lawn Plantation

Lodge Farm

Peartree Ct

Bull Hill

5

Cemy

Worthington

Worthington Field Farm

20

Callan's La

Smoile Farm

Works

Chy

4

PH

Cloud Hill View

Lountwood Farm

Lount

Works

Henry Dane Way
Vicarage Cl

Newbold

3

Works

PH

Valley View

Newbold Farm

19

Ashby Rd

Birch Coppice

Melbourne Rd

LE67

School La

Newbold CE Prim Sch

Ivanhoe Way

Rempstone Rd

B5324

2

New Lount (Nature Trail)

P

Gelsmoor Farm

Gelsmoor Rd

PH

Gelsmoor

1

Rough Park

Lower Moor La

Outwoods

B5324

Outwoods La

Acklow Rd

Dumbc

18

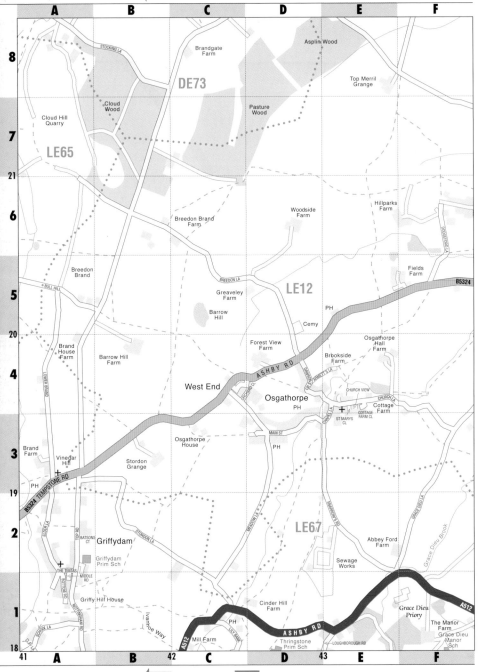

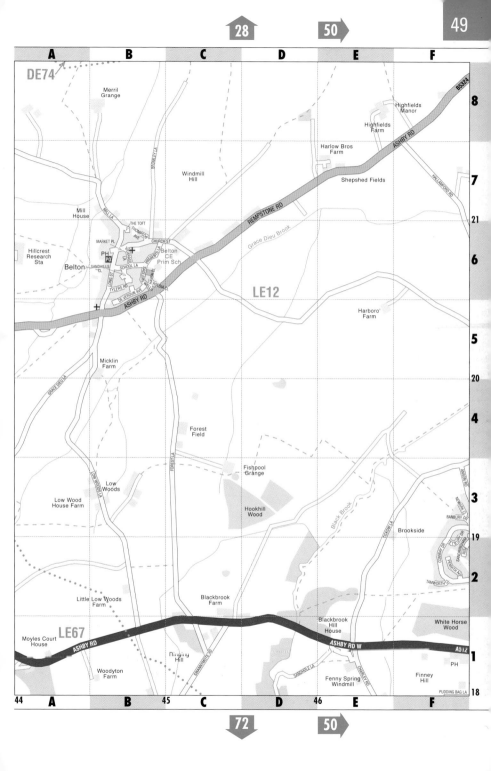

DE74

Merril Grange

Highfields Manor

Highfields Farm

B5324

ASHBY RD

Harlow Bros Farm

Windmill Hill

Shepshed Fields

HALLAMFORD RD

8

7

REMPSTONE RD

Grace Dieu Brook

Mill House

21

THE TOFT

MARKET PL

Hillcrest Research Sta

PH
PO

Belton
CE
Prim Sch

THORNHILL
AVE

CHURCH ST

BELL LA

THOMPSON

Belton

SANDHILLS
CL

SCHOOL LA

PIPER CL
ST

MARY'S CL

LE12

6

TYLERS RD

ST VERDUN AVE

ASHBY RD

Harboro' Farm

5

Micklin Farm

GRACE DIEU LA

20

Forest Field

4

FOREST LA

Low Woods

Fishpool Grange

ASTON RD

3

Low Wood House Farm

LOW WOODS LA

Hookhill Wood

Black Brook

NEWBRIDGE CT

BANBURY CT

Brookside

YEOMAN LA

19

CONWAY DR

DAVEY DR

PENISTA AVE

SANDHAM BRIDGE RD

2

TAMWORTH

Little Low Woods Farm

Blackbrook Farm

Blackbrook Hill House

White Horse Wood

LE67

Moyles Court House

ASHBY RD

Ringing Hill

ASHBY RD W

A512

PH

Finney Hill

1

Woodyton Farm

SWANNYMOTE RD

SANDHOLE LA

Fenny Spring Windmill

OAKLEY RD

PUDDING BAG LA

18

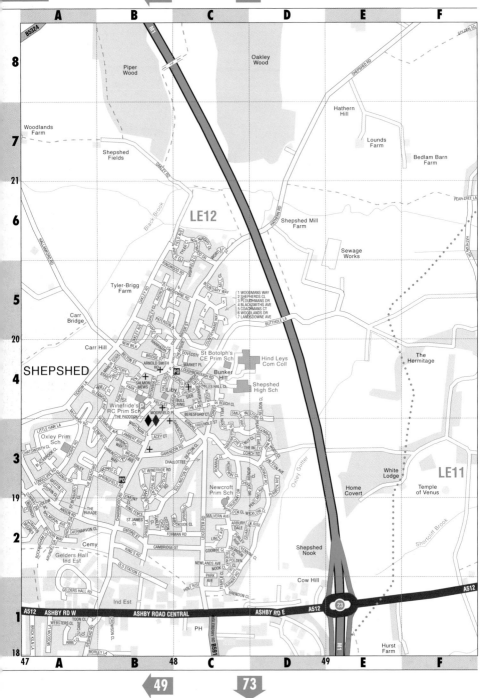

B5324

8

Piper
Wood

Oakley
Wood

SHEPSHED RD

Hathern
Hill

GOLDEN SQ

7

Woodlands
Farm

Shepshed
Fields

DARLEY RD

Lounds
Farm

Bedlam Barn
Farm

21

HALLBROOK RD

Black Brook

LE12

HATHERN RD

Shepshed Mill
Farm

PEAR-TREE LA

HATHERN RD

6

Tyler-Brigg
Farm

RINGWOOD RD

LANSDOWNE RD

OAKLEY RD

FIELD ST

NOEL HURST CT

WHARF LA

BOUNDARY WAY

Sewage
Works

5

Carr
Bridge

PATERSON RD

COURT WALK

COURTMANS WAY

1 WOODMANS WAY
2 SHEPHERDS CL
3 PLOUGHMANS DR
4 BLACKSMITHS AVE
5 COACHMANS CT
6 WOODLANDS DR
7 LANSDOWNE AVE

BUTTHOLE LA

20

Carr Hill

NEW WLK

HAWLEY RD

DOVECOTE

St Botolph's
CE Prim Sch

Hind Leys
Com Coll

The
Hermitage

SHEPSHED

FACTORY ST

BELTON ST
BRIDGE ST

Arnold Smith
HO

MARKET PL

LOUGHBOROUGH RD

Bunker
Hill

Shepshed
High Sch

4

GLENMORE

PARK RD

HALL CROFT

SALMON
MEWS

Lib

CHURCH ST

CHARNWOOD RD

CHARLES HALL CL

MILES HALL CL

Oxley Gutter

St Winefride's
RC Prim Sch

MOORFIELD PL

BULL
RING

BERESFORD CT

THE LANT

BEECH CL

The Paddock

WEAVERS

MARSHAL ST

LACEY CT

KIRKHILL AVE

FREEHOLD ST

SMITH CL

INLEY RD

MALVINA RD

CHARNWOOD RD

White
Lodge

LE11

3

Oxley Prim
Sch

LITTLE HAW LA

CHATSWORTH CL

DOILEY

FENWICK WAY

SPRINGFIELD RD

ST WINEFRIDE RD

CHALLOTTEE

GARENDON RD

HOLLOW RD

JOHNS CL

THE INLEYS

COACH RD

CARILLON CL

Home
Covert

Temple
of Venus

19

PINGLE CL

SHUTTLE CL

CHAPEL ST

DUMONT
CL

RING FENCE

Newcroft
Prim Sch

MILBURN
CL

POLLOCK CL

WICKLOW CL

Shortcliff Brook

ANSON RD

THE
PARADE

ST JAMES

OXFORD ST

BROOKSIDE CL

MALVERN AVE

LINLEY AVE

ARBURY
DALE

LINLEY RISE

SMITH CRES

Shepshed
Nook

2

FOX LOW WAY

CAERNARVON CL

KING'S RD

Cemy

FORMAN RD

CAMBRIDGE ST

COOMBE CL

POLDEN

NEWLANDS AVE

NOOK CL

PARK AVE

BRENDON CL

Cow Hill

A512

1

A512

ASHBY RD W

TOON CL

Gelders Hall
Ind Est

GELDERS HALL RD

OLD STATION CL

HOLT RISE

Ind Est

ASHBY ROAD CENTRAL

ASHBY RD E

A512

23

M1

Hurst
Farm

18

BRICK KILN LA

C MOSSOM

WEBSTERS CL

TOON CL

CANE CL

ABBE

MORLEY LA

PH

JEREMY RD

B591

47 A | **48** B | C | **48** D | **49** E | F

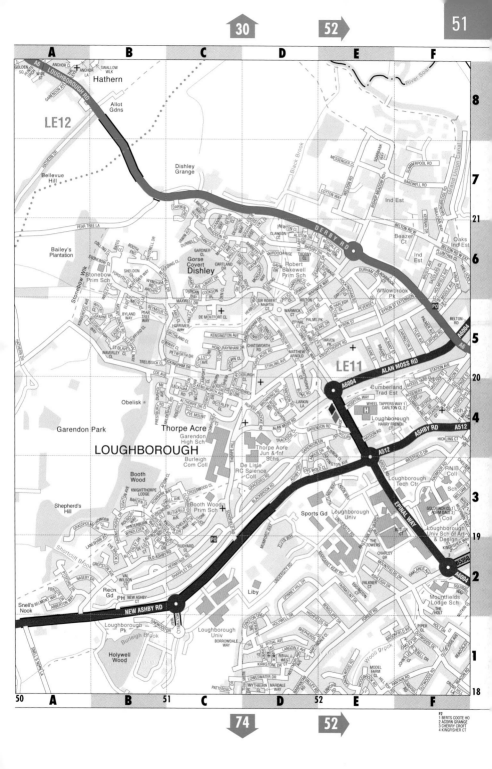

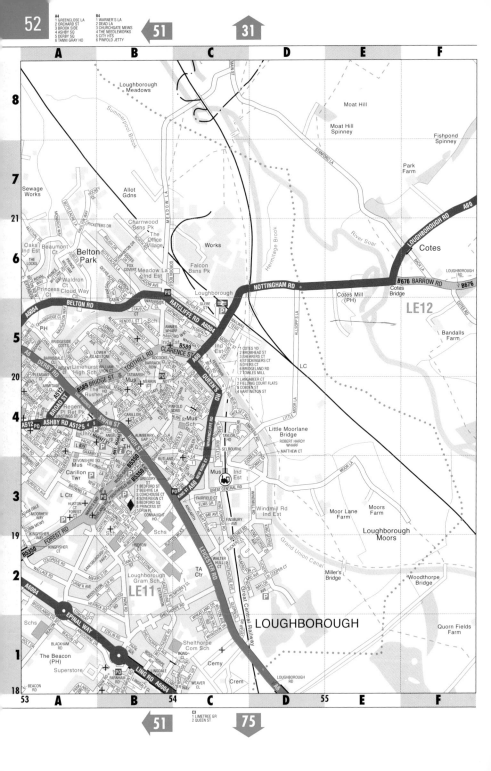

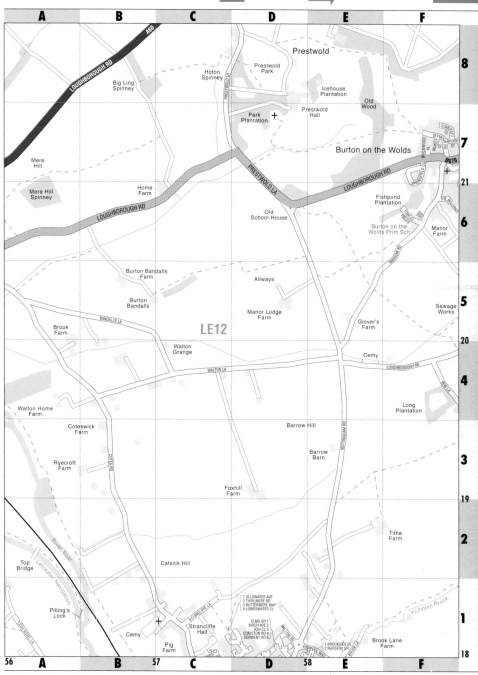

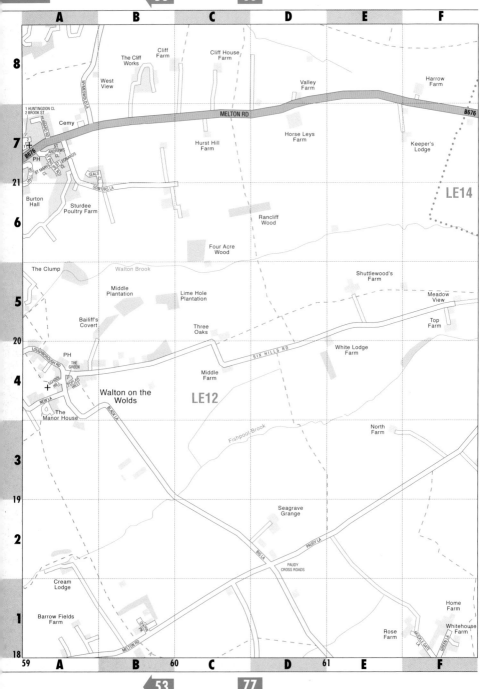

8

A | **B** | **C** | **D** | **E** | **F**

The Cliff Works
Cliff Farm
Cliff House Farm
West View
Valley Farm
Harrow Farm

WYMESWOLD LA

1 HUNTINGDON CL
2 BROOK ST

MELTON RD
B676

7

Cemy
Hurst Hill Farm
Horse Leys Farm
Keeper's Lodge

ST ANDREWS CL
ST LEONARDS
SEALS

21

ST MARYS CL

SOUTERS LA

Burton Hall
Sturdee Poultry Farm
Rancliff Wood

LE14

6

Four Acre Wood

The Clump
Walton Brook

Middle Plantation
Lime Hole Plantation
Shuttlewood's Farm
Meadow View

5

Bailiff's Covert
Three Oaks
Top Farm

20

LOUGHBOROUGH RD
PH
THE GREEN

SIX HILLS RD
White Lodge Farm

4

SCHOOL
HILL
POPLAR HILL

Middle Farm

NEW LA

Walton on the Wolds

LE12

The Manor House

BLACK LA

Fishpool Brook

North Farm

3

19

Seagrave Grange

2

BIG LA
PAUDY LA

PAUDY CROSS ROADS

Cream Lodge

Home Farm

1

Barrow Fields Farm

Rose Farm
Whitehouse Farm

MUCKLE GATE LA
GREEN LA

18

MELTON RD

59 **A** | **B** | 60 **C** | **D** | 61 **E** | **F**

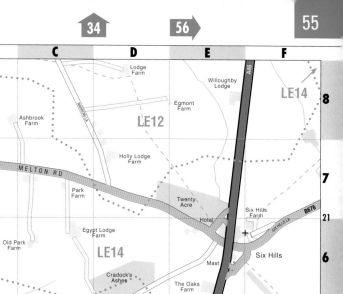

	A	B	C	D	E	F	

LE12

Burton Wolds

Ashbrook Farm

Lodge Farm

Willoughby Lodge

Egmont Farm

LE12

LE14

8

MELTON RD

Holly Lodge Farm

Seldom Seen Farm

Park Farm

Twenty Acre

Hotel

Six Hills Farm

B676

7

21

Old Park Farm

Egypt Lodge Farm

LE14

Cradock's Ashes

The Oaks Farm

Mast

Six Hills

6

Walton Thorns

Walton Thorns

Mount Pleasant Farm

Wolds Farm

Ragdale Wood

5

20

PAUDY LA

Lodge Farm

Seagrave Wolds

Thrusington Wolds Gorse

4

New York Farm

LE12

The Lodge

BERYCOTT LA

Bunker Hill Farm

Charlton Gorse Farm

3

19

LE7

2

OLD GATE RD

Thrussington Grange

Ck Brook

1

North Hill Farm

18

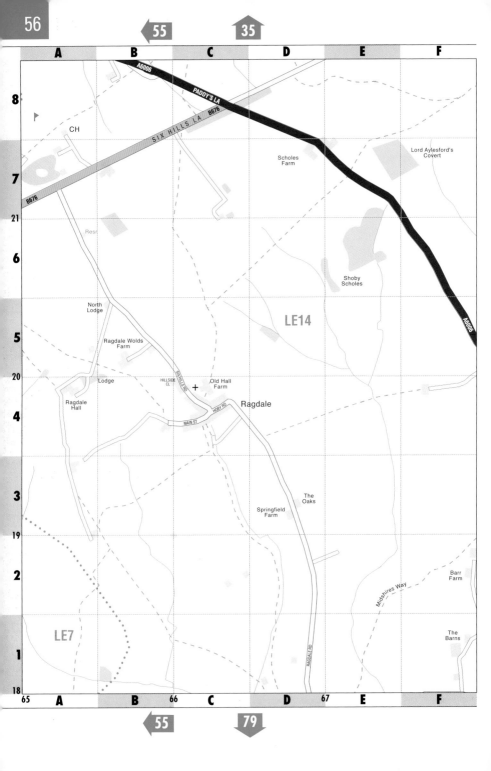

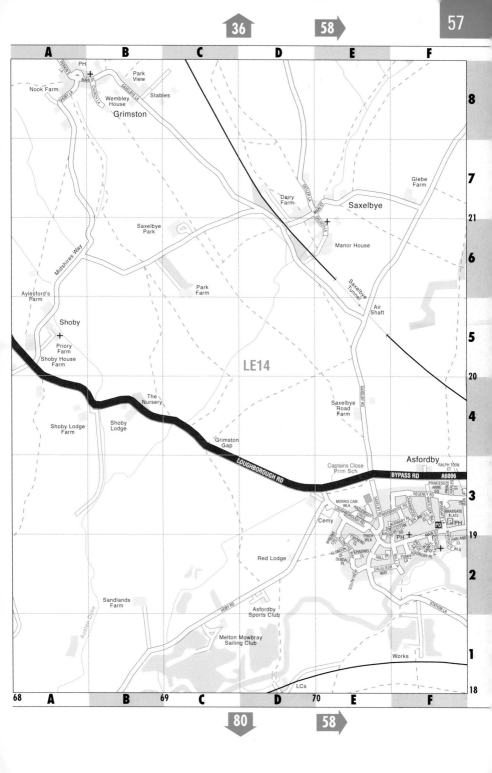

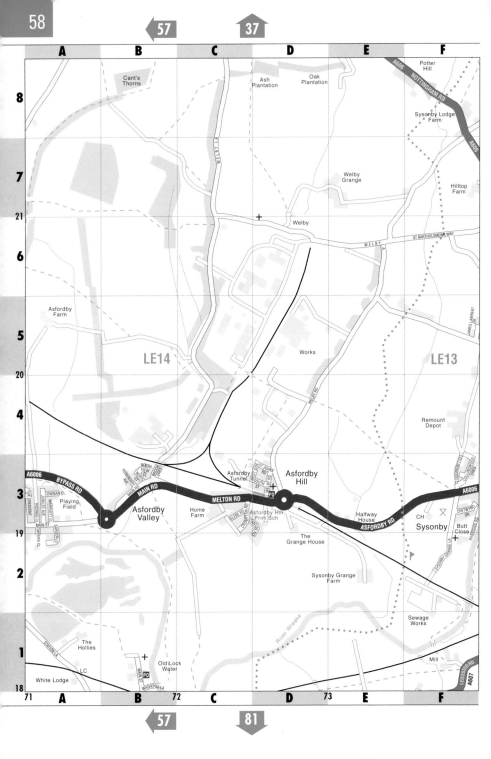

57
37

A   B   C   D   E   F

8

Potter
Hill

Cant's
Thorns

Ash
Plantation

Oak
Plantation

NOTTINGHAM RD

A606

Sysonby Lodge
Farm

A606

7

Welby
Grange

Hilltop
Farm

21

Welby

WELBY

ST BARTHOLOMEW'S WAY

6

Asfordby
Farm

LE14

Works

LE13

JAMES LAMBERT

5

20

Remount
Depot

4

A6006

BYPASS RD

MAIN RD

MELTON RD

NORTH
VIEW

Asfordby
Tunnel

ST JOHNS

SOUTH
ST

Asfordby
Hill

PO

ASFORDBY RD

A6006

Asfordby
Valley

Home Farm

Asfordby Hill
Prim Sch

Halfway
House

CH

Butt
Close

3

COWMAN CL

Playing
Field

JUBILEE AVE
MARRIOTT CL

GLEBE RD

Sysonby

CHETWYND

RIVERSIDE RD

19

CRESCENT

MAIN ST
SAXON

The
Grange House

LOCOMOTION CT
COL LIVERWOOD
DRIVE

2

The
Hollies

Sysonby Grange
Farm

ASFORDBY GRANGE LA

Sewage
Works

1

STATION LA

LC

Old Lock
Water

River Wreake

Mill

LEICESTER RD

A607

White Lodge

PO

WASHDYKE LA

18

71   A   B   72   C   D   73   E   F

57
81

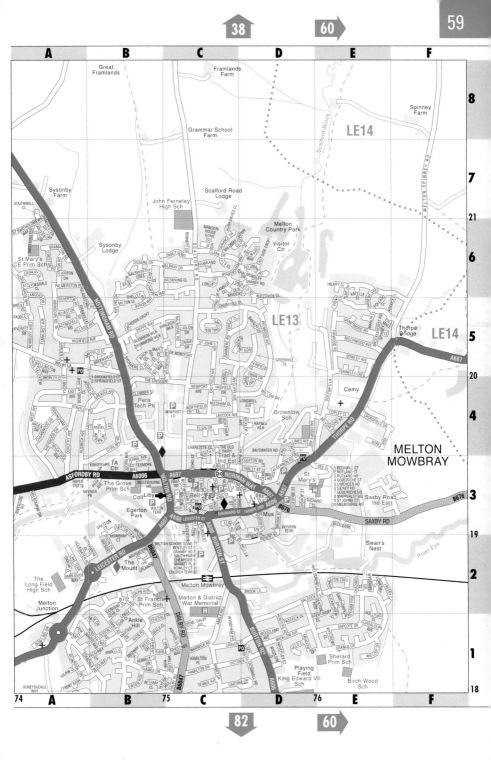

59 39

A B C D E F

8

West Lodge

Brentingby Wood

Pooles Lodge Farm

New Plantation

7

CH

Tumbledown Farm Park

Twin Lakes Park

21

Lodge Farm

Hills Barn Farm

6

LE13

Bell's Plantation

Ashleigh

Brentingby Lodge Farm

WOODLOUGA

5

LE14

Thorpe Arnold

Covermill Hill

A607

Church Farm

20

Rippons Plantation

Wyfordby Grange

Brentingby Lodge

4

L45 LA

Shipmans Barn Stud

B676

3

B676

Pinfold Lees Hill

Dovecot Nook Hill

Wyfordby

19

Woodbine Farm

LC

Brentingby

MAIN RD

Mill Hill

2

L45 LA

Brentingby Junction

West End Farm

The Hall

LC

LE13

River Eye

1

Burbage's Covert

Gravel Hole Spinney

18

77 A B 78 C D 79 E F

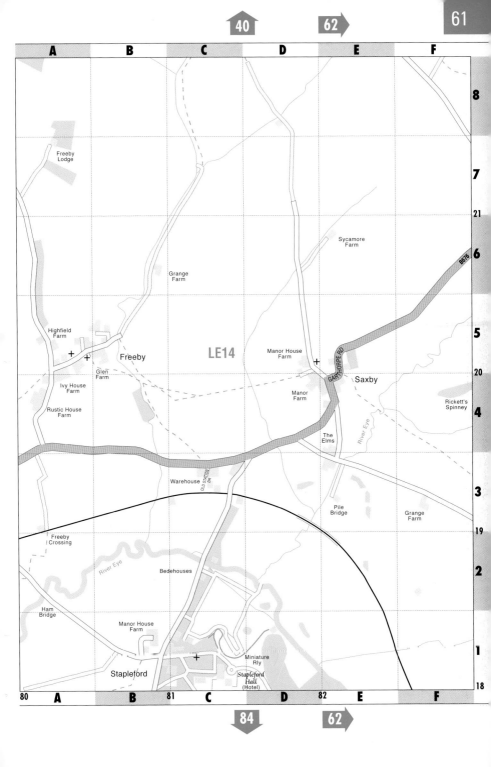

A B C D E F

8

Freeby
Lodge

7

21

Sycamore
Farm

6 B676

Grange
Farm

Highfield
Farm

5

Manor House
Farm

Freeby

LE14

GARTHORPE RD

Saxby

20

Glen
Farm

Ivy House
Farm

Manor
Farm

Rickett's
Spinney

4

Rustic House
Farm

River Eye

The
Elms

Warehouse

OLD STATION DR

Pile
Bridge

Grange
Farm

3

19

Freeby
Crossing

River Eye

Bedehouses

2

Ham
Bridge

Manor House
Farm

Miniature
Rly

1

Stapleford

Stapleford
Hall
(Hotel)

18

A **B** **C** **D** **E** **F**

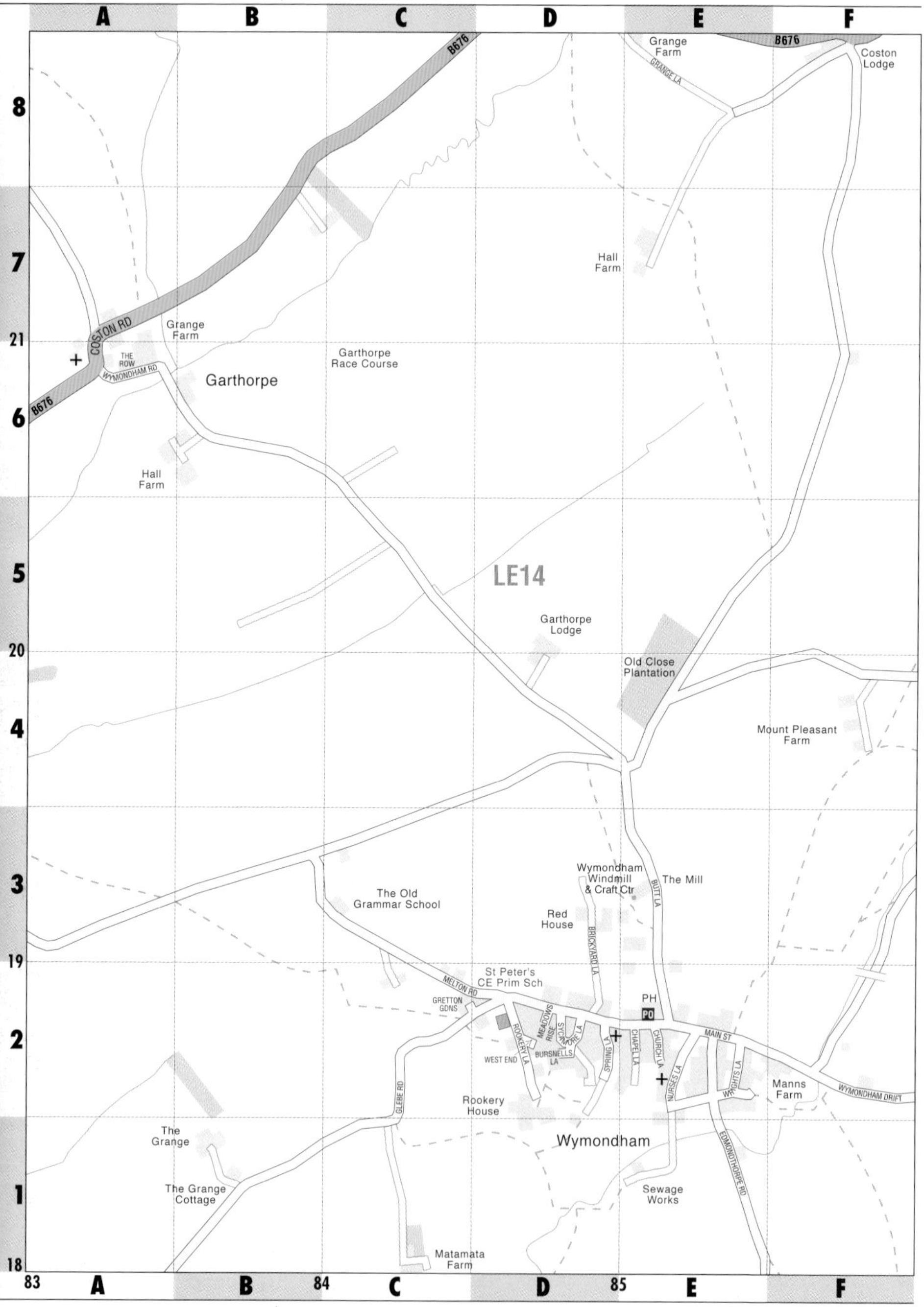

8

7

21

6

5

20

4

LE14

3

19

2

1

18

83 **A** **B** 84 **C** **D** 85 **E** **F**

B676

Grange
Farm

GRANGE LA

Coston
Lodge

B676

Hall
Farm

COSTON RD

Grange
Farm

THE
ROW
WYMONDHAM RD.

Garthorpe

Garthorpe
Race Course

B676

Hall
Farm

Garthorpe
Lodge

Old Close
Plantation

Mount Pleasant
Farm

The Old
Grammar School

Wymondham
Windmill
& Craft Ctr

The Mill

BUTT LA

Red
House

BRICKKILN LA

St Peter's
CE Prim Sch

MELTON RD

GRETTON
GDNS

PH

PO

MAIN ST

Manns
Farm

WYMONDHAM DRIFT

WEST END

ROOKERY LA

BURGNELLS
LA

ST JOHN'S

CHURCH LA

CHURCH LA

GLEBE RD

Rookery
House

Wymondham

EDMONTHORPE RD

Sewage
Works

The
Grange

The Grange
Cottage

Matamata
Farm

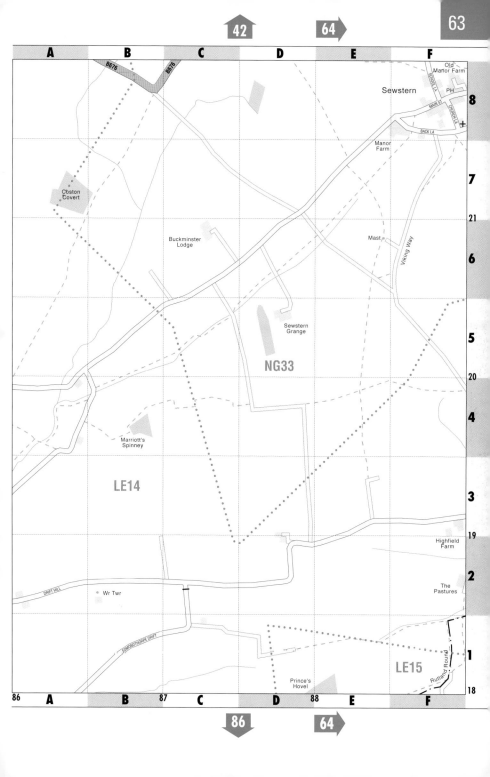

63
43

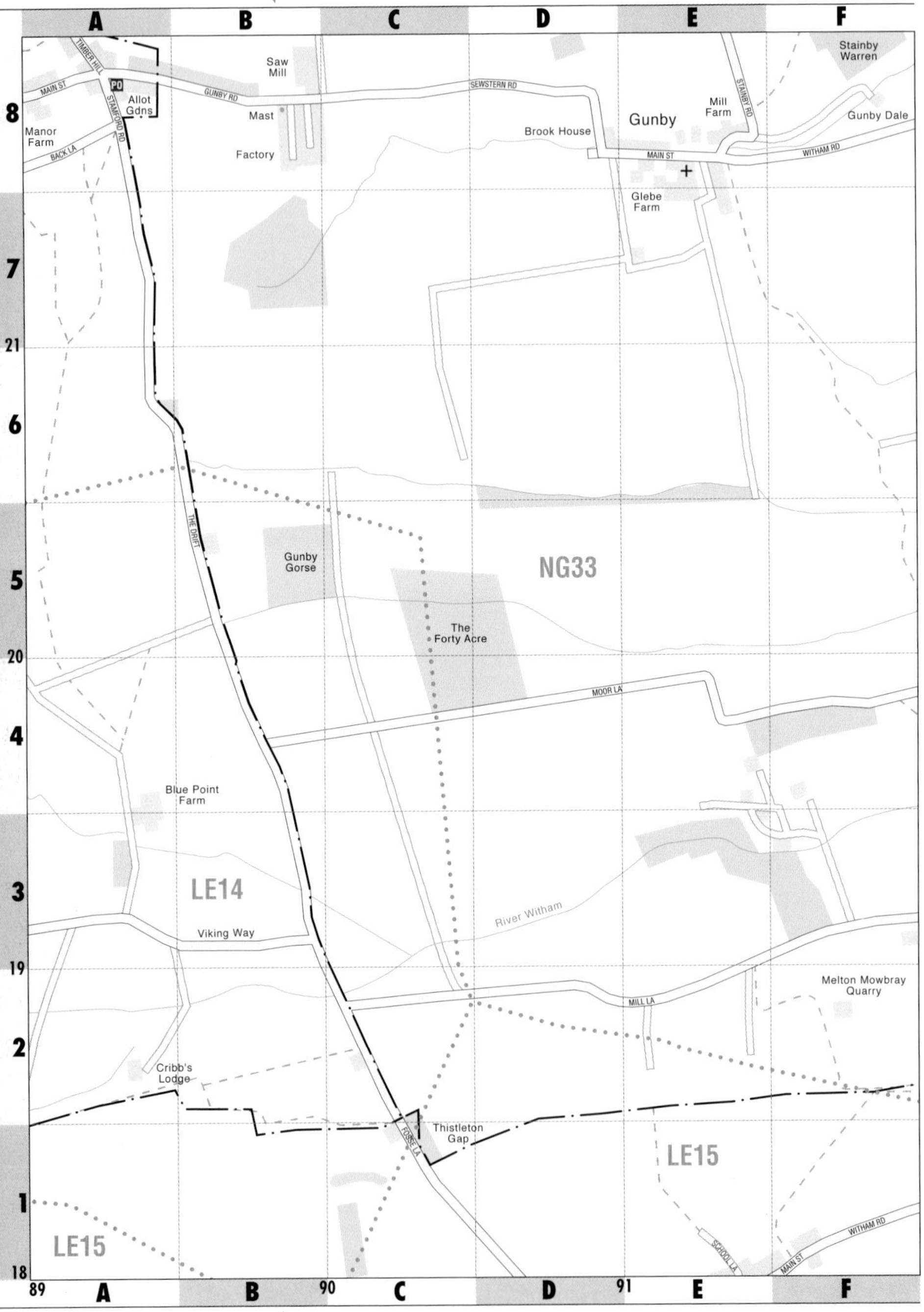

A **B** **C** **D** **E** **F**

8

TIMBER HILL
MAIN ST
PO
Allot Gdns
STATION ROAD
GUNBY RD
Saw Mill
Mast
SEWSTERN RD
Gunby
Mill Farm
STAINBY RD
Stainby Warren
Gunby Dale
WITHAM RD
Manor Farm
BACK LA
Factory
Brook House
MAIN ST
Glebe Farm
+

7

21

6

THE DRIFT

Gunby Gorse

NG33

5

20

The Forty Acre

MOOR LA

4

Blue Point Farm

3

LE14

River Witham

Viking Way

19

Melton Mowbray Quarry

MILL LA

2

Cribb's Lodge

Thistleton Gap
TURBINE ST

LE15

SPOOL LA
MAIN ST
WITHAM RD

1

LE15

18

89 **A** **B** 90 **C** **D** 91 **E** **F**

North Witham

HONEY POT LA

8

Mast
Black Bull
Farm

South Lodge
Farm Cottages
WOOLLEY'S LA

Hillview

BULL LA

7

Mickley
Cottage

21

Mickley
Wood

6

Temple
Hill

River Witham

NG33

Witham
Common

5

Battlebourn
Head

20

MOOR LA
UNWIN GN
LAUNDS
GN
THE
PARKSIDE
WIMBERLEY
WAY
WELLFIELD CL

Cemy

Sewage
Works

Woodbine
Farm

4

1 HALFORD CL
2 COVERLEY RD
3 HARRINGTON RD

South Witham

Fox Hill
(PH)

TOLLEMACHE FIELDS

South Witham
Com Prim Sch
PO

WATER LA
PRIORY

CHURCH ST
CHURCH CL
RUTLAND

Motel

MORKERY LA

HILL
VIEW
RD

Manor
Farm

HIGH ST
MARKET
CT
STATION AVE

PH

BROADGATE RD

South Witham
Nature Reserve

3

MILL LA

RAILWAY CL

THISTLE CL
PENGELLY CL

19

WITHAM RD

2

Green La

Morkery Wood

LE15

Stanton
Plantation

1

65

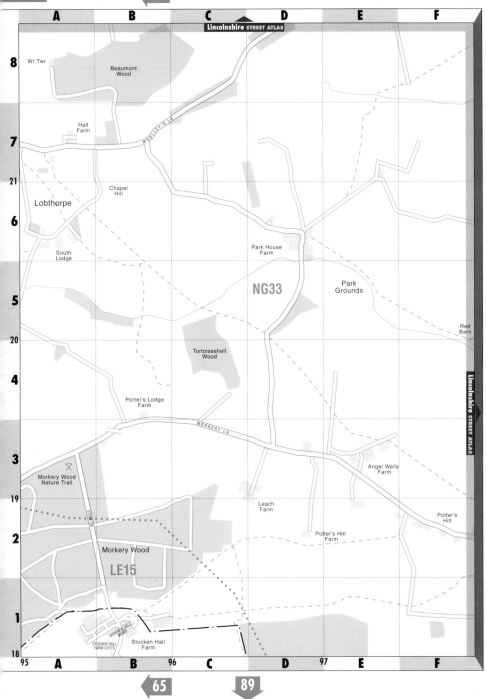

Lincolnshire STREET ATLAS

Lincolnshire STREET ATLAS

Wr Twr

Beaumont Wood

Hall Farm

WOOLLEY'S LA

Chapel Hill

Lobthorpe

South Lodge

Park House Farm

NG33

Park Grounds

Red Barn

Tortoiseshell Wood

Porter's Lodge Farm

MORKERY LA

Angel Wells Farm

Morkery Wood Nature Trail

Leach Farm

Potter's Hill

STUB LA

Potter's Hill Farm

Morkery Wood

LE15

STOCKEN HALL MEWS

STOCKEN HALL FARM COTTS

Stocken Hall Farm

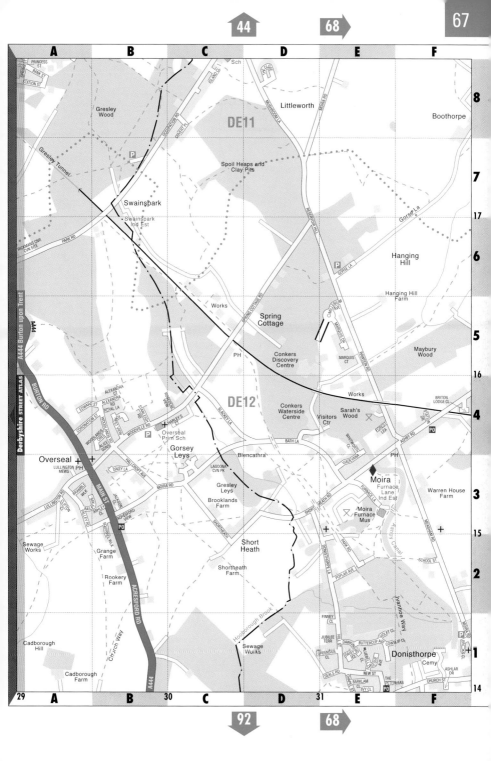

A B C D E F

8

Gresley
Wood

DE11

Littleworth

Boothorpe

Spoil Heaps and
Clay Pits

7

17

Swainspark

Swainspark
Ind Est

Gorse La

Hanging
Hill

6

Hanging Hill
Farm

Works

Spring
Cottage

Maybury
Wood

5

16

PH

Conkers
Discovery
Centre

MARQUIS
CT

DE12

Works

BRITON
LODGE CL

4

Conkers
Waterside
Centre

Visitors
Ctr

Sarah's
Wood

Overseal
Prim Sch

PO

Gorsey
Leys

Bath La

Blencathra

PH

Overseal

Moira

Furnace
Lane
Ind Est

Warren House
Farm

Gresley
Leys

Brooklands
Farm

Moira
Furnace
Mus

3

15

Short
Heath

Sewage
Works

Shortheath
Farm

2

Ivanhoe Way

Cadborough
Hill

Finney
Cl

Jubilee
Terr

PO

Donisthorpe

Cemy

1

Sewage
Works

14

Cadborough
Farm

Grange
Farm

Rookery
Farm

A B C D E F

A444 Burton upon Trent

Derbyshire STREET ATLAS

BURTON RD

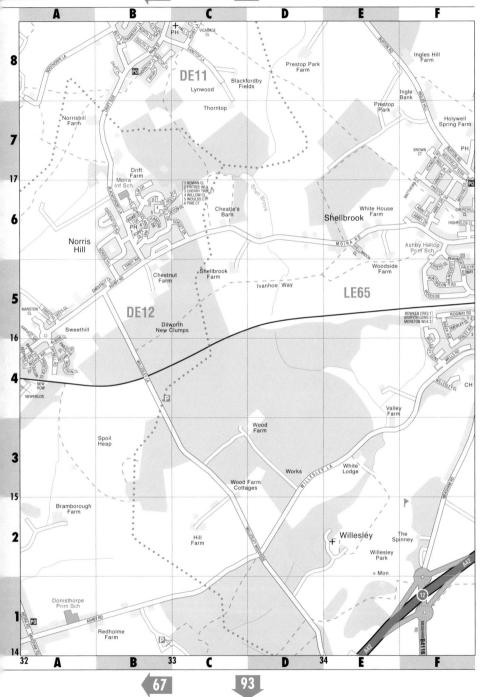

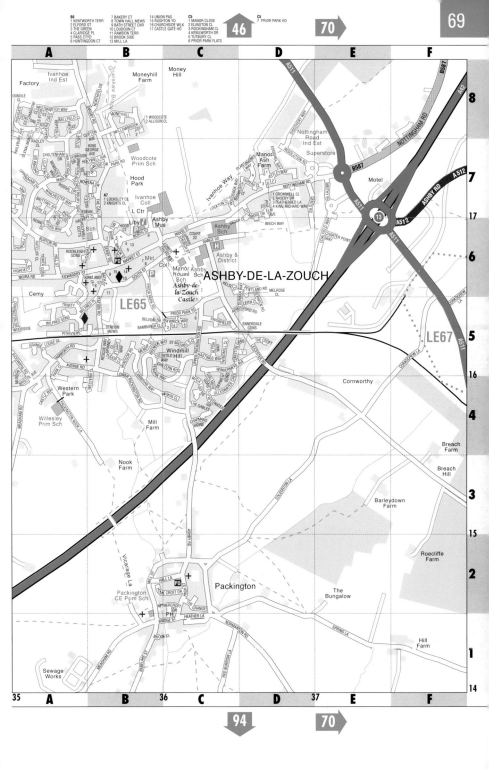

B6
1 KENTWORTH TERR
2 ELFORD ST
3 THE GREEN
4 CLARIDGE PL
5 PASS CTYD
6 HUNTINGDON CT

7 BAKERY CT
8 TOWN HALL MEWS
9 BATH STREET CNR
10 LOUGOUN CT
11 RAWDON TERR
12 BROOK SIDE
13 MILL LA

14 UNION PAS
15 RUSHTON YD
16 CHURCHSIDE WLK
17 CASTLE GATE HO

C5
1 MANOR CLOSE
2 ELVASTON CL
3 ROCKINGHAM CL
4 KENILWORTH DR
5 TUTBURY CL
6 PRIOR PARK FLATS

C5
7 PRIOR PARK HO

46

70

69

ASHBY-DE-LA-ZOUCH

LE65

LE67

Packington

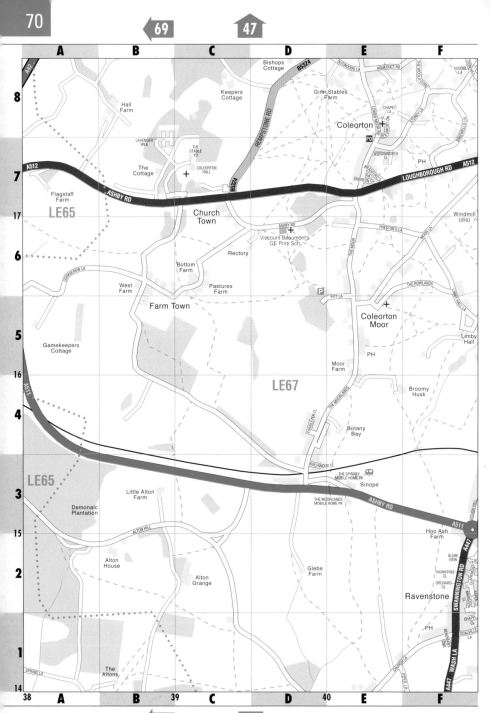

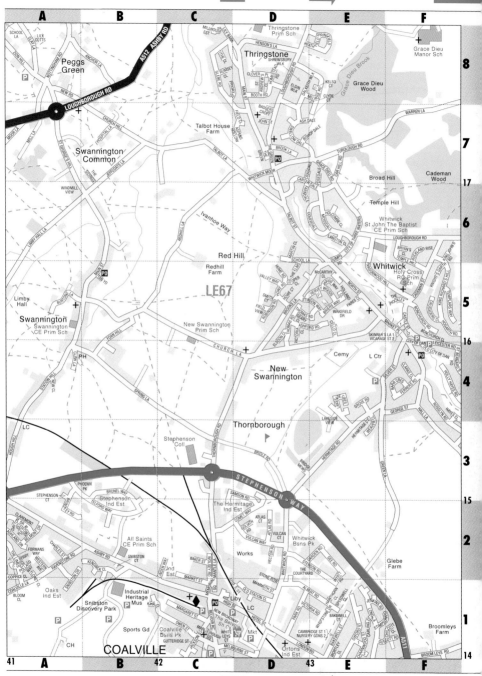

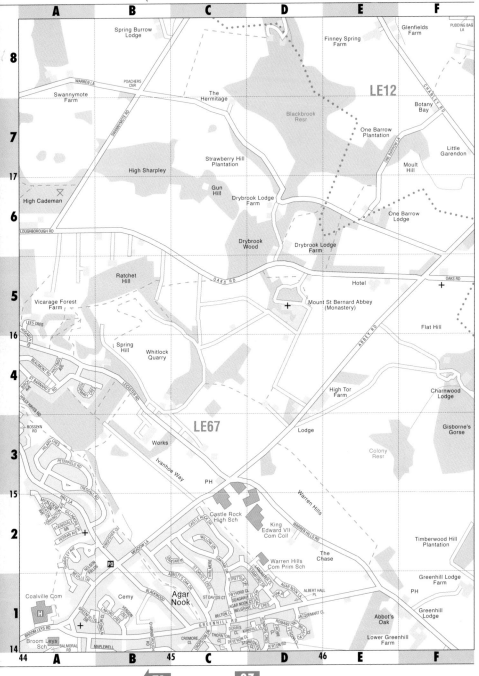

71
49

A **B** **C** **D** **E** **F**

8

Spring Burrow Lodge

Finney Spring Farm

Glenfields Farm

PUDDING BAG LA

WARREN LA

POACHERS CNR

LE12

Botany Bay

7

Swannymote Farm

The Hermitage

Blackbrook Resr

One Barrow Plantation

CHARNEY RD

Little Garendon

17

SWANNYMOTE RD

High Sharpley

Strawberry Hill Plantation

Moult Hill

6

High Cademan

Gun Hill

Drybrook Lodge Farm

ONE BARROW RD

One Barrow Lodge

LOUGHBOROUGH RD

Drybrook Wood

Drybrook Lodge Farm

5

Ratchet Hill

OAKS RD

Hotel

OAKS RD

Vicarage Forest Farm

Mount St Bernard Abbey (Monastery)

Flat Hill

LEES CRES

16

Spring Hill

Whitlock Quarry

ABBEY RD

4

BEAUMONT RD
ST BARNARD'S RD
HASTINGS RD
BIRCH AVE
FOXLEY HAYES RD

LEICESTER RD

High Tor Farm

Charnwood Lodge

ROSSLYN RD

LE67

Lodge

Gisborne's Gorse

3

HILARY CRES
PETERFIELD RD

Works

Ivanhoe Way

PH

Colony Resr

15

MICKLETON DR
HALL LA
TRESSALL RD

Warren Hills

2

STANSDALE
PERRAN AVE
DR

Castle Rock High Sch

CASTLE ROCK DR

WILLOW DR

King Edward VII Com Coll

WARREN HILLS RD

Timberwood Hill Plantation

MEADOW LA

KINGS CLOSE DR

OAKLAND DR

The Chase

SHAFTS RD
NEVILLE DR
SELSEY FIELDS

PO

OAKSMERE
ABBOTT'S OAK DR
THIRLMERE
STRETTON
LANGMERE
AGAR NOOK LA

Warren Hills Com Prim Sch

Greenhill Lodge Farm

BLACKROD

Agar Nook

ST CHAD'S DR

TWYFORD CL
SEAGRAVE CL
AGAR NOOK CT CL
BELGRAVE CL

AGAR NOOK CL

ALBERT HALL PL

PH

Greenhill Lodge

1

Coalville Com

Cemy

CHARNBOROUGH RD

ST DAVIDS CT
BELTON CL
THORNTON CL

DURRIS CL

ROMANS CRES
BRADGATE CRES
JACQUEMART CL

Abbot's Oak

H

GREENHILL RD
CROMORE CL

KIRKHILL CL
DEVERON CL
THORPE
AIRTON CL
STONEACRE

ROMANS

Lower Greenhill Farm

BROOM LEYS RD

Broom Leys Sch

BALMORAL RD

MAPLEWELL

14

44 **A** **B** **45** **C** **D** **46** **E** **F**

71
97

73 51

A B C D E F

8

7

17

6

5

16

4

3

15

2

1

14

Holywell Hall

Burleigh Wood

Nanpantan

CH

Lodge

Nanpantan Hall

The Home Farm

Buck Hill

Charnwood Hall

West Beacon Farm

Beacon Cottage

DEAN'S LA

CHARLEY RD

SHELLS NOOK LA

LONGCLIFFE RD

PH

NANPANTAN RD

Works

P

WOODHOUSE LA

AMBLESIDE CL
Holywell Prim Sch
GUILDFORD WAY
NICHOLSON RD
MONTAGUE DR
TYNEDALE RD
LEONFIELD RD
GARENDON RD
 ANNESLEY RD
CHICHESTER CL

EXMOOR CL
CERE DR
WHITEHALL RD

Brooke House Farm

Wood Brooke

LE11

LOUGHBOROUGH

Sports Ground

Out Woods

Out Woods Nature Reserve

Lodge
The Outwoods Nature Trail

Outwood Cottage
P

Blackbird's Nest

Longhill Farm

Thorntree Farm

LE12

Beacon Hill

The Beacon Hill Country Park

Beacon Plantation

Broombriggs Cottage Farm

Beacon Hill

P

P

BEACON RD

BREAKBACK RD

CH

P

Broombriggs Farm Nature Trail

Windmill Hill

Broombriggs Farm Country Park

Broombriggs Hill

Broombriggs House

Outwoods Farm

Moat House

Woodbrook Vale High Sch

ROSEWOOD WAY

Halfway House

Pocket Gate Farm

Hangingstone Farm

BROOK RD

Hangingstone Hills

Breakback Plantation

Brook Road Farm

PH

PATTISON ST
PERRY CL
HERRICK CL
LUCKETT RD
BIRD HILL RD
WINDMILL RD
PATERSON DR

HILL RISE 1
THE DRIVE 2

MILL RD

MARYWELL RD

PO

50 A B 51 C D 52 E F

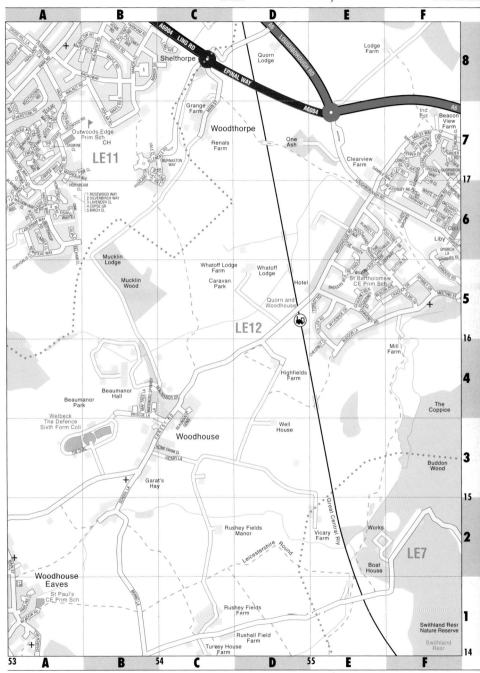

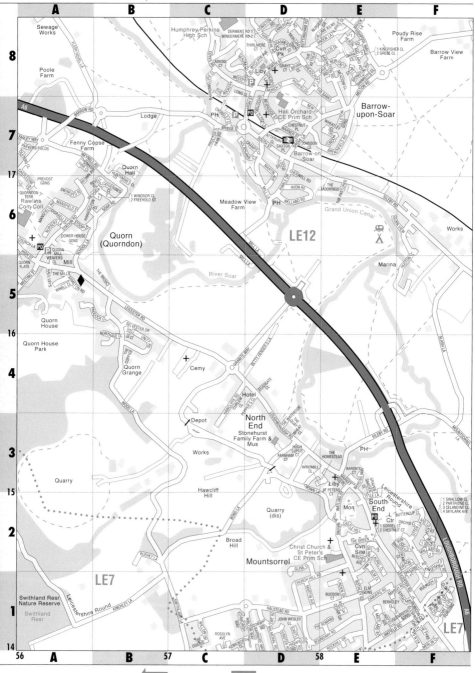

A B C D E F

8

Paudy Farm

MELTON RD

MUCKLE GATE LA

BANKS

GREEN LANE CL

WATER LA

CHURCH ST

BIG LA

Seagrave

KING ST

PO

Prim Sch

Cemy

SWAN ST

Hall Farm

HALL FARM CT

PH

Quebec House

7

Mast

17

Canbyfield Lodge

LE12

6

Sunrise Farm

Works

Hanover Lodge

HAYWELL

SILEBY RD

5

RUSHEY AVE

SEAGRAVE RD

Highgate Lodge

16

BARKING RD

Highgate Com Prim Sch

DRIVE

PRYOR RD

BRAMLEY CL

4

Sileby

Redlands Com Prim Sch

Sileby Memorial Park

PO

Bowling Green CL

WELLBROOK AVE

HIGHGATE RD

GREGORY'S

STANAGE RD

BARNARDS DR

AINSWORTH DR

1 NORTHILL CL
2 CLAIRE CT

C3
1 OLD TANNERY DR
2 SIMONS WLK
3 LAWSON CL
4 WILLET CL
5 CYGNET CL
6 JORDEAN CT

PH

Bsns Ctr

RATCLIFFE RD

3

MOUNTSORREL LA

THE MALTINGS

Liby

HARLEQUIN RD

Works

Chy

Cemy

PEAS HILL RD

Peas Hill Farm

15

Weir

Leicestershire Round

PRESTON CL

COSSINGTON RD

Blossom Farm

2

River Soar

Leicestershire Round

LE7

LE7

LC

1

Brook Farm

Glebe Lodge Farm

HUMBLE LA

14

59 A 60 B C 61 D E F

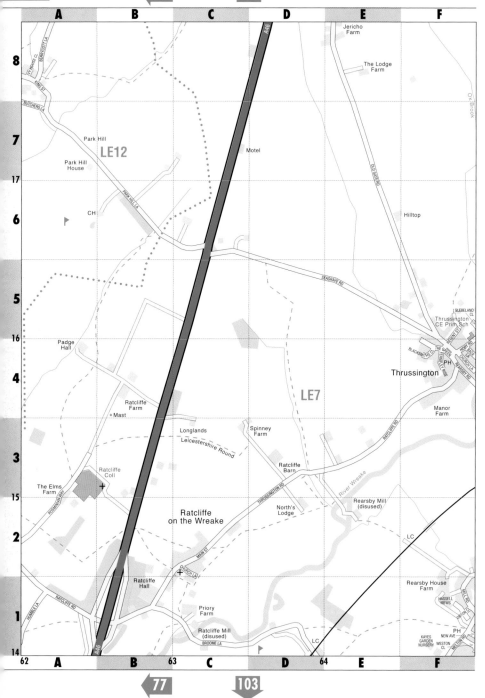

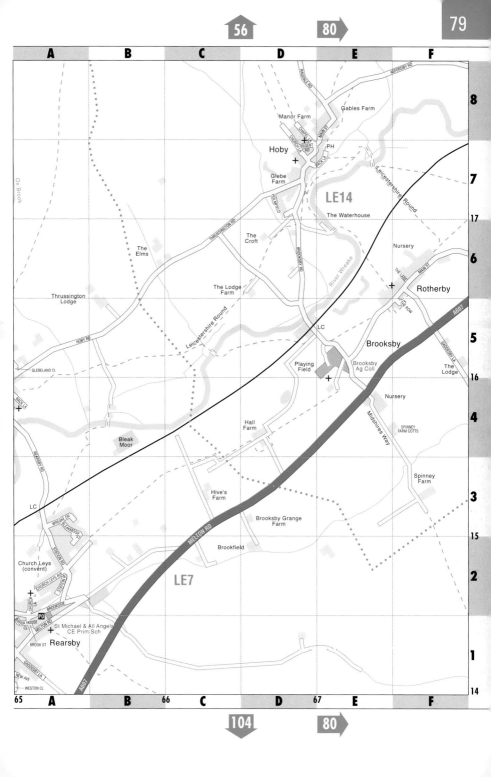

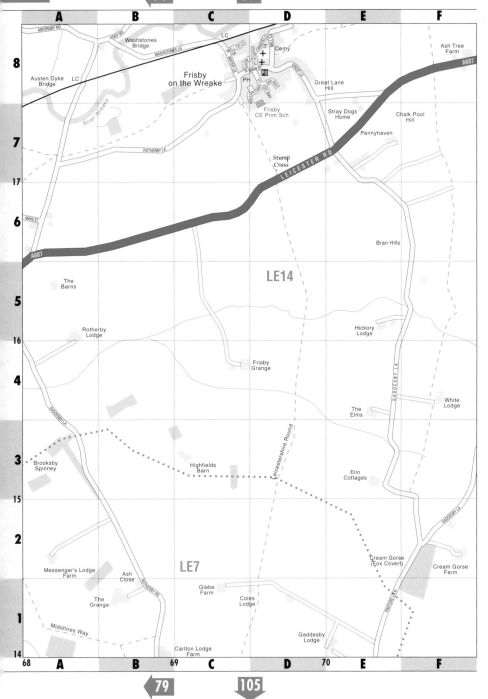

A   B   C   D   E   F

8

7

17

6

5

16

4

3

15

2

1

14

ASFORDBY RD

HOBY RD

Washstones
Bridge

WASHSTONES LA

LC

WELL END LD

WATER LA

Austen Dyke
Bridge

LC

Frisby
on the Wreake

River Wreake

ROTHERBY LA

Cemy

PH

PO

GREAT LA

Great Lane
Hill

Frisby
CE Prim Sch

Stray Dogs
Home

Pennyhaven

Chalk Pool
Hill

Ash Tree
Farm

A607

Stump
Cross

LEICESTER RD

Bran Hills

A607

MAIN ST

The
Barns

LE14

Rotherby
Lodge

Frisby
Grange

Hickory
Lodge

GADDESBY LA

The
Elms

White
Lodge

Brooksby
Spinney

GADDESBY LA

Highfields
Barn

Leicestershire Round

Elm
Cottages

GADDESBY LA

Messenger's Lodge
Farm

Ash
Close

LE7

ROTHERBY RD

The
Grange

Glebe
Farm

Coles
Lodge

Cream Gorse
(Fox Covert)

PASTURE LA

Cream Gorse
Farm

Midshires Way

Gaddesby
Lodge

Carlton Lodge
Farm

68

69

70

A   B   C   D   E   F

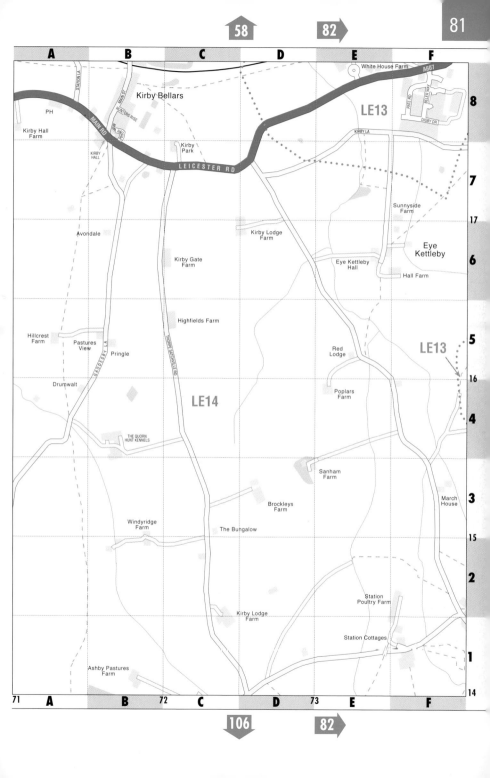

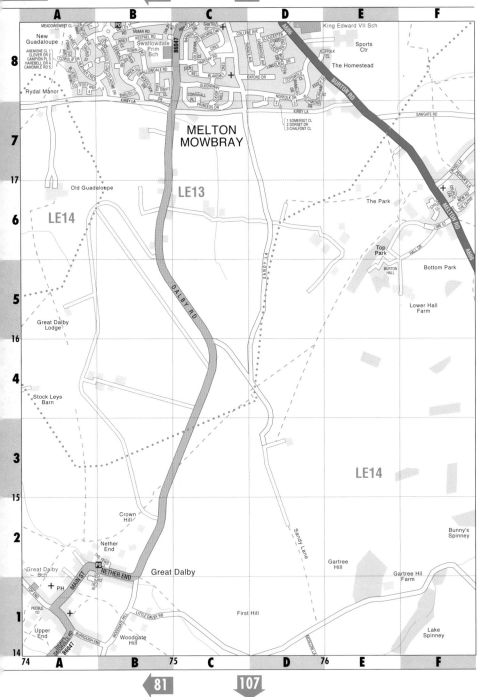

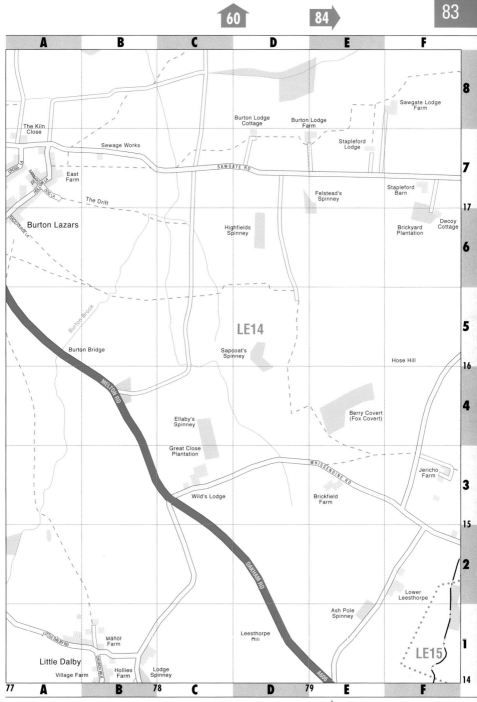

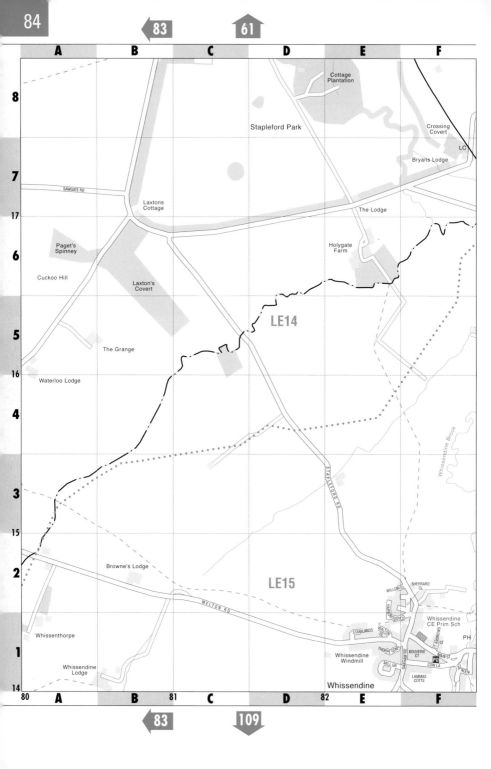

A   B   C   D   E   F

8

Cottage
Plantation

Stapleford Park

Crossing
Covert

LC

7

Bryans Lodge

SAWGATE RD

Laxtons
Cottage

17

The Lodge

Paget's
Spinney

Holygate
Farm

6

Cuckoo Hill

Laxton's
Covert

LE14

5

The Grange

16

Waterloo Lodge

4

Whissendine Brook

STAPLEFORD RD

3

15

Browne's Lodge

2

LE15

SHERRARD
CL

WILLOW CL

Whissendine
CE Prim Sch

MELTON RD

HARRI...
BOUGH...

PH

STANILANDS

MALTON
CL

ST ANDREWS CL

Whissenthorpe

THORPE CL

BOUVERIE
CT

DR RYLAND

MAIN ST

PO

1

Whissendine
Lodge

Whissendine
Windmill

MILL GR

COW LA

BROOK...

LAMMAS
COTTS

14

Whissendine

80   A   B   81   C   D   82   E   F

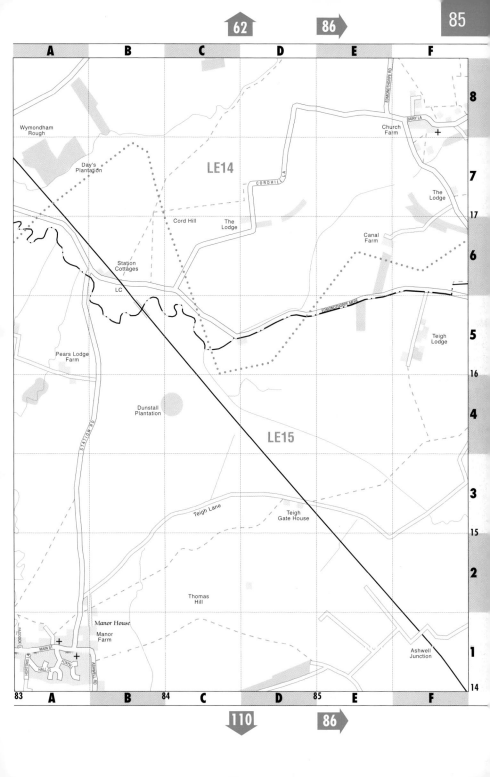

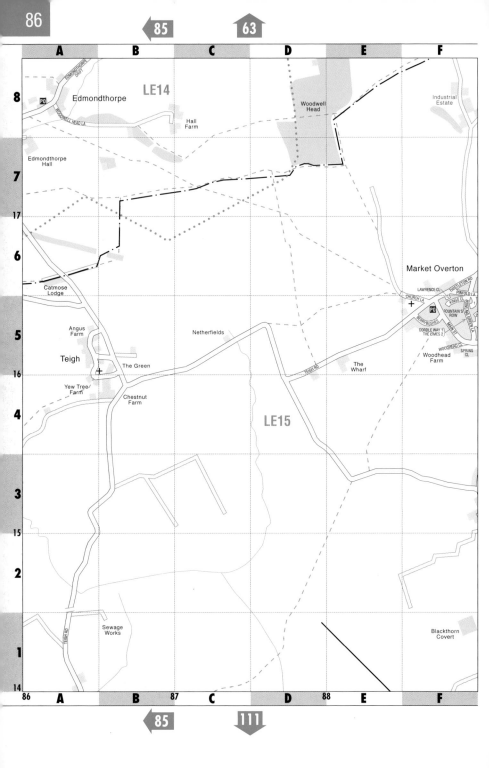

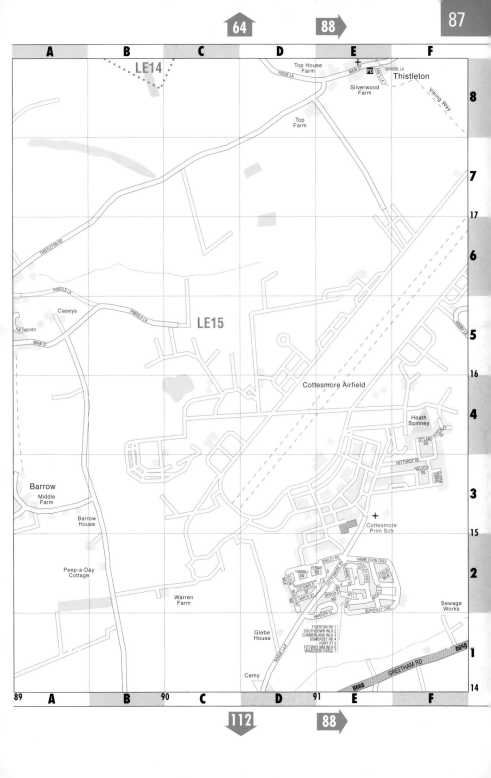

87

65

NG33

8

A B C D E F

7

17

Hooby
Lodge

NEW RD

6

HOOBY LA

5

16

The Viking Way

LE15

Ram Jam
Inn

B668

GREETHAM RD

CLIPSHAM RD

WALNUT
CL

SPINNEY
LA

PH

ROOKERY LA

CHURCH
LA

Stretton

4

Hotel

Greetham Lodge
Farm

3

White
House

15

STRETTON RD

Ye Olde
Greetham Inn

Greetham Wood
Near

2

CHURCH LA

SHEPHERD LA

GREAT LA

BULL LA

TITHE
BARN
ROW

LILY LA

Greetham
Quarry

PO

PH

NORTH BRICK
CL

LOCK'S CL

OAKHAM RD

MAIN ST

KIRK'S CL

BRIDGE LA

WHEAT SHEAF LA

Works

B668

1

Greetham

Brook
Farm

Mast

A1

14

92 A B 93 C D 94 E F

87

113

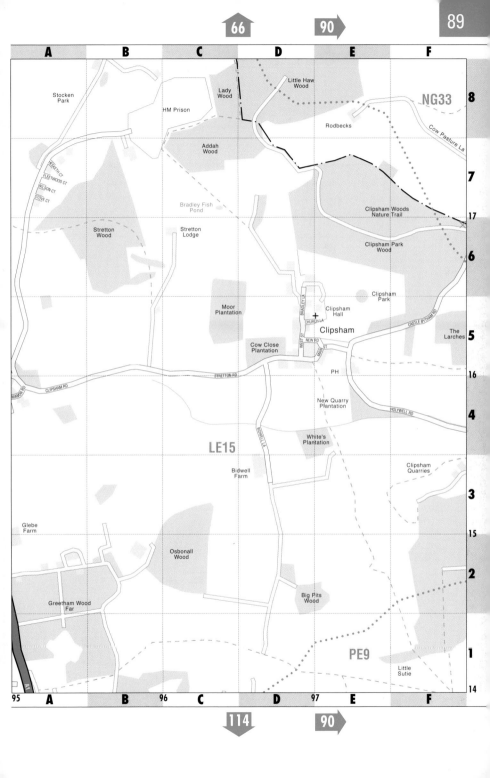

A   **B**   **C**   **D**   **E**   **F**

Stocken
Park

Lady
Wood

Little Haw
Wood

NG33

HM Prison

Rodbecks

Cow Pasture La

8

Addah
Wood

7

Clipsham Woods
Nature Trail

17

Bradley Fish
Pond

KENZIN CT
FLEETWOOD CT
WILSON CT
STOVE CT

Stretton
Wood

Stretton
Lodge

Clipsham Park
Wood

6

Clipsham
Park

Moor
Plantation

BRADLEY LA

Clipsham
Hall

CHURCH LA

Clipsham

CASTLE BYTHAM RD

The
Larches

5

Cow Close
Plantation

WEST ST

NEW RD

MAIN ST

STRETTON RD

PH

16

CLIPSHAM RD

New Quarry
Plantation

HOLYWELL RD

4

MAIN RD

BIDWELL LA

White's
Plantation

LE15

Clipsham
Quarries

Bidwell
Farm

3

Glebe
Farm

Osbonall
Wood

15

2

Greetham Wood
Far

Big Pits
Wood

PE9

Little
Sutie

1

N

14

95   **A**   **B**   96   **C**   **D**   97   **E**   **F**

89

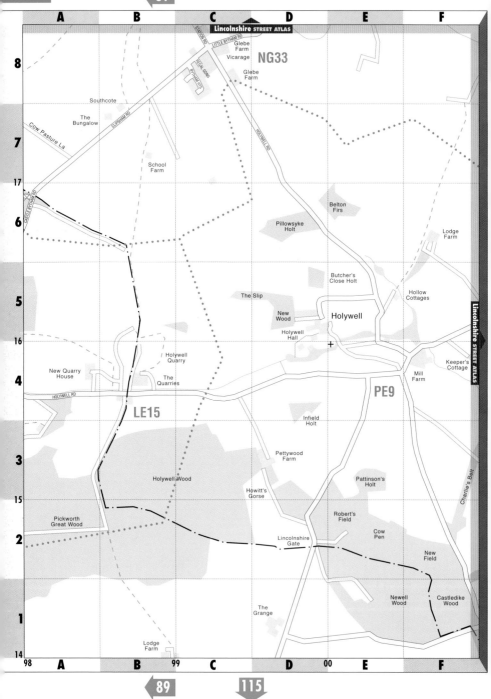

Lincolnshire STREET ATLAS

NG33

PE9

LE15

Lincolnshire STREET ATLAS

STATION RD
LITTLE BYTHAM RD
Glebe Farm
Vicarage
Glebe Farm
GLEBE GDNS
BY THE FLITTS
CLIPSHAM RD
Southcote
The Bungalow
Cow Pasture La
School Farm
HOLYWELL RD
CASTLE BYTHAM RD
Belton Firs
Pillowsyke Holt
Lodge Farm
Butcher's Close Holt
The Slip
Hollow Cottages
New Wood
Holywell
Holywell Hall
Keeper's Cottage
Holywell Quarry
New Quarry House
The Quarries
Mill Farm
HOLYWELL RD
Infield Holt
Pettywood Farm
Holywell Wood
Howitt's Gorse
Pattinson's Holt
Charlie's Belt
Pickworth Great Wood
Robert's Field
Cow Pen
Lincolnshire Gate
New Field
Newell Wood
Castledike Wood
The Grange
Lodge Farm

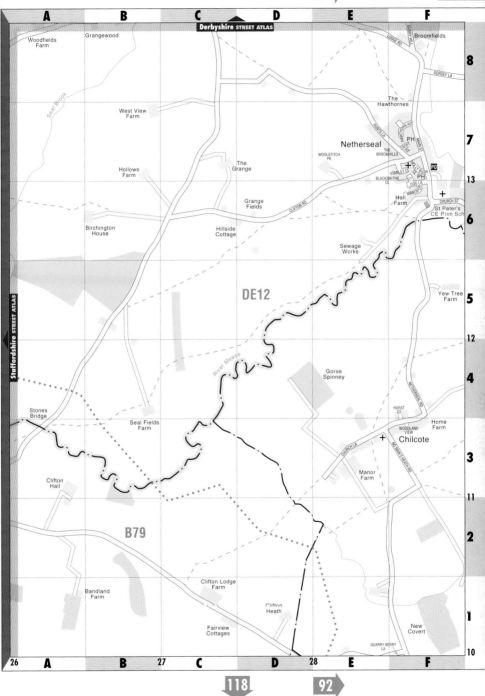

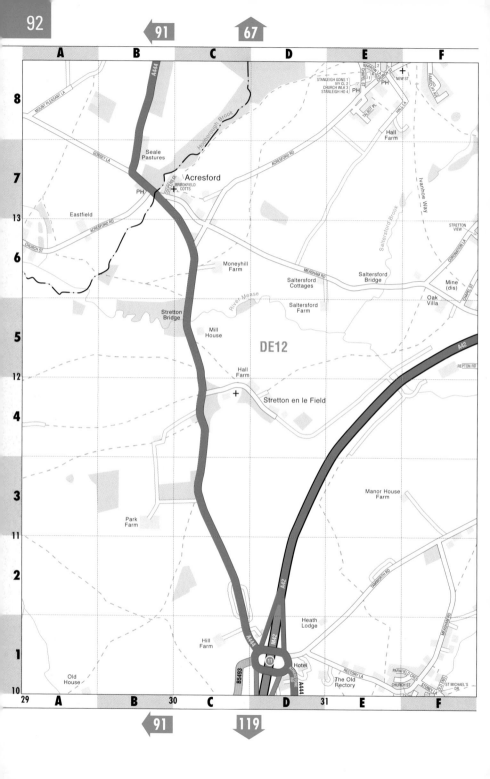

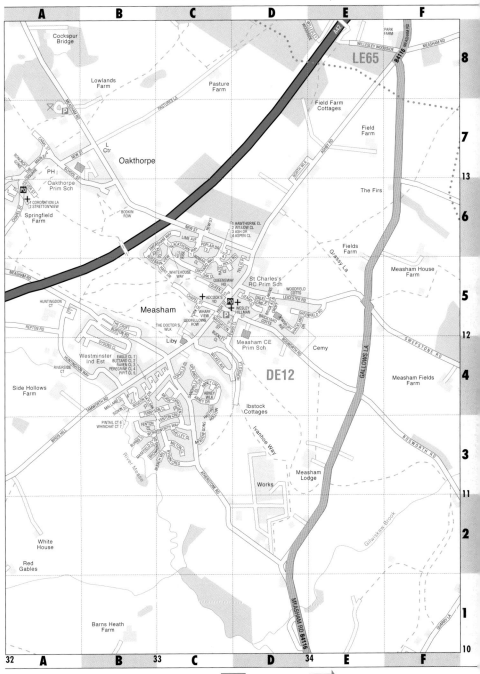

68
94

	A		B		C		D		E		F	

LE65

8

7

13

6

5

12

4

3

11

2

1

10

Cockspur Bridge

Lowlands Farm

Pasture Farm

Field Farm Cottages

Field Farm

PASTURE LA

WILLESLEY WOODSIDE

PARK FARM

MEASHAM RD

MEASHAM RD

CHESTNUT RD

CARR ST

NEW ST

SCHOOL ST

THE SQUARE

Oakthorpe

L Ctr

PH

Oakthorpe Prim Sch

CORONATION LA
STRETTON VIEW

Springfield Farm

CHAPEL ST

BODKIN ROW

NEW ST

NEW ST

LIME AVE

MEADOW WAY

BLACKTHORN WLK

BIRCH BANK

ROWAN WAY

ORCHARD WAY

HAZEL CT

TOLL ST

WHITEHOUSE WAY

OAK CL

POPLAR DR

1 HAWTHORNE CL
2 WILLOW CL
3 ASH DR
4 ASPEN CL

QUEENSWAY

QUEEN'S CT

ADCOCK'S YD

St Charles's RC Prim Sch

WOODFIELD COTTS

LEICESTER RD

Fields Farm

Grassy La

GRASSY LA

The Firs

Measham House Farm

Measham

Measham RD

HUNTINGDON CT

REPTON RD

THE CROFT

BURTON RD

DYSONS CL

Westminster Ind Est

HUNTINGDON WAY

RIVERSIDE CT

TAMWORTH RD

EAGLE CL 1
BUZZARD CL 2
RAVEN CL 3
PEREGRINE CL 4
PIPIT CL 5

WHARF VIEW

THE DOCTOR'S WLK

ODDFELLOWS ROW

Liby

RUSKIN CT

BLUNKET CL

ODDALLS CL

COPNALLS CL

WILSON CL

SANDOWELL CT

MALLARD CL

SISKIN CL

WICKS AVE

Measham CE Prim Sch

BOSWORTH RD

DE12

Cemy

ABBEY WLK

ABBEY DR

ASHBY CRES

NORRIS LA

MILTON CL

SWEPSTONE RD

GALLOWS LA

WESLEY HILLMAN

DALE GDNS
BRICKYARD COTTS

GREENFIELD DR

MASBURY CL

Measham Fields Farm

PINTAIL CT 6
WHINCHAT CT 7

FENTON CL

FENTON CRES

WORDSWORTH WAY

BURNS CL

MASEFIELD DR

BROWNING CL

BYRON CRES

KEATS CL

SHELLEY CL

BRIDGE HILL

River Mease

Side Hollows Farm

Ibstock Cottages

Ivanhoe Way

Works

Measham Lodge

Gilwiskaw Brook

BOSWORTH RD

White House

Red Gables

Barns Heath Farm

MEASHAM RD B4116

QUARRY LA

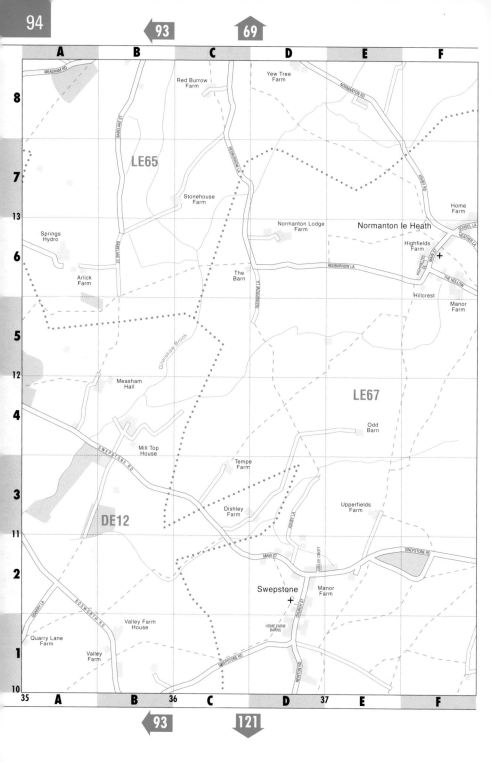

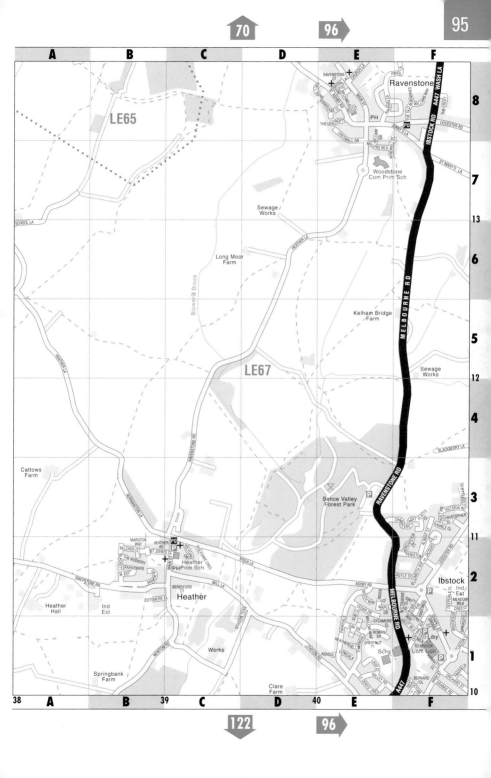

A B C D E F

8

7

Snibston

Grange
Farm

13

6

Berryhills
Farm

Smith's
Farm

Donington le Heath

5

12

River Sence

4

Blackberry
Farm

Blackberry La

3

Leicester Rd

11

2

Works

Clay Pit

Brookside
Ind
Est

Cemy

Pretoria Rd

Ibstock

Pig Farm

1

10

Pickering Grange
Farm

Belvoirdale
Com Prim Sch

St Clare's
RC Prim Sch

Scotlands
Ind Est

Charnwood
CT

Playing
Fields

Stephenson Way

Bardon Rd A511

Leicester Rd

St Mary's

Standard Hill

Frearson
Rd

Ash Tree
Rd

St Saviours

St Vincents
CL

Workspace
17

Harrison
PL

Stadium CL

Kemp Rd

Clifton Rd

North Ave

Moreton Ct

Cavendish Ave

Cameford CL

Berwick CL

Bardon Rd

The
Spinney

St Marys
Ct

Townsend La

Berryhill La

Hoyt's La

Meadow View

Tweentown

Manor Brook CL

PH

The Green

Allot
Gdns

Hugglescote
Com Prim Sch

Donington le Heath
Manor House

The Old
Surgery

Holly
Bank

St John's

Dennis St

Mill Lane

Peggs Grange

Grange Rd

Mill Pond

River Sence
Way

Recn Gd

Cemy

Grange Farm
Bsns Pk

Upper Grange
Farm

Louella
Stud

River Sence

The Elms

LE67

Broadmere Rd

Sports
Gd

South
Leicester
Ind Est

Midland Rd

Moira Rd

Chichester

Sherwood

Byron CL

Swinfen CL

Lawrence CL

Ibstock Rd

Ind Est

South St

Reveridge La

PH

Ellistown

Ellistown
Com Prim Sch

Rushes Way

St Christophers Pk
Cvn Site

Old School

Clay La

St Christophers Rd

East Cres

Victoria Rd B585

B585

Ellistown
Farm

Ellistown Terrace Rd

COALVILLE

Newbridge
High Sch

Hugglescote

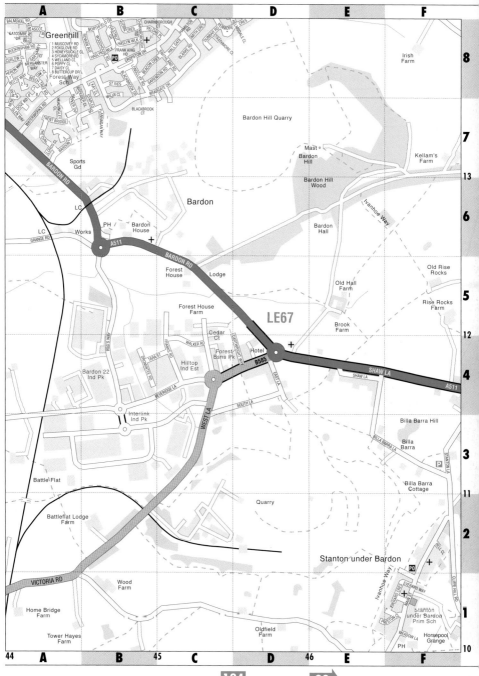

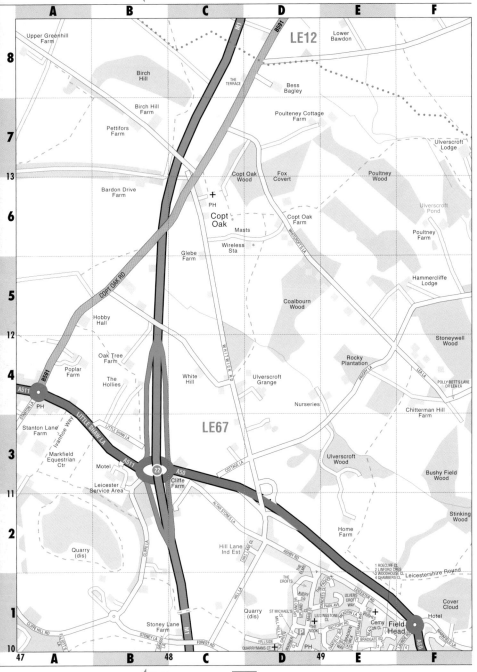

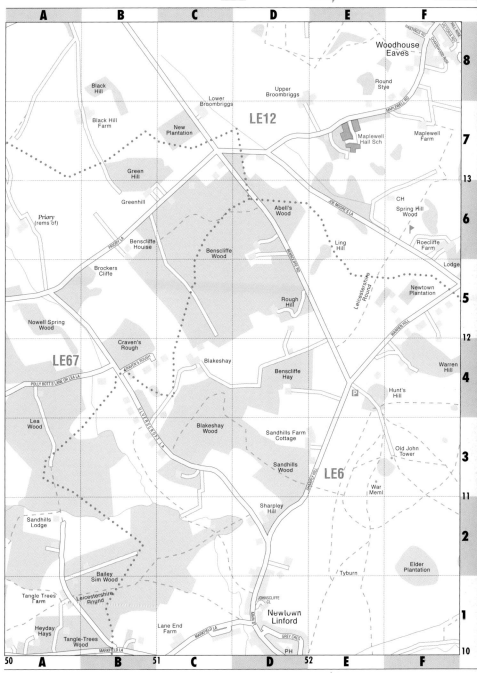

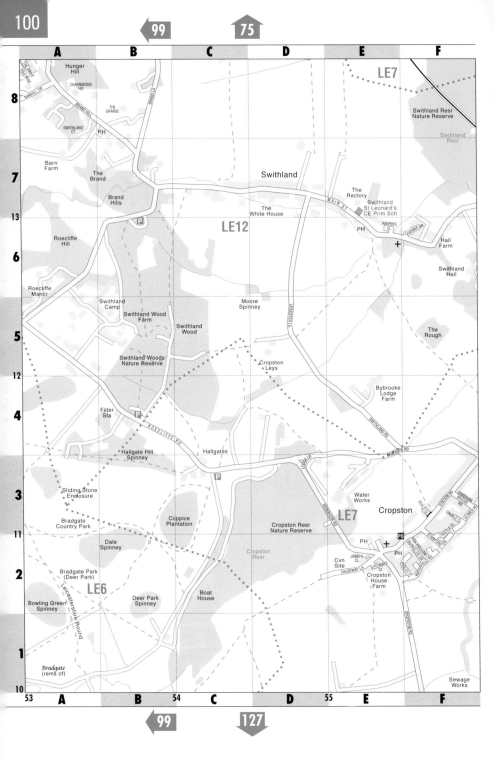

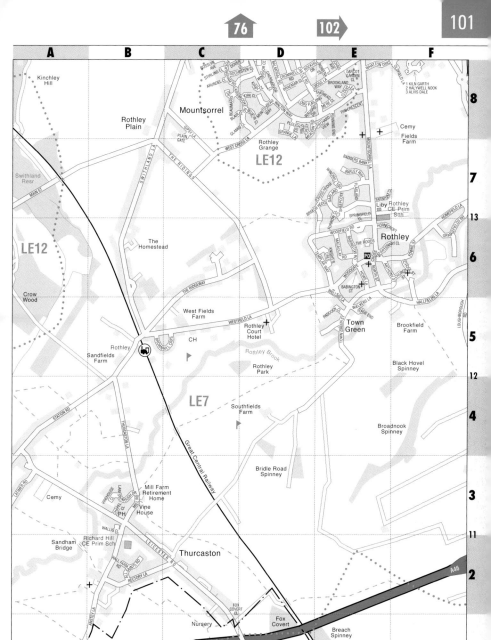

A   B   C   D   E   F

Kinchley
Hill

Rothley
Plain

Mountsorrel

Swithland
Resr

LE12

MAIN ST

THE RIDINGS

SWITHLAND LA

GIPSY LA
PLAIN
GATE

WEST CROSS LA

Rothley
Grange

LE12

ROSSLYN AVE
STIRLING CL
ARUNDEL CL
DOVER
ROCHESTER CL
YORK CL
GLAMIS

BOSWORTH RD
CROMWELL RD
BRAKEMAR CL
BUXTON CL
BRAXFIELD

HALFORD
CAMPHORARD
BILLSDON WAY
MONT'S BALL
PLOUGH
GRANGE LA

LONG FURLONG
CHURCHILL WAY
WHITE CRESCENT
MERE CL
CARPOT GARDEN CL
BROCKLAND
WAY
RUNNING END
ORCHARD
VIEW

MOUNTSORREL LA

WHATTON OAKS
SOMERS LA   1 KILN GARTH
2 HALYWELL NOOK
3 ALVIS DALE

Cmty
Fields
Farm   8

The
Homestead

Crow
Wood

THE RIDGEWAY

WESTFIELD LA

West Fields
Farm

CH

BADGERS BANK LA
PARLEY RD

BREECROSS ROAD
GARLAND
SHEEPCOTE
FERN
WINDMILL RD
RANDHILL
KNIGHTS

PEAK RD
WOODFIELD RD
HOMEFIELD
SPRINGFIELD
THE WOODS
MACKAY RD
KNIGHTS
RD
JOHNS MEAD

TARNCLIFF
Liby Rothley
CE Prim
Sch

Rothley

HOMEFIELD LA
GRASMERE DR

LE12

LEICESTER RD
BROADHILL CRES

Rothley
Sandfields
Farm

Rothley
Court
Hotel

Rothley Brook

Rothley
Park

WELLSIC LA
PADDOCK
WALKERS END
GORSE END

BABINGTON
CT
HALLFIELDS LA

HOMEFIELD NPT
GREENWAY CL
DOWN ST
CHURCH ST

PO

Town
Green

Brookfield
Farm

Black Hovel
Spinney

LOUGHBOROUGH RD

13

6

5

12

LE7

STATION RD

THURCASTON LA

Southfields
Farm

Broadnook
Spinney

4

Great Central Railway

Cmty

WINDMILL DR
LANE'S
CROFT
WALLIS CL
GROUP DR
PH

Mill Farm
Retirement
Home
Vine
House

Bridle Road
Spinney

3

11

Sandham
Bridge

LATIMER RD

Richard Hill
CE Prim Sch

Thurcaston

LEICESTER RD

HALL FARM RD
JAMES RD
RECTORY LA

+

A46

2

BRISTOL LA

FOX
COVERT

Nursery

ROWLANDSON CL
HOVERY
LA
LAWRENCE
FIELD CL

Fox
Covert

Breach
Spinney

LE4

HALLAM FIELDS RD

1

Park View
Riding Sch

A46

HARROWGATE DR

Birstall

10

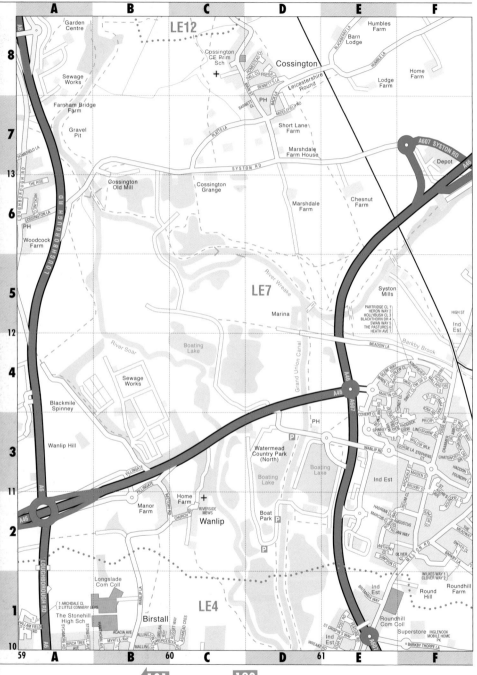

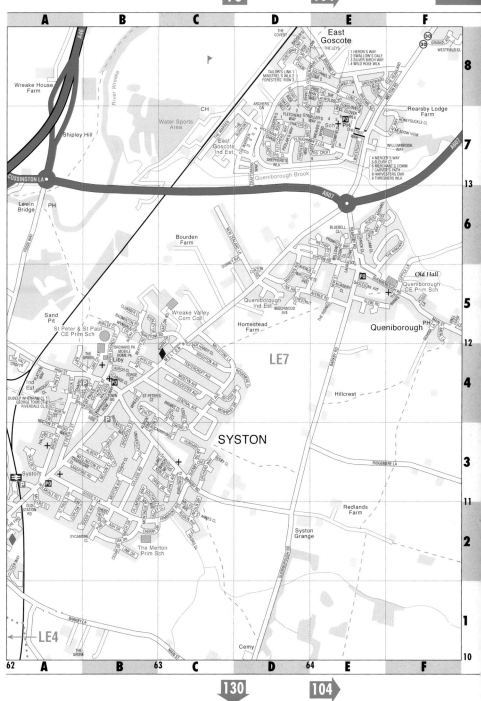

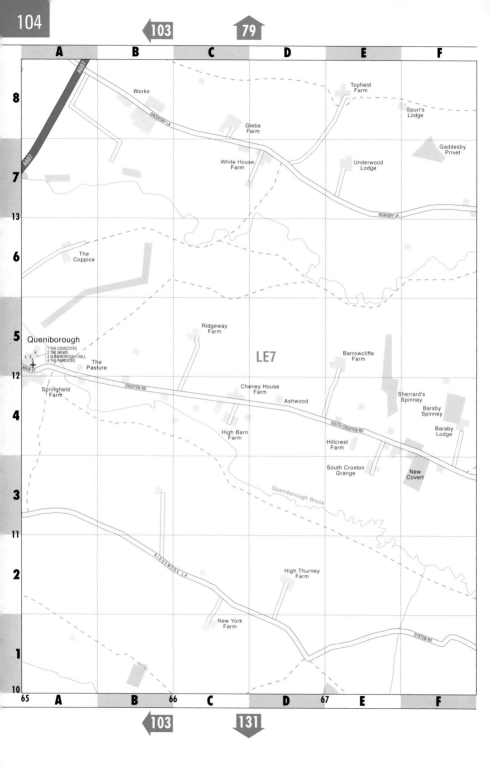

A   B   C   D   E   F

8

Works

Topfield
Farm

GADDESBY LA

Spurr's
Lodge

Glebe
Farm

Gaddesby
Privet

White House
Farm

7

Underwood
Lodge

A607

REARSBY LA

13

The
Coppice

6

Ridgeway
Farm

5

Queneborough

Barrowcliffe
Farm

1 THE DOVECOTES
2 THE MEWS
3 QUENIBOROUGH HALL
4 THE PADDOCKS

LE7

The
Pasture

MAIN ST

12

Springfield
Farm

CROXTON RD

Cheney House
Farm

Sherrard's
Spinney

Ashwood

Barsby
Spinney

4

SOUTH CROXTON RD

Barsby
Lodge

High Barn
Farm

Hillcrest
Farm

South Croxton
Grange

New
Covert

3

Queniborough Brook

11

RIDGEMERE LA

2

High Thurney
Farm

New York
Farm

SYSTON RD

1

10

65   A   B   66   C   D   67   E   F

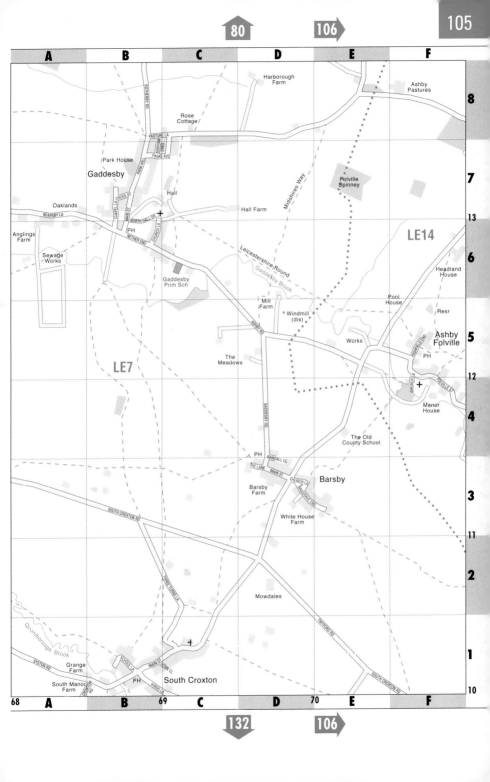

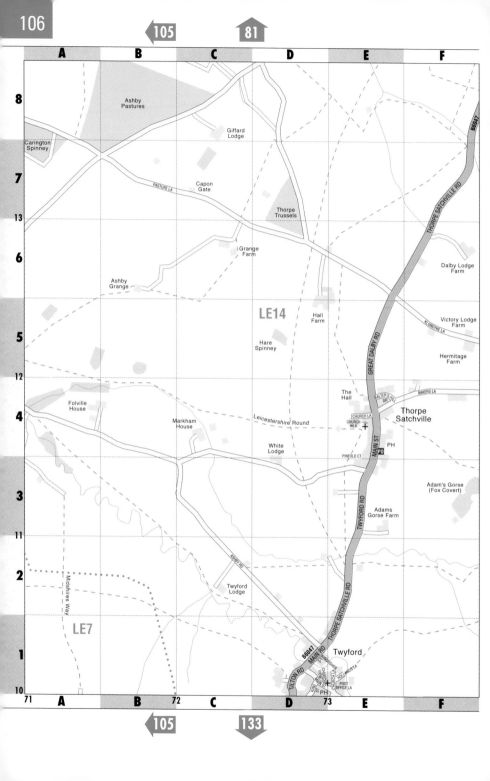

A **B** **C** **D** **E** **F**

8

Ashby
Pastures

Giffard
Lodge

Carington
Spinney

7

PASTURE LA

Capon
Gate

B6047

13

Thorpe
Trussels

6

Grange
Farm

Dalby Lodge
Farm

Ashby
Grange

LE14

Hall
Farm

Victory Lodge
Farm

KLONDYKE LA

5

Hare
Spinney

Hermitage
Farm

GREAT DALBY RD

12

The
Hall

SALTER'S HILL DR.

BAKERS LA

4

Folville
House

Leicestershire Round

CHURCH LA

Thorpe
Satchville

Markham
House

CHURCH
WLK

MAIN ST

White
Lodge

PO

PH

TWYFORD RD

PINFOLD CT

Adam's Gorse
(Fox Covert)

3

Adams
Gorse Farm

11

ASHBY RD

THORPE SATCHVILLE RD

2

Midshires Way

Twyford
Lodge

LE7

1

B6047

MAIN RD

TULTON RD

Twyford

CHURCH
VIEW
CL

KIRK
ST

PH

POST
OFFICE LA

HOLLANDS CL

POST
OFFICE

10

A 72 **C** **D** 73 **E** **F**

71 **A** **B** 72 **C** **D** **E** **F**

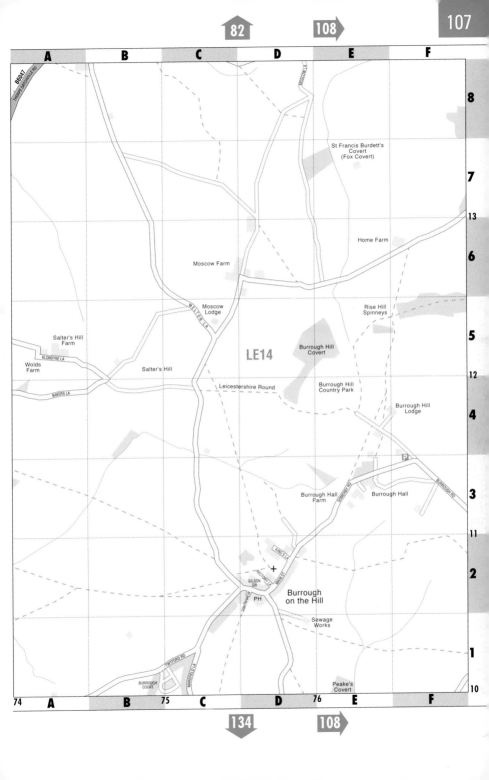

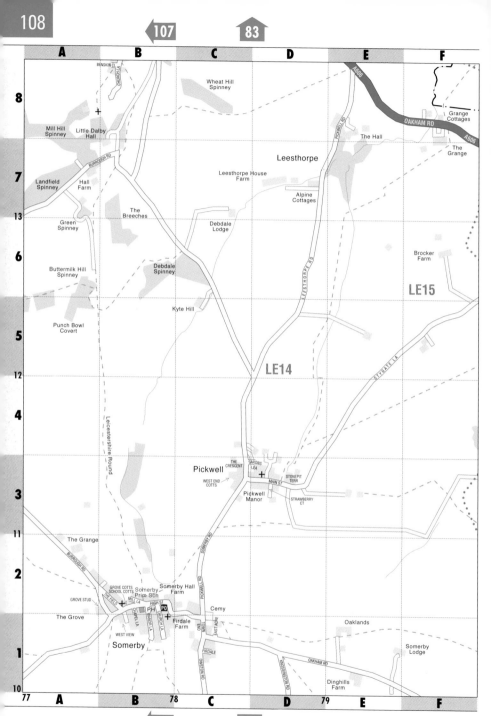

A   B   C   D   E   F

8

Wheat Hill
Spinney

BENSKIN CL

THORPE

A606

OAKHAM RD

Grange
Cottages

A606

Mill Hill
Spinney

Little Dalby
Hall

The Hall

The
Grange

Leesthorpe

7

BURROUGH RD

Landfield
Spinney

Hall
Farm

Leesthorpe House
Farm

POXWELL RD

13

The
Breeches

Alpine
Cottages

Debdale
Lodge

Green
Spinney

6

Buttermilk Hill
Spinney

Debdale
Spinney

LEESTHORPE RD

Brocker
Farm

LE15

Kyte Hill

5

Punch Bowl
Covert

STYGATE LA

12

LE14

4

Leicestershire Round

3

Pickwell

THE
CRESCENT

SAXONS
LEA

WEST END
COTTS

MAIN ST

STONEPIT
TERR

Pickwell
Manor

STRAWBERRY
CT

11

The Grange

BURROUGH RD

SOMERBY RD

2

GROVE COTTS
SCHOOL COTTS

Somerby
Prim Sch

Somerby Hall
Farm

PICKWELL RD

GROVE STUD

THE FIELD

MILL LA

HIGH ST

PH

PO

Cemy

Oaklands

The Grove

WEST VIEW

CHAPEL LA

CHURCH LA

Firdale
Farm

EAST ACRE

Somerby
Lodge

1

Somerby

DW RD

FIRDALE

KINGSTHORPE RD

OAKHAM RD

Dinghills
Farm

10

77   A   B   78   C   D   79   E   F

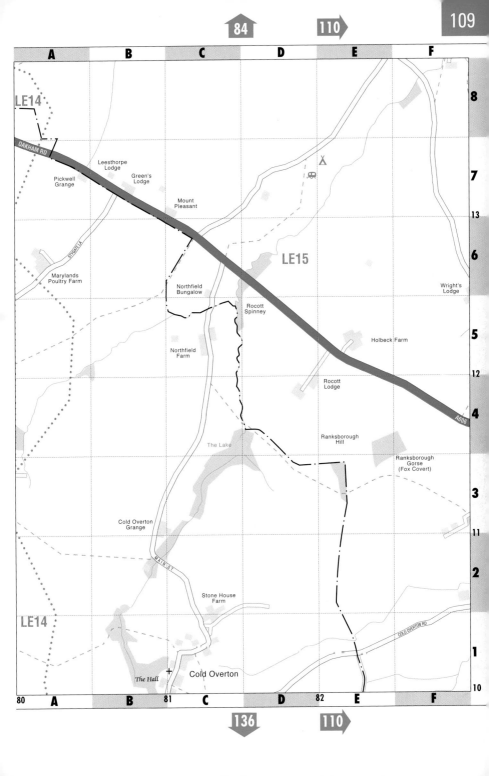

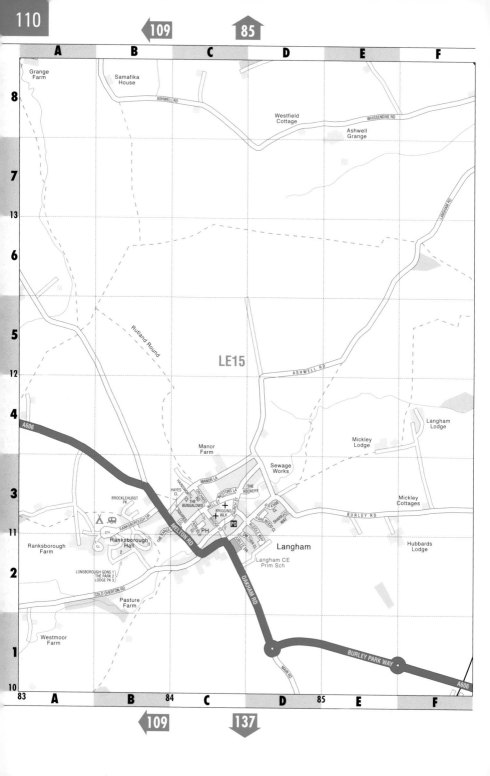

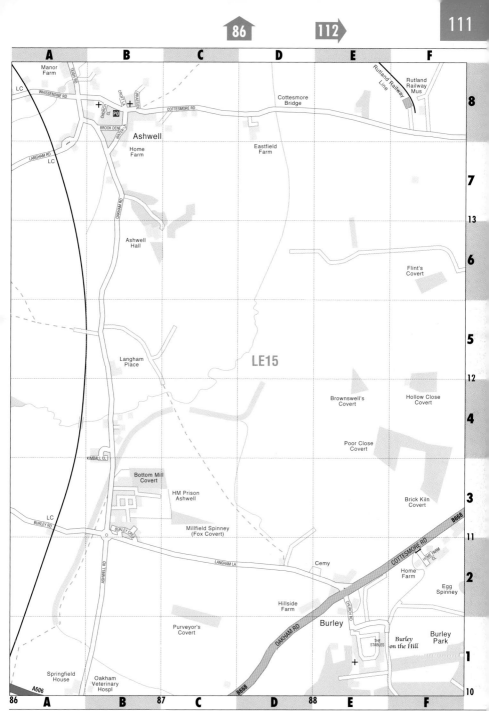

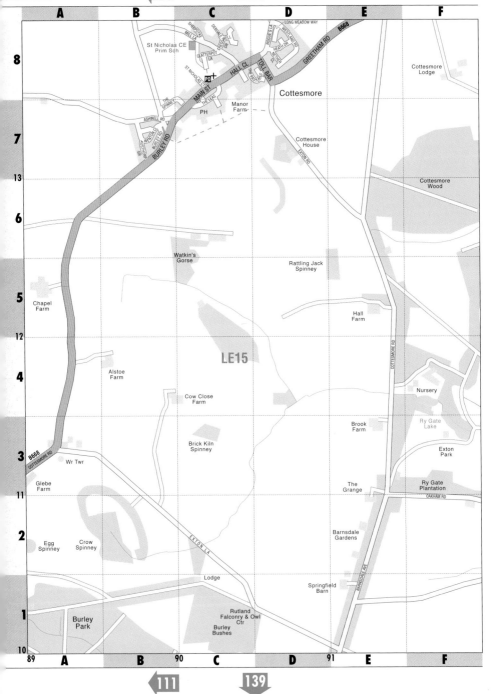

A B C D E F

8

7

13

6

5

12

4

3

11

2

1

10

St Nicholas CE Prim Sch

SHEEPCOTE
MILL LA
DERBAL RD
BELL
CLATTERPOT LA
ST NICHOLAS ST
THE SPINNEY
MAIN ST
ASHWELL RD
ASHTHORPE
EXTON RD
BURLEY RD
THE LEAS
PH
PO
HALL CL
TOLL BAR
THE POPLARS
POGUE'S LA
KEEL'S RD
HEATH DR
HEATH RD
LONG MEADOW WAY
GREETHAM RD
B668

Cottesmore

Manor Farm

Cottesmore House

Cottesmore Lodge

Cottesmore Wood

Watkin's Gorse

Rattling Jack Spinney

Hall Farm

Chapel Farm

LE15

Alstoe Farm

Cow Close Farm

Nursery

Ry Gate Lake

Brick Kiln Spinney

Brook Farm

Exton Park

B668
COTTESMORE RD

Wr Twr

Glebe Farm

The Grange

Ry Gate Plantation

OAKHAM RD

COTTESMORE RD

Egg Spinney

Crow Spinney

EXTON LA

Barnsdale Gardens

Lodge

Springfield Barn

BARNSDALE AVE

Rutland Falconry & Owl Ctr

Burley Bushes

Burley Park

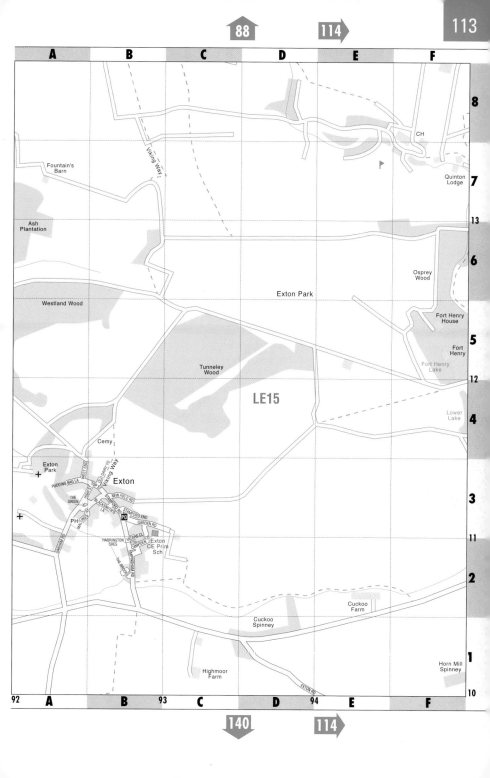

88
114

A B C D E F

8

Fountain's Barn

Viking Way

CH

Quinton Lodge

7

Ash Plantation

13

Osprey Wood

6

Westland Wood

Exton Park

Fort Henry House

Fort Henry

5

Tunneley Wood

Fort Henry Lake

12

LE15

Lower Lake

4

Cemy

Exton Park

Viking Way

Exton

Lower Lake

PUDDING BAG LA

WEST END

OLD DAIRY YD

TOP ST

NEW FIELD RD

STAMFORD END

THE GREEN

BLACKSMITH'S LA

PH

PO

STAMFORD END

GARDEN RD

3

11

OAKHAM RD

MAIN ST

HARRINGTON CRES

VICARS CL

CAMPDEN

Exton CE Prim Sch

EMPINGHAM RD

THE BRICKS

2

Cuckoo Farm

Cuckoo Spinney

Highmoor Farm

Horn Mill Spinney

1

EXTON RD

140
114

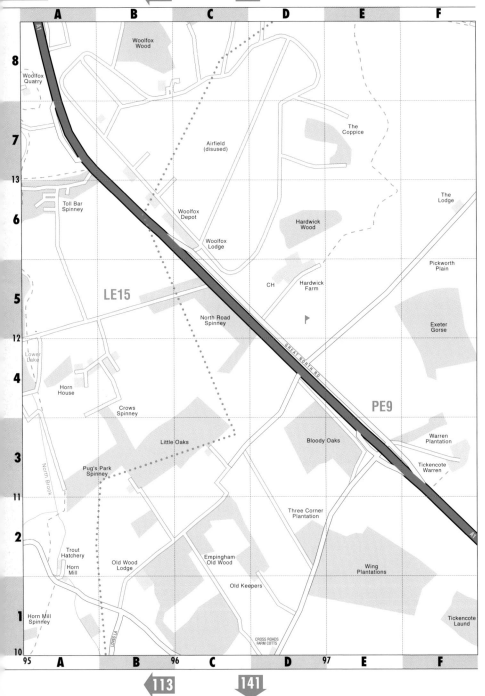

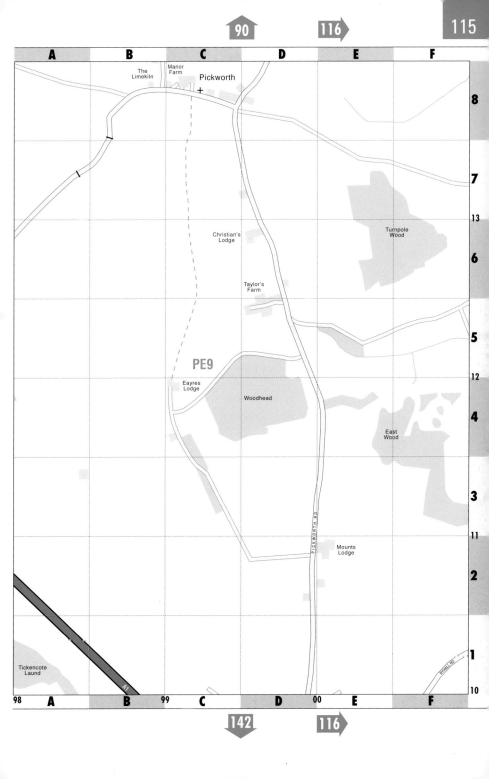

The Limekiln

Manor Farm

Pickworth

Christian's Lodge

Turnpole Wood

Taylor's Farm

PE9

Eayres Lodge

Woodhead

East Wood

PICKWORTH RD

Mounts Lodge

Tickencote Laund

A1

PITHALL RD

115

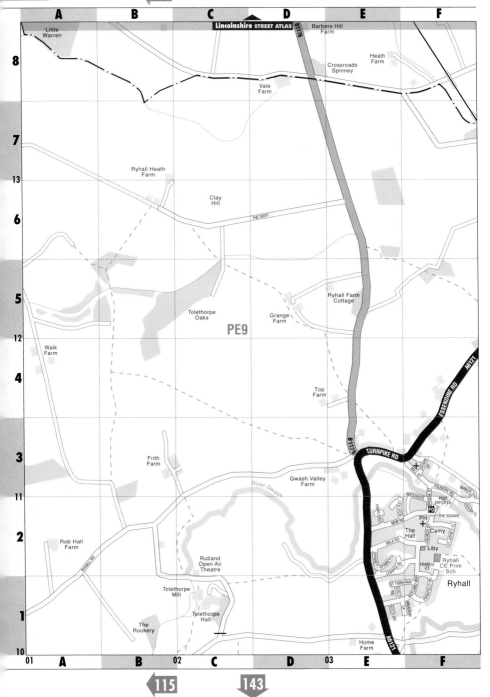

Lincolnshire STREET ATLAS

Little Warren

Barbers Hill Farm

Heath Farm

Crossroads Spinney

Vale Farm

Ryhall Heath Farm

Clay Hill

THE DRIFT

Ryhall Farm Cottage

Tolethorpe Oaks

PE9

Grange Farm

Walk Farm

Top Farm

Frith Farm

Gwash Valley Farm

River Gwash

TURNPIKE RD

B1176

ESSENDINE RD   A6121

Rob Hall Farm

RYHALL RD

Rutland Open Air Theatre

Tolethorpe Mill

Tolethorpe Hall

The Rookery

Home Farm

Ryhall CE Prim Sch

Ryhall

The Hall

Liby

Cemy

PO

POST OFFICE LA

PH

THE SQUARE

FRANCIS CT

A6121

B1176

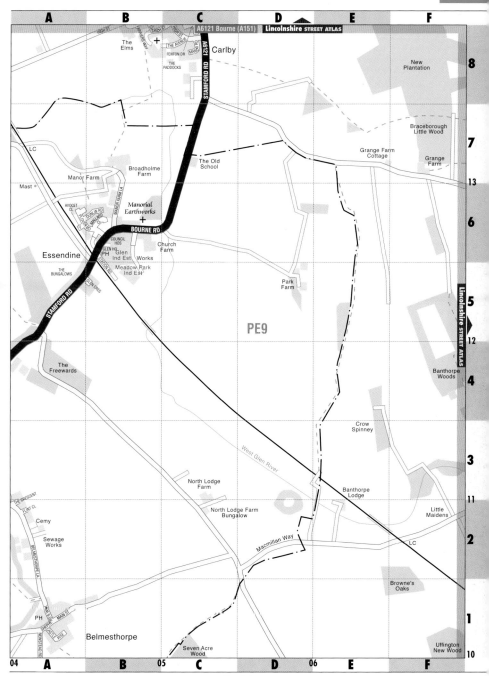

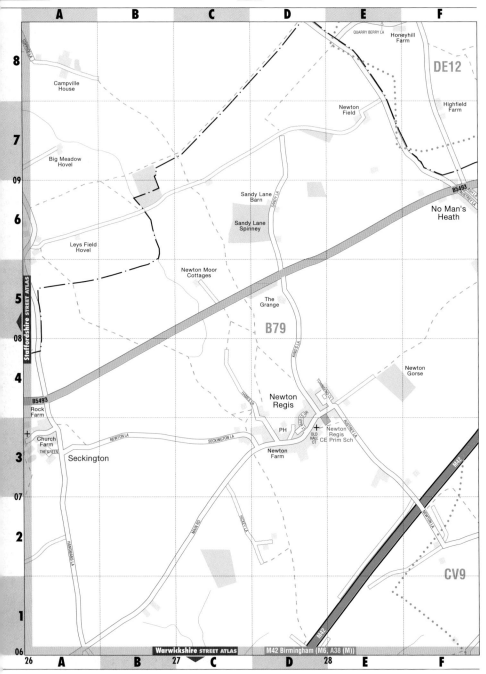

A B C D E F

8

Campville
House

DE12

Newton
Field

Honeyhill
Farm

QUARRY BERRY LA

Highfield
Farm

7

Big Meadow
Hovel

09

Sandy Lane
Barn

B5493

Sandy Lane
Spinney

No Man's
Heath

6

Leys Field
Hovel

Newton Moor
Cottages

5

The
Grange

B79

08

Staffordshire STREET ATLAS

Newton
Gorse

4

B5493

Rock
Farm

Newton
Regis

Church
Farm
THE GREEN

NEWTON LA

SECKINGTON LA

PH

Newton
Regis
CE Prim Sch

OLD
HALL
CT

3

Seckington

Newton
Farm

07

MAIN RD

HONEY LA

M42

2

HANDMANS LA

CV9

1

06

26

A

B

27

C

Warwickshire STREET ATLAS

D

M42 Birmingham (M6, A38 (M))

28

E

M42

F

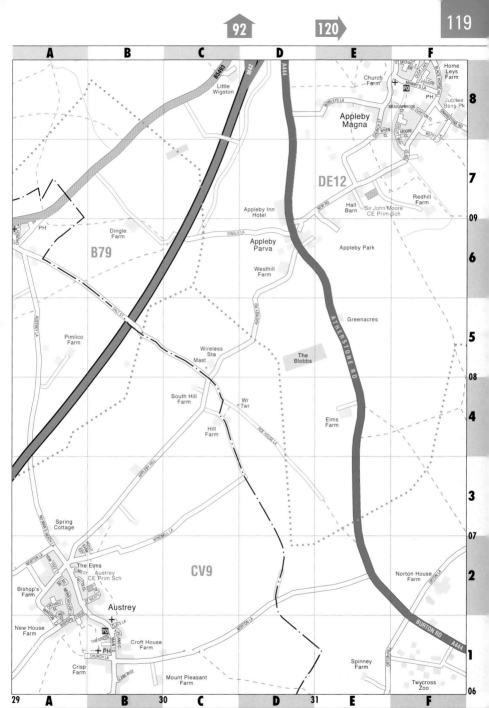

A **B** **C** **D** **E** **F**

B5493

M42

A444

St Michael's
Church
Church St
BLACK HORSE HILL
Home
Leys
Farm
MAWBY'S LA
HILLSIDE
PO
PH
Jubilee
Bsns Pk
MEADOWBROOK
GARTON CL
BOTT
GARDSTONE RD

8

Little
Wigston

Church
Farm

WINLEYS LA

Appleby
Magna

CHURCH ST
WREN CL
SCOTT LANE
MOORE CL
BOTT
LEST

7

DE12

NEW RD

Appleby Inn
Hotel

Hall
Barn

Sir John Moore
CE Prim Sch

Redhill
Farm

09

Dingle
Farm

DINGLE LA

Appleby
Parva

Appleby Park

+
PH

CHURCH LA

B79

AUSTREY LA

SALT ST

Westhill
Farm

DR LENS HILL

6

Greenacres

ATHERSTONE RD

Pimlico
Farm

Wireless
Sta
Mast

The
Blobbs

5

08

South Hill
Farm

Wr
Twr

Elms
Farm

4

APPLEBY HILL

RIDE HOUSE LA

Hill
Farm

Spring
Cottage

WINDMILL LA

MOLLY

3

07

NO MAN'S HEATH LA

NEWTON LA

PUMP TREE CL

ELMS CT

The Elms

Austrey
CE Prim Sch

CV9

Norton House
Farm

ORTON LA

2

Bishop's
Farm

ORCHARD

ST NICH'S

MAIN RD

MEADOW VIEW CL

Austrey
+

BELL'S LA

NORTON LA

New House
Farm

BISHOPS CLEEVE

PO
THE GREEN
MAIN D
CHURCH LA

Croft House
Farm

ORTON HILL

BURTON RD

A444

1

+ PH

Spinney
Farm

Crisp
Farm

GLEBE RISE

Mount Pleasant
Farm

Twycross
Zoo

06

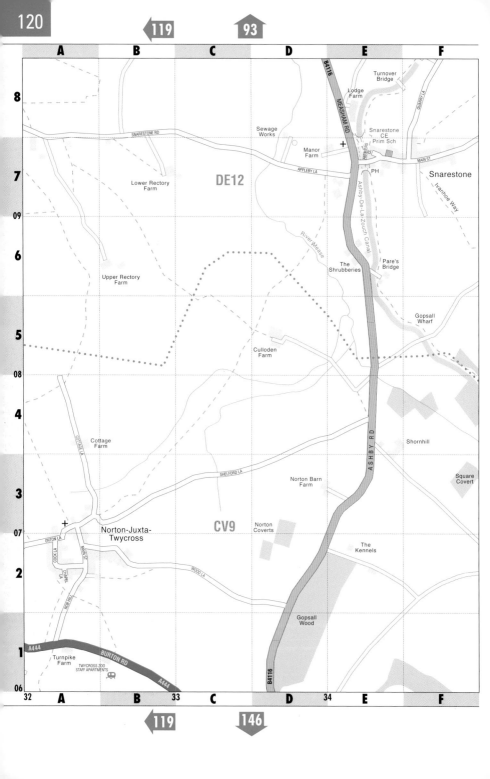

119
93
119
146

A B C D E F

8
7
09
6
5
08
4
3
07
2
1
06

32 A B 33 C D 34 E F

B4116
MEASHAM RD
Turnover Bridge
Lodge Farm
Snarestone CE Prim Sch
QUARRY LA
MAIN ST
Snarestone
PH
PH
Ivanhoe Way
Sewage Works
Manor Farm
APPLEBY LA
SNARESTONE RD
DE12
Lower Rectory Farm
River Mease
Ashby-De-La-Zouch Canal
The Shrubberies
Pare's Bridge
Gopsall Wharf
Upper Rectory Farm
Culloden Farm
ASHBY RD
Shornhill
Square Covert
Cottage Farm
SHELFORD LA
Norton Barn Farm
CV9
Norton Coverts
The Kennels
ORTON LA
Norton-Juxta-Twycross
CLOCK LA
MAIN ST
WOOD LA
CHAPEL LA
THE BOW
Gopsall Wood
A444
BURTON RD
Turnpike Farm
TWYCROSS ZOO STAFF APARTMENTS
A444
B4116

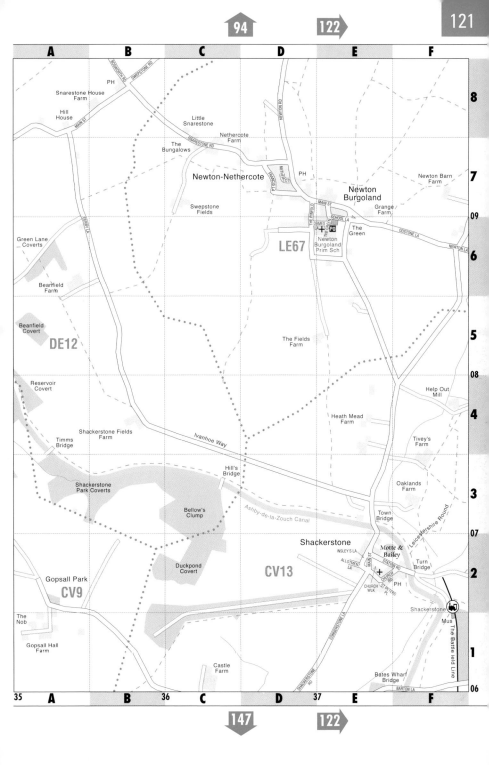

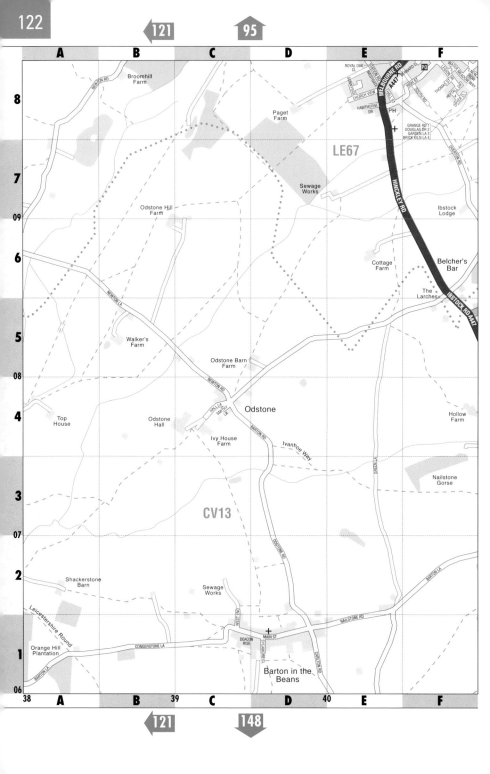

121
95

A B C D E F

8

Broomhill
Farm

NEWTON RD

ROYAL OAK
CL

SUTTON CL

SEXTON RD

PO

WATER MEADOW WAY

HIGH ST

THOMAS ST

LEGION CL

SOUTH RD

HEYLEN CL

GREEN CL

CHURCH VIEW

MELBOURNE RD A447

PH

HAWTHORNE
DR

+

GRANGE RD 1
DOUGLAS DR 2
GARDEN LA 3
BRICK KILN LA 4

Paget
Farm

LE67

7

Sewage
Works

Odstone Hill
Farm

09

Ibstock
Lodge

HINCKLEY RD

6

Cottage
Farm

Belcher's
Bar

NEWTON LA

The
Larches

IBSTOCK RD A447

5

Walker's
Farm

Odstone Barn
Farm

NEWTON RD

08

4

Top
House

Odstone
Hall

VALL LA

SMITHY
LA

Odstone

BARTON RD

Ivy House
Farm

Ivanhoe Way

GREEN LA

Hollow
Farm

3

CV13

07

Nailstone
Gorse

2

Shackerstone
Barn

Sewage
Works

BARTON LA

Leicestershire Round

WEST END

NAILSTONE RD

ODSTONE RD

CARLTON RD

1

Orange Hill
Plantation

BARTON LA

CONGERSTONE LA

DEACON
RISE

MAIN ST

SYCAMORE CL

+

Barton in the
Beans

06

38   39   40

A B C D E F

121
148

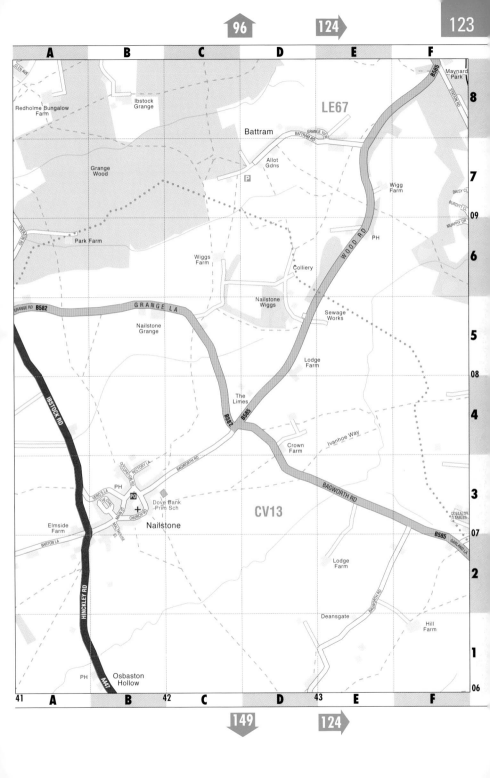

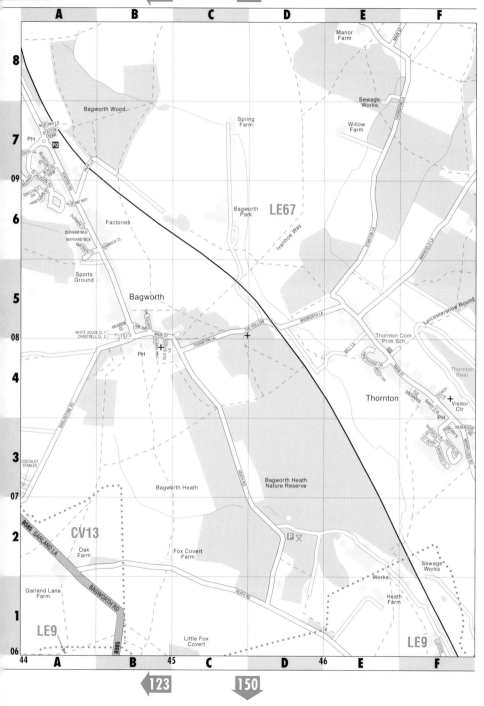

123
97

A   B   C   D   E   F

8

Manor
Farm

Bagworth Wood

Sewage
Works

Spring
Farm

7
NORTHFIELD
STATION
TERR
PH
PO

Willow
Farm

09

Bagworth
Park

LE67

6
Factories

Ivanhoe Way

DURHAM WLK
MAYNARD WLK
MATFORD CL
WARWICK CL

Leicestershire Round

5
Sports
Ground

Bagworth

Bagworth La

08
WHITE HOUSE CL 1
CHANTRELL CL 2
MEADOW
CL
LIME GR
THE SQUARE
MAIN ST

Thornton Com
Prim Sch

THE HOLLOW

THORNTON LA

4
PH

MILL LA

Thornton
Resr

Thornton

CHURCH
PH

Visitor
Ctr

BARLESTONE RD

3
COSTALOT
STABLES

RESERVOIR
RD

07

2
B585 GARLAND LA

CV13

Oak
Farm

Bagworth Heath

Bagworth Heath
Nature Reserve

HEATH RD

P

Sewage
Works

Fox Covert
Farm

Works

Heath
Farm

1
Garland Lane
Farm

BAGWORTH RD

HEATH RD

LE9

Little Fox
Covert

LE9

06
44 A   B   45 C   D   46 E   F

B585

123
150

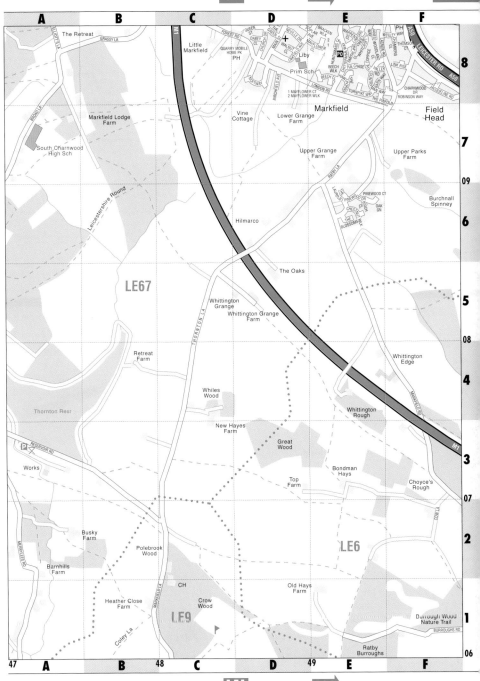

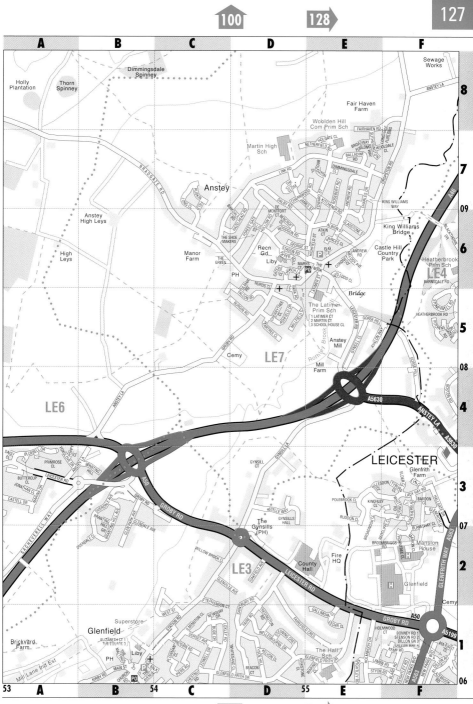

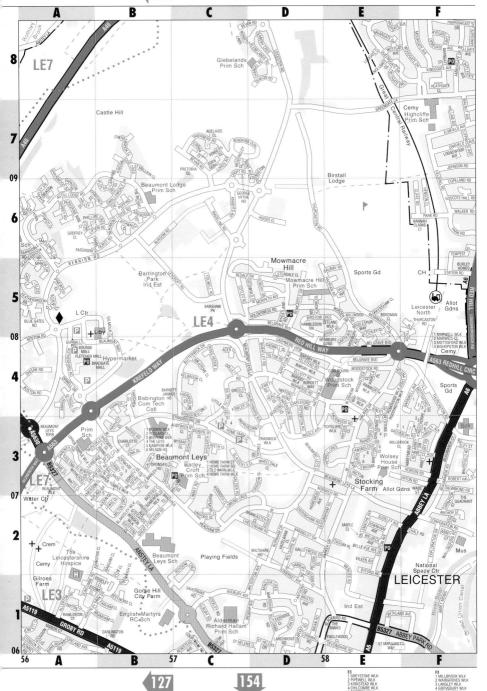

LE7

Castle Hill

Glebelands Prim Sch

Beaumont Lodge Prim Sch

Birstall Lodge

George Hythe Ho

Mowmacre Hill

Mowmacre Hill Prim Sch

Sports Gd

LE4

Barrington Park Ind Est

Barshaw Pk

L Ctr

BLUE GATES RD

Liby

Bourne Mall Fletcher Mall

Bradgate Mall

Hypermarket

KREFELD WAY

RED HILL WAY

BELGRAVE BVD

Leicester North

Allot Gdns

Belgrave Bvd

Belgrave Bvd

A563 REDHILL CIRC

Woodstock Prim Sch

Sports Gd

Babington Com Tech Coll

Prim Sch

Beaumont Leys

Home Farm

Barley Croft Prim Sch

Wolsey House Prim Sch

Stocking Farm

Allot Gdns

A50

B5327

LE7

Water Ctr

Beaumont Wlk

The Quadrant

ABBEY LA

Crem

Cemy

The Leicestershire Hospice

Gilroes Farm

LE3

Beaumont Leys Sch

Gorse Hill City Farm

Playing Fields

English Martyrs RC Sch

National Space Ctr

LEICESTER

Mus

A5119

GROBY RD

A5119

B5327

Alderman Richard Hallam Prim Sch

Ind Est

B5327 ABBEY PARK RD

A6

E3
1 GREYSTOKE WLK
2 PIPEWELL WLK
3 KIRKSTEAD WLK
4 CHILCOMBE WLK
5 BRETTON WLK
6 CANONSLEIGH WLK
7 SHELFORD WLK
8 ROBERTSBRIDGE WLK

F3
1 MILLBROOK WLK
2 WAINGROVES WLK
3 LANGLEY WLK
4 GROVEBURY WLK
5 MELCOMBE WLK
6 KIRKSCROFT WLK

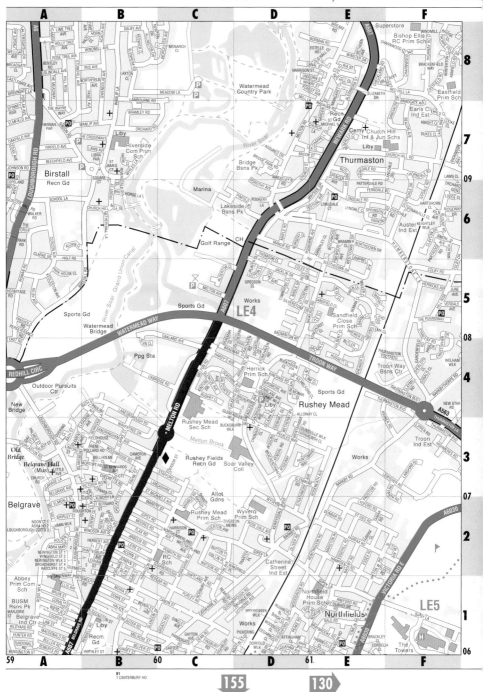

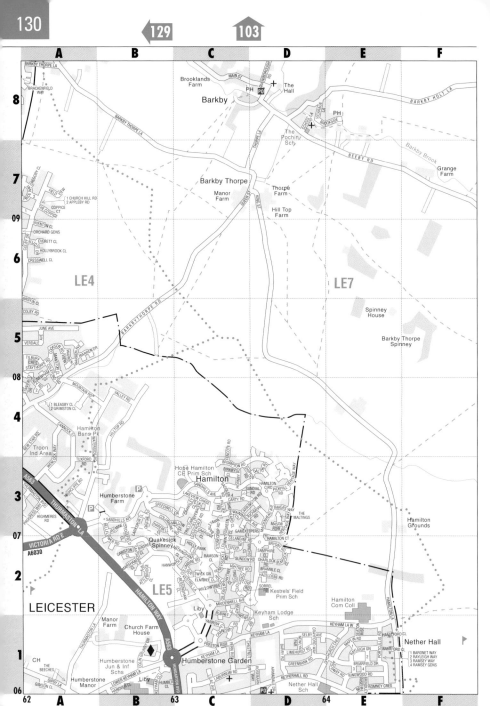

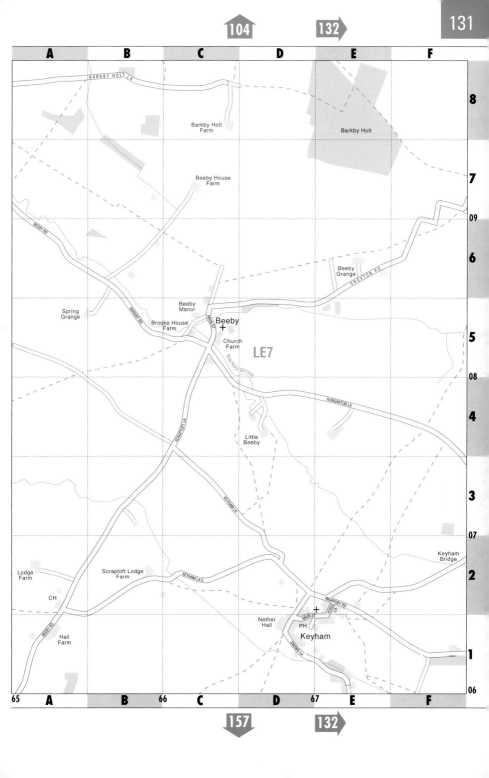

A   B   C   D   E   F

8

7

09

6

BARKBY HOLT LA

Barkby Holt
Farm

Barkby Holt

Beeby House
Farm

BEEBY RD

Beeby
Grange

CROXTON RD

Spring
Grange

BARKBY RD

Beeby
Manor

Brooke House
Farm

Beeby
+

Church
Farm

LE7

5

08

Barkby Brook

4

HUNGARTON LA

SCRAPTOFT LA

Little
Beeby

3

07

KEYHAM LA

Lodge
Farm

CH

Scraptoft Lodge
Farm

KEYHAM LA E

Keyham
Bridge

2

Hall
Farm

BEEBY RD

Nether
Hall

PH

INGARSBY RD

MAIN ST

GADDESBY LA

+

Keyham

SNOWS LA

1

06

65   66   67

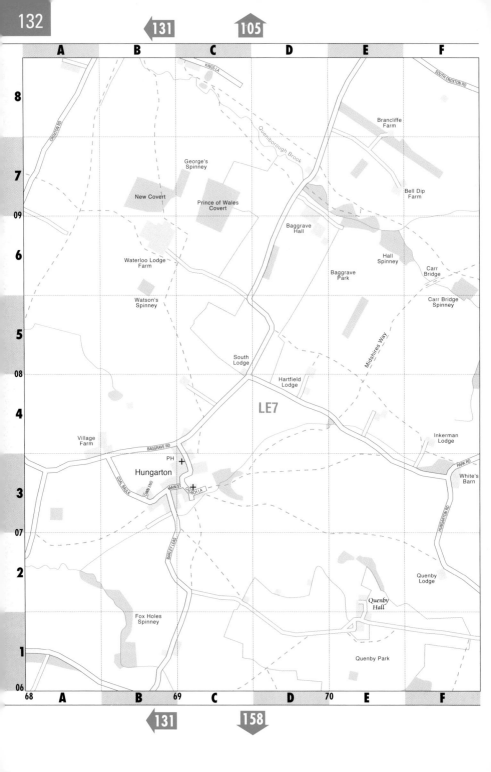

A **B** **C** **D** **E** **F**

8
7
09
6
5
08
4
3
07
2
1
06

KINGS LA
CROXTON RD
SOUTH CROXTON RD
Querinborough Brook
Brancliffe Farm
George's Spinney
New Covert
Prince of Wales Covert
Bell Dip Farm
Baggrave Hall
Hall Spinney
Carr Bridge
Waterloo Lodge Farm
Baggrave Park
Carr Bridge Spinney
Watson's Spinney
Midshires Way
South Lodge
Hartfield Lodge
LE7
Village Farm
BAGGRAVE RD
PH
Hungarton
Inkerman Lodge
PARK RD
White's Barn
COAL BRICK
TOWN END
MAIN ST
MOT LA
HUNGARTON RD
BARLEY LEAS
Quenby Lodge
Fox Holes Spinney
Quenby Hall
Quenby Park

68   A   B   69   C   D   70   E   F

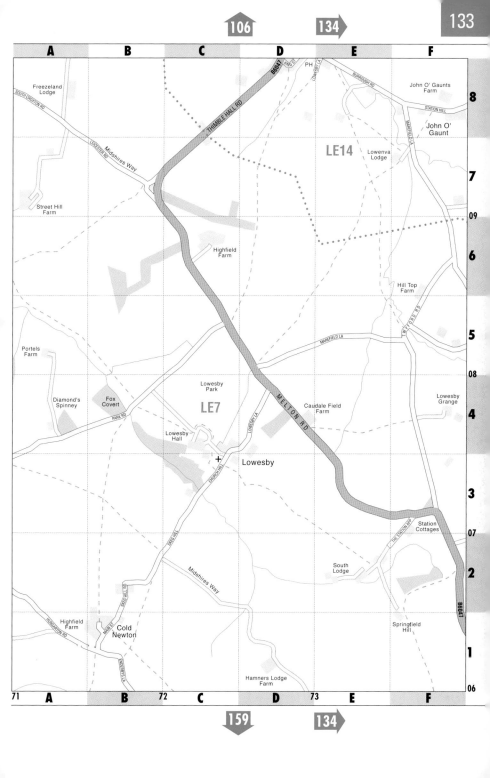

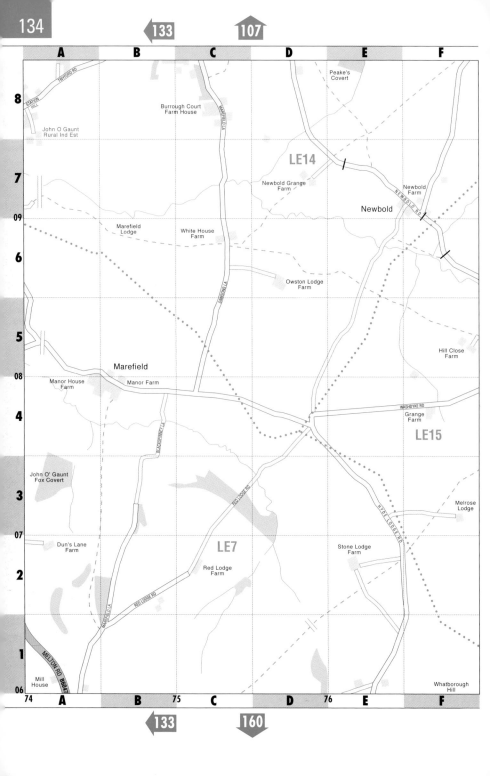

133
107

| | A | B | C | D | E | F |

8

STATION HILL

TWYFORD RD

John O Gaunt
Rural Ind Est

Burrough Court
Farm House

MAREFIELD LA

Peake's
Covert

LE14

Newbold Grange
Farm

Newbold
Farm

NEWBOLD RD

Newbold

7

09

Marefield
Lodge

White House
Farm

6

Owston Lodge
Farm

Hill Close
Farm

DIBBONS LA

5

Marefield

Manor House
Farm

Manor Farm

08

WASHDYKE RD

Grange
Farm

LE15

4

BLACKSPINNEY LA

John O' Gaunt
Fox Covert

3

RED LODGE RD

HYDE LODGE RD

Melrose
Lodge

Dun's Lane
Farm

07

LE7

Stone Lodge
Farm

2

MAREFIELD LA

RED LODGE RD

Red Lodge
Farm

1

MELTON RD BRIDGE

06

Mill
House

Whatborough
Hill

| 74 | A | | B | 75 | C | | D | 76 | E | | F |

133
160

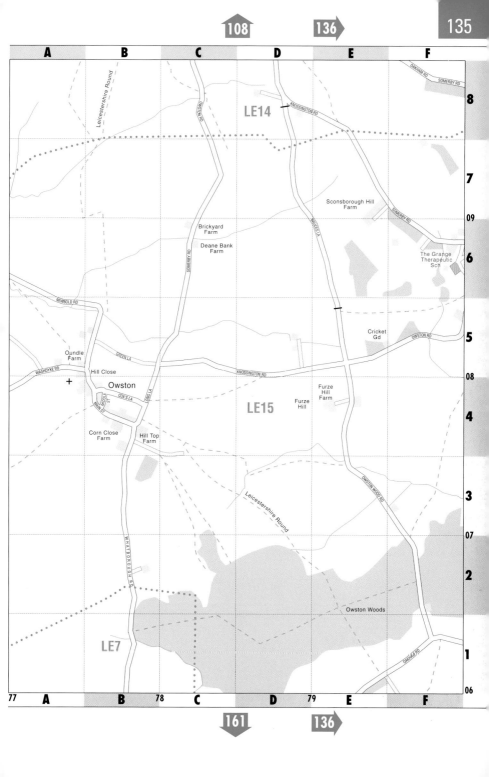

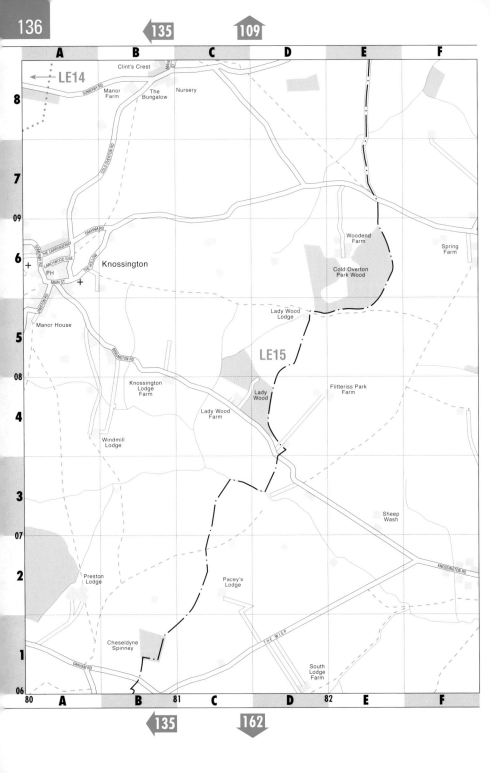

LE14

Clint's Crest

Manor
Farm

The
Bungalow

Nursery

8

SOMERBY RD

COLD OVERTON RD

7

09

OAKHAM RD

THE CARRIAGE WAY

LANCHWOOD RISE

6

PH

MAIN ST

THE PUNK

SOMERBY RD

Knossington

Woodend
Farm

Cold Overton
Park Wood

Spring
Farm

Manor House

5

08

OVERTON RD

BRAUNSTON RD

Knossington
Lodge
Farm

Lady Wood
Lodge

LE15

Lady
Wood

Flitteriss Park
Farm

4

Lady Wood
Farm

Windmill
Lodge

3

07

Sheep
Wash

2

Preston
Lodge

Pacey's
Lodge

KNOSSINGTON RD

Cheseldyne
Spinney

THE WISP

1

06

OAKHAM RD

South
Lodge
Farm

80 A B 81 C D 82 E F

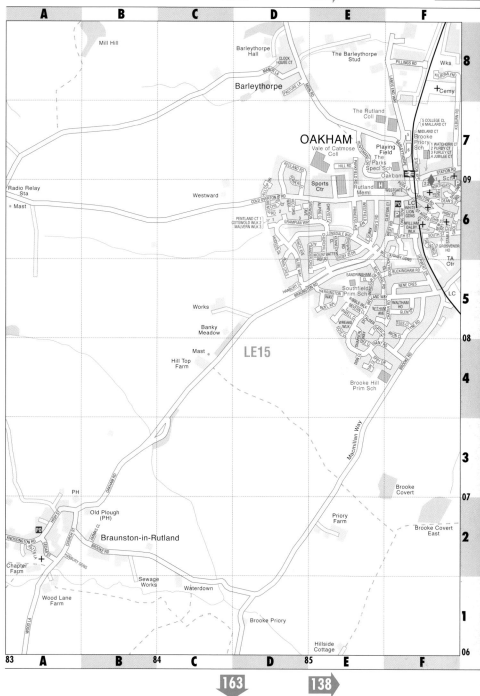

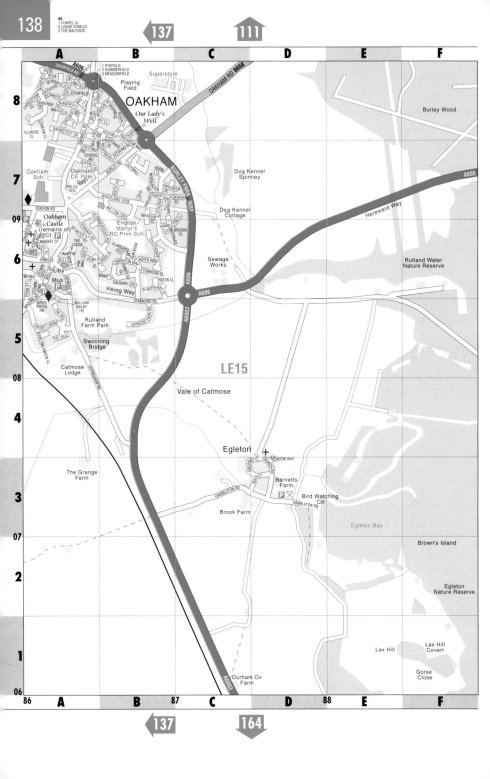

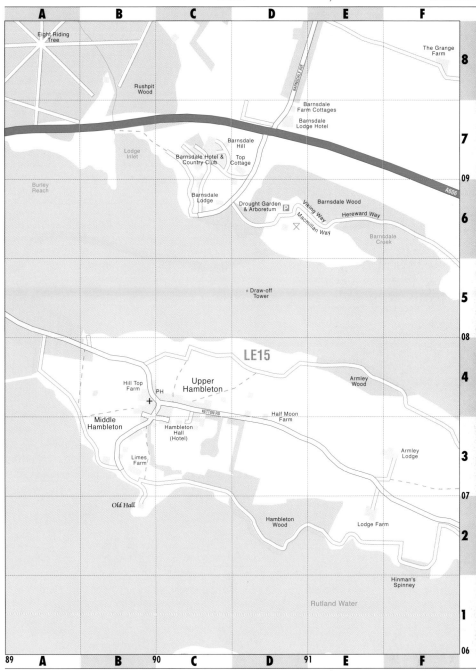

A B C D E F

8

Eight Riding
Tree

The Grange
Farm

Rushpit
Wood

BARNSDALE AVE

7

Barnsdale
Farm Cottages

Barnsdale
Lodge Hotel

Lodge
Inlet

Barnsdale
Hill

Barnsdale Hotel &
Country Club

Top
Cottage

09

A606

Burley
Reach

Barnsdale
Lodge

Drought Garden
& Arboretum

P

Barnsdale Wood

Viking Way

Macmillan Way

Hereward Way

6

Barnsdale
Creek

Draw-off
Tower

5

LE15

08

Hill Top
Farm

PH

Upper
Hambleton

Armley
Wood

4

Middle
Hambleton

KETTON RD

Half Moon
Farm

Hambleton
Hall
(Hotel)

Armley
Lodge

3

Limes
Farm

07

Old Hall

Hambleton
Wood

Lodge Farm

2

Hinman's
Spinney

Rutland Water

1

06

89 A B 90 C D 91 E F

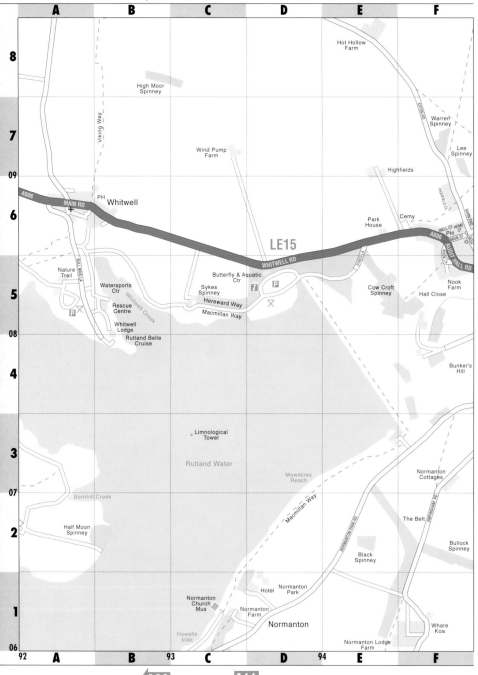

139
113

A   B   C   D   E   F

8

High Moor
Spinney

Hot Hollow
Farm

Warren
Spinney

Viking Way

EXTON RD

7

Wind Pump
Farm

Lee
Spinney

09

Highfields

HIGHFIELD CL

BARN RD

A606

MAIN RD   PH   Whitwell

Park
House

Cemy

WELL CT   HOME
CT

MAIN ST

AUDIT HALL RD

6

LE15

A606   PH   CHURCH

WHITWELL RD

Nature
Trail

BULL BRIG LA

Watersports
Ctr

Butterfly & Aquatic
Ctr

Sykes
Spinney

i   P

Cow Croft
Spinney

Hall Close

Nook
Farm

5

Whitwell Creek

Rescue
Centre

P

Hereward Way

Macmillan Way

Bunker's
Hill

08

Whitwell
Lodge

Rutland Belle
Cruise

4

Limnological
Tower

Normanton
Cottages

3

Rutland Water

Mowmires
Reach

Macmillan Way

07

Barnhill Creek

NORMANTON PARK RD

EMPINGHAM RD

The Belt

2

Half Moon
Spinney

Black
Spinney

Bullock
Spinney

Hotel

Normanton
Park

Whare
Koa

1

Normanton
Church
Mus

Normanton
Farm

Normanton

06

Howells
Inlet

Normanton Lodge
Farm

92   A   B   93   C   D   94   E   F

139
166

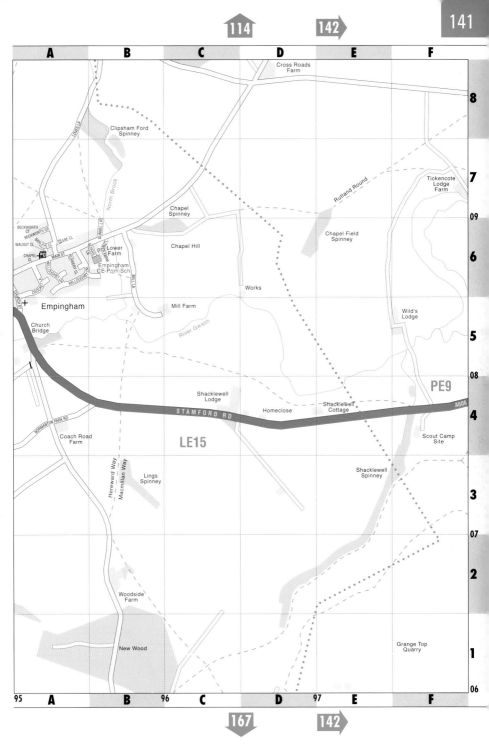

A B C D E F

8

Tickencote
Park

Tickencote

Mill
Pond

Tickencote
Hall

WEST
VIEW

WINDYRIDGE

Casterton
Bsns & Ent
Coll

Glebe
Barn

7

Sewage
Works

PH

Great Casterton
CE Prim Sch

09

Great Casterton

Ingthorpe
Farm

Ingthorpe

PH
Church
Farm

6

HOME
FARM CL

Toll Bar

1 LAVENDER WAY
2 BUTTERCUP CL

5

MEADOWSWEET

SWEETBRIAR

PH Quarry
Farm

08

Glebe
House

PE9

CLOVER GDNS 1
CORNFLOWER CL 2
MARIGOLD CL 3
SORREL CL 4
BRAMBLE GR 5

A606

STAMFORD RD

4

Tinwell Lodge
Farm Cottages

Sidney
House

GARDEN
CL

EMPINGHAM RD

CHESTNUT
GDNS

A606

3

Mast

The
Rookery

GREAT NORTH RD

07

Tinwell Lodge
Farm

2

Grange Top
Quarry

CASTERTON LA

Tinwell
House

A1

STEEPFIELD LA

Tinwell

TINWELL RD

A6121

HOLLA

1

Cvn
Site

PH

MILL
WELLAND
VIEW
THE
PADDOCKS

Mill
Farmhouse

Tinwell
Grange

The
Manor

A6121

06

River Welland

98 A B 99 C D 00 E F

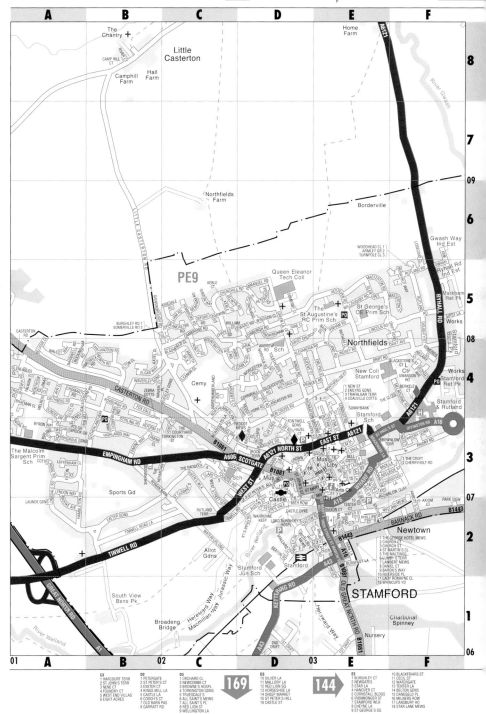

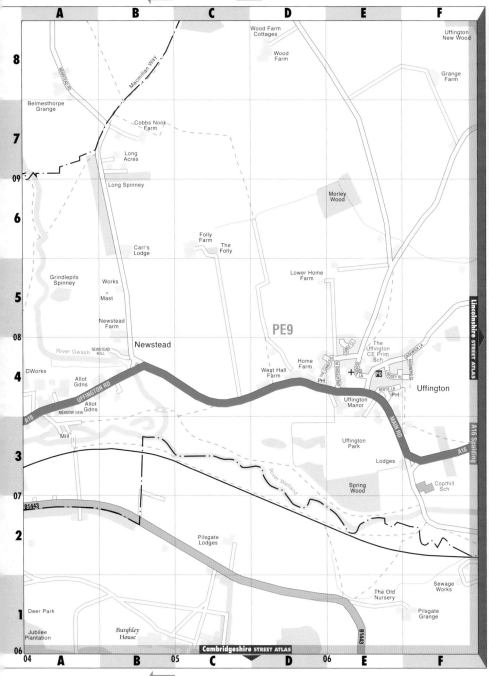

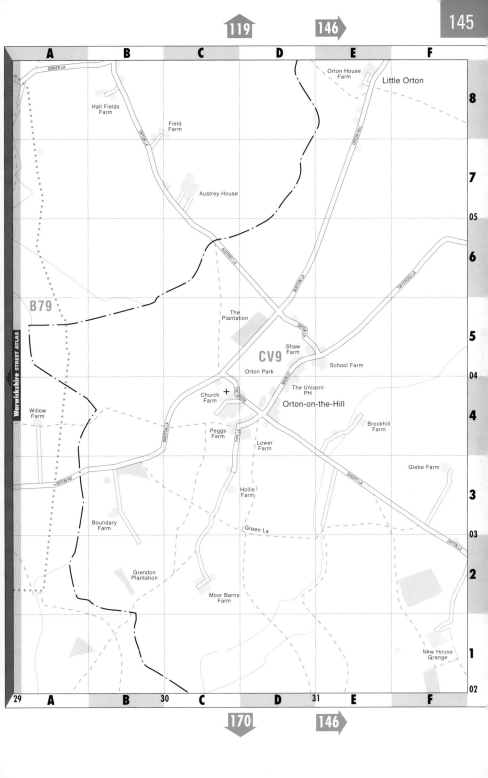

A B C D E F

CINDER LA

Orton House Farm

Little Orton

Hall Fields Farm

Field Farm

ORTON LA

8

Austrey House

ORTON HILL

7

05

AUSTREY LA

6

NORTON LA

TWYCROSS LA

B79

The Plantation

ORTON LA

5

Shaw Farm

School Farm

CV9

MAIN ST

04

Orton Park

The Unicorn PH

Church Farm

Orton-on-the-Hill

Willow Farm

4

THE GREEN

PIPE LA

WARTON LA

Peggs Farm

Lower Farm

Brookhill Farm

SHEEPY LA

Glebe Farm

ORTON RD

3

Hollis Farm

03

Boundary Farm

Green La

ORTON LA

2

Grendon Plantation

Moor Barns Farm

New House Grange

1

02

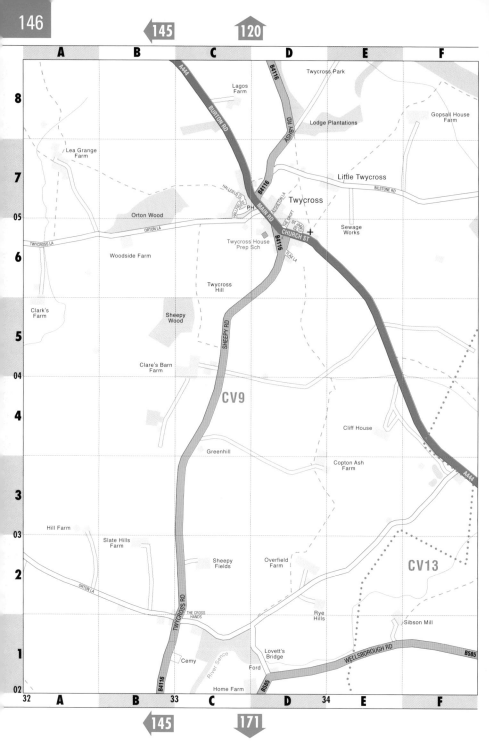

145
120

A   **B**   **C**   **D**   **E**   **F**

Twycross Park

Lagos
Farm

Lodge Plantations

Gopsall House
Farm

BURTON RD

A444

B4116

ASHBY RD

8

Lea Grange
Farm

7

Little Twycross

Bilstone Rd

HALLFIELD RD

B4116

MAIN RD

ASHETOLL LA

05

Orton Wood

PH

Twycross

THE BIGHT

Sewage
Works

ORTON LA

CHURCH ST

ST JAS
CEV

TWYCROSS LA

Twycross House
Prep Sch

B4116

+

6

Woodside Farm

Twycross
Hill

CLAX LA

Sheepy
Wood

5

SHEEPY RD

Clark's
Farm

Clare's Barn
Farm

04

CV9

4

Cliff House

Greenhill

Copton Ash
Farm

A444

3

Hill Farm

03

Slate Hills
Farm

Sheepy
Fields

Overfield
Farm

CV13

2

ORTON LA

THE CROSS
HANDS

Rye
Hills

Sibson Mill

TWYCROSS RD

Lovett's
Bridge

WELLSBOROUGH RD

B585

1

Cemy

River Sence

Ford

B585

02

B4116

Home Farm

32   **A**   **B**   **33**   **C**   **D**   **34**   **E**   **F**

145
171

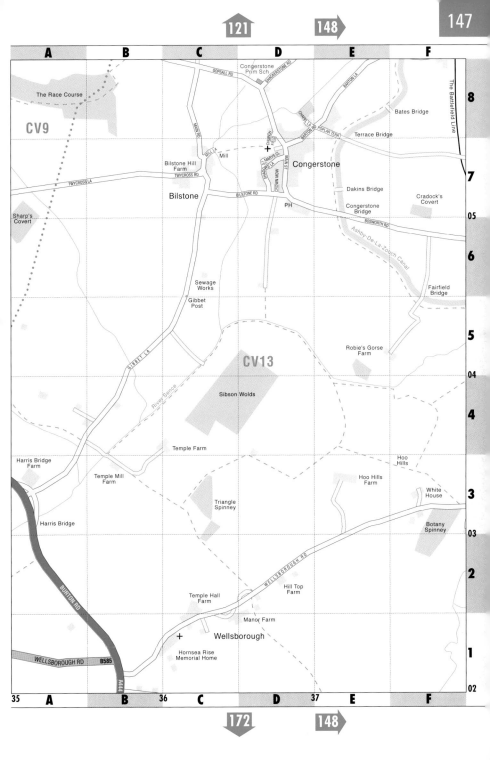

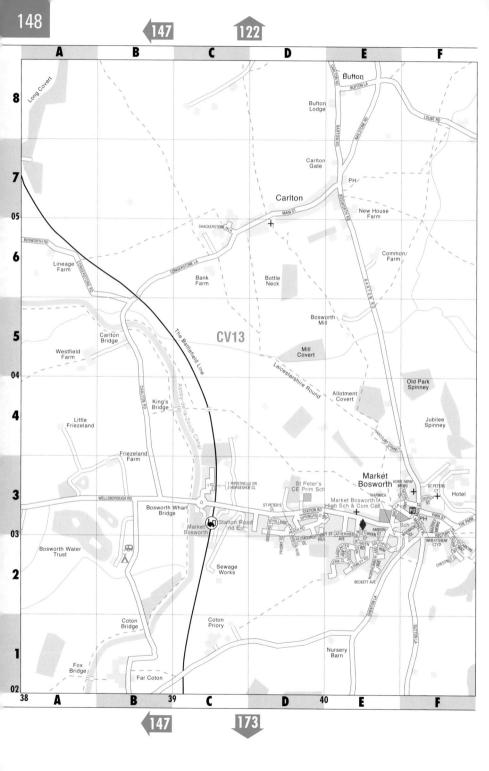

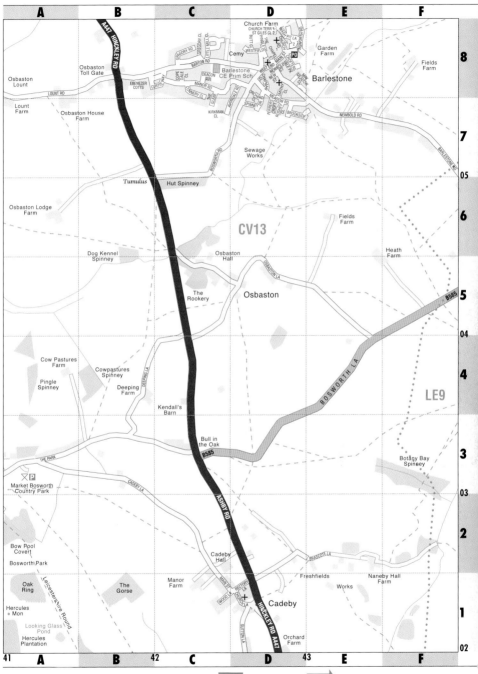

A B C D E F

8

7

05

6

5

04

4

3

03

2

1

02

41 A B 42 C D 43 E F

Osbaston Lount
Lount Farm
LOUNT RD
Osbaston House Farm
Osbaston Toll Gate
A447 HINCKLEY RD
EBENEZER COTTS
Osbaston Lodge Farm
Tumulus
Hut Spinney
Dog Kennel Spinney
The Rookery
Cow Pastures Farm
Cowpastures Spinney
Pingle Spinney
Deeping Farm
DEEPING LA
Kendall's Barn
Bull in the Oak
B585
THE PARK
Market Bosworth Country Park
CADEBY LA
Bow Pool Covert
Bosworth Park
Oak Ring
Leicestershire Round
Hercules Mon
The Gorse
Manor Farm
Looking Glass Pond
Hercules Plantation
Cadeby Hall
MAIN ST
ASHBY RD
RECTORY LA
DROVE LA
Cadeby
A447 HINCKLEY RD
SUTTON LA
Orchard Farm

Church Farm
CHURCH TERR
ST GILES CL
Cemy
Barlestone CE Prim Sch
GREGORY CL
LITTLE HILL CL
BARTON RD
DEACON AVE
MANOR RD
GORSE CL
CURTIS WAY
ANNERY CL
GLEBE
KIRKMAN CL
BARSDALE RD
WESTFIELD
SPINNEY DR
FERRERS
RECTORY
CROFT
BROOKSIDE
BOSWORTH RD
Sewage Works
CV13
Osbaston Hall
Osbaston
OSBASTON LA
Fields Farm
Garden Farm
Barlestone
PO
NEWBOLD RD
Fields Farm
BARLESTONE RD
Heath Farm
B585
BOSWORTH LA
LE9
Botany Bay Spinney
Naneby Hall Farm
BRASCOTE LA
Freshfields
Works

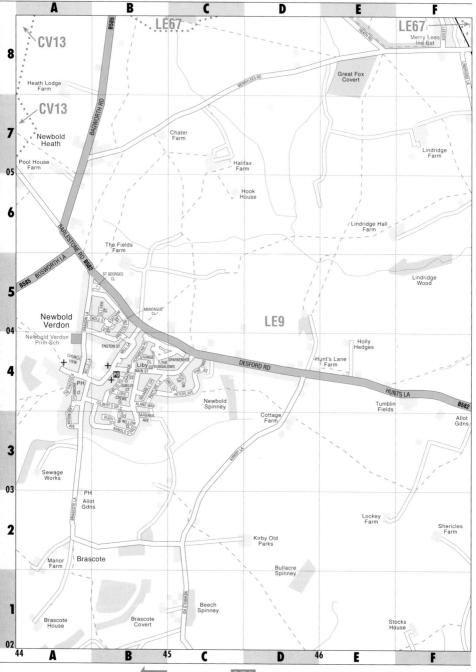

149
124

LE67

CV13

Heath Lodge Farm

CV13

Newbold Heath

Pool House Farm

BAGWORTH RD

B585

Merrilees Rd

LE67

Merry Lees Ind Est

Great Fox Covert

Chater Farm

Halifax Farm

Hook House

Lindridge Farm

Lindridge Hall Farm

Lindridge Wood

BARLESTONE RD

BOSWORTH LA

B585

B582

The Fields Farm

St Georges Cl

Montague Cl

LE9

Newbold Verdon

Newbold Verdon Prim-Sch

Enston St

Liby

Church View

PH

PO

Grange Cl

The Bungalows

Sparkenhoe

Desford Rd

Hunt's Lane Farm

Holly Hedges

Hunts La

B582

Newbold Spinney

Peters Ave

Alans Way

Gilbert's Dr

Barbara Ave

Willow Cl

Rugb

Arnold Cl

Tumblin Fields

Allot Gdns

Cottage Farm

Sewage Works

PH Allot Gdns

BRASCOTE LA

Kirby La

Lockey Farm

Shericles Farm

Brascote

Manor Farm

Kirby Old Parks

Bullacre Spinney

NEWBOLD RD

Brascote House

Brascote Covert

Beech Spinney

Stocks House

149
175

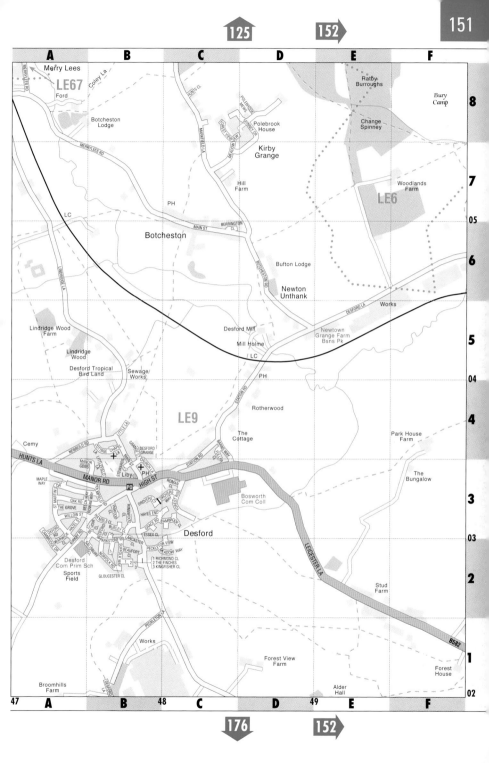

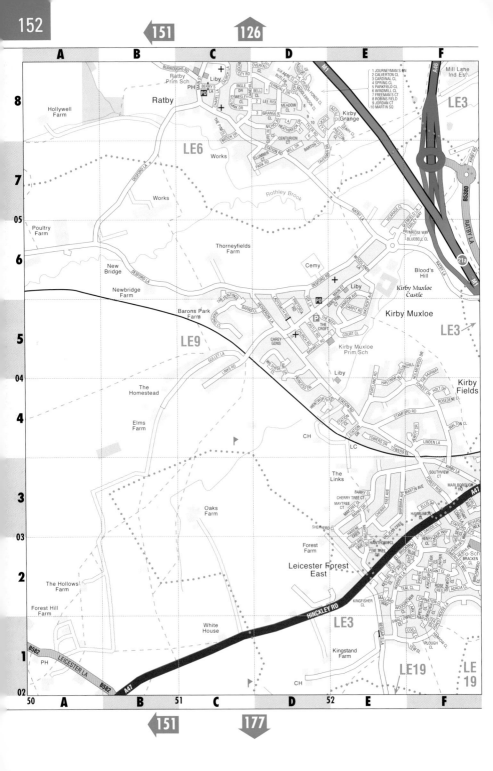

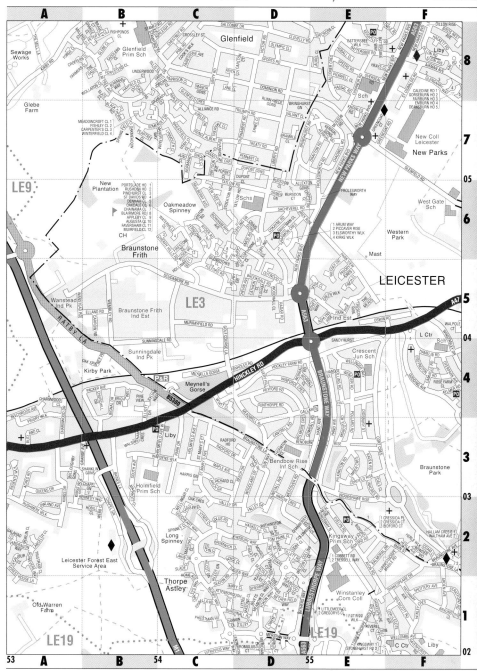

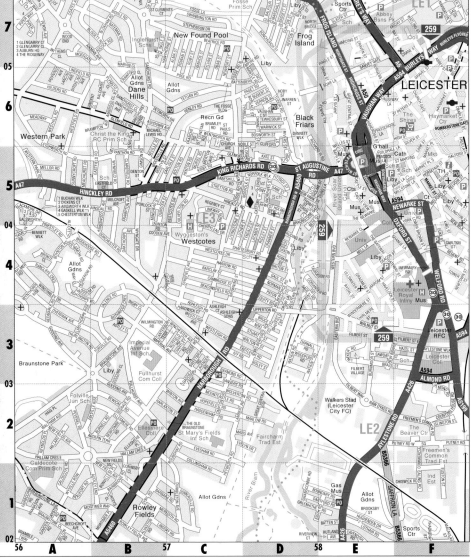

153

128

D4
1 WEST ST OPEN
2 THE RIVER BLDG
3 RIVER SOAR LIVING
D5
1 FREDERICK JACKSON HO
2 ARUNDEL HO

3 ANDREWES WLK
4 NORFOLK HO
5 MUSGROVE CL
6 COVENTRY ST
7 EARL HOWE TERR

179

For full street detail of the highlighted area see page 259.

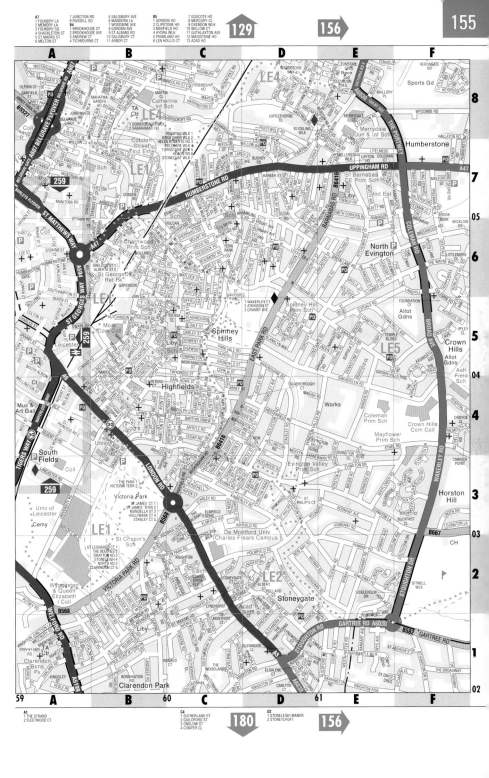

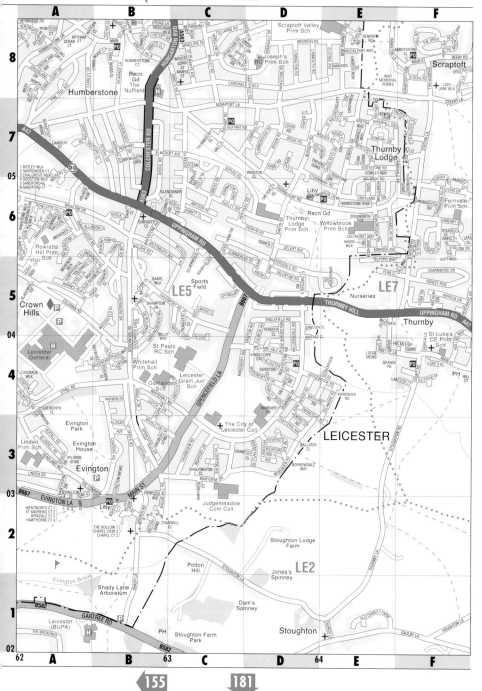

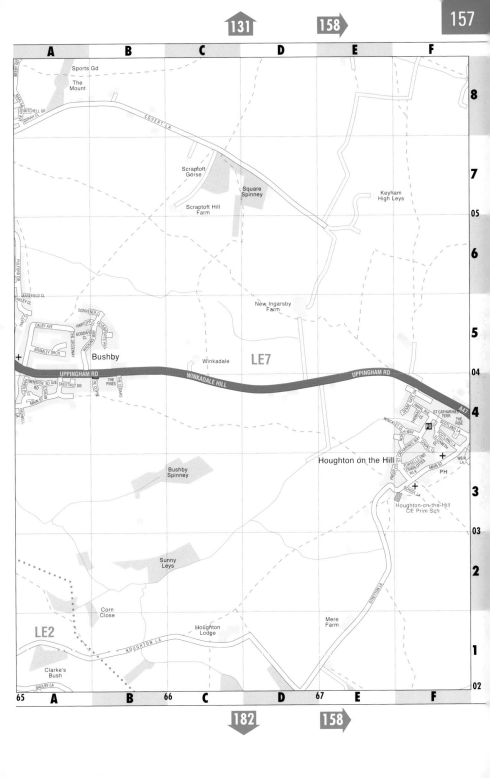

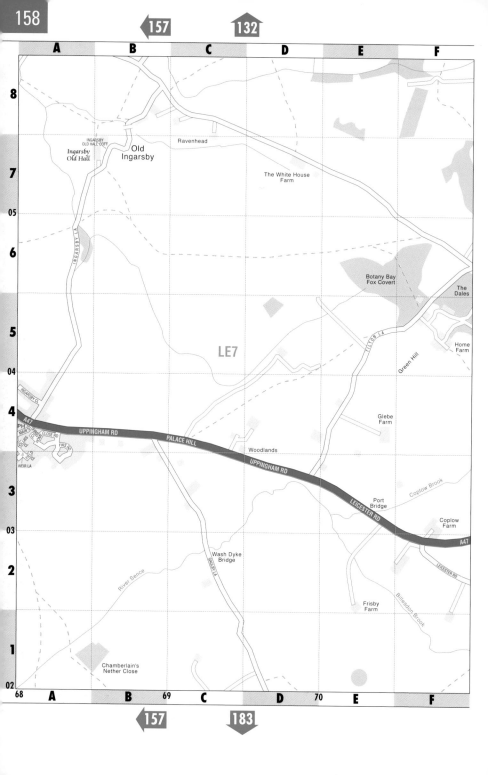

A   B   C   D   E   F

8

Ravenhead

INGARSBY OLD HALL COTT

Ingarsby Old Hall

Old Ingarsby

The White House Farm

7

05

INGARSBY LA

6

Botany Bay Fox Covert

The Dales

5

LE7

TILTON LA

Green Hill

Home Farm

04

INGARSBY CL

4

A47

Glebe Farm

PH

MAIN ST

CLOSE RD

HOME CL

HVAS RD

UPPINGHAM RD

PALACE HILL

Woodlands

UPPINGHAM RD

LEICESTER RD

Coplow Brook

WEIR LA

Port Bridge

Coplow Farm

3

03

River Sence

Wash Dyke Bridge

SHELBY LA

A47

LEICESTER RD

2

Frisby Farm

Billesdon Brook

1

Chamberlain's Nether Close

02

68   A   69   B   C   70   D   E   F

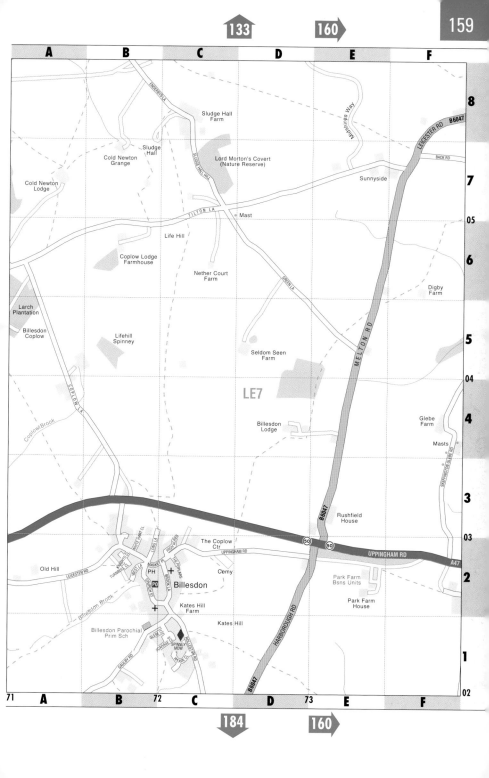

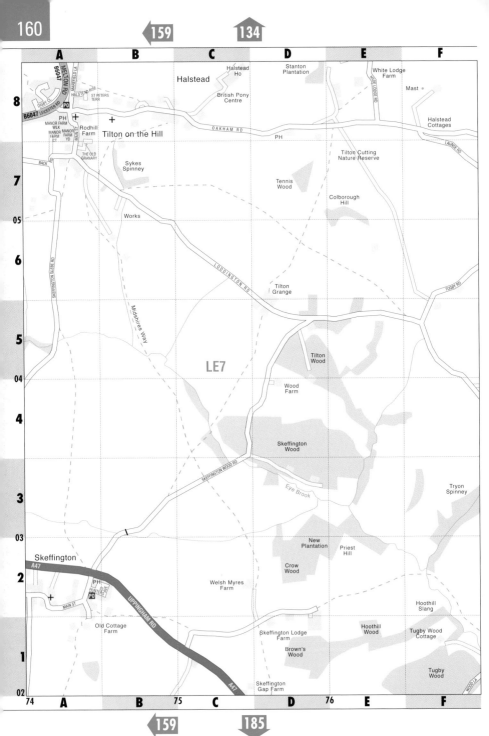

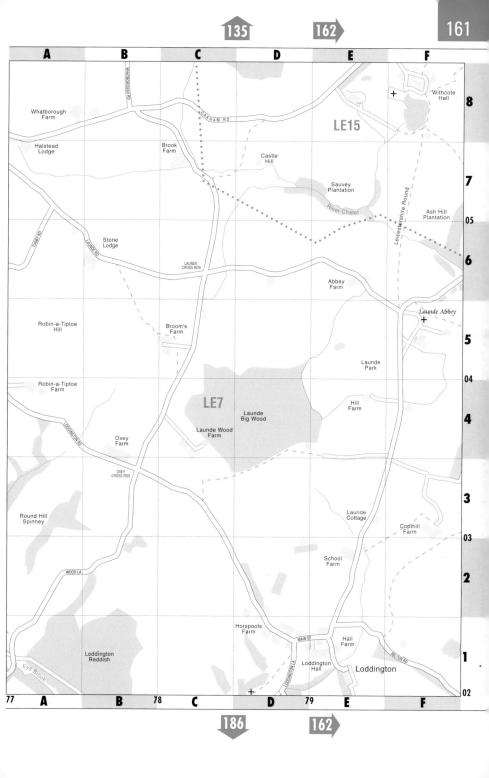

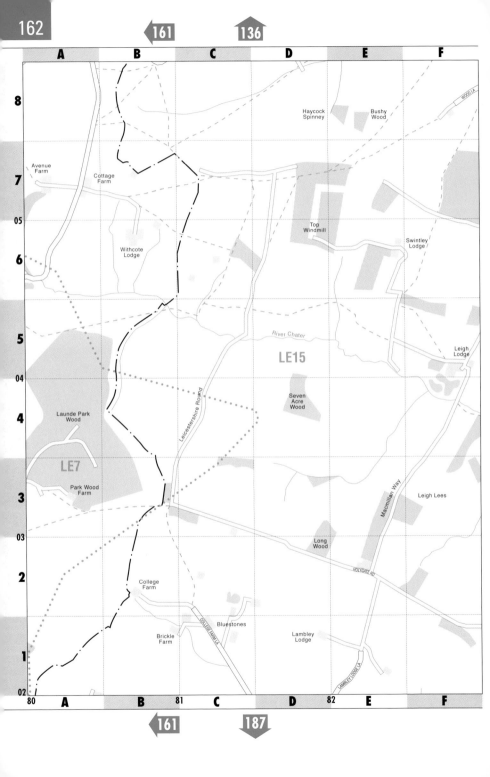

161
136

Avenue
Farm

Cottage
Farm

Haycock
Spinney

Bushy
Wood

WOOD LA

Withcote
Lodge

Top
Windmill

Swintley
Lodge

River Chater

LE15

Leigh
Lodge

Laude Park
Wood

Leicestershire Round

Seven
Acre
Wood

LE7

Macmillan Way

Leigh Lees

Park Wood
Farm

Long
Wood

HOLYGATE RD

College
Farm

Brickle
Farm

COLLEGE FARM LA

Bluestones

Lambley
Lodge

LAMBLEY LODGE LA

161
187

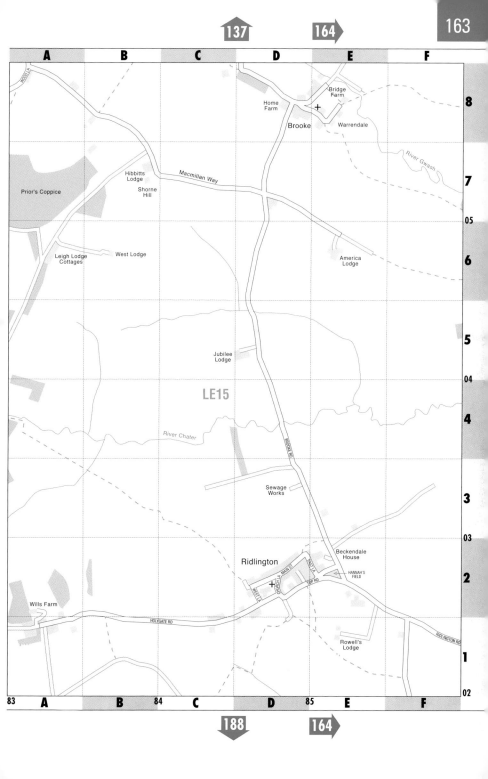

Bridge
Farm
Home
Farm
Brooke
Warrendale
River Gwash
Hibbitts
Lodge
Macmillan Way
Shorne
Hill
Prior's Coppice
Leigh Lodge
Cottages
West Lodge
America
Lodge
Jubilee
Lodge
LE15
River Chater
BROOKE RD
Sewage
Works
Beckendale
House
Ridlington
HANNAH'S
FIELD
Wills Farm
MAIN ST
WEST LA
CHURCH LA
EAST LA
TOP RD
HOLYGATE RD
Rowell's
Lodge
RIDLINGTON RD

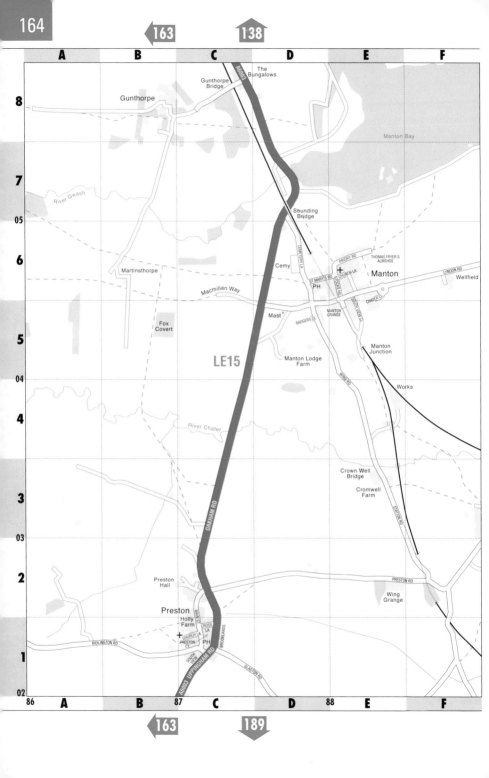

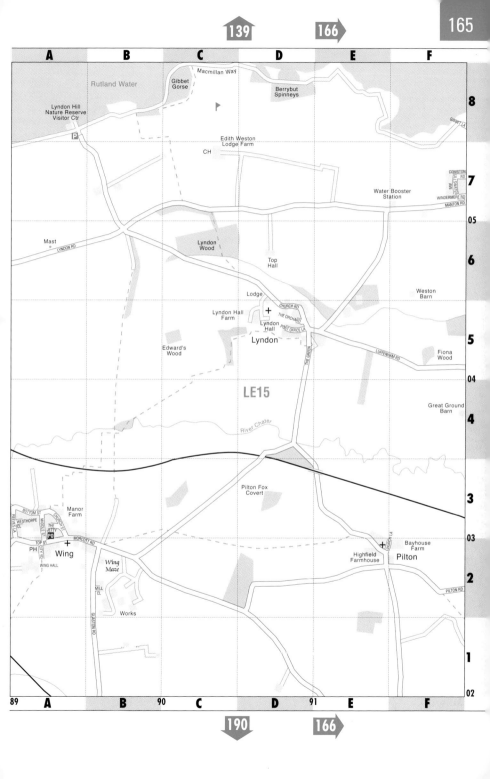

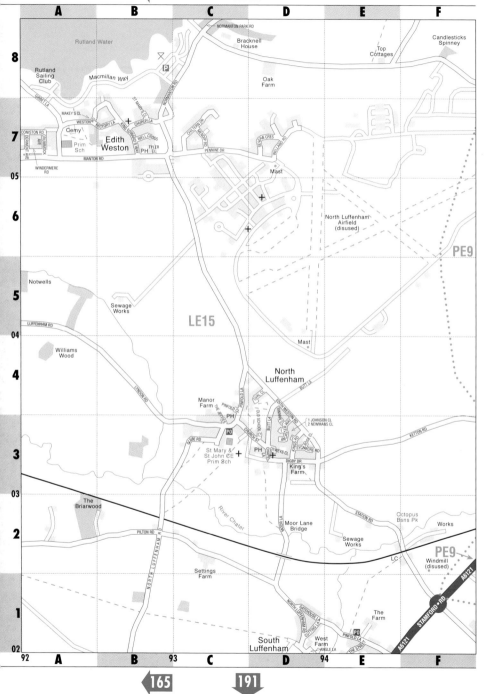

165
140

A B C D E F

8

Rutland Water

Candlesticks
Spinney

Normanton Park Rd

Bracknell
House

Top
Cottages

Rutland Sailing
Club

Macmillan Way

Oak
Farm

Gibbet La

St Mary's La

Weston Rd

Normanton Rd

Church La

7

Makey's Cl

Weston Rd

Victory La

King Edward's Way

Chilterns

Mendip Rd

Pennine Dr

Dejean Cres

Welland Rise

Coniston Rd
Derwent Ave
Drummock Ave

Cemy
Prim
Sch

Edith
Weston

Well Cross

PH
Tyler
Cl

Windermere
Rd

Manton Rd

05

Mast

+

+

6

North Luffenham
Airfield
(disused)

PE9

5

Notwells

Sewage
Works

LE15

Luffenham Rd

04

Mast

4

Williams
Wood

Lyndon Rd

North
Luffenham

Butt La

Manor
Farm

The Jefferies

PH

Pinfold Cl

Pinfold La

Oak La

Royal Preston Rd

Old School Cl

Butt La

Church La

1 Johnson Cl
2 Newmans Cl

Netton Rd

Edmore Rd

1 2

Ancaster Cl

3

Lane Rd

PO

St Mary &
St John CE
Prim Sch

+

PH

+

Dewey's Cl

Digby Dr

King's
Farm

Station Rd

Octopus
Bsns Pk

Works

03

The
Briarwood

River Chater

Moor Lane
Bridge

2

Pilton Rd

North Luffenham Rd

Sewage
Works

LC

PE9

Windmill
(disused)

Stamford Rd

A6121

A6121

1

Settings
Farm

North Luffenham Rd

Gatehouse La

The
Farm

02

South
Luffenham

West
Farm

Angle La

Pinfold La

PO

The Street

92 A B 93 C D 94 E F

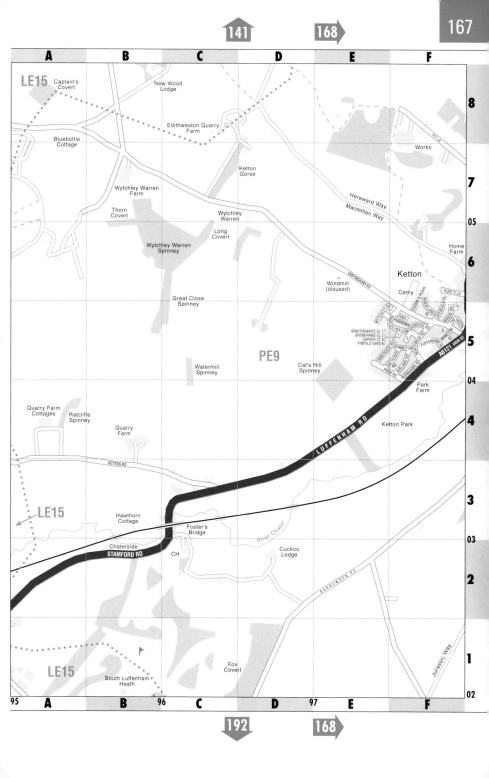

167
142

A B C D E F

8

7

05

6

5

04

4

3

03

2

1

02

98 A B 99 C D 00 E F

Works

STAMFORD RD

A6121

Tinwell Crossing

Home Wood

Keeper's Lodge

THE CRESCENT

The Firs

MOLESWORTH BGLWS

MANOR VIEW

PH

HIGH ST

Home Farm

PO

Ketton

Ketton CE Prim Sch

Liby

CHURCH

Aldgate

Sewage Works

Manor Farm

NEVILLE DAY CL

WEST FIELDS

WEST ST

River Welland

PE9

THE CRESCENT

WESTERN AVE

THE RETREAT

DEEP MORE

A43

LC

GEESTON RD

Geeston

MacMillan Way

Hereward Way

Jurassic Way

Collyweston Quarries Nature Reserve

STAMFORD RD

Windmill (dis)

Collyweston Bridge

Kilthorpe Grange

Sewage Works

KETTON RD

Nursery

SLATE DRIFT

Manor Farm

BACK LA

NEW RD

HALL YD

PO

HIGH ST

THE WALKS

PH

MAIN RD

Collyweston

THE DRIFT

COLLINS WAY

Cemy

Wr Twr

THE DROVE

A43

Vigo Woods

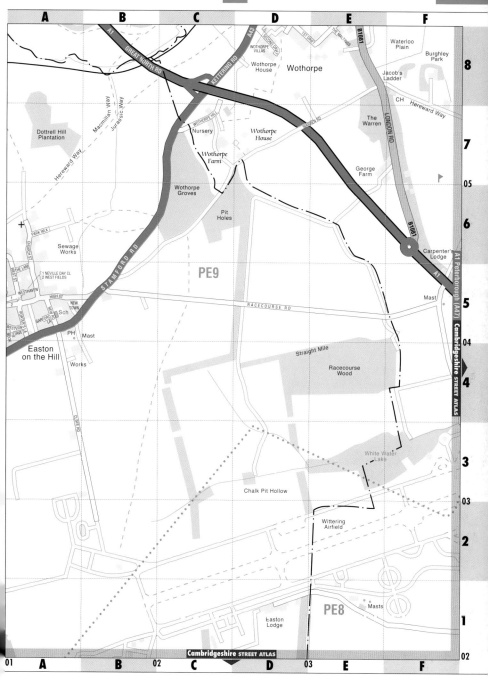

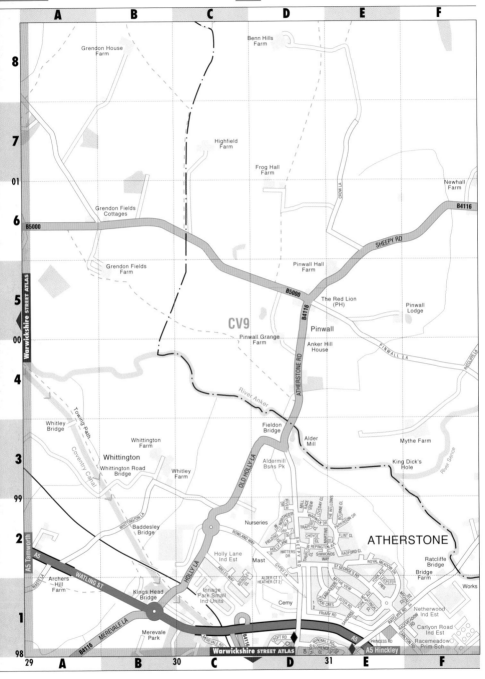

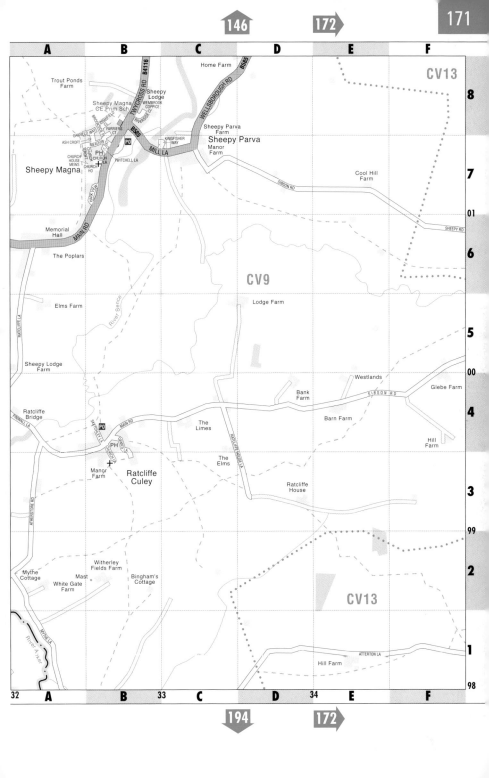

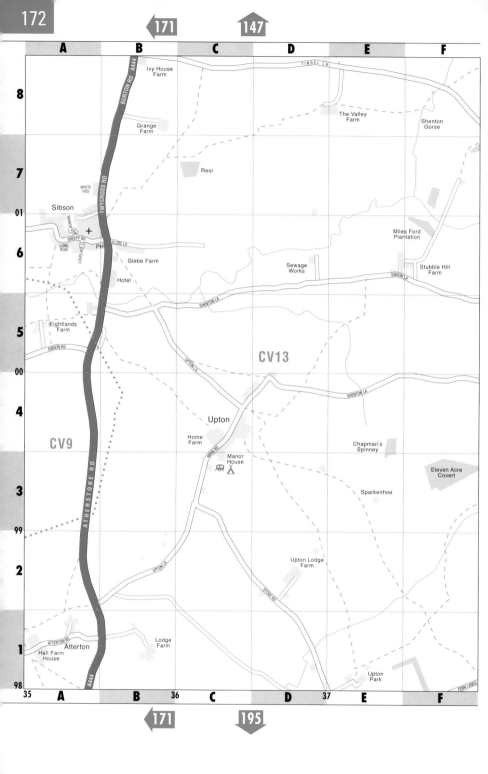

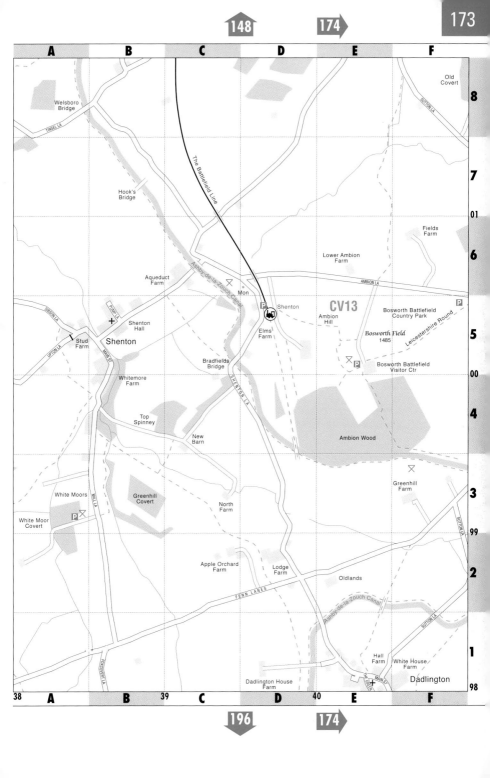

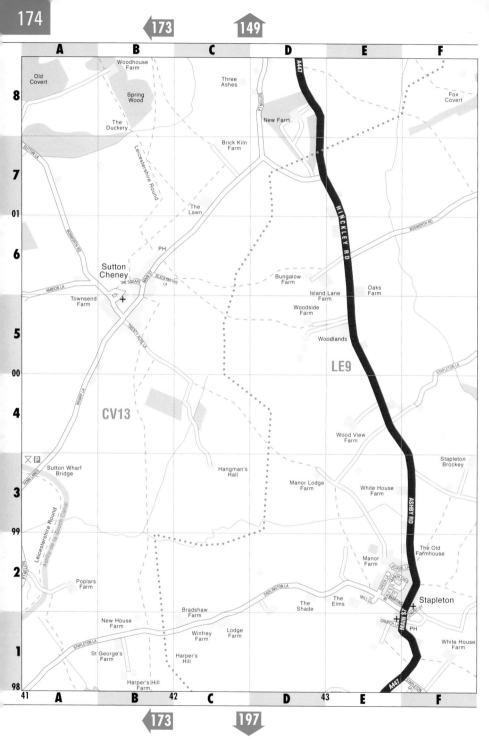

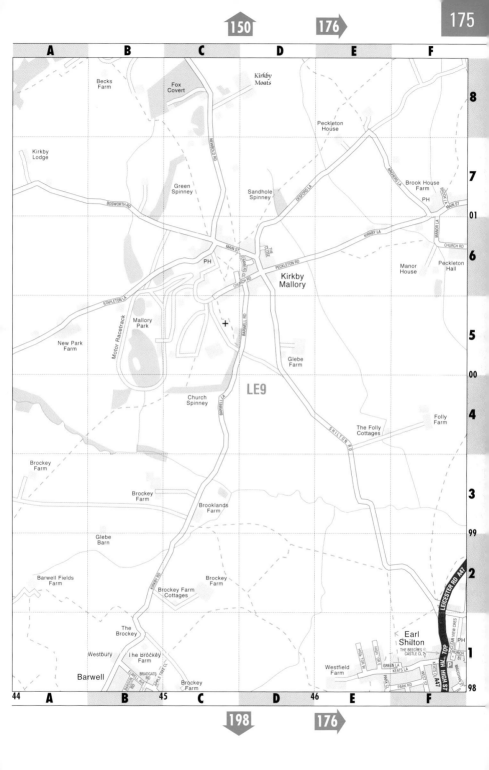

150
176

A B C D E F

8

Kirkby
Moats

Becks
Farm

Fox
Covert

Peckleton
House

7

Kirkby
Lodge

Green
Spinney

Sandhole
Spinney

NEWBOLD RD

DESFORD LA

BAGWORTH LA

Brook House
Farm

PH

MAIN ST

01

BOSWORTH RD

KIRKBY LA

MANOR LA

CHURCH RD

6

MAIN ST

THE CLOSE

STAMPERS CL

CHURCH RD

PH

PECKLETON RD

Kirkby
Mallory

Manor
House

Peckleton
Hall

STAPLETON LA

Mallory
Park

New Park
Farm

Motor Racetrack

BARWELL RD

+

Glebe
Farm

5

00

Church Spinney

LE9

SHILTON RD

The Folly
Cottages

Folly
Farm

4

BARWELL RD

Brockey
Farm

Brockey
Farm

Brooklands
Farm

3

99

Glebe
Barn

KIRKBY RD

Brockey
Farm

2

Barwell Fields
Farm

Brockey Farm
Cottages

The
Brockey

Westbury

The Brockey
Farm

BRADGATE
RD

TURVILLE LN

BARWELL LN

Westfield
Farm

HIGH TOP

GREEN LA

KEATS LA

PARK CL

PARK RD

CLEAR VIEW CRES

Earl
Shilton

THE BEECHES
CASTLE CL

PH

CHURCH

WEST ST

KEATS LA

HILL TOP

HIGH ST

LEICESTER RD A47

MAUGHAN ST

A47

1

Barwell

Brockey
Farm

98

44 A B 45 C D 46 E F

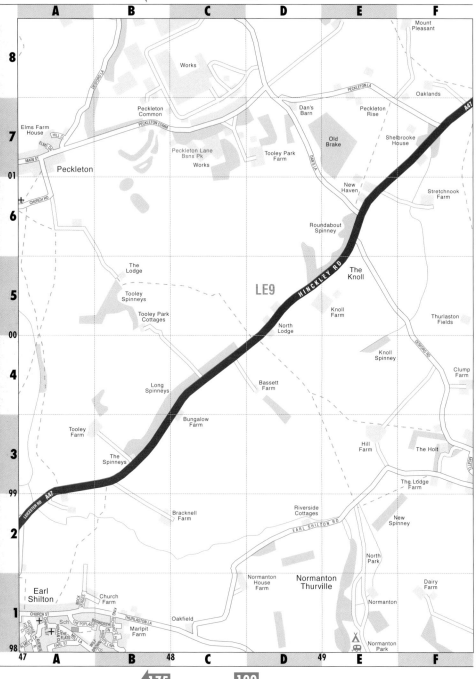

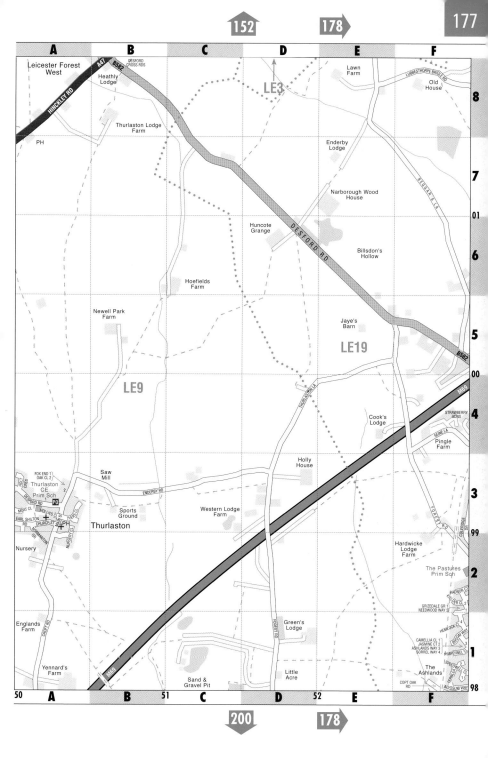

Leicester Forest West

Heathly Lodge

Thurlaston Lodge Farm

PH

DESFORD CROSS RDS

LE3

Lawn Farm

Old House

LUBBESTHORPE BRIDGE RD

Enderby Lodge

BEGGAR'S LA

Narborough Wood House

Huncote Grange

DESFORD RD

Billsdon's Hollow

Hoefields Farm

Newell Park Farm

Jaye's Barn

LE19

LE9

THURLASTON LA

00

M69

B582

Cook's Lodge

STRAWBERRY GDNS

SEINE LA

Pingle Farm

Holly House

FOX END 1
OAK CL 2

Thurlaston CE Prim Sch

Saw Mill

ENDERBY RD

Western Lodge Farm

FOREST RD

COLERIDGE

Hardwicke Lodge Farm

HOLLIES CL

EARL SHILTON RD

MOAT CL

DESFORD RD

SCRAMANTON CR

CHURCH ST
PH

NURSERY GT

Thurlaston

Sports Ground

The Pastures Prim Sch

RADNOR CL 1
KELLER CL 2

Nursery

GRIZEDALE GR 1
NEEDWOOD WAY 2

HEMLOCK CL

CROFT RD

Green's Lodge

CAMELLIA CL 1
JASMINE CT 2
ASHLANDS WAY 3
SORREL WAY 4

Englands Farm

FOREST RD

PRIMROSE CL

BROOM RD

PIMPERNEL

SPEEDWELL CL

FENNEL CL

Yennard's Farm

M69

Little Acre

The Ashlands

Sand & Gravel Pit

COPT OAK RD

ALYSSUM WAY

HINCKLEY RD

A47
B582

01

8

7

6

5

4

3

99

2

1

98

50   A   B   51   C   D   52   E   F

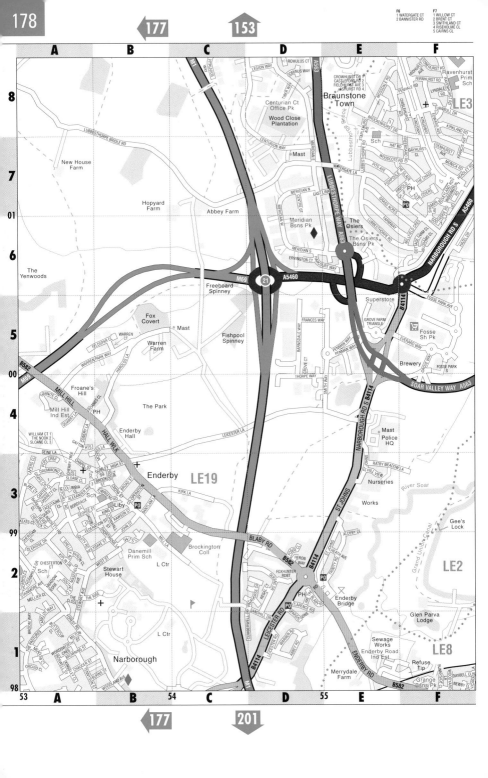

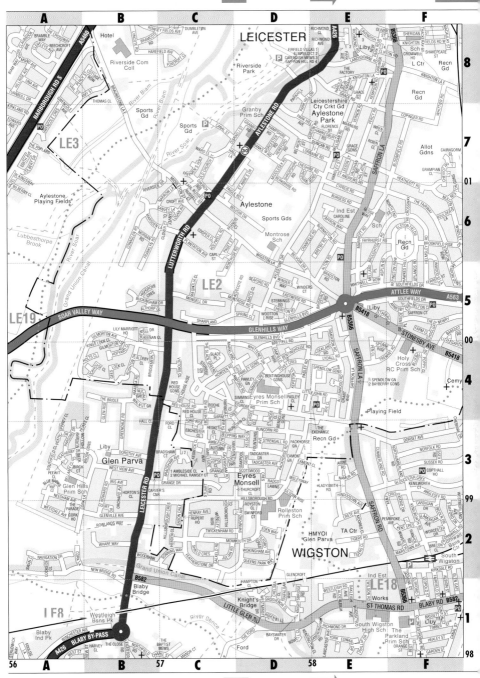

LEICESTER

LE3

LE2

LE19

LE18

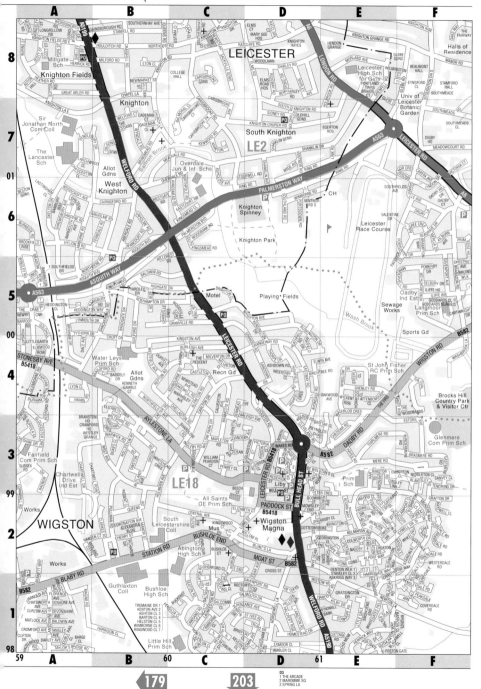

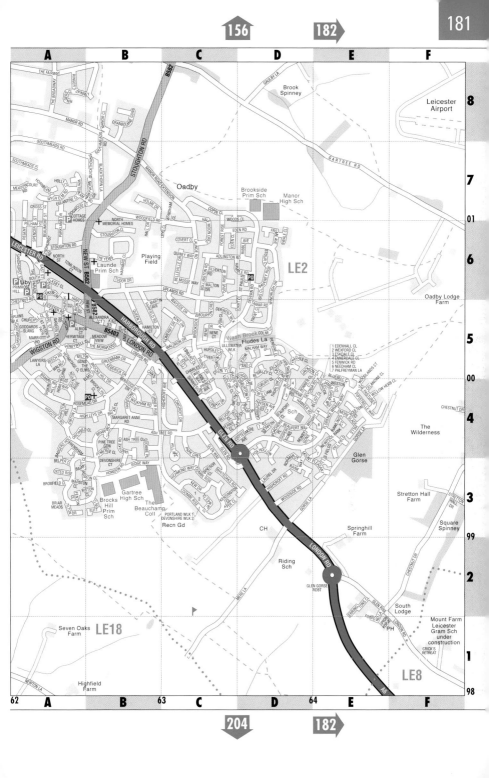

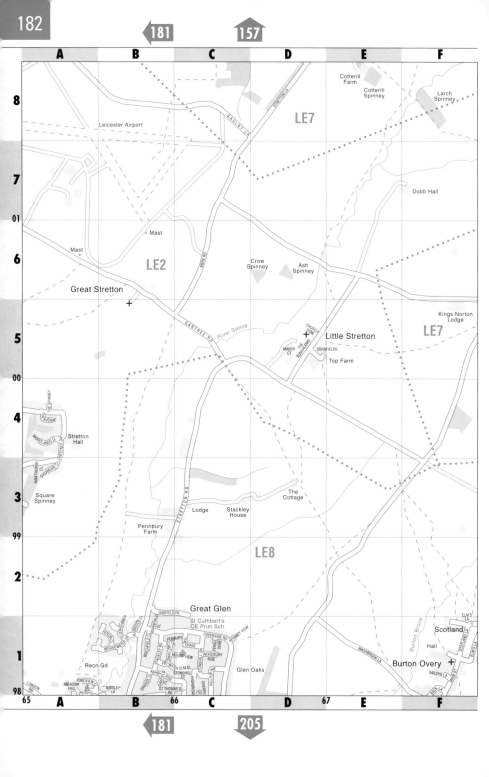

181
157

A   B   C   D   E   F

8

Cotterill Farm

Cotterill Spinney

Larch Spinney

Leicester Airport

GAULBY LA

STRETTON LA

LE7

7

Dobb Hall

01

Mast

6

Mast

MERE RD

Crow Spinney

Ash Spinney

LE2

Great Stretton

Kings Norton Lodge

GARTREE RD   River Sence

CHURCH WAY

Little Stretton

LE7

5

MANOR CT

BUILDINGS

CORNFIELDS

Top Farm

00

4

YEW SPINNEY

THE AVENUE

WOODLANDS CL   CHESTNUT DR

Stretton Hall

HAWTHORNE CL   SYCAMORE CL

3

Square Spinney

STRETTON RD

Lodge

Stackley House

The Cottage

Pennbury Farm

99

LE8

2

Great Glen

GARFIELD PK

St Cuthbert's CE Prim Sch

Burton Brook

ELM'S

Scotland

SCOTLAND RD

1

HIGH ST   BRIDGE WAY   BEECHES CL   STACKLEY RD

COVERSIDE RD   SPINNEY VIEW

PEMBURY   THE CHASE

MOUNT VIEW

FERNIE DENE

WOODBURY RISE

WASHBROOK LA

Hall

BAILEYS LA

MAIN ST

BACK LA

Burton Overy

Recn Gd

ASHBY CL   NYCH   ELM CL   STONEHILL

HILLTOP

GRANGE CL

MAGHBURGH

ABBO

ST THOMAS'S RD

Glen Oaks

MEADOW HILL   FORDVIEW

LONDON RD

BIRDLEY LA

98

65   A   B   66   C   D   67   E   F

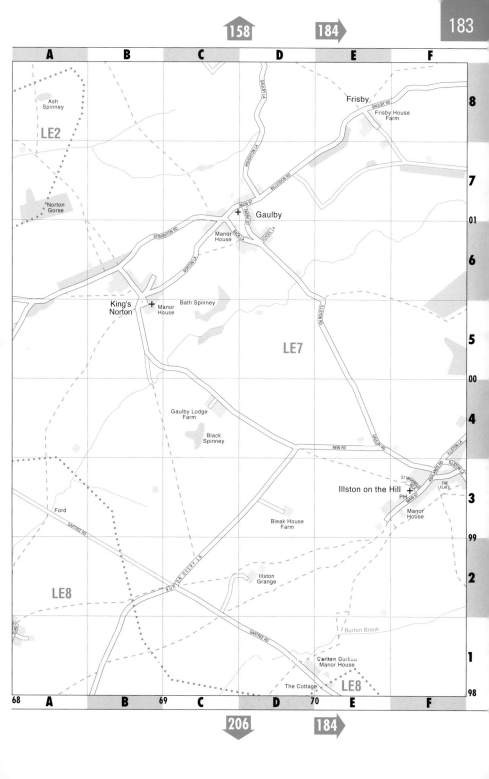

A B C D E F

8

Ash
Spinney

LE2

Frisby

GAULBY LA

Frisby House
Farm

GAULBY RD

7

Norton
Gorse

HOUGHTON LA

BILLESDON RD

01

MAIN ST

FRONT ST

Gaulby

STOUGHTON RD

Manor
House

BACK LA

SCHOOL LA

6

AGNTON LA

King's
Norton

Manor
House

Bath Spinney

LE7

ILLSTON RD

5

00

Gaulby Lodge
Farm

Black
Spinney

4

NEW RD

GAULBY RD

ILLSTON LA

ASH LANES RD

ILLSTON RD

St MICHAEL'S
WELL RD

Illston on the Hill

THE
FLATS

PH

MAIN ST

Manor
House

3

Ford

GARTREE RD

BURTON OVERY LA

Bleak House
Farm

99

LE8

Illston
Grange

2

GARTREE RD

Burton Brook

Carlton Curlieu
Manor House

1

LE8

The Cottage

98

183
159

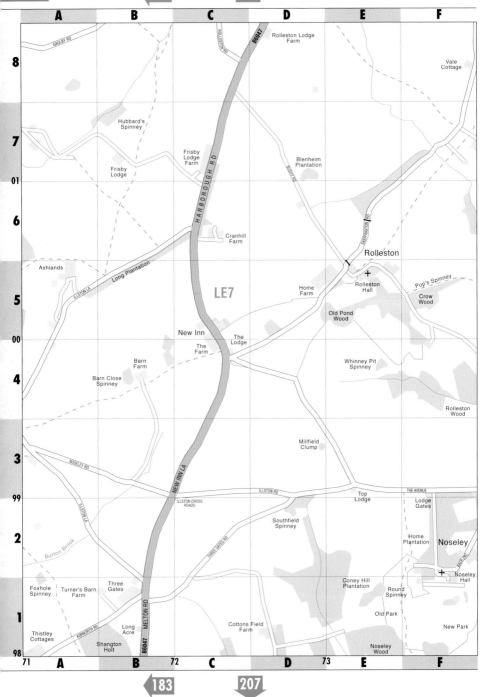

183
207

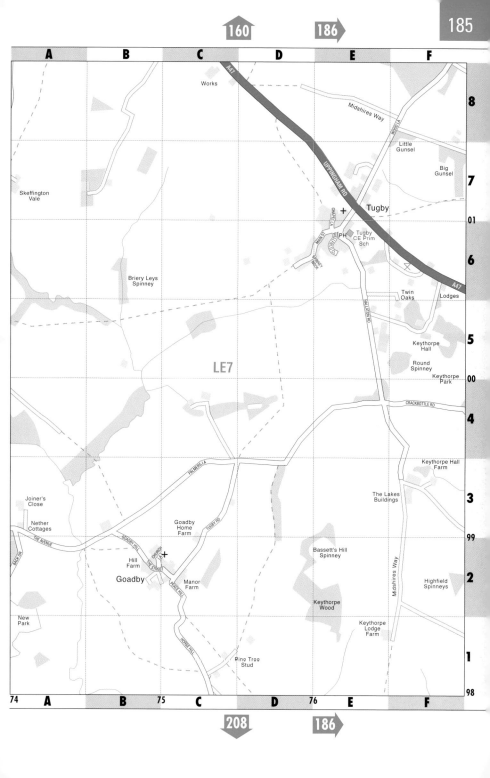

A B C D E F

8

Works

A47

Midshires Way

BROOK LA

Little
Gunsel

Big
Gunsel

7

UPPINGHAM RD

Skeffington
Vale

CHAPEL LA

+

Tugby

01

MAIN ST

PH

Tugby
CE Prim
Sch

A47

6

Briery Leys
Spinney

SPINNEY TRACK

Twin
Oaks

Lodges

HALLATON RD

Keythorpe
Hall

5

Round
Spinney

Keythorpe
Park

00

LE7

CRACKBOTTLE RD

4

Keythorpe Hall
Farm

PALMERS LA

The Lakes
Buildings

3

Joiner's
Close

TUGBY RD

Nether
Cottages

THE AVENUE

GOADBY HILL

Goadby
Home
Farm

99

BACK RD

Bassett's Hill
Spinney

Highfield
Spinneys

2

Hill
Farm

CHURCH LA

THE STREET

+

Goadby

Manor
Farm

PASTURE HILL

Keythorpe
Wood

Midshires Way

New
Park

HORSE HILL

Keythorpe
Lodge
Farm

1

Pine Tree
Stud

98

74 A B 75 C D 76 E F

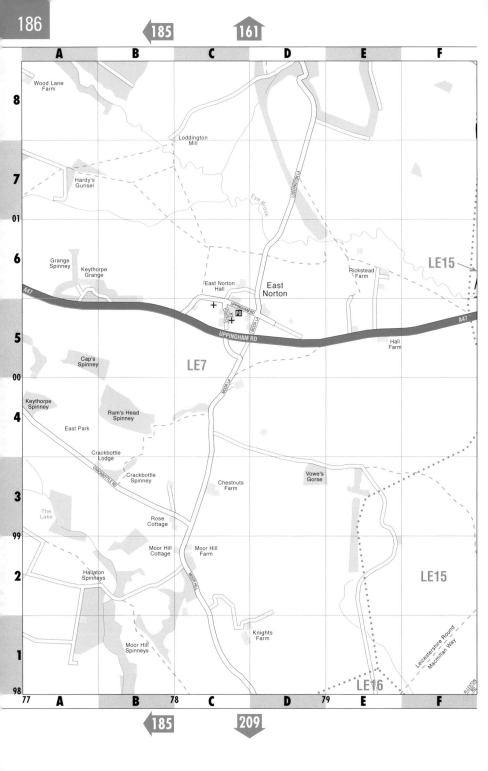

185
161

A B C D E F

8

Wood Lane
Farm

Loddington
Mill

7

Hardy's
Gunsel

01

Eye Brook

LODDINGTON LA

6

Grange
Spinney

Keythorpe
Grange

East Norton
Hall

East
Norton

Rickstead
Farm

LE15

A47

UPPINGHAM RD

PO

5

UPPINGHAM RD

Hall
Farm

A47

LE7

Cap's
Spinney

00

MOOR LA

Keythorpe
Spinney

Ram's Head
Spinney

4

East Park

Crackbottle
Lodge

CRACKBOTTLE RD

Crackbottle
Spinney

Chestnuts
Farm

Vowe's
Gorse

3

The
Lake

Rose
Cottage

99

Moor Hill
Cottage

Moor Hill
Farm

2

Hallaton
Spinneys

MOOR HILL

LE15

Knights
Farm

Moor Hill
Spinneys

1

Leicestershire Round
Macmillan Way

98

LE16

ALLEXTON
RD

77 A B 78 C D 79 E F

185
209

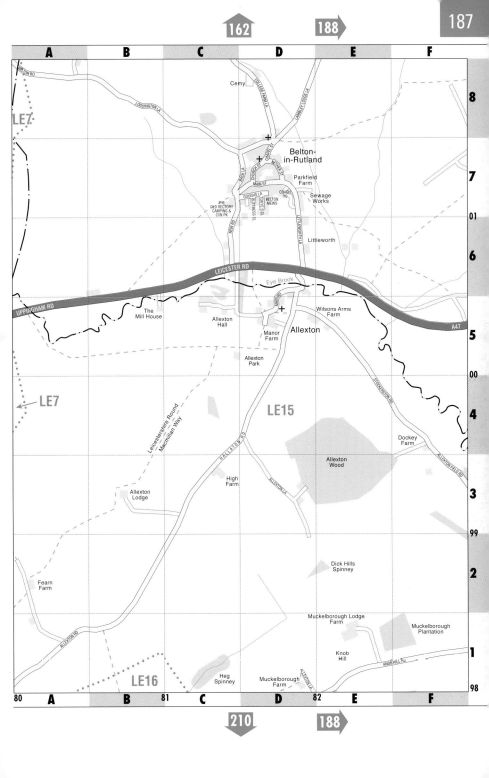

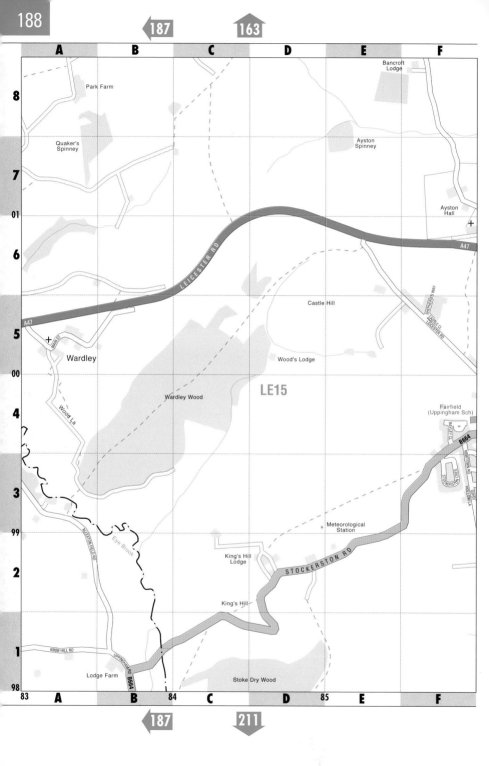

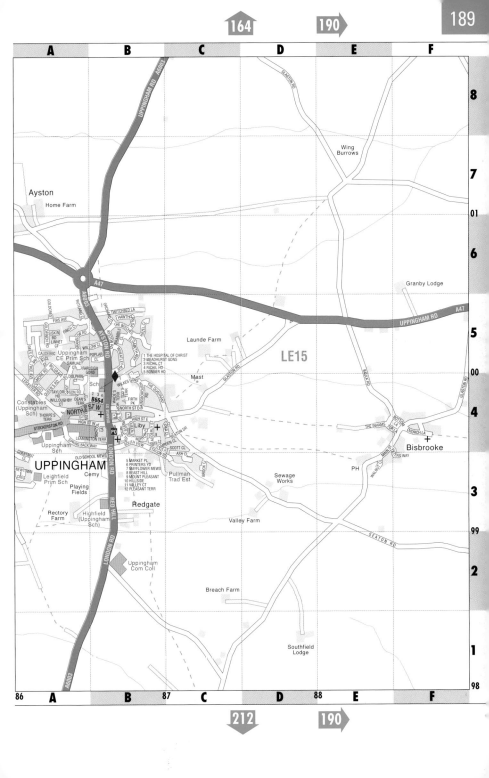

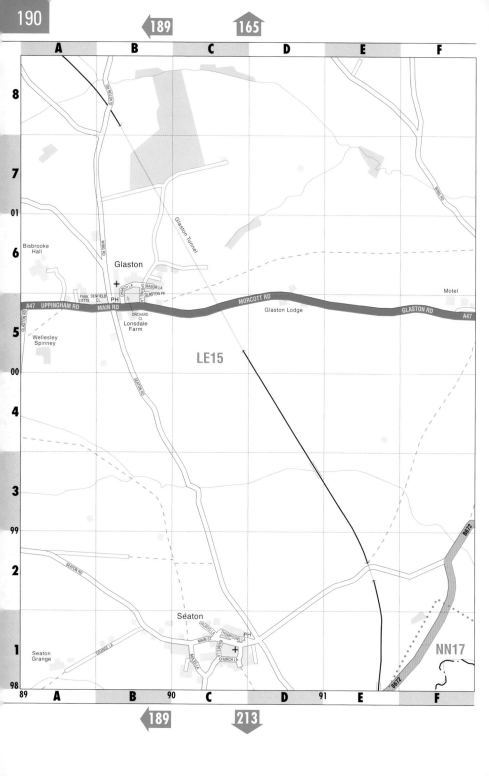

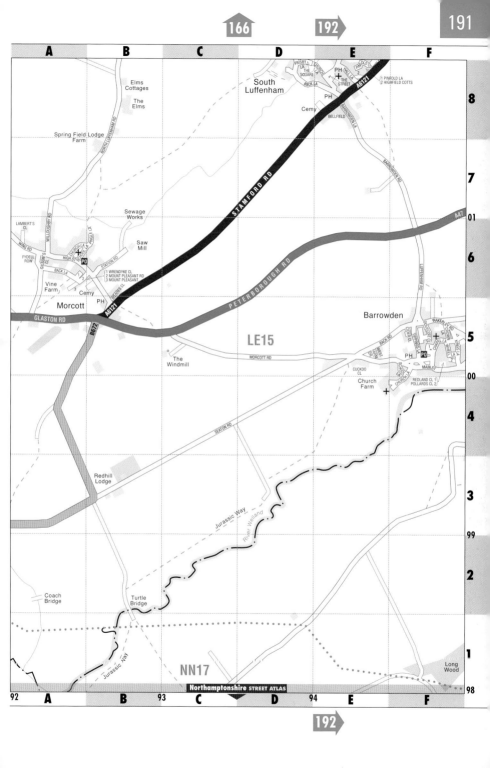

A B C D E F

8
7
01
6
5
00
4
3
99
2
1
98

Elms
Cottages

The
Elms

South
Luffenham

FRISBY LA | THE
SQUARE
BACK LA

PH | HALL
THE
STREET

1 PINFOLD LA
2 HIGHFIELD COTTS

A6121

PH

Cemy

BELLFIELD

BARROWDEN LA

Spring Field Lodge
Farm

STAMFORD RD

A47

BARNSDALE RD

Sewage
Works

LAMBERT'S
CL

WING RD

WILLOUGHBY RD

CHAPEL LA

CHURCH LA

HIGH ST

STATION RD

Saw
Mill

PETERBOROUGH RD

LUFFENHAM RD

FYDELL
ROW

GLEBE'S CL

BACK LA

PO

1 WRENDYKE CL
2 MOUNT PLEASANT RD
3 MOUNT PLEASANT

VICAR'S CL

Vine
Farm

Cemy

PH

Morcott

A6121

LE15

Barrowden

WAKERLEY RD

DOCTOR'S CL

KINGS LA

BACK RD

CHURCH LA

WEST
CL

SPRINGS LA

PH

PO

MAIN ST

REDLAND CL 1
POLLARDS CL 2

GLASTON RD

B672

The
Windmill

MORCOTT RD

CUCKOO
CL

Church
Farm

CHURCH CL

SOUTH VIEW

Redhill
Lodge

SEATON RD

Jurassic Way

River Welland

Coach
Bridge

Turtle
Bridge

Jurassic Way

NN17

Long
Wood

92   A   B   93   C   D   94   E   F

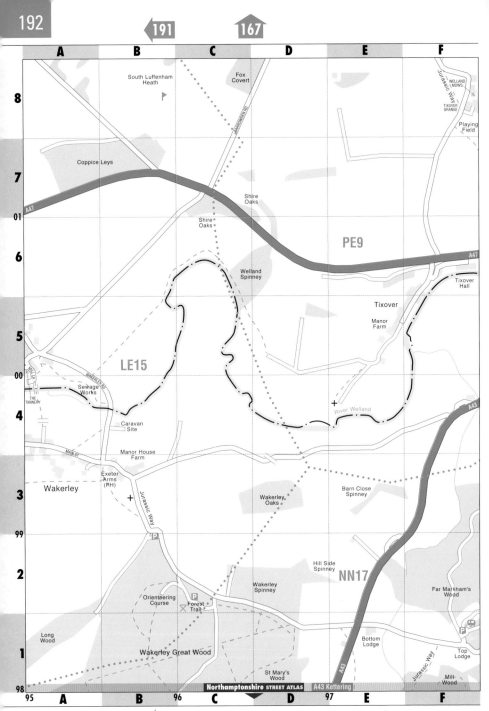

A B C D E F

8

South Luffenham Heath

Fox Covert

WELLAND MDWS.

Jurassic Way

TIXOVER GRANGE

Playing Field

7

Coppice Leys

A1

01

Shire Oaks

Shire Oaks

PE9

6

Welland Spinney

A47

Tixover Hall

Tixover

5

LE15

Manor Farm

00

Sewage Works

MELTON RD

WAKERLEY RD

THE TANNERY

4

Caravan Site

River Welland

A43

MAIN ST

Manor House Farm

3

Wakerley

Exeter Arms (PH)

Jurassic Way

Wakerley Oaks

Barn Close Spinney

99

P

Hill Side Spinney

NN17

2

Orienteering Course

P Forest Trail

Wakerley Spinney

Far Markham's Wood

Long Wood

P

Bottom Lodge

Top Lodge

1

Wakerley Great Wood

A43

Jurassic Way

Mill Wood

98

St Mary's Wood

95 A B 96 C D 97 E F

Sewage Works

Cuckoo Lodge

Vigo Woods

A47 Peterborough

8

River Welland

Quarry

Little Wood

7

01

Collyweston Great Wood

HIGHFIELD RD
STAMFORD RD
MILL ST
CHURCH LA
GREEN LA
QUEEN'S HILL
HIGH ST
CASTLE HILL

Duddington

Manor House

PH

PE9

6

Gregory's Lodge

Cemy

The Assarts

5

00

Gore Piece

Cambridgeshire STREET ATLAS

North Spinney

4

Noses Halt

Long Spinney

Jurassic Way

Little Wood

PE8

Cunnington's Spinney

Dales Wood

Peter's Nook

3

99

Dumb Bob Spinney

Buxton Wood

The Gullet

Westhay Wood

2

NN17

Great Watkinson

Old Sale

TOP LODGE

Jurassic Way

1

Stocklings

98

Hither Hazelwood

98   A   B   99   C   D   00   E   F

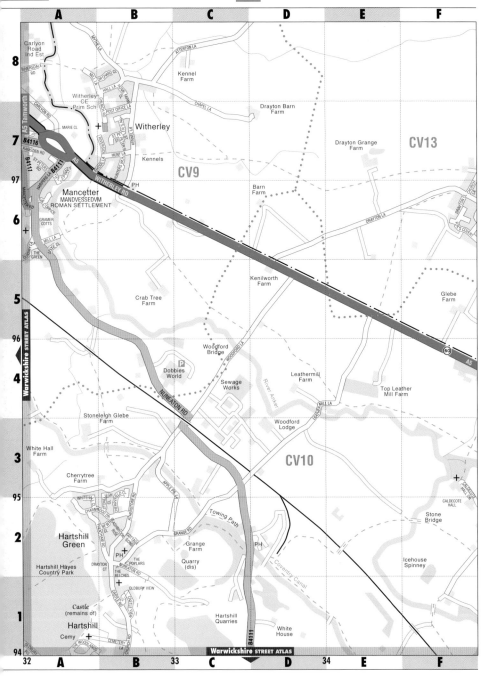

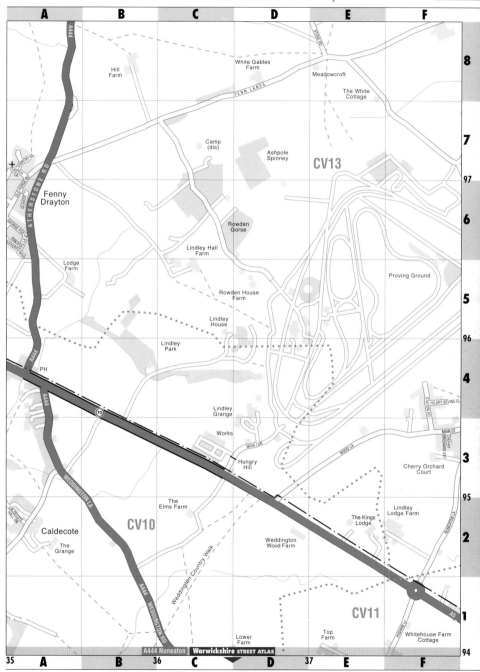

A   B   C   D   E   F

8

White Gables
Farm

Meadowcroft

Hill
Farm

The White
Cottage

7

Camp
(dis)

Ashpole
Spinney

CV13

97

Fenny
Drayton

Rowden
Gorse

6

Lindley Hall
Farm

Lodge
Farm

Proving Ground

Rowden House
Farm

5

Lindley
House

96

Lindley
Park

PH

4

Lindley
Grange

Hilary Bevins Cl

Works

Hungry
Hill

3

Cherry Orchard
Court

95

The
Elms Farm

Lindley
Lodge Farm

CV10

The Kings
Lodge

Caldecote

Weddington
Wood Farm

2

The
Grange

Weddington Country Walk

CV11

1

Lower
Farm

Top
Farm

Whitehouse Farm
Cottage

94

195
173

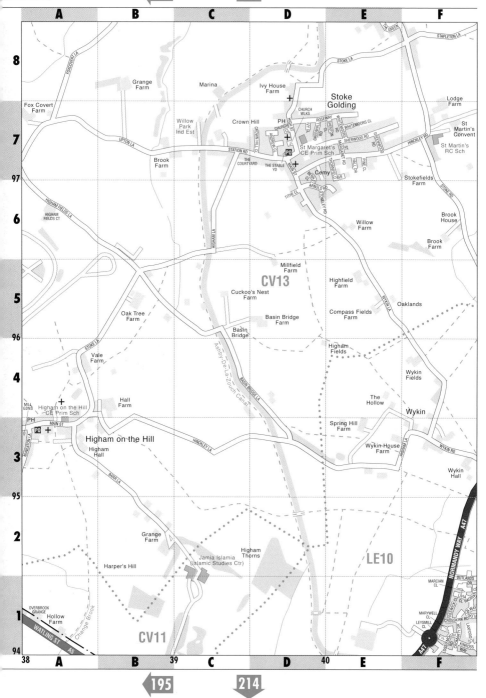

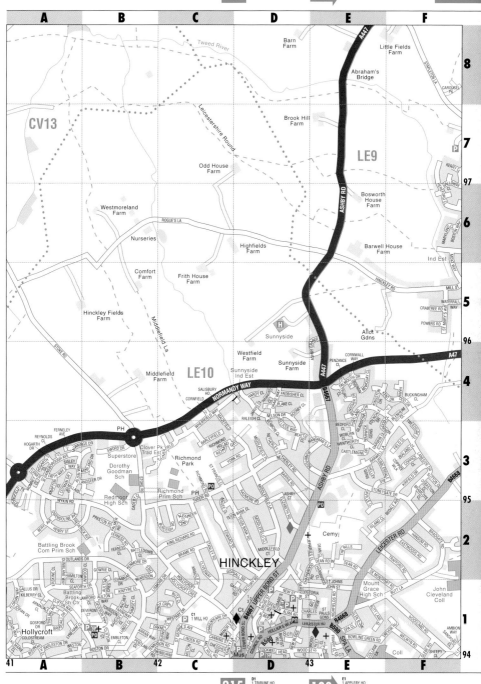

A B C D E F

CV13

Tweed River

Barn Farm

Little Fields Farm

A447

Abraham's Bridge

LE9

Brook Hill Farm

8

Leicestershire Round

Odd House Farm

P 7

97

ASHBY RD

Bosworth House Farm

Westmoreland Farm

ROGUE'S LA

Nurseries

Highfields Farm

Barwell House Farm

Ind Est 6

KERRY CL
OLD MILL

MARYLAND BOSTON RD

Comfort Farm

Frith House Farm

Hinckley Fields Farm

Middlefield La

Westfield Farm

Sunnyside

H Allot Gdns

Ind Est
MILL ST
WATERFALL WAY

CRABTREE RD
POWERS RD

ST MARY'S RD

A47

5

96

LE10

Middlefield Farm

Sunnyside Ind Est

Westfield Farm

Sunnyside Farm

ASHBY GRANGE

PENZANCE CL

Cornwall Way

A447

B4687

4

SALISBURY HO
CORNFIELD

NORMANDY WAY

HARDY CL
FROBISHER CL

BLAKE CL
NELSON DR
COWPER CL

WHARFEDALE RD
WYKEN RD
RALEIGH DR

BARLEYFIELD
RICHMOND RD

Buckingham CL

Bedford CL
WOBURN CL
WENTWORTH CL
CASTLEMAINE CL

WARWICK GDNS

TWEEDS CL

FERNELEY AVE
REYNOLDS CL
HOGARTH DR

PH

Clover Pk Trad Est
Superstore

Dorothy Goodman Sch

Richmond Park

Richmond Prim Sch

PH
PO

BEATTIE CL
HANGMAN'S LA

ASHBY RD

STONEYGATE DR

BORSALL RD

B4668

3

95

WYKIN RD
PRESTON RD

Redmoor High Sch

TUDOR RD

ST FRANCIS

YORK RD

RICHMOND RD

ASHBY CT

PO

LEICESTER RD

HENRY ST

King Richard Rd

BRAMB RD

STANLEY RD

PALMERS RD

TEIGN BANK RD

WOODLAND AVE

Cemy

+

2

Battling Brook Com Prim Sch

OUTLANDS DR
GOWRIE CL

BATTLEDOWN CL

BRAIME CL
CLOVERDALE

HINCKLEY

MIDDLEFIELD CT

DEAN RD W

Mount Grace High Sch

John Cleveland Coll

Gallus Dr
KILBERRY CL

Battling Brook Sch Ctr

MARSDON

TELCROFT CRES

CT 1 MILL HO

NEW ST

St Johns

JOHN ST

AMBION WAY

1

Gosford Dr
COLDSTREAM

Hollycroft

P
PO

EMBLETON CL

P

UPPER BOND ST

LINDEN RD

WOOD ST S AVE

LINDEN RD

B4667

HOLLIER'S WLK

CHARLES ST
PAULS GDNS

Mus

STOCKWELL HEAD
WOOD ST

SPA LA

B4668

B590

Bowling Green Rd

Coll

94

41 A B 42 C D 43 E F

D1
1 TRIBUNE HO
2 PRAETOR HO
3 JURIST HO
4 WELL LA
5 MANOR PL
6 BAINES LA
7 KING ST
8 WEAVERS CT
9 JUBILEE HO
10 QUEEN VICTORIA CT
11 CROWN CT
12 LAWRENCE HO

E1
1 APPLEBY HO
2 ST PETERS CT
3 BOSWORTH HO
4 PRIORY WLK

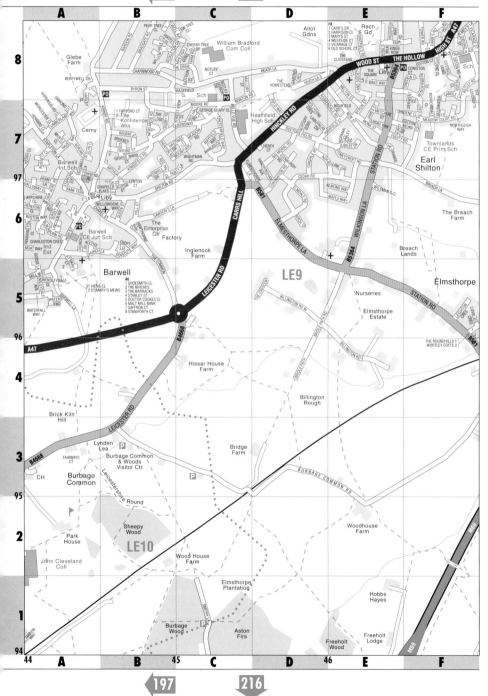

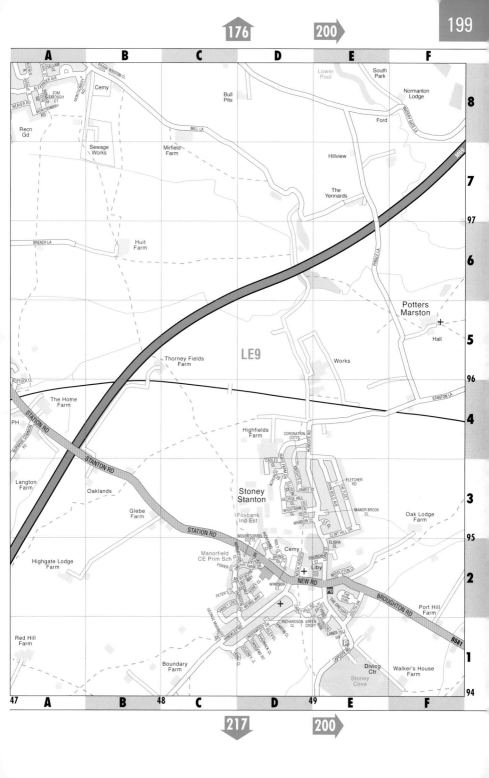

199
177
199
218

A B C D E F

8

7

97

6

5

96

4

3

95

2

1

94

50 A B 51 C D 52 E F

M69
Croft Rd
Watery Gate La
Sandpit Cotts
Croft La

Thurlaston Brook
Cemy
L Ctr
SPORTS FIELD LA
CHENEY CT 1
EUNICE AVE 2
Huncote Com Prim Sch
CRITCHLOW
DENMAN LA
LANGLEY CL
HOBILL CL
RISE CL
Springfield Farm
VETCH CL 1
COWSLIP CL 2
LOBELIA CL 3
CROP CL
Red Hill
WOODSIDE
BLAKENHALL CL
THORNBOROUGH CL
Huncote
Liby
COOPER CL
ROBOTHAM CL
Stone Quarry
Mill
MALT
CHICORY WY
PO
PH
THE GREEN
NARBOROUGH RD
CANET RD
RATCLIFFE
DUNCAN RD
SCHOOL
LECKLEY
Elms Farm
Huncote Rd
LE19

Thurlaston La

Hill Foot Farm
Croft Hill
Croft Quarry
Flash Farm
River Soar
B4114

Station La
Huncote Rd
Marston Rd
LE9
Church Farm
Cemy
PH
THE GREEN
HILL ST
DOVECOTE RD
Works
Fosse Farm
GUTHLAXTON GAP
Croft Rd

TERRACE COTTS
SPINNEY CT
SPINNEY
HOLLIER'S WAY
KENDALL'S AVE
SALISBURY AVE
WINTON AVE
CROXTON WAY
WINDSOR AVE
BALA RD
PO
Fosse House
Clarke's Spinney
Lowlands Farm
SCHOOL LA
BROUGHTON RD
BROCKEY AVE
CROFT
Depot
Bsns Pk
Three Boundary Farm
Croft CE Prim Sch
Croft Lodge Farm
Poplars Farm
COVENTRY RD
Ireland House Barn
Sewage Works
Paradise Spinney
LEICESTER RD
Sopers Bridge
Port Hill Farm
River Soar
Sutton Hill Farm
Sewage Works
Lodge Farm
Highland Farm
B581
Sopers Bridge Farm
BROUGHTON RD
B581
Fossefield Farm
B4114
Sutton Hill Bridge
Messenger's Barn
Sutton Farm
Walton Lodge Farm
Sutton Fields Farm

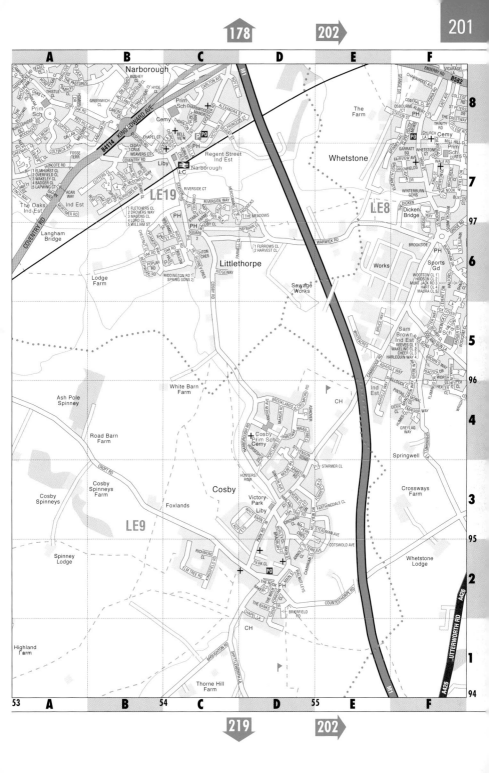

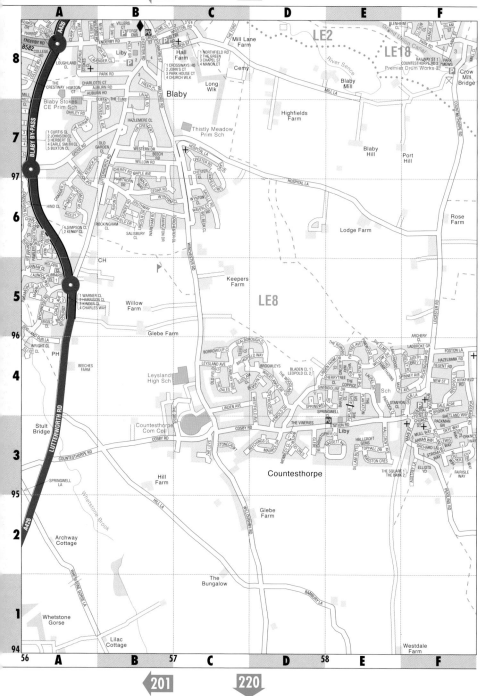

201
179

LE2

LE18

Grand Union Canal

Premier Drum Works

Crow Mill Bridge

River Sence

Mill Lane Farm

Cerny

Blaby Mill

1 NORTHFIELD RD
2 THE GREEN
3 CHAPEL ST
4 MANOR CT

Long Wlk

1 CROSSWAYS HO
2 JOHN'S CT
3 PARK HOUSE CT
4 CHURCH WLK

Hall Farm

Liby

ENDERBY RD

THE CRESTWAY

Blaby

Blaby Stokes CE Prim Sch

1 CURTIS CL
2 JOHNSON CL
3 HERBERT CL
4 EARLE SMITH CL
5 BUXTON CL

Thistly Meadow Prim Sch

Highfields Farm

Blaby Hill

Port Hill

Rose Farm

BLABY BY-PASS

B582

ENDERBY RD

COLLEGE

MILL MILE CL

HOSPITAL LA

Lodge Farm

LE8

Keepers Farm

CH

4 SIMPSON CL
2 KENNY CL

1 WARNER CL
2 HARRISON CL
3 KINDER CL
4 CHARLES WAY

Willow Farm

Glebe Farm

LUTTERWORTH RD

A426

BEECHES FARM

PH

WRIGHT CL

SCARBOROUGH CL

BORROWDALE CL

Leysland High Sch

BROADFIELD WAY

BROOMLEYS

1 BLADEN CL
2 LEOPOLD CL

ARCHERY CL

LADBROKE GR

FOSTON LA

HAZELBANK RD

REGENT RD

NEW ST

KIRKHILL

DALE ACRE

SHETLAND WAY

PACKMAN

SKYE WAY

ORKNEY CL

The Coppice

Sch

Countesthorpe Com Coll

Stult Bridge

COUNTESTHORPE RD

SPRINGWELL LA

WHETSTONE GORSE LA

WHETSTONE GORSE LA

Hill Farm

HILL LA

Whetstone Brook

The Vineries

Liby

HALLCROFT GDNS

TOPHALL DR

ORCHARD RD

Countesthorpe

ELLIOTS YD

THE SQUARE
THE BANK

FAIRISLE WAY

PEATLING RD

Archway Cottage

Glebe Farm

The Bungalow

BANBURY LA

Whetstone Gorse

Lilac Cottage

Westdale Farm

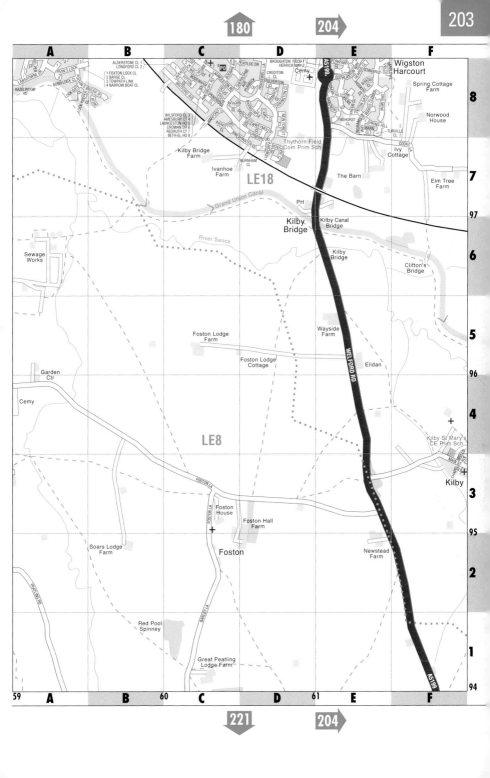

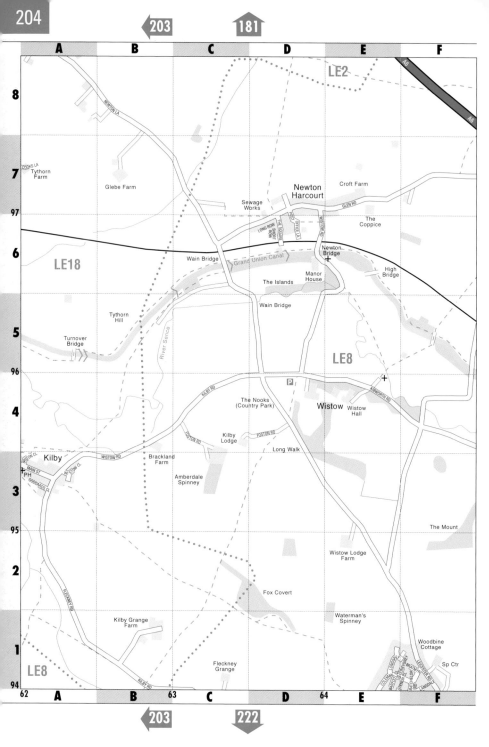

A   **B**   **C**   **D**   **E**   **F**

LE2

A6

8

NEWTON LA

7

COOKS LA
Tythorn
Farm

Glebe Farm

Croft Farm

Newton
Harcourt

Sewage
Works

97

THE SQUARE
LONG ROW
OFFICE LA.
PSET

GLEN RD

The
Coppice

6

LE18

Wain Bridge

Grand Union Canal

Newton
Bridge

High
Bridge

Manor
House

The Islands

Tythorn
Hill

River Sence

Wain Bridge

5

Turnover
Bridge

LE8

96

KILBY RD

The Nooks
(Country Park)

P

KIBWORTH RD

4

Wistow

Wistow
Hall

FOSTON RD

FOSTON RD

Kilby
Lodge

Long Walk

Kilby

WISTOW RD

Brackland
Farm

MAIN ST
WISTON CL
PH
GODDARDS CL
PRESTON CL

Amberdale
Spinney

3

95

The Mount

Wistow Lodge
Farm

2

FLECKNEY RD

Fox Covert

Waterman's
Spinney

Kilby Grange
Farm

Woodbine
Cottage

1

LE8

KILBY RD

Fleckney
Grange

Sp Ctr

COLTON CL
LONGFORD
STONHOUSE CL
BATH LA
TATTON CL
BRATBY LA
LAINGALE
LEICESTER RD

94

A   62   **B**   63   **C**   **D**   64   **E**   **F**

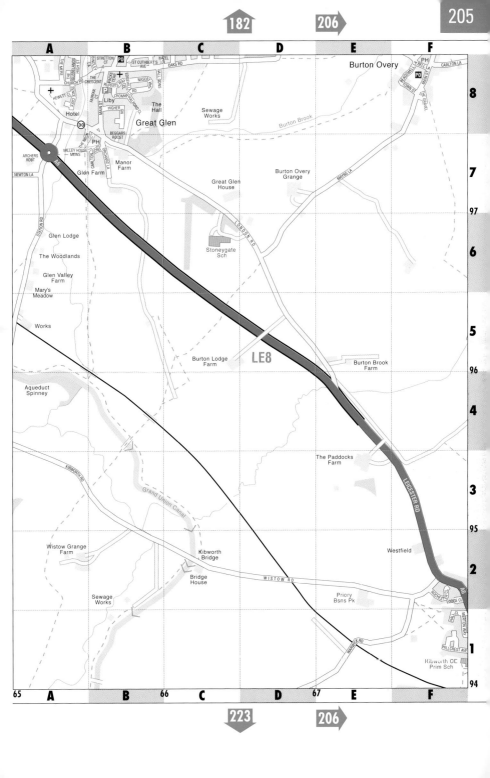

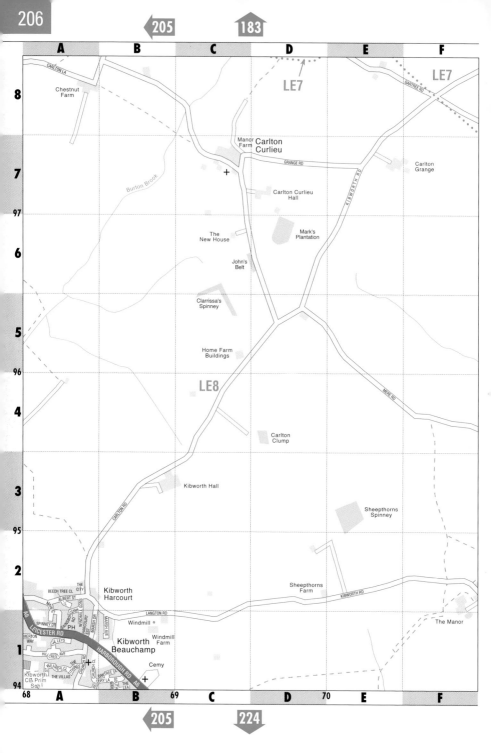

LE7

LE7

Chestnut
Farm

CARLTON LA

8

Burton Brook

GARTREE RD

Manor
Farm

Carlton
Curlieu

GRANGE RD

Carlton
Grange

7

Carlton Curlieu
Hall

97

KIBWORTH RD

The
New House

Mark's
Plantation

6

John's
Belt

Clarissa's
Spinney

5

Home Farm
Buildings

LE8

96

MERE RD

4

Carlton
Clump

3

Kibworth Hall

CARLTON RD

Sheepthorns
Spinney

95

2

BEECH TREE CL

THE
CITY

Kibworth
Harcourt

Sheepthorns
Farm

KIBWORTH RD

ALBERT ST

LANGTON RD

The Manor

Windmill

A6 LEICESTER RD

PH

MERTON
WAY

Kibworth
Beauchamp

Windmill
Farm

MARSH AVE

SPINNEY DR

HARBOROUGH RD A6

Cemy

Kibworth
CB Prim
Schl

THE VILLAS

THE LEA

1

94

68

69

70

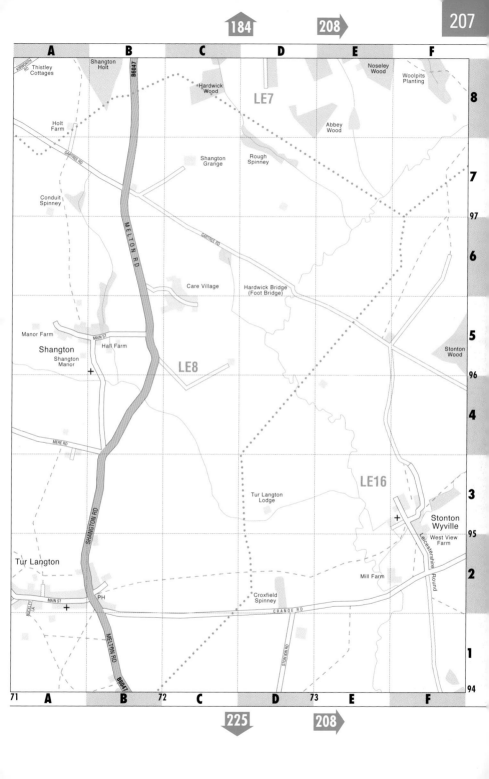

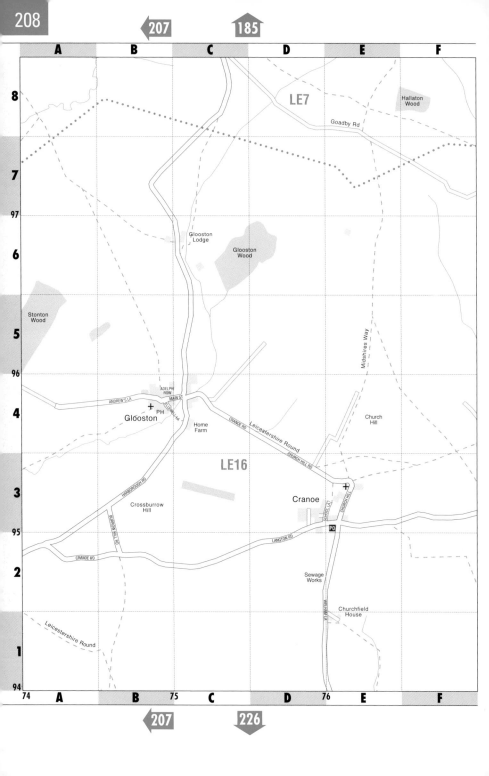

207

185

A　B　C　D　E　F

8

LE7

Hallaton
Wood

Goadby Rd

7

97

Glooston
Lodge

6

Glooston
Wood

Stonton
Wood

Midshires Way

5

96

ADELPHI
ROW

MAIN ST

ANDREW'S LA

PH

4

Glooston

Home
Farm

CRANOE RD

Leicestershire Round

CHURCH HILL RD

Church
Hill

LE16

3

HARBOROUGH RD

Crossburrow
Hill

Cranoe

CHURCH HILL RD

CHURCH ST

BURROW HILL RD

PO

95

CRANOE RD

LANGTON RD

2

Sewage
Works

Churchfield
House

WELHAM LA

Leicestershire Round

1

94

74　A　B　75　C　D　76　E　F

207

226

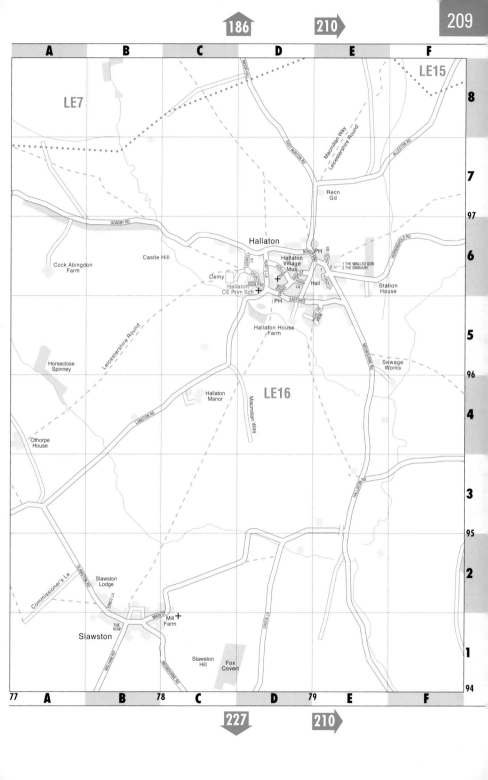

LE15

A B C D E F

LE7

8

7

97

6

Hallaton

Castle Hill

Cock Abingdon
Farm

Cemy

Hallaton
CE Prim Sch

Hallaton
Village
Mus

1 THE WALLED GDN
2 THE GRANARY

Hall

PH

EASTGATE

Station
House

5

Hallaton House
Farm

Horseclose
Spinney

Leicestershire Round

LE16

96

Hallaton
Manor

Macmillan Way

4

Othorpe
House

LANGTON RD

3

95

Slawston
Lodge

Commissioner's La

SLAPSTING RD

TONGS LA

MAIN ST

Mill
Farm

2

THE ROW

Slawston

WELHAM RD

MELBOURNE RD

Slawston
Hill

Fox
Covert

1

77 A 78 B C 79 D E F 94

MOOR HILL

EAST NORTON RD

Macmillan Way
Leicestershire Round

ALLEXTON RD

Recn
Gd

GOADBY RD

HORNINGHOLD RD

NORTH END
PH

HAZEL GR

HOG LA
HURN ST
HURN LA

MEDBOURNE RD

SEWAGE
Works

HALLATON RD

GREEN LA

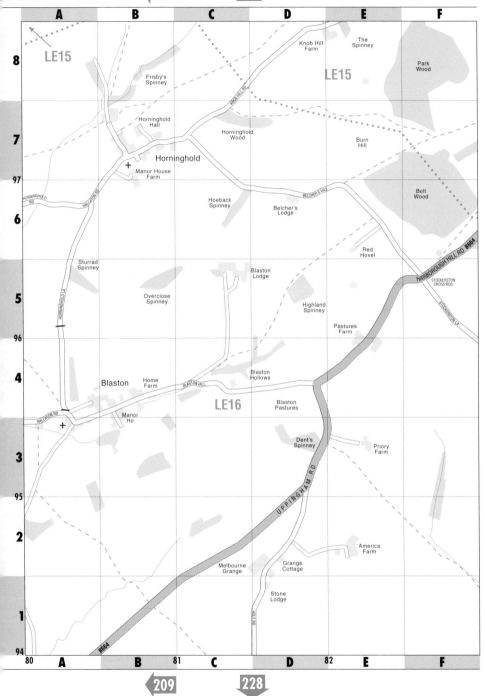

LE15

8

Frisby's
Spinney

Horninghold
Hall

7

Horninghold

Manor House
Farm

97

HORNINGHOLD
RD

HALLATON RD

6

Sturrad
Spinney

Overclose
Spinney

5

HORNINGHOLD LA

96

4

Blaston

Home
Farm

BLASTON HILL

LE16

HALLATON RD

3

95

2

94

B664

Knob Hill
Farm

The
Spinney

LE15

Park
Wood

KNOB HILL RD

Horninghold
Wood

Burn
Hill

Hoeback
Spinney

BELCHER'S HILL

Belcher's
Lodge

Bolt
Wood

Red
Hovel

HARBOROUGH HILL RD B664

Blaston
Lodge

Highland
Spinney

Pastures
Farm

STOCKERSTON
CROSS RDS

STOCKERSTON LA

Blaston
Hollows

Blaston
Pastures

Dent's
Spinney

Priory
Farm

UPPINGHAM RD

America
Farm

Grange
Cottage

HOLT RD

Melbourne
Grange

Stone
Lodge

Manor
Ho

80   A   B   81   C   D   82   E   F

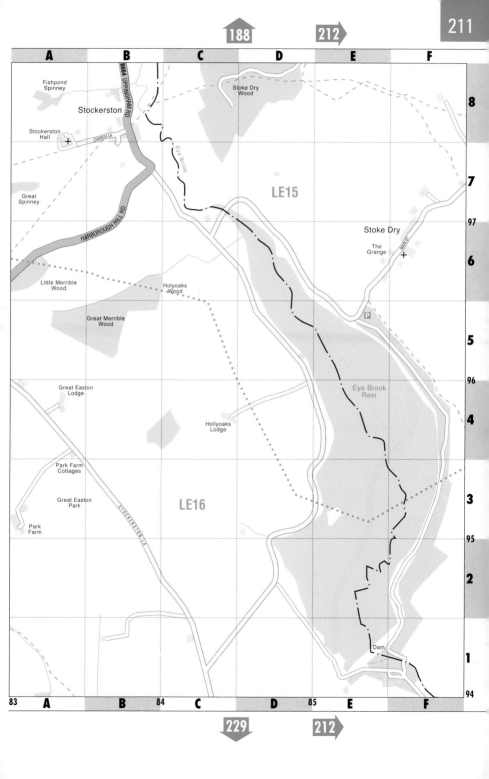

188
212

A　　B　　C　　D　　E　　F

Fishpond
Spinney

Stockerston

Stoke Dry
Wood

8

B664 UPPINGHAM RD

Stockerston
Hall

CHURCH LA

Eye Brook

LE15

7

97

Stoke Dry

Great
Spinney

HARBOROUGH HILL RD

The
Grange

MAIN ST

6

Little Merrible
Wood

Holyoaks
Wood

P

Great Merrible
Wood

5

96

Great Easton
Lodge

Eye Brook
Resr

4

Hollyoaks
Lodge

Park Farm
Cottages

STOCKERSTON LA

LE16

3

95

Great Easton
Park

Park
Farm

2

Dam

1

94

83　　A　　B　　84　　C　　D　　85　　E　　F

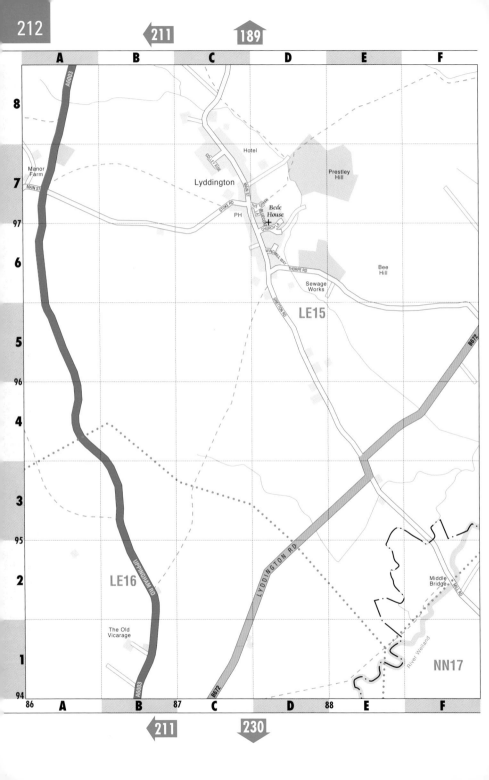

211
189

A   B   C   D   E   F

8

7

Manor
Farm

97

Lyddington

Hotel

MAIN ST

COLLEGE ST

STOKE RD

MAIN ST

THE GREEN

CHURCH ST

PH

Bede
House

CHURCH

Prestley
Hill

6

WINDMILL WAY

THORPE RD

Sewage
Works

Bee
Hill

GRETTON RD

LE15

5

B672

96

4

3

95

LYDDINGTON RD

2

LE16

UPPINGHAM RD

The Old
Vicarage

Middle
Bridge

BULL RD

1

B672

River Welland

NN17

94

86   A   B   87   C   D   88   E   F

A6003

A6003

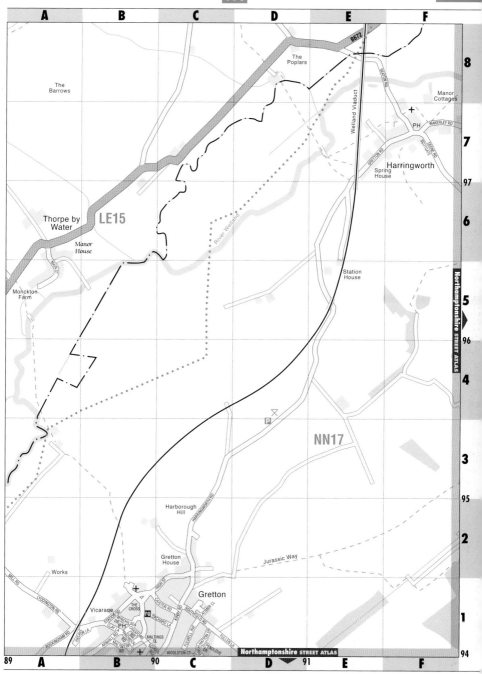

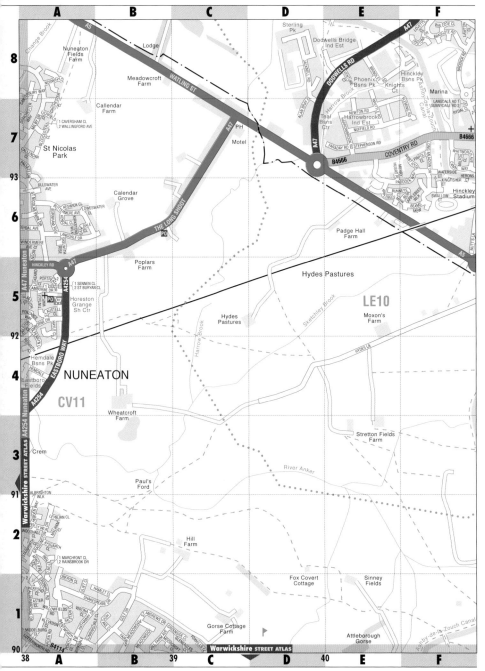

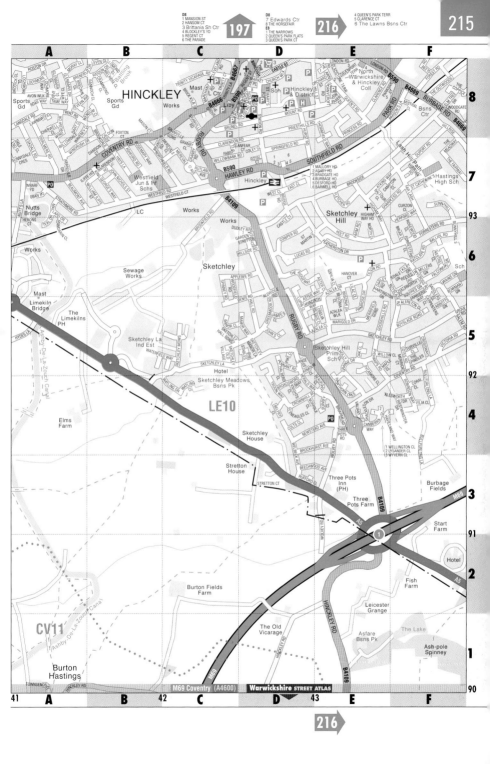

D8
1 MANSION ST
2 HANSOM CT
3 BRITTANIA Sh Ctr
4 BLOCKLEY'S YD
5 REGENT CT
6 THE PARADE

197

D8
7 Edwards Ctr
8 THE HORSEFAIR
E8
1 THE NARROWS
2 QUEEN'S PARK FLATS
3 QUEEN'S PARK CT

216

4 QUEEN'S PARK TERR
5 CLARENCE CT
6 The Lawns Bsns Ctr

215

A B C D E F

8

THE COPPICE
WOODGATE RD
Aston
Firs
Aston
Firs
CASTLEWOOD
MOBILE HOME PK
ASTON FIRS
CVN SITE
Averley House
Farm
HINCKLEY RD
B4669
HINCKLEY RD
B4669
SMITHY LA
LE9

BURBAGE RD
B578
Threeways
Farm
Threeways
SAPCOTE RD
The
Homestead
M69

7
THE FAIRWAY
WOODBANK
NEWBOLD RD
MEADOW DR
BATES CL
ASTILL BOROUGH CL
CHESTER CT
DORCHESTER RD
SHERIFF
ASTON FLAMVILLE RD
ASTON LA

93
HINCKLEY RD
STOCKING
LEYS
WOODS AVE
ELMINSTER CL
REGENCY
CT
CAMROSE AVE

6
FORRESTERS
RD
P
THE LEYS
ASHBURTON
CL
Leicestershire Round
1 GROSVENOR CRES
2 CEDAR CT
3 PILGRIMS GATE
Cottage
Farm
MANOR HOUSE CL
Manor
House
Pond
Spinney
Manor
Farm
Sch
Burbage
Cemy
Aston Flamville
SHARNFORD RD
HICKLEY RD

Church St
PO
Burbage
Sch
CHURCH
Liby
Oak
Farm
LYCHGATE LA
5
WINDSOR ST
HORSE
ORCHARD
BRITANNIA
LIBRARY
GATE CL
SAVILLE RD
LODGE CL
Lychgate
Farm
Lychgate
Farm
LE10

92
White House
Farm
Deepdale
Farm
Mickle Hill
Spinney
Mickle Hill

4
WOODLAND LA
Fields
Farm
IRONHOUSE LA
LUTTERWORTH RD
Mickle Hill
Farm

3
M69
Burbage
House
Orchard
Farm
Soar Brook

91
Soar Brook
Spinney

2
A5
Three Corner
Spinney
Hogue Hall
B4114

1
Ash-pole
Spinney
Crab-tree
Spinney
B578
A5
Lodge
Farm
COVENTRY RD
B4114
CHURCH
LA

90
44 A B 45 C D 46 E F

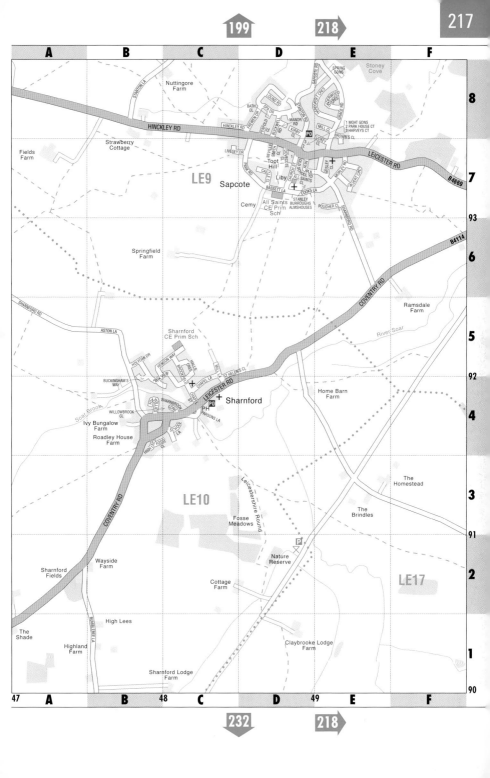

199
218
232
218

A **B** **C** **D** **E** **F**

8
7
93
6
5
92
4
3
91
2
1
90

47 48 49

Nuttingore Farm

Strawberry Cottage

Fields Farm

HINCKLEY RD

SPRING GDNS

Stoney Cove

1 MOAT GDNS
2 PARK HOUSE CT
3 HARVEYS CT

BATH CL

MANOR RD

KIRBY

PO

BROWN'S CL

LEICESTER RD

B4669

LIVESEY DR

Toot Hill

Liby

ALL SAINTS

WESLEY CL

LE9

Sapcote

Cemy

All Saints CE Prim Sch

STANLEY BURROUGHS ALMSHOUSES

POUGHER CL

HARRISON CL

B4114

Springfield Farm

COVENTRY RD

Ramsdale Farm

River Soar

SHARNFORD RD

ASTON LA

Sharnford CE Prim Sch

HOLYOAK DR

HEACOM WAY

VALE

BROOKFIELD

BUCKINGHAM'S WAY

CHAPEL LA

ST HELENS CL

LEICESTER RD

Sharnford

PH

PO

PARSONS LA

Home Barn Farm

Soar Brook

WILLOWBROOK CL

SHARNBROOK GDNS

SCHOOL LA

Ivy Bungalow Farm

Roadley House Farm

HIGH ST FOSSE CL

COVENTRY RD

LE10

The Homestead

The Brindles

Leicestershire Round

Fosse Meadows

91

P

Nature Reserve

LE17

Wayside Farm

Sharnford Fields

Cottage Farm

MARBLE LEE LA

High Lees

The Shade

Highland Farm

Sharnford Lodge Farm

Claybrooke Lodge Farm

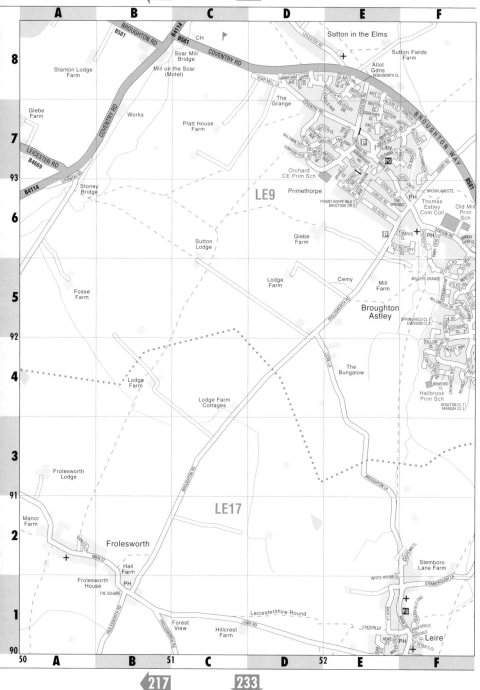

217
200

Sutton in the Elms

Sutton Fields Farm

Allot Gdns

Stanton Lodge Farm

BROUGHTON RD
B581
B4114
B581
CH
COVENTRY RD
Soar Mill Bridge
Mill on the Soar (Motel)
SOAR MILL LA
GRANTHAM
AVE
LEICESTER RD
KENILWORTH CL

Glebe Farm

LEICESTER RD
B4669
B4114
COVENTRY RD
Works
COVENTRY RD

The Grange

COVENTRY RD

KITE CL
KESTREL
FALCON CL
HARRIER
OSPREY
EAGLE

Platt House Farm

Stoney Bridge

BALDWIN CL
GORHAM RISE
SALLING RD

Orchard CE Prim Sch

LE9
Primethorpe
PRIMETHORPE WLK 1
BROCTONE DR 2

The Springs
PH

Liby
P
PO
CL

Thomas Estley Com Coll

Old Mill Prim Sch

Brooklands Cl

BROUGHTON WAY

Fosse Farm

Sutton Lodge

Glebe Farm

JUBILEE RD
SIX ACRES

ST MARYS CL
P
OLD RECTORY CL
CL
CH
STATION RD
MANOR

Millers Grange

Lodge Farm

Cemy

Mill Farm

Broughton Astley

STILES
MILLWOOD DR
BENFORD

92

Lodge Farm

The Bungalow

FROLESWORTH RD

LEIRE LA

Springfield Cl 1
Everson Cl 2

FALLOW

PLOVER

Lodge Farm Cottages

Hallbrook Prim Sch

BOULTON CL 1
FARADAY CL 2

Frolesworth Lodge

BROUGHTON LA

LE17

Manor Farm

Frolesworth

MAIN ST
KIRKBY RD

Hall Farm
PH

Stemboro Lane Farm

ANCHOR CL
STEMBROUGH LA

Frolesworth House
THE SQUARE

WHITE HOUSE CL

PO
BACK LA
MAIN ST

Forest View

Leicestershire Round
LEIRE RD

Hillcrest Farm

STATION LA

Leire
HOKE CT
PH
ST PETER'S CL

217
233

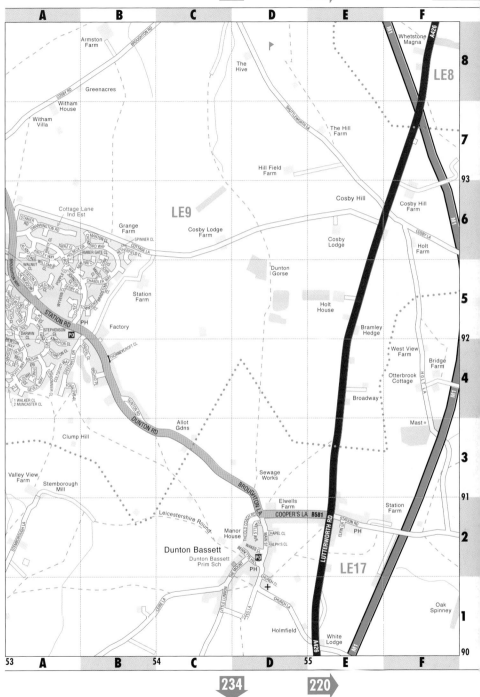

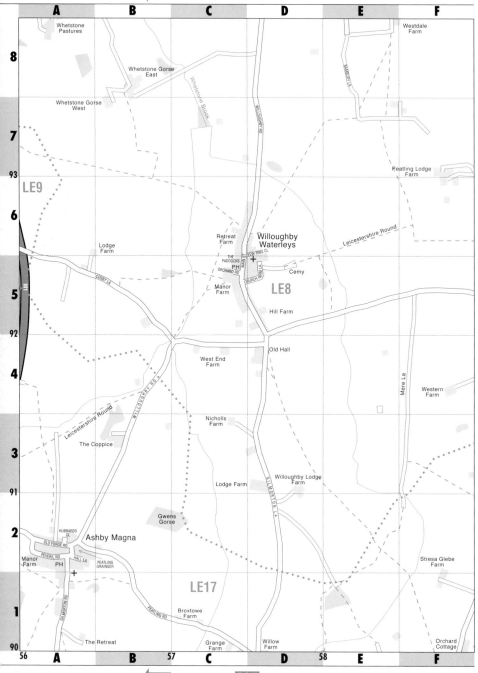

219
202
219
235

Whetstone
Pastures

Whetstone Gorse
East

Whetstone Block

Whetstone Gorse
West

Westdale
Farm

BANBURY LA

WILLOUGHBY RD

Peatling Lodge
Farm

LE9

Lodge
Farm

COSBY LA

Retreat
Farm

Willoughby
Waterleys

Leicestershire Round

THE
PADDOCKS
ORCHARD RD

PH

ST MARYS
YEW TREE CL
CHURCH RD

Cemy

LE8

Manor
Farm

Hill Farm

Old Hall

Mt

West End
Farm

Mere La

Western
Farm

WILLOUGHBY RD

Leicestershire Round

Nicholls
Farm

The Coppice

GILMORTON LA

Willoughby Lodge
Farm

Lodge Farm

Gwens
Gorse

HUBBARDS
CL

OLD FORGE RD

Ashby Magna

PEVERIL RD

Manor
Farm

PH

HALL LA

PEATLING
GRAINGER

Stresa Glebe
Farm

LE17

GILMORTON RD

Broxtowe
Farm

PEATLING RD

The Retreat

Grange
Farm

Willow
Farm

Orchard
Cottage

56   57   58

90 91 92 93
1 2 3 4 5 6 7 8
A B C D E F

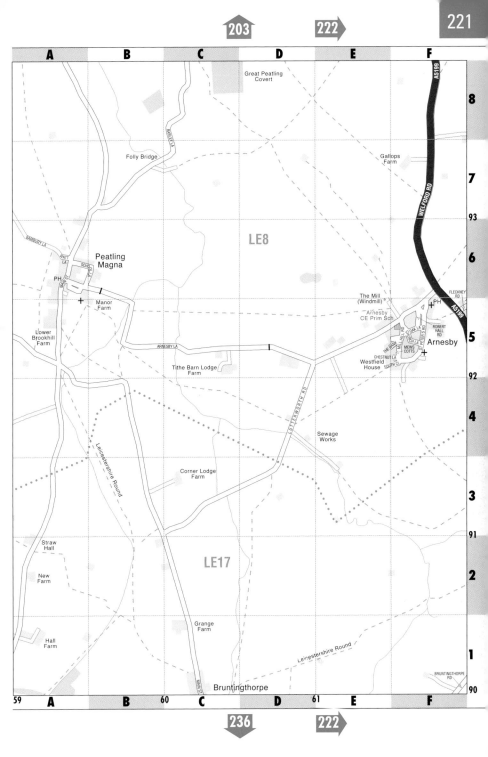

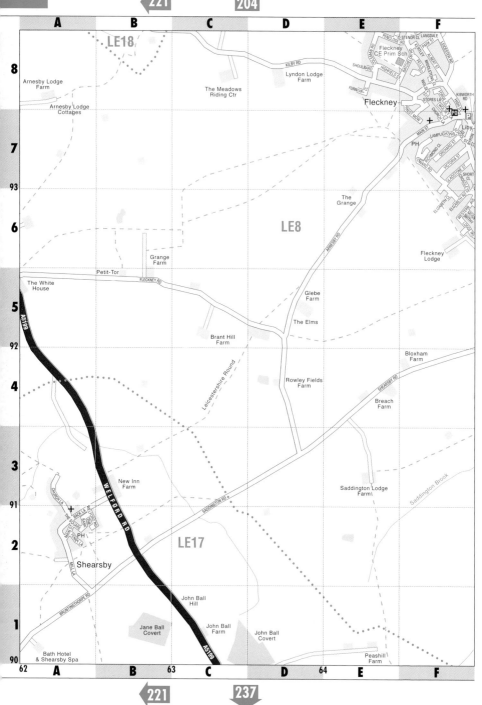

LE18

8

Arnesby Lodge
Farm

Arnesby Lodge
Cottages

7

93

6

The White
House

5

92

4

3

91

2

Shearsby

1

90

Bath Hotel
& Shearsby Spa

The Meadows
Riding Ctr

KILBY RD

Lyndon Lodge
Farm

PENCLOSE RD
STENOR CL LANGDALE
Fleckney
CE Prim Sch
PERKYN
PARK LA
LEVEL
LEICESTER RD
SHOULBARD
HIGHFIELD
MIDDLETON
MILL ST
WELLS
FURNIVAL
STORES LA
CHURCH
MAIN ST
KIBWORTH
RD
Fleckney
PO
P
Liby
PRIEST MDW
MAIN ST
LAMPLIGHT MDW
ORCHARD ST
PH
Liby
EDWARD ST
GLADSTONE ST
VICTORIA ST
SHORT
ELIZABETH CL
ELIZABETH RD
WESTERN
LODGE
WITH

Fleckney

The
Grange

LE8

ARNESBY RD

Fleckney
Lodge

Grange
Farm

Petit-Tor

FLECKNEY RD

Glebe
Farm

The Elms

Bloxham
Farm

Leicestershire Round

Brant Hill
Farm

Rowley Fields
Farm

SHEARSBY RD

Breach
Farm

Saddington Brook

New Inn
Farm

SADDINGTON RD

Saddington Lodge
Farm

WELFORD RD

CHURCH LA
BACK LA
THE SCHOOL
MAIN ST
BANK
PH
MILL ST
BRUNTINGTHORPE RD
MILL LA

LE17

John Ball
Hill

Jane Ball
Covert

John Ball
Farm

John Ball
Covert

Peashill
Farm

A5199

A5199

62 A 63 B D 64 E F

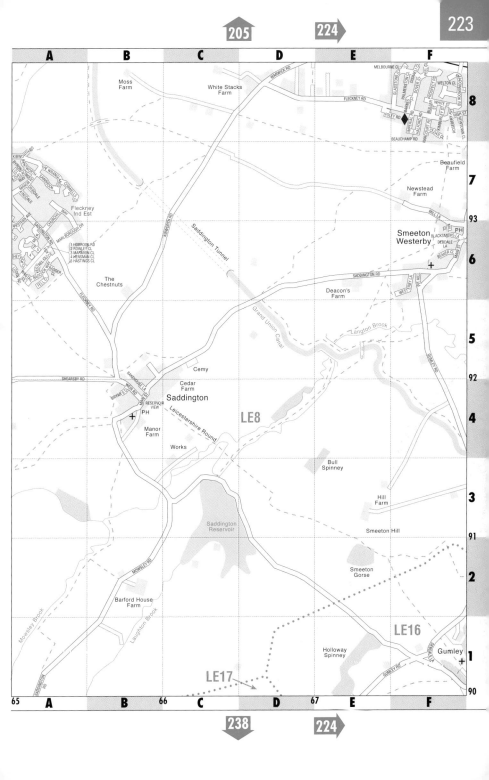

A · B · C · D · E · F

8

Moss Farm

White Stacks Farm

MELBOURNE CL
GLADSTONE ST · PALMERSTON RD · DOVER ST · PEEL ST
WELTON CL
MOXHOBROOK CL
WARWICK RD
FLECKNEY RD
FOLEY RD
IMPERIAL AV · BARNES CL · HALFORD ST · PROSPECT RD · BULLER RD · WHITE ST · HIGH ST
MARCOURT RD · KIMBERLEY RD · ASHBERRY · VALENTINE CL
BEAUCHAMP RD

7

Beaufield Farm

Newstead Farm

KIBWORTH RD
PYWELL RD
THE WRANGS · CHAPWELL · MERRICK RD
MAPLE · DALE
WESTERN · CADEBY · CHURCHILL · WAY
MARLBOROUGH · DR
1 HOBBROOK RD
2 ROWLEY CL
3 MARMION CL
4 MENSMAN CL
5 HASTINGS CL
HEYCOCK · FELL CL
COOKE RD
BLACKBIRD · BADGER

Fleckney Ind Est

MILL LA
93

Smeeton Westerby
BLACKSMITHS
DEBDALE LA
BEAKER CL
PH

The Chestnuts

KIBWORTH RD

Saddington Tunnel

SADDINGTON RD
+
WEST LA · PIT HILL
FERRY LA
GUMLEY RD

6

Deacon's Farm

FLECKNEY RD

Grand Union Canal

Langton Brook

5

92

SHEARSBY RD

BAGHOUSE LA
WEIR RD
BRYAN'S LA
RESERVOIR VIEW
PH

Cemy

Cedar Farm

Saddington

Leicestershire Round

LE8

4

Manor Farm

Works

Bull Spinney

Hill Farm

3

91

Saddington Reservoir

Smeeton Hill

MOWSLEY RD

Smeeton Gorse

2

Laughton Brook

Barford House Farm

LE16

Mowsley Brook

LE17

Holloway Spinney

GUMLEY RD

Gumley
+
1

SADDINGTON RD

65 · 66 · 67
90

A · B · C · D · E · F

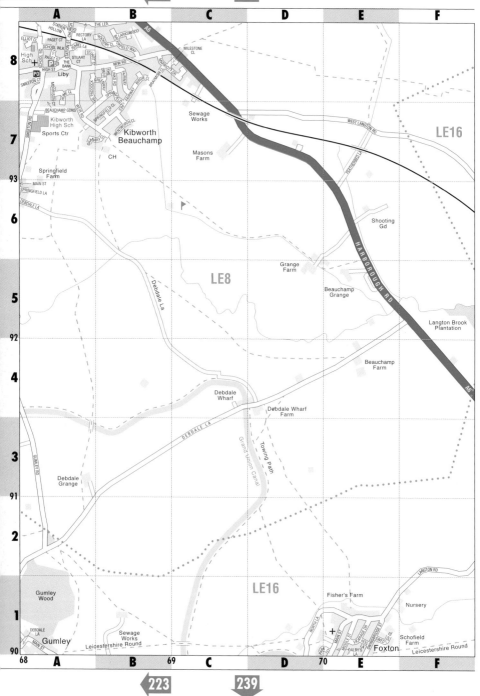

223
206
223
239

Station Hollow
THE LEA
THE LEA
RECTORY LA
LARKSWOOD
ELLIOT CL
PAGET CT
SCHOOL WLK
LABEL LA
RECTORY CT
ARFIELD WAY
A6
MILESTONE CL
High Sch
THE BANK
PAGET CT
HIGH ST
STUART CT
NEW RD
PO
Liby
MORRISON CT
High St
MILL CL
THE
BRAMWELL
THE
HADDOCK
PO
BREACH
NEW RD
SMEETON CT
BEAUCHAMP GDNS
MILL RD
SPRINGFIELD CL
WENTWORTH CL
CHURCH RD
SPINNEY
SEVERN WAY
ALBERT BRIDGE LA
Sewage
Works
Kibworth
High Sch
Kibworth
Beauchamp
WEST LANGTON RD
LE16
Sports Ctr
ST MARY
GLEBE
CH
Masons
Farm
Springfield
Farm
MAIN ST
SPRINGFIELD LA
DEBDALE LA
Shooting
Gd
HARBOROUGH RD
LE8
Debdale La
Grange
Farm
Beauchamp
Grange
Langton Brook
Plantation
Beauchamp
Farm
A6
Debdale
Wharf
DEBDALE LA
Debdale Wharf
Farm
Grand Union Canal
Towing Path
GUMLEY RD
Debdale
Grange
LE16
Gumley
Wood
Fisher's Farm
LANGTON RD
Nursery
NORTH LA
MILL ST
MAIN ST
DALBY'S
GALLOWTREE CL
BRIDGE CT
SWINGBRIDGE CT
Schofield
Farm
DEBDALE LA
MAIN ST
Gumley
Sewage
Works
Leicestershire Round
Foxton
Leicestershire Round

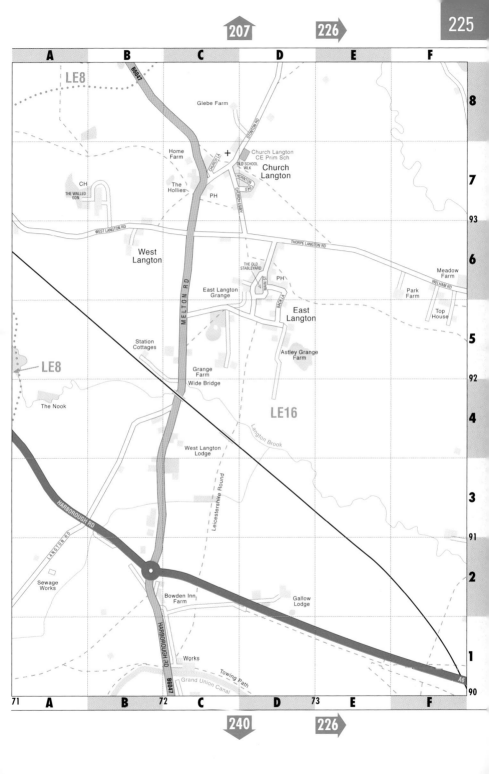

LE8

B6047

Glebe Farm

STRETTON RD

8

Home
Farm

CHURCH CL

+

Church Langton
CE Prim Sch

OLD SCHOOL
WLK

Church
Langton

THORNTON SPS

7

CH

THE WALLED
GDN

The
Hollies

PH

CHURCH HEADY

93

WEST LANGTON RD

THORPE LANGTON RD

West
Langton

6

MELTON RD

THE OLD
STABLEYARD

PH

SAINTS

Meadow
Farm

WELHAM RD

East Langton
Grange

BACK LA

East
Langton

Park
Farm

Top
House

Station
Cottages

Astley Grange
Farm

5

92

Grange
Farm

Wide Bridge

LE8

The Nook

LE16

Langton Brook

4

West Langton
Lodge

Leicestershire Round

3

HARBOROUGH RD

91

LANGTON RD

2

Sewage
Works

Bowden Inn
Farm

Gallow
Lodge

HARBOROUGH RD

B6047

Works

Towing Path

1

A6

Grand Union Canal

90

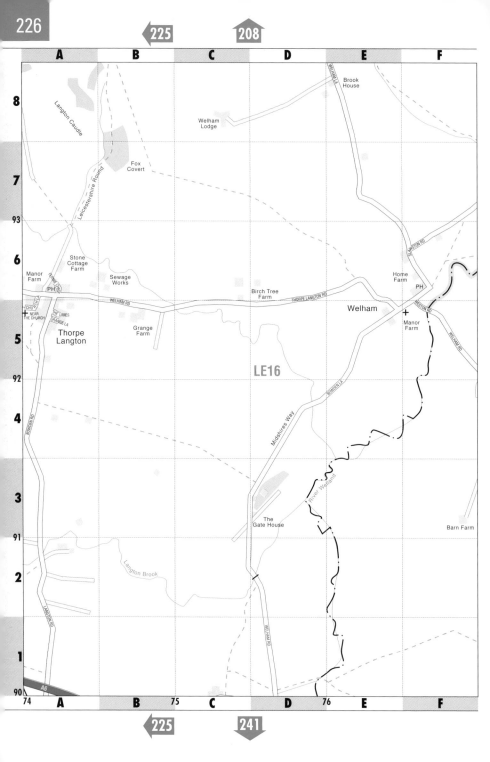

8

7

93

6

92

5

4

3

91

2

1

90

A   B   C   D   E   F

Langton Caudle

Fox
Covert

Leicestershire Round

Welham
Lodge

Brook
House

WELHAM LA

WESTON RD

Stone
Cottage
Farm

Manor
Farm

PH

PEAKE CLO

NEAR
THE CHURCH
THE LIMES
GRANGE LA

CHU

Thorpe
Langton

Sewage
Works

Grange
Farm

Birch Tree
Farm

WELHAM RD

THORPE LANGTON RD

Welham

Home
Farm

PH

Manor
Farm

WESTON RD

WELHAM RD

LE16

Midshires Way

BOWDEN LA

River Welland

The
Gate House

Barn Farm

Langton Brook

WELHAM RD

BOWDEN RD

LANGTON RD

A6

74   A   B   75   C   D   76   E   F

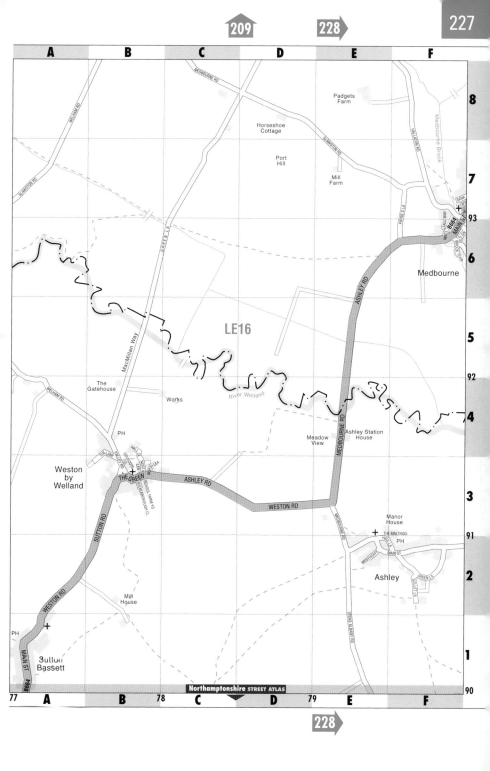

A B C D E F

8

Medbourne Rd
Padgets Farm
Horseshoe Cottage
Slawston Rd
Port Hill
Mill Farm
Halton Rd
Medbourne Brook

7

Payne's La
Slate La
Manor's Yd
B664
Main St
Brook Terr
93

6

Green La
Ashley Rd
Medbourne

LE16

5

92

The Gatehouse
Works
River Welland

4

Belham Rd
PH
Hall La
North Lea
Nonley Lea
Brackleborough Cl
School Farm Yd
The Lane
Valley Rd
Meadow View
Ashley Station House
Medbourne Rd

Weston by Welland
The Green
Ashley Rd
Weston Rd

3

Sutton Rd
Manor House
The Maltings
Hall La
PH
91

Mill House
Weston Rd
Green La
Valley La
Westcott La
Main St
Ashley

2

Stoke Albany Rd

PH
Main St
B664
Sutton Bassett

1

90

77 A 78 B C 79 D E F

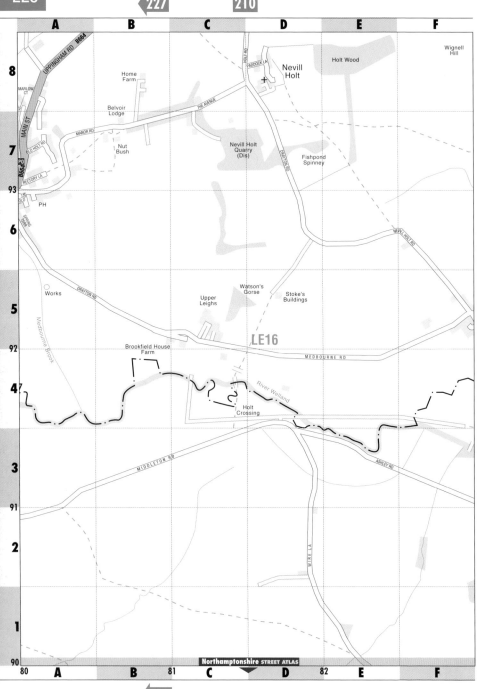

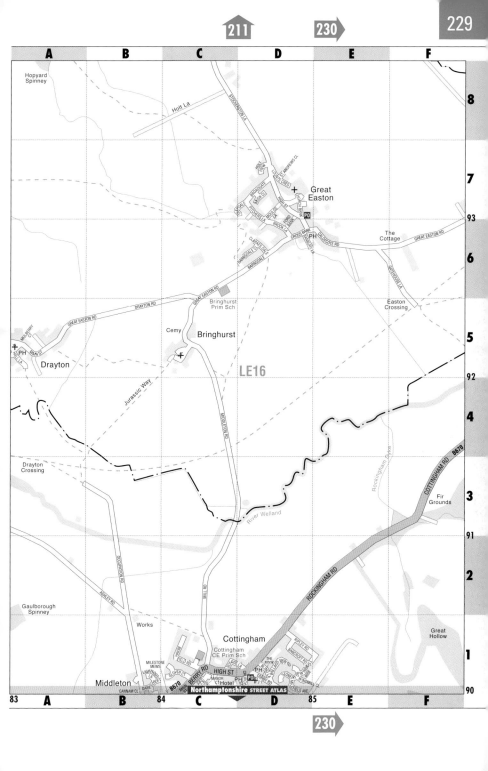

211
230

A   B   C   D   E   F

8

7

93

6

5

92

4

91

3

2

90

Hopyard
Spinney

Holt La

ROCKINGHAM LA

HIGH
VIEW

BROADGATE

PINFOLD

PRICHELS LA

WELL CT

MOLL ST

HIGH ST

CH ANTRY CRES

GT ANTRY CL

Great
Easton

BROOK LA

POND
WALK

PO

CROSS BANK

DEECOTE RD

The
Cottage

GREAT EASTON RD

PH

CLARKES CALS

BARNSDALE C L

BARNSDALE

DEECOTE LA

CH ANTRY LA

GREAT EASTON RD

DRAYTON RD

Bringhurst
Prim Sch

Easton
Crossing

DEECOTE LA

GREAT EASTON RD

Cemy

Bringhurst

MILL BERRY
CT

MAIN ST

PH

Drayton

LE16

Jurassic Way

MIDDLETON RD

Drayton
Crossing

River Welland

Rockingham Dyke

COTTINGHAM RD

B670

Fir
Grounds

ASHLEY RD

CORBY RD

Gaulborough
Spinney

Works

ROCKINGHAM RD

Great
Hollow

MILESTONE
MEWS

FIELD RD

GLOVER CT

CANNAM CL

B670

BERRY RD

Cottingham

Cottingham
CE Prim Sch

HIGH ST

MANOR
CT

Hotel

PO

PH

THE
NOOK

PH

HALFS RD

BANCROFT RD

WINDMILL
FIELD AVE

Middleton

MILL RD

Northamptonshire STREET ATLAS

83   A   B   84   C   D   85   E   F

230

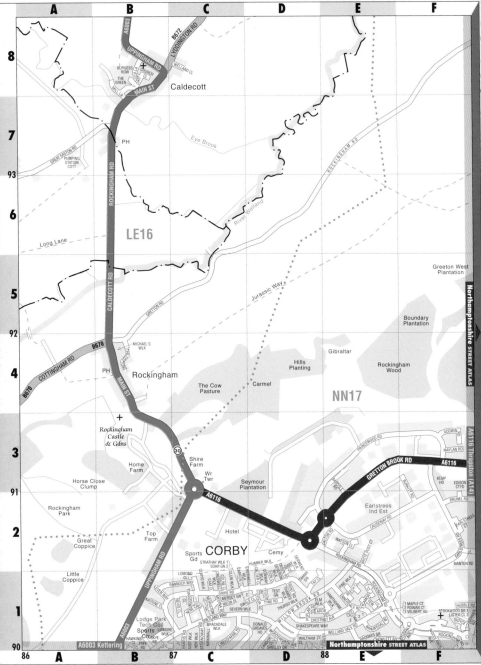

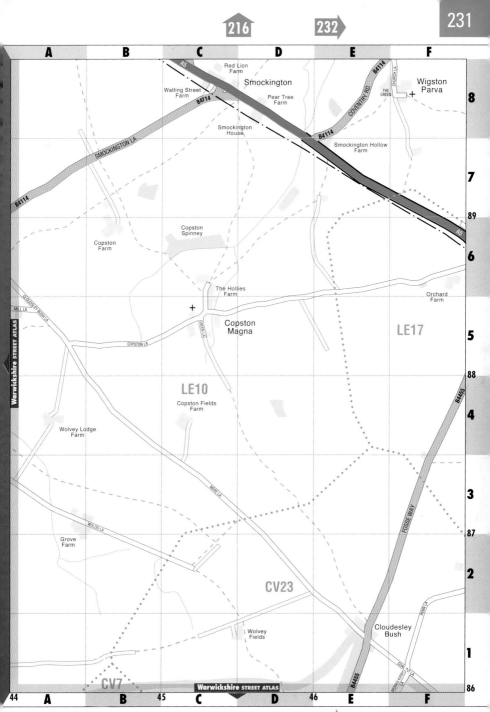

A   B   C   D   E   F

8

7

89

6

5

88

4

3

87

2

1

86

Red Lion Farm

Smockington

Watling Street Farm

Pear Tree Farm

B4114

Smockington House

B4114

Coventry Rd

Church La

The Green

Wigston Parva

Smockington Hollow Farm

Smockington La

B4114

A5

Copston Spinney

Copston Farm

The Hollies Farm

Orchard Farm

LE17

Copston Magna

Green La

Copston La

Gopsley Bush La

Mill La

Copston Fields Farm

LE10

Wolvey Lodge Farm

Mere La

Fosse Way

B4455

Wolds La

Grove Farm

CV23

Wolvey Fields

Cloudesley Bush

Finn La

B4455

Monks Kirby La

CV7

Warwickshire Street Atlas

Warwickshire STREET ATLAS

44   A   B   45   C   D   46   E   F

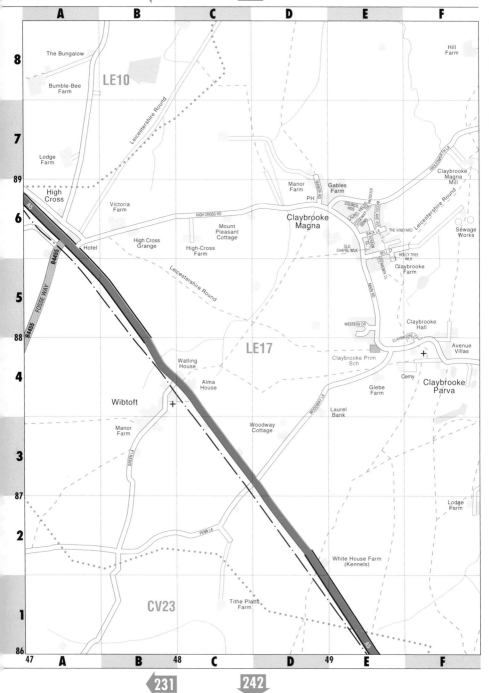

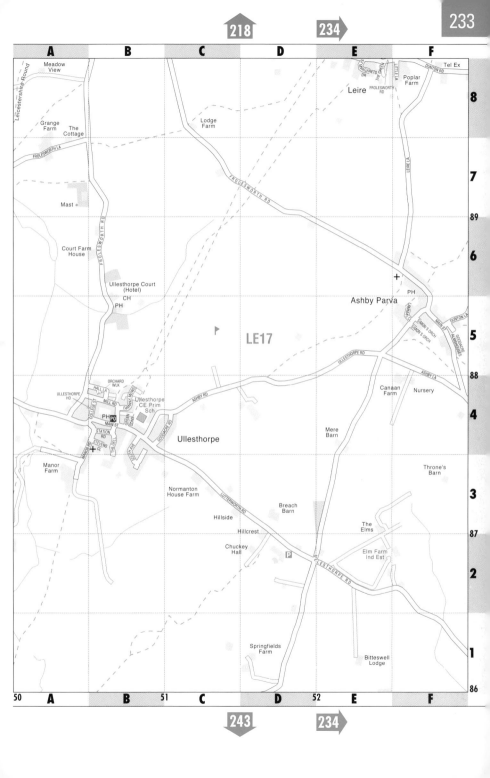

218
234
243
234

Meadow View

Grange Farm

The Cottage

FROLESWORTH LA

Mast

Court Farm House

FROLESWORTH RD

Lodge Farm

FROLESWORTH RD

Leire

LEIRE LA

ST MARGARETS DR

THE GREEN

FROLESWORTH RD

LITTLE LA

DUNTON RD

Tel Ex

Poplar Farm

DUNTON LA

Ullesthorpe Court (Hotel)

CH

PH

Ashby Parva

PH

SIMON'S DITCH

SIMON'S DITCH

CANAAN LA

MALT ST

GOODACRE MEWS

LE17

ULLESTHORPE RD

ASHBY LA

ORCHARD WLK

HALL LA

MILL RD

ULLESTHORPE RD

COLLEGE ST

GREEN GN

FOXWAY MEWS

Ullesthorpe CE Prim Sch

GOODACRE RD

Canaan Farm

Nursery

PH

PO

MAIN ST

STATION RD

STEVENS CL

THE CL

OVERTON LN

ASHBY RD

Ullesthorpe

Mere Barn

Throne's Barn

Manor Farm

MANOR RD

Normanton House Farm

LUTTERWORTH RD

Hillside

Breach Barn

The Elms

Hillcrest

Chuckey Hall

P

ULLESTHORPE RD

Elm Farm Ind Est

Springfields Farm

Bitteswell Lodge

50   51   52

86 87 88 89

1 2 3 4 5 6 7 8

A B C D E F

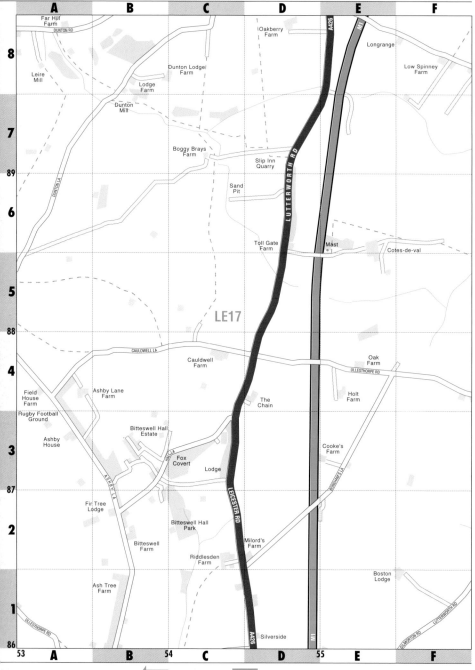

A B C D E F

8

7

89

6

5

88

4

3

87

2

1

86

53 A B 54 C D 55 E F

Far Hill Farm
DUNTON RD
Leire Mill
Lodge Farm
Dunton Mill
DUNTON LA
Dunton Lodge Farm
Oakberry Farm
Longrange
Low Spinney Farm
A26
M1
Boggy Brays Farm
Slip Inn Quarry
Sand Pit
LUTTERWORTH RD
Toll Gate Farm
Mast
Cotes-de-val
LE17
CAULDWELL LA
Cauldwell Farm
Oak Farm
ULLESTHORPE RD
Field House Farm
Ashby Lane Farm
The Chain
Holt Farm
Rugby Football Ground
Ashby House
Bitteswell Hall Estate
ASHBY LA
Fox Covert
HALL LA
Lodge
Cooke's Farm
BOSCHAM LA
Fir Tree Lodge
Bitteswell Hall Park
LEICESTER RD
Milord's Farm
Bitteswell Farm
Riddlesden Farm
Boston Lodge
Ash Tree Farm
ULLESTHORPE RD
A26
Silverside
M1
BELMORTON RD
LUTTERWORTH RD

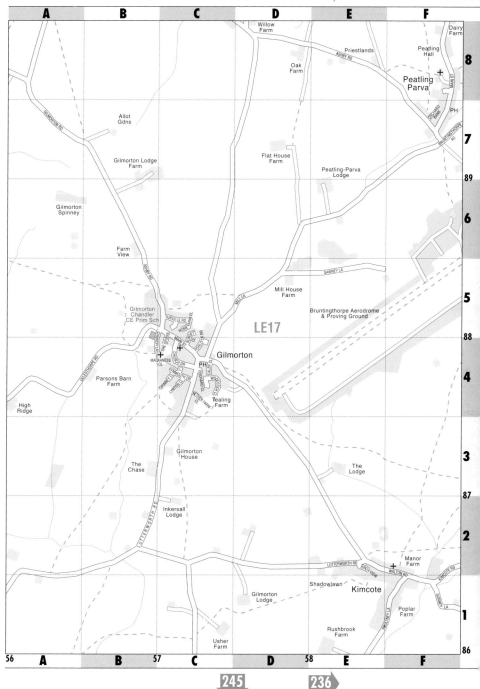

8

Dairy Farm

Willow Farm

Priestlands

ASHBY RD

Peatling Hall

Oak Farm

Peatling Parva

MAIN ST

PH

ORCHARD BANK

7

GILMORTON RD

Allot Gdns

Gilmorton Lodge Farm

Flat House Farm

Peatling-Parva Lodge

BRUNTINGTHORPE RD

89

Gilmorton Spinney

6

Farm View

ASHBY RD

MILL LA

GAWNEY LA

Mill House Farm

5

Gilmorton Chandler CE Prim Sch

LE17

Bruntingthorpe Aerodrome & Proving Ground

88

TURVILLE DR

HOME FARM

THE SIDINGS

MAIN ST

CHURCH DR

DUCTOR DR

Gilmorton

PH

4

ILKESTHORPE RD

MACKANESS CL

SPINNEY DR

LYNTOLN CL

DENMOUTH DR

CROMAT RD

ORCHARD GDNS

TALBT CL

WOODCOCK

DEXTER FARM CL

Parsons Barn Farm

Tealing Farm

High Ridge

3

Gilmorton House

The Chase

The Lodge

87

Inkersall Lodge

2

LUTTERWORTH RD

LUTTERWORTH RD

BIRCH VIEW

WALTON RD

Manor Farm

KIMCOTE RD

Shadowlawn

Kimcote

GURNEY LA

1

Gilmorton Lodge

SMOTHLY LA

Poplar Farm

Rushbrook Farm

Usher Farm

86

56   **A**   **B**   57   **C**   **D**   58   **E**   **F**

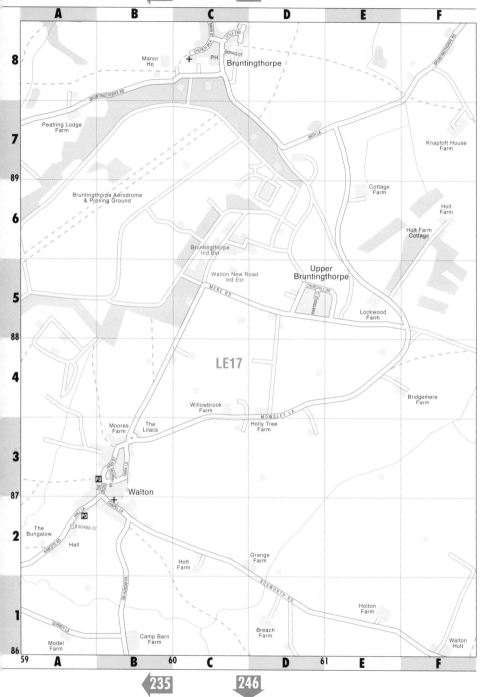

A B C D E F

8   Manor Ho   PH   MORRIS CT   **Bruntingthorpe**

CHURCH WK   MAIN ST   LITTLE END

BRUNTINGTHORPE RD

7   Peatling Lodge Farm   BATH LA   Knaptoft House Farm

89

6   Bruntingthorpe Aerodrome & Proving Ground   Cottage Farm   Holt Farm

Holt Farm Cottage

Bruntingthorpe Ind Est

Walton New Road Ind Est   **Upper Bruntingthorpe**   CHURCHILL DR   PARTRIDGE CL

5   MERE RD   Lockwood Farm

88

LE17

4   Bridgemere Farm

Willowbrook Farm   MOWSLEY LA

Moores Farm   The Lilacs   Holly Tree Farm

3

HEOX LA   PARK LA

87   PO   THE CROSS   **Walton**

2   The Bungalow   HILL LA   PO   OLD SCHOOL CL   CHAPEL LA

Hall   KIMCOTE RD   Holt Farm   Grange Farm

KILWORTH RD   BOSWORTH RD   Holton Farm

1   GURNEY LA   Camp Barn Farm   Breach Farm   Walton Holt

Model Farm

86

59   A   B   60   C   D   61   E   F

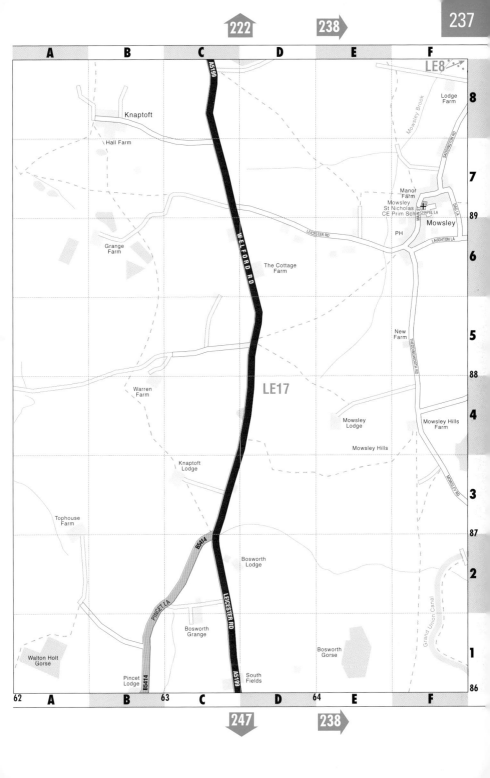

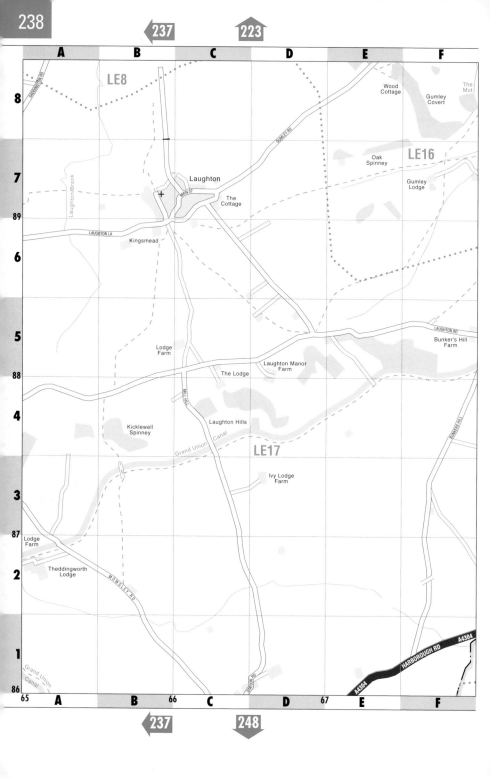

237
223

LE8

A B C D E F

8

Wood
Cottage

Gumley
Covert

The
Mot

DUMLEY RD

LE16

7

Oak
Spinney

Laughton

Gumley
Lodge

The
Cottage

LaughtonBrook

89

LAUGHTON LA

Kingsmead

6

5

Lodge
Farm

Laughton Manor
Farm

LAUGHTON RD

Bunker's Hill
Farm

88

The Lodge

4

MILL HILL

Kicklewell
Spinney

Laughton Hills

Grand Union Canal

LE17

BURGESS HILL

Ivy Lodge
Farm

3

87

Lodge
Farm

Theddingworth
Lodge

MOWSLEY RD

2

1

HARBOROUGH RD

A4304

A4304

86

Grand Union
Canal

65 A B 66 C D 67 E F

237
248

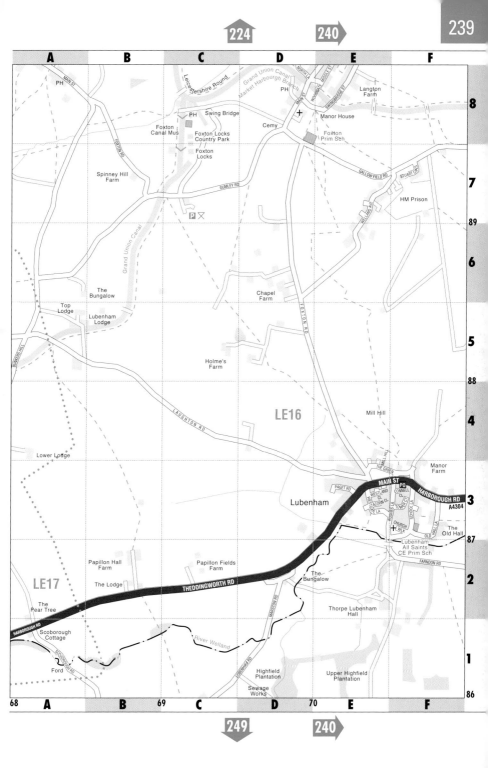

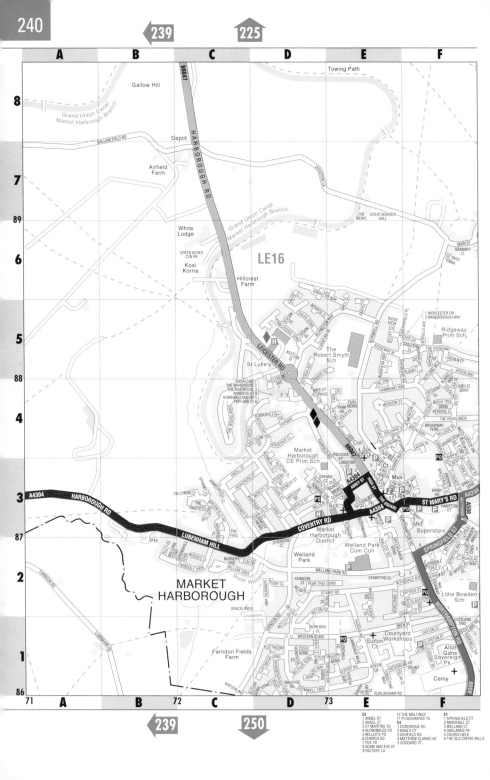

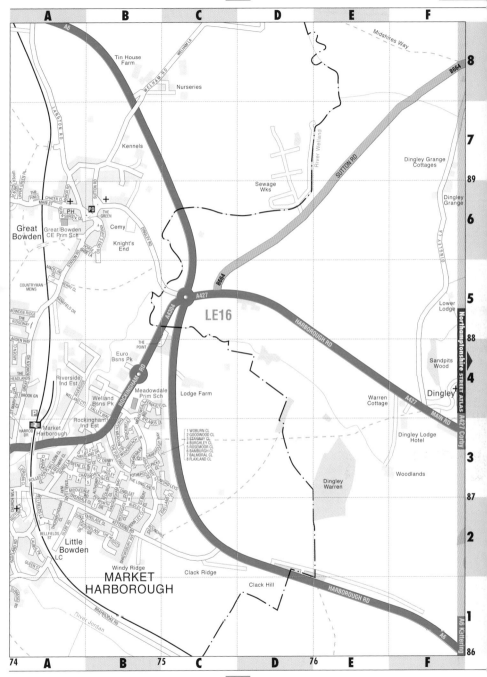

A   B   C   D   E   F

Midshires Way

B664

Tin House Farm

WELHAM RD

WELHAM LK

Nurseries

7

River Welland

Dingley Grange Cottages

89

Kennels

Sewage Wks

SUTTON RD

Dingley Grange

6

LANGTON RD

THE PINES
UPPER GREEN
CHATER CL
MAIN ST
PH
SBROOK CL
PO

SUTTON RD

KNIGHTS END RD

THE GREEN
Cemy

Great Bowden

Great Bowden CE Prim Sch

Knight's End

DINGLEY RD

DINGLEY LA

Lower Lodge

5

COUNTRYMAN MEWS
BOWDEN RIDGE
THE RIDGEWAY
ARDEN WAY
MADELINE
BERRY CL
BARKFIELD DR
STROUD RD

B664

A427

LE16

HARBOROUGH RD

88

Northamptonshire STREET ATLAS Corby

4

ARDEN CL
THE HEADLANDS
GREAT BOWDEN RD
CLEBROOK GDN

THE POINT
Euro Bsns Pk

ROCKINGHAM RD

THE POINT
Meadowdale Prim Sch
Lodge Farm

Sandpits Wood

Dingley

MAIN RD
A427

A6

A4304

Riverside Ind Est
Welland Bsns Pk
Rockingham Ind Est

Warren Cottage

HARROD DR
Market Harborough

1 WOBURN CL
2 GOODWOOD CL
3 STANWAY CL
4 BURGHLEY CL
5 ROSEMOOR CL
6 BAMBURGH CL
7 BALMORAL CL
8 FLAXLAND CL

Dingley Lodge Hotel

3

CHURCH WALK

DENBY

STAMFORD LEYS

Woodlands

87

Dingley Warren

BELLFIELDS ST

Little Bowden
LC

KETTERING RD

2

QUEEN ST
SCOTT RD

Windy Ridge
MARKET HARBOROUGH

Clack Ridge

Clack Hill

HARBOROUGH RD

A6 Kettering

River Jordan
BRAYBROOKE RD

1

86

74   A   B   75   C   D   76   E   F

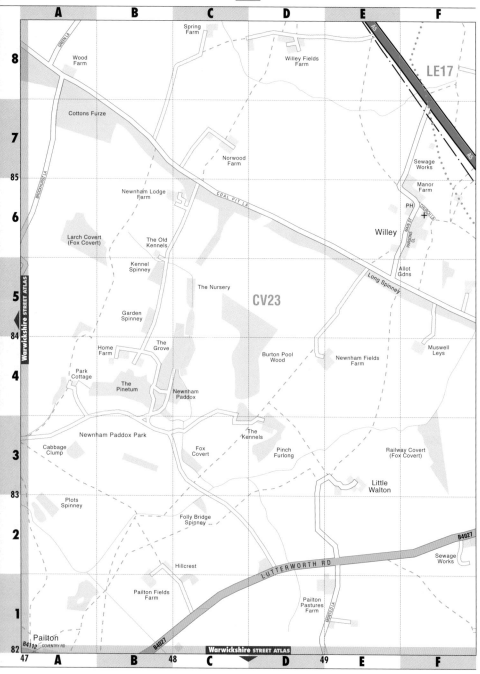

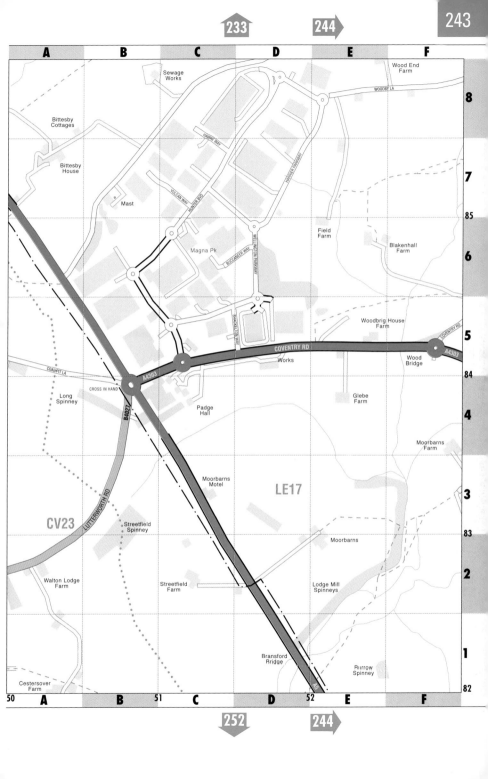

A B C D E F

8
7
85
6
5
84
4
3
83
2
1
82

Wood End Farm

WOODBY LA

Sewage Works

Bittesby Cottages

HAVRIE WAY

Bittesby House

VULCAN WAY

HUNTER RD

HARRIER PARKWAY

Mast

Magna Pk

BUCCANEER WAY

WELLINGTON PARKWAY

Field Farm

Blakenhall Farm

Woodbrig House Farm

SHACKLETON WAY

COVENTRY RD

Works

Wood Bridge

COVENTRY RD

A4303

COALPIT LA

A4303

CROSS IN HAND

Long Spinney

B4027

Padge Hall

Glebe Farm

Moorbarns Farm

LUTTERWORTH RD

Moorbarns Motel

LE17

Moorbarns

Streetfield Spinney

CV23

Walton Lodge Farm

Streetfield Farm

Lodge Mill Spinneys

Bransford Bridge

Burrow Spinney

A5

Cestersover Farm

50 A B 51 C D 52 E F

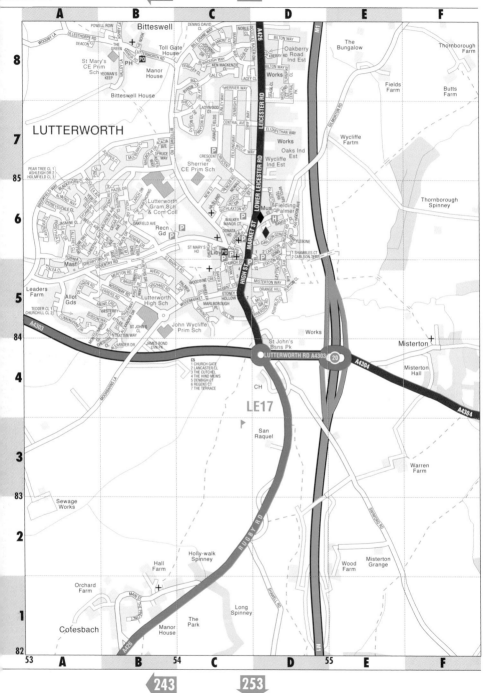

LUTTERWORTH

Bitteswell

LE17

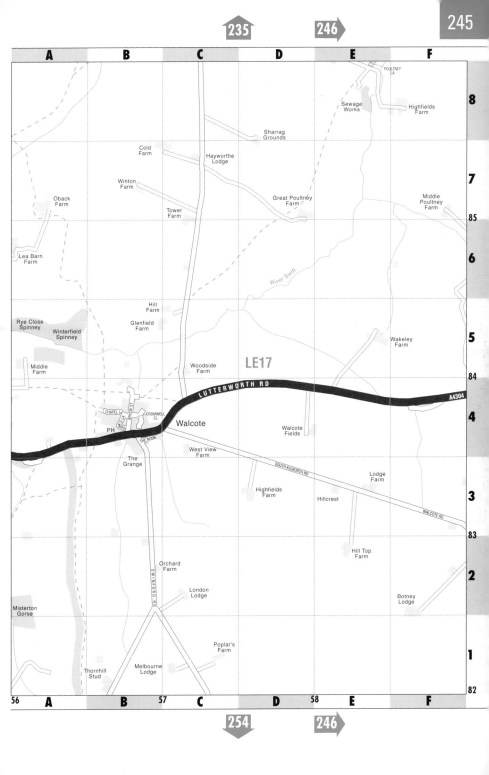

POULTNEY LA

Sewage
Works

Highfields
Farm

Sharrag
Grounds

Cold
Farm

Hayworthe
Lodge

Winton
Farm

Great Poultney
Farm

Middle
Poultney
Farm

Oback
Farm

Tower
Farm

Lea Barn
Farm

River Swift

Hill
Farm

Rye Close
Spinney

Winterfield
Spinney

Glenfield
Farm

Wakeley
Farm

LE17

Middle
Farm

Woodside
Farm

LUTTERWORTH RD

A4304

CHAPEL LA

CROMWELL
CL

Walcote

PH

THE NOOK

Walcote
Fields

West View
Farm

The
Grange

SOUTH KILWORTH RD

Lodge
Farm

Highfields
Farm

Hillcrest

WALCOTE RD

SWINFORD RD

Orchard
Farm

Hill Top
Farm

London
Lodge

Botney
Lodge

Misterton
Gorse

Poplar's
Farm

Thornhill
Stud

Melbourne
Lodge

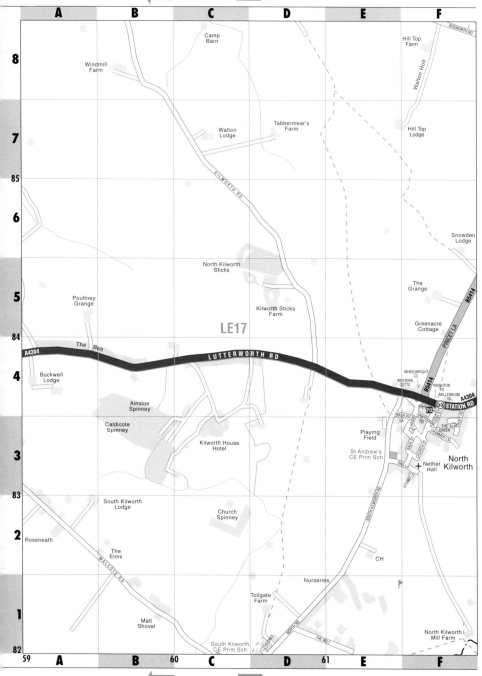

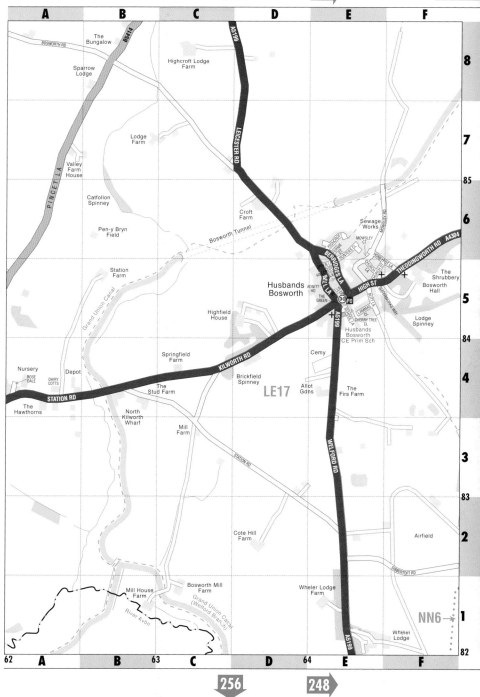

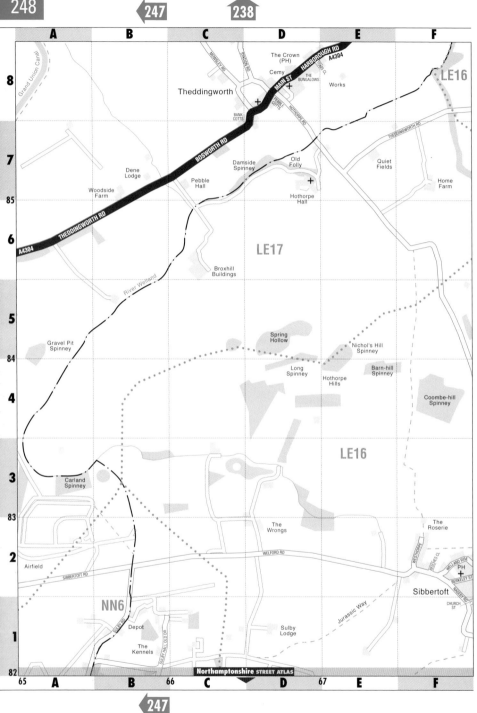

Grand Union Canal

8

Theddingworth

The Crown (PH)

Cemy

HARBOROUGH RD
A4304

MAIN ST

The Bungalows

Works

LE16

MORRIS RD
SHEARS RD

PLACE CL

PEBBLE COTTS

HOTHORPE RD

BANK COTTS

7

BOSWORTH RD

THEDDINGWORTH RD

Dene Lodge

Damside Spinney

Old Folly

Quiet Fields

Home Farm

Pebble Hall

Woodside Farm

85

Hothorpe Hall

6

THEDDINGWORTH RD

A4304

LE17

River Welland

Broxhill Buildings

5

Spring Hollow

Nichol's Hill Spinney

Gravel Pit Spinney

84

Long Spinney

Barn-hill Spinney

Hothorpe Hills

Coombe-hill Spinney

4

LE16

3

Carland Spinney

83

The Wrongs

The Roserie

2

Airfield

WELFORD RD

WESTHORPE

BEEVES CL

WELLAND RISE

PH

BERKELEY ST

RUSHEY CL

Sibbertoft

SIBBERTOFT RD

CHURCH ST

NN6

1

Depot

SELBY RD

SELBY HILL OLD DR

The Kennels

Sulby Lodge

Jurassic Way

82

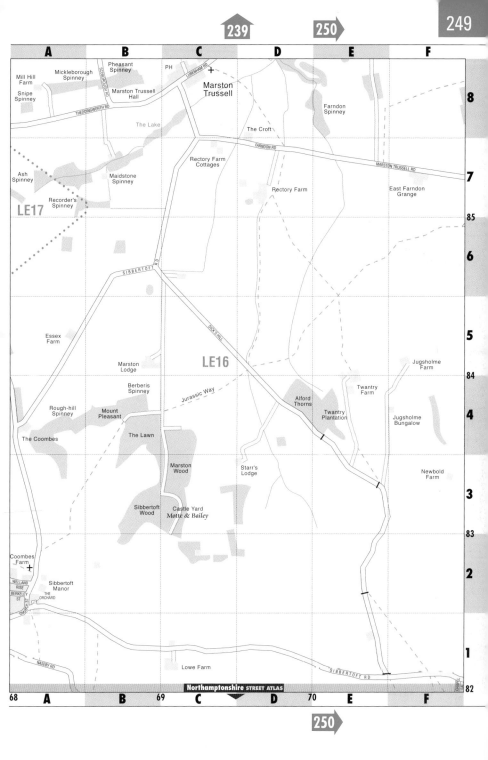

A   B   C   D   E   F

Mill Hill
Farm
Mickleborough
Spinney
Pheasant
Spinney
PH
Marston
Trussell

8

Snipe
Spinney
Marston Trussell
Hall
Farndon
Spinney

THEDDINGWORTH RD
SCHOOL/OLD RD
LUBENHAM RD

The Lake
The Croft

Ash
Spinney
Maidstone
Spinney
Rectory Farm
Cottages
FARNDON RD
MARSTON TRUSSELL RD

7

Recorder's
Spinney
Rectory Farm
East Farndon
Grange

LE17

85

SIBBERTOFT RD

6

Essex
Farm

5

Jugsholme
Farm

Marston
Lodge

LE16

84

Berberis
Spinney
DICK'S HILL
Jurassic Way
Twantry
Farm

Rough-hill
Spinney
Mount
Pleasant
Alford
Thorns
Twantry
Plantation

4

Jugsholme
Bungalow

The Coombes
The Lawn

Marston
Wood
Starr's
Lodge
Newbold
Farm

3

Sibbertoft
Wood
Castle Yard
Motte & Bailey

83

Coombes
Farm

2

WELLAND
RISE
Sibbertoft
Manor

BERKELEY
ST
THE
ORCHARD

CHAPEL
NASEBY RD

SIBBERTOFT RD

1

Lowe Farm

CHAPEL

82

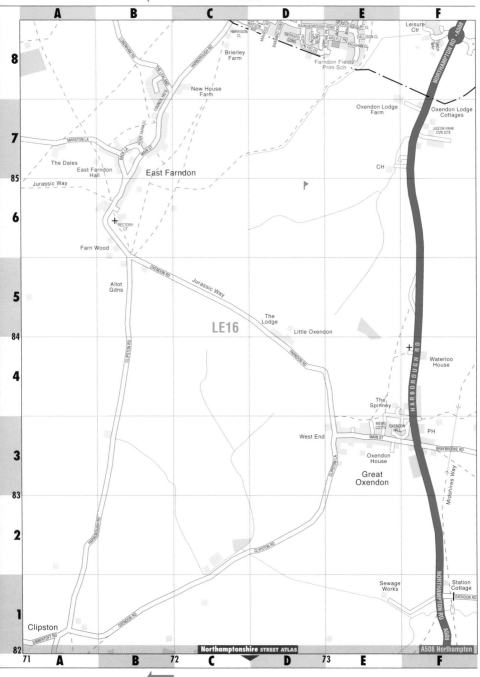

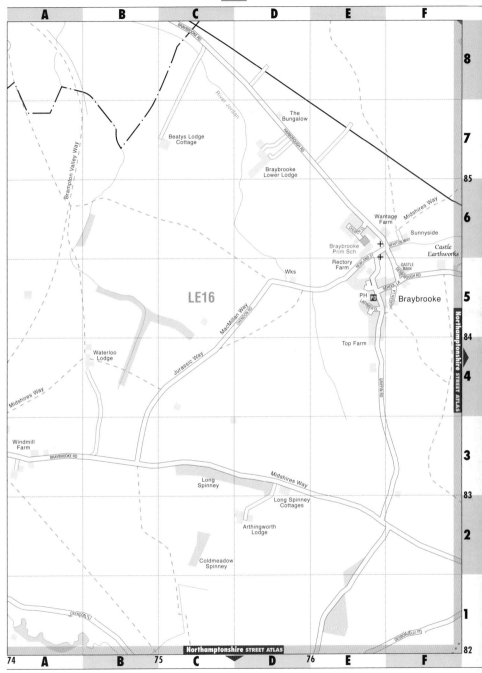

A   **B**   **C**   **D**   **E**   **F**

8

BRAYBROOKE RD

River Jordan

The Bungalow

7

HARBROUGH RD

Brampton Valley Way

Beatys Lodge Cottage

Braybrooke Lower Lodge

85

Midshires Way

6

Wantage Farm

Sunnyside

CHURCH CL

Braybrooke Prim Sch

NEWTON WAY

Castle Earthworks

Rectory Farm

NEWLAND ST

CASTLE BANK

LE16

Wks

CASTLE YD

PLOUGH RD

MacMillan Way

OXENDON RD

SCHOOL LA

5

PH

PO

GRISELL LA

Braybrooke

LATIMER CL

84

Waterloo Lodge

Jurassic Way

Top Farm

4

Midshires Way

GRIFFIN RD

Windmill Farm

3

BRAYBROOKE RD

Midshires Way

83

Long Spinney

Long Spinney Cottages

Arthingworth Lodge

2

Coldmeadow Spinney

1

OXENDON LA

DESBOROUGH RD

82

74   **A**   **B**   75   **C**   **D**   76   **E**   **F**

Northamptonshire STREET ATLAS

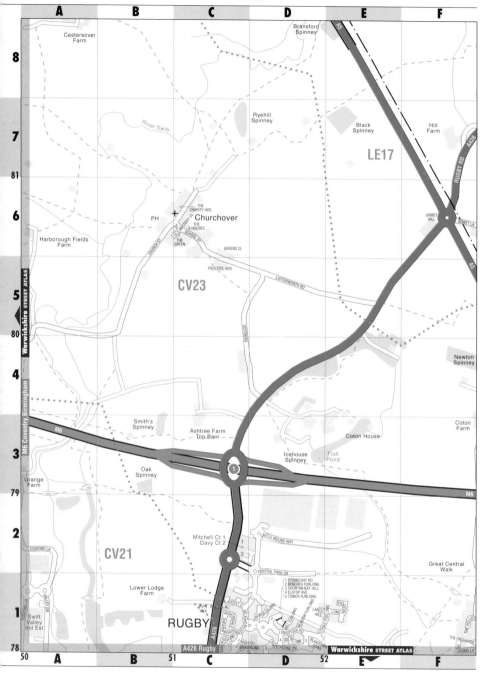

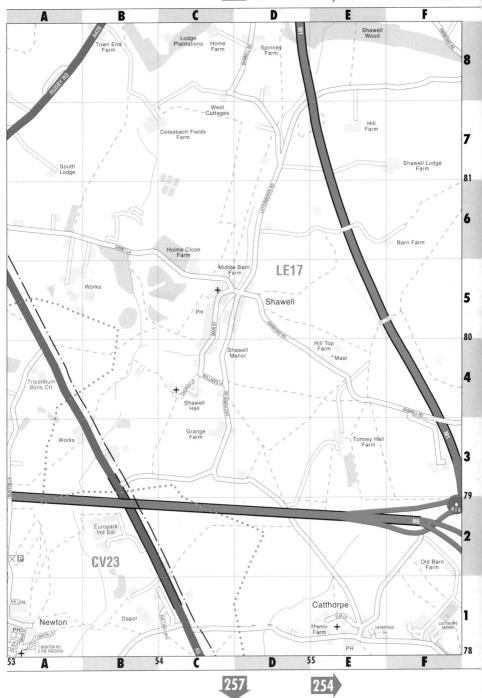

A B C D E F

8

7

81

6

5

80

4

3

79

2

1

78

RUGBY RD
A426
Town End Farm
Lodge Plantations
Home Farm
Spinney Farm
M1
Shawell Wood
SWINFORD RD
West Cottages
Cotesbach Fields Farm
SHAWELL RD
Hill Farm
South Lodge
Shawell Lodge Farm
LUTTERWORTH RD
GIBBET LA
Holme Close Farm
Barn Farm
Middle Barn Farm
LE17
Works
PH
Shawell
MAIN ST
Hill Top Farm
SWINFORD RD
Mast
Shawell Manor
Tripontium Bsns Ctr
BULLACES LA
CATTHORPE RD
Shawell Hall
CHURCH LA
Works
Grange Farm
Tomley Hall Farm
SHAWELL RD
M1
NEWTON LA
A14
M6
Europark Ind Est
CV23
Old Barn Farm
HOLTEND CRES
THE LEYS
A5
Newton
PH
LITTLE LONDON LA
Depot
Catthorpe
ELM LA
Manor Farm
HERMITAGE LA
CATTHORPE MANOR
PH
1 NEWTON RD
2 THE PADDOCK

53 A 54 B C 55 D E F
78

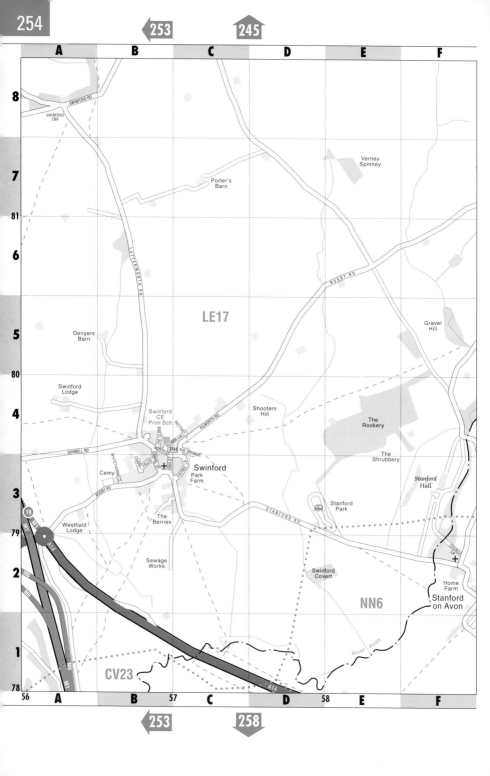

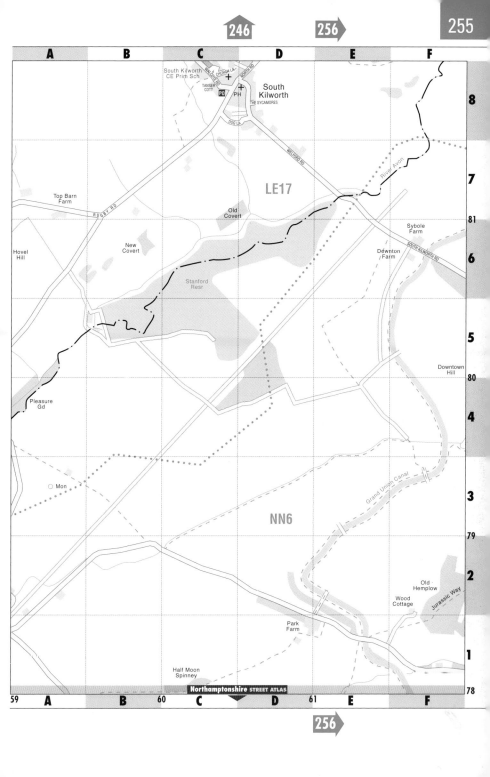

8

South Kilworth
CE Prim Sch

South
Kilworth

THE SYCAMORES

LE17

7

81

Top Barn
Farm

RUGBY RD

Old
Covert

Sybole
Farm

Downton
Farm

SOUTH KILWORTH RD

6

Hovel
Hill

New
Covert

Stanford
Resr

5

Downtown
Hill

80

Pleasure
Gd

4

Grand Union Canal

Mon

3

NN6

79

Old
Hemplow

2

Wood
Cottage

Jurassic Way

Park
Farm

1

Half Moon
Spinney

78

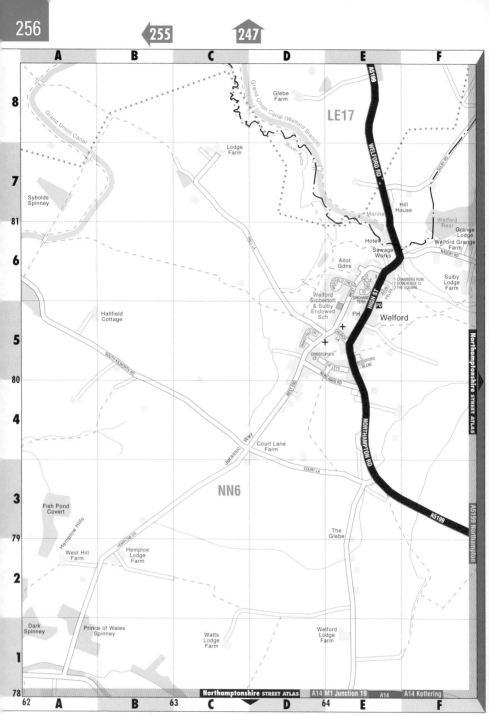

LE17

NN6

Northamptonshire STREET ATLAS

A5199 Northampton

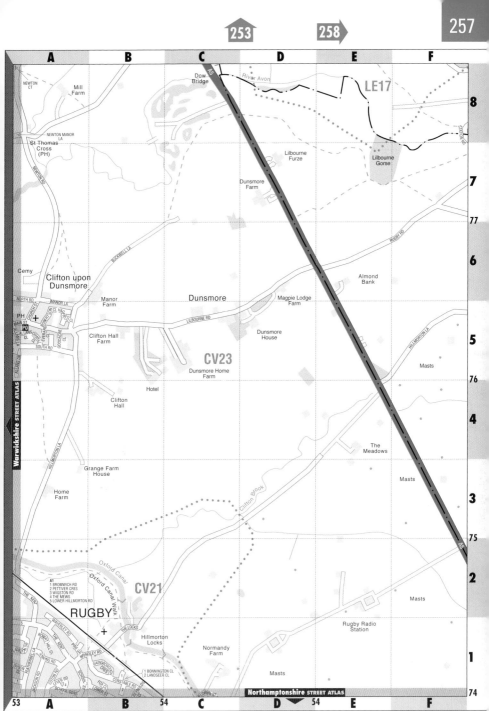

River Avon

A14

8

7
STATION RD
STATION RD

77
RUGBY RD
HORSEPOOL
THE GREEN
CHAPEL
The Green Farm
GREEN FARM CL
STONEHO
Sewage Works

6
Lilbourne
Lilbourne Fields Farmhouse
Lilbourne Lodge
Clarkes Farm
YELVERTOFT RD
Lodge Farm
HILLMORTON LA

5
Mast
CV23

76
Mast

4
Mast
Mast

Mast

3
Mast
Mast
Mast
Radio Station
Mast

75
Mast
Mast
NN6

2
A5
Mast
Mast
Mast
Shenley Farm
New House Farm
Crick Lodge

1
Mast
A5

74
Mast
M1

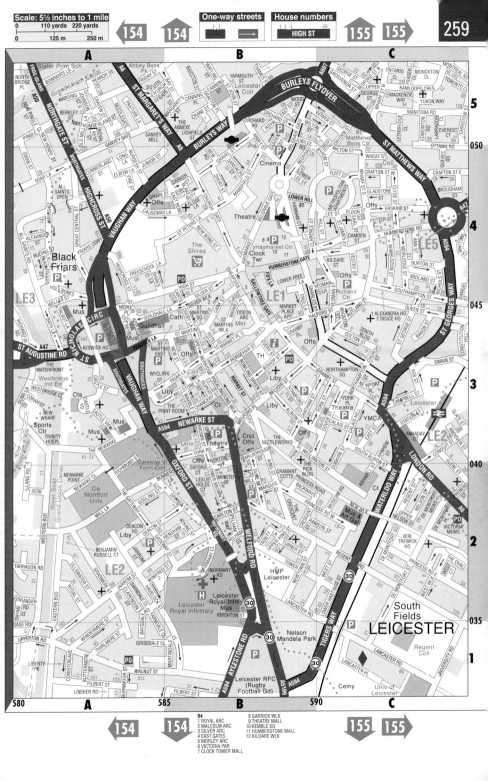

Index

Place name May be abbreviated on the map

Location number Present when a number indicates the place's position in a crowded area of mapping

Locality, town or village Shown when more than one place has the same name

Postcode district District for the indexed place

Page and grid square Page number and grid reference for the standard mapping

Church Rd 6 Beckenham BR2.........53 C6

Cities, towns and villages are listed in CAPITAL LETTERS   Public and commercial buildings are highlighted in magenta
Places of interest are highlighted in blue with a star★

Abbreviations used in the index

Acad	**Academy**	Comm	**Common**	Gd	**Ground**	L	**Leisure**
App	**Approach**	Cott	**Cottage**	Gdn	**Garden**	La	**Lane**
Arc	**Arcade**	Cres	**Crescent**	Gn	**Green**	Liby	**Library**
Ave	**Avenue**	Cswy	**Causeway**	Gr	**Grove**	Mdw	**Meadow**
Bglw	**Bungalow**	Ct	**Court**	H	**Hall**	Meml	**Memorial**
Bldg	**Building**	Ctr	**Centre**	Ho	**House**	Mkt	**Market**
Bsns, Bus	**Business**	Ctry	**Country**	Hospl	**Hospital**	Mus	**Museum**
Bvd	**Boulevard**	Cty	**County**	HQ	**Headquarters**	Orch	**Orchard**
Cath	**Cathedral**	Dr	**Drive**	Hts	**Heights**	Pal	**Palace**
Cir	**Circus**	Dro	**Drove**	Ind	**Industrial**	Par	**Parade**
Cl	**Close**	Ed	**Education**	Inst	**Institute**	Pas	**Passage**
Cnr	**Corner**	Emb	**Embankment**	Int	**International**	Pk	**Park**
Coll	**College**	Est	**Estate**	Intc	**Interchange**	Pl	**Place**
Com	**Community**	Ex	**Exhibition**	Junc	**Junction**	Prec	**Precinct**

Prom	**Promenade**
Rd	**Road**
Recn	**Recreation**
Ret	**Retail**
Sh	**Shopping**
Sq	**Square**
St	**Street**
Sta	**Station**
Terr	**Terrace**
TH	**Town Hall**
Univ	**University**
Wk, Wlk	**Walk**
Wr	**Water**
Yd	**Yard**

Index of towns, villages, streets, hospitals, industrial estates, railway stations, schools, shopping centres, universities and places of interest

260 1st–All

1st Drift PE9 . . . . 169 D8
5 Houses The CV23 . . . . . 252 C6

A

Abberton Way LE11 . . . . . . 51 A2
Abbey Bsns Pk LE4 . . . . . 154 E7
Abbey Cl
Ashby-de-la-Z LE65 . . . . . 68 F6
Shepshed LE12 . . . . 50 A1
Abbey Court Rd LE4 . . . . 128 F3
Abbey Ct LE4 . . . . 128 F2
Abbey Dr
Ashby-de-la-Z LE65 . . . . . 68 F6
Leicester LE4 . . . . 128 F3
Shellbrook LE65 . . . . 68 F6
Abbey Gate LE4 . . . . . . 154 E7
Abbey La
Leicester LE4 . . . . 128 F2
Sedgebrook NG32 . . . . 8 F8
Abbey Lodge Cl 1
DE11 . . . . 44 A7
Abbey Mdws LE4 . . . . . . 128 F3
Abbeymead Rd LE4 . . . . 128 F3
ABBEY PARK 128 F3
Abbey Park Rd LE4 . . . . 154 F8
Abbey Park St LE4 . . . . 155 A8
Abbey Prim Com Sch
LE4 . . . . 129 A1
Abbey Rd
Coalville LE67, LE12 . . . . . 72 C4
Narborough LE19 . . . . . . 178 D1
Abbey Rise LE4 . . . . . . 128 F3
Abbey St
Leicester LE1 . . . . 259 B5
Market Harborough
LE16 . . . . 240 E3
Abbots Cl LE5 . . . . 156 B8
Abbots Ct LE5 . . . . 156 B8
Abbotsford Cl LE7 . . . . .
Abbotsford Rd
Ashby-de-la-Z LE65 . . . . . 69 C5
Leicester LE5 . . . . 155 F7
Abbot's Rd N LE5 . . . . . 156 B8
Abbots Rd S LE5 . . . . . 156 C8
Abbotts Cl
Swadlincote DE11 . . . . . . 44 A6
Syston LE7 . . . . 102 F3
Abbott's Cl PE9 . . . . . . 143 F2

Abbotts Gn LE10 . . . . . . 215 F5
Abbott's Oak Dr LE67 . . . 72 C1
Abbotts Rd DE11 . . . . . . 44 A6
Abbott St NG10 . . . . 10 D6
Abelles Way CV9 . . . . . . 170 C2
Aberdale Rd LE2 . . . . . . 180 B6
Aberdeen Cl PE9 . . . . . . 142 F4
Aber Rd LE2 . . . . 155 D2
Abingdon Rd
Leicester LE2 . . . . 155 B4
Melton Mowbray LE13 . . . . 59 A5
Abington High Sch
LE18 . . . . 180 C2
Abington Rd LE18 . . . . . 180 C2
AB KETTLEBY 37 D2
Ab Kettleby Com Prim Sch
LE14 . . . . 37 C3
Abney Cres DE12 . . . . . . 93 C4
Abney Dr DE12 . . . . 93 C4
Abney St LE5 . . . . 155 C4
Abney Wlk DE12 . . . . . . 93 C4
Acacia Ave
Birstall LE4 . . . . 129 B8
Lutterworth LE17 . . . . . 244 B7
Swadlincote DE11 . . . . . . 44 B7
Acacia Cl LE3 . . . . 152 F2
Acacia Dr DE73 . . . . 26 A8
Acan Way LE19 . . . . 201 A7
Acer Cl
Leicester LE4 . . . . 128 C4
Loughborough LE11 . . . . . 75 A7
Narborough LE19 . . . . . 201 A7
Achurch Cl LE9 . . . . . . 199 D3
Acorn Cl
Birstall LE4 . . . . 129 A6
Lubenham LE16 . . . . . . 239 E3
Acorn Grange 2 LE11 . . 51 F2
Acorn St LE4 . . . . 129 A6
Acorn Way LE18 . . . . . . 180 E2
Acre La DE72 . . . . 16 C8
ACRESFORD 92 C7
Acresford Rd
Donisthorpe DE12 . . . . . . 92 D7
Nethersea1 DE12 . . . . . . 92 B6
Overseal DE12 . . . . 67 B2
Acresford View DE12 . . . . 67 B3
Acres Rd LE3 . . . . 153 A3
Acres Rise LE13 . . . . 59 E4
Acton Ave NG10 . . . . 10 E6
Acton Cl NG10 . . . . 10 E6
Acton Gr NG10 . . . . 10 E6
Acton Rd NG10 . . . . 10 E6
Acton Road Ind Est
NG10 . . . . 10 E6

Acton St NG10 . . . . 10 E6
Adam Dale LE11 . . . . . . 52 A3
Adam & Eve St 8
LE16 . . . . 240 E3
Adamswood Cl LE16 . . . . 240 C3
Adcock Cl LE13 . . . . 59 F5
Adcock Rd LE3 . . . . 154 B7
Adcocks Cl LE11 . . . . . . 52 B5
Adcock's Yd DE12 . . . . . 93 C5
Adcote Cl LE9 . . . . 198 A6
Adderley Rd LE2 . . . . . . 155 B1
Adderly St LE15 . . . . . . 189 B4
Adelaide Cl LE4 . . . . . . 128 C7
Adelaide St LE15 . . . . . 189 B4
Adelphi Row LE16 . . . . . 208 B4
Adkins Ct LE12 . . . . 76 C8
Adlington Rd LE2 . . . . . 181 C6
Admiral Ct LE16 . . . . . . 240 D3
Adnitt Ho LE17 . . . . . . 247 E5
Adrian Dr LE9 . . . . 198 A7
Aeropark The* DE74 . . . . 17 A1
Afton Cl LE9 . . . . 51 B3
Agar Nook Ct LE67 . . . . . 72 D1
Agar Nook La LE67 . . . . . 72 D1
Aikman Ave LE3 . . . . . . 154 B7
Aikman Cl LE3 . . . . 154 A7
Aingarth LE11 . . . . 52 C3
Ainsdale Cl LE8 . . . . . . 223 A7
Ainsdale Rd LE3 . . . . . . 154 B5
Ainsworth Dr LE12 . . . . . 77 E4
Ainsworth Wlk LE3 . . . . 154 A5
Aintree Cl LE5 . . . . 156 D4
Aintree Cres LE2 . . . . . . 180 F6
Airedale Cl
Leire LE17 . . . . 218 F1
Long Eaton NG10 . . . . . . 10 A6
Airedale Rd PE9 . . . . . . 143 C5
Aisne Rd LE18 . . . . 179 E3
Alan Bray Cl LE10 . . . . . 214 D7
Alan Cl LE4 . . . . 129 B4
Aland Gdns LE9 . . . . . . 219 A6
Alan Moss Rd LE11 . . . . . 51 F5
Alans Way LE19 . . . . . . 150 B4
Albany Cl LE16 . . . . 240 F4
Albany Rd LE16 . . . . . . 240 F4
Albany St LE11 . . . . 52 B3
Albany The LE2 . . . . 155 C3
Alberta St LE5 . . . . 155 B6
Albert Ave LE12 . . . . 77 D4
Albert Ct
Leicester LE2 . . . . 155 D2

Albert Ct continued
Whetstone LE8 . . . . 201 F8
Albert Hall Pl LE67 . . . . . 72 D1
Albert Pl LE11 . . . . 52 B3
Albert Prom LE11 . . . . . . 52 C3
Albert Rd
Breaston DE72 . . . . 9 B7
Coalville LE67 . . . . 71 E1
Hinckley LE10 . . . . 197 D1
Leicester LE2 . . . . 155 C2
Long Eaton NG10 . . . . . . 10 D8
Market Harborough
LE16 . . . . 240 F3
Stamford PE9 . . . . 143 E3
Swadlincote DE11 . . . . . . 44 A2
Albert St
Bottesford NG13 . . . . 3 A3
Fleckney LE8 . . . . 222 F8
Heather LE67 . . . . 95 F3
Kibworth Beauchamp
LE8 . . . . 206 A2
Loughborough LE11 . . . . . 52 B3
Melton Mowbray LE13 . . . . 59 D1
Syston LE7 . . . . 103 B3
ALBERT VILLAGE 44 C1
Albert Village Com Prim
Sch DE11 . . . . 44 C1
Albion Cl DE12 . . . . 68 A4
Albion Ct LE2 . . . . 181 A5
Albion Par LE7 . . . . 103 B3
Albion Rd
Long Eaton NG10 . . . . . . 10 F8
Sileby LE12 . . . . 77 C2
Albion St
Anstey LE7 . . . . 127 E6
Leicester LE1 . . . . 259 B3
Leicester, Oadby LE2 . . . . 181 A5
Syston LE7 . . . . 103 B3
Wigston LE18 . . . . 179 F1
Woodville DE11 . . . . 44 F2
Albrighton Wlk CV11 . . . 214 A2
Alcester Dr LE5 . . . . . . 156 B6
Alcott Cl LE3 . . . . 154 A4
Aldeby Cl
Leicester LE2 . . . . 179 B4
Narborough LE19 . . . . . 178 D5
Alderbrooke Dr CV11 . . 214 A1
Alder Cl LE3 . . . . 152 F2
Alder Cres LE17 . . . . . . 244 B6
Alder Ct CV9 . . . . 170 D1
Alderleigh Rd LE2 . . . . 179 B1
Alderman Richard Hallam
Prim Sch LE4 . . . . 128 C1

Aldermill Bsns Pk
CV9 . . . . 170 D3
Alderstone Dr LE18 . . . . 203 C8
Alderton Cl LE4 . . . . . . 129 C5
ALDGATE 168 B5
Aldgate Ave LE5 . . . . . . 156 B3
Aldgate Ct PE9 . . . . . . 168 A5
Aldin Way LE10 . . . . . . 197 A3
Aldridge Rd LE10 . . . . . 215 D6
Aldwinkles Yd 4
LE16 . . . . 240 E3
Alesworth Dr LE10 . . . . 215 F4
Alexander Ave
Earl Shilton LE9 . . . . . . 199 A8
Enderby LE19 . . . . 178 A3
Alexander Cres LE15 . . . 137 E6
Alexander Dr LE12 . . . . 244 B5
Alexander Gdns LE10 . . 197 C2
Alexander Rd LE12 . . . . . 75 F7
Alexander St LE3 . . . . . 259 A4
Alexandra Bldg LE18 . . . 180 B2
Alexandra Ct
Leicester, Oadby LE2 . . . 181 B5
Overseal DE12 . . . . 67 B4
Alexandra Ho LE1 . . . . 259 C4
Alexandra Rd
Leicester LE2 . . . . 155 D1
Long Eaton NG10 . . . . . . 10 D8
Overseal DE12 . . . . 67 B4
Stamford PE9 . . . . 143 D4
Swadlincote DE11 . . . . . . 44 B3
Alexandra St
Narborough LE19 . . . . . 201 C8
Thurmaston LE4 . . . . . . 129 E8
Alfred St LE1 . . . . 52 B5
Alfreton Cl LE10 . . . . . . 215 F5
Alfreton Rd LE18 . . . . . 180 C4
Algernon Rd LE13 . . . . . 59 D3
Alice Gdns
Overseal DE12 . . . . 67 B4
Whetstone LE8 . . . . 201 F5
Allandale Rd LE2 . . . . . 155 E1
Allandale Rd LE2 . . . . . 155 E1
Allans Cl CV23 . . . . 257 A5
Allans Dr CV23 . . . . 257 A5
Allans La CV23 . . . . 257 A5
Allen Ave LE12 . . . . 75 F7
Allendale Rd LE11 . . . . . 75 B7
Allenwood Rd LE2 . . . . 179 E4
Allerton Dr LE3 . . . . . . 128 A1
ALLEXTON 187 D5
Allexton Field Rd
LE15 . . . . 188 A2
Allexton Gdns LE3 . . . . 153 D6

Allexton La
Allexton LE15 187 D3
Stockerston LE15 187 D1
Allexton Rd LE15 209 F7
Allfrey Cl LE17 244 A6
Alliance Rd LE3 153 C7
ALLINGTON 4 E5
Allington Dr LE4 129 B8
Allington Gdns NG32 4 F4
Allington Rd NG32 4 E2
Allington St LE4 155 B8
Allington with Sedgebrook CE Prim Sch NG32 4 F5
Allinson Cl LE5 156 A6
Allison Ave DE11 44 B3
Allison Cl LE65 69 B8
Allotment La CV13 121 E2
Alloway Cl LE4 129 D4
All Saints CE Prim Sch
Coalville LE67 71 B2
Sapcote LE9 217 D7
Wigston LE18 180 C2
All Saints Cl
Asfordby LE14 57 F2
Sapcote LE9 217 D7
All Saint's Mews 6 PE9 143 D3
All Saints Open LE1 259 A4
All Saints' Pl 7 PE9 143 D3
All Saints Rd
Leicester LE3 259 A4
Thurcaston LE7 101 B2
All Saints' St PE9 143 D3
Allsopp's La LE11 52 D5
Alma Rd LE10 197 D1
Alma St
Leicester LE3 154 C7
Melbourne DE73 26 A7
Almey's La LE9 176 A1
Almond Cl
Countesthorpe LE8 202 E4
Loughborough LE11 75 A6
Almond Gr DE11 44 A5
Almond Rd LE2 154 F3
Almond Way
Bagworth LE67 124 A6
Earl Shilton LE9 198 E6
Lutterworth LE17 244 A6
Alpine Cl LE15 137 E6
Alport Way LE18 180 E2
Alsthorpe Rd LE15 138 B7
Alston Dr LE11 51 D6
Altar Stones La LE67 98 C2
Althorp Cl
Leicester LE2 179 B5
Market Harborough LE16 241 B3
Althorpe Dr LE11 51 C4
Alton Hill LE67 70 B3
Alton Rd LE2 179 E6
Alton Way LE65 69 C5
Alvaston Rd
Leicester LE3 154 B1
Melton Mowbray LE13 59 A5
Alvecote Rd LE2 179 D5
Alvington Way LE16 240 D5
Alvis Dale LE7 101 F8
Alwyne Cl LE15 138 A6
Alyssum Way LE19 177 F1
Amadis Rd LE4 128 A4
Amanda Rd LE2 179 B4
Ambassador Rd
Diseworth DE74 28 B7
Leicester LE5 156 A6
Amber Gate Cl LE9 219 A6
Ambergate Dr LE4 128 F8
Amberley Cl LE4 129 E6
Amberwood DE11 44 A5
Ambion Ct CV13 148 E2
Ambion La CV13 173 E6
Ambion Rise CV13 148 D2
Ambion Way LE10 197 F1
Ambler Cl LE18 180 D1
Ambleside
Barwell LE9 198 C7
Leicester LE2 155 C2
Ambleside Cl
Leicester LE2 179 C3
Loughborough LE11 74 C8
Ambleside Dr LE2 179 C3
Ambleside Way
Leicester LE2 179 C3
Melton Mowbray LE13 59 A2
Ambrose Cl LE3 154 B6
Amersham Rd LE4 128 D1
Amersham Way DE12 93 C6
Amesbury Ct LE18 203 C8
Amesbury Rd LE18 203 C8
Amhurst Cl LE3 127 F1
Amis Cl LE11 51 C5
Amos Rd LE3 153 D6
Amsden Rise LE9 218 E7
Amyson Rd LE5 156 C6
Amy St LE3 179 B8
Ancaster Rd PE9 143 C5
Ancaster Way LE15 166 D3
Anchor Cl
Hathern LE12 51 A8
Swadlincote DE11 44 C4
Anchor La
Hathern LE12 51 A8
Peggs Green LE67 71 B8
Anchor St LE4 128 F2
Andover St LE2 259 C3
Andrew Ave LE9 201 D4
Andrew Cl CV13 196 D7
Andrew Ct 3 LE2 155 B4
Andrewes Cl LE3 154 D5
Andrewes St LE3 154 D5
Andrewes Wlk 3 LE3 154 D5
Andrew Macdonald Cl LE16 240 F3
Andrew Rd
Anstey LE7 127 E7
Stamford PE9 143 D4
Andrews Cl LE12 218 F2
Andrew's La LE16 208 B4
Aneford Rd LE4 129 E1
Anemone Cl LE13 82 A8
Angela Dr LE5 156 B4
Angel Ct 2 LE16 240 E3
Angel St 1 LE16 240 E3
Angel Yd LE11 52 B4
Angle La LE15 166 D1
Anglesey Rd LE18 179 F3
Anglian Water Bird Watching Ctr* LE15 138 D3
Angus Cl
Leicester LE7 156 F6
Stamford PE9 142 F4
Angus Dr LE11 51 E4
Angus Rd LE9 198 A6
Ankle Hill LE13 59 C1
Anne Rd PE9 143 C4
Annexe The LE1 259 B5
Annies Wharf LE11 52 B5
Ann St LE1 259 C4
Ann's Way LE2 181 C5
Annwell La LE65 45 E2
ANNWELL PLACE 45 E1
Anson Rd
Diseworth DE74 28 B8
Shepshed LE12 50 A3
Anstee Rd NG10 10 C5
ANSTEY 127 C7
Anstey La
Groby LE6 127 B3
Groby LE6 127 B4
Leicester LE4 128 B2
Thurcaston LE7 101 B1
Anthony Cl LE7 102 E2
Anthony Dr LE7 156 F5
Anthony Rd LE4 128 D1
Anthony St LE7 101 F6
Antill Cl LE14 57 F3
Antringham Cl LE5 130 C2
Apiary Gate DE74 17 B3
Apollo Cl LE2 155 B5
Apollo Ct LE2 155 B5
Applebee Rd LE10 215 D6
Applebees Mdw LE10 214 E6
Applebees Wlk LE10 214 F6
Appleby Cl LE3 153 C6
Appleby Hill CV9 119 B3
Appleby Ho 1 LE10 197 E1
Appleby La DE12 120 D7
APPLEBY MAGNA 119 E8
APPLEBY PARVA 119 D6
Appleby Rd LE4 130 A7
Applegate LE1 259 A3
Apple Pie La CV10 194 B3
Appleton Ave LE4 128 D4
Appleton Dr LE12 33 B3
Apple Tree Cl LE9 175 B1
Approach The LE5 155 F4
Aqueduct Rd LE67 70 E8
Aquitaine Cl LE19 178 A3
Arbor Ct 11 LE2 155 B4
Arbor Rd LE9 200 D4
Arbour Rd LE4 129 B2
Arbury Dale LE12 50 C2
Arcade The 1 LE18 180 D3
Archdale Cl LE4 102 A1
Archdale St LE7 102 F3
Archdeacon La LE1 154 F7
Archer Cl
Leicester LE4 129 E4
Loughborough LE11 51 B6
Archers' Gn LE7 103 D7
Archers La LE9 175 F7
Archers Rdbt LE8 205 A7
Archery Cl LE8 202 F4
Archway Rd LE5 130 E1
Ardath Rd LE4 129 C1
Arden Ave LE3 153 F1
Arden Cl LE16 241 A4
Arden Dr LE13 59 A4
Arden Rd CV11 214 A1
Arden Way LE16 240 F5
Ardern Terr LE3 154 B2
Argosy Rd DE74 28 E8
Arguile Pl LE10 197 C1
Argyle Pk LE16 250 E8
Argyle St LE67 95 F2
Argyll Way PE9 143 B3
Arkwright Ho LE9 218 E7
Armadale Cl LE10 197 A1
Armadale Dr LE5 156 D8
Armadale Gn LE5 156 C8
Armett's La LE12 48 E4
Armitage Cl LE11 52 A4
Armley Gr PE9 143 F5
Armour Cl LE10 215 D5
Armson Ave LE9 152 E5
Armston Rd
Cosby LE9 201 D3
Quorn (Quorndon) LE12 76 A5
Arncliffe Cl CV11 214 A2
Arncliffe Rd LE5 156 C8
Arndale LE18 180 F1
ARNESBY 221 F5
Arnesby CE Prim Sch LE8 221 F5
Arnesby Cres LE2 179 F5
Arnesby La LE8 221 C5
Arnesby Rd LE8 222 E6
Arnhem St LE1 259 C3
Arnhill Rd NN17 213 B1
Arnold Ave
Long Eaton NG10 10 A4
Wigston LE18 180 A1
Arnold Cl LE9 201 D2
Arnold Cres NG10 10 A4
Arnold Rd CV13 196 D6
Arnold's Cres LE9 150 B3
Arnold Smith Ho LE12 50 B4
Arnold St LE1 155 B7
Arnside Cl DE11 44 C1
Arran Rd
Leicester LE4 129 D4
Stamford PE9 142 F4
Arran Way
Countesthorpe LE8 202 F3
Hinckley LE10 197 B1
Arreton Cl LE2 180 C7
Arthur St
Barwell LE9 198 B7
Loughborough LE11 52 A3
Artisan Rd LE14 36 B5
Arum Way LE3 153 D6
Arundel Ave DE74 16 E5
Arundel Cl LE12 101 C8
Arundel Gr LE12 50 A2
Arundel St 2 LE3 154 D5
Ascot Dr LE67 97 A8
Ascot Rd LE4 129 B2
Ascott Dr DE11 44 A7
Asfare Bsns Pk LE10 215 E1
ASFORDBY 57 F3
ASFORDBY HILL 58 D3
Asfordby Hill Prim Sch LE14 58 D3
Asfordby Pl LE14 57 F2
Asfordby Rd
Hoby LE14 79 F8
Melton Mowbray LE13, LE14 58 E3
Asfordby St LE5 155 D6
ASFORDBY VALLEY 58 B3
Asha Ho LE4 129 A2
Asha Margh LE4 129 A2
Ashbourne Dr DE11 44 A1
Ashbourne Rd LE18 180 C4
Ashbourne St LE2 155 C5
Ashbrook Rise CV10 194 B2
Ashburton Cl LE10 216 A6
Ashburton Rd LE67 96 C6
Ashby Cres LE11 51 D3
Ashby Ct LE10 197 D3
ASHBY-DE-LA-ZOUCH 69 C6
Ashby-de-la-Zouch Castle* LE65 69 C6
Ashby-de-la-Zouch CE Prim Sch LE65 69 B6
Ashby & District Hospl LE65 69 C6
ASHBY FOLVILLE 105 F5
Ashby Glade LE5 156 C5
Ashby Grange LE10 197 E5
Ashby Hill Top Prim Sch LE65 68 F6
Ashby Ho LE10 215 D7
Ashby La
Bitteswell LE17 234 B3
Blackfordby DE11 68 C8
Swepstone LE67 94 D3
ASHBY MAGNA 220 A2
Ashby Mus* LE65 69 B6
ASHBY PARVA 233 F5
Ashby Rd
Ashby-de-la-Z LE65, LE67 70 B7
Barwell LE9 197 E6
Blackfordby DE11, LE65 45 D2
Breedon on t H DE73 26 E2
Cadeby CV13 149 C2
Coalville LE67 70 E3
Coleorton LE67 70 D6
Diseworth DE74 28 C7
Donisthorpe DE12 68 A1
Gaddesby LE7 105 D5
Gilmorton LE17 235 B5
Hinckley LE10 197 E3
Ibstock LE67 95 E2
Kegworth DE74 18 A2
Kegworth DE74 18 B2
Loughborough LE11 51 F4
Markfield LE67 98 D2
Measham DE12 93 E7
Melbourne DE73 26 A6
Moira DE12 67 F4
Moira, Norris Hill DE12 68 B5
Newbold LE67 47 D2
Normanton Le H LE67 94 F7
Osgathorpe LE67 48 D4
Packington LE65 69 C2
Peatling Parva LE17 235 E8
Ravenstone LE67 95 E8
Rempstone LE12 32 B6
Shepshed LE12 49 F8
Snarestone DE12 120 E4
Stapleton LE9 174 F3
Thringstone LE67 48 D1
Twyford LE14 106 C2
Ullesthorpe LE17 233 C4
Ashby Rd E LE12 50 D1
Ashby Rd W LE12 49 E1
Ashby Rise LE8 182 B1
Ashby Road Central LE12 50 B1
Ashby Sch LE65 69 C6
Ashby Sq 4 LE11 52 A4
Ash Cl
Aston-on-T DE72 16 B7
Barrow-u-S LE12 53 D1
Ratby LE6 126 B1
Uppingham LE15 189 C3
Ashclose Ave LE2 180 C6
Ash Croft CV9 171 B7
Ash Ct LE6 126 E2
Ashdale LE67 95 E1
Ash Dale LE67 71 D7
Ashdown Ave LE3 154 B6
Ashdown Cl LE11 51 C5
Ashdown Rd LE18 180 D4
Ash Dr
Measham DE12 93 C6
Syston LE7 103 B2
Ashfield LE15 138 A8
Ashfield Dr
Anstey LE7 127 D5
Moira DE12 68 B6
Ashfield Rd
Leicester LE2 155 D3
3 Market Harborough LE16 240 E4
Thurmaston LE4 129 F8
Ash Field Sch LE5 155 F4
Ashford Ct LE2 155 D1
Ashford Rd
Hinckley LE10 215 B7
Leicester LE2 155 A1
Whitwick LE67 71 D5
Ash Gr
Blaby LE8 202 B8
Bottesford NG13 2 F3
Hathern LE12 30 A2
Long Eaton NG10 10 C6
Melton Mowbray LE13 59 B5
Mountsorrel LE12 76 E1
Ashington Cl LE3 154 B8
Ash La B79 118 F6
Ashland Dr LE67 71 A2
Ashlands Rd LE7 183 F3
Ashlands Way LE19 177 F1
Ashlar Dr DE12 67 F1
Ashleigh Ct LE3 154 C3
Ashleigh Dr
Loughborough LE11 51 E2
Lutterworth LE17 244 A6
Ashleigh Gdns
Barwell LE9 198 C8
Leicester LE3 154 C3
Ashleigh Rd
Glenfield LE3 153 C8
Leicester LE3 154 C3
ASHLEY 227 F2
Ashley Cl DE12 67 B3
Ashley Rd
Medbourne LE16 227 E6
Middleton LE16 229 B2
Weston by W LE16 227 C3
Ashley Way LE16 241 B3
Ashlyns Rise LE3 153 E5
Ashmead Cres LE4 102 C1
Ashmount Sch LE11 52 A1
Ashover Cl LE9 201 D4
Ashover Rd LE5 155 D4
Ash Pl PE9 142 F4
Ash Rd
Croft LE9 200 D3
Earl Shilton LE9 198 D7
Ash St LE5 155 C7
Ashthorpe Rd LE3 154 A4
Ashton Cl
Leicester, Oadby LE2 181 B3
Melton Mowbray LE13 59 C1
Wigston LE18 180 C1
Ash Tree Cl LE2 181 B4
Ashtree Gdns PE9 168 D2
Ashtree Rd LE5 130 C2
Ash Tree Rd LE67 96 B7
Ash-Tree Rd LE9 201 D3
Ash Tree Rd LE2 181 C4
Ashurst Cl LE18 203 E8
Ashurst Rd LE3 178 F8
Ashview Cl NG10 10 A8
Ashville Way LE8 201 E4
Ash Way LE14 80 D8
ASHWELL 111 B8
Ashwell Rd
Cottesmore LE15 112 B7
Langham LE15 110 D5
Oakham LE15 111 B2
Whissendine LE15 110 B8
Ashwell St LE1 259 C2
Ash Wlk LE12 31 D8
Askrigg Way LE18 180 E2
Aspen Ave LE11 75 A7
Aspen Cl
Measham DE12 93 C6
Ravenstone LE67 70 F2
Aspen Dr LE8 202 E4
Aspens Hollow LE67 71 D7
Aspen Way LE17 244 B7
Asplin Rd LE2 179 E5
Asquith Bvd LE2, LE12 180 B5
Asquith Way LE2 180 B5
Assheton La CV9 146 D7
Assured Dr LE4 129 D7
Aster Cl
Hinckley LE10 215 E6
Nuneaton CV11 214 A1
Aster Way LE10 215 D6
Astill Cl LE6 152 E8
Astill Dr LE4 128 F5
Astill Lodge Rd LE4 128 A6
Astley Cl
Leicester LE3 154 B3
Astley Cl *continued*
Market Harborough LE16 240 D1
Astley Rd LE9 198 F8
Astley Way LE65 69 D7
Aston Dr DE11 44 A7
Aston Firs Cvn Site LE9 216 E8
ASTON FLAMVILLE 216 E6
Aston Flamville Rd LE10 216 C7
Aston Hall Dr DE72 16 A7
Aston Hill LE2 180 A8
Aston La
Aston Flamville LE10 216 D7
Aston-on-T DE72 16 C8
Hinckley LE10 216 A6
Sharnford LE10 217 B5
ASTON-ON-TRENT 16 B8
Aston-on-Trent Prim Sch DE72 16 A8
Astron Bsns Pk DE11 44 A3
ATHERSTONE 170 E2
Atherstone Cl LE2 181 D4
Atherstone Rd
Appleby Magna DE12 119 E5
Atherstone CV9 170 D4
Fenny Drayton CV10, CV13 195 A6
Hartshill Green CV10 194 B2
Loughborough LE11 75 A7
Measham DE12 93 C3
Ratcliffe Culey CV9 171 A3
Sibson CV9, CV13 172 A3
Atkin Ct LE7 127 E6
Atkinson Rd LE65 68 F7
Atkinson St LE5 155 D6
Atkins St LE2 259 B2
Atkins Way LE10 215 E7
Atlas Cl LE2 155 B5
Atlas Ct LE67 71 D2
Atlas Rd LE67 71 D2
Attenborough Cl
Braunstone Town LE3 153 C1
Wigston LE18 180 E4
ATTERTON 172 A1
Atterton La CV9, CV13 171 E1
Atterury Cl LE12 76 D7
Attewell Cl DE72 9 B7
Attfield Dr LE8 201 F7
Attingham Cl LE4 129 D1
Attlebridge Cl LE5 130 B2
Attlee Cl LE17 244 B5
Attlee Way LE2 179 E5
Auburn Ho
Blaby LE8 202 A8
Leicester LE3 154 A7
Auburn Rd LE8 202 B8
Auden Cl LE4 128 B2
Audens Way DE11 44 C6
Audit Hall Rd LE15 140 F5
Audley Cl LE16 241 B2
Audley End LE3 154 B1
Augusta Cl LE3 153 C6
Augustus Cl LE7 102 E2
Ault Dene DE11 44 E4
Aulton Cres LE10 197 B1
Aulton Way LE10 197 B1
Aumberry Gap LE11 52 B4
Auriga St LE16 240 F2
Austen Ave NG10 10 C5
Auster Ind Est LE4 129 F6
Austhorp Gr LE15 112 B7
Austin Friar's La PE9 143 D2
Austin Rise LE5 156 D8
Austins Cl LE16 240 D3
Austin St PE9 143 D2
AUSTREY 119 B2
Austrey CE Prim Sch CV9 119 B2
Austrey La
Countesthorpe LE8 202 F3
Newton Regis B79 118 E3
No Man's Heath B79 119 A5
Orton-on-t-H CV9 145 C6
Austrey Rd DE12 119 D5
Austwick Cl LE4 128 C3
Autumn Rd LE2 179 C3
Avalon Way LE7 127 E5
Avebury Ave LE4 128 C1
Aveland Rd PE9 167 F5
Avenue Cl LE7 103 E5
Avenue Gdns LE2 155 C1
Avenue N LE9 199 A8
Avenue Prim Sch LE2 155 B1
Avenue Rd
Ashby-de-la-Z LE65 69 A5
Coalville LE67 96 D8
Leicester LE2 155 C1
Queniborough LE7 103 E5
Sileby LE12 77 D3
Avenue Road Extension LE2 155 B1
Avenue S LE9 199 A8
Avenue The
Blaby LE8 202 A8
Broughton Astley LE9 218 E7
Carlby PE9 117 C8
Glenfield LE3 127 B1
Leicester LE2 155 C2
Leicester, Oadby LE2 182 A4
Medbourne LE16 228 C8
Noseley LE7 184 F3
Averham Cl DE11 44 A3
Averil Rd LE5 156 B7

Avery Cl LE17 . . . . **244** B5
Avery Dr
Markfield LE67 . . . . **98** D1
Syston LE7 . . . . **103** B5
Avery Hill LE3 . . . . **153** D4
Avington Cl LE3 . . . . **128** A2
Avoca Cl LE5 . . . . **156** B6
Avocet Cl
Essendine PE9 . . . . **117** A6
Rugby CV23 . . . . **252** C1
Avon Cl
Leicester, Oadby LE2 . . . . **181** C5
Oakham LE15 . . . . **137** F5
Swadlincote DE11 . . . . **44** B6
Avondale Cl NG10 . . . . **10** A6
Avondale Rd
Barlestone CV13 . . . . **149** D8
Wigston LE18 . . . . **180** D4
Avon Dr LE8 . . . . **201** F7
Avon Fields NN6 . . . . **256** E6
Avon Rd
Barrow-u-S LE12 . . . . **76** D6
Leicester LE3 . . . . **153** E2
Melton Mowbray LE13 . . . . . . **59** B1
Avonside Dr LE5 . . . . **155** F5
Avon St LE2 . . . . **155** B4
Avon Vale Rd LE11 . . . . **52** C1
Avon Wlk LE10 . . . . **215** A8
Axbridge Cl LE4 . . . . **128** D1
Axiom Ct PE9 . . . . **143** F2
AYLESTONE **179** D6
Aylestone Dr LE2 . . . . **179** D5
Aylestone La LE18 . . . . **180** B3
AYLESTONE PARK **179** E7
Aylestone Rd LE2 . . . . **179** D7
Aylestone Wlk LE2 . . . . . . **154** F3
Aylmer Rd LE3 . . . . **153** F4
Ayr Cl PE9 . . . . **143** A4
Ayrshire Cl LE9 . . . . **198** A6
Aysgarth Cl CV11 . . . . **214** A2
Aysgarth Rd LE4 . . . . **128** C3
AYSTON **189** A7
Ayston Rd
Leicester LE3 . . . . **154** A1
Uppingham LE15 . . . . **189** B5
Azad Ho 囗 LE2 . . . . **155** B5
Azalea Cl
Hinckley LE10 . . . . **215** E5
Lutterworth LE17 . . . . **244** A5
Azalea Dr LE10 . . . . **215** E6
Azalea Wlk LE10 . . . . **215** E5

B

Babelake St LE65 . . . . **94** B8
Babingley Dr LE4 . . . . **128** D2
Babington Com Tech Coll
LE4 . . . . **128** B3
Babington Rd LE7 . . . . **101** E6
Babington Rd
Barrow-u-S LE12 . . . . **76** E8
Rothley LE7 . . . . **101** E6
Babington Row LE4 . . . . . **180** A5
Back Dr LE7 . . . . **185** A2
Back La
Allington NG32 . . . . **4** F5
Belton-in-R LE15 . . . . **187** D7
Burton Overy LE8 . . . . **182** F1
Castle Donington DE74 . . . . . **17** A6
Claybrooke Magna
LE17 . . . . **232** E6
Collyweston PE8 . . . . **168** D2
Cossington LE7 . . . . **102** D7
Cotes LE12 . . . . **52** F6
East Farndon LE16 . . . . **250** B7
East Langton LE16 . . . . **225** D6
Gaulby LE7 . . . . **183** C6
Harston NG32 . . . . **15** A4
Hoby LE14 . . . . **79** E7
Leire LE17 . . . . **218** E1
Long Clawson LE14 . . . . **20** C3
Market Bosworth CV13 . . . . **148** E3
Morcott LE15 . . . . **191** A6
Sewstern NG33 . . . . **63** F8
Shearsby LE17 . . . . **222** A2
Sileby LE7 . . . . **77** C3
Skillington NG33 . . . . **43** B8
South Luffenham LE15 . . . . . **191** D8
Stamford PE9 . . . . **143** E3
Stonesby LE14 . . . . **40** E6
Thrussington LE7 . . . . **78** F4
Willoughby-on-t-W LE12 . . . . **34** D7
Back Rd
Barrowden LE15 . . . . **191** E5
Tilton on t H LE7 . . . . **160** A7
Back St
Buckminster NG33 . . . . **42** D2
North Kilworth LE17 . . . . **246** F3
Saltby LE14 . . . . **24** E1
Backway The LE16 . . . . . . **240** F2
Badcock Way LE8 . . . . **223** A6
Baddely Dr LE18 . . . . **180** B4
Baden Rd LE5 . . . . **155** E3
Badgerbrook Prim Sch
LE8 . . . . **201** F5
Badger Cl
Fleckney LE8 . . . . **223** A6
Narborough LE19 . . . . **201** A7
Badger Ct LE11 . . . . **74** D8
Badger Dr LE8 . . . . **201** F5
Badgers Bank LE7 . . . . . . **101** E7
Badgers Cl
Leicester LE4 . . . . **128** B3
Manton LE15 . . . . **164** D5

Badger's Cnr LE7 . . . . **103** D8
Badgers Croft LE67 . . . . . . **71** D7
Badgers Holt LE2 . . . . **181** A4
Badgers Wlk LE12 . . . . **75** E5
Badmington Rd LE4 . . . . . **129** D5
Badminton Rd
Leicester LE4 . . . . **129** D5
Syston LE7 . . . . **103** B5
Baggrave End LE7 . . . . . . **105** D3
Baggrave Rd LE7 . . . . **132** B4
Baggrave St LE5 . . . . **155** D6
Bagley Cl LE11 . . . . **51** C6
BAGWORTH **124** B5
Bagworth Heath Nature
Reserve* LE67 . . . . **124** D3
Bagworth La LE67 . . . . . . **124** D5
Bagworth Rd
Barlestone CV13 . . . . **123** E2
Barlestone CV13 . . . . **123** E3
Nailstone CV13 . . . . **123** C3
Newbold Verdon LE9 . . . . . . **150** B7
Bailey Ave DE12 . . . . **67** A3
Bailey Cl LE11 . . . . **74** D8
Baileys Croft LE12 . . . . **34** D7
Baileys La LE8 . . . . **182** F1
Bainbridge Rd
Leicester LE3 . . . . **154** B1
Loughborough LE11 . . . . **52** C1
Wigston LE18 . . . . **180** E1
Bain Cl LE9 . . . . **143** E5
Baines Ct LE15 . . . . **138** A6
Baines La
Braunstone Town LE3 . . . . . **153** B3
Seaton LE15 . . . . **190** C1
Baines' La 囗 LE10 . . . . . . **197** D1
Bakehouse La LE8 . . . . . . **223** B4
Baker Ave LE65 . . . . **68** F5
Baker's La LE4 . . . . **106** F4
Baker's La NG13 . . . . **6** F4
Baker St
Coalville LE67 . . . . **71** C2
Lutterworth LE17 . . . . **244** C5
Swadlincote DE11 . . . . **44** C3
Bakers Way LE5 . . . . **130** D3
Bakery Cl LE9 . . . . **201** D2
Bakery La LE9 . . . . **200** A2
Bakewell Cl LE67 . . . . **71** E1
Bakewell Dr DE74 . . . . **17** A2
Bakewell Rd
Long Eaton NG10 . . . . **10** E5
Loughborough LE11 . . . . **51** F7
Wigston LE18 . . . . **180** C4
Bakewells La LE67 . . . . **70** F8
Bakewell St
Coalville LE67 . . . . **71** E1
Leicester LE2 . . . . **155** C6
Bala Rd LE9 . . . . **200** D4
Balcombe Ave LE3 . . . . . . **154** B6
Balderstone Cl LE5 . . . . . . **156** A6
Baldock's La LE13 . . . . **59** D2
Baldwin Ave LE18 . . . . **180** A1
Baldwin Rise LE9 . . . . **218** D7
Bale Rd LE4 . . . . **129** E1
Balfour Cl LE10 . . . . **215** E7
Balfour Gdns LE16 . . . . . . **240** D1
Balfour St LE3 . . . . **154** D7
Balgrave Gr LE4 . . . . **128** B3
Balk Rd PE9 . . . . **116** E2
Balk The LE3 . . . . **127** B1
Balladine Rd LE7 . . . . **127** E7
Ballards Cl LE4 . . . . **128** B3
Ballater Cl LE5 . . . . **156** D3
Balliol Ave LE7 . . . . **103** C2
Balliol Rd LE10 . . . . **215** F6
Balmoral Ave LE12 . . . . . . **50** A2
Balmoral Cl
Leicester LE2 . . . . **180** C7
Market Harborough
LE16 . . . . **241** B2
Balmoral Ct DE74 . . . . **17** D5
Balmoral Dr LE13 . . . . **153** E2
Balmoral Rd
Coalville LE67 . . . . **97** A8
Earl Shilton LE9 . . . . **198** D7
Melton Mowbray LE13 . . . . . **59** C5
Mountsorrel LE12 . . . . **101** D8
Oakham LE15 . . . . **137** E5
Baltimore Cl 囗 DE11 . . . . **44** A7
Bambrook Cl LE9 . . . . **151** C3
Bamburgh Cl
Ashby-de-la-Z LE65 . . . . **69** B5
Market Harborough
LE16 . . . . **241** B3
Bambury La
Countesthorpe LE8 . . . . **202** D1
Peatling Magna LE8 . . . . **221** A6
Bampton Way LE2 . . . . . . **180** A6
Bampton Cl LE18 . . . . **203** D8
Bampton St LE11 . . . . **52** B3
Banbury Dr
Melton Mowbray LE13 . . . . . **82** D8
Shepshed LE12 . . . . **49** F3
Banbury La LE16 . . . . **229** D6
Bancroft Rd LE16 . . . . **229** D1
Bandalls La LE12 . . . . **53** B5
Banff Cl LE15 . . . . **138** B6
Bankart Ave LE2 . . . . **155** E1
Bank Cotts LE14 . . . . **248** C8
Bankfield Dr LE16 . . . . . . **241** A5
Banks Cl LE12 . . . . **77** C3
Bankside LE5 . . . . **156** E8
Banks Rd LE2 . . . . **179** D7
Bank St
Long Eaton NG10 . . . . **10** E7
Lutterworth LE17 . . . . **244** C5
Swadlincote DE11 . . . . **67** A8

Banks The
Barrow-u-S LE12 . . . . **76** B8
Cosby LE9 . . . . **201** D2
Bank Terr LE9 . . . . **198** A6
Bank The
Arnesby LE8 . . . . **221** F5
Countesthorpe LE8 . . . . **202** F4
Kibworth Beauchamp
LE8 . . . . **224** A8
Shearsby LE17 . . . . **222** A2
Banky Mdw LE10 . . . . **216** A7
Bannerman Rd LE5 . . . . . . **155** E3
Bannister Rd 囗 LE3 . . . . . **178** F6
Bantlam La LE19 . . . . **178** B3
Baptist Mews The
LE8 . . . . **179** C1
Baptist Wlk LE10 . . . . **197** D1
Barbara Ave
Leicester Forest East
LE9 . . . . **152** E3
Leicester LE5 . . . . **156** B7
Newbold Verdon LE9 . . . . . . **150** B3
Barbara Cl LE19 . . . . **178** A3
Barbara Rd LE3 . . . . **154** B1
Barclay La LE3 . . . . **154** C4
Barden Cl LE11 . . . . **51** B3
Bardolph St E LE4 . . . . . . **155** C8
Bardolph St LE4 . . . . **155** B8
Barden Rd
Barwell LE9 . . . . **198** B8
Leicester LE4 . . . . **128** C4
Bardsey Cl LE10 . . . . **197** B1
Bardsley Rd NN17 . . . . **230** E3
Barfoot Cl LE8 . . . . **204** E1
Barfoot Rd LE2 . . . . **179** F5
Barford Cl LE18 . . . . **203** C8
Barge Cl LE18 . . . . **180** A1
BARKBY **130** C8
Barkby Holt La LE7 . . . . . . **130** F8
Barkby La LE7 . . . . **103** A1
Barkby Rd
Beeby LE7 . . . . **131** B5
Leicester LE4 . . . . **129** E3
Queniborough LE7 . . . . **103** E4
Syston LE7 . . . . **103** C3
Barkby Thorpe La
LE4 . . . . **130** B8
Barkbythorpe Rd LE4,
LE7 . . . . **130** B5
Barker Cres LE13 . . . . **82** C8
Barkers Field LE14 . . . . **20** C3
Barker St LE5 . . . . **155** D7
Barkestone La NG13 . . . . **6** E6
BARKESTONE-LE-VALE
. . . . **6** C2
Barkford Cl LE7 . . . . **130** E1
Barklam Cl DE12 . . . . **67** E1
Barleston Dr LE4 . . . . **197** A1
BARLESTONE **149** E8
Barlestone CE Prim Sch
CV13 . . . . **149** C8
Barlestone Rd
Bagworth LE67, CV13 . . . . . **124** A4
Newbold Verdon LE9 . . . . . . **150** A6
Barley Cl LE3 . . . . **153** C7
Barley Croft Prim Sch
LE4 . . . . **128** C3
Barleyfield LE10 . . . . **197** C3
Barley La LE8 . . . . **221** C8
Barley Leas LE7 . . . . **132** B2
BARLEYTHORPE **137** D8
Barleythorpe Rd LE15 . . **137** F7
Barley Way LE7 . . . . **101** E7
Barling Rd LE5 . . . . **155** E8
Barlow Rd LE15 . . . . **137** F6
Barmouth Ave LE2 . . . . . . **180** A6
Barmstedt Dr LE15 . . . . . . **138** A8
Barnabas Rd LE5 . . . . **155** E7
Barnack Rd PE9 . . . . **143** F2
Barnard Cl
Burton Lazars LE14 . . . . **83** A7
Leicester LE2 . . . . **155** B5
Barnard Gdns LE16 . . . . . . **250** D8
Barnards Dr LE12 . . . . **77** E4
Barnard Way LE12 . . . . **76** D1
Barnby Ave LE18 . . . . **180** C4
Barn Cl
Castle Donington DE74 . . . . . **17** B3
Long Eaton NG10 . . . . **10** B5
Wigston LE18 . . . . **203** E8
Barn End
Empingham LE15 . . . . **140** F6
Skillington NG33 . . . . **43** B8
Barnes Cl
Kibworth Beauchamp
LE8 . . . . **223** F8
Leicester LE4 . . . . **129** E5
Barnes Heath Rd LE5 . . . **156** A5
Barnet Cl LE4 . . . . **181** A3
Barnett Cl LE7 . . . . **102** D7
Barnett Janner Ho
LE4 . . . . **128** C4
Barnfield Cl
Great Glen LE8 . . . . **182** B1
Long Whatton LE12 . . . . **29** B4
Barngate Cl
Birstall LE4 . . . . **128** F8

Bargate Cl *continued*
Melton Mowbray LE13 . . . . . **59** D5
Barn Hill PE9 . . . . **143** D3
Barnley Cl LE8 . . . . **202** E4
Barns Cl LE9 . . . . **152** C5
Barnsdale LE15 . . . . **229** D6
Barnsdale Ave LE15 . . . . . **112** E1
Barnsdale Cl
Great Easton LE16 . . . . **229** D8
Loughborough LE11 . . . . **52** A5
Barnsdale Gdns*
LE15 . . . . **112** E2
Barnsdale Rd LE4 . . . . **127** F5
Barnsdale Way LE19 . . . . **178** D5
Barnstaple Cl LE18 . . . . . **203** D8
Barnstaple Rd LE5 . . . . . . **156** D3
Barnstone La NG13 . . . . **5** A5
Barns Way LE9 . . . . **151** C4
Barn Way LE67 . . . . **125** E8
Barnwell Ave LE4 . . . . **128** F4
Barnwell Rd PE9 . . . . **143** A4
Baronet Way LE5 . . . . **130** E1
Barons Cl LE9 . . . . **152** C5
Baron's Ct LE12 . . . . **76** E3
Baron St LE1 . . . . **259** C3
Barons Way LE12 . . . . **76** E3
Baron's Way PE9 . . . . **143** E2
Barrack Row LE11 . . . . **52** B5
Barracks The 囗 LE9 . . . . . **198** A6
Barradale Ave LE12 . . . . . . **77** C4
Barratt Cl LE2 . . . . **155** D2
Barr Cres LE67 . . . . **71** F4
Barrett Dr LE11 . . . . **51** D6
Barrie Rd LE10 . . . . **197** D3
Barrington Ct LE2 . . . . **30** B6
Barrington Park Ind Est
LE4 . . . . **128** B5
Barrington Rd LE2 . . . . . . **155** E1
Barr La CV13 . . . . **196** B3
Barroon DE74 . . . . **17** B3
BARROW **87** A3
Barrowcliffe Cl LE12 . . . . . **76** C8
Barrow Cres LE7 . . . . **105** B7
BARROWDEN **191** F5
Barrowden La LE15 . . . . . **191** C5
Barrowden Rd
Ketton PE9 . . . . **167** E2
South Luffenham LE15 . . . . . **191** F7
Barrow-u-Soar Sta
LE12 . . . . **76** D7
Barrow Rd
Burton o t W LE12 . . . . **53** F6
Cotes LE12 . . . . **52** F6
Quorn (Quorndon) LE12 . . . . **76** A7
Sileby LE12 . . . . **77** B4
Barrow St LE11 . . . . **52** B4
BARROW-UPON-SOAR
. . . . **76** E7
Barry Cl LE3 . . . . **152** E3
Barry Dr
Leicester Forest East
LE9 . . . . **152** E3
Syston LE7 . . . . **103** C4
Barry Rd LE5 . . . . **130** D1
Barrys Cl DE11 . . . . **44** F3
BARSBY **105** E3
Barsby Dr LE11 . . . . **51** D6
Barsby Wlk LE4 . . . . **128** D4
Barshaw Pk LE4 . . . . **128** C5
Barston St LE1 . . . . **259** B5
Bartholomew St LE2 . . . . **155** C4
Bartles Hollow PE9 . . . . . **167** F5
Barton Cl
Ratby LE6 . . . . **152** D7
Wigston LE18 . . . . **180** C1
BARTON IN THE BEANS
. . . . **122** D1
Barton La
Congerstone CV13 . . . . **121** F1
Nailstone CV13 . . . . **122** F2
Barton Rd
Barton in B CV13 . . . . **148** E8
Carlton CV13 . . . . **148** E6
Congerstone CV13 . . . . **147** D8
Leicester LE3 . . . . **154** C8
Odstone CV13 . . . . **122** D4
Osbaston CV13 . . . . **149** C8
BARWELL **198** A6
Barwell Ho LE10 . . . . **215** D7
Barwell Inf Sch LE9 . . . . . **198** A7
Barwell La
Barwell LE9 . . . . **198** A5
Hinckley LE10 . . . . **197** E3
Kirkby Mallory LE9 . . . . **175** C4
Barwell Newlands Com
Prim Sch LE9 . . . . **198** C8
Barwell Rd
Kirby Muxloe LE9 . . . . **152** D3
Kirkby Mallory LE9 . . . . **175** D5
Basin Bridge La CV13 . . . **196** C4
Baslow Cl NG10 . . . . **10** A5
Baslow Rd LE5 . . . . **155** D4
Bassett Ave LE8 . . . . **202** E3
Bassett La LE9 . . . . **217** D7
Bassett St
Leicester LE3 . . . . **154** D7
Wigston LE18 . . . . **179** F1
Batchelor Rd LE8 . . . . **222** F8
Bateman Rd LE3 . . . . **154** B7
Bates Cl
Loughborough LE11 . . . . **51** B6
Market Harborough
LE16 . . . . **240** E5
Bath Cl LE9 . . . . **217** D8
Bath La
Bruntingthorpe LE17 . . . . . . **236** D7

Bath La *continued*
Leicester LE3 . . . . **259** A3
Moira DE12 . . . . **67** D4
Bath Row PE9 . . . . **143** D2
Bath St
Ashby-de-la-Z LE65 . . . . **69** B6
Leicester LE4 . . . . **129** B4
Market Harborough
LE16 . . . . **240** E1
Syston LE7 . . . . **103** A4
Bath Street Cnr 囗
LE65 . . . . **69** B6
Bathurst Rd LE5 . . . . **156** D4
Batsons Cl LE67 . . . . **48** A2
Battenberg Rd LE3 . . . . . . **154** D6
Batten St LE2 . . . . **154** E1
Battersbee Rd LE3 . . . . . . **153** E8
Battersbee Way LE3 . . . . . **153** E8
Battersbee Wlk LE3 . . . . . **153** E8
Battledown Cl LE10 . . . . . **197** B2
Battlefield Line Mus The*
CV13 . . . . **121** F1
Battlefield Line The*
Market Bosworth
CV13 . . . . **148** C5
Shackerstone CV13 . . . . **121** F1
Battleflat Dr LE67 . . . . **96** E3
Battling Brook Com Prim
Sch LE10 . . . . **197** B2
Battling Brook Sh Ctr
LE10 . . . . **197** B1
BATTRAM **123** D8
Battram Rd LE67 . . . . **123** D8
Baulk Rd LE15 . . . . **189** E4
Baxter Gate LE11 . . . . **52** B4
Baxters Cl LE4 . . . . **128** B3
Bayberry Gdns LE2 . . . . . **179** E4
Baycliff Cl LE3 . . . . **154** B8
Bayham Cl LE15 . . . . **156** B5
Bayleaf Cl LE5 . . . . **188** F4
Bayleys Cl LE15 . . . . **141** A6
Bayliss Cl LE9 . . . . **75** F7
Baysdale LE18 . . . . **180** F2
Bayswater Dr LE2 . . . . **179** D1
Bayswater Rd LE13 . . . . **59** D4
Beacon Ave
Loughborough LE11 . . . . **51** F1
Quorn (Quorndon) LE12 . . . . **75** E5
Thurmaston LE4 . . . . **129** F7
Beacon Cl
Groby LE6 . . . . **126** F2
Leicester LE4 . . . . **128** A6
Markfield LE67 . . . . **98** C1
Beacon Cres LE67 . . . . **97** B8
Beacon Dr LE15 . . . . **127** D1
Beacon Dr LE12 . . . . **74** D2
Beacon Hill Ctry Pk The*
LE12 . . . . **74** D2
Beacon Rd
Loughborough LE11 . . . . **52** A1
Woodhouse Eaves LE12 . . . . **74** D1
Beaconsfield Rd
Leicester LE3 . . . . **154** C4
Melton Mowbray LE13 . . . . . **59** A5
Beaconsfield St NG10 . . . . **10** E7
Beacon View
Bagworth LE67 . . . . **124** A7
Bottesford NG13 . . . . **3** B3
Beadmans Cnr LE67 . . . . . . **70** F1
Beadswell La LE8 . . . . **205** F8
Beaker Cl LE4 . . . . **128** A5
Beale's G LE7 . . . . **174** E2
Beal St LE2 . . . . **155** B6
Beamont Cl LE17 . . . . **244** C8
Beams Mdw LE10 . . . . **214** F6
Beardsley Rd LE12 . . . . **75** E6
Beards Rd DE11 . . . . **44** A6
Bearsdon Cres LE10 . . . . **197** B2
Beast Hill LE15 . . . . **189** B4
Beatrice Rd LE3 . . . . **154** C7
Beattie Cl LE10 . . . . **197** D3
Beatty Ave LE5 . . . . **155** E7
Beatty Rd
Leicester LE5 . . . . **155** E7
Syston LE7 . . . . **103** B5
Beauchamp Coll The
LE2 . . . . **181** B3
Beauchamp Gdns
LE8 . . . . **224** A7
Beauchamp Rd LE10 . . . . **223** F8
Beaufort Ave LE11 . . . . **75** A4
Beaufort Cl
Desford LE9 . . . . **151** B2
Hinckley LE10 . . . . **215** E4
Leicester, Oadby LE2 . . . . . . **181** D4
Beaufort Rd
Cottesmore LE15 . . . . **87** D2
Leicester LE3 . . . . **154** A1
Beaufort Way LE2 . . . . **181** D4
Beaumanor Dr LE12 . . . . . . **75** C4
Beaumanor Gdns LE12 . . . **75** C4
Beaumanor Rd LE4 . . . . . . **128** F3
Beaumaris Cres LE12 . . . . . **50** A2
Beaumaris Rd LE12 . . . . . . **101** C8
Beaumont Ave
Ashby-de-la-Z LE65 . . . . **68** F5
Hinckley LE10 . . . . **215** A7
Beaumont Gdns LE13 . . . . **59** C5
Beaumont Gn
Coleorton LE67 . . . . **70** E8
Groby LE6 . . . . **126** F2
Beaumont Hall LE2 . . . . . **180** F8
BEAUMONT LEYS **128** C3

Beaumont Leys Cl
LE4 . . . . 128 D3
Beaumont Leys La
LE4 . . . . 128 C4
Beaumont Leys Sch
LE4 . . . . 128 B2
Beaumont Leys Terr
LE4 . . . . 128 A3
Beaumont Lodge Prim Sch
LE4 . . . . 128 B6
Beaumont Lodge Rd
LE4 . . . . 128 B6
Beaumont Rd
Barrow-u-S LE12 . . . . . . 76 C8
Leicester LE5 . . . . 155 C6
Loughborough LE11 . . . . 75 B8
Whitwick LE67 . . . . 72 A4
Beaumont St LE2 . . . . . 181 A6
Beaumont Way LE4 . . . 128 B4
Beaumont Wlk LE4 . . . . 128 A3
Beauville Dr LE4 . . . . . . 128 A3
Beaver Cl LE8 . . . . 201 F5
Beaver Ctr The LE2 . . . . 154 F2
Beazer Ct LE1 . . . . 51 F6
Beck Cl LE2 . . . . 179 A3
Beckett Ave CV13 . . . . 148 E2
Beckett Rd LE5 . . . . 155 C3
Beckingham Rd LE2 . . . 155 C3
BECKINGTHORPE 3 A3
Beckmill Ct LE13 . . . . 59 D3
Beckmill La LE13 . . . . . . 59 D3
Beckworth Ct LE15 . . . . 141 A6
Beckworth Gr LE15 . . . . 141 A6
Bedale Ave LE10 . . . . . 197 F2
Bedale Cl LE67 . . . . 96 C8
Bedale Dr LE5 . . . . 128 C5
Bedale St LE15 . . . . 87 E2
Bede Ho* LE15 . . . . 212 D7
Bede Island Rd LE2 . . . 259 A2
Bede St LE3 . . . . 154 D5
Bedford Cl
Desford LE9 . . . . 151 B3
Hinckley LE10 . . . . 197 E3
Kegworth DE74 . . . . 18 D1
Bedford Rd LE18 . . . . . 180 A3
Bedford St N LE1 . . . . . 259 C5
Bedford St S LE1 . . . . . 259 B4
Bedford Sq LE11 . . . . 52 B3
Bedford St LE11 . . . . 52 B3
BEEBY 131 C5
Beeby Cl LE7 . . . . 103 C3
Beeby Rd
Barkby LE7 . . . . 130 E7
Leicester LE5 . . . . 155 D6
Scraptoft LE7 . . . . 131 A1
Beech Ave
Breaston DE72 . . . . 9 F8
East Leake LE12 . . . . 31 D8
Groby LE6 . . . . 126 E1
Lutterworth LE17 . . . . . 244 A6
Melbourne DE73 . . . . 26 B8
Ravenstone LE67 . . . . . . 95 E8
Beech Cl
Corby NN17 . . . . 230 E1
Markfield LE67 . . . . 125 E8
Shepshed LE12 . . . . 50 C4
Beechcroft Ave LE3 . . . 179 A8
Beechcroft Rd LE2 . . . . 155 C1
Beech Ct LE18 . . . . 180 C5
Beech Dr
Blackfordby DE11 . . . . . . 45 B2
Bottesford NG13 . . . . 3 C2
Braunstone Town LE3 . . 153 B3
Ryhall PE9 . . . . 116 E1
Syston LE7 . . . . 103 B2
Thornton LE67 . . . . 124 E4
Beeches Ave LE12 . . . . . 76 E2
Beeches Cl LE16 . . . . . . 248 E5
Beeches Farm LE8 . . . . 202 A4
Beeches Rd LE11 . . . . . . 52 C3
Beeches The
Earl Shilton LE9 . . . . . . 175 F1
Hartshill Green CV10 . . 194 B2
Leicester, Clarendon Park
LE2 . . . . 155 B2
Leicester, Humberstone
Garden LE5 . . . . 130 A1
Uppingham LE15 . . . . . 189 B5
Beechfield Ave LE4 . . . 129 A4
Beechfield Cl LE8 . . . . . 182 B1
Beech Gr PE9 . . . . 142 F4
Beechings Cl LE8 . . . . . 202 D3
Beech Rd
Blaby LE8 . . . . 202 B7
Leicester, Oadby LE2 . . 181 A5
Oakham LE15 . . . . 138 D7
Beech St LE5 . . . . 155 C7
Beech Tree Cl LE8 . . . . 206 A4
Beech Tree Rd LE67 . . . . 97 A8
Beech Way
Ashby-de-la-Z LE65 . . . . 69 D6
Desford LE9 . . . . 151 A3
Ibstock LE67 . . . . 95 E2
Beech Wlk LE67 . . . . . . 125 E8
Beechwood Ave
Hinckley LE10 . . . . 215 D3
Leicester Forest East
LE3 . . . . 153 A4
Melton Mowbray LE13 . . 59 E5
Quenniborough LE7 . . . 103 D5
Thurmaston LE4 . . . . . . 129 E6
Beechwood Cl LE16 . . . 156 C5
Beechwood Rd LE19 . . 201 B6
Beehive Ave DE12 . . . . . 68 A4
Beehive La LE11 . . . . 52 B3
Bee Hives The DE11 . . . . 44 A7

Beggar's La
Enderby LE19 . . . . 177 F7
Leicester Forest East
LE3 . . . . 152 E1
Beggars Roost LE8 . . . 205 B7
Begonia Cl
Hinckley LE10 . . . . 215 E5
Leicester Forest East
LE3 . . . . 152 F2
Begonia Dr LE10 . . . . . 215 E5
Belcher Cl LE8 . . . . 95 B2
BELCHER'S BAR 122 F6
Belcher's Hill LE16 . . . . 210 D6
Beler Way LE13 . . . . 81 F8
Belfield Gdns NG10 . . . . 10 E7
Belfield Rd DE11 . . . . . . 44 B5
Belfry Cl LE17 . . . . 215 D4
Belfry Dr LE3 . . . . 153 D5
BELGRAVE 129 A2
Belgrave Ave LE4 . . . . . 129 A3
Belgrave Bvd
Leicester LE4 . . . . 128 D5
Leicester LE4 . . . . 128 E4
Belgrave Circ LE1 . . . . 155 A8
Belgrave Cl LE67 . . . . . . 72 D1
Belgrave Ct ▣ LE5 . . . 130 C3
Belgrave Flyover LE1,
LE4 . . . . 155 A8
Belgrave Gate
Leicester LE1 . . . . 155 A7
Leicester LE1 . . . . 259 B5
Belgrave Hall (Mus)*
LE4 . . . . 129 A3
Belgrave Ind Ctr LE4 . . 129 A1
Belgrave Rd
Leicester LE4 . . . . 81 F8
Uppingham LE15 . . . . . 189 A5
Belgrave St Peter's CE
Prim Sch LE4 . . . . 128 F3
Bellamy Cl LE1 . . . . 179 A3
Bell Ave DE72 . . . . 16 A7
Bell Cl
Broughton Astley LE9 . . 219 A4
Ratby LE6 . . . . 152 D8
Stanton u B LE67 . . . . . . 97 F2
Bell Cotts PE9 . . . . 143 E3
Bell Ctr The LE13 . . . . . . 59 C3
Belleville Dr LE2 . . . . . 181 C6
Belle Vue Ave LE4 . . . . 128 E2
Belle Vue Rd LE9 . . . . . 198 C7
Bellfield LE15 . . . . 191 E8
Bellfields La LE16 . . . . . 241 A2
Bellfields St LE16 . . . . . 241 A2
Bellflower Rd LE5 . . . . . 130 B3
Bellholme Cl LE4 . . . . . 129 B3
Bell La
Burton Overy LE8 . . . . 205 E8
Husbands Bosworth
LE17 . . . . 247 E5
Leicester LE5 . . . . 155 B6
Narborough LE19 . . . . . 201 C7
Bells La LE9 . . . . 150 A4
Bell St
Claybrooke Magna
LE17 . . . . 232 E6
Lutterworth LE17 . . . . . 244 D5
Wigston LE18 . . . . 180 D3
Bell View LE19 . . . . 201 C8
BELMESTHORPE 117 A7
Belmesthorpe La PE9 . . 117 A2
Belmont Ave DE72 . . . . . 9 E8
Belmont Dr LE67 . . . . . . 71 A2
Belmont Prim Sch
DE11 . . . . 44 C4
Belmont St
Leicester LE2 . . . . 179 D7
Swadlincote DE11 . . . . . 44 C4
Belmont Way LE11 . . . . . 51 A2
Belper Cl
Leicester, Oadby LE2 . . 181 A3
Wigston LE18 . . . . 203 A8
Belper St LE4 . . . . 129 B1
BELTON 49 A6
Belton CE Prim Sch
LE12 . . . . 49 B6
Belton Cl
Coalville LE67 . . . . 72 C1
Leicester LE17 . . . . 179 F5
Belton Gdns ▥ PE9 . . . 143 E3
Belton Mews LE67 . . . . 187 D7
BELTON PARK 52 A6
Belton Rd
Leicester LE3 . . . . 154 A1
Loddington LE7 . . . . . . 161 F1
Loughborough LE11 . . . . 52 A5
Belton Rd W LE11 . . . . . 51 F6
Belton Rd W Extension
LE11 . . . . 51 F7
Belton St
Shepshed LE12 . . . . 50 B4
Stamford PE9 . . . . 143 D2
Belt The LE17 . . . . 246 D1
Belvedere Rd DE11 . . . . 44 F2
BELVOIR 14 E8
Belvoir Ave
Ab Kettleby LE14 . . . . . . 37 C2
Bottesford NG13 . . . . 3 A1
Belvoir Castle (restored)*
NG32 . . . . 14 D8
Belvoir Cl
Breaston DE72 . . . . 9 D7
Desford LE9 . . . . 151 B3
Leicester, Oadby LE2 . . 181 C4
Long Eaton NG10 . . . . . 10 E5
Mountsorrel LE12 . . . . . 101 D8

Belvoir Cl continued
Stamford PE9 . . . . 143 A4
Belvoir Cres DE11 . . . . . 44 A6
Belvoirdale Com Prim Sch
LE67 . . . . 96 D8
Belvoir Dr
Ashby-de-la-Z LE65 . . . . 69 B5
Leicester LE2 . . . . 179 D6
Loughborough LE11 . . . . 74 F7
Syston LE7 . . . . 103 C4
Belvoir Dr E LE2 . . . . . . 179 D6
Belvoir High Sch NG13 . . 3 A1
Belvoir La NG32 . . . . 8 B1
Belvoir Rd
Bottesford NG13 . . . . 7 B7
Coalville LE67 . . . . 96 C8
Eaton NG32 . . . . 13 E2
Redmile NG13 . . . . 7 A3
Woolsthorpe by B NG32 . 15 E7
Belvoir Sh Ctr The
LE67 . . . . 71 C1
Belvoir Sq LE15 . . . . 87 F3
Belvoir St
Leicester LE1 . . . . 259 B3
Melton Mowbray LE13 . . 59 E4
Belvoir Way LE12 . . . . . . 50 A2
Beman Cl LE1 . . . . 259 E5
Bembridge Cl LE4 . . . . 154 D8
Bembridge Rd LE4 . . . . 154 D8
Benbow Ave DE73 . . . . . 26 A8
Benbow Cl LE10 . . . . . . 197 D4
Benches Furlong
CV23 . . . . 252 D1
Bencroft Cl LE7 . . . . . . 127 D6
Bendbow Rise LE3 . . . . 153 E3
Bendbow Rise Inf Sch
LE3 . . . . 153 D3
Benenden Way LE65 . . . . 69 A7
Benford Cl LE12 . . . . . . 218 F4
Benjamin Russell Ct
LE2 . . . . 259 A2
Bennet Cl CV13 . . . . . . 196 D7
Bennett Dr LE13 . . . . 59 C6
Bennett Rise LE9 . . . . . 200 E8
Bennetts Hill LE17 . . . . 219 D2
Bennett's La LE17 . . . . 102 D8
Bennett St NG10 . . . . . . 10 D8
Bennett Way LE18 . . . . 180 A1
Bennett Wlk LE3 . . . . . 154 A4
Bennion Rd
Bushby LE7 . . . . 157 A4
Leicester LE4 . . . . 128 A5
Benscliffe Dr LE11 . . . . . 51 E2
Benscliffe Gdns LE7 . . 179 D3
Benscliffe Rd LE6 . . . . . . 99 D5
Benskin Cl LE14 . . . . . . 108 B8
Benskins Oval LE8 . . . . 128 C7
Benskin Wlk LE4 . . . . . 128 B2
Benskyn Cl LE8 . . . . . . 202 D4
Benson St LE5 . . . . 155 E5
Bentburn Ho LE3 . . . . . 154 A7
Bentinghouse Gdns
LE2 . . . . 179 D4
Bentinghouse Rd LE2 . . 179 D4
Bentley Cl LE11 . . . . 52 C4
Bentley Dale DE11 . . . . . 45 A3
Bentley Rd
Birstall LE4 . . . . 129 A8
Castle Donington DE74 . . 16 F4
Bentley St
Melton Mowbray LE13 . . 59 C3
Stamford PE9 . . . . 143 E4
Beresford Ct
Heather LE67 . . . . 95 C2
Shepshed LE12 . . . . 50 C4
Beresford Dr LE2 . . . . . 180 D8
Beresford Rd NG10 . . . . 10 A5
Berford Cl LE9 . . . . 218 F5
Berkeley Ave NG10 . . . . 10 C6
Berkeley Cl
Leicester, Oadby LE2 . . 181 D5
Mountsorrel LE12 . . . . . . 76 F1
Berkeley Ct PE9 . . . . . . 143 F4
Berkeley Rd LE11 . . . . . . 74 C8
Berkeley St LE16 . . . . . 248 F2
Berkley St LE1 . . . . 259 A5
Berkshire Rd LE2 . . . . . 179 D7
Bernard Cl LE1 . . . . 95 F1
Bernard Ct DE11 . . . . . . 44 D3
Bernard St DE11 . . . . . . 44 D3
Berners St LE2 . . . . 155 C5
Berridge Dr LE2 . . . . . . 181 A4
Berridge La LE14 . . . . . 129 B3
Berridges La LE17 . . . . 247 E5
Berridge St LE1 . . . . . . 259 B3
Berrington Cl
Botcheston LE9 . . . . . . 151 C6
Leicester LE5 . . . . 155 E8
Berrisford St LE67 . . . . . 96 D8
Berry Ave DE73 . . . . 27 A3
Berrybushes LE15 . . . . . 86 F5
Berrybut Way PE9 . . . . 143 F5
Berry Cl
Great Bowden LE16 . . . 241 A5
Ravenstone LE67 . . . . . . 71 A2
Berrycott La LE12 . . . . . 55 B3
Berry Field Rd LE16 . . . 229 C1
Berryhill La LE67 . . . . . . 96 B6
Berry Rd LE16 . . . . 229 C1
Berry's La LE6 . . . . 152 C8
Berrywell Dr LE9 . . . . . 198 A8
Bertie La PE9 . . . . 144 E4
Berts Coote Ho ▯
LE1 . . . . 51 F2
Bert's Way NG32 . . . . . . 24 B7
Berwick Rd LE65 . . . . . . 69 D5
Beryl Ave LE10 . . . . 197 A2
BESCABY 23 E1

Bescaby La LE14 . . . . . . 40 B7
Bessingham Cl LE5 . . . 130 C2
Best Cl LE18 . . . . 179 F1
Bestwood Cl LE3 . . . . . 128 B1
Beth-El Ho LE18 . . . . . 203 C8
Betty Henser's La LE12 . . 76 D4
Bevan Rd
Leicester LE4 . . . . 128 C7
Leicester LE4 . . . . 128 D8
Beveridge La
Bardon LE67 . . . . 97 C4
Ellistown LE67 . . . . 96 E3
Beveridge St LE12 . . . . . 76 D7
Beverley Ave LE4 . . . . . 129 B1
Beverley Cl LE67 . . . . . . 96 E3
Beverley Dr LE9 . . . . . . 218 E7
Beverley Gdns PE9 . . . 143 C4
Beverley Rd DE74 . . . . . 28 D8
Bevington Cl LE8 . . . . . 126 B1
Bewcastle Gr LE4 . . . . 128 D5
Bewicke Rd LE3 . . . . . . 154 E3
Bexhill Rise LE5 . . . . . . 156 E7
Biam Way LE3 . . . . 179 A8
Bickley Ave LE13 . . . . . . 59 D4
Biddle Rd
Leicester LE3 . . . . 154 B7
Littlethorpe LE19 . . . . . 201 C6
Biddulph Ave LE2 . . . . 155 C4
Biddulph St LE2 . . . . . . 155 C4
Bideford Cl LE18 . . . . . 203 D7
Bideford Rd LE5 . . . . . . 156 D3
Bidford Cl LE3 . . . . 153 E2
Bidford Ct LE3 . . . . 153 E2
Bidford Rd LE3 . . . . 153 E2
Bidwell La LE15 . . . . 89 D4
Biggin Hill Rd LE5 . . . . 156 B3
Biggin St LE11 . . . . 52 B4
Biggin The DE74 . . . . 17 B3
Bigg's Cl LE8 . . . . 202 A5
Big La
Barrow-u-S LE12 . . . . . . 54 D2
Seagrave LE12 . . . . 77 E8
Bignal Dr LE3 . . . . 153 B4
Bilberry Cl LE17 . . . . . . 179 A6
Billa Barra La LE67 . . . . 97 E3
Bill Crane Way LE17 . . 244 C8
BILLESDON 159 C2
Billesdon Cl LE3 . . . . . . 127 E3
Billesdon Parochial Prim
Sch LE7 . . . . 159 B1
Billesdon Rd LE7 . . . . . 183 D7
Billington Cl LE4 . . . . . 128 A3
Billington Rd E LE9 . . . 198 E4
Billington Rd W LE9 . . . 198 D5
Bilsdale Rd LE18 . . . . . 180 F1
BILSTONE 147 C7
Bilstone Rd
Congerstone CV13 . . . . 147 D3
Twycross CV9 . . . . 146 F8
Bilton Way LE17 . . . . . . 244 D8
Bindley La LE3 . . . . 182 B1
Bingley Rd LE19 . . . . . . 201 C6
Bintree Cl LE5 . . . . 130 B2
Birch Ave
Barrow-u-S LE12 . . . . . . 53 D1
Swadlincote DE11 . . . . . 44 A7
Birch Cl
Earl Shilton LE9 . . . . . . 198 D6
Leicester LE4 . . . . 129 D1
Loughborough LE11 . . . . 75 A6
Markfield LE67 . . . . 125 E6
Melton Mowbray LE13 . . 59 B5
Birch Cl LE2 . . . . 179 A3
Birches The ▤ LE9 . . . 198 A6
Birchfield Ave LE67 . . . 125 D8
Birch Rd PE9 . . . . 142 F5
Birch Tree Ave LE4 . . . 102 A1
Birch Tree Gdns LE16 . 240 F5
Birchtree Rd LE18 . . . . 180 D4
Birch View LE17 . . . . . . 235 E2
Birchwood Ave
Long Eaton, Breaston
NG10 . . . . 10 A7
Long Eaton, New Sawley
NG10 . . . . 10 C5
Birchwood Cl
Coleorton LE67 . . . . 70 D3
Leicester Forest East
LE3 . . . . 152 F2
Syston LE7 . . . . 103 C3
Bird Wood Sch LE13 . . . 59 E1
Bird Hill Rd LE12 . . . . . . 74 F1
Birdie Cl LE8 . . . . 224 B8
Birds La LE14 . . . . 13 A3
Birds Nest Ave LE4 . . . 154 A8
Birkby Cl LE5 . . . . 130 C3
Birkdale Ave LE2 . . . . . 155 D1
Birkdale Cl CV11 . . . . . 214 A1
Birkdale Cl LE5 . . . . . . 156 A2
Birkdale Rd LE7 . . . . . . 127 D6
Birkenshaw Rd LE3 . . . 128 A1
Birsmore Ave LE4 . . . . 129 D4
BIRSTALL 128 F8
Birstall Rd LE4 . . . . 129 B5
Birstall St LE1 . . . . 155 B4
Birstow Cres LE4 . . . . . 128 C3
Birtley Coppice LE16 . . 240 D4
BISBROOKE 189 F4
Bishop Cl LE10 . . . . 250 E8
Bishop Dale LE67 . . . . . . 71 D7
Bishopdale Cl NG10 . . . . 10 A6
Bishop Ellis RC Prim Sch
LE4 . . . . 129 F8
Bishop Meadow Rd
LE11 . . . . 51 E7
Bishops Cleeve CV9 . . . 119 A1

Bishops Ct DE73 . . . . . . 26 B7
Bishop's Ct DE73 . . . . . . 26 A7
Bishops Gate DE11 . . . . 44 E2
Bishop St
Leicester LE1 . . . . 259 B3
Loughborough LE11 . . . . 52 C5
Melton Mowbray LE13 . . 59 D3
Bishopston Wlk LE4 . . . 128 F4
Bisley St LE3 . . . . 154 D3
BITTESWELL 244 B8
Bitteswell Rd LE17 . . . 244 B7
BLABY 202 B8
Blaby By-Pass LE8 . . . . 202 A7
Blaby Ind Pk LE8 . . . . . 179 A1
Blaby Rd
Narborough LE19 . . . . . 178 D2
Wigston LE18 . . . . 180 A1
Blaby Stokes CE Prim Sch
LE8 . . . . 202 A7
Blackberry La
Cossington LE7 . . . . 77 F1
Ibstock LE67 . . . . 96 A4
Blackbird Ave LE4 . . . . 154 E8
Blackbird Rd LE4 . . . . . 154 D8
Blackbrook Cl LE12 . . . . 50 A3
Blackbrook Ct
Coalville LE67 . . . . 97 B8
Loughborough LE11 . . . . 51 E6
Blackbrook Dr LE67 . . . . 97 B8
Blackbrook Rd LE11 . . . 51 D3
Blackburn Rd LE9 . . . . 198 A6
Blackett Ave LE3 . . . . . 154 A8
Blackett Dr LE67 . . . . . . 95 B2
BLACKFORDBY 45 C1
Blackfordby La LE12 . . . 68 B6
Blackfordby St Margaret's
CE Prim Sch LE15 . . . . 45 C1
BLACK FRIARS 259 A4
Blackfriars St
Leicester LE3 . . . . 259 A4
10 Stamford PE9 . . . . . 143 E3
Blackham Rd LE11 . . . . . 52 A1
Blackmore Dr LE3 . . . . 154 A5
Blacksmith End LE14 . . . 13 A3
Blacksmith Pl ▮ LE15 . 130 C3
Blacksmiths Ave LE12 . . 50 C5
Blacksmiths Cl
Nether Broughton
LE14 . . . . 36 D8
Nethersale DE12 . . . . . . 91 F7
Thrussington LE7 . . . . . . 78 F4
Blacksmiths La
Smeeton Westerby
LE8 . . . . 223 F6
Sutton Cheney CV13 . . 174 B6
Blacksmith's La
Exton LE15 . . . . 113 B3
Woodville DE11 . . . . 44 F3
Blackspinney La LE7 . . 134 B4
Blackstone's Ct PE9 . . 143 F4
Blackthorn Dr
Lutterworth LE17 . . . . . 244 A6
Melbourne DE73 . . . . . . 26 A8
Blackthorn Dr
Leicester LE4 . . . . 128 A6
Syston LE7 . . . . 102 F3
Blackthorn La LE2 . . . . 181 B7
Black Thorn Rd LE3 . . . 153 B7
Blackthorn Way LE2 . . . 93 C6
Blackwell Cl LE18 . . . . 180 C1
Blackwell La DE73 . . . . . 26 B7
Blackwood LE67 . . . . . . 72 B1
Bladen Cl LE8 . . . . 202 D4
Blair Cl LE12 . . . . 101 C8
Blairmore Rd LE3 . . . . 153 C6
Blaise Gr LE4 . . . . 129 D1
Blake Cl LE10 . . . . 197 D4
Blake Dr LE11 . . . . 51 E5
Blakemore Rd DE73 . . . . 26 B8
Blakeney Cres LE13 . . . . 82 C8
Blakenhall Cl LE19 . . . 200 F8
Blakenhall Rd LE5 . . . . 156 A5
Blakeshay Cl LE3 . . . . . 127 F2
Blakesley Rd LE18 . . . . 180 E3
Blakesley Wlk LE4 . . . . 128 B2
Blake St LE1 . . . . 259 B4
Blanch Croft DE73 . . . . . 26 B7
Blandford Ave NG10 . . . 10 B6
Bland Rd LE3 . . . . 127 F1
Blankley Dr LE2 . . . . . . 155 D1
Blanklyn Ave LE5 . . . . . 155 D5
Blankney Rd LE5 . . . . . . 87 E2
Blashfield Cl PE9 . . . . . 143 D4
BLASTON 210 B4
Blaston Hill LE16 . . . . . 210 C4
Blaston Rd LE16 . . . . . . 209 C2
Blaydon Cl LE3 . . . . . . 154 B8
Bleach Mill La LE3 . . . . 93 C3
Bleakmoor Cl LE7 . . . . . 79 A3
Bleasby Cl LE4 . . . . 130 A4
Blenheim Cl
Hinckley LE10 . . . . 197 F4
Loughborough LE11 . . . . 51 C4
3 Swadlincote DE11 . . . . 44 A7
Wigston LE18 . . . . 202 F8
Blenheim Cres LE9 . . . 218 D7
Blenheim Rd LE4 . . . . . 129 B8
Blenheim Way
Leicester LE4 . . . . 128 E4

Blenheim Way continued
Market Harborough
LE16 . . . . .240 E5
Blenheim Wlk LE13 . . . . . . .59 B5
Bley Ave LE12 . . . . .31 D8
Blickling Wlk LE5 . . . . . .155 E8
Blind La
Breaston DE72 . . . . .9 D8
Cottingham LE16 . . . . . . .229 D1
Blissett Rd LE3 . . . . .154 B7
Blithfield Ave LE11 . . . . . .51 C3
Blockley's Yd 4 LE10 . . .215 D8
Bloom CE LE67 . . . . .71 A2
Bloomfield Rd LE2 . . . . . .179 F7
Blossom Rd LE3 . . . . . . .154 A4
Blossoms The LE67 . . . . .125 E6
Blount Rd LE4 . . . . .129 F6
Bloxams Cl LE3 . . . . .178 F6
Bloxham Rd LE3 . . . . . . .154 B7
Bloxsom Cl LE67 . . . . . . .124 A7
Blue Banks Ave LE2 . . . . .179 A3
Bluebell Cl
Donisthorpe DE12 . . . . .67 E1
Kirby Muxloe LE9 . . . . . . .152 E6
Leicester, Oadby LE2 . . . . .181 E4
Queniborough LE7 . . . . . . .103 E6
Bluebell Dr
Groby LE6 . . . . .127 A3
Leicester LE2 . . . . .179 F4
Loughborough LE11 . . . . . . .51 F1
Bluebell La LE16 . . . . . . .208 B4
Bluebell Rd PE9 . . . . .142 F5
Bluebell Row LE13 . . . . . . .82 A8
Blueberry Way DE11 . . . . . .44 F3
Bluecoat La LE15 . . . . . . .212 D7
Bluecoat Sch The
PE9 . . . . .143 D4
Blue Gates Rd LE4 . . . . . .128 A5
Blue Pots Cl LE3 . . . . . . .152 F2
Blue Pots La NG32 . . . . . . .22 F7
Blue Town NG33 . . . . .43 B8
Blundell Rd LE5 . . . . .156 A3
Blunt's La LE18 . . . . .180 D2
Blyth Ave LE13 . . . . .59 B2
Blyth Ct DE74 . . . . .17 B4
Boathouse The LE16 . . . . .240 D4
Bob Trewick Ho LE1 . . . . .259 C2
Bodenham Cl LE18 . . . . . .203 C8
Bodicoat Cl LE18 . . . . . . .201 F5
Bodkin Row DE12 . . . . .93 B6
Bodkin Wlk LE4 . . . . .128 B3
Bodmin Ave LE18 . . . . . . .180 D1
Bodmin Cl LE10 . . . . .197 E4
Bodnant Ave LE5 . . . . . . .155 E3
Bodycote Cl LE9 . . . . .218 F5
Bofols Rd LE4 . . . . .36 A5
Boilerhouse Rd LE14 . . . . .36 A4
Bollard's La LE12 . . . . .30 A7
Bollington Rd LE2 . . . . . .181 C6
Bolsover St LE5 . . . . .155 E6
Bolton La LE14 . . . . .20 F7
Bolton Rd LE3 . . . . .154 C5
Bolus Rd LE3 . . . . .153 C2
Bombard Rd LE14 . . . . . . .36 A5
Bonchurch Cl LE67 . . . . . . .71 F5
Bonchurch Rd LE67 . . . . . .71 F5
Bonchurch St LE3 . . . . . .154 D7
Boncroft Gdns DE12 . . . . . .93 A7
Bond Cl LE11 . . . . .52 C1
Bondgate DE74 . . . . .17 B3
Bond La LE12 . . . . .76 C2
Bondman Cl LE4 . . . . .128 E5
Boneham's La LE17 . . . . . .234 E3
Bonner Cl LE2 . . . . .181 D4
Bonner Ho LE15 . . . . .189 A4
Bonners La LE2 . . . . .259 B2
Bonney Rd LE3 . . . . .154 A8
Bonnington Cl CV21 . . . . .257 B1
Bonnington Rd LE2 . . . . . .155 B1
Bonsall Ct NG10 . . . . .10 F8
Bonsall St
Leicester LE5 . . . . .155 C4
Long Eaton NG10 . . . . .10 E8
Bonville Pl LE3 . . . . .154 B1
Booth Cl LE5 . . . . .156 B5
Booth End LE11 . . . . .51 B6
BOOTHORPE 67 A8
Boothorpe La DE11 . . . . . . .68 A8
Booth Rd LE67 . . . . .71 D8
Booth Wood Prim Sch
LE11 . . . . .51 C3
Bordeaux Cl LE18 . . . . . . .178 A3
Border Dr LE4 . . . . .128 C5
Borlace St LE3 . . . . .154 D6
Borough St
Castle Donington DE74 . . . . .17 B4
Kegworth DE74 . . . . .18 D2
Borough The LE10 . . . . . . .215 D8
Borrowcup Cl LE8 . . . . . . .202 C4
Borrowdale Cl LE9 . . . . . .198 F7
Borrowdale Dr NG10 . . . . .10 A6
Borrowdale Way
Leicester LE5 . . . . .156 D5
Loughborough LE11 . . . . . . .51 D1
Borrowell DE74 . . . . .71 D8
Bostock Cl LE9 . . . . .199 A4
Boston Rd LE4 . . . . .128 A4
Boston Way LE9 . . . . .198 A6
Boswell St LE19 . . . . .178 A1
Bosworth Battlefield Ctry
Pk* CV13 . . . . .173 F5
Bosworth Battlefield
Visitor Ctr* CV13 . . . . .173 E5
Bosworth Cl
Ashby-de-la-Z LE65 . . . . . . .69 D7

Bosworth Cl continued
Hinckley LE10 . . . . .197 A1
Bosworth Com Coll
LE9 . . . . .151 C3
Bosworth Field*
CV13 . . . . .173 E5
Bosworth Gn LE9 . . . . . . .176 B1
Bosworth Ho 3 LE10 . . . .197 E1
Bosworth La CV13 . . . . . .149 E4
Bosworth Rd
Barlestone CV13 . . . . .149 C7
Carlton CV13 . . . . .148 E7
Castle Donington DE74 . . . . .16 F3
Congerstone CV13. . . . . . .147 E6
Kirkby Mallory LE9 . . . . . .175 B7
Measham DE12 . . . . .93 D4
Sutton Cheney CV13 . . . . .174 A6
Theddingworth LE17 . . . . .248 C7
Walton LE17 . . . . .236 D1
Bosworth St LE13 . . . . . .154 D6
Bosworth Water Trust*
CV13 . . . . .148 A2
Bosworth Way NG10 . . . . .10 E5
BOTCHESTON 151 B6
Botcheston Rd LE9 . . . . . .151 D6
Bothe Cl NG10 . . . . .10 C6
Botley Wlk LE5 . . . . .156 A6
BOTTESFORD 3 C3
Bottesford CE Prim Sch
NG13 . . . . .3 A2
Bottesford La NG13 . . . . . . .2 C5
Bottesford Rd NG32 . . . . . . .4 D4
Botteshale La LE14 . . . . . .52 B6
Bottom Gn LE14 . . . . .19 A1
Bottom La LE15 . . . . .189 F4
Bottom Rd LE67 . . . . .48 A1
Bottom St
Allington NG32 . . . . .4 F5
Wing LE15 . . . . .165 A3
Bott's La DE12 . . . . .119 F7
Botts Way LE67 . . . . .97 A8
Boulder La LE12 . . . . .179 F6
Boulter Cres LE18 . . . . . .180 D3
Boulton Cl LE2 . . . . .218 F4
Boulton St LE2 . . . . .181 E4
BOUNDARY 45 C2
Boundary Rd
Leicester LE2 . . . . .154 E1
Lutterworth LE17 . . . . . . .244 D6
Mountsorrel LE12 . . . . .76 E1
Boundary Way LE12 . . . . . .50 C5
Bourne Cl CV9 . . . . .170 E2
Bourne Ct DE73 . . . . .26 A7
Bourne Mall LE4 . . . . . . .128 A4
Bourne Rd PE9 . . . . .117 B6
Bourne Sq DE72 . . . . .9 E7
Bourne Way DE11 . . . . . . .44 D4
Bourton Cres LE2 . . . . . . .181 C5
Bouverie Ct LE15 . . . . .84 F1
Bowbridge Gdns NG13 . . . .3 A3
Bowbridge La NG13 . . . . . . .2 F3
Bowden La
Market Harborough
LE16 . . . . .240 E4
Welham LE16 . . . . .226 E4
Bowden Rd LE16 . . . . .226 A4
Bowden Ridge LE16 . . . . .241 A5
Bowder Ho LE3 . . . . .153 F2
Bowens Ct DE11 . . . . .44 F3
Bowhill Gr LE5 . . . . .156 E7
Bowhill Way LE5 . . . . . . .156 E7
Bowker Cres LE65 . . . . . . .68 F5
Bowler Ct LE11 . . . . .52 C4
Bowley Ave LE13 . . . . .59 E5
Bowley Ct LE3 . . . . .59 C3
Bowleys La DE12 . . . . . . .119 E8
Bowley The DE74 . . . . .28 B5
Bowling Gn LE13 . . . . .59 A1
Bowling Green Cl
Oakham LE15 . . . . .138 A5
Sileby LE12 . . . . .77 D4
Bowling Green La LE15 . . .86 F5
Bowling Green Rd
LE1 . . . . .197 E1
Bowling Green St
LE1 . . . . .259 B3
Bowman Gn LE10 . . . . . . .215 F6
Bowmans Way
Glenfield LE3 . . . . .153 B8
Sedgebrook NG32 . . . . .8 F8
Bowmars La LE3 . . . . .259 A5
Box Cl DE11 . . . . .44 E3
Boyer's Orch LE14 . . . . . .12 B3
Boyer St LE11 . . . . .52 C4
Boyers Wlk LE3 . . . . .152 F3
Boynton Rd LE3 . . . . .154 A4
Boyslade Rd LE10 . . . . . . .215 F6
Boyslade Road E
LE10 . . . . .215 F5
Brabazon Rd LE2 . . . . . . .180 F5
Bracadale Wlk NN17 . . . .230 C1
Bracken Cl
Coalville LE67 . . . . .96 C6
Leicester Forest East
LE3 . . . . .152 F2
Leicester LE5 . . . . .156 B4
Bracken Dale LE7 . . . . . . .157 F6
Brackenfield Way
LE4 . . . . .130 A8
Bracken Hill LE6 . . . . .126 B6
Brackenthwaite LE4 . . . . .129 D3
Bracken Way LE67 . . . . . . .98 E1
Bracken Wlk LE67 . . . . . .125 E8
Brackley Cl LE4 . . . . .129 D3
Bradbourne Rd LE5 . . . . . .155 D5
Bradbury Cl LE9 . . . . .201 D2
Braddon Rd LE11 . . . . .51 C6

Bradford Cl LE5 . . . . .155 E5
Bradford's La LE67 . . . . . . .70 E7
Bradgate Ave LE4. . . . . . .129 F7
Bradgate Cl
Leicester LE7. . . . . .156 E5
North End LE12 . . . . .76 D4
Ratby LE6. . . . . .77 C3
Bradgate Ctry Pk* LE7,
LE6. . . . . .100 A2
Bradgate Dr
Coalville LE67 . . . . .97 C8
Ratby LE6. . . . . .126 C1
Wigston LE18. . . . . .180 B5
Bradgate Flats LE14 . . . . .57 F3
Bradgate Hill LE6 . . . . . . .126 B4
Bradgate Ho LE10 . . . . . . .215 D7
Bradgate La LE14 . . . . .57 F3
Bradgate Mall LE4. . . . . . .128 B4
Bradgate Rd
Barwell LE9 . . . . .198 B8
Cropston LE7 . . . . .100 E4
Hinckley LE10 . . . . .197 F2
Loughborough LE11. . . . . . .74 E8
Markfield LE67 . . . . .98 B1
Newtown Linford LE6 . . . . .127 B7
Bradgate St LE4 . . . . .154 D8
Brading Rd LE3. . . . . .154 C8
Bradley La LE15 . . . . .89 D5
Bradshaw Ave LE2 . . . . . .179 C3
Bradshaw St LE2 . . . . . . .179 C3
Bradshaw St NG10 . . . . . . .10 B5
Bradstone Cl LE2 . . . . . . .219 B5
Bradston Rd LE2 . . . . .179 E5
Braemar Cl
Leicester LE4 . . . . .129 C4
Mountsorrel LE12 . . . . . . .101 D8
Stamford PE9. . . . . .143 A4
Braemar Dr LE4 . . . . .129 D4
Braeside LE15 . . . . .111 B8
Braids Ct LE2 . . . . .180 E8
Brailsford Rd LE18 . . . . . .180 A3
Braithewaite Cl PE9 . . . . .167 F5
Bramall Ct LE5 . . . . .155 E8
Bramall Rd LE5 . . . . .155 E7
Bramber Cl LE4 . . . . .129 E5
Bramble Cl
Hamilton LE5 . . . . .130 D2
Leicester LE3 . . . . .153 D7
Loughborough LE11. . . . . . .51 E5
Uppingham LE15 . . . . .189 B5
Bramble Dr LE9 . . . . .150 B4
Bramble Gr PE9. . . . . .142 F4
Brambles Rd LE67 . . . . . . .96 C6
Bramble Way LE3. . . . . . .179 A8
Brambling Cl CV23. . . . . . .252 C1
Brambling Rd LE4 . . . . . .128 D5
Brambling Way LE2. . . . . .181 A4
Bramcote Cl LE10. . . . . . .197 F3
Bramcote Rd
Leicester LE3. . . . . .179 B8
Loughborough LE11. . . . . . .74 F7
Wigston LE18. . . . . .180 C4
Bramham Ave LE9 . . . . . .179 D5
Bramham Ct LE3. . . . . . . .128 B1
Bramley Cl
Broughton Astley LE9 . . . .218 E7
Market Harborough
LE16 . . . . .240 F5
Moira DE12 . . . . .68 A4
Sileby LE12. . . . . .77 D4
Wymeswold LE12 . . . . .33 D3
Bramley Ct LE3 . . . . .153 B8
Bramley Orch LE7 . . . . . . .157 A5
Bramley Rd
Birstall LE4 . . . . .129 B7
Hinckley LE10 . . . . .215 F6
Leicester, Oadby LE2 . . . . .181 B4
Long Eaton NG10 . . . . .10 C5
Brampton Ave LE3 . . . . . .154 B6
Brampton Rd LE13. . . . . . .59 A6
Brampton Way LE2 . . . . . .180 F6
Brancaster Cl LE4 . . . . . .128 D2
Brand Hill LE12 . . . . .100 A8
Brand La LE12. . . . . .75 B1
Brandon Rd LE67 . . . . . . .128 B1
Brandon St LE4. . . . . .155 B8
Bransdale Cl NG10. . . . . . .10 B6
Bransdale Rd LE18. . . . . . .180 F2
BRANSTON 23 C7
Branston Ave LE12 . . . . . . .76 E8
Branston Cres LE13 . . . . . .59 E2
Branston Ho LE18 . . . . . . .180 B3
Branston La NG32 . . . . . . .23 D4
Branting Hill LE6. . . . . . . .126 B3
Branting Hill Ave LE6 . . . .126 B3
Branting Hill Gr LE3 . . . . .127 B3
BRASCOTE. 150 A2
Brascote La
Cadeby CV13 . . . . .149 E2
Newbold Verdon LE9 . . . . .150 A2
Brascote Rd LE10 . . . . . . .214 F8
Bratmyr LE8 . . . . .202 F6
Braunstone Ave LE3 . . . . .154 B3
Braunstone Cl LE3 . . . . . .154 B3
BRAUNSTONE FRITH 153 E5
Braunstone Frith Ind Est
LE3 . . . . .153 B6
Braunstone Frith Inf Sch
LE3 . . . . .153 D6
Braunstone Frith Jun Sch
LE3 . . . . .153 D6
Braunstone Gate LE3 . . . .154 D5
Braunstone La
Braunstone Town
LE3 . . . . .153 D3
Leicester LE3. . . . . .154 A1

Braunstone Lane E LE2,
LE3 . . . . .179 B8
BRAUNSTONE TOWN 178 E8
Braunstone Way LE3. . . . .153 E4
BRAUNSTONE-IN-RUTLAND
. . . . .137 B2
Braunston Rd
Knossington LE15 . . . . . . .136 B5
Oakham LE15. . . . . .137 D5
BRAYBROOKE 251 F5
Braybrooke Prim Sch
LE16 . . . . .251 E6
Braybrooke Rd
Great Oxendon LE16 . . . . . .251 A3
Leicester LE4 . . . . .129 E1
Market Harborough
LE16 . . . . .241 B1
Braymish Cl LE8. . . . . . . .224 B8
Brazenose La PE9 . . . . . . .143 E3
Brazil St LE2 . . . . .154 E3
Breachfield Rd LE12 . . . . .76 E7
Breach La LE9 . . . . .198 F6
Breachprint Rd LE67 . . . . .96 D7
Breadcroft La LE12 . . . . . .76 D8
Breadsall Cl DE11 . . . . . . .44 A7
Breakback Rd LE12 . . . . . .74 E3
BREASTON 9 D7
Breaston Ind Est DE72 . . . .9 C7
Brechin Cl LE10 . . . . .215 A8
Brecknock Dr NG10 . . . . . .10 A7
Brecon Cl
Long Eaton NG10 . . . . .10 A8
Wigston LE18. . . . . .179 F2
Bredon Cl 5 NG10 . . . . . . .10 A8
Breech Hedge LE7 . . . . . . .101 E2
Breedon Ave LE18 . . . . . .180 C3
Breedon La
Osgathorpe LE12 . . . . .48 C5
Worthington LE65 . . . . .47 F6
BREEDON ON THE HILL 26 E2
Breedon on the Hill St
Hardulph's CE Prim Sch
DE73 . . . . .26 F2
Breedon St LE2. . . . . .155 C5
Brendon Cl LE12. . . . . .50 C1
Brendon Way LE65. . . . . . .69 B5
Brenfield Dr LE10 . . . . . . .215 A8
Brentland Dr LE4 . . . . . . .178 F7
BRENTINGBY 60 C2
Brentingby Cl LE13 . . . . . .59 E1
Brent Knowle Gdns
LE5. . . . . .156 D5
Brentnall Cl NG10. . . . . . . .10 B5
Brentwood Rd LE2 . . . . . .155 A1
Bretby Bsns Pk DE15. . . . . .44 A8
Bretby Hts DE11 . . . . .44 A8
Bretby Rd LE2 . . . . .179 E6
Bretby View DE11 . . . . . . .45 A4
Breton Cl LE18 . . . . .204 A3
Brettell Rd LE2 . . . . .179 D4
Bretton Cl LE4 . . . . .128 E3
Bretton Wlk 5 LE4. . . . . .128 E3
Breward Way LE13. . . . . . .59 D6
Brewer Cl LE4. . . . . .129 E5
Brewery Row LE12. . . . . . .14 E8
Brex Rise LE3 . . . . .153 D6
Breydon Ind Ctr NG10. . . . .10 F7
Brian Rd LE4 . . . . .128 D1
Brians Cl LE7 . . . . .103 C4
Brianway The LE5. . . . . . .155 F7
Briar Cl
Blackfordby DE11 . . . . .68 B8
Coalville LE67 . . . . .96 C7
Hinckley LE10 . . . . .215 F6
Leicester, Oadby LE2 . . . . .181 B4
Briarfield Dr LE15 . . . . . . .130 E1
Briar Gate NG10 . . . . .10 C8
Briargate Dr LE4 . . . . . . .128 E8
Briarmead LE10 . . . . .215 E4
Briar Meads LE2 . . . . .181 B3
Briar Rd LE5 . . . . .156 D2
Briar Wlk LE2. . . . . .181 B4
Brick Kiln Croft DE12 . . . . .93 D5
Brick Kiln La
Ibstock LE67 . . . . .122 F8
Shepshed LE12 . . . . .50 A1
Brick Kiln St LE10 . . . . . . .215 D8
Brickman Cl LE3. . . . . .152 F2
Brickwood Pl LE12 . . . . . . .53 F7
Brickyard Cotts DE12 . . . . .93 D5
Brickyard La
East Leake LE12 . . . . .31 A8
Wymondham LE14 . . . . .62 D3
Bridegate La LE14 . . . . . . .19 B6
Bridevale Rd LE2. . . . . . . .179 D4
Bridge Bsns Pk LE4. . . . . .129 D7
Bridge Cl
Swadlincote DE11 . . . . .44 C2
Thurmaston LE4 . . . . .129 E7
Bridge Fields DE72 . . . . . . .9 C7
Bridge Fields LE8 . . . . . . .18 E3
Bridge Ho LE11 . . . . .52 B4
Bridge Jun Sch LE15 . . . . .155 C7
Bridge La
Greetham LE15 . . . . .88 B1
Witherley CV9 . . . . .194 B7
Bridgeland Rd LE12 . . . . . .52 C5
Bridgemere Cl LE2 . . . . . .179 D4
Bridge Mews LE67 . . . . . . .71 D3
Bridge Park Rd LE4 . . . . . .129 D7
Bridge Rd
Coalville LE67 . . . . .96 D8
Hinckley LE10 . . . . .197 D1
Leicester LE5 . . . . .155 D7
Bridgeside Cotts LE11 . . . .52 A5

Bridge St
Barrow-u-S LE12 . . . . .76 C7
Langham LE15 . . . . .110 C3
Long Eaton NG10 . . . . .10 D8
Loughborough LE11. . . . . . .52 A4
Packington LE65 . . . . .69 C1
Ryhall PE9 . . . . .116 F2
Swadlincote DE11 . . . . .50 B4
Swadlincote DE11 . . . . .44 C2
Bridgewater Dr LE8 . . . . .182 B1
Bridge Way LE8 . . . . .201 F7
Bridle Cl
Croft LE9 . . . . .200 C3
Melton Mowbray LE13. . . . . .59 A5
Bridle Path Rd LE9 . . . . . .198 D5
Bridle Rd LE67 . . . . .71 D3
Bridlespur Way LE4 . . . . .128 E5
Bridle The LE2 . . . . .179 B4
Bridport Cl LE18 . . . . .180 D1
Brierfield Rd LE9 . . . . .201 D2
Briers Cl LE19 . . . . .201 B7
Briers Way LE67. . . . . .71 E5
Briggins Wlk LE15 . . . . . . .110 C3
Brightman Ho DE11. . . . . . .44 B5
Brighton Ave
Syston LE7 . . . . .103 C4
Wigston LE18. . . . . .180 D5
Brighton Cl LE18 . . . . .180 C5
Brighton Rd LE5 . . . . .155 E8
Brightside Ave LE13 . . . . . .59 A4
Brightside Rd LE5 . . . . . . .155 E4
Brightwell Dr LE3 . . . . . . .153 B4
Brindle Path LE19 . . . . . . .198 D4
Brindley Cl
Coalville LE67 . . . . .71 A2
Hinckley LE10 . . . . .214 E8
Rugby CV21 . . . . .257 B1
Brindley Rise LE3 . . . . . . .130 E1
Brindle Path LE19 . . . . . . .199 D2
Brindley Rd
Atherstone CV9 . . . . .170 C1
Stoney Stanton LE9 . . . . . .199 D2
Brindley Rd
Coalville LE67 . . . . .71 A2
Hinckley LE10 . . . . .214 E8
Brindley Rise LE3 . . . . . . .130 E1
BRINGHURST 229 C5
Bringhurst Gn LE3 . . . . . . .153 E7
Bringhurst Prim Sch
LE16 . . . . .229 C6
Bringhurst Rd LE3 . . . . . . .153 D7
Brington Cl LE18 . . . . .180 E2
Brinks The LE18 . . . . .76 B5
Brinsmead Rd LE2 . . . . . . .180 B7
Brisco Ave LE11 . . . . .51 F6
Briscoe La LE12 . . . . .75 B4
Bristol Ave
Ashby-de-la-Z LE65 . . . . . . .69 A4
Leicester LE4 . . . . .128 D1
Britannia Rd LE10 . . . . . . .216 A5
Britannia St
Leicester LE1 . . . . .155 A4
Shepshed LE12 . . . . .50 B4
Britannia Way LE4 . . . . . .102 E1
Britannia Wlk LE16 . . . . . .240 F2
Britford Ave LE18 . . . . . . .203 C8
British Pony Ctr*
LE7. . . . . .160 C8
British School Gdns
LE13 . . . . .59 C3
Briton Lodge Cl LE67 . . . . .67 F4
Briton St LE3 . . . . .154 D4
Brittania Sh Ctr 3
LE10 . . . . .215 D8
Brittany Ave LE65 . . . . . . .69 A7
Brixham Dr LE2, LE18 . . . . .180 A5
Brixworth Rise LE5 . . . . . .156 E6
Broad Ave LE5 . . . . .155 F5
Broadbent Cl LE18 . . . . . .201 F7
Broadfield Way LE8 . . . . .202 C4
Broadford Cl LE4 . . . . .129 D4
Broadgate LE16 . . . . .220 D7
Broadgate Cl LE16 . . . . . .129 A8
Broadgate Rd NG33 . . . . . . .65 C3
Broadhill Rd DE74 . . . . . . .18 C2
Broadhurst St LE4 . . . . . . .129 B2
Broad La LE67 . . . . .125 A7
Broad Mdw LE18. . . . . . . .180 E1
Broadmead Rd LE8. . . . . . .202 A6
Broad Rushes DE74 . . . . . . .17 B6
Broad St
Coalville LE67 . . . . .96 D8
Enderby LE19. . . . . .178 B3
Long Eaton NG10 . . . . .10 D7
Loughborough LE11. . . . . . .52 A4
Stamford PE9. . . . . .143 E3
Syston LE7. . . . . .103 A3
Broadsword Way
LE10 . . . . .215 D4
Broadway
Loughborough LE11. . . . . . .75 B8
Syston LE7. . . . . .103 A3
Broadway Furlong
LE7. . . . . .127 C7
Broadway Rd LE5 . . . . . . .155 D2
Broadway Terr LE16. . . . . .240 F4
Broadway The
Leicester LE2 . . . . .156 A1
Market Harborough
LE16 . . . . .240 F4
Brockenhurst Dr LE18 . . . .178 E8
Brockey Cl LE19 . . . . .198 B7
Brockhurst Ave LE10 . . . . .215 D4
Brockhurst Cl LE23 . . . . . .242 A6
Brockington Coll
LE19 . . . . .178 C2
Brocklehurst Rd LE15. . . . .110 B3
Brocklehurst Rd LE15 . . . . .59 E5
Brocklesby Way LE5 . . . . .156 E6
Brocks Hill Cl LE2 . . . . . . .181 B4
Brocks Hill Country Pk &
Visitor Ctr* LE2 . . . . . .180 F4

Brocks Hill Dr LE2 181 B5
Brocks Hill Prim Sch
LE2 181 B3
Broctone Cl LE9 219 B5
Broctone Dr LE9 218 E7
Brodick Cl LE10 215 A8
Brodick Rd LE10 214 F8
Bromhead St LE11 52 C5
Bromley La LE12 49 B7
Brompton Rd LE5 130 C3
Bromwich Cl LE3 153 C2
Bromwich Rd 1
CV21 257 A1
Bronte Cl
Leicester LE3 154 A4
Long Eaton NG10 10 A7
Bronze Barrow Cl
LE18 180 F1
Brook Bank LE5 155 F7
Brook Cl
Long Eaton NG10 10 E5
Packington LE65 69 B1
Uppingham LE15 189 C3
Brook Cres LE14 58 B3
Brook Ct LE8 202 F4
Brookdale LE10 215 B7
Brookdale Rd
Hartshorne DE11 45 A4
Leicester LE3 153 D5
Brook Dene LE15 111 B8
Brook Dr LE6 152 C8
BROOKE 163 D8
Brooke Ave PE9 143 A2
Brooke Cl LE15 138 B7
Brooke Hill Prim Sch
LE15 137 E4
Brooke House Coll
LE16 240 E4
Brooke Priory Sch
LE15 137 F7
Brooke Rd
Braunston-in-R LE15 137 B2
Oakham LE15 137 F4
Ridlington LE15 163 D4
Brookes Ave LE9 200 C3
Brookes Gr NN17 230 E1
Brook Farm Ct
Hoton LE12 32 D2
Willoughby-on-t-W LE12 34 C7
Brookfield LE10 217 C5
Brookfield Ave
Loughborough LE11 51 E1
Syston LE7 103 B3
Brookfield Cotts DE12 92 C7
Brookfield Ct LE13 59 B5
Brookfield Rd
Hinckley LE10 215 C6
Market Harborough
LE16 240 C3
Brookfield Rise LE2 179 F6
Brookfield St
Melton Mowbray LE13 59 B5
Syston LE7 103 B3
Brookfield Way
Kibworth Beauchamp
LE8 224 B8
Lutterworth LE17 244 A6
Brook Gdns LE2 179 B3
Brookhouse Ave 2
LE2 155 B4
Brook House Cl LE7 79 A1
Brook House Mews
DE11 44 A7
Brookhouse St 1
LE2 155 B4
Brook La
Asfordby LE14 57 F2
Barrow-u-S LE12 76 E8
Billesdon LE7 159 C2
Great Easton LE16 229 D6
Loughborough LE11 74 D8
Melton Mowbray LE13 59 D2
Peckleton LE9 175 F7
Thringstone LE67 71 D7
Brookland Rd LE2 155 A1
Brooklands LE15 164 C1
Brooklands Cl
Broughton Astley LE9 218 F6
Whetstone LE8 201 F7
Brooklands Gdns
LE16 240 E2
Brooklands Prim Sch
NG10 10 D6
Brooklands Rd LE9 201 D4
Brookland Way LE12 101 E8
Brook Rd
Leicester LE5 156 D7
Woodhouse Eaves LE12 74 E4
BROOKSBY 79 E5
Brooksby Ag Coll LE14 79 E5
Brooksby Cl LE2 181 A6
Brooksby Dr LE2 181 A6
Brooksby Melton Coll
(King Street Annexe)
LE13 59 C3
Brooksby Melton Coll
(Melton Campus)
LE13 59 B3
Brooksby Rd LE14 79 D6
Brooksby St LE2 154 E1
Brooks Cl DE12 67 F1
Brookside
Barkby LE7 130 E8
Barlestone CV13 149 D7
Diseworth DE74 28 C5
East Leake LE12 31 E8
Hinckley LE10 215 E7
Leicester LE5 155 D3
Brookside continued
Rearsby LE7 79 A2
Syston LE7 103 B4
Whetstone LE8 201 F6
Brook Side
12 Ashby-de-la-Z LE65 69 B6
3 Loughborough LE11 52 A4
Brookside Ave LE12 31 E8
Brookside Cl
Barrow-u-S LE12 53 D1
Long Eaton NG10 10 B8
Shepshed LE12 50 C2
Brookside Cres LE67 95 F1
Brookside Dr LE2 181 C5
Brookside Ho LE67 96 A2
Brookside Ind Est LE67 96 A2
Brookside Pl CV9 171 B8
Brookside Prim Sch
LE2 181 D7
Brookside Rd LE11 74 D8
Brooks La LE67 71 D5
Brook St
Ashby-de-la-Z LE65 69 B6
Burton o t W LE12 53 F7
Enderby LE19 178 B3
Hartshorne DE11 45 A7
Huncote LE9 200 D7
Melton Mowbray LE13 59 D3
Rearsby LE7 79 A1
Shepshed LE12 50 C5
Sileby LE12 77 C3
Swadlincote DE11 44 A3
Syston LE7 103 A4
Thurmaston LE4 129 D7
Walcote LE17 245 B4
Whetstone LE8 201 F7
Wymeswold LE12 33 D3
Brooks The LE15 113 B2
Brook Terr LE16 227 F6
Brookvale High Sch
LE6 126 D2
Broom Ave LE11 75 A7
Broombriggs Farm Ctry
Pk* LE12 74 E1
Broombriggs Farm Nature
Trail* LE12 74 F1
Broombriggs Rd LE3 127 F3
Broome Ave LE7 103 E8
Broome La LE7 78 C1
Broomfield LE7 103 E7
Broomfield Com Prim Sch
LE7 103 E7
Broomhills Rd LE19 200 F8
Broomhills The DE12 91 F7
Broomleys LE8 202 D4
Broom Leys Ave LE67 96 F8
Broom Leys Rd LE67 72 A1
Broom Leys Sch LE67 72 A1
Broom Way LE19 177 F1
Brosdale Dr LE10 197 A1
Brouder Cl LE67 97 A8
Brougham St LE1 259 C4
BROUGHTON ASTLEY
218 E5
Broughton Cl
Anstey LE7 127 E7
Loughborough LE11 51 C4
Broughton Field LE18 203 E8
Broughton La
Dunton Bassett LE17 219 D2
Leire LE17 218 E3
Long Clawson LE14 20 A2
Broughton Rd
Cosby LE9 201 C1
Croft LE9 200 C3
Frolesworth LE17 218 C3
Leicester LE2 179 E6
Stoney Stanton LE9 199 F2
Broughton St LE67 96 D8
Broughton Way LE9 218 F7
Brown Ave LE12 76 A6
Brown Ct LE65 68 F7
Browne's Hospl 3
PE9 143 D3
Brownhill Cres LE7 101 C5
Browning Cl LE13 59 C6
Browning Dr DE12 93 C3
Browning Rd
Loughborough LE11 51 D4
Oakham LE15 137 E6
Swadlincote DE11 44 C5
Browning St
Leicester LE3 154 C4
Narborough LE19 178 A1
Brownlow Cres LE13 82 C8
Brownlow Quay PE9 143 E3
Brownlow Sch LE13 59 D4
Brownlow St PE9 143 E3
Brownlow Terr PE9 143 E3
Brown's Cl LE9 217 E8
Browns La LE11 52 A3
Brown's Rd NG10 10 E8
Brown's Way LE8 201 F5
Broxburn Cl LE4 129 D4
Broxfield Cl LE2 181 A3
Bruces La LE14, LE15 135 E6
Bruce St LE3 154 D3
Bruce Way LE8 201 E5
Bruin St LE4 129 A1
Bruins Wlk LE2 180 F5
Brunel Ave LE3 154 A8
Brunel Rd
Corby NN17 230 F2
Hinckley LE10 215 C8
Brunel Way LE67 71 B3
Brunswick St LE1 155 B6
BRUNTINGTHORPE 236 C8
Bruntingthorpe
Aerodrome & Proving
Ground LE17 236 B6
Bruntingthorpe Ind Est
LE17 236 C6
Bruntingthorpe Rd
Peatling Parva LE17 236 B8
Shearsby LE17 222 A1
Brunt La DE11 44 F3
Brush Dr LE11 52 B6
Brushfield Ave LE12 77 D4
Bruxby St LE7 102 F3
Bryan Cl LE12 76 D8
Bryan's Cl LE67 71 F6
Bryar's Cl LE8 223 B4
Bryngarth Cres LE5 156 B7
Bryony Rd LE5 130 D2
Buccaneer Way LE17 243 D6
Buchan Wlk LE3 154 A5
Buckfast Cl
Leicester LE5 155 F3
Wigston LE18 180 C1
Buckhaven Cl LE4 129 D4
Buckingham Cl
Groby LE6 126 E2
Hinckley LE10 197 F4
Buckingham Dr
Leicester LE2 179 B5
Loughborough LE11 51 C5
Buckingham Rd
Coalville LE67 96 F8
Countesthorpe LE8 202 F4
Oakham LE15 137 F5
Buckingham's Way
LE9 217 B4
Buckland Rd LE5 155 D8
Buckley Cl
Measham DE12 93 C4
Woodville DE11 44 F2
Buckley La LE8 207 A2
BUCKMINSTER 42 D2
Buckminster Cl LE13 59 E2
Buckminster La NG33 43 A6
Buckminster Prim Sch
NG33 42 E1
Buckminster Rd
Leicester LE3 154 D8
Sproxton LE14 41 F5
Stainby NG33 43 C2
Bucksburn Wlk LE4 129 D4
Buck's La LE12 30 A7
Buckwell La CV23 257 B6
Buckwell Rd LE9 217 D8
Buddon Cl LE3 127 E3
Buddon Ct LE12 76 E1
Buddon La LE12 75 E5
Bude Dr LE3 127 C1
Bude Rd LE18 180 D1
BUFTON 148 E8
Bufton La CV13 148 E8
Bullaces La LE17 253 C4
Bull Brig La LE15 140 A5
Buller Rd LE4 129 A1
Buller St LE8 223 F8
Bullfield Cl LE15 88 B2
Bullfinch Cl LE15 138 A8
Bullfurlong La LE10 215 F4
Bull Head St LE18 180 D3
Bull Hill LE12, LE65 48 A5
Bull La
Ketton PE9 168 A6
North Witham NG33 65 C7
Oakham LE15 138 A6
Bull Ring LE12 50 B4
Bull's Head Row DE73 26 E6
Bullrush Cl LE12 76 F1
Bulstrode Pl DE74 18 C2
Bulwer Rd LE2 155 B1
Bumblebee La LE9 217 B1
Bungalows The
Essendine PE9 117 A5
Langham LE15 110 C3
Little Stretton LE2 182 D5
Newbold Verdon LE9 150 B4
Theddingworth LE17 248 D8
Bunkers Hill LE17 238 F4
Bunneys Mdw LE10 214 E6
BURBAGE 216 B6
Burbage CE Inf Sch
LE10 216 A5
Burbage Cl LE11 51 E6
Burbage Comm*
LE10 198 A3
BURBAGE COMMON 198 A3
Burbage Common Rd
LE9 198 D3
Burbage Common &
Woods Visitor Ctr*
LE10 198 B3
Burbage Ho LE10 215 D7
Burbage Jun Sch
LE10 215 F6
Burbage Rd LE10 216 A7
Burchnall Rd LE3 153 D1
Burden La LE14 12 B3
Burder St LE11 52 C5
Burdet Cl LE3 153 E1
Burdett Cl LE17 235 C4
Burdetts Cl LE14 82 A1
Burdett Way LE4 128 D4
Burditt Cl LE67 123 F7
Burdock Cl LE5 130 D2
Burfield Ave LE11 52 A3
Burfield St LE4 155 B8
Burford Cl LE16 240 D1
Burgess Rd
Coalville LE67 96 C8
Leicester LE2 179 E6
Burgess Row LE16 230 B8
Burgess St
Leicester LE1 259 A4
Wigston LE18 180 D3
Burghley Circ LE15 87 E2
Burghley Cl
Great Casterton PE9 142 E7
Market Harborough
LE16 241 A3
Burghley Ct 1 PE9 143 E3
Burghley Ho* PE9 144 B1
Burghley La PE9 143 E2
Burghley Rd PE9 143 C5
Burgin Rd LE7 127 D5
Burgins La LE14 40 A7
Burkitt Rd NN17 230 F3
Burleigh Ave LE18 180 C4
Burleigh Com Coll
LE11 51 C3
Burleigh Rd
Hinckley LE10 197 C2
Loughborough LE11 52 A4
BURLEY 111 E1
Burley Cl
Cosby LE9 201 D3
Desford LE9 151 B3
Burley Cres LE15 111 B3
Burley Homes LE4 128 F5
Burley Park Way
LE15 138 C7
Burley Rd
Cottesmore LE15 112 B7
Langham LE15 110 E3
Oakham LE15 138 B7
Ryhall PE9 116 E1
Burley Rise DE74 18 D1
Burleys Flyover LE1 259 B5
Burleys Way LE1 259 B5
Burlington Cl DE72 9 D8
Burlington Rd LE2 155 C1
Burnaby Ave LE5 155 D6
Burnaby Pl LE14 57 F3
Burnaston Rd LE2 179 E6
Burnaston Way LE12 75 C7
Burnell Rd LE3 154 B2
Burneston Way LE18 180 E2
Burnet Cl LE5 130 C2
Burney La DE73 26 C2
Burnham Cl LE18 203 D7
Burnham Dr
Leicester LE4 128 D2
Whetstone LE8 201 F6
Burnham Rise CV11 214 A6
Burnhams Rd PE9 167 F5
Burnmill Rd LE16 240 E5
Burnmoor St LE2 154 E3
Burns Cl
Measham DE12 93 B3
Melton Mowbray LE13 59 B6
Burnside Rd
Broughton Astley LE9 218 F5
Leicester LE2 180 A6
Burns Rd
Loughborough LE11 51 D4
Stamford PE9 143 B4
Burns St
Leicester LE2 180 A8
Narborough LE19 178 B1
Burnsway LE10 197 C1
Burrough Ct LE14 107 B1
Burrough End LE14 82 A1
Burrough Hill Ctry Pk*
LE14 107 E4
BURROUGH ON THE HILL
107 D2
Burrough Rd
Little Dalby LE14 108 A7
Somerby LE14 108 A2
Twyford LE14 133 E8
Burroughs Rd LE6 126 A1
Burrough Way LE17 244 C8
Burrough Wood Nature
Trail* LE6 125 F1
Burrow Hill Rd LE16 208 B3
Burrows Cl LE19 201 B7
Burrows The
East Goscote LE7 103 D7
Narborough LE19 201 A8
Bursdon Cl LE3 153 D6
Bursdon Ct LE3 153 D6
Bursnells La LE14 62 D2
Bursom Rd LE4 128 B6
Burton Cl
Harby LE14 12 A3
Leicester, Oadby LE2 181 D4
Lutterworth LE17 244 D5
Burton Hall LE14 82 E5
BURTON HASTINGS 215 A1
Burton La LE12 33 B3
BURTON LAZARS 83 A6
BURTON ON THE WOLDS
53 F7
Burton on the Wolds Prim
Sch LE12 53 F6
BURTON OVERY 182 F1
Burton Overy La LE7,
LE8 183 C2
Burton Rd
Ashby-de-la-Z LE65 69 A6
Measham DE12 93 B5
Melton Mowbray LE13 59 D1
Orton-on-t-H CV9 119 F1
Overseal DE12 67 A4
Sileby LE12 77 C3
Swadlincote DE11 44 D6
Twycross CV9 146 C8
Wellsborough CV13 147 A2
Burtons La LE67 71 A5
Burton's La NG32 4 F5
Burton St
Leicester LE1 259 C4
Loughborough LE11 52 B2
Melton Mowbray LE13 59 C2
Burton Wlk LE12 31 E8
Burton Wlks LE11 52 B2
BURTON WOLDS 55 A8
Bury Cl LE16 229 C1
Buscot Cl LE4 155 D8
BUSHBY 157 B5
Bushby Rd LE5 155 D7
Bushey Cl LE19 201 B8
Bush Lock Cl LE18 203 A8
Bushloe Ct LE18 180 C2
Bushloe End LE18 180 C2
Bushloe High Sch
LE18 180 B1
Bushnell Cl LE9 219 A4
Bushy Cl NG10 10 B6
Bushy Rd LE7 184 D7
BUSM Bsns Pk LE4 129 A1
Buswells Lodge Prim Sch
LE4 128 A3
Butchers La LE12 78 A7
Butcombe Rd LE4 128 D1
Bute Cl LE10 197 C1
Bute Way LE8 202 F3
Butler Cl
Leicester LE4 129 E4
Ratby LE6 152 D8
Butler Ct LE11 51 F3
Butler Gdns LE16 240 C1
Butler Way LE12 77 D2
Butt Cl
Barlestone CV13 149 D8
Wigston LE18 180 E1
Butt Close La LE1 259 B4
Buttercup Ave DE12 67 E1
Buttercup Cl
Groby LE6 127 A3
Mountsorrel LE12 76 F2
Narborough LE19 178 A1
Stamford PE9 142 F5
Buttercup Dr LE67 97 A8
Buttercup Rd LE11 75 A6
Butterley Dr LE11 51 B2
Buttermere Ave CV11 214 A6
Buttermere Cl LE13 59 B2
Buttermere St LE2 259 A1
Buttermere Way LE12 53 C1
Butterwick Dr LE4 128 C4
Butthole La LE12 50 D5
Butt La
Blackfordby DE11 45 A1
Hinckley LE10 197 F1
Husbands Bosworth
LE17 247 E5
Normanton on S LE12 30 F4
North Luffenham LE15 166 D3
Wymondham LE14 62 E3
Butt Lane Cl LE10 197 E1
Buttress Cl LE15 187 D7
Butts Cl CV9 119 A2
Butts The LE14 24 E1
Buxton Cl
Swadlincote DE11 44 A7
Whetstone LE8 201 F7
Buxton St LE2 155 C6
Buzzard Cl
Broughton Astley LE9 218 F7
Measham DE12 93 B4
Byfield Dr LE18 180 E2
Byford Rd LE4 128 E2
Byland Way LE11 51 B5
Bypass Rd LE14 57 F3
Byre Cres LE9 218 F5
Byron Cl
Fleckney LE8 223 A7
Lutterworth LE17 244 C8
Narborough LE19 178 A2
Byron Cres DE12 93 C3
Byron Ct LE8 222 F7
Byron Rd DE11 44 C6
Byron St Extension
LE11 51 F5
Byron St
Barwell LE9 198 B8
Earl Shilton LE9 198 E7
Leicester LE1 259 C4
Loughborough LE11 51 E5
Byron Way
Melton Mowbray LE13 59 B5
Stamford PE9 143 A3
Byrton Dr LE67 96 C4
Bytham Hts NG33 90 C8
Byway Rd LE5 155 E2

C

Cabin Leas LE11 52 B5
CADEBY 149 D1
Cadeby Cl LE10 197 B3
Cadeby La CV13 149 B3
Cademan Cl LE2 180 B7
Cademan Ct LE2 180 B7
Cademan St LE67 71 F5
Cadles Cl LE9 199 D3
Cadle St LE9 150 B5
Caernarvon Cl
Mountsorrel LE12 101 D8
Shepshed LE12 50 A2
Cairngorm Cl LE2 179 F7
Cairns Cl 5 LE3 178 F7

Cairnsford Rd LE2 . . . . 180 B6
Caistor Rd NN17 . . . . 213 C1
Caithness Rd PE9 . . . . 143 A4
Calais Hill LE1 . . . . 259 C3
Calais St LE1 . . . . 259 C3
CALDECOTE 195 A2
Caldecote Com Prim Sch
LE3 . . . . 154 A1
Caldecote Hall CV10 . . . . 194 F2
Caldecote Hall Dr
CV10 . . . . 194 F3
Caldecote Rd
Great Easton LE16 . . . . 229 E6
Leicester LE3 . . . . 154 A1
CALDECOTT 230 C8
Caldecott Cl LE18 . . . . 180 F2
Caldecott Rd LE16 . . . . 230 B5
Calder Cl
Corby NN17 . . . . 230 D1
Oakham LE15 . . . . 137 E5
Calderdale Dr NG10 . . . . 10 A6
Calder Rd LE4 . . . . 128 C3
Caldon Cl LE10 . . . . 215 B8
Caldwell St LE11 . . . . 52 A4
Caledine Rd LE3 . . . . 154 A8
Caledonian Rd PE9 . . . . 143 B4
Calgary Cres LE15 . . . . 138 B6
Calgary Rd LE1 . . . . 155 A7
Calke Cl LE11 . . . . 75 A6
Calke Rd DE73 . . . . 26 A6
Callan Cl LE19 . . . . 201 A8
Callan's La LE65 . . . . 46 D7
Callendar Cl CV11 . . . . 214 A7
Callis The LE65 . . . . 69 B7
Caloe Cl LE12 . . . . 77 E3
Calver Hey Rd LE4 . . . . 128 B3
Calvert Cres LE19 . . . . 217 E7
Calverton Ave LE18 . . . . 180 C4
Calverton Cl LE16 . . . . 152 D8
Camborne Cl LE18 . . . . 180 C1
Camborne Dr CV11 . . . . 214 A5
Cambourne Rd LE10 . . . . 216 A6
Cambrian Cl LE9 . . . . 201 D2
Cambrian Way
Ashby-de-la-Z LE65 . . . . 69 A3
Swadlincote DE11 . . . . 44 A3
Cambridge Ave LE13 . . . . 82 D8
Cambridge Cl LE7 . . . . 103 C3
Cambridge Dr LE9 . . . . 151 A2
Cambridge Rd
Cosby LE8, LE9 . . . . 201 E5
Stamford PE9 . . . . 143 C5
Cambridge St
Coalville LE67 . . . . 71 E1
Leicester LE3 . . . . 154 C4
Loughborough LE11 . . . . 52 B5
Shepshed LE12 . . . . 50 B2
Cam Cl NN17 . . . . 230 C1
Camden Rd LE3 . . . . 154 A4
Camden St LE1 . . . . 259 C4
Camelford Rd LE67 . . . . 96 C7
Camellia Cl LE9 . . . . 177 F1
Camelot Way LE19 . . . . 178 A1
Cameron Ave LE4 . . . . 129 B3
Camfield Rise LE2 . . . . 179 D4
Camomile Rd LE13 . . . . 82 B8
Campbell Ave LE4 . . . . 129 E5
Campbell St LE1 . . . . 259 C3
Campden Cl
Exton LE15 . . . . 113 B2
Uppingham LE15 . . . . 189 B4
Camp Hill Ct PE9 . . . . 143 B8
Campion Cl LE19 . . . . 201 A8
Campion Gr PE9 . . . . 142 F5
Campion Hill DE74 . . . . 17 A4
Campion Pl LE13 . . . . 82 A8
Campion Wlk LE4 . . . . 128 B3
Campton Cl LE10 . . . . 215 C2
Camrose Cl LE15 . . . . 138 B6
Camville Rd LE3 . . . . 153 F4
Canada Fields LE17 . . . . 244 C7
Canal Bank
Shardlow DE72 . . . . 9 A1
Canal La
Harby LE14 . . . . 12 D5
Hose LE14 . . . . 20 E8
Long Clawson LE14 . . . . 20 C6
Canalside LE16 . . . . 240 D4
Canal St
Leicester LE2 . . . . 179 C7
Oakthorpe DE12 . . . . 93 A7
Thurmaston LE4 . . . . 129 E8
Wigston LE18 . . . . 179 F1
Canal Way LE10 . . . . 214 F7
Canberra Way LE10 . . . . 215 E4
Candle La LE7 . . . . 198 F8
Cank St LE1 . . . . 259 B4
Cannam Cl
Middleton LE16 . . . . 229 B1
Whetstone LE8 . . . . 202 A5
Canner Cl DE11 . . . . 45 A2
Canning Pl LE1 . . . . 259 B5
Canning St
Hinckley LE10 . . . . 197 C1
Leicester LE1 . . . . 259 B5
Canning Way LE11 . . . . 51 C6
Cannock Cl LE67 . . . . 96 D4
Cannock St LE4 . . . . 130 A4
Cannock Way NG10 . . . . 10 F7
Canon Cl LE2 . . . . 181 B5
Canons Cl LE19 . . . . 201 B8
Canonsleigh Rd LE4 . . . . 128 E3

Canonsleigh Wlk [6]
LE4 . . . . 128 E3
Canon St LE1 . . . . 129 C1
Canterbury Dr
Ashby-de-la-Z LE65 . . . . 69 A7
Melton Mowbray LE13 . . . . . . 59 A6
Canterbury Rd LE4 . . . . 129 B1
Canterbury Terr LE3 . . . . 154 B3
Canterbury Way CV11 . . . . . . 214 A8
Cantrell Rd LE3 . . . . 153 D3
Canvey Cl LE18 . . . . 180 F3
Capendale Cl PE9 . . . . 167 F5
Capers Cl LE19 . . . . 178 A3
Capesthorne Cl LE5 . . . . 155 D8
Captains Close Prim Sch
LE14 . . . . 57 E3
Cara Cl LE2 . . . . 180 C8
Carbery Cl LE2 . . . . 181 D4
Cardigan Dr LE18 . . . . 179 F2
Cardinal Cl LE5 . . . . 152 D8
Cardinals Wlk LE5 . . . . 156 C8
Carey Cl LE18 . . . . 203 D8
Carey Gdns LE9 . . . . 152 D5
Carey Hill Rd LE9 . . . . 199 D2
Carey Rd LE9 . . . . 200 D7
Careys Cl LE1 . . . . 259 A3
Carfax Ave LE2 . . . . 180 F7
Car Hill Rd LE67 . . . . 71 E1
Carillon Ct LE1 . . . . 52 B4
Carillon Tower & War
Meml* LE11 . . . . 52 A3
Carington St LE11 . . . . 51 F5
Carisbrooke Ave LE2 . . . . . . 180 C7
Carisbrooke Cl LE2 . . . . 180 C7
Carisbrooke Gdns
LE2 . . . . 180 C8
Carisbrooke Pk LE2 . . . . 180 C7
Carisbrooke Rd
Leicester LE2 . . . . 180 C7
Mountsorrel LE12 . . . . 101 D8
Carisbrooke Gr PE9 . . . . 143 A3
CARLBY 117 C8
Carlin Cl DE72 . . . . 9 E8
Carling Cl LE67 . . . . 71 E1
Carlisle St LE3 . . . . 154 C5
Carl Moult Ho DE11 . . . . 44 A2
Carlson Gdns LE17 . . . . 244 D6
Carlson Terr LE17 . . . . 244 D6
Carl St LE2 . . . . 179 C6
CARLTON 148 D7
Carlton Ave LE19 . . . . 201 C8
Carlton Cl LE11 . . . . 51 F4
Carlton Ct
Glenfield LE3 . . . . 153 D8
Leicester LE2 . . . . 155 D1
Carlton Dr LE18 . . . . 180 C4
Carlton Gdns LE8 . . . . 205 B7
Carlton La LE8 . . . . 205 F8
Carlton Rd
Barton in t B CV13 . . . . 122 D1
Carlton CV13 . . . . 148 B4
Kibworth Beauchamp
LE8 . . . . 206 B3
Long Eaton NG10 . . . . 10 B5
Carlton St LE1 . . . . 259 B2
Carlyon Ct LE19 . . . . 152 E5
Carlyon Rd
Atherstone CV9 . . . . 170 F1
Atherstone, Mancetter
CV9 . . . . 194 A7
Carlyon Road Ind Est
Atherstone CV9 . . . . 170 F1
Atherstone CV9 . . . . 194 A8
Carmen Gr LE6 . . . . 126 C3
Carnation Cl LE3 . . . . 152 F2
Carnation St LE4 . . . . 128 F2
Carnegie Cres LE13 . . . . 59 E6
Carnival Way DE74 . . . . 17 B4
Carnoustie Rd LE3 . . . . 153 D6
Caroline Cl LE2 . . . . 179 E6
Carousel Pk LE9 . . . . 197 F8
Carpenters Cl LE10 . . . . 215 F5
Carpenter's Cl LE3 . . . . 153 B7
Carpe Rd LE4 . . . . 129 D1
Carrfield Ave NG10 . . . . 10 F8
Carrfields La LE14 . . . . 80 D8
Carriageway The
LE15 . . . . 136 A6
Carrick Point LE5 . . . . 155 F4
Carrington Rd LE5 . . . . 130 C3
Carron Cl NN17 . . . . 230 C1
Carrow Rd LE3 . . . . 153 B5
Carrs Cl DE74 . . . . 17 A3
Carr's Dr [1] LE9 . . . . 198 F8
Carrs Hill LE9 . . . . 198 C6
Carr's Rd LE9 . . . . 198 F8
Carter Cl
Enderby LE19 . . . . 178 A3
Long Eaton NG10 . . . . 10 B6
Carter Dale LE67 . . . . 71 D7
Carter St LE4 . . . . 155 C8
Cartland Dr LE11 . . . . 51 C6
Carts La LE1 . . . . 259 B4
Cartwright Dr LE2 . . . . 181 A5
Cartwright St LE11 . . . . 52 C5
Cartwright Way LE67 . . . . 97 C4
Carty Rd LE5 . . . . 130 C3
Carver Ct PE9 . . . . 167 F5
Carver's Cnr LE2 . . . . 179 B3
Carver's Path LE7 . . . . 103 C7
Casewick La PE9 . . . . 144 F4
Cashmore View LE4 . . . . 128 D4
Castell Dr LE4 . . . . 128 C2
Casterton Bsns & Ent Coll
PE9 . . . . 142 E7
Casterton La PE9 . . . . 142 E2
Casterton Rd PE9 . . . . 143 B4

Castle Bank LE16 . . . . 251 F5
Castle Bytham Rd LE15 . . . . . 89 F5
Castle Cl
Bottesford NG13 . . . . 3 D2
Earl Shilton LE9 . . . . 175 F1
Sapcote LE9 . . . . 217 D7
Uppingham LE15 . . . . 188 F5
Castle Ct LE10 . . . . 215 D6
Castledine Ave LE12 . . . . 76 A6
Castledine St Extension
LE11 . . . . 52 B2
Castledine St
Loughborough LE11 . . . . 52 B2
Quorn (Quorndon) LE12 . . . . . 75 F6
Castle Donington Com
Coll LE74 . . . . 17 C3
Castle Dyke PE9 . . . . 143 D2
Castle Fields LE4 . . . . 128 A5
Castleford Rd LE3 . . . . 178 E8
Castlegate Ave LE4 . . . . 128 F8
Castle Gate Ho [7] LE65 . . . . 69 B6
Castle Hill
Castle Donington DE74 . . . . . . 17 B4
East Leake LE12 . . . . 31 F8
Mountsorrel LE12 . . . . 76 E2
Castle La
Melbourne DE73 . . . . 26 B7
[5] Stamford PE9 . . . . 143 D2
Castlemaine Dr LE10 . . . . . . 197 E3
Castle Mews LE12 . . . . 75 F6
Castle Mews The [5]
DE11 . . . . 44 A7
Castle Mills DE73 . . . . 26 B7
Castle Mound Way
CV23 . . . . 252 D2
Castle Rd
Hartshill CV10 . . . . 194 B1
Kirby Muxloe LE9 . . . . 152 D5
Mountsorrel LE12 . . . . 101 D8
Castle Rise
Belmesthorpe PE9 . . . . 117 A1
Groby LE6 . . . . 126 F2
Castle Rock Dr LE67 . . . . 72 C2
Castle Rock High Sch
LE67 . . . . 72 C2
Castle St
Hinckley LE10 . . . . 215 D8
Leicester LE1 . . . . 259 A3
Melbourne DE73 . . . . 26 B7
[6] Stamford PE9 . . . . 143 D3
Whitwick LE67 . . . . 71 F5
Castleton Rd LE18 . . . . 180 C4
Castle View
Hartshill CV10 . . . . 194 B1
Leicester LE1 . . . . 259 B4
Castle View Rd NG13 . . . . 7 C8
Castle Way LE65 . . . . 69 A4
Castlewood Mobile Home
Pk LE9 . . . . 216 D8
Castle St LE1 . . . . 259 A3
Caswell Cl LE4 . . . . 128 D4
Caters Cl LE7 . . . . 127 D6
Catesby St LE3 . . . . 154 D5
Catharine Rise DE11 . . . . 44 A1
Catherine Inf Sch LE4 . . . . . 155 B8
Catherine Jun Sch
LE4 . . . . 155 B8
Catherines Cl LE2 . . . . 76 B6
Catherine St LE4 . . . . 129 C1
Catherine Street Ind Est
LE4 . . . . 129 D2
Cathkin Cl LE3 . . . . 153 D5
Catmose Park Rd
LE15 . . . . 138 B5
Catmose St LE15 . . . . 138 A6
CATTHORPE 253 C1
Catthorpe Manor
LE17 . . . . 253 F1
Catthorpe Rd LE17 . . . . 253 C4
Cattle Market LE11 . . . . 52 B3
Cauby Cl LE12 . . . . 77 E3
Caudebec Cl LE15 . . . . 189 A5
Caudle Cl LE7 . . . . 100 F3
Cauldwell La LE17 . . . . 234 B4
Causeway La
Cropston LE7 . . . . 100 C2
Leicester LE1 . . . . 259 A4
Causeway Rd NN17 . . . . 230 E2
Cavalry Cl LE13 . . . . 59 A6
Cavendish Cl
Castle Donington DE74 . . . . . . 17 A2
Shardlow DE72 . . . . 9 A2
[9] Swadlincote DE11 . . . . . . 44 A7
Cavendish Cres LE67 . . . . 96 C7
Cavendish Ct LE2 . . . . 180 C7
Cavendish Mews LE2 . . . . . . 179 E8
Cavendish Rd LE2 . . . . 179 E8
Cave Rd LE12 . . . . 76 E8
Caversham Cl CV11 . . . . 214 A7
Caversham Rd LE2 . . . . 179 C3
Cawdell Dr LE12 . . . . 29 D2
Cawsand Rd LE18 . . . . 180 C1
Cawston Cl LE5 . . . . 130 B2
Caxton Pl LE12 . . . . 76 D7
Caxton St LE16 . . . . 240 F1
Cecil Ct [1] PE9 . . . . 143 E3
Cecilia Rd LE2 . . . . 155 B2
Cecil Rd LE2 . . . . 155 B6
Cedar Ave
Birstall LE4 . . . . 129 A7
East Leake LE12 . . . . 31 D8
Long Eaton NG10 . . . . 10 C5
Lutterworth LE17 . . . . 244 B6
Wigston LE18 . . . . 180 D2
Cedar Cl
Ashby-de-la-Z LE65 . . . . 69 C6
Glenfield LE3 . . . . 127 E1

Cedar Cl continued
Kibworth Beauchamp
LE8 . . . . 223 F8
Uppingham LE15 . . . . 189 C4
Cedar Cres LE19 . . . . 201 B7
Cedar Croft DE72 . . . . 16 A7
Cedar Ct LE67 . . . . 97 C5
Cedar Ct
Corby NN17 . . . . 230 E1
Groby LE6 . . . . 126 F2
Hinckley LE10 . . . . 216 A6
Leicester LE5 . . . . 156 A8
Cedar Dr
Ibstock LE67 . . . . 95 E2
Market Bosworth CV13 . . . . 148 F2
Melton Mowbray LE13 . . . . . . 59 B5
Syston LE7 . . . . 103 B2
Cedar Gr
Moira DE12 . . . . 68 B6
Mountsorrel LE12 . . . . 76 E1
Swadlincote DE11 . . . . 44 A7
Cedar Rd
Blaby LE8 . . . . 202 B6
Castle Donington DE74 . . . . . . 17 B2
Earl Shilton LE9 . . . . 198 D7
Leicester LE2 . . . . 155 C4
Loughborough LE11 . . . . 52 A4
Stamford PE9 . . . . 142 F4
Cedars Cl LE2 . . . . 155 C3
Cedar St LE15 . . . . 137 A2
Cedars The
Bushby LE7 . . . . 157 B4
Leicester LE2 . . . . 180 B7
Cedarwood Cl LE4 . . . . 129 D1
Celandine Cl
Leicester, Oadby LE2 . . . . . . 181 E4
Mountsorrel LE12 . . . . 76 F2
Celandine Dr LE13 . . . . 82 B8
Celandine Pl DE11 . . . . 44 E4
Celandine Rd LE5 . . . . 130 C2
Cello Cl LE67 . . . . 71 E5
Celt St LE3 . . . . 154 D4
Cemetery La
Hartshill CV10 . . . . 194 B1
Manton LE15 . . . . 164 D6
Cemetery Rd
Sileby LE12 . . . . 77 D3
Whetstone LE8 . . . . 201 F7
Central Ave
Ibstock LE67 . . . . 95 F1
Leicester LE2 . . . . 155 C2
Lutterworth LE17 . . . . 244 C7
Shepshed LE12 . . . . 50 B3
Syston LE7 . . . . 103 C4
Wigston LE18 . . . . 180 C2
Central Ct LE18 . . . . 201 F8
Central Park Dr CV23 . . . . . . 252 D2
Central Pk LE17 . . . . 244 D8
Central Rd
Coalville LE67 . . . . 96 D7
Leicester LE3 . . . . 154 D7
Central St LE8 . . . . 202 F4
Centre Ct LE19 . . . . 178 D7
Centurian Ct Office Pk
LE19 . . . . 178 D8
Centurion Ct LE6 . . . . 152 D8
Centurion Way LE19 . . . . 178 D7
Century Ct LE5 . . . . 156 C6
Chadderton Cl LE2 . . . . 180 A7
CHADWELL 39 C5
Chadwell Cl
Asfordby LE14 . . . . 57 E2
Melton Mowbray LE13 . . . . . . 59 E2
Chadwell Rd LE3 . . . . 153 E7
Chadwick Dr LE5 . . . . 150 B4
Chadwick Wlk LE4 . . . . 128 D3
Chaffinch Cl
Leicester LE4 . . . . 128 B6
Oakham LE15 . . . . 138 B8
Chainama Ct LE3 . . . . 153 C6
Chainbridge Cl LE11 . . . . 52 A5
Chale Rd LE4 . . . . 128 F2
Chalfont Cl LE13 . . . . 82 D7
Chalfont Dr LE12 . . . . 77 C1
Chalgrove Wlk LE5 . . . . 156 A6
Challottee LE8 . . . . 50 C3
Chalmondley Dr LE13 . . . . 59 D6
Chalvington Cl LE5 . . . . 156 C3
Chambers Cl LE67 . . . . 125 F8
Chambers Row NN6 . . . . 256 E6
Champion Cl LE15 . . . . 156 B5
Chancel Rd LE4 . . . . 128 D8
Chancery St LE1 . . . . 259 B3
Chandlers Croft LE67 . . . . 95 F3
Chandler Way LE9 . . . . 219 B5
Chandos St LE2 . . . . 155 C4
Channing Way LE67 . . . . 96 C4
Chantrell Cl LE67 . . . . 124 B5
Chantry Cl
Huncote LE9 . . . . 200 D7
Long Eaton NG10 . . . . 10 A4
Melbourne DE73 . . . . 26 B7
Chapel Bar LE12 . . . . 33 C3
Chapel Cl
Ab Kettleby LE14 . . . . 37 C2
Dunton Bassett LE17 . . . . . . 219 D2
Empingham LE15 . . . . 141 A6
Houghton on t h LE7 . . . . . . 157 F4
Kilby LE18 . . . . 203 F3
Moira DE11 . . . . 44 C1
[1] Oakham LE15 . . . . 138 A6
Ravenstone LE67 . . . . 70 F1
Syston LE7 . . . . 103 A4
Thurcaston LE7 . . . . 101 B3

Chapel Flats LE9 . . . . 198 B6
Chapel Gn LE3 . . . . 153 B3
Chapel Hill
Groby LE6 . . . . 126 C3
Woolsthorpe by B NG32 . . . . 15 B8
Chapel La
Ab Kettleby LE14 . . . . 37 C2
Barrowden LE15 . . . . 191 F5
Clipston LE16 . . . . 249 F1
Colerton LE67 . . . . 70 E8
Congerstone CV13 . . . . 147 D8
Cosby LE9 . . . . 201 D2
Croxton Kerrial NG32 . . . . . . 24 A7
Desford LE9 . . . . 151 B4
Gaddesby LE7 . . . . 105 B7
Granby NG13 . . . . 5 B5
Hoby LE14 . . . . 79 D8
Hose LE14 . . . . 20 F8
Ketton PE9 . . . . 168 A5
Leicester LE2 . . . . 180 B8
Lilbourne CV23 . . . . 258 A6
Mowsley LE17 . . . . 237 F7
Nether Broughton LE14 . . . . . 36 C8
North Luffenham LE15 . . . . . 166 D3
Norton–JCV7 CV9 . . . . 120 A2
Old Dalby LE14 . . . . 35 E4
Osgathorpe LE12 . . . . 48 E3
Ratby LE6 . . . . 152 C8
Sharnford LE10 . . . . 217 C4
Somerby LE14 . . . . 108 B2
Stathern LE14 . . . . 13 A3
Tugby LE7 . . . . 185 E6
Upper Broughton LE14 . . . . . 19 A1
Walcote LE17 . . . . 245 A4
Walcote LE17 . . . . 236 B2
Willoughby-on-t-W LE12 . . . . 34 D7
Witherley CV9 . . . . 194 C7
Wymondham LE14 . . . . 62 E2
Chapel Rise LE65 . . . . 47 F5
Chapel Row NG33 . . . . 43 B8
Chapel St
Barkestone-le-V NG13 . . . . 6 B2
Barlestone CV13 . . . . 149 B8
Barwell LE9 . . . . 198 B6
Belton-in-R LE15 . . . . 187 D7
Blaby LE8 . . . . 179 C1
Bottesford NG13 . . . . 3 B3
Donisthorpe DE12 . . . . 92 A8
Earl Shilton LE9 . . . . 176 A1
Eaton NG32 . . . . 22 F6
Enderby LE19 . . . . 178 A3
Ibstock LE67 . . . . 95 F1
Leicester LE2 . . . . 181 A5
Long Eaton NG10 . . . . 10 E7
Lutterworth LE17 . . . . 244 C6
Measham DE12 . . . . 93 C5
Melbourne DE73 . . . . 26 B7
Melton Mowbray LE13 . . . . . . 59 C3
Oakthorpe DE12 . . . . 93 A6
Sharnford LE10 . . . . 217 C4
Shepshed LE12 . . . . 50 B5
Smisby LE65 . . . . 45 F3
Stapleton LE9 . . . . 174 F1
Swadlincote, Church Gresley
DE11 . . . . 44 A1
Swinford LE17 . . . . 254 B3
Syston LE7 . . . . 103 B4
Woodville DE11 . . . . 44 F2
Chapel View LE15 . . . . 156 B2
Chapel Yard PE9 . . . . 143 E3
Chaplin Cl LE2 . . . . 77 C3
Chaplin Ct LE3 . . . . 153 D3
Chapman Cl CV13 . . . . 149 D8
Chapmans Mdws LE65 . . . . . . 69 C4
Chapman St LE12 . . . . 52 C4
Chappell Cl LE4 . . . . 129 E7
Charity Hos The CV23 . . . . . 252 C6
Charlecote Ave LE3 . . . . 153 F1
Charles Dr LE7 . . . . 127 E7
Charles Hall Cl LE4 . . . . 50 C4
Charles Rd PE9 . . . . 143 C5
Charles St
Hinckley LE10 . . . . 197 E1
Leicester LE1 . . . . 259 B4
Long Eaton NG10 . . . . 10 D6
Loughborough LE11 . . . . 52 B5
Market Harborough
LE16 . . . . 240 D3
Ravenstone LE67 . . . . 71 A2
Sileby LE12 . . . . 77 C2
Swadlincote DE11 . . . . 44 B2
Charleston Cl DE11 . . . . 44 B2
Charleston Cres LE9 . . . . 198 A6
Charles Way
Leicester, Oadby LE2 . . . . . . 181 C5
Whetstone LE8 . . . . 201 E5
Charley Dr LE11 . . . . 51 E2
Charley Rd
Shepshed LE12 . . . . 72 F7
Woodhouse Eaves LE12 . . . . . 73 F2
Charlock Dr PE9 . . . . 142 F4
Charlock Rd LE5 . . . . 130 D2
Charlotte Ct
Blaby LE8 . . . . 202 A8
Leicester LE2 . . . . 128 B3
Charlotte St LE13 . . . . 59 C3
Charlottes Wlk LE7 . . . . 157 F3
Charlton Cl LE8 . . . . 202 A6
Charnborough Cl LE67 . . . . . . 97 B8
Charnborough Rd LE67 . . . . . 97 B8
Charnia Gr LE12 . . . . 100 F6
Charnor Rd LE3 . . . . 153 E8
Charnwood Cl
Asfordby LE14 . . . . 57 F3
Castle Donington DE74 . . . . . . 17 C2
Long Eaton NG10 . . . . 10 B4
Sutton Bonington LE12 . . . . . 30 C5

Charnwood Ave *continued*
Thurmaston LE4. . . . . 129 F8
Whetstone LE8 . . . . 201 F8
Charnwood Bsns Pk
LE11. . . . . 52 B6
Charnwood Cl
Hinckley LE10 . . . . 197 E2
Leicester Forest East
LE3 . . . . 153 A4
Thurmaston LE4. . . . . 129 F8
Charnwood Ct LE67. . . . . . 96 E8
Charnwood Dr
Hartshill Green CV10. . . . . . 194 B2
Leicester Forest East
LE3 . . . . 153 A3
Markfield LE67. . . . . 125 F8
Melton Mowbray LE13. . . . . 59 A4
Thurnby LE7. . . . . 156 F5
Charnwood Fields
LE12. . . . . 30 C5
Charnwood Ho LE12. . . . 100 A8
Charnwood Ind Units LE2,
LE5. . . . . 155 B6
Charnwood Manor
LE19. . . . . 201 C8
Charnwood Mus*
LE11. . . . . 52 A4
Charnwood Prim Sch
LE2. . . . . 155 B6
Charnwood Rd
Anstey LE7 . . . . 127 D7
Barwell LE9 . . . . 198 B8
Hinckley LE10 . . . . 197 D2
Loughborough LE11. . . . . . . 52 B2
Shepshed LE12 . . . . 50 B2
Charnwood Rise LE12. . . 99 F8
Charnwood St
Coalville LE67 . . . . 71 E1
Leicester LE5. . . . . 155 C6
Charteris Cl LE11. . . . . . . 51 D6
Charter Point Way
LE65. . . . . 69 E6
Charter St LE1. . . . . 154 F7
Charters The PE9 . . . . . . 144 E4
Chartley Rd LE3. . . . . 154 C3
Chartwell Dr LE18 . . . . . 180 A3
Chartwell Drive Ind Est
LE18. . . . . 180 A3
Chartwell Point LE18 . . 180 B3
Chase The
Braunstone Town LE3 . . . . . 178 F7
Great Glen LE8 . . . . 103 D8
Great Glen LE8 . . . . 205 C7
Markfield LE67. . . . . 125 E8
Chater Cl
Great Bowden LE16. . . . . . . 241 A6
Leicester LE5. . . . . 156 D7
Manton LE15. . . . . 164 E6
Chater La PE9 . . . . 168 A7
Chater Mews PE9. . . . . . . 168 A7
Chater Rd LE15 . . . . 137 F5
Chatham St LE1. . . . . 259 B3
Chatsworth Ave LE8 . . . . 180 A1
Chatsworth Cl
Hinckley LE10 . . . . 215 F6
Shepshed LE12 . . . . 50 A3
Chatsworth Dr
Market Harborough
LE16 . . . . 241 B3
Syston LE7. . . . . 102 F3
Chatsworth Rd
Loughborough LE11. . . . . . . 51 D5
Stamford PE9. . . . . 143 B4
Swadlincote DE11. . . . . 44 A6
Chatsworth St LE2 . . . . . 155 C6
Chatteris Ave LE5. . . . . . 156 D3
Chaucer St
Leicester LE2. . . . . 155 C3
Narborough LE19. . . . . 178 A1
Chaveney Cl LE12. . . . . . . 75 E5
Chaveney Rd LE12 . . . . . . 75 E5
Chaveney Wlk LE12 . . . . . 75 E5
Cheapside
Leicester LE1. . . . . 259 B4
Melton Mowbray LE13. . . . . 59 C3
Checketts Cl LE4 . . . . 129 B2
Checketts Rd LE4 . . . . . . 129 B3
Checkland Rd LE4 . . . . . . 129 E8
Cheddar Rd LE18 . . . . 180 E3
Cheer Cl LE8 . . . . 201 F4
Chelker Way LE11 . . . . 51 C3
Chellaston La DE72. . . . . . 16 A8
Chellaston Rd LE18 . . . . . 180 C4
Chelsea Cl LE2. . . . . 179 D1
Cheltenham Dr LE65. . . . . 69 A7
Cheltenham Rd LE4. . . . . 128 D2
Cheney Ct LE9. . . . . 200 D8
Cheney End LE9 . . . . 200 D7
Cheney Rd LE4 . . . . 130 A4
Chepstow Rd LE2. . . . . . . 155 C3
Cheriborough Rd DE74. . . . 17 A3
Cheriton Rd LE2 . . . . 179 D5
Cherrybrook Cl LE1 . . . . . 178 F7
Cherry Cl
Breaston DE72. . . . . 9 E8
Loughborough LE11. . . . . . . 75 A7
Cherry Croft LE11. . . . . . . 51 F7
Cherry Dr LE7 . . . . 103 B2
Cherryfield Cl CV10. . . . . 194 B2
Cherry Gr LE8 . . . . 182 C1
Cherry Hills Rd LE3. . . . . 153 C6
Cherryholt La PE9. . . . . . 143 F3
Cherryholt Rd PE9. . . . . . 143 E3
Cherryleas Dr LE3 . . . . . . 154 C4
Cherry Orchard Est
CV13. . . . . 195 F3
Cherry Rd LE8. . . . . 202 B7

Cherry St LE18 . . . . 180 B2
Cherrytree Ave LE17. . . . 244 A5
Cherry Tree Ave LE9 . . . . 152 E3
Cherrytree Cl
Anstey LE7. . . . . 127 D5
Countesthorpe LE8 . . . . . . 202 E4
Cherry Tree Cl LE17. . . . . 247 E5
Cherry Tree Ct
Leicester Forest East
LE9 . . . . 152 E3
Moira DE12 . . . . 68 B6
Cherry Tree Dr
Barwell LE9 . . . . 198 B8
Plungar NG13 . . . . 6 A1
Cherry Tree Gr LE19. . . . 178 A3
Cherry Tree Mews
DE11 . . . . 44 F2
Cherwell Cl LE10 . . . . 215 A8
Cherwell Rd LE12. . . . . . . 76 D7
Cherwell Wlk NN17. . . . . 230 C1
Cheshire Cl LE17 . . . . 244 B4
Cheshire Dr LE18 . . . . 180 A3
Cheshire Gdns LE2 . . . . . 179 D7
Cheshire Rd LE2. . . . . 179 D7
Chester Cl
Blaby LE8. . . . . 202 C7
Leicester LE1. . . . . 155 B7
Loughborough LE11. . . . . . . 51 F3
Chesterfield Ave NG10 . . . 10 F7
Chesterfield Rd LE5 . . . . 155 D4
Chesterfield Way LE19 . . 198 C7
Chester Gdns DE11 . . . . . 44 B2
Chester Rd LE8. . . . . 202 C7
Chesterton Ct LE19 . . . . . 178 A2
Chesterton Wlk LE3 . . . . 154 A5
Chestnut Ave
Corby NN17. . . . . 230 D1
Leicester LE5. . . . . 130 D1
Leicester, Oadby LE2 . . . . . 181 A5
Lutterworth LE17. . . . . 244 A6
Swadlincote DE11. . . . . 44 B6
Chestnut Cl
Bottesford NG13. . . . . 3 C3
Broughton Astley LE9 . . . . 219 A5
Ibstock LE67 . . . . 95 E1
Littlethorpe LE19. . . . . 201 B6
Market Bosworth CV13. . . 148 F2
Moira DE12 . . . . 68 B5
Queniborough LE7 . . . . . . 103 D5
Quorn (Quorndon) LE12. . . 75 E4
Shepshed LE12 . . . . 50 C3
Syston LE7. . . . . 103 B2
Uppingham LE15 . . . . 189 A3
Chestnut Ct LE12. . . . . . . 76 E2
Chestnut Dr
Bagworth LE67 . . . . 124 A6
Bushby LE7. . . . . 157 A4
Leicester, Oadby LE2 . . . . . 182 A4
Chestnut Gdns PE9 . . . . . 142 F3
Chestnut Gn DE11 . . . . . . 44 B2
Chestnut Gr LE67. . . . . . . 97 B8
Chestnut La LE8 . . . . 221 F5
Chestnut Pl LE12 . . . . 76 D7
Chestnut Rd
Glenfield LE3 . . . . 153 C8
Oakham LE15. . . . . 138 A7
Chestnut St LE11. . . . . . . 52 A4
Chestnuts The
Countesthorpe LE8 . . . . . . 202 E4
Long Eaton NG10. . . . . 10 A8
Chestnut Way
East Goscote LE7 . . . . 103 E7
Melton Mowbray LE13. . . . . 59 C1
Chestnut Wlk
Groby LE6. . . . . 126 F2
Market Harborough
LE16 . . . . 241 B2
Chettle Rd LE3 . . . . 154 A7
Chetwynd Dr LE13 . . . . . . 58 F3
Chevin Ave LE3 . . . . 153 D5
Cheviot Cl
Oakham LE15. . . . . 137 E6
Swadlincote DE11. . . . . 44 A3
Cheviot Dr LE12 . . . . 50 C3
Cheviot Rd
Leicester LE2. . . . . 179 F7
Long Eaton NG10. . . . . 10 A8
Cheyne La PE9. . . . . 143 E3
Chichester Cl
Ellistown LE67 . . . . 96 C4
Loughborough LE11. . . . . . . 74 C8
Nuneaton CV11. . . . . 214 A7
Chilcombe Cl LE4 . . . . . . 128 E3
Chilcombe Wlk LE4
LE4. . . . . 128 E3
CHILCOTE 91 F3
Chilcott Cl LE67 . . . . 71 F1
Child Cl LE14. . . . . 82 F6
Chiltern Ave
Cosby LE9 . . . . 201 D2
Shepshed LE12 . . . . 50 D3
Chiltern Cl
Market Harborough
LE16 . . . . 240 F5
Oakham LE15. . . . . 137 D6
Chiltern Dr LE15. . . . . 166 C7
Chiltern Gn LE2 . . . . 180 A6
Chiltern Rd DE11 . . . . 44 A3
Chiltern Rise LE65 . . . . . . 69 C5
Chislehurst Ave LE3 . . . . 178 F8
Chiswick Dr LE11 . . . . 51 C4
Chiswick Rd LE2 . . . . 154 F1
Chitterman Way LE67 . . . 125 E8
Chorley Wood Rd
LE5. . . . . 156 D4
Choyce Cl CV9. . . . . 170 D2
Chrisett Cl LE15 . . . . 156 B6
Christ Church Cl PE9 . . . 143 D4

Christ Church & St Peter's
CE Prim Sch LE12. . . . . 76 E2
Christie Dr LE11. . . . . 51 D6
Christopher Cl
Countesthorpe LE8 . . . . . . 202 E3
Heather LE67. . . . . 95 F3
Christopher Ct NN6. . . . . 256 D5
Christopher Dr LE4. . . . . 129 F4
Christow St LE1. . . . . 155 B7
Christ the King RC Prim
Sch LE3. . . . . 154 B6
Chrysanthemum Ct
DE11 . . . . 44 A5
Church Ave
Leicester LE3. . . . . 154 C5
Long Eaton NG10. . . . . 10 A4
Swadlincote DE11. . . . . 44 B3
Church Bank LE8 . . . . 229 D7
Church Cl
Ashwell LE15. . . . . 111 B8
Barwell LE9 . . . . 198 A6
Blackfordby DE11. . . . . 45 B1
Braybrooke LE16 . . . . 251 E6
Broughton Astley LE9 . . . . 218 F6
Caldecott LE16. . . . . 230 B8
Dunton Bassett LE17. . . . . 219 D1
Hinckley LE10 . . . . 216 A5
Hose LE14 . . . . 20 F7
Kibworth Beauchamp
LE8. . . . . 206 A1
Lutterworth LE17. . . . . 244 C6
Stoke Golding CV13. . . . . . 196 D7
Syston LE7. . . . . 103 B4
Church Cnr NG13 . . . . 6 B4
Church Croft CV9 . . . . 171 B7
Church Cswy LE16 . . . . . . 225 C7
Church Ct PE9 . . . . 143 E2
Church Dr
Gilmorton LE17 . . . . 235 C4
Markfield LE67. . . . . 125 D8
Church End LE14 . . . . 19 D1
Church Farm La LE8 . . . . 220 D5
Church Field CV13. . . . . . 147 D8
Churchgate LE16 . . . . 209 D6
Church Gate
Kegworth DE74 . . . . 18 D2
Leicester LE1. . . . . 259 B4
Loughborough LE11. . . . . . . 52 B4
[1] Lutterworth LE17. . . . . 244 C5
Shepshed LE12 . . . . 50 C4
Churchgate Mews [3]
LE11. . . . . 52 B4
CHURCH GRESLEY 44 B2
Church Gresley Inf Sch
DE11 . . . . 44 B2
Church Hill
Bagworth LE67 . . . . 124 B4
Birstall LE4 . . . . 129 B6
Cranoe LE16 . . . . 208 E3
Knipton NG32 . . . . 14 E3
Scraptoft LE7 . . . . 156 F8
Swannington LE67 . . . . 71 B7
Tilton on t LE7 . . . . 133 C3
Woodhouse Eaves LE12. . . . 75 A1
Church Hill CE Jun Sch
LE4. . . . . 129 F7
Church Hill Inf Sch
LE4. . . . . 129 F7
Church Hill Rd
Cranoe LE16 . . . . 208 D3
Mountsorrel LE12. . . . . 76 D1
Thurmaston LE4. . . . . 129 F7
Church Ho CV9. . . . . 171 B7
Church House Mews
CV9. . . . . 171 B7
Churchill Cl
Ashby-de-la-Z LE65 . . . . . . 69 A6
Breaston DE72. . . . . 9 D8
Leicester, Oadby LE2 . . . . . 181 A5
Lutterworth LE17. . . . . 244 A5
Melton Mowbray LE13. . . . . 59 C5
Churchill Dr
Leicester Forest East
LE3 . . . . 153 B4
Upper Bruntingthorpe
LE17 . . . . 236 D5
Churchill Rd
Oakham LE15. . . . . 137 E6
Stamford PE9. . . . . 143 C5
Churchill St LE2. . . . . 155 B4
Churchill Way LE8 . . . . . . 223 A7
Church La
Ab Kettleby LE14 . . . . 37 C3
Anstey LE7. . . . . 127 D6
Arnesby LE8. . . . . 221 F5
Asfordby LE14 . . . . 57 F2
Ashby Folville LE14 . . . . . . 105 F4
Austrey CV9. . . . . 119 B1
Barrowden LE15 . . . . 191 F4
Barrow-u-S LE12 . . . . 76 D8
Barsby LE7. . . . . 105 D3
Billesdon LE7 . . . . 159 B5
Bisbrooke LE15 . . . . 189 F4
Bottesford NG13. . . . . 3 B3
Cadeby CV13 . . . . 149 D1
Caldecott LE16. . . . . 230 B8
Castle Donington DE74 . . . . 17 B3
Chilcote DE12 . . . . 91 E3
Church Langton LE16. . . . . 225 C7
Clipsham LE15. . . . . 89 D5
Croxton Kerrial NG32 . . . . 24 B2
Desford LE9 . . . . 151 B3
Duddington PE9 . . . . 193 B6
Dunton Bassett LE17. . . . . 219 D1
East Norton LE7. . . . . 186 C5
Eaton NG32 . . . . 22 F7
Edith Weston LE15. . . . . . . 166 B7
Fenny Drayton CV13 . . . . . 194 F6

Church La *continued*
Fleckney LE8 . . . . 222 F7
Frisby on t W LE14 . . . . 80 D8
Gaddesby LE7 . . . . 105 B6
Gilmorton LE17 . . . . 235 B4
Glaston LE15 . . . . 190 B6
Goadby LE7 . . . . 185 B2
Greetham LE15 . . . . 88 A2
Grimston LE14. . . . . 57 B8
Hemington DE74 . . . . 17 E4
Hoby LE14 . . . . 79 D7
Hungarton LE7 . . . . 132 C3
Husbands Bosworth
LE17 . . . . 247 E5
Leicester LE2. . . . . 180 B7
Leicester, Stoughton
LE2. . . . . 156 E1
Little Dalby LE14 . . . . 108 B8
Long Clawson LE14 . . . . . . 20 C3
Lyddington LE15 . . . . 212 D6
Manton LE15. . . . . 164 E6
Market Overton LE15. . . . . 86 F5
Morcott LE15. . . . . 191 A6
Muston NG13. . . . . 7 F8
Narborough LE19. . . . . 201 C8
No Man's Heath B79 . . . . . 119 A6
Old Dalby LE14 . . . . 35 E4
Osgathorpe LE12. . . . . 48 E4
Pilton LE15. . . . . 165 E2
Plungar NG13 . . . . 5 F1
Preston LE15 . . . . 164 C1
Quorn (Quorndon) LE12. . . 76 A6
Ratby LE6. . . . . 152 C8
Ratcliffe Culey CV9 . . . . . . 171 B3
Ratcliffe on t W LE7. . . . . . 78 C2
Ravenstone LE67 . . . . 70 E1
Rearsby LE7. . . . . 79 A2
Redmile NG13 . . . . 6 F3
Ridlington LE15 . . . . 163 D2
Saxelbye LE14 . . . . 57 E6
Seaton LE15. . . . . 190 C1
Sedgebrook NG32 . . . . 4 F1
Sewstern NG33 . . . . 63 F8
Shawell LE17 . . . . 253 C4
Shearsby LE17 . . . . 222 A3
Sheepy Magna CV9 . . . . . . 171 B7
Somerby LE14 . . . . 108 B1
South Kilworth LE17 . . . . . 255 C8
South Luffenham LE15. . . . 191 E8
South Witham NG33 . . . . . . 65 B3
Sproxton LE14 . . . . 41 F6
Stamford PE9. . . . . 143 E2
Stoney Stanton LE9 . . . . . . 199 E2
Swadlincote DE11. . . . . 44 B1
Swadlincote, Lower Midway
DE11 . . . . 44 C4
Swadlincote, Newhall
DE11 . . . . 44 A6
Swepstone LE67 . . . . 94 D2
Thurlaston LE9 . . . . 177 A3
Thurmaston LE4. . . . . 129 D7
Twycross CV9 . . . . 146 D6
Wing LE15. . . . . 165 A3
Worthington LE65 . . . . 47 F6
Wymeswold LE12. . . . . 33 C3
Church Terr
Barlestone CV13 . . . . 149 D8
Melton Mowbray LE13. . . . . 59 C3
CHURCH TOWN 70 C7
Church View
Bottesford NG13. . . . . 3 B3
Breaston DE72. . . . . 9 D7
Ibstock LE67 . . . . 122 E8
Narborough LE19. . . . . 201 C8
Newbold Verdon LE9 . . . . . 150 A4
Osgathorpe LE12. . . . . 48 E4
Twyford LE14. . . . . 106 D1
Churchward Ave LE4. . . . 128 D4
CHURCH WILNE 9 B4
Church Wlk
Blaby LE8. . . . . 202 B8
Bruntingthorpe LE17 . . . . . 236 C8
Donisthorpe DE12 . . . . 92 E8
Hinckley LE10 . . . . 215 D8
Hose LE14 . . . . 20 F7
Little Dalby LE14 . . . . 83 B1
Lubenham LE16 . . . . 239 F3
Market Harborough
LE16 . . . . 241 A2
Shackerstone CV13 . . . . . . 121 E2
Thorpe Satchville LE14 . . . 106 E4
Church Wlks CV13. . . . . . 196 D7
Cider Cl LE15. . . . . 191 F5
Cinder La CV9. . . . . 145 A8
Circle The LE5. . . . . 155 C6
Citrus Gr DE74. . . . . 18 C3
City Hts [5] LE1. . . . . 52 B4
City Of Dan LE67 . . . . 71 F4
City of Leicester Coll The
LE5. . . . . 156 C3
City Of Three Waters
LE1. . . . . 71 E6
City Rd LE14 . . . . 12 F3
City The
Blackfordby DE11. . . . . 45 A2
Kibworth Beauchamp
LE8. . . . . 206 A2
Woodville LE12 . . . . 44 F1
City Yd LE15. . . . . 165 A2
Civic Way DE11. . . . . 44 B4
Claire Ct LE12. . . . . 77 E3
Clamp Dr DE11. . . . . 44 B3
Clapgun St DE74. . . . . 17 B3
Clare Cl PE9. . . . . 143 C3
Clarefield Rd LE3 . . . . . . 154 B5
Clare Gr LE3 . . . . 153 D2
Claremont Dr
Market Harborough
LE16 . . . . 241 A3

Claremont Dr continued
Ravenstone LE67 . . . . .70 F2
Claremont St LE4 . . . . 129 A3
Clarence Ct 5 LE10 . . . . . 215 E8
Clarence Dr LE67 . . . . .96 F8
Clarence Rd
Hinckley LE10 . . . . 215 E8
Long Eaton NG10 . . . . .10 C6
Narborough LE19 . . . . 178 D2
Clarence St
Leicester LE1 . . . . .259 B4
Loughborough LE11 . . . . .52 C5
Market Harborough
LE16 . . . . .240 F3
Clarendon Bsns Pk
LE2 . . . . 155 A1
Clarendon Ct LE2 . . . . 155 B2
Clarendon Ho LE10 . . . . . . 215 B7
CLARENDON PARK 155 B1
Clarendon Park Rd
LE2 . . . . 155 B1
Clarendon Rd LE10 . . . . . . 215 C7
Clarendon St LE2 . . . . 259 A2
Claresholm Cres
LE15 . . . . 138 B6
Claridge Pl 4 LE65 . . . . . . .69 B6
Clark Dr LE13 . . . . .59 C6
Clarke Cl LE67 . . . . .71 F4
Clarke Dr NG10 . . . . .10 A4
Clarke Gr LE4 . . . . 129 A6
Clarke Rd LE67 . . . . .97 C8
Clarkes Dale LE16 . . . . 229 D6
Clarkes La DE72 . . . . .16 B8
Clarke Rd LE18 . . . . 180 B2
Clarke St
Leicester LE4 . . . . 129 B3
Market Harborough
LE16 . . . . .240 D3
Clark Gdns LE8 . . . . 202 A8
Clatterpot La LE15 . . . . 112 C8
Clawson Cl LE11 . . . . .51 D6
Clawson La
Ab Kettleby LE14 . . . . .37 D4
Hickling LE14 . . . . .19 D7
Long Clawson LE14 . . . . . . .21 C1
Upper Broughton LE14 . . . . . 19 E1
Claxton Rise LE14 . . . . .20 C2
Claybrook Ave LE3 . . . . . . 179 A8
Claybrooke Ct LE17 . . . . . 232 F5
CLAYBROOKE MAGNA
 . . . . 232 D6
CLAYBROOKE PARVA
 . . . . 232 F4
Claybrooke Prim Sch
LE17 . . . . 232 E4
Clay Cl DE11 . . . . .44 D5
Claydon Rd LE5 . . . . 155 E8
Claye St NG10 . . . . .10 E7
Clay La
Ellistown LE67 . . . . .96 E2
Gretton NN17 . . . . 213 B1
Peggs Green LE67 . . . . .71 A8
Claymar Dr DE11 . . . . .44 A7
Claymill Rd LE4 . . . . 129 F4
Clay St
Draycott DE72 . . . . .9 A7
Wymeswold LE12 . . . . .33 C3
Clayton Dr LE4 . . . . 129 F6
Clear View Cres LE9 . . . . . 175 F1
Cleeve Mount LE11 . . . . .51 C4
Clematis Cl LE4 . . . . 128 A5
Clement Ave LE4 . . . . 129 A3
Clements Gate DE74 . . . . . .28 D6
Clevedon Cres LE4 . . . . . . 155 E8
Cleveland Ave
Draycott DE72 . . . . .9 A7
Long Eaton NG10 . . . . .10 F8
Cleveland Cl DE11 . . . . .44 B3
Cleveland Rd
Hinckley LE10 . . . . 215 C8
Loughborough LE11 . . . . .74 F7
Wigston LE18 . . . . 180 D3
Cleveleys Ave LE3 . . . . . . 179 A8
Cliff Ave LE11 . . . . .51 F5
Cliff Cres PE9 . . . . 143 D3
Cliffe Hill Rd LE67 . . . . .98 A1
Cliffe House Mews
LE8 . . . . 201 F8
Cliffe La LE67 . . . . .98 B2
Cliffe Rd
Birstall LE4 . . . . 128 F6
Easton o t H PE9 . . . . 169 A3
Clifford Cl NG10 . . . . .10 A4
Clifford Rd LE11 . . . . .51 F5
Clifford St
Leicester LE3 . . . . 154 D6
Long Eaton NG10 . . . . .10 E7
Wigston LE18 . . . . 179 F1
Cliff Rd
Stamford PE9 . . . . 143 D3
Woolsthorpe By N NG32 . . . .8 C1
Cliffwood Ave LE4 . . . . . . 128 F7
Clifton Ave
Ashby-de-la-Z LE65 . . . . . . .69 B8
Long Eaton NG10 . . . . .10 F7
Clifton Cl
Overseal DE12 . . . . .67 A3
Swadlincote DE11 . . . . .44 A2
Clifton Ct
Hinckley LE10 . . . . 197 B1
Oakham LE15 . . . . 137 F6
Clifton Dr
Ashby-de-la-Z LE65 . . . . . . .69 A7
Wigston LE18 . . . . 180 A1

Clifton Rd
Leicester LE2 . . . . 179 F8
Netherseal DE12 . . . . .91 D6
Cliftonthorpe LE65 . . . . .46 B1
Clifton Thorpe Mdws
LE65 . . . . .46 B1
CLIFTON UPON
DUNSMORE 257 A6
Clifton Way LE10 . . . . 197 A1
Clink La LE67 . . . . .71 A4
Clint Hill Dr LE9 . . . . 199 E3
Clipper Rd LE4 . . . . 129 F3
CLIPSHAM 89 E5
Clipsham Rd
Castle Bytham LE33 . . . . . . .90 B7
Stretton LE15 . . . . .89 A7
Clipsham Woods Nature
Trail* LE15 . . . . .89 E7
CLIPSTON 250 A1
Clipstone Cl LE18 . . . . 180 C2
Clipstone Gdns LE18 . . . . 180 C2
Clipstone Ho 2 LE2 . . . . . 155 B5
Clipston La LE16 . . . . 250 E3
Clipston Rd
East Farndon LE16 . . . . 250 B4
Great Oxendon LE16 . . . . . 250 D2
Clipston St LE16 . . . . 240 F1
Clivesway LE10 . . . . 215 A8
Clock House Ct LE15 . . . . 137 D8
Clock Tower Mall 7
LE1 .259 B4
Cloisters The LE9 . . . . 198 E8
Close The
Anstey LE7 . . . . 127 D7
Barwell LE9 . . . . 198 B7
Blaby LE8 . . . . 179 B1
Burton Lazars LE14 . . . . . . .82 F6
Easton o n H PE9 . . . . 168 F4
Kirkby Mallory LE9 . . . . 175 D6
Narborough LE9 . . . . 178 A2
Ratby LE6 . . . . 126 C1
Stamford PE9 . . . . 143 F4
Swadlincote DE11 . . . . .67 D8
Swinford LE17 . . . . 254 B4
CLOUDESLEY BUSH 231 E1
Cloud Hill View LE67 . . . . .47 E3
Cloud Lea LE12 . . . . 101 E8
Cloudsley Bush La
LE10 . . . . 231 A5
Cloud Way Ct LE11 . . . . . . .52 A6
Clovelly Rd
Glenfield LE3 . . . . 153 D8
Leicester LE5 . . . . 155 F4
Clover Cl LE19 . . . . 201 A8
Cloverdale DE11 . . . . .44 B7
Cloverdale Rd LE5 . . . . . . 130 C3
Clover Dr LE13 . . . . .82 B8
Cloverfield LE10 . . . . 197 C3
Clover Gdns PE9 . . . . 142 E4
Clover La LE12 . . . . .76 F1
Clover Pk Trad Est
LE10 . . . . 197 B3
Clover Pl LE67 . . . . .71 D8
Clover Way LE67 . . . . 103 A2
Clover Wlk LE7 . . . . 103 E7
Clowbridge Dr LE11 . . . . . .51 C1
Clumber Cl
Loughborough LE11 . . . . .75 A6
Syston LE7 . . . . 103 B5
Clumber Ct LE6 . . . . 152 D7
Clumber Rd LE18 . . . . 155 E6
Clumber St
Long Eaton NG10 . . . . .10 E7
Melton Mowbray LE13 . . . . .59 B4
Clun Wlk NN17 . . . . 230 C1
Clutsom Rd LE67 . . . . .96 C7
Clwyd Wlk NN17 . . . . 230 C1
Clyde Ct LE67 . . . . .71 E8
Clydesdale Cl LE13 . . . . . . .59 A6
Clyde St LE1 . . . . 259 C4
Coach Ho LE15 . . . . 187 D7
Coachhouse Mews 4
DE11 . . . . .44 A7
Coachmans Ct LE12 . . . . . .50 C5
Coachouse Ct LE11 . . . . . . .52 B3
Coach Rd LE12 . . . . .50 D3
Coal Baulk LE7 . . . . 132 B3
Coalbourn Cl LE4 . . . . 128 E4
Coales Ave LE8 . . . . 202 A5
Coales Gdns LE16 . . . . 240 D5
Coalfield Way LE65 . . . . . . .69 E6
Coal La
Hartshorne DE11,
DE12 . . . . .45 D8
Hose LE14 . . . . .20 F8
Coal Pit La
Cloudesley Bush
CV23 . . . . 231 F1
Willey CV23 . . . . 242 C6
COALVILLE 96 D7
Coalville Bsns Pk LE67 . . .71 C1
Coalville Com Hospl
LE67 . . . . .72 A1
Coalville Cotts PE9 . . . . . 143 E4
Coalville La LE67 . . . . .71 A1
Coatbridge Ave LE4 . . . . . 129 D4
Coates Ave LE3 . . . . 154 A7
Cobbett Rd LE3 . . . . 153 D2
Cobden Ho LE11 . . . . .52 C4
Cobden Prim Sch LE11 . . .52 C4
Cobden St
Leicester LE1 . . . . 155 B7
Long Eaton NG10 . . . . .10 E7
Loughborough LE11 . . . . .52 C4
Cobden Street Ind Est
LE1 . . . . 155 B7
Cobleas NG32 . . . . .15 B7
Cobwells Cl LE8 . . . . 223 A7

Cockcharme Gapp
DE74 . . . . .17 B6
Cock La CV9 . . . . 120 A2
Cockleys NG10 . . . . .10 C6
Cockshut La DE73 . . . . .26 A8
Cockshut Lane Bsns Ctr
DE73 . . . . .26 A7
Coe Ave LE11 . . . . .51 B5
Cokayne Rd LE3 . . . . 153 D6
Colbert Dr LE3 . . . . 179 A7
Colby Dr LE4 . . . . 130 A6
Colby Rd LE4 . . . . 129 F5
Colchester Rd LE5 . . . . . . 156 B7
COLD NEWTON 133 B1
COLD OVERTON 109 C1
Cold Overton Rd
Knossington LE15 . . . . 136 B7
Langham LE15 . . . . 110 B2
Oakham LE15 . . . . 137 D6
Coldstream Cl LE10 . . . . . 197 A1
Colebrook Cl LE5 . . . . 155 E3
Coleford Rd LE4 . . . . 130 A5
Coleman Cl LE5 . . . . 155 F7
Coleman Ct LE5 . . . . 155 F7
Coleman Prim Sch
LE5 . . . . 155 C4
Coleman Rd
Fleckney LE8 . . . . 204 E1
Leicester LE5 . . . . 156 A5
COLEORTON 70 E8
Coleorton Hall LE67 . . . . . .70 C7
Coleorton La LE65 . . . . .69 D3
COLEORTON MOOR 70 E5
Coleridge Dr LE19 . . . . . . 178 A2
Coles Cl LE4 . . . . 130 C3
Coles Lo LE15 . . . . 215 D7
Colgrove Rd LE11 . . . . .52 A2
Colindale Ave LE4 . . . . 129 A8
Colin Grundy Dr LE5 . . . . 130 B1
Collaton Rd LE18 . . . . 180 C1
College Ave
Leicester LE2 . . . . 155 B4
Melton Mowbray LE13 . . . . .82 C8
College Cl
Coalville LE67 . . . . .96 C8
Great Casterton PE9 . . . . . 142 E7
Oakham LE15 . . . . 137 F7
College Farm La
LE15 . . . . 187 D8
College Hall LE10 . . . . 180 C8
College Ho LE18 . . . . 202 A8
College La LE10 . . . . 197 E1
College Rd
Sutton Bonington LE12 . . . .30 A8
Syston LE7 . . . . 103 B3
Whetstone LE8 . . . . 202 A8
College St
Leicester LE2 . . . . 155 B4
Ullesthorpe LE17 . . . . 233 B4
Collett Rd LE4 . . . . 128 C4
Collier Row LE19 . . . . 212 C7
Colliers Way LE67 . . . . .96 E2
Colliery Rd DE11 . . . . .44 A1
Colliery Row DE11 . . . . .44 A1
Colling Cl LE11 . . . . .51 B6
Collingham Rd LE3 . . . . . . 154 C1
Collingwood Cl LE13 . . . . .58 F3
Collingwood Cres LE13 . . .58 F3
Collingwood Dr LE12 . . . . .77 D4
Collingwood Rd NG10 . . . .10 E6
Collin Pl LE4 . . . . 129 C2
Collins Cl LE3 . . . . 153 D2
Collyns Way PE9 . . . . 168 D2
COLLYWESTON 168 D2
Colne Cl
Corby NN17 . . . . 230 C1
Leicester, Oadby LE2 . . . . 181 D5
Colonel's La LE14 . . . . .19 A1
Colsterdale Cl LE4 . . . . . . 128 D5
Colsterworth Rd
Skillington NG33 . . . . .43 C7
Stainby NG33 . . . . .43 F3
COLSTON BASSETT 11 A6
Colston La LE14 . . . . .11 E4
Coltbeck Ave LE19 . . . . . . 201 A7
Coltfoot Way LE13 . . . . .82 A8
Colthurst Way LE5 . . . . . . 156 A6
Colton St LE1 . . . . 259 C3
Colts Cl LE10 . . . . 215 D4
Coltsfoot Cl DE11 . . . . .44 F4
Coltsfoot Rd LE5 . . . . 130 C2
Coltsfoot Way LE9 . . . . . . 219 A4
Columbia Cl LE9 . . . . 178 A3
Columbine Cl LE13 . . . . . . .59 A6
Columbine Rd LE5 . . . . . . 130 B3
Colwell Rd LE3 . . . . 153 F3
Combe Cl LE3 . . . . 154 C8
Comet Cl LE3 . . . . 154 B7
Comet Way LE67 . . . . .71 D2
Commerce St DE73 . . . . . . .26 A7
Commercial Sq LE1 . . . . . 154 F1
Common Rd DE11 . . . . .44 C2
Common Side DE11 . . . . . . .44 C2
Common The
Barwell LE9 . . . . 198 B5
Leicester LE5 . . . . 156 A3
Compass Rd LE8 . . . . 156 D7
Compton Ave DE72 . . . . . . .16 A8
Compton Cl LE11 . . . . .74 C8
Compton Dr LE9 . . . . 200 D8
Compton Rd LE3 . . . . 154 C2
Conaglen Rd LE2 . . . . 179 B6
Condon Rd LE12 . . . . .76 B4
Conduit Cl LE19 . . . . 218 F7
Conduit Rd PE9 . . . . 143 E4
Conduit St LE2 . . . . 259 C3
Cone La LE15 . . . . 155 C3
Coneries The LE11 . . . . . . .52 B4

Conery La LE19 . . . . 178 A4
Coneygrey LE8 . . . . 204 F1
CONGERSTONE 147 D7
Congerstone La
Barton in t B CV13 . . . . 122 B1
Carlton CV13 . . . . 148 C6
Shackerstone CV13 . . . . . . 121 C1
Congerstone Prim Sch
CV13 . . . . 147 D8
Congerstone Rd
LE3 . . . . 148 A6
Conifer Cl
4 Leicester LE2 . . . . 155 C4
Lutterworth LE17 . . . . 244 B6
Coninsby Cl LE13 . . . . 154 B1
Coniston Ave LE2 . . . . 259 A1
Coniston Cl LE9 . . . . 198 F8
Coniston Cres LE11 . . . . . .51 D1
Coniston Gdns LE65 . . . . . .69 C5
Coniston Rd
Barrow-u-S LE12 . . . . .76 D8
Edith Weston LE15 . . . . . . 166 A7
Melton Mowbray LE13 . . . . .59 A6
Coniston Way LE9 . . . . . . 200 D4
Conkers Discovery Ctr*
DE12 . . . . .67 D5
Conkers Waterside Ctr*
DE12 . . . . .67 D4
Connaught Ho LE11 . . . . . .52 B3
Connaught Rd LE16 . . . . . 240 F4
Connaught St LE2 . . . . 155 B4
Connell Cl LE16 . . . . 239 F3
Constable Ave LE4 . . . . . . 155 B8
Constable Rd CV21 . . . . . 257 B1
Constables (Uppingham
Sch) LE15 . . . . 189 A4
Constance Rd LE5 . . . . . . 155 D5
Constitution Hill LE1 . . . . 259 C3
Convent Cl LE13 . . . . .59 B2
Convent Dr LE67 . . . . .96 D8
Conway Cl LE11 . . . . .51 C5
Conway Dr
Melton Mowbray LE13 . . . . .59 C5
Shepshed LE12 . . . . .49 F2
Conway Rd
Leicester LE2 . . . . 155 D3
Long Eaton NG10 . . . . .10 F8
Mountsorrel LE12 . . . . .76 D1
Conway St NG10 . . . . .10 F8
Conway Wlk NN17 . . . . . . 230 D1
Cooch's Ct 6 PE9 . . . . . . 143 D2
Cooden Ave LE3 . . . . 154 B4
Cooke Cl
Braunstone Town
LE3 . . . . 153 D2
Thurmaston LE4 . . . . 129 F7
Cooke's Dr LE9 . . . . 218 E6
Cooks Dr DE74 . . . . .17 A3
Cooks La
Sapcote LE9 . . . . 217 D7
Wigston LE18 . . . . 203 F7
Cookson Pl LE11 . . . . .51 C6
Cookson Rd LE4 . . . . 130 A5
Cook's Wlk LE3 . . . . 153 C8
Coombe Cl LE12 . . . . .50 C2
Coombe Pl LE2 . . . . 181 B4
Coombe Rise LE2 . . . . 181 C3
Co-operative St LE19 . . . 178 B3
Co-operative St NG10 . . . .10 E6
Cooper Cl
Huncote LE9 . . . . 200 E8
Leicester LE2 . . . . 179 C6
Whitwick LE67 . . . . .71 D5
Cooper Ct LE11 . . . . .52 D2
Cooper Gdns LE2 . . . . 181 C6
Cooper La LE6 . . . . 152 D8
Coopers Cl DE12 . . . . .92 B7
Cooper's La LE17 . . . . 219 D2
Cooper's Nook LE7 . . . . . . 103 D7
Copdale Rd LE5 . . . . 155 E5
Cope Dale Cl CV13 . . . . . . 149 C8
Copeland Ave LE3 . . . . . . 128 A1
Copeland Cres LE11 . . . . . .51 D5
Copeland Rd LE4 . . . . 128 F6
Copestake Cl NG10 . . . . . .10 A7
Cophills Cl LE12 . . . . .93 C4
Copinger Rd LE2 . . . . 179 F7
Copley Cl LE13 . . . . .59 E4
Coplow Ave LE5 . . . . 155 E2
Coplow Cres LE7 . . . . 103 A2
Coplow La LE7 . . . . 159 A4
Coppice Cl
Hinckley LE10 . . . . 197 F3
Ravenstone LE67 . . . . .71 A2
Coppice Ct LE4 . . . . 130 A7
Coppice Ho DE11 . . . . .44 E1
Coppice La
Newton Regis B79 . . . . 118 A8
Queniborough LE7 . . . . . . 103 F5
Coppice Rd PE9 . . . . 116 E2
Coppice Side DE11 . . . . . . .44 C3
Coppice The
Atherstone CV9 . . . . 194 A6
Countesthorpe LE8 . . . . . 202 E4
Hinckley LE10 . . . . 215 F8
Markfield LE67 . . . . 125 E8
Narborough LE19 . . . . 201 A8
Quorn (Quorndon) LE12 . . .76 B4
Thurmaston LE4 . . . . 130 A7
Coppice Wlk LE10 . . . . . . 197 F3
Copse Cl
Coalville LE67 . . . . .96 C7
Leicester Forest East
LE3 . . . . 152 F1
Long Eaton NG10 . . . . .10 B8

Copse Cl continued
Leicester, Oadby LE2 . . . . 181 C7
Copse Gr LE11 . . . . .75 A6
Copse Rise DE11 . . . . .44 B7
Copseside Cl 8 NG10 . . . .10 A8
Copse The LE7 . . . . 157 B4
Copsey Croft Ct NG10 . . . .10 F7
Copson St LE67 . . . . .96 A1
Copston La LE10 . . . . 231 B5
COPSTON MAGNA 231 C5
Copthall Ho LE18 . . . . 179 F3
Copthill Sch PE9 . . . . 144 F3
Copthorne Cl LE13 . . . . . . 153 D6
COPT OAK 98 C6
Copt Oak Rd
Copt Oak LE67 . . . . .98 B5
Narborough LE19 . . . . 200 F8
Narborough LE19 . . . . 201 A8
Corah Cl LE17 . . . . 157 A8
Corah St LE3 . . . . 259 A3
Coral Cl LE10 . . . . 215 F4
Coral St LE4 . . . . 129 A1
Corbet Cl LE4 . . . . 128 B3
CORBY 230 C2
Corby Rd LE16 . . . . 229 D1
Cordelia Cl LE5 . . . . 155 E8
Cordell Rd LE11 . . . . .51 D6
Cordery Rd LE5 . . . . 156 B3
Cordhill La LE14 . . . . .85 D7
Cordle Way LE15 . . . . .86 F5
Cordonnier Ct LE19 . . . . . 219 A4
Cordwell Cl DE74 . . . . .16 F3
Corfield Rise LE3 . . . . 153 E3
Coriander Rd LE2 . . . . 154 D4
Cork Ho LE2 . . . . 179 A2
Cork La LE2 . . . . 179 A2
Corkscrew La
Ashby-de-la-Z LE65 . . . . . . .69 F5
Coleorton LE67 . . . . .70 A6
Cork St LE5 . . . . 155 C5
Cornfield LE10 . . . . 197 C4
Cornfield Cl LE19 . . . . 201 C7
Cornfields LE2 . . . . 182 D5
Cornflower Cl PE9 . . . . . . 142 E4
Cornhall Bldgs 5
PE9 . . . . 143 E3
Cornwall Bsns Ctr
LE18 . . . . 179 F2
Cornwallis Ave LE4 . . . . . 128 B2
Cornwallis Cl NG10 . . . . . .10 C6
Cornwall Pl LE13 . . . . .82 C8
Cornwall Rd
Leicester LE4 . . . . 128 D1
Stamford PE9 . . . . 143 D4
Wigston LE18 . . . . 179 F2
Cornwall St LE19 . . . . 178 B3
Cornwall Way LE10 . . . . . 197 B4
Coronation Ave
Broughton Astley LE9 . . . . 218 E6
Long Clawson LE14 . . . . . . .20 B2
Moira DE12 . . . . .68 B6
Wigston LE18 . . . . 180 D2
Coronation Ct DE73 . . . . . .26 B8
Coronation Cotts LE9 . . . 199 D3
Coronation La DE12 . . . . . .92 F6
Coronation Rd LE9 . . . . . . 198 D7
Coronation St
Overseal DE12 . . . . .67 A4
Swadlincote DE11 . . . . .44 A5
Coronet Cl LE7 . . . . 127 E6
Corporation Rd LE4 . . . . . 128 F2
Corshaw Wlk LE5 . . . . 155 D8
Cort Cres LE3 . . . . 153 E3
Corydalis Cl LE11 . . . . .75 A6
COSBY 201 C3
Cosby La LE8, LE9 . . . . . . 220 B5
Cosby Prim Sch LE9 . . . . 201 C3
Cosby Rd
Broughton Astley LE9 . . . . 219 A8
Countesthorpe LE8 . . . . . 202 B3
Littlethorpe LE19 . . . . 201 C6
Cosford La
Rugby CV21 . . . . 252 A3
Rugby CV23 . . . . 252 A2
COSSINGTON 102 C8
Cossington CE Prim Sch
LE7 . . . . 102 C8
Cossington La
Rothley LE7 . . . . 102 A6
Syston LE7 . . . . 103 A2
Cossington Rd LE12 . . . . . .77 C2
Cossington St LE4 . . . . . . 129 B1
Costalot Stables LE67 . . . 124 A3
Costello Cl LE67 . . . . .95 F3
COSTON 41 D1
Coston Rd
Buckminster NG33 . . . . .42 D2
Garthorpe LE14 . . . . .62 A7
Sproxton LE14 . . . . .41 F5
COTES 52 F6
COTESBACH 244 A1
Cotes Dr LE11 . . . . .52 B6
Cotes Rd
Barrow-u-S LE12 . . . . .53 B3
Hinckley LE10 . . . . 215 F5
Cotes Yd LE11 . . . . .52 C5
Cothelstone Ave LE11 . . . .51 C5
Cotley Cres LE15 . . . . .87 E2
Cotley Rd LE4 . . . . 130 A5
Cotman Dr LE10 . . . . 197 A3
Coton Park Dr CV23 . . . . 252 C1
Coton Rd
Churchover CV23 . . . . 252 C5
Rugby CV21 . . . . 257 A1
Cotsmore Cl LE67 . . . . .95 F2
Cotswold Ave LE9 . . . . . . 201 E2
Cotswold Cl
2 Long Eaton NG10 . . . . .10 B8

Cotswold Cl continued
Loughborough LE11 . . . . . . .51 D3
Melton Mowbray LE13 . . . . .82 D8
Swadlincote DE11 . . . . .44 A3
Cotswold Gn LE4 . . . . 128 D5
Cotswold St LE15 . . . . .87 D2
Cotswold Way LE65 . . . . . . .69 B5
Cotswold Wlk LE15 . . . . . 137 D6
Cottage Cl
Ratby LE6 . . . . 126 D1
Swadlincote DE11 . . . . .44 A7
Cottage Farm Cl
Braunstone Town LE3 . . . . 178 F6
Osgathorpe LE12 . . . . .48 E4
Cottage Gardens Cl
LE12 .30 A1
Cottage Gdns
Earl Shilton LE9 . . . . 198 F8
Hartshill Green CV10 . . . . . 194 B2
Cottage Homes LE2 . . . . . 181 A7
Cottage La
Broughton Astley LE9 . . . . 219 B6
Desford LE9 . . . . 151 B4
Markfield LE67 . . . . .98 C3
Norton-J-T CV9 . . . . 120 A4
Cottage Lane Ind Est
LE9 . . . . 219 A6
Cottage Rd LE18 . . . . 180 E1
Cottage Row LE18 . . . . . . 179 B8
Cottagers Cl LE2 . . . . 179 F5
Cottesbrooke Cl LE18 . . . . 180 D2
COTTESMORE 112 D8
Cottesmore Ave
Leicester, Oadby LE2 . . . . . 181 D4
Melton Mowbray LE13 . . . . .59 B3
Cottesmore Dr LE11 . . . . . .74 F8
Cottesmore Prim Sch
LE15 . . . . .87 E3
Cottesmore Rd
Ashwell LE15 . . . . 111 C8
Burley LE15 . . . . 111 F2
Cottesmore LE15 . . . . .87 E2
Exton LE15 . . . . 112 E4
Leicester LE5 . . . . 155 D7
Stamford PE9 . . . . 143 A3
Uppingham LE15 . . . . 189 A4
COTTINGHAM 229 C1
Cottingham CE Prim Sch
LE16 . . . . 229 C1
Cottingham Rd LE16 . . . . . 230 A4
Cotton Cl
Broughton Astley LE9 . . . . 219 A5
Leicester LE4 . . . . 129 D5
Cotton Croft LE12 . . . . .50 B2
Cotton Ct LE9 . . . . 198 F8
Cotton Mews LE9 . . . . 198 F7
Cottons The LE16 . . . . 230 B4
Cotton Way LE11 . . . . .51 E2
Coulson Cl LE8 . . . . 202 A6
Coulter Cl LE7 . . . . 156 F8
Council Hos
Claybrooke Magna
LE17 . . . . 232 C6
Essendine PE9 . . . . 117 B6
Council Ho's LE16 . . . . 250 B8
Council Rd LE10 . . . . 197 D1
Council St LE17 . . . . 244 C6
COUNTESTHORPE 202 D3
Countesthorpe Com Coll
LE8 . . . . 202 C3
Countesthorpe Rd
Countesthorpe LE8,
LE18 . . . . 202 F7
Whetstone LE8, LE9 . . . . . 201 E2
Wigston LE18 . . . . 179 F1
Counting House Rd
LE2 . . . . 154 F2
Country Bridge Mobile
Home Pk LE12 . . . . .30 A3
Countryman Mews
LE16 . . . . 241 A5
Countrymans Way
LE12 . . . . .50 C5
Countryman's Way
LE7 . . . . 103 E8
Countryman Way
LE67 . . . . 125 E8
Court 22 LE65 . . . . .69 C6
Court Cl LE9 . . . . 152 E5
Courtenay Rd LE3 . . . . 154 C8
Court La NN6 . . . . 256 D3
Court Rd
Glen Parva LE2 . . . . 179 B2
Thurnby LE7 . . . . 156 F4
Court St DE11 . . . . .44 E3
Courtyard The
Coalville LE67 . . . . .71 D2
Lockington DE74 . . . . .17 F4
Stamford PE9 . . . . 143 C3
Stoke Golding CV13 . . . . . 196 C7
Waltham on t W LE14 . . . . .40 A7
Courtyard Workshops
LE16 . . . . 240 E1
Coventry Cl DE11 . . . . .44 D6
Coventry Rd
Broughton Astley LE9 . . . . 218 D7
Croft LE9 . . . . 200 D3
Hinckley LE10 . . . . 215 B7
Hinckley, Sketchley Hill
LE10 . . . . 215 F5
Lutterworth LE17 . . . . 244 B5
Market Harborough
LE16 . . . . 240 D3
Narborough LE19 . . . . 201 B7
Pailton CV23 . . . . 242 A1
Sapcote LE9 . . . . 218 B7
Sharnford LE10 . . . . 217 B3
Willey LE17 . . . . 243 D5

Coventry St 6 LE3 . . . . . 154 D5
Coverack Wlk LE5 . . . . 156 A4
Coverdale LE67 . . . . .71 E6
Coverdale Rd LE18 . . . . . . 180 F1
Coverley Rd NG33 . . . . .65 B4
Coverside Rd NG8 . . . . 182 C1
Covert Cl
Leicester, Oadby LE2 . . . . . 181 C6
Syston LE7 . . . . 102 E3
Covert La LE7 . . . . 157 B8
Covert Pl DE11 . . . . .67 C8
Covert The LE7 . . . . 103 D8
Covett Way LE3 . . . . 153 E5
Cowdall Rd LE3 . . . . 153 E3
Cowdray Cl LE11 . . . . .52 A1
Cow La
Ratby LE6 . . . . 125 F2
Whissendine LE15 . . . . .84 F1
Cowley Way LE5 . . . . 156 E7
Cowman Cl LE14 . . . . .58 A3
Cowper Rd LE10 . . . . 215 D6
Cow Row NG33 . . . . .42 D2
Cowslip Cl
Donisthorpe DE12 . . . . .67 E1
Narborough LE19 . . . . 200 F8
Cowslip Dr LE13 . . . . .82 A8
Cowslip Mdw DE72 . . . . . . .9 A7
Cox Dr NG13 . . . . .2 F3
Cox's La LE15 . . . . 135 B4
Crabtree Cl DE74 . . . . .17 A2
Crabtree Cnr LE2 . . . . 180 A5
Crabtree Rd
Barwell LE9 . . . . 197 F5
Skillington NG33 . . . . .43 C6
Crackbottle Rd LE7 . . . . . . 186 B3
Crackthorne Dr CV23 . . . . 252 D1
Cradock Dr LE12 . . . . .75 F5
Cradock Rd LE2 . . . . 155 B2
Cradock St
Leicester LE1 . . . . 155 B6
Loughborough LE11 . . . . . . .52 B4
Crafton St E LE1 . . . . 259 C4
Crafton St W LE1 . . . . 259 C4
Craftsmans Way LE1 . . . . 103 D7
Cragdale LE67 . . . . .71 D7
Craig Gdns LE3 . . . . 153 D6
Craighill Rd LE2 . . . . 180 B8
Craig St NG10 . . . . .10 E7
Cramant Cotts LE1 . . . . . . 259 B2
Crammond Cl LE10 . . . . . . 215 B8
Cramps Cl LE12 . . . . .76 D7
Cranberry Cl LE1 . . . . 153 D2
Cranbourne Gdns
LE2 . . . . 181 B8
Cranbrook Rd LE7 . . . . 156 F6
Craneley Ct 2 LE5 . . . . . . 130 C3
Crane-Ley Rd LE6 . . . . 126 E3
Cranesbill Rd LE5 . . . . 130 C1
Crane St LE1 . . . . 259 B5
Cranfield Rd LE2 . . . . 179 D6
Cranfleet Way NG10 . . . . . .10 B7
Cranmer Cl LE8 . . . . 202 A6
Cranmer Dr LE7 . . . . 102 E3
Cranmere Rd LE13 . . . . . . .59 C5
Cranmer La LE17 . . . . 246 F3
Cranmer St
Leicester LE3 . . . . 154 D4
Long Eaton NG10 . . . . .10 D8
CRANOE 208 D3
Cranoe Rd
Glooston LE16 . . . . 208 C4
Slawston Wyville LE16,
LE8 . . . . 207 D2
Cransley Cl LE5 . . . . 130 C3
Cranstone Cres LE3 . . . . . 153 C7
Crantock Cl LE5 . . . . 156 D3
Cranwell Cl LE5 . . . . 156 B2
Craven Cl LE11 . . . . .74 F7
Craven's Rough LE67 . . . . .99 B4
Craven St
Leicester LE1 . . . . 259 A5
Melton Mowbray LE13 . . . . .59 C1
Crawford Cl LE3 . . . . 154 B6
Crawford Ho LE18 . . . . . . 180 B3
Crawshaw Cl LE12 . . . . . . .29 C3
Craxford Rd NN17 . . . . 213 B1
Crayburn Ho LE3 . . . . 154 A8
Crayford Way LE5 . . . . 130 D1
Craythorne Cl DE11 . . . . . .44 A7
Craythorne Way LE18 . . . . 180 F2
Creaton Cl LE12 . . . . 180 E2
Creaton Rd LE18 . . . . 180 E2
Crediton Cl LE18 . . . . 203 D8
Crescent Cl LE16 . . . . 240 F4
Crescent Ho LE17 . . . . 244 C8
Crescent Jun Sch
LE3 . . . . 153 C4
Crescent Rd
Coalville LE67 . . . . .96 C7
Lutterworth LE17 . . . . 244 C7
Crescent St LE1 . . . . 259 B2
Crescent The
Allington NG32 . . . . .4 F4
Asfordby LE14 . . . . .58 A3
Blaby LE0 . . . . 202 B7
Breaston DE72 . . . . .9 F8
Breedon on t H DE73 . . . . .26 E2
Easton o t H PE9 . . . . 168 F5
Elmesthorpe LE9 . . . . 198 D5
Great Glen LE8 . . . . 205 B8
Ketton PE9 . . . . 168 A7
Leicester LE3 . . . . 259 B2
Market Harborough
LE16 . . . . 240 F4
Melton Mowbray LE13 . . . . .59 B4
Mountsorrel LE12 . . . . 101 D4
Old Dalby LE14 . . . . .36 B6
Pickwell LE14 . . . . 108 C3

Crescent The continued
Ryhall PE9 . . . . 117 A2
Saltby LE14 . . . . .24 E1
Stathern LE14 . . . . .13 A2
Wigston LE18 . . . . 180 C4
Cressida Ct LE3 . . . . 153 E2
Cressida Pl LE3 . . . . 153 E2
Cresswell Cl LE4 . . . . 130 A6
Cresswell Dr LE15 . . . . . . 112 C8
Cresswell The LE8 . . . . . . 201 F8
Creswell Dr LE67 . . . . .98 D8
Creswell Wlk NN17 . . . . . . 230 C1
Crete Ave LE18 . . . . 179 E2
Cricket Cl LE4 . . . . 128 C6
Cricket Lawns LE15 . . . . . 138 A5
Crick's Retreat LE2 . . . . . . 181 F1
Critchlow Rd LE9 . . . . 200 D8
Crockett La LE15 . . . . 141 A6
CROFT 200 D3
Croft Ave LE2 . . . . 179 C6
Croft CE Prim Sch
LE9 . . . . 200 C3
Croft Cl
Barwell LE9 . . . . 198 B6
Nethersal DE12 . . . . .91 F7
Croft Dr LE18 . . . . 180 B4
Crofters Cl LE3 . . . . 153 B8
Crofters Dr LE5 . . . . 156 A7
Crofters Vale Pk
CV13 . . . . 149 D8
Croft Gdns LE14 . . . . .35 E4
Croft Hill Rd LE9 . . . . 200 C7
Croft La
Ashwell LE15 . . . . 111 B8
Leicester LE9 . . . . 200 A7
Croft Rd
Atherstone CV9 . . . . 170 D1
Cosby LE9 . . . . 201 B3
Thurlaston LE9 . . . . 177 A1
Crofts The LE67 . . . . .98 D1
Croft The
Ashby-de-la-Z LE65 . . . . . . .69 D5
Draycott DE72 . . . . .9 A4
Kegworth DE74 . . . . .18 D2
Kirby Muxloe LE9 . . . . 152 E5
Measham DE12 . . . . .93 B5
Stamford PE9 . . . . 143 F3
Twycross CV9 . . . . 146 D6
Croftway LE67 . . . . 125 D8
Croft Way LE9 . . . . 219 A5
Cromarty Cl LE4 . . . . 129 D3
Cromarty Dr LE10 . . . . 196 F1
Cromarty Rd PE9 . . . . 143 A4
Cromer St LE2 . . . . 155 C3
Cromford Ave LE18 . . . . . . 180 A1
Cromford Cl NG10 . . . . .10 A5
Cromford Rd LE2 . . . . 201 D4
Cromford St LE2 . . . . 155 C4
Cromford Way LE9 . . . . . . 219 B6
Cromore Cl LE67 . . . . .72 C1
Crompton Rd LE14 . . . . . . .58 C3
Cromwell Cl
Ashby-de-la-Z LE65 . . . . . . .69 D7
Walcote LE17 . . . . 245 B4
Cromwell Cres LE16 . . . . . 240 D1
Cromwell Ho LE2 . . . . 179 F8
Cromwell Rd
Great Glen LE8 . . . . 205 B8
Melton Mowbray LE13 . . . . .59 D1
Mountsorrel LE12 . . . . 101 D8
Croome Cl LE11 . . . . .52 C1
CROPSTON 100 E3
Cropston Ave LE11 . . . . . . .51 B2
Cropston Cl LE3 . . . . 153 D6
Cropston Dr LE67 . . . . .97 B8
Cropston Rd
Anstey LE7 . . . . 127 F7
Cropston LE7 . . . . 100 F1
Cropston Resr Nature
Reserve* LE7 . . . . 100 D3
Cropthorne Ave LE5 . . . . . 155 F5
Crosby Rd LE16 . . . . 240 F1
Cross Bank LE16 . . . . 229 D6
Crossfield Dr LE3 . . . . .59 E4
Cross Gn LE7 . . . . 101 E6
Cross Hands The CV9 . . . . 146 C1
Cross Hedge LE7 . . . . 101 E7
Cross Hedge Cl LE4 . . . . . 128 C4
Cross Hill Cl LE12 . . . . .34 D7
Cross Hill Cl LE12 . . . . .33 C3
Cross Hill La LE11 . . . . .75 A8
Cross In Hand LE12 . . . . . 243 B4
Cross Keys Gn LE5 . . . . . . 156 C7
Crosskirk Rd LE10 . . . . . . 196 F1
Cross La
Burton Lazars LE14 . . . . . . .82 F7
Mountsorrel LE12 . . . . 101 D8
Preston LE15 . . . . 164 C1
Crossland Row LE10 . . . . . 216 A6
Crossley Cl LE12 . . . . .76 C7
Crossley St LE3 . . . . 154 C8
Crossley St LE3 . . . . 154 C8
Cross St LE9 . . . . 155 C1
Cross Roads Farm Cotts
PE9 . . . . 114 D3
Crossroads Farm Mus*
LE14 . . . . .22 A5
Cross St
Blaby LE8 . . . . 202 B8
Breedon on t H DE73 . . . . .26 F2
Enderby LE19 . . . . 178 B3
Gaddesby LE7 . . . . 105 B7
Hathern LE12 . . . . .30 A1
Leicester LE4 . . . . 129 A1

Cross St continued
Leicester, Oadby LE2 . . . . . 181 A7
Long Eaton NG10 . . . . .10 E8
Loughborough LE11 . . . . . . .52 C5
Market Harborough
LE16 . . . . 240 F2
Syston LE7 . . . . 103 B3
Wigston LE18 . . . . 180 D2
Cross The
Enderby LE9 . . . . 178 B3
Gretton NN17 . . . . 213 B1
Hallaton LE16 . . . . 209 D6
Walton LE17 . . . . 236 B3
Crossways LE10 . . . . 215 F5
Crossways Ho LE8 . . . . . . 202 B8
Crossways The LE4 . . . . . . 129 B7
Crossway The
Braunstone Town LE3 . . . . 179 A8
Leicester LE2 . . . . 179 C8
Crossways Cl LE11 . . . . . . .51 C3
Crossword Cl LE11 . . . . . . .51 C3
Crowan Dr LE18 . . . . 203 C8
Crowfoot Way LE9 . . . . . . 218 F4
Crowhill Rd CV11 . . . . 214 A1
Crowhurst Dr LE3 . . . . 178 E8
Crow La
Atherstone CV9 . . . . 170 C6
Leicester LE3 . . . . 154 D4
Crown Bsns Pk LE14 . . . . . .36 B5
Crown Cl NG10 . . . . .10 A7
Crown Ct 11 LE10 . . . . . . 197 D1
Crown Gdns LE15 . . . . 138 A6
Crown Hill Cl CV13 . . . . . . 196 D7
Crownhill Rd LE10 . . . . . . 215 D4
CROWN HILLS 156 A5
Crown Hills Ave LE5 . . . . . 155 E5
Crown Hills Com Coll
LE5 . . . . 155 F4
Crown Hills Rise LE5 . . . . 155 E5
Crown La
Barrowden LE15 . . . . 191 F5
Mountsorrel LE12 . . . . .76 D3
Crown Mdw CV13 . . . . . 147 D7
Crown St
Oakham LE15 . . . . 138 A6
Ryhall PE9 . . . . 116 F3
Stamford PE9 . . . . 143 D3
Crowsfurlong CV23 . . . . . . 252 D1
Crowson Cl LE12 . . . . .50 B1
CROXTON KERRIAL 24 B7
Croxton Kerrial CE Prim
Sch NG32 . . . . .24 A7
Croxton La NG32 . . . . .15 B2
Croxton Rd
Queniborough LE7 . . . . . . 104 B4
Saltby LE14 . . . . .24 D3
South Croxton LE7 . . . . . . 132 A8
Croyde Cl LE5 . . . . 155 F4
Croyland Gn LE5 . . . . 156 E6
Crummock Ave LE15 . . . . . 166 A7
Crusaders Cl LE67 . . . . . . .71 F5
Cuckoo Cl LE15 . . . . 191 E5
Cufflin Cl LE16 . . . . 152 D8
Cuffling Cl LE3 . . . . 153 D6
Cuffling Dr LE3 . . . . 153 D6
Culham Ave LE5 . . . . 155 D8
Culver Rd LE3 . . . . 153 D6
Culworth Dr LE18 . . . . 180 C2
Cumberland Rd
Loughborough LE11 . . . . . . .51 F4
Wigston LE18 . . . . 179 E3
Cumberland St LE1 . . . . . . 259 A4
Cumberland Trad Est
LE11 . . . . .51 F4
Cumberland Way LE9 . . . . 198 A2
Cumberwell Dr LE67 . . . . . .87 E2
Cumberwell Dr LE19 . . . . . 178 C1
Cumbrae Dr LE10 . . . . 197 B2
Cumbrian Way LE12 . . . . . .50 D3
Cunnery Cl CV13 . . . . 149 C8
Cunningham Dr LE17 . . . . 244 A5
Curlew Cl
Coalville LE67 . . . . .97 A8
North End LE12 . . . . .76 C4
Syston LE7 . . . . 102 E4
Curlew Wlk LE5 . . . . 155 C7
Curteys Cl LE5 . . . . 155 B7
Curtis Cl LE8 . . . . 201 F7
Curtis Way CV13 . . . . 149 C8
Curzon Ave
Birstall LE4 . . . . 129 A6
Wigston LE18 . . . . 180 A1
Curzon Cl
Hinckley LE10 . . . . 215 F7
Queniborough LE7 . . . . . . 103 D5
Curzon Rd LE2 . . . . 179 E7
Curzon St
Ibstock LE67 . . . . .95 F1
Leicester LE1 . . . . 155 B7
Loughborough LE11 . . . . . . .52 A4
Cutchel The 3 LE17 . . . 244 C5
Cutters Cl LE18 . . . . 201 B7
Cutting La LE15 . . . . 166 D1
Cuttings The LE16 . . . . . . 156 F6
Cutting The DE11 . . . . .44 F4
Cygnet Cl
5 Sileby LE12 . . . . .77 C3
Syston LE7 . . . . 102 F4
Cypress Cl LE11 . . . . .75 A7
Cyprus Rd LE2 . . . . 179 E6
Cyril St LE3 . . . . 179 A8

Cross St continued
Enderby LE19 . . . . 178 B2
Leicester, Oadby LE2 . . . . . 181 A7
Long Eaton NG10 . . . . .10 E8
Loughborough LE11 . . . . . . .52 C5
Market Harborough
LE16 . . . . 240 F2
Syston LE7 . . . . 103 B3
Wigston LE18 . . . . 180 D2

D

Dabey Cl LE67 . . . . 125 D8
DADLINGTON 173 F1
Dadlington La LE9 . . . . 174 D2
Dag La
Mowsley LE17 . . . . 237 F7
North Kilworth LE17 . . . . . 246 F3
Dahlia Cl LE10 . . . . 215 E6
Dairy Cotts LE17 . . . . 247 A4
Dairy La
Edmondthorpe LE14 . . . . . .85 F8
Hose LE14 . . . . .20 F7
Daisy Cl
Bagworth LE67 . . . . 124 A7
Coalville LE67 . . . . .97 A8
Donisthorpe DE12 . . . . .67 E1
Groby LE6 . . . . 127 A3
Daisy La DE12 . . . . .67 B3
Dakota Rd DE74 . . . . .28 B8
Dakyn Rd LE5 . . . . 156 D6
Dalby Ave
Birstall LE4 . . . . 129 B8
Bushby LE7 . . . . 157 A5
Dalby Dr LE6 . . . . 126 F3
Dalby Rd
Anstey LE7 . . . . 127 D7
Melton Mowbray LE13,
LE14 . . . . .82 B5
Dalby La LE14 . . . . 224 F1
DALBY WOLDS 35 A1
Dale Acre LE8 . . . . 202 F4
Dale Ave LE18 . . . . 180 A4
Dale Cl DE72 . . . . .9 D8
Dale End Cl LE10 . . . . 215 A2
Dale Gdns LE12 . . . . .93 D5
Dales Cl LE12 . . . . .32 E5
Dale St LE2 . . . . 155 C5
Dales The LE8 . . . . 202 C4
Dalestorth St NG32 . . . . . . .4 F5
Dalgliesh Way LE14 . . . . . .57 C2
Dalkeith Rd LE4 . . . . 129 D4
Dalkeith Wlk LE67 . . . . . . .71 D8
Dalley Cl LE7 . . . . 103 B2
Dallison Cl LE16 . . . . 250 E8
Dalliwell LE14 . . . . .13 A2
Dalton Rd
Corby NN17 . . . . 230 E2
Hamilton LE5 . . . . 130 D3
Dames La LE64 . . . . 121 E6
Damson Ct LE10 . . . . 215 B7
Dances Dr LE2 . . . . 128 D2
Dandees Cl LE67 . . . . .98 E1
Danegeld Pl PE9 . . . . 143 E3
Danehill LE6 . . . . 152 C8
DANE HILLS 154 B6
Danehurst Ave LE3 . . . . . . 154 B6
Danemill Prim Sch
Enderby LE19 . . . . 178 B2
Enderby LE19 . . . . 178 B3
Danesholl Rd LE3 . . . . 154 D5
Dane St LE3 . . . . 154 C5
Danet Ct LE9 . . . . 143 E2
Dannett St LE3 . . . . 154 C8
Dannett Wlk LE3 . . . . 154 C8
Dan's La LE14 . . . . 176 D7
Danver's La LE12 . . . . .50 C4
Danvers Rd
Leicester LE3 . . . . 154 C3
Mountsorrel LE12 . . . . .76 E1
Darby Way LE9 . . . . 201 A7
Darcy Gdns LE13 . . . . .59 C6
Darenth Dr LE4 . . . . 128 A3
Darescroft LE16 . . . . 229 B1
Dare's Wlk LE10 . . . . 197 D1
Darien Way LE3 . . . . 153 D2
Darker St LE1 . . . . 259 B4
Darklands La DE11 . . . . . . .44 A4
Darklands Rd DE11 . . . . . . 180 A1
Darley Cl DE11 . . . . .44 A1
Darley Dr NG10 . . . . .10 A5
Darley Rd
Blaby LE8 . . . . 202 A7
Hinckley LE10 . . . . 215 E6
Darley St LE2 . . . . 155 C5
Darlington Rd LE3 . . . . . . 154 A8
Darnall Rd LE2 . . . . 179 E6
Darsway DE74 . . . . .16 F4
Dart Cl
Corby NN17 . . . . 230 D2
Hinckley LE10 . . . . 215 A8
Leicester, Oadby LE2 . . . . . 181 D5
Dartford Rd LE2 . . . . 154 E1
Darwen Cl LE13 . . . . .82 A8
Darwin Cl
Braunstone Town LF3 . . . . 153 C1
Broughton Astley LE9 . . . . 219 A5
Hinckley LE10 . . . . 197 E3
Stamford PE9 . . . . 143 C5
Darwin Cres LE11 . . . . .51 C7
Darwin Rd NG10 . . . . .10 B5
Dashwood Rd LE2 . . . . 155 C3
Dauphine Cl LE67 . . . . .72 D1
Davenport Ave LE2 . . . . . . 180 F5
Davenport Rd
Leicester LE5 . . . . 156 C5
Wigston LE18 . . . . 180 D1
Davenport Terr LE10 . . . . . 215 E8

Davett Cl LE5. . . . . .156 B6
David Ave LE4 . . . . .128 E5
David Lees Cl LE67 . . . . . . .96 E3
David Royce Ho LE15 . . .138 A6
Davies Cl LE16. . . . . .240 D5
Davison Cl LE5 . . . . .156 A6
Davis Rd DE11. . . . . .44 B4
Davy Ct CV23 . . . . .252 C2
Dawkins Rd DE12. . . . . . . .67 E1
Dawlish Cl LE5 . . . . .156 D5
Dawsons La LE7, LE14 . . .134 C6
Dawson's La LE9 . . . . .198 B6
Dawson's Rd LE12 . . . . . . .48 D4
Daybell Cl
  Bottesford NG13 . . . . .3 B3
  Whetstone LE8 . . . . .178 F1
Daybell Rd DE12. . . . . .68 A4
Day St LE4 . . . . .129 A3
Dayton Cl LE67 . . . . .71 A2
Deacon Ave CV13 . . . . . . .149 C8
Deacon Cl
  Bitteswell LE17 . . . . .244 A8
  Market Harborough
  LE16 . . . . .240 D5
  Shepshed LE12 . . . . .50 C3
Deacon Ho LE2 . . . . .259 A2
Deacon Rd LE4 . . . . .128 D8
Deacon Rise CV13 . . . . . . .122 C1
Deacon St LE2. . . . . .259 A2
Deacon's Workshop
  (Mus)★ LE1 . . . . .259 A3
Dead La 🔒 LE11. . . . . . . .52 B4
Dean Cl LE10 . . . . .197 E2
Deancourt Rd LE2 . . . . . . .180 B6
Deane Gate Dr LE7 . . . . . .157 F4
Deanery Cres LE4. . . . . . . .128 D8
Deane St LE11. . . . . .51 E5
Dean Rd
  Hinckley LE10 . . . . .197 E2
  Leicester LE4 . . . . .129 C1
Dean Rd W LE10. . . . . .197 E2
Deansburn Ho LE3. . . . . . .153 F8
Deanside Dr LE11. . . . . . . .51 E6
Dean's La LE12 . . . . .74 B3
Dean's St LE15 . . . . .137 F6
Dean's Terr LE15. . . . . .189 A4
Debdale LE15. . . . . .112 C8
Debdale Hill LE14. . . . . . . .35 E4
Debdale La
  Gumley LE16 . . . . .224 C3
  Smeeton Westerby LE8 . .224 A6
Debdale Pl LE14 . . . . .57 E2
Deben Rd NN17 . . . . .230 D1
Dee Cl
  Melton Mowbray LE13. . . . .59 E3
  Oakham LE15. . . . . .137 E4
Deeming Dr LE12. . . . . . . .75 F7
Deene Cl LE16. . . . . .241 A3
Deene Rd NN17. . . . . .213 F7
Deepdale
  Great Easton LE16. . . . . . .229 D7
  Leicester LE5. . . . . .155 F6
Deepdale Cl LE67. . . . . . . .95 F2
Deepdale Rd NG10. . . . . . .10 A5
Deepdene Cl DE11. . . . . . .44 C1
Deeping La CV13 . . . . .149 B4
Deep Side PE9. . . . . .168 F4
Deepway The LE12. . . . . . .75 E5
Deers Acre LE11. . . . . .52 B6
Degens Way LE67 . . . . .96 B7
De Havilland Way
  LE10 . . . . .215 E4
Deighton Way LE11. . . . . . .51 C6
De-La-Bere Cres
  LE10. . . . . .216 A6
Delamere Rd LE13 . . . . . . .59 D6
Delamere Cl DE72 . . . . .9 D8
Delaware Rd LE5 . . . . .156 E4
De Lisle Cl LE16 . . . . .240 D2
De Lisle Ct LE11. . . . . .51 B2
De Lisle RC Science Coll
  LE11. . . . . .51 D3
Dell The
  Oakham LE15. . . . . .138 A5
  Lillesthorpe LE17 . . . . . . .233 B4
Delph The DE73 . . . . .26 F2
Delven La DE74. . . . . .17 B3
De Montfort University
  (Charles Frears Campus)
  LE2 . . . . .155 C2
De Montfort LE13. . . . . . . .59 C5
De Montfort Cl LE11 . . . . . .51 C5
De Montfort Ct
  Anstey LE7 . . . . .127 D6
  Leicester LE2. . . . . .155 C2
De Montfort Mews
  LE1. . . . . .259 C2
De Montfort Pl LE1. . . . . .259 C2
De Montfort Rd LE10 . . . . .197 E1
De Montfort Sq LE1. . . . . .259 C2
De Montfort St LE1. . . . . .259 C2
De Montfort Univ
  Leicester LE1. . . . . .259 B3
  Leicester LE2. . . . . .259 A2
Dempsey Cl LE17 . . . . . . .244 C8
Denacre Ave LE18 . . . . . . .180 A1
Denbigh Cl 🔒 LE17 . . . . .244 C5
Denbigh Pl LE17. . . . . . . .244 C7
Denbydale LE18 . . . . .180 F1
Denegate Ave LE4 . . . . . . .128 F8
Denfield Cl LE15. . . . . . . .190 B5
Denham Cl LE13. . . . . . . .153 C6
Denis Cl LE3 . . . . .154 A5
Denis Rd LE10. . . . . .215 D5
Deniston Ave LE9. . . . . . . .218 D7

Denman La LE9. . . . . .200 D8
Denmark Rd LE2 . . . . .179 E8
Dennead Ave LE18 . . . . . .180 C4
Dennis David Cl LE17 . . . .244 C8
Dennis St LE67 . . . . .96 D6
Denstone Cl LE65. . . . . . . .69 A8
Denton La
  Harston NG32 . . . . .15 C4
  Sedgebrook NG32 . . . . .8 F6
Denton Rise LE13. . . . . . . .59 E2
Denton St LE3. . . . . .154 B5
Denton Wlk LE18 . . . . . . .180 E2
Dents Rd LE65. . . . . .69 D7
Derby Cl LE9 . . . . .219 A5
Derby La DE12. . . . . .121 A6
Derby Rd
  Ashby-de-la-Z LE65 . . . . . .69 B6
  Aston-on-T DE72 . . . . .16 A8
  Draycott DE72 . . . . .9 A7
  Hathern LE12. . . . . .29 F2
  Hinckley LE10 . . . . .197 D1
  Kegworth DE74 . . . . .18 C2
  Long Eaton NG10. . . . . . . .10 D8
  Long Eaton, Wilsthorpe
  NG10. . . . . .10 B8
  Loughborough LE11. . . . . .51 E6
  Melbourne DE73 . . . . .26 A8
  Smisby LE65 . . . . .46 A4
  Swadlincote DE11. . . . . . .44 C3
  Ticknall DE11, DE73. . . . . .45 F7
Derbyshire Dr DE74. . . . . .17 B4
Derby Sq 🔒 LE11 . . . . . . .52 A4
Derrys Hollow LE67. . . . . . .96 E3
Derry Wlk LE4 . . . . .128 E4
Dersingham Rd LE4. . . . . .128 E2
De Ruthyn Cl DE12. . . . . . .68 A4
Derwent Ave LE15 . . . . . . .166 A7
Derwent Cl
  Earl Shilton LE9 . . . . .198 F8
  Swadlincote DE11. . . . . . .44 A1
Derwent Dr
  Loughborough LE11. . . . . .51 D1
  Melton Mowbray LE13. . . . .59 B1
  Oakham LE15. . . . . .137 F5
Derwent Gdns LE65. . . . . .69 C5
Derwent Rd LE12. . . . . . . .76 D8
Derwent St
  Draycott DE72 . . . . .9 A7
  Leicester LE2. . . . . .155 C5
  Long Eaton NG10. . . . . . . .10 C6
Derwent Street Ind Est
  NG10. . . . . .10 C6
Derwent Wlk
  Corby NN17 . . . . .230 D2
  Leicester, Oadby LE2 . . . .181 C5
Desborough Rd
  Braybrooke LE16 . . . . . . .251 F5
  Great Oxendon LE16 . . . . .251 F1
DESFORD 151 C3
Desford Com Prim Sch
  LE9 . . . . .151 A2
Desford Cross Roads
  LE9. . . . . .177 B8
Desford Grange LE9 . . . . .151 B4
Desford Ho LE10. . . . . . . .215 D7
Desford La
  Kirkby Mallory LE9. . . . . . .175 D7
  Peckleton LE9 . . . . .176 B8
  Ratby LE6, LE9 . . . . .152 B7
Desford Rd
  Enderby LE9, LE19. . . . . . .177 D6
  Kirby Muxloe LE9. . . . . . . .152 D6
  Narborough LE19. . . . . . .201 B8
  Newbold Verdon LE9. . . . . .150 D4
  Thurlaston LE9. . . . . .176 F4
Desford Tropical Bird
  Land★ LE9 . . . . .151 B5
Deuce Ho LE1 . . . . .259 C4
Devana Ave LE67 . . . . .96 F8
Devana Rd LE2. . . . . .155 C3
Devenports Hill LE7 . . . . .157 B5
De Verdon Rd LE17 . . . . . .244 A5
De Verdun Ave LE12. . . . . .49 B6
Deveron Cl LE67. . . . . .72 C1
Deveron Ct LE10. . . . . . . .197 B1
Deveron Way LE10. . . . . . .197 B1
Deveron Wlk NN17. . . . . .230 D1
Devitt Way LE9 . . . . .218 F4
Devon Cl DE12 . . . . .68 C6
Devonia Rd LE2 . . . . .181 D4
Devon La NG13 . . . . .3 B3
Devonshire Ave LE18. . . . .180 A1
Devonshire Ct LE2. . . . . . .181 B3
Devonshire La LE11. . . . . . .52 B3
Devonshire Rd LE4 . . . . . .128 E1
Devonshire Sq LE11. . . . . .52 B3
Devonshire Wlk LE2. . . . . .181 C3
Devon Way LE5 . . . . .155 F5
Devon Wlk LE15 . . . . .87 D2
Deweys Cl LE15. . . . . .166 D3
Dexters Cl LE2 . . . . .76 A7
Dickens Cl LE3 . . . . .154 A5
Dickens Dr
  Melton Mowbray LE13. . . . .59 B6
  Stamford PE9. . . . . .143 A3
  Swadlincote DE11. . . . . . .44 C5
Dicken The LE8 . . . . .201 F7
Dickinson Way LE4 . . . . . .129 F7
Dickman's La LE14. . . . . . .12 B3
Dick's Hill LE16. . . . . .249 C5
Didcott Way DE12 . . . . . . .119 F8
Didsbury St LE3 . . . . .153 E3
Dieppe Way LE18 . . . . .59 B5
Digby Cl
  Leicester LE3. . . . . .154 B3
  Tilton on t H LE7 . . . . . . .160 A8

Digby Dr
  Melton Mowbray LE13. . . . .81 F8
  North Luffenham LE15. . . .166 D3
  Oakham LE15. . . . . .137 E6
Digby Ho LE2 . . . . .180 F7
Dillon Gn LE3 . . . . .127 F1
Dillon Rd LE3 . . . . .153 F8
Dillon Rise LE3 . . . . .153 F8
Dillon Way LE3 . . . . .127 F1
Dimmingdale Cl LE7 . . . . .127 E7
Dingle La B79, DE12. . . . . .119 C6
DINGLEY 241 F4
Dingley Ave LE4 . . . . .129 C1
Dingley La LE16 . . . . .241 F6
Dingley Link LE18. . . . . . . .180 E3
Dingley Terr LE16. . . . . . . .240 F3
Dinmore Grange DE11. . . . .45 B6
Discovery Way LE65 . . . . . .69 D8
DISEWORTH 28 C5
Diseworth CE Prim Sch
  DE74 . . . . .28 C6
Diseworth Rd DE74 . . . . . .17 A1
Diseworth St LE2 . . . . . . .155 C5
DISHLEY 51 C6
Disney Cl LE9 . . . . .199 D2
Disraeli Cl LE18 . . . . .223 F8
Disraeli St
  Leicester LE2. . . . . .179 D7
  Quorn (Quorndon) LE12. . . .76 A6
Ditchling Ave LE3 . . . . . . .154 A6
Dixie Gram Sch The
  CV13 . . . . .148 F3
Dixon Dr LE2 . . . . .155 C3
Dixon Dr (Lakeside)
  LE13 . . . . .59 B2
Dobbies World★ CV9 . . . .194 B4
Dobney Ave LE7 . . . . .103 C6
Doctor Cookes Cl 🔒
  LE9. . . . . .198 A6
Doctors Fields LE7 . . . . . .198 D7
Doctor's La
  Breedon on t H DE73. . . . . .26 F2
  Melton Mowbray LE13. . . . .59 E4
Doctor's Wlk The DE12. . . .93 C5
Doddridge Rd 🔒
  LE16 . . . . .240 E4
Dodgeford La LE12 . . . . . . .48 F6
Dodwells Bridge Ind Est
  LE10. . . . . .214 B8
Dodwells Rd LE10 . . . . . . .214 E8
Dog & Gun La LE8 . . . . . .201 F5
Dog La
  Burton Lazars LE14. . . . . . .83 A7
  Netherseal DE12 . . . . .91 F6
  South Kilworth LE17 . . . . .255 C8
  Wilson DE73 . . . . .26 E6
Dogwood Ct LE2. . . . . . . .181 A7
Dolphin Ct LE15 . . . . .189 A4
Dominion Rd
  Glenfield LE3 . . . . .153 D8
  Swadlincote DE11. . . . . . .44 B5
Dominus Way LE19 . . . . . .178 D8
Domont Cl LE12 . . . . .50 B3
Donald Cl LE4 . . . . .129 F4
Donald Greaves Ho
  NN17. . . . . .230 D1
Donaldson Rd LE4 . . . . . .155 A8
Donata Ho LE17 . . . . .244 C6
Doncaster Rd LE4 . . . . . . .129 B1
Don Cl
  Corby NN17. . . . . .230 D1
  Oakham LE15. . . . . .137 E4
Donington Cvn Pk
  DE74 . . . . .17 A3
Donington Dr
  Ashby-de-la-Z LE65 . . . . . .68 F5
  Woodville DE11. . . . . .44 E1
Donington Grand Prix
  Collection Mus★
  DE74 . . . . .27 D8
Donington La
  Castle Donington DE72,
  DE74 . . . . .17 C7
  Castle Donington DE72,
  DE74 . . . . .17 C8
DONINGTON LE HEATH . . .96 B5
Donington le Heath Manor
  Ho★ LE67. . . . . .96 C6
Donington Park Motor
  Racing Circuit★
  DE74 . . . . .16 C1
DONISTHORPE 67 F1
Donisthorpe La LE12 . . . . .67 E2
Donisthorpe Prim Sch
  DE12 . . . . .68 A1
Donnett Cl LE5 . . . . .156 B6
Donnington Park Motor
  Racing Circuit★
  DE74 . . . . .27 C8
Donnington St LE2 . . . . . .155 C5
Dorchester Cl
  Blaby LE8. . . . . .202 B6
  Wigston LE18. . . . . .203 D8
Dorchester Rd
  Hinckley LE10 . . . . .216 B7
  Leicester LE4. . . . . .154 B4
Dorchester Way CV11. . . . .214 A7
Dore Rd LE5 . . . . .155 C4
Dorfold Wlk LE4 . . . . .129 D1
Dorian Rise LE13 . . . . .59 B2
Dormer Ct LE7 . . . . .30 A1
Dorothy Ave
  Glen Parva LE2 . . . . .179 B3
  Melton Mowbray LE13. . . . .59 A4
  Thurmaston LE4. . . . . . . .129 D6

Dorothy Goodman Sch
  LE10. . . . . .197 B3
Dorothy Rd LE5. . . . . .155 D5
Dorset Ave
  Glenfield LE3 . . . . .127 C1
  Wigston LE18. . . . . .179 F3
Dorset Dr
  Melton Mowbray LE13. . . . .82 D7
  Moira DE12 . . . . .68 C6
Dorset St LE4 . . . . .155 A8
Double Rail Cl LE18. . . . . .180 A1
Doudney Cl LE9 . . . . .199 D1
Doughty St PE9. . . . . .143 F5
Douglas Bader Dr
  LE17. . . . . .244 D8
Douglas Dr LE13 . . . . .122 F8
Douglas Jane Cl LE13. . . . .59 A4
Douglas Rd LE16. . . . . . . .240 F4
Dove Bank Prim Sch
  CV13 . . . . .123 B3
Dove Cl
  Hinckley LE10 . . . . .215 A8
  Oakham LE15. . . . . .137 E5
  Woodville DE11. . . . . .44 F3
Dovecote
  Castle Donington DE74 . . . .17 B3
  Shepshed LE12 . . . . .50 C4
  Tonge DE73 . . . . .27 B3
Dovecote Cl
  Barrowden LE15 . . . . .191 F5
  Sapcote LE9. . . . . .217 D7
  Weston by W LE16. . . . . . .227 B3
Dovecote Rd LE9 . . . . . . .200 C5
Dovecote St LE12 . . . . .30 A1
Dovecote The LE7 . . . . . . .104 A5
Dovecotes The LE2 . . . . . . .26 F2
Dovecote Way LE9 . . . . . .198 B6
Dovedale Ave
  Blaby LE8. . . . . .202 B7
  Long Eaton NG10. . . . . . . .10 A7
Dovedale Cl LE13 . . . . .59 B1
Dovedale Ct NG10 . . . . . . .10 A7
Dovedale Prim Sch
  NG10. . . . . .10 B6
Dovedale Rd
  Leicester LE2. . . . . .155 E1
  Thurmaston LE4. . . . . . . .129 E7
Dovehouse Cl NN6. . . . . .256 E6
Dove La NG10 . . . . .10 C8
Dovelands Prim Sch
  LE3. . . . . .154 B5
Dover Cl LE12 . . . . .101 D8
Dove Rd
  Coalville LE67 . . . . .97 A7
  Diseworth DE74. . . . . .28 C8
Dove Rise LE2 . . . . .181 C6
Dover St
  Kibworth Beauchamp
  LE8 . . . . .223 F8
  Leicester LE1. . . . . .259 C3
Dower House Gdns
  LE12. . . . . .76 A4
Downham Ave LE4 . . . . . .128 E2
Downing Cres PE9 . . . . . .143 D5
Downing Dr LE5 . . . . .156 D4
Downside Dr LE65 . . . . . . .69 A7
Down St LE4 . . . . .129 B1
Dowry Furlong Wildlife
  Area★ LE6. . . . . .126 E4
Doyle Cl LE11 . . . . .51 D6
Drage Cl LE17 . . . . .244 D8
Dragon La LE9 . . . . .150 A5
Dragon St NG13 . . . . .5 B5
Dragwell DE74. . . . . .18 D2
Drake Way LE10 . . . . .197 D4
Draper St LE2 . . . . .155 C3
DRAYCOTT 9 B6
Draycott Com Prim Sch
  DE72 . . . . .9 A7
Draycott Mills DE72. . . . . . .9 A7
Draycott Rd
  Breaston DE72. . . . . .9 C7
  Long Eaton NG10. . . . . . . .10 A4
DRAYTON 229 A5
Drayton Cl CV13 . . . . .194 B5
Drayton Ct CV10 . . . . .194 B2
Drayton Ho LE2. . . . . .155 B2
Drayton La CV13. . . . . . . .194 C6
Drayton Rd
  Bringhurst LE16. . . . . . . .229 B5
  Drayton LE16. . . . . .228 D7
  Leicester LE3. . . . . .153 E7
  Medbourne LE16 . . . . . . .228 A5
Drayton St DE11. . . . . .44 C4
Dribdale LE8 . . . . .223 A7
Drift Ave PE9 . . . . .143 F4
Drift Cl DE11. . . . . .68 B8
Drift Gdns PE9 . . . . .143 F5
Drift Hill
  Redmile NG13 . . . . .6 F4
  Wymondham LE14 . . . . . . .63 A2
Drift Rd PE9. . . . . .143 E4
Drift Side DE11. . . . . .68 B7
Drift The
  Collyweston PE9 . . . . . . .168 D2
  Denton NG32 . . . . .15 E3
  Essendine PE9 . . . . .116 D6
  Sewstern NG33. . . . . .42 F2
  Thistleton NG33. . . . . .64 B5
Drinkstone Rd LE5. . . . . . .155 E5
Drive, Dalby Rd LE13. . . . . .59 C1
Drive The
  Barwell LE9 . . . . .198 C8
  Birstall LE4 . . . . .128 F5
  Countesthorpe LE8 . . . . . .202 C4
  Kibworth Beauchamp
  LE8 . . . . .224 B8
  Scraptoft LE7. . . . . .156 F8

Drive continued
  Woodhouse Eaves
  LE12 . . . . .100 A8
Driveway The LE7. . . . . . . .157 A5
Drome Cl LE67 . . . . .72 D1
Dromintee Rd LE67 . . . . . .97 B4
Dronfield St LE5 . . . . .155 C5
Drought Gdn &
  Arboretum★
  LE15. . . . . .139 D6
Drovers Ct LE9 . . . . .151 B3
Drovers Way
  Desford LE9. . . . . .151 C3
  Narborough LE19. . . . . . .201 B7
Drove The PE9 . . . . .168 D1
Druid St LE10 . . . . .197 D1
Drumcliff Rd LE5 . . . . .156 E6
Drummond Rd
  Enderby LE19. . . . . .178 A3
  Leicester LE4. . . . . .128 F3
Drummond Wlk LE13 . . . . .59 B5
Drury La LE2 . . . . .180 F6
Drurys La LE15 . . . . .190 C1
Dryden Cl DE12. . . . . .93 C4
Dryden St LE1 . . . . .259 C5
Dryer Cl LE67. . . . . .122 F8
Dry Pot La LE12 . . . . .28 F2
Du Cane Cl LE12 . . . . .50 A1
Duck Lake DE12 . . . . .119 F8
DUDDINGTON 193 B6
Dudlestone Cl LE5 . . . . . .156 A5
Dudley Ave LE5 . . . . .156 C6
Dudley Cl LE5 . . . . .156 C6
Dudley Ct LE12 . . . . .77 C3
Dudley Ho LE5 . . . . .156 C6
Dudley Rise LE10 . . . . . . .215 D6
Dudley Whenham Cl
  LE7 . . . . .103 A4
Duffield Ave LE18. . . . . . . .180 B4
Duffield Cl NG10. . . . . .10 A5
Duffield St LE2 . . . . .155 C5
Dukes Cl
  Thurmaston LE4. . . . . . . .129 F7
  Wigston LE18. . . . . .180 B3
Dukes Dr LE2 . . . . .155 C2
Dukes Dr Flats LE2 . . . . . .155 C2
Dukes Rd LE14 . . . . .36 B6
Duke St
  Leicester LE1. . . . . .259 B2
  Loughborough LE11. . . . . .52 B5
  Melton Mowbray LE13. . . . .59 E4
Dulverton Cl
  Loughborough LE11. . . . . .74 D8
  Wigston LE18. . . . . .203 D8
Dulverton Rd
  Leicester LE3. . . . . .154 C5
  Melton Mowbray LE13. . . . .59 A5
Dumbleton Ave LE3. . . . . .154 C1
Dumps Rd LE67. . . . . .71 E6
Dunbar Rd
  Coalville LE67 . . . . .97 C8
  Leicester LE4. . . . . .129 E2
Dunbar Way LE65. . . . . . . .69 D6
Dunblane Ave LE4 . . . . . . .129 D4
Dunblane Way LE10. . . . . .197 A2
Duncan Ave LE19 . . . . . . .200 D7
Duncan Rd LE2 . . . . .179 E7
Duncan Way LE11. . . . . . . .51 C6
Duncombe Rd LE3 . . . . . .128 A1
Dundee Dr PE9 . . . . .143 A4
Dundee Rd
  Blaby LE8. . . . . .202 B6
  Swadlincote DE11. . . . . . .44 D5
Dundonald Rd LE4. . . . . . .129 A1
Dunholme Ave LE11 . . . . . .51 B4
Dunholme Rd LE4 . . . . . . .129 E1
Dunire Cl LE4 . . . . .128 C3
Dunkirk St LE1 . . . . .259 C3
Dunley Way LE17 . . . . . . .244 C7
Dunlin Rd
  Essendine PE9. . . . . .117 B6
  Leicester LE5. . . . . .155 C7
Dunmore Rd LE16 . . . . . .241 A1
Dunn Dr NG10. . . . . .10 B7
Dunnicliffe La DE73. . . . . . .26 A7
Dunnsmoor La DE11. . . . . .44 E7
Dunns La LE3 . . . . .259 A3
Dunslade Cl LE16. . . . . . .241 B2
Dunslade Gr LE16. . . . . . .241 B2
Dunslade Rd LE16 . . . . . .241 A2
DUNSMORE 257 C6
Dunsmore Cl LE11. . . . . . .74 D8
Dunsmore Way DE11. . . . . .44 D5
Dunstall Ave LE3 . . . . . . .153 D3
Dunster Rd LE12. . . . . .76 D1
Dunster St LE3 . . . . .154 B5
Dunston Cl NG10 . . . . .10 F7
Dunsville Wlk LE4 . . . . . . .129 D3
DUNTON BASSETT 219 C2
Dunton Bassett Prim Sch
  LE17. . . . . .219 D2
Dunton La LE17. . . . . .234 A6
Dunton Rd
  Broughton Astley LE17,
  LE9 . . . . .219 B3
  Leire LE17 . . . . .234 A8
Dunton St
  Leicester LE3. . . . . .154 D7
  Wigston LE18. . . . . .179 F1
Dupont Cl LE3 . . . . .153 D7
Dupont Gdns LE3 . . . . . . .153 D7
Duport Rd LE10 . . . . .215 F7
Durham Ave LE4 . . . . .128 C7
Durham Cl
  Bagworth LE67 . . . . .124 A6
  Melton Mowbray LE13. . . . .82 D8
  Swadlincote DE11. . . . . . .44 E5
Durham Dr LE18. . . . . . . .180 A4

Durham Rd LE11 . . . 51 E6
Durham Wlk LE67 . . . 124 A6
Durnford Rd LE18 . . . 203 D7
Durrell Cl LE11 . . . 51 C6
Durris Cl LE67 . . . 72 C1
Durston Cl LE5 . . . 156 D4
Duxbury Rd LE5 . . . 155 E7
Dwyer Cl LE7 . . . 102 F2
Dwyers Cl LE14 . . . 58 A3
Dyers Ct LE11 . . . 52 C5
Dysart Way LE1 . . . 155 B7
Dyson Cl
Lutterworth LE17 . . . 244 C7
Rugby CV21 . . . 257 A1
Dysons Cl DE12 . . . 93 B4

E

Eagle Cl
Broughton Astley LE9 . . . 218 E7
Measham DE12 . . . 93 B4
Eagles Dr LE13 . . . 82 B8
Eaglesfield LE17 . . . 218 F1
Eaglesfield End LE17 . . . 218 E1
Ealing Rd LE2 . . . 154 F1
Eamont Cl LE2 . . . 179 D3
Eamont Gn LE2 . . . 179 D3
Earle Smith Cl LE8 . . . 202 A7
Earl Howe St LE2 . . . 155 C4
Earl Howe Terr 7
LE3 . . . 154 D5
Earl Russell St LE2 . . . 179 C6
Earls Cl LE4 . . . 129 F7
Earls Cl Ind Est LE4 . . . 129 F7
EARL SHILTON . . . 198 F7
Earl Shilton Rd LE9 . . . 176 D2
Earls Rd LE14 . . . 36 B6
Earl St
Earl Shilton LE9 . . . 176 A1
Leicester LE1 . . . 259 C4
Earlstrees Ct NN17 . . . 230 F2
Earlstrees Ind Est
NN17 . . . 230 E2
Earlstrees Rd NN17 . . . 230 F2
Earls Way LE4 . . . 129 F7
Earlswood Cl DE72 . . . 9 D8
Earlswood Rd LE5 . . . 156 D4
Easby Cl LE11 . . . 51 B5
Easedale Cl CV11 . . . 214 A6
East Acre LE14 . . . 108 C1
East Ave
Leicester LE2 . . . 155 C2
Melton Mowbray LE13 . . . 59 A4
Syston LE7 . . . 103 C4
Whetstone LE8 . . . 201 F8
East Bond St LE1 . . . 259 B4
Eastboro Fields CV11 . . . 214 A4
Eastboro Way CV11 . . . 214 A4
East Cl LE10 . . . 215 D7
Eastcourt Rd LE2 . . . 180 C6
East Cres LE67 . . . 96 E2
East End LE14 . . . 20 D4
East End Dr DE11 . . . 44 C4
Eastern Bvd LE2 . . . 259 A2
EAST FARNDON . . . 250 B7
Eastfield Ave LE13 . . . 59 C4
Eastfield Ct LE3 . . . 154 B5
Eastfield Prim Sch
LE4 . . . 129 F8
Eastfield Rd
Leicester LE3 . . . 154 B5
Swadlincote DE11 . . . 44 C6
Thurmaston LE4 . . . 129 F8
Eastgate LE16 . . . 209 D5
East Gates 4 LE1 . . . 259 B4
East Gn LE9 . . . 198 A6
EAST GOSCOTE . . . 103 E8
East Goscote Ind Est
LE7 . . . 103 C7
EASTHORPE . . . 3 B1
Easthorpe La
Muston NG13 . . . 3 E1
Redmile NG13 . . . 6 F4
Easthorpe Rd NG13 . . . 3 C2
Easthorpe View NG13 . . . 3 C2
East La
Bardon LE67 . . . 97 D4
Ridlington LE15 . . . 163 E2
EAST LANGTON . . . 225 D5
EAST LEAKE . . . 31 E8
Eastleigh Rd LE3 . . . 154 D3
East Link LE19 . . . 178 E7
East Link Rd LE11 . . . 51 E2
Eastmere Rd LE18 . . . 180 F3
EAST NORTON . . . 186 D6
East Norton Rd LE16 . . . 209 D7
Easton Garford CE Sch
PE9 . . . 169 A5
EASTON ON THE HILL
. . . 169 A4
East Orch LE12 . . . 77 C1
East Park Rd LE5 . . . 155 D5
East Rd
Birstall LE4 . . . 129 A3
Wymeswold LE12 . . . 33 E4
East Side Croft LE13 . . . 59 D6
East St
Leicester LE1 . . . 259 C3
Leicester, Oadby LE2 . . . 181 A6
Long Eaton NG10 . . . 10 F8
Market Harborough
LE16 . . . 240 D3
Stamford PE9 . . . 143 E3
Eastway DE74 . . . 17 B3
Eastway Rd LE18 . . . 180 D4
EASTWELL . . . 22 B6

East Wlk
Ibstock LE67 . . . 95 F1
Ratby LE6 . . . 126 C1
Eastwood Rd LE2 . . . 179 D5
Eastwoods Rd LE10 . . . 197 F2
EATON . . . 22 E6
Eaton Ct NG32 . . . 22 F7
Eaton Grange Dr NG10 . . . 10 A8
Eaton Rd DE74 . . . 17 B3
Ebchester Cl LE2 . . . 179 C3
Ebchester Rd LE2 . . . 179 C4
Ebenezer Cotts CV13 . . . 149 B8
Edale Cl
Leicester LE3 . . . 153 E3
Long Eaton NG10 . . . 10 B6
Edale Gn LE10 . . . 215 F6
Eddystone Rd LE5 . . . 156 E7
Edelin Rd LE11 . . . 52 B1
Eden Cl
Leicester, Oadby LE2 . . . 181 C6
Loughborough LE11 . . . 51 C5
Edendale Dr LE10 . . . 197 E4
Edendale Rd LE13 . . . 82 B8
Eden Gdns LE4 . . . 128 C7
Edenhall Cl
Leicester LE4 . . . 129 D3
Leicester, Oadby LE2 . . . 181 D4
Edenhurst Ave LE3 . . . 178 F7
Eden Rd LE2 . . . 181 D6
Edensor St LE4 . . . 129 C3
Eden Way LE2 . . . 179 D2
Edgbaston Cl LE4 . . . 128 D7
Edgcote Ct LE5 . . . 155 E8
Edgecote Dr DE11 . . . 44 A7
Edgefield Cl LE5 . . . 130 B2
Edgehill Cl LE8 . . . 205 B8
Edge Hill Ct NG10 . . . 10 D4
Edgehill Rd LE4 . . . 129 E2
Edgehill Way LE65 . . . 69 D7
Edgeley Cl LE3 . . . 128 B1
Edgeley Rd LE8 . . . 202 F4
Edinburgh Cl LE16 . . . 240 F4
Edinburgh Rd
Earl Shilton LE9 . . . 198 D7
Stamford PE9 . . . 143 D5
Edinburgh Way LE12 . . . 76 C1
Edison Ctyd NN17 . . . 230 F3
Edith Ave LE3 . . . 179 A7
EDITH WESTON . . . 166 B7
Edith Weston Prim Sch
LE15 . . . 166 A7
Edith Weston Rd
LE15 . . . 166 D4
Edmonds Cl PE9 . . . 143 F4
Edmonds Dr PE9 . . . 168 A5
EDMONDTHORPE . . . 86 A8
Edmondthorpe Drift
LE14 . . . 63 B1
Edmondthorpe Mere
LE15 . . . 85 E5
Edmondthorpe Rd
LE14 . . . 62 E1
Edmonton Rd LE1 . . . 259 C5
Edmonton Way LE15 . . . 138 B6
Edward Ave LE3 . . . 178 F8
Edward Cl LE2 . . . 181 C5
Edward Dr LE2 . . . 179 E1
Edward Rd
Fleckney LE8 . . . 222 F7
Leicester LE2 . . . 155 B2
Long Eaton NG10 . . . 10 D8
Market Harborough
LE16 . . . 240 D5
Stamford PE9 . . . 143 D5
Edwards Ctr 7 LE10 . . . 215 D8
Edward St
Anstey LE7 . . . 127 E7
Hartshorne DE11 . . . 45 A3
Hinckley LE10 . . . 197 C2
Leicester LE5 . . . 155 C7
Loughborough LE11 . . . 52 A5
Moira DE11 . . . 44 C1
Overseal DE12 . . . 67 A4
Egerton Ave LE4 . . . 128 E2
Egerton Hos LE2 . . . 180 E7
Egerton Rd LE13 . . . 59 D3
Egerton View LE13 . . . 59 B3
Eggington Ct LE11 . . . 51 E2
Egginton St LE5 . . . 155 C5
Eglantine Cl LE2 . . . 181 A7
EGLETON . . . 138 C4
Egleton Nature Reserve*
LE15 . . . 138 F2
Eider Cl LE8 . . . 201 F4
Eight Acres 6 PE9 . . . 143 C3
Eileen Ave LE4 . . . 128 E2
Elbow La LE1 . . . 259 A4
Elder Cl LE3, LE7 . . . 127 F3
Elder La LE67 . . . 48 A2
Eldon St LE1 . . . 259 C4
Eleanor Cl PE9 . . . 143 C4
Elfin Gr LE17 . . . 219 E2
Elford St 2 LE65 . . . 69 B6
Elgar Dr NG10 . . . 10 B5
Elgar Way PE9 . . . 143 B4
Elgin Ave LE3 . . . 153 F8
Elgin Dr LE13 . . . 59 C4
Elgin Wlk LE67 . . . 71 D8
Eliot Cl
Long Eaton NG10 . . . 10 B5
Loughborough LE11 . . . 51 B6
Elisha Cl LE9 . . . 199 E2
Elizabethan Way
LE17 . . . 244 D7
Elizabeth Ave LE67 . . . 95 F2
Elizabeth Cl
Fleckney LE8 . . . 222 F6
Houghton on t H LE7 . . . 157 F4

Elizabeth Cres LE18 . . . 180 B4
Elizabeth Ct
Glenfield LE3 . . . 127 B1
Wigston LE18 . . . 180 D2
Elizabeth Dr
Leicester, Oadby LE2 . . . 181 C4
Thurmaston LE4 . . . 129 E8
Elizabeth Gdns LE8 . . . 201 F7
Elizabeth Rd
Fleckney LE8 . . . 222 F6
Hinckley LE10 . . . 197 D2
Stamford PE9 . . . 143 D4
Elizabeth St LE5 . . . 155 E5
Elizabeth Way LE15 . . . 189 B5
Elizabeth Woodville Prim
Sch LE6 . . . 126 E3
Ellaby Rd LE11 . . . 51 D6
Elland Rd LE3 . . . 153 B5
Ellesmere Coll LE3 . . . 154 B2
Ellesmere Pl LE3 . . . 154 B2
Ellesmere Rd LE3 . . . 154 B2
Elliot Cl
Kibworth Beauchamp
LE8 . . . 224 A8
Leicester, Oadby LE2 . . . 181 E4
Whetstone LE8 . . . 202 A4
Elliots Yd LE8 . . . 202 F3
Elliott Dr
Leicester Forest East
LE3 . . . 153 B4
Thurmaston LE4 . . . 130 A6
Elliott Rd LE4 . . . 128 D4
Elliott's La LE67 . . . 125 A8
Ellis Ave LE4 . . . 129 A1
Ellis Cl
Barrow-u-S LE12 . . . 76 E8
Ellistown LE67 . . . 96 E3
Glenfield LE3 . . . 153 B8
Long Eaton NG10 . . . 10 C6
Quorn (Quorndon) LE12 . . . 75 F7
Ellis Dr LE9 . . . 152 F3
Ellis Fields LE2 . . . 181 E3
Ellison Ave DE72 . . . 16 A7
Ellison Cl
Stoney Stanton LE9 . . . 199 D3
Wigston LE18 . . . 202 F8
Ellis St LE7 . . . 127 D6
ELLISTOWN . . . 96 D3
Ellistown Com Prim Sch
LE67 . . . 96 E3
Ellistown Terrace Rd
LE67 . . . 96 E1
Ellwood Cl LE5 . . . 156 B4
Elm Ave
Ashby-de-la-Z LE65 . . . 69 D7
Long Eaton NG10 . . . 10 C8
Lutterworth LE17 . . . 244 B6
Elm Cl
Groby LE6 . . . 126 F2
Ibstock LE67 . . . 95 E2
Mountsorrel LE12 . . . 76 E1
Oakham LE15 . . . 138 B7
Elmcroft Ave LE5 . . . 156 B7
Elmcroft Rd LE17 . . . 246 F3
Elm Ct LE7 . . . 127 E6
Elmdale Rd LE9 . . . 198 D6
Elmdale St LE4 . . . 129 A2
Elm Dr LE16 . . . 240 C2
ELMESTHORPE . . . 198 F5
Elmesthorpe La LE9 . . . 198 D6
Elmfield Ave
Birstall LE4 . . . 128 F7
Leicester LE2 . . . 155 C3
Elmfield Ct LE2 . . . 179 E8
Elmfield Gdns LE2 . . . 155 C3
Elm Gdns LE12 . . . 76 E1
Elm Gr DE12 . . . 68 B6
Elmhirst Rd LE17 . . . 244 B5
Elmhurst Ave LE13 . . . 59 A5
Elmhurst Cl LE19 . . . 201 A7
Elm La
Catthorpe CV23 . . . 253 E1
Eaton NG32 . . . 22 F6
Elms Cl
Leicester, Oadby LE2 . . . 181 B5
Rempstone LE12 . . . 32 D5
Elms Ct
Austrey CV9 . . . 119 A2
Leicester LE2 . . . 180 D8
Elmsdale Rd DE11 . . . 45 A4
Elms Dr
Austrey CV9 . . . 119 A2
Peckleton LE9 . . . 176 A7
Quorn (Quorndon) LE12 . . . 75 F5
Elms Farm Ind Est
LE17 . . . 233 E2
Elms Gr
Barrow-u-S LE12 . . . 53 D1
Loughborough LE11 . . . 52 C3
Elm's La LE8 . . . 182 F1
Elmsleigh Ave LE2 . . . 155 D1
Elmsleigh Cl DE11 . . . 44 B6
Elmsleigh Dr DE11 . . . 44 B6
Elmsleigh Gr DE11 . . . 44 B6
Elmsleigh Inf Sch
DE11 . . . 44 B6
Elms Rd
Leicester LE2 . . . 180 D8
Melton Mowbray LE13 . . . 59 C3
Elms Road Hos LE2 . . . 180 D8
Elm St PE9 . . . 143 E3
Elms The
Blaby LE8 . . . 202 B7
Countesthorpe LE8 . . . 202 E4
Leicester, Oadby LE2 . . . 181 B5
Markfield LE67 . . . 98 D2
Whitwick LE67 . . . 71 D5
Elmsthorpe Rise LE3 . . . 154 A3

Elm Tree Ave LE3 . . . 153 B8
Elmtree Cl LE5 . . . 130 C2
Elm Tree Dr LE10 . . . 215 F8
Elm Tree Rd LE9 . . . 201 C2
Elm Wlk NN17 . . . 230 D1
Elmwood Row LE2 . . . 180 A4
Elsadene Ave LE4 . . . 129 B3
Elsalene Cl LE6 . . . 126 C5
Elsalene Ct LE2 . . . 155 D1
Elsalene Dr LE6 . . . 126 C5
Elsdon Cl LE67 . . . 71 D5
Elsham Cl LE3 . . . 153 D5
Elstead La DE11 . . . 45 B1
Elston Fields LE2 . . . 179 F6
Elstop Ave CV23 . . . 252 D1
Elstree Ave LE5 . . . 156 E8
Elsworthy Wlk LE3 . . . 153 D6
Elton Cl PE9 . . . 143 B4
Elton & Orston Sta
NG13 . . . 2 A5
Elton Way LE67 . . . 96 E2
Elvaston Cl 2 LE65 . . . 69 C5
Elvaston Dr NG10 . . . 10 A4
Elvaston St DE72 . . . 9 B7
Elvyn Way LE11 . . . 51 D2
Elwell Ave LE9 . . . 175 B1
Elwells Ave LE17 . . . 219 D2
Elwin Ave LE18 . . . 180 D4
Ely Cl DE11 . . . 44 D6
Emberton Cl LE18 . . . 180 F3
Embleton Cl LE10 . . . 197 B1
Emburn Ho LE3 . . . 153 F8
Emerson Cl LE4 . . . 128 A3
Emlyns Gdns PE9 . . . 143 E4
Emlyns St PE9 . . . 143 E4
Emmanuel Rd PE9 . . . 143 D5
Emperor Way LE8 . . . 201 F4
EMPINGHAM . . . 141 A5
Empingham CE Prim Sch
LE15 . . . 141 B6
Empingham Rd
Empingham LE15 . . . 140 F2
Exton LE15 . . . 113 B2
Ketton PE9 . . . 167 E6
Stamford PE9 . . . 143 B3
Empire Rd LE3 . . . 154 D7
Empress Rd LE11 . . . 52 D4
ENDERBY . . . 178 B3
Enderby Rd
Blaby LE8 . . . 202 B8
Thurlaston LE9 . . . 177 B3
Whetstone LE8, LE19 . . . 178 E1
Enderby Road Ind Est
LE8 . . . 178 E1
Enderbys La LE7 . . . 159 B8
Englefield Rd LE5 . . . 156 D5
Englewood Cl LE4 . . . 128 D1
English Martyr's RC Prim
Sch LE15 . . . 138 B7
English Martyrs RC Sch
LE4 . . . 128 B1
Ennerdale Cl LE2 . . . 181 D4
Ennerdale Gdns LE65 . . . 69 D5
Ennerdale Rd
Barrow-u-S LE12 . . . 76 D8
Corby NN17 . . . 230 E1
Ensbury Gdns LE5 . . . 156 B3
Ensor Cl
Nuneaton CV11 . . . 214 A6
Swadlincote DE11 . . . 44 D5
Enston St LE9 . . . 150 B4
Enterprise Ctr The
LE9 . . . 198 B6
Epinal Ct LE11 . . . 51 D5
Epinal Way LE11 . . . 51 F3
Epping Dr LE13 . . . 59 C5
Epping Way LE2 . . . 179 D3
Epsom Rd LE4 . . . 129 B2
Equity Rd
Earl Shilton LE9 . . . 198 E7
Enderby LE19 . . . 178 A2
Leicester LE3 . . . 154 D4
Equity Rd E LE9 . . . 198 F7
Erdyngton Rd LE3 . . . 153 F4
Erith Rd LE2 . . . 154 E1
Ermine Cl PE9 . . . 143 B3
Ermine Rise PE9 . . . 142 D7
Ermine Way PE9 . . . 143 B3
Ernee Cl LE3 . . . 153 D7
Ernest Hall Way DE11 . . . 44 C4
Erringtons Cl LE2 . . . 181 E2
Erskine Cl LE10 . . . 197 A2
Erskine St LE1 . . . 259 C4
Ervington Ct LE19 . . . 178 D6
Ervin's Lock LE18 . . . 203 A8
Ervin Way LE7 . . . 103 E6
Escolme Cl DE11 . . . 44 D4
Eskdale Cl
Leicester, Oadby LE2 . . . 181 D4
Long Eaton NG10 . . . 10 B5
Eskdale Rd
Hinckley LE10 . . . 215 A7
Leicester LE4 . . . 128 D3
ESSENDINE . . . 117 A6
Essendine Rd PE9 . . . 116 F4
Essex Cl
Desford LE9 . . . 151 B3
Melton Mowbray LE13 . . . 82 D8
Essex Gdns LE16 . . . 240 D1
Essex Rd
Leicester LE4 . . . 129 E2
Stamford PE9 . . . 143 D4
Wigston LE18 . . . 179 F3
Estelle Ho LE4 . . . 129 E8
Estima Cl LE2 . . . 180 C8
Estley Rd LE9 . . . 218 E7
Estoril Ave LE18 . . . 180 F3
Ethel Rd LE5 . . . 155 E4

Eton Cl
Ashby-de-la-Z LE65 . . . 69 A8
Leicester LE2 . . . 180 B8
Eunice Ave LE9 . . . 200 D7
Eureka Prim Sch DE11 . . . 44 D5
Eureka Rd DE11 . . . 44 D5
Euro Bsns Pk LE16 . . . 241 B4
Europark Ind Est
CV23 . . . 253 B2
Euston St LE2 . . . 154 F1
Evelyn Dr LE3 . . . 154 D2
Evelyn Rd LE3 . . . 153 E2
Everard Cl CV23 . . . 257 A5
Everard Cres LE67 . . . 97 F1
Everard Way
Braunstone Town
LE19 . . . 178 F5
Stanton u B LE67 . . . 97 F1
Everest Ct LE1 . . . 155 B7
Everest Dr LE13 . . . 59 A5
Everett Cl LE4 . . . 130 A6
Everson Cl LE9 . . . 218 F5
Every St LE1 . . . 259 B3
Evesham Rd LE3 . . . 154 C2
EVINGTON . . . 156 A3
Evington Cl LE5 . . . 155 E3
Evington Ct LE5 . . . 156 A3
Evington Dr LE5 . . . 155 E3
Evington La
Leicester, Evington
LE5 . . . 156 A2
Leicester LE5 . . . 155 E3
Evington Mews LE5 . . . 156 B3
Evington Parks Rd
LE2 . . . 155 D3
Evington Pl LE2 . . . 155 C4
Evington Rd LE2 . . . 155 C3
Evington St LE2 . . . 155 B5
Evington Valley Gdns
LE5 . . . 155 D4
Evington Valley Prim Sch
LE5 . . . 155 D3
Evington Valley Rd
LE5 . . . 155 D4
Ewden Rise LE13 . . . 59 B1
Excalibur Cl LE3 . . . 153 A2
Excelsior Dr DE11 . . . 44 E2
Exchange The LE2 . . . 179 E4
Exeter Cl DE11 . . . 44 E6
Exeter Ct 3 PE9 . . . 143 D2
Exeter Gdns PE9 . . . 143 B2
Exeter Rd LE18 . . . 180 B4
Exmoor Ave LE4 . . . 154 E8
Exmoor Cl
Ellistown LE67 . . . 96 D4
Loughborough LE11 . . . 74 D8
Wigston LE18 . . . 180 D1
Exploration Dr LE4 . . . 128 F2
EXTON . . . 113 B3
Exton CE Prim Sch
LE15 . . . 113 B3
Exton Cl PE9 . . . 143 A3
Exton La LE15 . . . 112 C2
Exton Rd
Cottesmore LE15 . . . 112 D7
Empingham LE15 . . . 140 F8
Leicester LE5 . . . 155 E7
Eyebrook Cl LE5 . . . 130 C3
Eye Brook Cl LE11 . . . 51 B2
EYE KETTLEBY . . . 81 F6
Eynsford Cl LE2 . . . 180 F8
EYRES MONSELL . . . 179 D3
Eyres Monsell Prim Sch
LE2 . . . 179 D4

F

Fabis Cl DE11 . . . 44 A3
Fabius Cl LE10 . . . 215 C7
Facers La LE7 . . . 156 F8
Factory La 9 LE16 . . . 240 E3
Factory Rd LE10 . . . 197 D1
Factory St
Loughborough LE11 . . . 52 C3
Shepshed LE12 . . . 50 B4
Factory The LE2 . . . 179 E8
Fair Acre Rd LE9 . . . 198 A6
Fairbourne Rd LE3 . . . 154 A1
Fairburn Ho LE3 . . . 153 F8
Faircharm Trad Est
LE3 . . . 154 D2
Fairefield Cres LE3 . . . 127 D1
Faire Rd LE3 . . . 127 D1
Fairestone Ave LE3 . . . 153 C8
Fairfax Cl
Ashby-de-la-Z LE65 . . . 69 D7
Leicester LE4 . . . 129 E2
Fairfax Ct LE8 . . . 205 B8
Fairfax Rd
Leicester LE4 . . . 129 E2
Market Harborough
LE16 . . . 240 E1
Fairfield LE67 . . . 95 F1
Fair Field LE14 . . . 40 A6
Fairfield Cl
Langham LE15 . . . 110 C3
Melton Mowbray LE13 . . . 59 D5
Fairfield Com Prim Sch
LE18 . . . 180 A3
Fairfield Cres NG10 . . . 10 B4
Fairfield Ct
Coalville LE67 . . . 96 C6
Loughborough LE11 . . . 52 C3

Fairfield Rd
Coalville LE67 . . . .**96** C7
Leicester, Oadby LE2 . . . . .**181** B5
Market Harborough
 LE16 . . . .**240** D4
Fairfield Sch LE11 . . . .**52** B3
Fairfield St
Leicester LE5 . . . .**155** C5
Wigston LE18 . . . .**179** F1
Fairfield Terr DE11 . . . . . .**44** F3
Fairfield (Uppingham Sch)
 LE15 . . . .**188** F4
Fairford Ave LE5 . . . .**156** B3
Fairhaven Rd LE7 . . . .**127** E8
Fairholme Rd LE2 . . . .**180** B6
Fairside Way LE8 . . . .**202** F3
Fair Lea Cl NG10 . . . .**10** D6
Fair Mead LE12 . . . .**101** E8
Fairmeadows Way
 LE11 . . . .**75** A7
Fairmount Dr LE11 . . . .**51** E2
Fairstone Hill LE2 . . . .**181** B4
Fair View LE15 . . . .**138** B6
Fairview Ave LE8 . . . .**201** F7
Fairway
Kibworth Beauchamp
 LE8 . . . .**224** B8
Market Harborough
 LE16 . . . .**240** D4
Nuneaton CV11 . . . .**214** B1
Fairway Mdws LE17 . . . . .**233** B4
Fairway Rd LE12 . . . .**50** D3
Fairway Rd S LE12 . . . .**50** C1
Fairways Ct LE9 . . . .**198** A3
Fairway The
Blaby LE8 . . . .**202** A7
Hinckley LE10 . . . .**215** F7
Kirby Fields LE9 . . . .**152** F5
Leicester, Aylestone
 LE2 . . . .**179** F6
Leicester LE2 . . . .**181** A8
Falcon Bsns Pk LE11 . . . . .**52** C6
Falcon Cl
Broughton Astley LE9 . . . .**218** E7
Leicester Forest East
 LE3 . . . .**152** E2
Falconer Cres LE3 . . . . . .**153** E8
Falconers Gn LE10 . . . . . .**215** F6
Falcon Rd LE7 . . . .**127** D5
Falcon St LE11 . . . .**52** C5
Falcon Way DE11 . . . .**44** F3
Faldo Cl LE4 . . . .**129** E5
Faldo Dr LE13 . . . .**59** C6
Falkirk Cl PE9 . . . .**143** A4
Falkner Ct LE11 . . . .**51** E2
Fallow Cl
Broughton Astley LE9 . . . .**218** F4
Whetstone LE8 . . . .**201** F5
Fallowfield Rd LE5 . . . . . .**156** D4
Falmouth Cl CV11 . . . . . .**214** A5
Falmouth Dr
Hinckley LE10 . . . .**197** E4
Wigston LE18 . . . .**180** D1
Falmouth Rd LE5 . . . .**156** A4
Falstaff Cl CV11 . . . .**214** A1
Fane Cl PE9 . . . .**143** D5
Faraday Cl LE9 . . . .**218** F4
Faraday Ct LE2 . . . .**259** C3
Faraday Rd LE10 . . . .**214** E7
Far Croft PE9 . . . .**9** D8
Faringdon Ave LE17 . . . . .**244** D6
Far La LE12 . . . .**30** D4
Far Lash LE10 . . . .**215** F7
Farleigh Ave LE18 . . . . . .**180** D3
Farleigh Cl LE9 . . . .**218** E7
Farleigh Gdns LE15 . . . . .**189** A5
Farleigh (Uppingham Sch)
 LE15 . . . .**189** B5
Farley Rd LE2 . . . .**180** D8
Farley Way
Kirby Muxloe LE9 . . . .**152** F6
Quorn (Quorndon) LE12 . . .**75** F7
Farm Cl
Birstall LE4 . . . .**129** B7
Leicester LE2 . . . .**179** F5
Littlethorpe LE19 . . . .**201** C7
Long Eaton NG10 . . . .**10** E5
Farmers Cl LE3 . . . .**153** B8
Farmhouse Cl NG13 . . . . . .**3** A3
Farm La LE67 . . . .**96** B6
Farm Rd
Barwell LE9 . . . .**198** C8
Hinckley LE10 . . . .**215** B6
FARM TOWN **70** B5
Farmway LE3 . . . .**178** E6
Farndale
Whitwick LE67 . . . .**71** D6
Wigston LE18 . . . .**180** F2
Farndale Cl
Leicester LE2 . . . .**259** A2
Long Eaton NG10 . . . .**10** A4
Farndale View LE18 . . . . . .**74** E8
Farndale View Rd LE16 . . .**240** C2
Farndon Ct LE16 . . . .**240** D2
Farndon Dr LE9 . . . .**199** D2
Farndon Fields Prim Sch
 LE16 . . . .**250** E8
Farndon Rd
Great Oxendon LE16 . . . . .**250** D4
Lubenham LE16 . . . .**239** F2
Market Harborough
 LE16 . . . .**240** D1
Marston Trussell LE16 . . .**249** D7
Farneway LE10 . . . .**197** B1
Farnham Cl LE7 . . . .**101** E7

Farnham Ct LE12 . . . .**76** D3
Farnham Rd LE11 . . . .**75** B8
Farnham St
Leicester LE5 . . . .**155** C6
Quorn (Quorndon) LE12 . . .**75** F6
Farnworth Cl LE4 . . . .**129** D3
Farrier La LE4 . . . .**128** B4
Farriers Cl
Snarestone DE12 . . . .**120** E7
Wymeswold LE12 . . . .**33** B4
Farriers Ct CV9 . . . .**171** B8
Farriers Way
Carlby PE9 . . . .**117** B8
Hinckley LE10 . . . .**215** F6
Stathern LE14 . . . .**13** A3
Farriers' Way LE7 . . . .**103** D7
Farringdon St LE5 . . . . . .**155** C7
Farr Wood Cl LE6 . . . .**126** E3
Far St LE12 . . . .**33** C4
Farthing Ct NG10 . . . .**10** B7
Farthingdale Cl LE19 . . . .**201** E3
Farthings The LE12 . . . . . .**30** A1
Fastnet Rd LE5 . . . .**156** E7
Faversham Cl LE3 . . . . . .**153** C6
Fayrhurst Rd LE2 . . . .**179** E6
Fearn Cl DE72 . . . .**10** A7
Fearon St LE11 . . . .**51** F4
Featherbed La
Ashby-de-la-Z LE65 . . . . . .**69** D7
Rugby CV21 . . . .**257** A1
West Langton LE8 . . . . . .**224** E7
Featherby Dr LE9 . . . .**179** A3
Featherston Dr LE10 . . . .**215** E6
Featherstone Dr LE12 . . .**179** C2
Feature Rd LE4 . . . .**102** E1
Federation St LE19 . . . . .**178** A3
Feldspar Cl LE17 . . . .**244** C7
Feldspar Ct LE19 . . . .**178** B5
Fell Cl LE8 . . . .**223** A6
Felley Way LE3 . . . .**154** C8
Felstead Rd LE4 . . . .**128** D4
Fencote Rd LE5 . . . .**130** C3
Fen La NG23 . . . .**1** F7
Fennel St LE11 . . . .**52** B4
Fennes Cl LE14 . . . .**128** C7
Fenn Lanes
Dadlington CV13 . . . .**173** D2
Fenny Drayton CV13 . . . .**195** D8
FENNY DRAYTON **195** A6
Fenny La LE17 . . . .**222** A2
Fenton Ave DE11 . . . .**45** B1
Fenton Cl
Leicester, Oadby LE2 . . . .**181** A3
Measham DE12 . . . .**93** B3
Fenton Cres DE12 . . . .**93** C3
Fenton Dr PE9 . . . .**117** C8
Fenwick Rd LE2 . . . .**181** E4
Fermain Cl LE5 . . . .**156** D5
Fern Bank LE5 . . . .**155** C6
Fern Cl LE7 . . . .**156** E5
Fern Cres LE6 . . . .**126** D4
Ferndale LE67 . . . .**95** E1
Ferndale Dr LE16 . . . .**152** D8
Ferndale Gr LE10 . . . .**215** A7
Ferndale Rd
Leicester LE2 . . . .**180** B6
Thurmaston LE4 . . . .**129** E6
Ferndene Dr NG10 . . . .**10** A7
Ferndown Cl LE3 . . . .**153** C6
Ferneley Ave LE10 . . . . . .**197** A3
Ferneley Cres LE13 . . . . . .**59** E5
Ferneley Rise LE7 . . . .**78** F4
Ferness Cl LE10 . . . .**197** B2
Ferness Rd LE10 . . . .**197** B2
Fernfield Cl LE16 . . . .**241** B4
Fernhurst Rd LE3 . . . .**178** F8
Fernie Ave LE13 . . . .**59** B3
Fernie Chase LE16 . . . . . .**226** A6
Fernie Cl LE2 . . . .**181** C4
Fernie Cl LE17 . . . .**247** E6
Fernie Dene LE8 . . . .**182** C1
Fernie Rd
Leicester LE5 . . . .**155** D7
Market Harborough
 LE16 . . . .**240** F3
Fernie Sq LE15 . . . .**87** D2
Fernlea LE19 . . . .**177** F1
Fern Ley Cl LE16 . . . .**241** B2
Fernleys Cl LE4 . . . .**128** B3
Fern Rise LE5 . . . .**130** C1
Fernvale Prim Sch
 LE7 . . . .**156** F6
Ferrars Ct LE3 . . . .**153** D2
Ferrers Cl
Ashby-de-la-Z LE65 . . . . . .**68** F5
Castle Donington DE74 . . .**17** A3
Oakham LE15 . . . .**137** D6
Ferrers Croft CV13 . . . . . .**149** D7
Ferrers Ctr for Arts &
 Crafts★ LE65 . . . .**46** F7
Ferrers Rd LE2 . . . .**180** D8
Ferrers Rise LE6 . . . .**126** E3
Ferrous Cl LE4 . . . .**155** C8
Ferryman Rd LE11 . . . .**52** C5
Festival Ave
Breaston DE72 . . . .**9** C2
Thurmaston LE4 . . . .**129** E6
Festival Dr LE11 . . . .**52** A6
Fettes Cl LE65 . . . .**69** A8
Field Ave LE12 . . . .**50** C6
Field Cl
Breaston DE72 . . . .**9** F7
Hinckley LE10 . . . .**197** F3
Houghton on t H LE7 . . . .**158** A3
Littlethorpe LE19 . . . .**201** C7

Field Cl continued
Melton Mowbray LE13 . . . . .**59** D1
Thringstone LE67 . . . .**71** D7
Field Court Rd LE6 . . . . . .**126** F3
Field Crest LE12 . . . .**101** D8
Fieldfare Wlk LE5 . . . .**155** C7
Fieldgate Cres LE4 . . . . . .**128** E8
FIELD HEAD **98** F1
Fieldhead Cl LE16 . . . . . .**240** C3
Fieldhouse Rd LE4 . . . . . .**129** B3
Fieldhurst Ave LE3 . . . . . .**178** E8
Fielding Cl LE9 . . . .**170** D2
Fielding Palmer Hospl
 LE7 . . . .**244** D6
Fielding Rd LE4 . . . .**128** F6
Field La
Blackfordby DE11 . . . .**45** C2
Tonge DE73 . . . .**27** B3
Fields Farm Cl LE12 . . . . . .**34** D7
Fields Farm Rd NG10 . . . . .**10** E5
Field St LE12 . . . .**50** B4
Field The LE14 . . . .**108** B2
Field View
Syston LE7 . . . .**102** E3
Thurmaston LE4 . . . .**130** A7
Whitwick LE67 . . . .**71** D5
Field Way LE9 . . . .**198** D7
Fieldway Cres LE8 . . . . . .**182** B1
Fieldway Rd LE18 . . . .**218** F5
Fieldwork Rd LE14 . . . .**36** A5
Fife Cl PE9 . . . .**142** F4
Filbert St E LE2 . . . .**154** F3
Filbert St LE2 . . . .**259** A1
Filbert Village LE2 . . . . . .**154** E3
Filbert Way LE2 . . . .**154** E2
Fillingate LE7 . . . .**102** B3
Filsham Rd LE3 . . . .**178** B1
Finch Cl
Leicester LE5 . . . .**153** E5
Uppingham LE15 . . . .**189** A5
Woodville DE11 . . . .**44** F3
Finches The
Desford LE9 . . . .**151** B2
Market Overton LE15 . . . . .**87** A5
Finch-Hatton Dr
 NN17 . . . .**213** C1
Finch Way LE9 . . . .**201** A7
Fineacres LE14 . . . .**57** E3
Fineshade Ave LE14 . . . . .**154** C8
Finkey St LE15 . . . .**137** F6
Finney Cl DE12 . . . .**67** E1
Finns La NG23 . . . .**14** E3
Finsbury Ave
Loughborough LE11 . . . . . .**52** C3
Sileby LE12 . . . .**77** E3
Finsbury Rd LE4 . . . .**129** C1
Finson Cl LE18 . . . .**180** D3
Fiona Dr LE7 . . . .**156** F5
Firdale LE14 . . . .**108** C1
Firestone Cl LE3 . . . .**153** C6
Firfield Ave
Birstall LE4 . . . .**129** A7
Breaston DE72 . . . .**9** E8
Firfield Prim Sch DE72 . . . .**9** F7
Firfield Villas LE2 . . . . . .**179** E8
Fir Rd PE9 . . . .**142** F5
Firs Ave LE15 . . . .**189** A5
Firs Cl LE7 . . . .**158** A4
Firs Rd LE7 . . . .**158** A4
Firs St NG10 . . . .**10** A4
Firs The
Market Harborough
 LE16 . . . .**240** C3
Syston LE7 . . . .**103** A2
Wigston LE18 . . . .**180** E4
Firth Pk LE15 . . . .**189** B4
Firtree Ave LE18 . . . .**244** B6
Fir Tree Ave LE8 . . . .**202** E4
Firtree Cl LE9 . . . .**198** B8
Fir Tree Cl LE18 . . . .**180** C5
Firtree La LE17 . . . .**254** C3
Fir Tree La LE6 . . . .**126** E4
Firtree Wlk
Moira DE12 . . . .**68** B6
Moira LE12 . . . .**68** B6
Fir Tree Wlk LE16 . . . . . .**240** E4
Firwood Rd LE13 . . . .**59** E5
Fisher Cl
Cossington LE7 . . . .**102** D8
Stoney Stanton LE9 . . . . .**199** C2
Fishley Cl LE3 . . . .**153** B7
Fishpond La NG13 . . . .**6** C2
Fishponds Cl LE3 . . . .**153** B8
Fishpond Way LE11 . . . . . .**75** A6
Fishpools LE3 . . . .**178** E7
Fishpool Way LE12 . . . . . .**76** E8
Fish Well Cl NG33 . . . .**43** B8
Fitzroy St LE3 . . . .**154** D5
Fitzwilliam Cl LE2 . . . . . .**181** D4
Fitzwilliam Rd PE9 . . . . . .**143** C5
Fitzwilliam Wlk LE15 . . . . .**87** E2
Flagstaff Rd LE16 . . . . . .**156** D7
Flamborough Rd LE5 . . . .**156** D7
Flamingo Dr LE8 . . . .**201** F4
Flamville Rd LE10 . . . . . .**216** B5
Flanagan Way LE3 . . . .**97** B7
Flatholme Rd LE5 . . . . . .**156** E8
Flats La CV9 . . . .**119** B1
Flats The
Earl Shilton LE9 . . . .**176** A1
Illston on t H LE7 . . . . . .**183** F3
Flatten Way LE7 . . . .**103** A4
Flatts Cl LE67 . . . .**95** F3
Flavel Ct CV9 . . . .**119** A1
Flaxfield Cl LE6 . . . .**126** F3
Flax La CV9 . . . .**146** D6
Flaxland Cl LE16 . . . .**101** E7

Flaxland Cl LE16 . . . .**241** B3
Flaxland Cres LE12 . . . . . .**77** C2
Flax Rd LE4 . . . .**129** B2
FLECKNEY **222** E8
Fleckney CE Prim Sch
 LE8 . . . .**222** E8
Fleckney Ind Est LE8 . . . .**223** A7
Fleckney Rd
Arnesby LE8 . . . .**221** F5
Fleckney LE8 . . . .**223** A6
Kibworth Beauchamp
 LE8 . . . .**222** E8
Kilby LE18 . . . .**204** A2
Saddington LE8 . . . .**222** D4
Fleet St LE1 . . . .**259** C4
Fleet The LE9 . . . .**199** E3
Fleetwood Cl LE16 . . . . . .**240** D1
Fleetwood Ct
2 Leicester LE2 . . . .**155** A1
Stretton LE15 . . . .**89** A7
Fleetwood Gdns LE16 . . .**240** D1
Fleetwood Rd LE2 . . . . . .**155** A1
Fleming Ave NG13 . . . .**3** C3
Fleming Cl LE11 . . . .**51** D6
Fleming Rd LE10 . . . .**214** F7
Flesh Hovel La LE12 . . . . .**76** A8
Fletcher Mall LE4 . . . . . .**128** A4
Fletcher Rd
Hinckley LE10 . . . .**215** E7
Stoney Stanton LE9 . . . . .**199** E3
Fletchers Cl LE19 . . . .**201** B7
Fletcher St NG10 . . . .**10** D8
Fletchers' Way LE7 . . . . .**103** D7
Fletcher's Way LE7 . . . . .**103** D7
Fleury Ct LE17 . . . .**103** E7
Flint Cl
Atherstone CV9 . . . .**170** E2
Ryhall PE9 . . . .**117** A2
Flora St LE3 . . . .**154** D5
Florence Ave LE18 . . . . . .**180** A1
Florence Cl CV9 . . . .**170** D1
Florence Rd LE5 . . . .**155** C6
Florence St LE7 . . . .**179** E7
Florence Wragg Way
 LE2 . . . .**181** E4
Floret Cl LE67 . . . .**71** A2
Florian Way LE10 . . . .**197** A1
Florin Gdns NG10 . . . .**10** B7
Floyd Cl LE4 . . . .**128** E5
Fludes Ct LE2 . . . .**181** C5
Foan Hill LE67 . . . .**71** B5
Foley Rd LE8 . . . .**223** E8
Folville Jun Sch LE3 . . . . .**154** B2
Folville Rise LE3 . . . .**154** B2
Folville St LE1 . . . .**105** F4
Fontwell Dr LE2 . . . .**179** B5
Fontwell Gdns PE9 . . . . .**143** D3
Forbes Cl
Glenfield LE3 . . . .**153** C7
Long Eaton NG10 . . . .**10** E6
Ford Bank LE16 . . . .**229** D6
Ford Cl LE2 . . . .**179** C3
Fordice Cl LE67 . . . .**96** C7
Ford Rise LE2 . . . .**179** C3
Ford The LE2 . . . .**179** D1
Fordview Cl LE8 . . . .**182** A1
Forest Ave LE4 . . . .**129** E8
Forest Bsns Pk LE67 . . . . .**97** C4
Forest Cl
Groby LE6 . . . .**126** D3
Melton Mowbray LE13 . . . .**59** C5
Forest Ct LE11 . . . .**52** A3
Forest Dr
Kirby Fields LE9 . . . .**152** F4
Sileby LE12 . . . .**77** C4
Foresters Cl LE3 . . . .**153** D8
Foresters' Row LE7 . . . . .**103** D8
Forest Gate LE67 . . . .**72** C3
Forest Gdns PE9 . . . .**142** F5
Forest House La LE3 . . . . .**152** F2
Forest La LE12 . . . .**49** C4
Forest Lodge Prim Sch
 LE3 . . . .**153** E8
Forest Rise
Desford LE9 . . . .**152** E8
Groby LE6 . . . .**126** E3
Leicester Forest East
 LE9 . . . .**152** F3
Leicester, Oadby LE2 . . . .**181** C6
Thurnby LE7 . . . .**156** F5
Forest St LE12 . . . .**50** C4
Forest View
Botcheston LE9 . . . .**151** C8
Groby LE6 . . . .**126** E3
Overseal DE12 . . . .**67** B4
Forest Way Sch LE67 . . . . .**97** A8
Forge Cl
Fleckney LE8 . . . .**222** F8
Glenfield LE3 . . . .**153** A8
Forge Cnr LE8 . . . .**205** B8
Forge End LE7 . . . .**101** E5
Forge Rd LE12 . . . .**50** C4
Forman Cl DE11 . . . .**44** B4
Forman Rd LE12 . . . .**50** C2
Formans Way LE7 . . . .**71** A2
Forrester Cl
Coleorton LE67 . . . .**70** D4

Forrester Cl continued
Cosby LE9 . . . .**201** E3
Forresters Cl LE10 . . . . . .**215** F6
Forresters Rd LE10 . . . . . .**215** F6
Forryan Cl LE7 . . . .**201** D2
Forryan Rd LE10 . . . .**215** F7
Forryans Cl LE18 . . . .**203** E8
Forsells End LE7 . . . .**157** F3
Forsyth Cl LE11 . . . .**51** B6
Forsythia Cl LE17 . . . .**244** A6
Forth Cl LE15 . . . .**137** E5
Forties La LE65 . . . .**45** F3
Fort Rd LE12 . . . .**76** F2
Forty Foot La DE73 . . . . . .**26** F7
Fosbrook Dr DE74 . . . .**16** F4
Fosbrooke Cl LE67 . . . . . .**95** E8
Fosbrooke Dr NG10 . . . . . .**10** D5
Fosse Bldg The LE3 . . . . .**154** C6
Fosse Cl
Hinckley LE10 . . . .**216** A5
Narborough LE19 . . . . . .**178** D2
Sharnford LE10 . . . .**217** B4
Fosse La
Leicester LE3 . . . .**154** C7
Thistleton LE15 . . . .**64** C1
Fosse Park Ave LE19 . . . .**178** F5
Fosse Park S LE19 . . . . . .**178** F5
Fosse Prim Sch LE3 . . . . .**154** D7
Fosse Rd Central LE3 . . . .**154** C6
Fosse Rd N LE3 . . . .**154** C6
Fosse Rd S LE3 . . . .**154** C3
Fosse Sh Pk LE19 . . . . . .**178** F5
Fosse Terr LE19 . . . .**201** A7
Fosse Way
Cloudesley Bush
 CV23 . . . .**231** F3
Syston LE7 . . . .**102** F3
Fosseway Gdns LE17 . . . .**232** E6
Foster Rd DE11 . . . .**44** F2
FOSTON **203** C2
Foston Gate LE18 . . . .**203** E8
Foston La LE8 . . . .**203** C3
Foston Rd
Allington NG32 . . . .**4** F6
Wistow LE8 . . . .**204** D4
Fothergill Cl LE16 . . . .**241** A6
Foulds La LE8 . . . .**179** A1
Foundation Ct LE5 . . . . . .**155** F5
Foundry Ct 4 PE9 . . . . . .**143** C3
Foundry La
1 Leicester LE1 . . . .**155** A7
Syston LE7 . . . .**102** F3
Foundry Rd
Ryhall PE9 . . . .**116** F3
Stamford PE9 . . . .**143** C3
Foundry Sq 3 LE1 . . . . . .**155** A7
Fountains Ave LE2 . . . . . .**179** D3
Fountain's Row LE15 . . . . .**86** F5
Fount Ct LE16 . . . .**240** F1
Four Lane Ends DE11 . . . . .**44** A6
Fowke St LE7 . . . .**101** F6
Fowler Cl LE4 . . . .**128** C4
Fowler Rd LE67 . . . .**96** C7
Foxbank Ind Est LE17 . . . .**199** D3
Fox Cl
Fleckney LE8 . . . .**223** A6
Long Eaton NG10 . . . .**10** C6
Rugby CV21 . . . .**257** B1
Foxcote Dr LE11 . . . .**51** A2
Fox Covert
Loughborough LE11 . . . . . .**52** B6
Whetstone LE8 . . . .**201** F5
Fox Covert Cl LE7 . . . . . .**101** C2
Foxcovert La CV13 . . . . . .**196** A8
Foxcroft Cl LE3 . . . .**179** C8
Fox Dale PE9 . . . .**143** B4
Fox End LE9 . . . .**177** A3
Foxfield Cl LE17 . . . .**244** D5
Foxfield Way LE15 . . . . . .**138** A8
Foxglove Ave
Donisthorpe DE12 . . . .**67** C2
Melton Mowbray LE13 . . . .**82** A8
Foxglove Cl
Broughton Astley LE9 . . . .**219** A4
East Goscote LE7 . . . . . .**103** E8
Mountsorrel LE12 . . . .**76** F2
Narborough LE19 . . . . . .**201** A8
Foxglove Dr LE6 . . . .**127** A3
Foxglove Rd
Coalville LE67 . . . .**97** A8
Hamilton LE5 . . . .**130** C2
Stamford PE9 . . . .**142** E5
Foxhill LE15 . . . .**85** A1
Foxhill Dr LE2 . . . .**179** A3
Foxhills DE74 . . . .**18** C1
Foxhills Cl CV11 . . . .**214** C1
Foxholes Rd LE3 . . . .**153** D4
Fox Hollies LE10 . . . .**217** B4
Fox Hollow
Cropston LE7 . . . .**100** F2
East Goscote LE7 . . . . . .**103** D8
Leicester, Oadby LE2 . . . .**181** D4
Foxhunter Dr LE2 . . . .**180** F6
Foxhunter Rdbt LE19 . . . .**178** D2
Fox La
Kirby Muxloe LE9 . . . . . .**152** D5
Leicester LE1 . . . .**259** B4
Foxon St LE3 . . . .**154** D5
Foxon Way LE3 . . . .**153** D1
Foxpond La LE2 . . . .**181** E2
Fox's Covert CV13 . . . . . .**194** F6
Fox St LE1 . . . .**259** C3
FOXTON **224** E1
Foxton Canal Mus★
 LE16 . . . .**239** C8
Foxton Cl LE16 . . . .**215** B7
Foxton Lock Cl LE18 . . . .**203** A8

Foxton Locks Ctry Pk*
  LE16 . . . 239 C8
Foxton Prim Sch
  LE16 . . . 239 D8
Foxton Rd
  Foxton LE16 . . . 239 B7
  Lubenham LE16 . . . 239 D5
Fox Yd **7** LE16 . . . 240 E3
Frain Gdns DE73 . . . 26 F2
Framland Dr LE13 . . . 59 C6
Framland Ho **8** LE2 . . . 155 B5
Frampton Ave LE3 . . . 154 B5
Frances Way LE19 . . . 178 D5
Franche Rd LE3 . . . 154 C6
Francis Ave LE3 . . . 178 F7
Francis Ct
  Leicester LE2 . . . 179 C6
  Ryhall PE9 . . . 116 F2
Francis La LE7 . . . 51 C6
Francis La LE11 . . . 121 D7
Francis St LE2 . . . 155 D1
Francis Way LE67 . . . 96 C3
Frank Bodicote Way
  DE11 . . . 44 D4
Frank Booton Cl LE9 . . . 199 B8
Frank King Ho LE7 . . . 97 B8
Franklin Way LE1 . . . 201 C4
Franklyn Rd LE2 . . . 179 B6
Frank's La LE17 . . . 245 B4
Frankson Ave LE3 . . . 154 A1
Franks Rd LE67 . . . 97 C6
Fraser Cl LE1 . . . 259 C5
Frearson Rd LE67 . . . 96 B7
Frederick Ave
  Hinckley LE10 . . . 197 B2
  Kegworth DE74 . . . 18 C3
Frederick Cl LE7 . . . 103 E6
Frederick Jackson Ho **1**
  LE3 . . . 154 D5
Frederick Rd LE5 . . . 155 C6
Frederick St
  Long Eaton NG10 . . . 10 F7
  Loughborough LE11 . . . 52 A3
  Wigston LE18 . . . 180 D3
  Woodville DE11 . . . 44 F3
Fredscott Cl LE5 . . . 156 E7
Freeboard Rd LE3 . . . 178 F7
FREEBY . . . 61 B5
Freeby Cl LE13 . . . 59 E2
Freehold Rd LE4 . . . 129 A5
Freehold St
  Leicester LE1 . . . 155 B7
  Loughborough LE11 . . . 52 C4
  Quorn (Quorndon) LE12 . . . 76 B6
  Shepshed LE12 . . . 50 C3
Free La LE1 . . . 259 B4
Freeman Rd N LE5 . . . 155 F7
Freeman's Ct LE6 . . . 152 D8
Freeman's La LE10 . . . 216 A5
Freemantle Rd LE2 . . . 155 E1
Freeman Way LE12 . . . 75 F7
Freemen's Common Rd
  LE2 . . . 154 F2
Freemen's Common Trad
  Est LE2 . . . 154 F2
Freemen's Holt LE2 . . . 179 C7
Freer Cl
  Blaby LE8 . . . 202 B8
  Houghton on t H LE7 . . . 157 F3
  Wigston LE18 . . . 203 E8
Freeschool La LE1 . . . 259 A4
Freesia Cl LE11 . . . 75 A6
French Rd LE5 . . . 155 C7
Frensham Cl LE2 . . . 181 A4
Freshney Cl LE13 . . . 59 B1
Freshwater Cl LE18 . . . 203 D7
Freswick Cl LE4 . . . 196 F1
Freven Dr LE9 . . . 217 D8
Frewin St LE5 . . . 155 E7
Friar La LE1 . . . 259 B3
Friars Cswy LE1 . . . 259 A4
Friar St NG10 . . . 10 D7
Friary Cl LE10 . . . 197 E1
Friary Croft DE11 . . . 44 A7
Friary Rd CV9 . . . 170 D1
Friday St LE2 . . . 259 B5
Friendship Ho LE4 . . . 155 C8
Frinton Ave LE5 . . . 156 D5
FRISBY . . . 183 E8
Frisby Ave NG10 . . . 10 E6
Frisby CE Prim Sch
  LE14 . . . 80 D7
Frisby La LE15 . . . 191 D8
FRISBY ON THE WREAKE
  . . . 80 C8
Frisby Rd
  Barwell LE9 . . . 198 B7
  Leicester LE5 . . . 155 D8
Friswell La LE9 . . . 198 A7
Fritchley Cl LE9 . . . 200 E7
Frith Cl LE3 . . . 153 C8
Frith Way LE10 . . . 197 A3
Froanes Cl LE19 . . . 178 A4
Frobisher Cl LE10 . . . 197 D4
FROG ISLAND . . . 259 B5
Frog Island LE1 . . . 259 A5
Frog La NG13 . . . 12 F8
FROLESWORTH . . . 218 B2
Frolesworth La LE17 . . . 232 F7
Frolesworth Rd
  Ashby Parva LE17 . . . 233 D7
  Broughton Astley LE9 . . . 218 E5
  Leire LE17 . . . 233 E8
  Ullesthorpe LE17 . . . 233 B6
Frolesworth Way LE3 . . . 153 C6
Frome Ave LE2 . . . 181 D6

Front St
  Birstall LE4 . . . 129 B6
  Gaulby LE7 . . . 183 D7
Frost Fields DE74 . . . 17 B4
Fulbeck Ave LE5 . . . 156 D5
Fulford Rd LE3 . . . 153 C5
Fullen La NN17 . . . 213 C1
Fuller Cl LE9 . . . 151 C4
Fullhurst Ave LE3 . . . 154 B2
Fullhurst Com Coll
  LE3 . . . 154 B3
Fulmar Rd LE7 . . . 127 D6
Fulton Dr LE67 . . . 71 A2
Fulwell Ave NN17 . . . 213 C1
Fulwood Dr NG10 . . . 10 A7
Furley Ct LE15 . . . 137 F6
Furlongs Cl LE7 . . . 103 C3
Furlongs The LE16 . . . 241 B3
Furnace La DE12 . . . 67 E3
Furnace Lane Ind Est
  DE12 . . . 67 E3
Furnival Cl LE18 . . . 222 E8
Furrow Cl LE7 . . . 101 E7
Furrows Cl LE19 . . . 201 C7
Fydell Row LE15 . . . 191 A6
Fyfe Rd NN17 . . . 230 B1

G

Gables Ct LE17 . . . 218 A2
Gables Lea LE12 . . . 30 B6
Gables The LE65 . . . 69 C4
GADDESBY . . . 105 B7
Gaddesby Ave LE3 . . . 154 C3
Gaddesby La
  Frisby on t W LE14 . . . 80 E4
  Kirby Bellars LE14 . . . 81 B5
  Rearsby LE7 . . . 104 B8
  Rotherby LE14, LE7 . . . 80 A4
Gaddesby Prim Sch
  LE7 . . . 105 C6
Gaddesby Rd LE7 . . . 105 D4
Gainsborough Ave
  LE10 . . . 197 A3
Gainsborough Cl NG10 . . . 10 E5
Gainsborough Cres
  CV21 . . . 257 B1
Gainsborough Rd
  Kibworth Beauchamp
  LE8 . . . 206 A1
  Leicester LE2 . . . 180 B8
  Stamford PE9 . . . 143 B5
  Uppingham LE15 . . . 189 B4
Galahad Cl LE3 . . . 153 A2
Galby St LE5 . . . 155 D8
Gale Cl LE17 . . . 244 C8
Gallards Hill LE3 . . . 153 E4
Galleywood Dr LE4 . . . 128 D2
Gallico Cl LE11 . . . 51 D6
Gallimore Cl LE3 . . . 154 A7
Galloway Cl LE9 . . . 197 F7
Gallow Field Rd LE16 . . . 239 E7
Gallows La DE12 . . . 93 E4
Gallowtree Gate LE1 . . . 259 B4
Gallus Dr LE10 . . . 197 A1
Galsworthy Cres LE13 . . . 59 B6
Galsworthy Ct LE3 . . . 154 A5
Galway Rd LE4 . . . 128 E5
Gamble Cl LE67 . . . 75 F7
Gamble Way LE12 . . . 75 F7
Gamekeepers Ct LE5 . . . 130 C3
Gamel Rd LE5 . . . 156 B6
Gamel Wlk LE5 . . . 156 B5
Ganton Rd LE3 . . . 153 C6
Gaol St LE15 . . . 137 F6
Garden Cl
  Hinckley LE10 . . . 215 D6
  Leicester, Oadby LE2 . . . 181 A5
  Stamford PE9 . . . 142 F3
Garden Cres DE74 . . . 17 B3
Gardenfield Rd LE14 . . . 129 F4
Garden La
  Ibstock LE67 . . . 122 F8
  Melton Mowbray LE13 . . . 59 A5
Garden Rd
  Coalville LE67 . . . 71 C2
  Exton LE15 . . . 113 B3
  Hinckley LE10 . . . 197 D1
Garden Row DE74 . . . 18 D3
Garden St
  Leicester LE1 . . . 259 B5
  Thurmaston LE4 . . . 129 E7
  Wigston LE18 . . . 179 F1
Gardiner St LE16 . . . 240 C3
Gardner Cl LE11 . . . 51 C6
Garden Rd LE4 . . . 153 B4
Garendon Cl LE12 . . . 50 C3
Garendon Gn LE11 . . . 51 D4
Garendon High Sch
  LE11 . . . 51 C4
Garendon Rd
  Coalville LE67 . . . 97 C8
  Loughborough LE11 . . . 51 D4
  Shepshed LE12 . . . 50 B3
Garendon St LE2 . . . 155 B6
Garendon Way LE6 . . . 126 E2
Garfield Ave DE72 . . . 9 A7
Garfield Pk LE8 . . . 182 B2
Garfield Rd LE67 . . . 96 C7
Garfield St LE4 . . . 155 A8
Garfit Rd LE9 . . . 152 E5
Garford La LE9 . . . 151 B5
Gargamey Cl LE67 . . . 97 A8
Garland LE7 . . . 101 E7
Garland Cres LE3 . . . 154 B8
Garland La CV13 . . . 124 A2
Garnett Cres LE2 . . . 179 C4

Garratt Rd **6** PE9 . . . 143 D2
Garratt Sq LE8 . . . 201 F7
Garrick Wlk **8** LE1 . . . 259 B4
Garsdale LE18 . . . 180 F7
Garsington Wlk LE5 . . . 156 A6
Garth Ave LE4 . . . 128 E4
GARTHORPE . . . 62 B6
Garthorpe Dr LE13 . . . 59 E2
Garthorpe Rd LE14 . . . 61 E5
Garth St LE15 . . . 87 D2
Garton Cl DE12 . . . 119 F8
Garton Rd LE11 . . . 52 B3
Gartree Cres LE8 . . . 198 D8
Gartree Ct LE13 . . . 82 C8
Gartree Dr LE13 . . . 59 D1
Gartree High Sch LE2 . . . 181 B3
Gartree Rd
  Carlton Curlieu LE8,
  LE8 . . . 206 F8
  Great Stretton LE2 . . . 182 C5
  Leicester LE2 . . . 156 A1
Gascoigne Ave LE7 . . . 103 E5
Gaskell Wlk LE3 . . . 154 A5
Gas La
  Stamford PE9 . . . 143 E3
  Wigston LE18 . . . 180 C1
Gas Mus* LE2 . . . 154 E1
Gasny Ave DE74 . . . 17 B5
Gas St
  Leicester LE1 . . . 154 F7
  Stamford PE9 . . . 143 E3
Gas Wlk LE14 . . . 12 B3
Gatcombe Dr LE67 . . . 97 A8
Gatehouse La
  Great Easton LE16 . . . 229 F6
  South Luffenham PE9 . . . 166 D1
Gateway St LE2 . . . 259 A2
Gateway The LE2 . . . 259 A2
Gateway VI Form Coll
  LE2 . . . 259 A3
GAULBY . . . 183 D7
Gaulby La
  Houghton on t H LE7 . . . 158 C2
  Leicester LE2 . . . 156 F1
  Little Stretton LE2, LE7 . . . 182 C8
Gaulby Rd
  Billesdon LE7 . . . 183 E8
  Illston on t H LE7 . . . 183 E4
Gaul St LE3 . . . 154 D4
Gavin Cl LE3 . . . 153 C2
Gavin Dr LE11 . . . 51 D6
Gawney La LE17 . . . 235 E5
Gayhurst Cl
  Braunstone Town LE3 . . . 178 F7
  Wigston LE18 . . . 180 E2
Gayton Ave LE4 . . . 129 C1
Gayton Hts LE19 . . . 178 A4
Geary Cl
  Narborough LE19 . . . 201 B7
  Ratby LE6 . . . 152 E8
  Whitwick LE67 . . . 71 D5
Gedding Rd
  Kibworth Beauchamp
Geddington Rd LE5 . . . 155 C6
Geddington Cl LE18 . . . 180 E2
Gedge Way LE7 . . . 179 E6
Gee Rd LE67 . . . 71 E2
Gees Lock Cl LE2 . . . 179 B4
GEESTON . . . 168 B4
Geeston Rd PE9 . . . 168 B5
Gelders Hall Ind Est
  LE12 . . . 50 A1
Gelders Hall Rd LE12 . . . 50 A1
Gelert Ave LE5 . . . 156 A5
Gelscoe La LE12, DE73 . . . 27 C1
GELSMOOR . . . 47 F1
Gelsmoor Rd LE67 . . . 47 F1
George Ave NG10 . . . 10 D5
George Foster Cl LE9 . . . 176 A1
George Fox La CV13 . . . 195 A6
George Geary Cl LE9 . . . 198 C7
Georgeham Cl LE18 . . . 180 D1
George Hill Cl LE9 . . . 199 D3
George Holmes Bsns Pk
  DE11 . . . 44 A4
George Holmes Way
  DE11 . . . 44 A3
George Hotel Mews The
  PE9 . . . 143 E2
George Mythe Ho Ave . . . 128 C7
George Mariott Cl
  LE9 . . . 199 C1
George St
  Anstey LE7 . . . 127 D6
  Barwell LE9 . . . 198 B6
  Enderby LE19 . . . 178 A3
  Hinckley LE10 . . . 215 D8
  Leicester LE1 . . . 259 C5
  Loughborough LE11 . . . 51 F4
  Lutterworth LE17 . . . 244 C6
  Melbourne DE73 . . . 26 A7
  Melton Mowbray LE13 . . . 59 D3
  Swadlincote DE11 . . . 44 A1
  Whitwick LE67 . . . 71 F4
George Toon Ct LE7 . . . 103 A4
George Ward Ct LE9 . . . 198 B7
Georgina Ct DE74 . . . 17 B4
Gerrard Cres DE74 . . . 18 D1
Gerrard Gdns LE16 . . . 250 D8
Gertrude Rd DE72 . . . 9 A7
Gervas Rd LE5 . . . 156 C7
Geveze Way LE9 . . . 219 A4
Ghaus St LE17 . . . 252 F6
Gibbet La
  Bilstone CV13 . . . 147 B5
  Edith Weston LE15 . . . 166 A7
  Shawell LE17 . . . 253 B6
Gibbons Cl LE4 . . . 155 A8

Gibb St NG10 . . . 10 E7
Gibson Cl LE18 . . . 180 D3
Gibson Dr CV21 . . . 257 A1
Gibson Rd LE3 . . . 77 D4
Gibson's La LE14 . . . 35 C2
Gibson Way LE17 . . . 244 A5
Giffard Ct LE16 . . . 240 D3
Gifford Cl LE5 . . . 156 B3
Gilbert Cl
  Leicester LE4 . . . 129 E4
  Market Harborough
  LE16 . . . 241 B2
Gilbert's Dr LE8 . . . 150 B4
Giles Cl LE12 . . . 76 B5
Gillam Butts LE8 . . . 202 E3
Gillamore Dr LE67 . . . 72 A2
Gillbank Dr LE6 . . . 152 C8
Gilliver Gdns DE72 . . . 9 A7
Gilliver St
  Leicester LE2 . . . 180 B8
  Newbold Verdon LE9 . . . 150 B5
Gillman Rd LE3 . . . 154 A8
Gilmore Cl LE15 . . . 138 A8
GILMORTON . . . 235 C4
Gilmorton Ave LE2 . . . 179 B4
Gilmorton Chandler CE
  Prim Sch LE17 . . . 235 B5
Gilmorton La LE8 . . . 220 D2
Gilmorton Rd
  Ashby Magna LE17 . . . 235 A4
  Lutterworth LE17 . . . 244 E7
Gilmour Cl LE4 . . . 128 B5
Gilpin Cl LE13 . . . 59 A1
Gilson Gn LE14 . . . 107 D2
Gilson's Cl LE11 . . . 191 A6
Gilstead Cl LE7 . . . 156 F4
Gimson Ave LE9 . . . 201 D3
Gimson Cl LE5 . . . 130 A1
Gimson Rd LE3 . . . 154 B5
Gipsy Hollow La LE15 . . . 188 F3
Gipsy La
  Leicester LE4 . . . 129 D2
  Mountsorrel LE12 . . . 101 C8
  Stamford PE9 . . . 143 F5
Gipsy Nook LE14 . . . 40 E2
Gipsy Rd LE4 . . . 129 B2
Girton Way PE9 . . . 143 C5
Gisborough Way LE1 . . . 51 B5
Gisbourne Ct LE5 . . . 156 A2
Glade The LE3 . . . 178 F7
Gladstone Ave
  Loughborough LE11 . . . 52 B5
  Melton Mowbray LE13 . . . 59 B5
Gladstone Cl LE10 . . . 197 E4
Gladstone St
  Anstey LE7 . . . 127 C6
  Fleckney LE8 . . . 222 F7
  Hathern LE12 . . . 30 A1
  Ibstock LE67 . . . 95 F1
  Kibworth Beauchamp
  LE8 . . . 223 F8
  Leicester LE1 . . . 259 C4
  Long Eaton NG10 . . . 10 C6
  Loughborough LE11 . . . 52 B5
  Lutterworth LE17 . . . 244 D6
  Market Harborough
  LE16 . . . 240 F2
  Wigston LE18 . . . 180 D3
Glaisdale Cl LE4 . . . 128 A3
Glaisdale Rd LE4 . . . 180 E1
Glamis Cl LE12 . . . 101 D8
Glamorgan Ave LE18 . . . 179 F2
GLASTON . . . 190 B6
Glaston Pk LE15 . . . 190 B5
Glaston Rd
  Bisbrooke LE15 . . . 189 F4
  Preston LE15 . . . 164 C1
  Uppingham LE15 . . . 189 C5
  Wing LE15 . . . 165 B1
Glazebrook Rd LE3 . . . 154 A8
Glazebrook Sq LE3 . . . 154 A8
Glean Cl LE19 . . . 218 F4
Glebe Cl
  Billesdon LE7 . . . 159 C1
  Empingham LE15 . . . 141 A6
  Glenfield LE3 . . . 153 B8
  Leicester LE2 . . . 180 E7
  Mountsorrel LE12 . . . 76 D2
  Wigston LE18 . . . 180 D3
Glebe Dr LE8 . . . 202 D3
Glebe Gdns LE2 . . . 180 F8
Glebe Ho LE8 . . . 202 B8
Glebe La CV13 . . . 172 B6
Glebelands Prim Sch
  LE4 . . . 128 D8
Glebelands Rd LE4 . . . 128 D8
Glebelands The LE8 . . . 205 A8
Glebe Rd
  Asfordby Hill LE14 . . . 58 C3
  Broughton Astley LE9 . . . 218 E6
  Groby LE6 . . . 126 E3
  Leicester, Oadby LE2 . . . 180 F8
Glebe St
  Leicester LE2 . . . 259 C2
  Loughborough LE11 . . . 52 C5
  Swadlincote DE11 . . . 44 B3

Glebe The CV13 . . . 149 C8
Glebe View LE67 . . . 70 F2
Glebe Way
  Oakham LE15 . . . 137 D5
  Syston LE7 . . . 102 A4
Glenalmond Cl LE65 . . . 69 A8
Glen Ave LE67 . . . 123 A8
Glen Bank LE10 . . . 197 E1
Glenbarr Ave LE4 . . . 154 D8
Glenbarr Cl LE10 . . . 215 A8
Glenbarr Dr LE10 . . . 215 A8
Glenborne Rd LE2 . . . 180 A4
Glencoe Ave LE4 . . . 129 C4
Glen Cres
  Essendine PE9 . . . 117 B5
  Stamford PE9 . . . 143 C5
Glencroft LE2 . . . 179 D1
Glendale Ave LE3 . . . 127 B3
Glendon Cl LE14 . . . 57 E2
Glendon St LE4 . . . 129 B1
Glendower Cl LE3 . . . 156 B6
Glen Dr LE15 . . . 137 F5
Gleneagles Ave LE4 . . . 129 D4
Gleneagles Cl
  Hinckley LE10 . . . 215 D4
  Nuneaton CV11 . . . 214 C1
  Stamford PE9 . . . 143 A4
Gleneagles Wlk LE4 . . . 129 C4
GLENFIELD . . . 153 C8
Glenfield Cres LE3 . . . 153 C8
Glenfield Frith Dr
  LE3 . . . 127 D1
Glenfield Hospl LE3 . . . 127 F2
Glenfield Lane **3** LE9 . . . 152 F7
Glenfield Prim Sch
  LE3 . . . 153 B8
Glenfield Rd
  Leicester LE3 . . . 154 B6
  Long Eaton NG10 . . . 10 D5
Glenfield Rd E LE3 . . . 154 B6
Glenfields LE12 . . . 50 B3
Glenfrith Cl
  Leicester LE3 . . . 127 F3
  Mountsorrel LE12 . . . 76 F1
Glenfrith Gdns LE12 . . . 76 F1
Glenfrith Way LE3 . . . 127 F2
Glengarry Cl LE3 . . . 154 A7
Glengarry Ct LE3 . . . 154 A7
Glengarry Way LE3 . . . 153 A8
Glen Gorse LE8 . . . 179 F1
Glen Gorse Rdbt LE2 . . . 181 E2
Glenhills Bvd LE2 . . . 179 D5
Glen Hills Prim Sch
  LE2 . . . 179 A3
Glenhills Way LE2 . . . 179 D5
Glen Ho PE9 . . . 117 B6
Glen Ind Est PE9 . . . 117 B6
Glenmere Com Prim Sch
  LE18 . . . 180 F3
Glenmore Ave LE2 . . . 50 B4
Glenmore Rd LE4 . . . 129 D3
Glen Park Ave LE3 . . . 127 B3
GLEN PARVA . . . 179 B3
Glen Rd
  Leicester, Oadby LE2 . . . 181 C4
  Newton Harcourt LE8 . . . 204 E7
Glen Rise
  Glen Parva LE2 . . . 179 B4
  Leicester, Oadby LE2 . . . 181 E2
Glenrothes Cl LE3 . . . 153 C5
Glen St LE8 . . . 129 B2
Glenville Ave
  Glenfield LE3 . . . 127 C2
  Glen Parva LE2 . . . 179 C2
Glen Way
  Coalville LE67 . . . 96 F7
  Leicester, Oadby LE2 . . . 181 C4
Glenwood Cl LE2 . . . 155 D1
GLOOSTON . . . 208 B4
Glossop St LE5 . . . 155 C4
Gloucester Ave
  Melton Mowbray LE13 . . . 82 D8
  Syston LE7 . . . 103 C4
Gloucester Cl
  Leicester LE2 . . . 151 B2
  Nuneaton CV11 . . . 214 A7
Gloucester Cres
  Melton Mowbray LE13 . . . 82 D8
  Wigston LE18 . . . 179 F3
Gloucester Rd PE9 . . . 143 C4
Glover Ct
  Cottingham LE16 . . . 229 C1
  Leicester LE2 . . . 179 C6
Glover Rd DE74 . . . 17 B4
Glyn Cl LE9 . . . 198 B8
GOADBY . . . 185 B2
Goadby Hill LE7 . . . 185 B2
GOADBY MARWOOD . . . 22 C1
Goadby Rd
  Hallaton LE16 . . . 209 B6
  Waltham on t W LE14 . . . 40 A7
Goddard Cl LE7 . . . 157 A5
Goddard Ct **5** . . . 240 E4
Goddards Cl
  Kilby LE18 . . . 204 A3
  Leicester LE4 . . . 128 B3
  Leicester, Oadby LE2 . . . 180 F5
Goddards Slang LE67 . . . 103 E5
Godfrey Cl LE4 . . . 128 A6
Godsons Hill CV13 . . . 148 D3
Godson Wlk LE15 . . . 156 A6
Godwin Ave LE18 . . . 180 D2
Godwin Rd NN17 . . . 230 F3
Goldcrest LE15 . . . 189 A5

274 Gol–Gwe

Golden Sq LE12 51 A8
Goldfinch Cl LE11 51 F3
Goldfinch Rd LE15 189 A5
Goldhill LE18 180 A4
Goldhill Gdns LE2 180 D7
Goldhill Rd LE2 180 D7
Golding Cl LE11 51 B6
Goldsmith Rd LE3 154 A4
Goldspink Cl LE13 82 C8
Golf Course La LE3 153 C5
Golf Dr CV11 214 B1
Goliath Rd LE67 71 D2
Gonerby La NG32 4 F5
Goodacre Almshouses
LE17 233 F5
Goodacre Cl CV23 257 A5
Goodacre Rd LE17 233 C4
Goode's Ave LE7 103 B2
Goode's La LE7 103 B3
Goodheart Way LE3 153 C2
Gooding Ave LE3 154 A3
Gooding Cl LE3 154 B3
Goodriche Ho LE13 59 D3
Goodriche St LE13 59 D3
Goods Yard Cl LE11 51 F4
Goodwood Cl LE16 241 B3
Goodwood Cres LE5 156 B4
Goodwood Rd LE5 156 B4
Goosehills Rd LE10 215 E5
Goose La LE9 198 A5
Gopsall Rd
Congerstone CV13 147 C8
Hinckley LE10 197 D2
Gopsall St LE2 155 B5
Gordon Ave 8 LE2 155 B4
Gordon Ho 1 LE2 155 B5
Gordon Rd LE11 52 B6
Gores La LE16 241 A3
Gorham Rise LE9 218 D7
Gorseburn Ho LE3 153 F8
Gorse Hill
Anstey LE7 127 E5
Anstey LE7 127 F5
Gorse Hill City Farm*
LE4 128 B1
Gorse La
Leicester, Oadby LE2 181 D3
Moira DE12 67 E6
Syston LE7 102 F3
Gorse Rd LE67 96 C6
Gorsey La DE12 92 A7
GORSEY LEYS 67 C4
Gorsty Cl LE4 128 B3
Goscote Dr LE17 244 C6
Goscote Hall Rd LE4 128 F6
Goscote Ho 7 LE2 155 B5
Goseley Ave DE11 45 A4
Goseley Cres DE11 45 A4
GOSELEY DALE 45 A5
Gosford Dr LE10 197 A1
Goshawk Cl LE9 218 F7
Gosling St LE2 259 A2
Gotham St LE2 155 B4
Gough Rd LE5 155 E6
Goughs La LE15 187 D7
Goward St LE16 240 E3
Gower St LE1 259 C5
Gowrie Cl LE10 197 B2
Grace Ct LE2 179 E8
Grace Dieu La LE67,
LE12 48 F2
Grace Dieu Manor Sch
LE67 71 F8
Gracedieu Rd LE11 51 D3
Grace Dieu Rd LE67 71 E7
Grace Gdns LE2 179 E7
Gracelands LE16 240 C2
Grace Rd
Desford LE9 151 B3
Leicester LE2 179 E8
Sapcote LE9 217 E8
Grafton Dr LE18 180 F2
Grafton Pl LE1 259 B5
Grafton Rd LE11 51 E6
Graham Rise LE11 51 D6
Graham St LE1 155 B6
Gramer Cotts CV9 194 A6
Grampian Cl LE2 179 F7
Grampian Way
Long Eaton NG10 10 A8
Oakham LE15 137 D6
Granary Cl
Glenfield LE3 153 C8
Kibworth Beauchamp
LE8 224 B7
Market Harborough
LE16 240 F6
Granary The LE16 209 E6
GRANBY 5 C5
Granby Ave LE5 155 D6
Granby Cl LE10 215 C7
Granby Ct 4 LE5 130 C3
Granby Dr NG13 3 A2
Granby Hill NG13 5 B6
Granby Ho LE13 59 C3
Granby La
Granby NG13 5 A7
Plungar NG13 5 E2
Granby Pl LE1 259 B3
Granby Prim Sch LE2 179 D7
Granby Rd
Hinckley LE10 215 C7
Leicester LE2 179 D7
Melton Mowbray LE13 59 D6
Granby St
Leicester LE1 259 C3
Loughborough LE11 52 A4
Grange Ave
Breaston DE72 9 D8
Leicester Forest East
LE3 153 B3
Rearsby LE7 103 F8
Grange Bsns Pk LE8 178 F1
Grange Cl
Ashby-de-la-Z LE65 69 A5
Glenfield LE3 153 B8
Great Glen LE8 182 B1
Langham LE15 110 D3
Leicester LE2 179 C3
Melbourne DE73 26 B8
Newbold Verdon LE9 150 B4
Ratby LE6 152 D8
Grange Ct LE9 151 B4
Grange Dr
Castle Donington DE74 17 A3
Glen Parva LE2 179 C3
Hinckley LE10 215 E5
Long Eaton NG10 10 F8
Melton Mowbray LE13 59 E1
Whetstone LE8 201 F8
Grange Farm Bsns Pk
LE67 96 E5
Grange Farm Cl DE74 17 D5
Grangefields Dr LE7 101 F6
Grange La
Coston LE14 62 E8
Leicester LE2 259 B2
Mountsorrel LE12 101 D8
Nailstone CV13 123 B5
Seaton LE15 190 B1
Thorpe Langton LE16 226 A5
Thurnby LE7 156 E4
Grange Pk
Leicester LE7 156 E4
Long Eaton NG10 10 F8
Grange Prim Sch NG10 10 F8
Granger Ct LE11 52 A4
Grange Rd
Broughton Astley LE9 218 E7
Carlton Curlieu LE8 206 D7
Coalville LE67 96 E6
Hartshill Green CV10 194 C2
Ibstock LE67 95 F1
Long Eaton NG10 10 F8
Nailstone CV13 123 A5
Shepshed LE12 50 A3
Wigston LE18 180 D4
Grange St LE11 52 A5
Grange The
Earl Shilton LE9 198 E7
Packington LE65 69 C2
Woodhouse Eaves LE12 100 B8
Grange Therapeutic Sch
The LE15 135 F6
Grange View LE67 123 E8
Grangeway Rd LE18 180 D4
Granite Cl LE19 178 A4
Granite Way LE12 76 C4
Grantham Ave LE9 218 D8
Grantham Rd
Bottesford NG13 3 D2
Leicester LE5 156 C8
Skillington NG33 43 B8
Grant Way LE2 179 E4
Grantwood Rd LE13 59 E5
Granville Ave LE2 180 F6
Granville Com Sch
DE11 44 E4
Granville Cres LE18 180 B5
Granville Ct DE11 44 C4
Granville Gdns LE10 215 C8
Granville Rd
Hinckley LE10 215 C8
Leicester LE1 155 B4
Melton Mowbray LE13 59 A5
Wigston LE18 180 C5
Granville St
Loughborough LE11 52 A4
Market Harborough
LE16 240 F2
Woodville DE11 44 E3
Grapes Garden Cl LE12 76 E3
Grape St LE1 259 B4
Grasmere LE67 72 C2
Grasmere Cl LE12 76 D8
Grasmere Rd
Loughborough LE11 74 F7
Wigston LE18 180 F3
Grasmere St LE2 259 A2
Grass Acres LE3 178 E7
Grassholme Dr LE11 51 A3
Grassington Cl LE4 128 C4
Grassington Dr
Nuneaton CV11 214 A2
Wigston LE18 180 E1
Grassy La LE67 125 B8
Gravel St LE1 259 B4
Gravel The LE8 205 F8
Gray La LE12 77 D2
Grays Cl DE74 17 B3
Grays Ct
Barrow-u-S LE12 76 D8
Narborough LE19 178 A3
Gray St LE11 52 B2
Grayswood Dr LE4 128 A6
Great Arler Rd LE2 180 A8
GREAT BOWDEN 241 A6
Great Bowden CE Prim
Sch LE16 241 A6
Great Bowden Hall
LE16 240 E7
Great Bowden Rd
LE16 241 A4
GREAT CASTERTON 142 E7
Great Casterton CE Prim
Sch PE9 142 E7
Great Central Railway
Mus* LE11 52 C3
Great Central Rd LE11 52 C3
Great Central Rly*
Birstall LE4 128 E7
Mountsorrel LE7 75 E2
Great Central St LE1 259 A4
Great Central Way
LE3 154 D2
Great Central Wlk*
CV23 252 F2
Great Cl NG33 65 B4
GREAT DALBY 82 B2
Great Dalby Rd LE14 106 E5
Great Dalby Sch LE14 82 A1
GREAT EASTON 229 D7
Great Easton Rd
Bringhurst LE16 229 C6
Caldecott LE16 230 A7
Drayton LE16 229 A5
Great Easton LE16 229 F6
Greatford Rd PE9 144 E4
GREAT GLEN 205 B8
Great La
Frisby on t W LE14 80 D8
Greetham LE15 88 B2
Great Meadow Rd
LE4 128 B2
Great North Rd
Great Casterton PE9 114 D4
Stamford PE9 142 F3
Wothorpe PE9 169 B8
GREAT OXENDON 250 E3
GREAT STRETTON 182 B6
GREAT WILNE 9 C2
Greaves Ave
Melton Mowbray LE13 59 B4
Old Dalby LE14 36 C6
Grebe Cl LE12 76 E8
Grebe Way LE8 201 F5
Greedon Rise LE12 77 C4
Greenacre Dr LE5 156 B5
Green Acres Cvn Pk
LE16 240 C6
Greenacres Dr LE17 244 B6
Green Bank LE13 59 E3
Greenbank Dr LE2 181 B5
Greenbank Rd LE5 130 D1
Greenclose La 1 LE11 52 A4
Greencoat Cl LE3 153 E7
Greencoat Rd LE3 153 E7
Green Croft LE9 199 E1
Greendale Rd LE2 179 B3
Green Farm Cl CV23 258 A6
Greenfield Prim Sch
LE8 202 E4
Greenfield Rd
Measham DE12 93 E5
Oakham LE15 138 A8
Greenfields LE8 201 F7
Greenfields Dr LE67 72 A1
Greengate La LE4 128 E7
Green Gdns LE17 233 B4
GREENHILL 97 A8
Green Hill LE12 30 A1
Greenhill Cl
Melton Mowbray LE13 59 D5
Narborough LE19 201 A7
Greenhill Dr LE9 198 B7
Greenhill Rd
Coalville LE67 72 C1
Leicester LE2 155 B1
Stoke Golding CV13 196 D7
Green Hill Rise LE12 30 A2
Greenhithe Rd LE2 154 D1
Green La
Ashley LE16 227 F2
Barton in t B CV13 122 E3
Braybrooke LE16 251 F5
Copston Magna LE10 231 C5
Countesthorpe LE8 202 F4
Duddington PE9 193 B6
Earl Shilton LE9 175 F1
Easthorpe NG13 3 C1
Goadby Marwood LE14 22 E3
Granby NG13 5 C5
Harby LE14 12 C2
Husbands Bosworth
LE17 247 E5
Market Harborough
LE16 240 E1
North Kilworth LE17 246 F3
Owston LE15 135 B5
Seagrave LE12 77 F8
Stamford PE9 143 D5
Stapleton LE9 174 E2
Tilton on t H LE7 159 D6
Upper Broughton LE14 19 B4
Weston by W LE16 227 C6
Whitwick LE67 71 E3
Wibtoft LE17 232 B3
Wilson DE73 26 E5
Greenland Ave LE5 156 A8
Greenland Dr LE5 156 A8
Green Lands DE11 44 B7
Green Lane Cl
Leicester LE5 155 F6
Seagrave LE12 77 F8
Green Lane Inf Sch
LE5 155 C7
Green Lane Rd LE5 155 E6
Greenlawn Wlk LE3 154 D8
Green Leas DE72 16 A8
Greenmoor Rd LE10 215 D5
Green Rd LE9 218 E7
Greens Cl CV23 252 C6
Greenside Cl
Donisthorpe DE12 67 E1
Long Eaton NG10 10 E7
Nuneaton CV11 214 C1
Greenside Pl LE2 179 F5
Greenslade LE13 59 D3
Greensward LE7 103 E8
Green The
Allington NG32 4 F5
Anstey LE7 127 C6
3 Ashby-de-la-Z LE65 69 B6
Aston-on-T DE72 16 B8
Atherstone CV9 194 A6
Austrey CV9 119 B1
Barkestone-le-V NG13 6 B3
Bitteswell LE17 244 B8
Blaby LE8 202 C8
Breedon on t H DE73 26 E2
Caldecott LE16 230 B8
Castle Donington DE74 17 A3
Churchover CV23 252 C6
Coalville LE67 96 C5
Croft LE9 200 C5
Dadlington CV13 196 E8
Diseworth DE74 28 B5
Draycott DE72 9 A7
Exton LE15 113 A3
Great Bowden LE16 241 B6
Hathern LE12 30 A1
Hickling LE14 19 C6
Hose LE14 20 F7
Huncote LE9 200 D7
Husbands Bosworth
LE17 247 E5
Ketton PE9 167 F5
Leire LE17 233 E8
Lilbourne CV23 258 A6
Long Whatton LE12 29 C3
Lubenham LE16 239 E3
Lyddington LE15 212 D7
Lyndon LE15 165 D5
Markfield LE67 98 D1
Mountsorrel LE12 76 E2
Muston NG13 7 F8
Newton Burgoland
LE67 121 E6
North Kilworth LE17 246 F3
Old Dalby LE14 35 E4
Orton-on-t-H CV9 145 C4
Seckington B79 118 A3
Stathern LE14 13 A3
Stonesby LE14 40 E6
Syston LE7 103 B4
Thringstone LE67 71 D7
Thrussington LE7 78 F4
Walton on t W LE12 54 A4
Weston by W LE16 227 B3
Wigston Parva LE10 231 E8
Greenway LE8 224 B8
Greenway Cl LE7 101 E6
Greenway The LE4 129 A2
Greenwich Cl
Leicester LE3 128 B1
Narborough LE19 201 B8
Green Wlk LE3 153 E5
Greenwood Rd
Leicester LE5 155 F6
Stoke Golding CV13 196 E7
GREETHAM 88 A1
Greetham Rd
Cottesmore LE15 87 F1
Stretton LE15 88 F4
Gregory Ave DE72 9 C8
Gregory Cl
Barlestone CV13 149 C8
Thurmaston LE4 130 A7
Gregory Rd CV13 149 C8
Gregorys Cl LE3 153 D1
Gregory St LE11 52 B3
Gregson Cl
Leicester LE4 129 D5
Swadlincote DE11 44 B5
Grendon Cl LE18 180 E3
Grenehams Cl PE9 167 F5
Grenfell Rd LE2 180 E8
Grenville Gdns LE16 240 D1
Gresley Cl
Leicester, Beaumont Leys
LE4 128 C4
Leicester, Thurnby LE7 156 F6
Gresley Dr PE9 143 D2
Gresley Woodlands
DE11 44 A2
Gresley Wood Rd DE11 44 A2
Gretna Way LE5 156 E7
GRETTON 213 C1
Gretton Brook Rd
NN17 230 E3
Gretton Ct LE13 59 B3
Gretton Gdns LE14 62 C2
Gretton Rd
Harringworth NN17 213 E7
Lyddington LE15 212 D5
Rockingham LE16 230 B5
Grewcock Cl LE17 232 E6
Grey Cl LE6 126 F3
Grey Cres LE6 99 D1
Grey Friars LE1 259 B3
Greylag Way LE8 201 F4
Greyland Paddock
LE6 126 F3
Greys Dr LE6 126 E2
Greystoke Cl LE4 128 E3
Greystoke Prim Sch
LE19 201 C8
Greystoke Wlk 1 LE4 128 E3
Greystone Ave LE5 156 B6
Griffin Cl
Hamilton LE4 130 A5
Shepshed LE12 50 A3
Griffin Rd LE16 251 E4
Griffith Gdns LE65 68 F5
Griffiths Cl LE15 138 A8
GRIFFYDAM 48 B2
Griffydam Prim Sch
LE67 48 A2
Griggs Rd LE11 75 B8
Grimes Gate DE74 28 C6
GRIMSTON 57 B8
Grimston Cl LE4 130 A4
Grisedale Cl LE2 259 A1
Grittar Cl LE18 180 E3
Grizedale Gr LE19 177 F2
GROBY 126 D3
Groby Com Coll LE6 126 D2
Groby La LE6 126 E7
Groby Rd
Anstey LE7 127 C5
Glenfield LE3 127 C3
Leicester LE3 128 A1
Ratby LE6 126 D1
Grocot Rd LE5 156 A3
Grosvenor Ave
Breaston DE72 9 F8
Long Eaton NG10 10 A4
Grosvenor Cl LE2 179 D1
Grosvenor Cres
Hinckley LE10 216 A6
Leicester, Oadby LE2 180 F7
Grosvenor Ho LE15 137 F6
Grosvenor St LE1 259 C5
Grovebury Rd LE4 128 F3
Grovebury Wlk 4
LE4 128 F3
Grove Cotts LE14 108 B2
Grove Ct LE19 178 D5
Grove Farm Triangle
LE19 178 E5
Grove La LE12 76 D7
Grove Pk LE10 216 A6
Grove Prim Sch The
LE13 59 B3
Grove Rd
Hinckley LE10 216 A6
Leicester LE5 155 C6
Loughborough LE11 51 E3
Whetstone LE8 202 A7
Whitwick LE67 71 E4
Grove St DE11 44 B4
Grove Stud LE14 108 A2
Grove The
Asfordby LE14 57 E3
Breaston DE72 9 F8
Desford LE9 151 A3
Hinckley LE10 215 C8
Syston LE7 103 A1
Grove Way LE19 178 F5
Guadaloupe Ave LE13 59 E1
Guestwick Gn LE5 130 C2
Guild Cl LE7 100 F3
Guildford Ave DE11 44 E6
Guildford Way LE11 74 C8
Guildhall La LE1 259 A3
Guilford Dr LE18 180 B5
Guilford Rd LE2 155 E1
Guilford St 2 LE2 155 C4
Guinea Cl NG10 10 A7
Guinevere Way LE3 153 A2
Gullet La
Ashley LE16 227 F2
Kirby Muxloe LE9 152 C5
Gumbrill Ho LE5 156 A6
GUMLEY 224 A1
Gumley Rd
Foxton LE16 239 C7
Laughton LE16, LE17 238 D8
Smeeton Westerby LE8 223 F5
Gumley Sq LE19 178 B3
GUNBY 64 E8
Gunby Hill DE12 91 F8
Gunby Rd
North Witham NG33 65 A8
Sewstern NG33 64 B8
Stainby NG33 43 E1
Gunnel La LE15 141 B6
Gunnsbrook Cl LE16 241 A6
GUNTHORPE 164 B8
Gunthorpe Cl LE15 138 B7
Gunthorpe Rd LE3 153 D4
Gurnall Rd LE4 128 A4
Gurney Cres LE19 201 C6
Gurney La LE17 236 A1
Guscott Rd LE67 71 E1
Guthlaxton Ave
11 Leicester LE2 155 B5
Lutterworth LE17 244 C6
Guthlaxton Coll LE18 180 B2
Guthlaxton Gap LE9,
LE19 200 F5
Guthlaxton St LE2 155 B5
Guthlaxton Way LE18 180 E1
Guthridge Cres LE3 154 B3
Gutteridge St LE67 96 C8
Gwash Cl PE9 116 F2
Gwash Way PE9 143 F5
Gwash Way Ind Est
PE9 143 F6
Gwencole Ave LE3 179 A8
Gwencole Cres LE3 179 A7
Gwendolen Rd LE5 155 E4
Gwendolin Ave LE4 129 B8
Gwendoline Ave LE10 197 A2
Gwendoline Dr LE8 202 E4

Gynsill Cl LE7 . . . . 127 E5
Gynsill Cl LE7 . . . . 127 D3
Gynsill La LE7 . . . . 127 D3
Gynsills Hall LE7 . . . . 127 D3
Gypsy La CV9 . . . . 170 D2

H

Hackett Cl LE65 . . . . 69 B7
Hackett Rd LE3 . . . . 153 F8
Haddenham Rd LE3 . . . . 154 C2
Haddon Cl LE7 . . . . 102 F3
Haddonian Rd LE16 . . . . 240 E1
Haddon Rd PE9 . . . . 143 B4
Haddon St LE2 . . . . 155 C6
Haddon Way
  Long Eaton NG10 . . . . . . 9 F4
  Loughborough LE11 . . . . 75 A6
Hades La LE12 . . . . 34 D4
Hadfield Cl CV23 . . . . . . 257 A5
Hadfield Dr LE13 . . . . . . 59 C4
Hadrian Cl
  Hinckley LE10 . . . . 196 F1
  Syston LE7 . . . . 102 E2
Hadrian Rd
  Leicester LE4 . . . . 128 E5
  Thurmaston LE4 . . . . . . 129 E7
Hagley Cl LE16 . . . . 241 B3
Haig Pl LE3 . . . . 154 A2
Hailebury Ave LE65 . . . . . 69 A8
Hailey Ave LE11 . . . . 51 C5
Hainsworth Cl LE15 . . . . 110 C3
Halberd Cl LE10 . . . . 215 D5
Halcroft Rise LE18 . . . . . 180 D1
Half Croft The LE7 . . . . . 103 A4
Half Moon Cres LE2 . . . . 181 C6
Halford Cl
  Great Glen LE8 . . . . . . 205 B8
  South Witham NG33 . . . 65 B4
  Whetstone LE8 . . . . . . 201 F6
Halford Rd LE8 . . . . 223 F8
Halford St
  Leicester LE1 . . . . 259 C3
  Syston LE7 . . . . 103 A3
Halifax Dr LE4 . . . . 128 E4
Halkin St LE4 . . . . 129 B1
Hallam Ave LE4 . . . . 128 F7
Hallam Cl LE9 . . . . 199 A8
Hallam Cres E LE3 . . . . . 154 A2
Hallam Fields DE74 . . . . 17 B2
Hallam Fields Rd LE4 . . . 102 A1
Hallamford Rd LE12 . . . . 50 A6
HALLATON 209 D6
Hallaton CE Prim Sch
  LE16 . . . . 209 D6
Hallaton Rd
  Allexton LE15 . . . . 187 C4
  Horninghold LE16 . . . . 210 A6
  Leicester LE5 . . . . 155 F8
  Medbourne LE16 . . . . 227 F7
  Slawston LE16 . . . . . . 209 E3
  Tugby LE7 . . . . 185 E5
Hallaton St LE2 . . . . 179 E7
Hallaton Village Mus*
  LE16 . . . . 209 D6
Hallbrook Prim Sch
  LE9 . . . . 218 F4
Hallbrook Rd LE9 . . . . . . 218 F4
Hall Cl
  Blackfordby DE11 . . . . 68 C8
  Cossington LE7 . . . . . 102 D8
  Cottesmore LE15 . . . . . 112 C8
  Glen Parva LE2 . . . . . . 179 B3
  Kibworth Beauchamp
    LE8 . . . . 205 F1
  Weston by W LE16 . . . 227 B4
  Whissendine LE15 . . . . 85 A1
Hall Croft LE12 . . . . 50 B4
Hallcroft Ave
  Countesthorpe LE8 . . . 202 E3
  Overseal DE12 . . . . . . 67 B3
Hallcroft Gdns LE8 . . . . 202 E3
Hall Dr
  Asfordby LE14 . . . . 57 E2
  Burton Lazars LE14 . . . 82 F6
  Burton o t W LE12 . . . 54 A7
  Leicester, Oadby LE2 . . 181 B6
  Stoke Golding CV13 . . . 196 F7
Halley Cl LE4 . . . . 128 A6
Hall Farm Cl
  Castle Donington DE74 . 17 B3
  Queniborough LE7 . . . 103 F5
  Swadlincote DE11 . . . . 44 C4
Hall Farm Cres LE9 . . . . 219 A5
Hall Farm Rd LE12 . . . . 77 F7
Hall Farm Rd
  Swadlincote DE11 . . . . 44 C4
  Thurcaston LE7 . . . . . 101 B2
Hallfield Cl CV9 . . . . 146 C2
Hallfields LE7 . . . . 101 F5
Hall Gate
  Coalville LE67 . . . . . . 97 C8
  Diseworth DE74 . . . . . 28 C6
Hallgate Dr LE3 . . . . 127 F3
Hall Gdns
  East Leake LE12 . . . . . 31 F8
  Great Glen LE8 . . . . . . 205 B8
  Hemington DE74 . . . . 17 D4
  Ravenstone LE67 . . . . . 95 D8
Hall La
  Ashby Magna LE17 . . . 220 A2
  Ashley LE16 . . . . 227 E2
  Bitteswell LE17 . . . . . 234 C3
  Coalville LE67 . . . . . . 72 A2
  Donisthorpe DE12 . . . . 92 E8
  Drayton LE16 . . . . . . 229 A5

Hall La continued
  Eastwell LE14 . . . . 22 B5
  Leicester LE2 . . . . 179 C7
  Odstone CV13 . . . . . . 122 C4
  Packington LE65 . . . . . . 69 C2
  South Luffenham LE15 . . 191 E8
  Stainby NG33 . . . . 43 D2
  Ullesthorpe LE17 . . . . 233 B4
  Walton LE17 . . . . 236 A2
  Welford NN6 . . . . 256 D6
  Witherley CV9 . . . . . . 194 B8
Hall Leys LE12 . . . . 76 A5
Hall Orchard CE Prim Sch
  LE12 . . . . 76 D7
Hall Orchard La LE14 . . . 80 D8
Hall Rd
  Hinckley LE10 . . . . . . 215 D5
  Scraptoft LE7 . . . . . . 156 F8
Hall Sch The LE3 . . . . . . 127 E1
Halls Cres LE10 . . . . . . 217 C5
Hall St
  Ibstock LE67 . . . . . . 122 E8
  Swadlincote DE11 . . . . 44 A2
Hall Wlk LE9 . . . . 178 B4
Hall Wood Cl DE11 . . . . 44 A2
Hall Yd PE9 . . . . 168 C2
Halsbury St LE2 . . . . . . 155 D3
HALSTEAD 160 C8
Halstead Rd LE10 . . . . . 76 D1
Halstead Rise LE7 . . . . . 160 A8
Halstead St LE5 . . . . . . 155 D6
Halter Slade LE18 . . . . . 180 E1
Halywell Nook LE7 . . . . 101 F8
Hamble Cl LE10 . . . . . . 151 B3
Hambledon Cres
  Cottesmore LE15 . . . . . 87 E2
  Loughborough LE11 . . . 74 F8
Hambledon Gn LE4 . . . . 128 D5
Hamble Rd LE4 . . . . . . 181 D6
Hambleton Cl
  Leicester Forest East
    LE3 . . . . 152 F2
  Oakham LE15 . . . . . . 138 B6
Hambleton Rd
  Egleton LE15 . . . . . . 138 C3
  Stamford PE9 . . . . . . 143 A2
Hamelin Rd LE3 . . . . . . 153 F4
Hames La B79 . . . . 118 D3
Hamilford Cl LE7 . . . . . 130 E1
HAMILTON 130 C3
Hamilton Bsns Pk
  LE4 . . . . 130 A4
Hamilton Circ LE5 . . . . 130 D3
Hamilton Cl LE10 . . . . . 197 A2
Hamilton Com Coll
  LE3 . . . . 130 E2
Hamilton Ct
  Melton Mowbray LE13 . . 59 C1
  Swadlincote DE11 . . . . 44 C5
Hamilton Gr DE11 . . . . 44 D5
Hamilton La LE7 . . . . . . 130 E2
Hamilton Pl LE13 . . . . . 59 C1
Hamilton Rd
  Coalville LE67 . . . . . . 97 C8
  Long Eaton NG10 . . . . 10 D8
Hamilton St LE2 . . . . . . 155 B4
Hamilton Way LE5 . . . . 130 B2
Hamlet Cl CV11 . . . . . . 214 B1
Hammercliffe Rd LE5 . . 155 C8
Hammond Way LE16 . . 240 E4
Hampden Rd LE4 . . . . . 129 E2
Hampshire Rd LE2 . . . . 179 D7
Hampstead Cl LE19 . . . 201 B8
Hampton Cl
  Coalville LE67 . . . . . . 96 F8
  Glen Parva LE2 . . . . . . 179 D1
  Wigston LE18 . . . . . . 180 D2
Hampton Ct LE16 . . . . . 240 F3
Hanbury Cl LE15 . . . . . 137 D5
Hanbury Gdns LE15 . . . 137 A2
Hanbury Rd LE5 . . . . . . 156 D4
Hand Ave LE3 . . . . 153 E3
Hand Cl LE3 . . . . 153 E4
Handley St LE2 . . . . . . 179 E7
Hand's Wlk NG13 . . . . 3 A2
Hanford Way LE11 . . . . 52 B5
Hanger Bank DE72 . . . . 16 B8
Hangmans La B79 . . . . 118 A2
Hangman's La LE10 . . . 197 E3
Hannah Clarke Ct LE4 . . 128 F6
Hannah Par LE4 . . . . . . 129 A7
Hannah's Field LE15 . . . 163 E2
Hannam Ct LE1 . . . . . . 259 B4
Hanover Cl LE3 . . . . . . 130 B1
Hanover Ct
  Hinckley LE10 . . . . . . 215 E6
  Loughborough LE11 . . . 51 D5
Hanover Dr LE12 . . . . . 77 D4
Hansen Ct LE18 . . . . . . 180 B2
Hansom Ct [2] LE1 . . . . 215 D8
Hansom Rd LE1 . . . . . . 197 F2
Hanworth Cl LE5 . . . . . 130 C2
Haramead Bsns Ctr
  LE1 . . . . 259 B5
Haramead Rd LE1 . . . . 155 B7
Harborough Dr LE15 . . . 84 E1
Harborough Hill Rd
  LE15 . . . . 211 B6
Harborough Rd
  Billesdon LE7 . . . . . . 184 C6
  Braybrooke LE16 . . . . 251 D7
  Clipston LE16 . . . . . . 250 A4
  Dingley LE16 . . . . . . 241 D5
  Dingley LE16 . . . . . . 241 E1

Harborough Rd continued
  East Farndon LE16 . . . 250 C8
  Glooston LE16 . . . . . . 208 B3
  Great Oxendon LE16 . . 250 F4
  Kibworth Beauchamp LE8,
    LE16 . . . . 224 E5
  Leicester, Oadby LE2 . . 181 B5
  Lubenham LE16 . . . . . 240 A3
  Market Harborough
    LE16 . . . . 240 C7
  Theddingworth LE17 . . 238 F1
HARBY 12 B3
Harby CE Prim Sch
  LE14 . . . . 12 B3
Harby La
  Harby NG13 . . . . 11 B5
  Hose LE14 . . . . 20 F7
  Plungar NG13 . . . . . . 12 E6
  Stathern LE14 . . . . . . 12 F3
Harcourt Cl LE7 . . . . . . 103 A4
Harcourt Est LE8 . . . . . 206 A1
Harcourt Pl DE74 . . . . 17 B4
Harcourt Rd
  Kibworth Beauchamp
    LE8 . . . . 223 F8
  Wigston LE18 . . . . . . 180 E1
Harcourt Spinney
  CV13 . . . . 148 E4
Harcourt St LE16 . . . . . 240 D3
Harcourt Terr [1] PE9 . . 143 C3
Harcourt Way LE19 . . . 178 D6
Hardacre Cl DE73 . . . . 26 A8
Hardie Cres LE3 . . . . . . 153 D2
Harding St LE1 . . . . . . 259 A5
Hardwick Cl LE15 . . . . 138 B7
Hardwick Cres LE7 . . . 102 F3
Hardwick Ct
  Leicester LE3 . . . . . . 154 C3
  Long Eaton NG10 . . . . 9 F4
Hardwicke Rd LE10 . . . 51 C4
Hardwick Rd LE18 . . . 200 F8
Hardwick Rd
  Gretton NN17 . . . . . . 213 B1
  Leicester LE5 . . . . . . 156 E4
  Stamford PE9 . . . . . . 143 B4
Hardy Cl
  Hinckley LE10 . . . . . . 197 D4
  Long Eaton NG10 . . . . 10 D6
Hardy's Ave LE4 . . . . . . 129 C4
Harebell Cl
  Hamilton LE5 . . . . . . 130 B3
  Swadlincote DE11 . . . . 44 E4
Harebell Dr LE13 . . . . 82 A8
Harecroft Cres LE19 . . . 217 E8
Harefield Ave LE3 . . . . 179 C8
Harene Cres LE9 . . . . . 152 E3
Hare Pie View LE16 . . . 209 E5
Harewood Cl LE15 . . . . 110 D3
Harewood St LE5 . . . . 155 D4
Harker Dr LE67 . . . . . . 97 A7
Harland Cl
  Asfordby LE14 . . . . . . 57 F2
  Cosby LE9 . . . . 201 D3
Harlaxton St LE3 . . . . . 154 C2
Harlech Cl LE11 . . . . . . 51 E5
Harlech Wlk LE15 . . . . 59 C5
Harleigh Rd LE12 . . . . 77 C2
Harlequin Way LE8 . . . 201 F4
Harles Acres LE14 . . . . 19 C6
Harley Cl LE12 . . . . . . 50 B2
Harley's Ct DE12 . . . . 67 C4
Harolds La LE19 . . . . . . 178 B5
Harold St LE2 . . . . 179 E8
Harpers La CV9 . . . . . . 194 A7
Harratts Cl LE17 . . . . . 95 F1
Harrier Cl
  Broughton Astley LE9 . . 218 E2
  Cottesmore LE15 . . . . . 87 E1
Harrier Parkway
  LE17 . . . . 243 D7
Harriman Cl LE12 . . . . 50 B4
Harrimans Dr DE72 . . . 9 F8
Harrington Cl LE12 . . . 76 A6
Harrington Cres LE13 . . 113 B2
Harrington Rd
  Shepshed LE12 . . . . . 50 C3
  South Witham LE15 . . . 65 B4
  Wigston LE18 . . . . . . 180 E3
Harrington St
  Draycott DE72 . . . . . . 9 A7
  Leicester LE3 . . . . . . 155 C8
  Long Eaton NG10 . . . . 10 B8
Harrington Way LE15 . . 137 E5
HARRINGWORTH . . . 213 F7
Harringworth Rd
  Gretton NN17 . . . . . . 213 C2
  Leicester LE5 . . . . . . 156 B5
Harris Cl LE9 . . . . 219 A5
Harris Gn LE3 . . . . . . 153 C3
Harrison Cl
  [2] Earl Shilton LE9 . . 198 F8
  Glenfield LE3 . . . . . . 153 C8
  Market Harborough
    LE16 . . . . 250 D8
  Whetstone LE8 . . . . . 202 A5
  Wigston LE18 . . . . . . 180 B1
Harrison Ct LE4 . . . . . . 129 C2
Harrison Pl LE67 . . . . . 96 C8
Harrison Rd LE4 . . . . . 129 B2
Harrisons Row LE7 . . . 103 B4
Harrison St LE4 . . . . . . 129 C4
Harris Rd
  Corby NN17 . . . . 230 C1
  Leicester LE4 . . . . . . 128 B3
Harrod Dr LE16 . . . . . . 241 A4
Harrogate Rd LE4 . . . . 129 C1
Harrogate Way LE18 . . 180 E2

Harrop Cl LE8 . . . . 202 E7
Harrowbrook Ind Est
  LE10 . . . . 214 E7
Harrowbrook Rd
  LE10 . . . . 214 E7
Harrow Cl
  Ashby-de-la-Z LE65 . . . 69 A8
  Leicester Forest East
    LE3 . . . . 152 F1
Harrowden Ct LE5 . . . . 156 A6
Harrowden Rise LE5 . . . 156 A6
Harrowgate Dr LE4 . . . 101 F1
Harrow Rd
  Leicester LE4 . . . . . . 154 C4
  Swadlincote DE11 . . . . 44 B7
Harry French Ct LE11 . . 51 E4
Harston Rd NG32 . . . . 15 F5
Hart Cl LE8 . . . . 201 F5
Hart Dr DE12 . . . . . . 93 C5
Hartfield Rd LE5 . . . . . 156 D8
Hartington Gn LE10 . . . 215 E6
Hartington Rd LE12 . . . 155 C6
Hartington St LE11 . . . 52 C4
Hartland Dr
  Market Harborough
    LE16 . . . . 241 B3
  Melton Mowbray LE13 . 82 C8
Hartopp Cl LE7 . . . . . . 157 A5
Hartopp Rd
  Leicester LE2 . . . . . . 155 B1
  Melton Mowbray LE13 . 82 C8
Hart Rd LE5 . . . . 155 C6
Hartshill CE Prim Sch
  CV10 . . . . 194 A2
Hartshill Hayes Cty Pk*
  CV10 . . . . 194 A2
Hartshill Rd DE11 . . . . 45 A4
Hartshorn Cl LE4 . . . . 129 F6
HARTSHORNE 45 B6
Hartshorne CE Prim Sch
  DE11 . . . . 45 B6
Hartshorne Rd DE11 . . 44 F3
Hartside Gdns [1] NG10 . 10 A8
Harvard Cl LE1 . . . . . . 181 B6
Harvest Cl
  Leicester LE4 . . . . . . 128 B3
  Littlethorpe LE19 . . . 201 D6
Harvester Cl LE13 . . . . 152 F2
Harvesters Cnr LE7 . . . 103 E7
Harvest Gr DE12 . . . . 68 A5
Harvest Hill LE11 . . . . 44 B7
Harvest Way LE9 . . . . 218 F4
Harvey Cl
  Barwell LE9 . . . . 198 A8
  Blaby LE8 . . . . 179 B1
Harvey Rd DE74 . . . . . 17 D7
Harveys Ct LE10 . . . . . 217 D7
Harwin Rd LE5 . . . . . . 156 B4
Harwood Dr LE10 . . . 197 F4
Haskell Cl LE3 . . . . . . 153 D2
Haslemere Rd NG10 . . 10 B8
Haslyn Wlk LE67 . . . . . 97 B8
Hassal Rd LE3 . . . . . . 153 E8
Hassell Mews LE7 . . . . 78 F1
Hastings Ave LE67 . . . 72 A4
Hastings Cl
  Breedon on t H DE73 . . 26 E2
  Fleckney LE8 . . . . . . 223 A6
Hastings Dr LE9 . . . . . 198 C7
Hastings High Sch
  LE10 . . . . 215 F7
Hastings Hollow DE12 . 93 C4
Hastings Rd
  Kirby Fields LE9 . . . . . 152 E4
  Leicester LE5 . . . . . . 155 D8
  Swadlincote DE11 . . . . 44 B3
  Woodhouse Eaves LE12 . 99 F8
Hasting St LE11 . . . . . . 52 A4
Hasting St DE74 . . . . . 17 B2
Hastings The
  Braunstone Town
    LE3 . . . . 153 D1
  Ibstock LE67 . . . . . . 95 F2
Hastings Way LE65 . . . 69 C5
Hastings Wlk LE63 . . . 153 E1
Hathaway Ave LE3 . . . 153 F1
Hathaway Dr CV11 . . . 214 A1
Hatherleigh Rd LE5 . . . 155 F3
HATHERN 30 C5
Hathern CE Prim Sch
  LE12 . . . . 30 C5
Hathern Cl LE12 . . . . 30 A1
Hathern Dr LE11, LE12 . 50 F6
Hathern Rd
  Long Whatton LE12 . . 29 D3
  Shepshed LE12 . . . . . 50 D6
Hathern Turn LE12 . . . 29 F2
Hathernware Ind Est
  LE12 . . . . 30 C5
Hathersage Ave NG10 . 9 F5
Hat Rd LE3 . . . . 178 E7
Hattern Ave LE4 . . . . . 128 D4
Hatters Dr CV9 . . . . . . 170 D2
Hatton Crofts NG10 . . 10 C6
Hatton Cl DE73 . . . . . 26 A7
Hatton La NN17 . . . . . 213 B1
Haulton Dr LE74 . . . . . 17 A4
Havelock St
  Leicester LE2 . . . . . . 259 A2
  Loughborough LE11 . . 51 F4
Haven Cl
  Belton LE12 . . . . 49 B6
  Leicester Forest East
    LE3 . . . . 152 F2
Haven Pk LE11 . . . . . . 51 E5
Haven Rd CV13 . . . . . 148 E2

Haven Wlk LE5 . . . . . . 156 E6
Hawarden Ave LE5 . . . 155 F7
Hawcliffe Rd LE12 . . . 76 C4
Hawk Cl LE12 . . . . . . 218 E7
Hawker Rd LE2 . . . . . . 181 D4
Hawkesbury Rd LE2 . . . 179 F7
Hawkes Hill LE7 . . . . . 179 F5
Hawke Way LE17 . . . . . 243 C7
Hawkins Cl
  Corby NN17 . . . . 230 B1
  Hinckley LE10 . . . . . . 197 D4
Hawley Cl LE67 . . . . . . 96 E6
Hawley Rd LE10 . . . . . 215 D7
Hawthorn Ave
  Birstall LE4 . . . . 129 B8
  Breaston DE72 . . . . . . 9 F8
  Netherseal DE12 . . . . . 91 F7
Hawthorn Cl
  Coalville LE67 . . . . . . 71 E1
  Leicester Forest East
    LE9 . . . . 152 E2
  Old Dalby LE14 . . . . . 35 E4
Hawthorn Cres LE10 . . 215 E4
Hawthorn Dr
  Blaby LE8 . . . . 202 B6
  Melton Mowbray LE13 . 59 C5
  Uppingham LE15 . . . . 189 B5
Hawthorne Ave
  Hathern LE12 . . . . . . 30 A2
  Long Eaton NG10 . . . . 10 C6
Hawthorne Cl
  Leicester, Oadby LE2 . . 182 A3
  Measham DE12 . . . . . 93 C5
Hawthorne Ct LE5 . . . 156 A2
Hawthorne Dr
  Ibstock LE67 . . . . . . 122 E8
  Leicester LE5 . . . . . . 156 A3
  Thornton LE67 . . . . . 124 E4
Hawthorne Rd LE17 . . 246 F3
Hawthorne St LE3 . . . 154 C2
Hawthorne Way LE9 . . 198 B6
Hawthorn Wlk NN17 . . 230 E1
Hawthorn Gr LE2 . . . . 181 B7
Hawthorn Rd
  Bagworth LE67 . . . . . 124 A6
  Castle Donington DE74 . 17 B5
  Mountsorrel LE12 . . . 76 E2
Hawthorn Rise LE4 . . . 126 F3
Hawthorns The
  Countesthorpe LE8 . . . 202 E4
  Leicester LE2 . . . . . . 155 D1
  Lutterworth LE17 . . . 244 B6
  Markfield LE67 . . . . . 125 E8
Haybarn Cl LE19 . . . . . 201 D6
Haybrooke Rd LE12 . . . 77 D4
Hayden Ave LE2 . . . . . 181 D4
Hayden Cl LE4 . . . . . . 128 E3
Haydon Rd LE11 . . . . . 51 E4
Hayes Ave DE72 . . . . . 9 B7
Hayes Cl
  Langham LE15 . . . . . . 110 C3
  Whitwick LE67 . . . . . 71 F4
Hayes Cotts LE13 . . . . 59 A3
Hayes Gdns LE8 . . . . . 151 B3
Hayes Rd LE16 . . . . . . 180 C3
Hayfield Cl LE3 . . . . . . 153 B8
Hayhill LE12 . . . . 77 A5
Hayle Cl CV11 . . . . . . 214 A5
Hayling Cres LE5 . . . . 156 A8
Haymarket LE1 . . . . . . 259 B4
Haymarket Ctr LE1 . . . 259 B4
Haymeadow Cl LE17 . . 74 F8
Haynes Rd LE5 . . . . . . 155 E7
Hays La LE10 . . . . . . 215 B7
Hay Wain La DE11 . . . 44 B7
Hayward Ave LE11 . . . 52 C2
Haywood Cl LE5 . . . . . 156 B4
Haywoods Rd DE11 . . . 44 C1
Hazeland Cl LE17 . . . . 244 C6
Hazelbank Cl LE4 . . . . 128 D2
Hazelbank Rd LE2 . . . . 202 F4
Hazel Cl
  Birstall LE4 . . . . 129 B8
  Great Glen LE8 . . . . . . 205 B8
  Littlethorpe LE19 . . . 201 C6
  Measham DE12 . . . . . 93 C5
  Swadlincote DE11 . . . . 44 A5
  Uppingham LE15 . . . . 189 B5
Hazeldene Rd LE5 . . . . 130 D2
Hazel Dr
  Braunstone Town LE3 . . 178 F6
  Lutterworth LE17 . . . 244 B6
Hazel Gr
  Hallaton LE16 . . . . . . 209 E6
  Moira DE12 . . . . 68 B6
  Stamford PE9 . . . . . . 142 F4
Hazelhead Rd LE7 . . . 127 D6
Hazelnut Cl LE5 . . . . . 156 B4
Hazel Prim Sch LE2 . . . 154 F3
Hazel Rd LE11 . . . . . . 75 A8
Hazelrigg Cl DE74 . . . 16 F4
Hazel St
  Desford LE9 . . . . 151 A3
  Leicester LE2 . . . . . . 154 F3
Hazel Way LE8 . . . . . . 198 A7
Hazelwood Rd
  Leicester LE5 . . . . . . 155 D3
  Wigston LE18 . . . . . . 180 A1
Hazlemere Cl LE8 . . . 202 B7
Hazlewood Cres LE14 . 57 E3
Heacham Dr LE4 . . . . 128 C7
Headingley Cl
  Corby NN17 . . . . 97 A7
  Leicester LE4 . . . . . . 128 C7

Headland Rd LE5 . . . . 156 A3
Headlands The LE16 . . . . 240 F4
Headland The LE7 . . . . 103 F8
Headley Rd LE3 . . . . 128 F7
Heafield Dr DE74 . . . . 18 C2
Healey St LE18 . . . . 179 F1
Healy Cl LE4 . . . . 128 D4
Heanor St LE1 . . . . 259 A5
Heards Cl LE18 . . . . 203 E8
Hearthcote Rd DE11 . . . . 44 A3
Hearth St LE16 . . . . 240 D3
Heath Ave
  Narborough LE19 . . . . . . 178 E2
  Syston LE7 . . . . 102 F3
Heathbrook Dr LE6 . . . . . 152 D8
Heathcoat St LE11 . . . . . . 52 A4
Heathcote Dr LE12 . . . . . . 77 D4
Heathcott Rd LE7 . . . . . . 179 F7
Heath Ct LE9 . . . . 198 D7
Heath Dr LE15 . . . . 112 D8
HEATH END 46 C7
HEATHER 95 C2
Heatherbrook Prim Sch
  LE4 . . . . 127 F6
Heatherbrook Rd LE4 . . 128 A5
Heather Cres
  Breaston DE72 . . . . 9 F7
  Melton Mowbray LE13 . . 82 A8
Heather Ct LE99 . . . . 170 D1
Heatherdale LE67 . . . . 95 E1
Heather Ho LE67 . . . . 95 C2
Heather La
  Normanton Le H LE67 . . 95 A5
  Packington LE65 . . . . 69 C1
  Ravenstone LE67 . . . . 95 D6
Heather Prim Sch
  LE67 . . . . 95 C2
Heather Rd LE2 . . . . 180 A8
Heather Way LE8 . . . . . . 202 F3
Heathfield LE67 . . . . 71 E8
Heathfield High Sch
  LE9 . . . . 198 C7
Heathfield Rd LE18 . . . . 180 D5
Heathgate Cl LE4 . . . . . . 128 F8
Heath Gdns DE72 . . . . 10 A8
Heath La B
  Blackfordby DE11 . . . . . . 45 C2
  Earl Shilton LE9 . . . . 198 D8
  Hartshorne DE11 . . . . 45 E4
  Smisby LE65 . . . . 46 B6
  Wyville NG32 . . . . 25 F8
Heath La S LE9 . . . . 198 D8
Heathley Cl LE3 . . . . 152 F2
Heathley Park Dr LE3 . . 128 A1
Heath Rd
  Bagworth LE67 . . . . 124 C3
  Market Bosworth CV13 . . 148 D3
Heawood Way LE3 . . . . . 153 D1
Heays Cl LE3 . . . . 153 F8
Hebden Cl LE2 . . . . 179 C2
Hebden Way CV11 . . . . . 214 A2
Hecadeck La LE14 . . . . . . 36 C8
Hector Rd LE67 . . . . 71 D2
Hectors Way LE15 . . . . . 137 D6
Heddington Cl LE2 . . . . . 180 A5
Heddington Way LE2 . . . 180 A5
Hedge Gr DE11 . . . . 44 B7
Hedge Rd LE67 . . . . 96 C7
Hedgerow La LE9 . . . . . . 152 D5
Hedgerow Rd LE3 . . . . . . 154 A4
Hefford Gdns LE4 . . . . . . 128 D4
Heighton Cres LE19 . . . . 201 C6
Helena Cres LE4 . . . . 128 F4
Helen Roberts Ho
  LE5 . . . . 155 C7
Helmsdale Cl LE67 . . . . . . 97 C8
Helmsley Rd LE2 . . . . . . 179 F6
Helston Cl
  Nuneaton CV11 . . . . 214 A5
  Wigston LE18 . . . . 180 C1
Hemdale CV11 . . . . 214 A4
Hemdale Bsns Pk
  CV11 . . . . 214 A4
HEMINGTON 17 D5
Hemington Ct DE74 . . . . . 17 C5
Hemington Hill DE74 . . . 17 C4
Hemington La DE74 . . . . . 17 C4
Hemington Prim Sch
  DE74 . . . . 17 D5
Hemington Rd LE65 . . . . 156 D3
Hemlock Cl LE19 . . . . . . 177 F1
Hemplow Dr NN6 . . . . . . 256 B2
Hendon Grange LE2 . . . . 180 E8
Henley Cres LE3 . . . . 153 F1
Henley Rd LE3 . . . . 154 C6
Henray Ave LE2 . . . . 179 C2
Henry Cl LE3 . . . . 153 F8
Henry Dane Way LE67 . . . 47 E3
Henry St LE10 . . . . 197 A2
Henshaw St LE2 . . . . 259 B2
Hensman Cl LE8 . . . . 223 A6
Henson Cl LE4 . . . . 128 F6
Henson's La LE67 . . . . 71 D8
Henson Way LE10 . . . . . . 217 C5
Henton Rd LE3 . . . . 154 C5
Hepworth Rd DE11 . . . . . . 44 E1
Herald Way LE10 . . . . . . 215 D4
Herbert Ave LE4 . . . . 129 B2
Herbert Cl LE8 . . . . 202 A7
Herbert St LE11 . . . . 52 B5
Herdsmans Cl LE19 . . . . 201 C7
Hereford Cl LE19 . . . . . . 197 F6
Hereford Cres DE11 . . . . . 44 D6
Hereford Rd LE2 . . . . 179 D7
Hereward Dr LE7 . . . . . . 156 F5

Herford Way LE10 . . . . . 215 F6
Heritage Cl DE11 . . . . 44 C3
Heritage Way LE5 . . . . . 130 D3
Herle Ave LE3 . . . . 153 F2
Herle Wlk LE3 . . . . 153 F2
Hermitage Cl
  Catthorpe CV23 . . . . 253 E1
  Leicester, Oadby LE2 . . 181 A5
Hermitage Ct
  Leicester, Oadby LE2 . . 181 A5
  Whitwick LE67 . . . . 71 E3
Hermitage Ind Est The
  LE67 . . . . 71 C2
Hermitage Park Way B
  DE11 . . . . 44 A7
Hermitage Rd
  Birstall LE4 . . . . 129 A5
  Loughborough LE11 . . . . . 51 C2
  Whitwick LE67 . . . . 71 E3
Hermitage The PE9 . . . . 143 C3
Heron Cl
  Great Glen LE8 . . . . 182 B1
  Mountsorrel LE12 . . . . . . 76 F2
  Syston LE7 . . . . 44 F3
Heronagate Rd LE5 . . . . 156 A8
Heron Rd
  Barrow-u-S LE12 . . . . 76 E8
  Leicester LE5 . . . . 155 C7
  Oakham LE15 . . . . 138 B8
Herons Ct LE10 . . . . 215 A7
Heron's Way LE7 . . . . . . 103 E8
Heron Way
  Coalville LE67 . . . . 97 A8
  Narborough LE19 . . . . . . 178 D2
  Syston LE7 . . . . 102 F4
Herrick Cl
  Enderby LE19 . . . . 178 A3
  Sileby LE12 . . . . 77 B3
Herrick Dr LE7 . . . . 156 F5
  Herrick Prim Sch LE4 . . 129 D4
Herrick Rd
  Leicester LE2 . . . . 180 A8
  Loughborough LE11 . . . . . 52 B2
  Woodhouse Eaves LE12 . . 74 F2
Herricks Ave LE4 . . . . . . 129 F5
Herrick Way LE18 . . . . . 180 E1
Herriot Way LE11 . . . . 51 D5
Herschell St LE2 . . . . 155 C3
Herthull Rd LE5 . . . . 156 C6
Hervey Woods LE67 . . . . 71 E5
Hesilrige Wlk LE5 . . . . . 156 B8
Hesketh Ave LE2 . . . . . . 179 C3
Hesketh Cl LE2 . . . . 179 C3
Hesketh Cl LE15 . . . . 89 A7
Hewes Cl LE2 . . . . 179 B3
Hewett Cl LE8 . . . . 205 A8
Hewitt Dr LE9 . . . . 152 F4
Hextall Dr LE67 . . . . 122 F8
Hextall Rd LE5 . . . . 156 A3
Hexter Cl LE8 . . . . 201 F4
Heybridge Rd LE4 . . . . . 155 F8
Heybrook Ave LE8 . . . . . 202 A7
Heycock Cl LE8 . . . . 223 A6
Heyford Rd LE3 . . . . 153 D4
Heygate St LE16 . . . . . . 240 E4
Hey St NG10 . . . . 10 C4
Heythrop Cl LE2 . . . . 181 A5
Heythrop Rd LE15 . . . . . . 87 F3
Heyworth Rd LE3 . . . . . . 154 C1
HICKLING 19 C7
Hickling Cl LE7 . . . . 102 A6
Hickling Ct LE11 . . . . 51 F4
Hickling Dr LE12 . . . . 77 D4
Hickling La
  Long Clawson LE14 . . . . . 20 A4
  Upper Broughton LE14 . . 19 A2
Hickling Rd LE14 . . . . 19 B8
Hidcote Rd LE2 . . . . 181 A4
Higgs Cl LE5 . . . . 156 A5
High Acres LE7 . . . . 159 C2
Higham Fields Ct
  CV13 . . . . 196 A6
Higham Fields La
  CV13 . . . . 196 A6
Higham La
  Hinckley LE10 . . . . 196 F3
  Stoke Golding CV13 . . . . 196 C6
HIGHAM ON THE HILL
  . . . . 196 A3
Higham on the Hill CE
  Prim Sch CV13 . . . . . . 196 A4
Higham Way LE10 . . . . . 215 E7
Higham Way Ho LE10 . . 215 E7
Highbridge LE2 . . . . 77 C3
Highbrow LE8 . . . . 182 C1
Highbury Rd LE4 . . . . . . 155 C8
Highcliffe Prim Sch
  LE4 . . . . 128 F7
Highcliffe Rd LE5 . . . . . . 130 A3
High Cres PE9 . . . . 142 D7
Highcroft LE7 . . . . 247 E6
Highcroft Ave LE2 . . . . . 181 A4
Highcroft Cl NG10 . . . . . . 10 E5
Highcroft Rd LE2 . . . . . . 181 D3
HIGH CROSS 232 A6
High Cross Rd LE17 . . . . 232 C6
Highcross St
  Leicester LE1 . . . . 259 A4
  Market Harborough
  LE16 . . . . 240 C3
Higher Gn LE8 . . . . 205 B8
Highfield PE9 . . . . 193 B7
Highfield Ave LE13 . . . . . . 59 A5
Highfield Cl
  Empingham LE15 . . . . . . 140 F6
  Sheepy Magna CV9 . . . . 171 B8
  Shepshed LE12 . . . . 50 C5
Highfield Cotts LE15 . . . 191 E8

Highfield Cres
  Croxton Kerrial NG32 . . . 24 B7
  Wigston LE18 . . . . 180 A4
Highfield Ct LE9 . . . . 198 E7
Highfield Dr LE18 . . . . . . 180 D4
Highfield End LE14 . . . . . 105 F5
Highfield Rd
  Groby LE6 . . . . 126 C2
  Swadlincote DE11 . . . . . . 44 B3
HIGHFIELDS 155 C4
Highfields
  Barrow-u-S LE12 . . . . 76 D8
  Thornton LE67 . . . . 124 F3
Highfields Cl
  Ashby-de-la-Z LE65 . . . . . 68 F6
  Normanton Le H LE67 . . 94 F6
Highfields Dr LE11 . . . . . . 51 E1
Highfields Prim Sch
  LE2 . . . . 155 B5
Highfields Rd
  Hinckley LE10 . . . . 197 E1
  Mountsorrel LE12 . . . . . . 76 D1
Highfield St
  Anstey LE7 . . . . 127 E6
  Coalville LE67 . . . . 96 C7
  Earl Shilton LE9 . . . . 198 E7
  Fleckney LE8 . . . . 222 E8
  Leicester LE2 . . . . 155 B4
  Market Harborough
  LE16 . . . . 240 D3
  Stoney Stanton LE9 . . . . 199 D3
  Swadlincote DE11 . . . . . . 44 B3
Highfield (Uppingham
  Sch) LE15 . . . . 189 B3
Highgate
  Ashby-de-la-Z LE65 . . . . . 69 A8
  Leicester LE2 . . . . 180 A4
Highgate Ave LE4 . . . . . 128 E8
Highgate Cl NG13 . . . . . . 12 F8
Highgate Com Prim Sch
  LE7 . . . . 77 D4
Highgate Dr LE2 . . . . 180 B5
Highgate La LE13 . . . . 13 A7
Highgate Rd LE12 . . . . . . 77 D3
Highgrove Cl LE67 . . . . . . 96 F8
Highgrove Cres LE2 . . . . 179 B5
Highgrove Gdns PE9 . . . 143 A3
Highland Ave LE9 . . . . . . 152 E2
Highland Dr LE11 . . . . 75 B6
Highlands PE9 . . . . 116 E2
Highlands Way PE9 . . . . 143 B3
High Lees LE12 . . . . 217 B4
High Mdw LE12 . . . . 30 A1
Highmeres Rd LE4 . . . . . 129 F3
High St E LE15 . . . . 189 A4
High St W LE15 . . . . 189 A4
High St
  Barrow-u-S LE12 . . . . 76 D7
  Barwell LE9 . . . . 198 A6
  Bottesford NG32 . . . . 3 A2
  Braunston-in-R LE15 . . . 137 A2
  Carlby PE9 . . . . 117 B8
  Carlby PE9 . . . . 117 C8
  Castle Donington DE74 . . 17 A2
  Coalville LE67 . . . . 71 C1
  Collyweston PE9 . . . . . . 168 D2
  Cottingham LE16 . . . . . . 229 C1
  Desford LE9 . . . . 151 B3
  Duddington PE9 . . . . . . 193 B6
  Earl Shilton LE9 . . . . 198 F8
  Easton o t H PE9 . . . . . . 169 A5
  Enderby LE19 . . . . 178 B3
  Exton LE15 . . . . 113 A3
  Fleckney LE8 . . . . 222 F8
  Great Easton LE16 . . . . . 229 D7
  Great Glen LE8 . . . . 205 A8
  Gretton NN17 . . . . 213 C1
  Hallaton LE16 . . . . 209 D6
  Husbands Bosworth
  LE17 . . . . 247 E5
  Ibstock LE67 . . . . 122 F8
  Kegworth DE74 . . . . 18 C2
  Ketton PE9 . . . . 168 A6
  Kibworth Beauchamp
  LE8 . . . . 224 A8
  Leicester, Evington LE5 . . 156 B2
  Leicester LE1 . . . . 259 B4
  Leicester, Oadby LE2 . . . 181 A5
  Long Eaton NG10 . . . . . . 10 E8
  Loughborough LE11 . . . . . 52 B4
  Lutterworth LE17 . . . . . . 244 C5
  Market Harborough
  LE16 . . . . 240 E3
  Measham DE12 . . . . 93 C5
  Melbourne DE73 . . . . 26 A7
  Melton Mowbray LE13 . . 59 C3
  Morcott LE15 . . . . 191 A6
  North Kilworth LE17 . . . . 246 F4
  Oakham LE15 . . . . 137 F6
  Packington LE65 . . . . 69 C2
  Quorn (Quorndon) LE12 . . 75 F6
  Sileby LE12 . . . . 77 C3
  Somerby LE14 . . . . 108 B2
  South Witham NG33 . . . . 65 B3
  Stamford PE9 . . . . 143 E3
  Staunton in t V NG13 . . . . 1 B4
  Stoke Golding CV13 . . . . 196 D7
  Swadlincote, Church Gresley
  DE11 . . . . 44 C3
  Swadlincote, Newhall
  DE11 . . . . 44 B8
  Swinford LE17 . . . . 254 B3
  Syston LE7 . . . . 103 A4
  Waltham on t W LE14 . . . 40 A6
  Walton LE17 . . . . 236 B3
  Welford NN6 . . . . 256 E6
  Whetstone LE8 . . . . 201 F7
  Woodville DE11 . . . . 44 F2

High Street St Martin's
  PE9 . . . . 143 E2
High Tor E LE9 . . . . 175 E1
High Tor W LE9 . . . . 175 E1
Highway Rd
  Leicester LE5 . . . . 155 C2
  Thurmaston LE4 . . . . . . 129 F8
Hilary Bevins Cl CV13 . . 195 F4
Hilary Cl LE13 . . . . 59 E6
Hilary Cres
  Coalville LE67 . . . . 72 A3
  Groby LE6 . . . . 126 D3
Hilcot Gn LE3 . . . . 153 C2
Hilders Rd LE3 . . . . 154 A6
Hildyard Rd LE4 . . . . 129 A1
Hilary Cl PE9 . . . . 143 F4
Hilary Pl LE3 . . . . 154 A2
Hillberry Cl LE19 . . . . . . 201 A8
Hill Cl LE9 . . . . 176 A7
Hillcrest Ave
  Kibworth Beauchamp
  LE8 . . . . 206 A1
  Market Harborough
  LE16 . . . . 240 D4
Hillcrest Dr LE12 . . . . 75 B7
Hillcrest La LE17 . . . . . . 247 E5
Hillcrest Rd LE2 . . . . 180 C6
Hillcroft Cl LE4 . . . . 129 F8
Hillcroft Rd LE5 . . . . 155 C5
Hill Ct LE7 . . . . 156 F4
Hill Dr LE17 . . . . 244 C5
Hill Farm Ave CV11 . . . . 214 B1
Hill Field LE2 . . . . 181 E4
Hill Gdns LE16 . . . . 240 C3
Hillier Rd LE15 . . . . 130 C3
Hill La
  Countesthorpe LE8 . . . . 202 B2
  Markfield LE67 . . . . 98 C1
Hill Lane Cl LE67 . . . . 98 D2
Hill Lane Ind Est LE67 . . 98 C2
Hillmorton La
  Clifton u D CV23 . . . . . . 257 A4
  Lilbourne CV23 . . . . 257 F5
Hill Rd
  Oakham LE15 . . . . 137 E7
  Orston NG13 . . . . 2 A6
Hillrise LE10 . . . . 215 F8
Hill Rise
  Birstall LE4 . . . . 129 A8
  Leicester LE4 . . . . 129 F5
  Measham DE12 . . . . 93 C6
  Woodhouse Eaves
  LE12 . . . . 100 A8
Hillrise Ave LE3 . . . . 179 A8
Hillsborough Cl LE2 . . . 179 C2
Hillsborough Cres
  LE2 . . . . 179 C2
Hillsborough Rd LE2 . . . 179 D3
Hillside
  Appleby Magna DE12 . . . 119 F8
  Castle Donington DE74 . . 17 B4
  Kegworth DE74 . . . . 18 D1
  Market Bosworth CV13 . . 148 D3
  Markfield LE67 . . . . 98 D1
  Uppingham LE15 . . . . . . 189 B4
Hillside Ave
  Melton Mowbray LE13 . . 59 B5
  Wigston LE18 . . . . 180 D1
Hillside Cl LE14 . . . . 56 C4
Hillside Ct DE73 . . . . 26 F2
Hillside Dr NG10 . . . . 10 B8
Hillside Rd
  Hinckley LE10 . . . . 215 D6
  Market Harborough
  LE16 . . . . 240 F4
Hillside Wlk by N NG32 . . . 8 B1
Hills Rd DE72 . . . . 9 C8
Hill St
  Ashby-de-la-Z LE65 . . . . . 69 A6
  Barwell LE9 . . . . 198 B6
  Croft LE9 . . . . 200 C5
  Donisthorpe DE12 . . . . . . 67 E1
  Hinckley LE10 . . . . 215 E8
  Leicester LE1 . . . . 259 C4
  Newbold Verdon LE9 . . . 150 B5
  Swadlincote, Church Gresley
  DE11 . . . . 44 C3
Hill Top
  Castle Donington DE74 . . 17 A1
  Earl Shilton LE9 . . . . 175 F1
Hilltop Ave LE8 . . . . 182 C1
Hilltop Cl LE9 . . . . 137 D6
Hilltop Ind Est LE67 . . . . 97 C4
Hilltop Rd LE5 . . . . 130 B4
Hill Top Rd LE1 . . . . 74 F8
Hill View LE19 . . . . 178 E3
Hill View Dr LE9 . . . . . . 201 D3
Hill View Rd NG33 . . . . . 65 B3
Hill Way LE2 . . . . 181 C4
Hilton Cl
  Long Eaton NG10 . . . . 9 F4
  Swadlincote DE11 . . . . . . 44 A7
Hilton Gdns DE72 . . . . . . 16 A7
HINCKLEY 197 C2
Hinckley Bsns Pk
  LE10 . . . . 214 F8
Hinckley & District Hospl
  LE10 . . . . 215 D8
Hinckley & District Mus*
  LE10 . . . . 197 D1
Hinckley La CV13 . . . . . . 196 C3
Hinckley Rd
  Aston Flamville LE10 . . . 216 E6
  Barwell LE9 . . . . 197 E5
  Burton Hastings CV11 . . 215 A1
  Burton Hastings CV11,
  LE10 . . . . 215 D1

Hinckley Rd continued
  Burton Hastings LE10 . . . 215 E1
  Earl Shilton LE9 . . . . 198 D7
  Hinckley LE10 . . . . 216 A6
  Hinkley, Burbage LE9 . . 216 D8
  Ibstock LE67 . . . . 122 E7
  Kirkby Mallory LE9 . . . . 174 E6
  Leicester Forest East LE3,
  LE9 . . . . 152 D2
  Leicester LE3 . . . . 153 D4
  Leicester, Westcotes
  LE3 . . . . 154 C5
  Nailstone CV13 . . . . 123 A2
  Nuneaton CV11 . . . . 214 A5
  Sapcote LE9 . . . . 217 B8
  Stoke Golding CV13 . . . 196 F7
  Thurlaston LE9 . . . . 176 C5
  Hinckley Sta LE10 . . . . . 215 D7
Hind Ave DE72 . . . . 9 C8
Hind Cl LE8 . . . . 202 A6
Hind Leys Com Coll
  LE12 . . . . 50 D4
Hind Mews The 4
  LE17 . . . . 244 C5
Hindoostan Ave LE18 . . 179 E2
Hinks Ave LE7 . . . . 156 F8
Hipwell Cres LE4 . . . . . . 128 E3
HMYOI Glen Parva
  LE2 . . . . 179 D2
Hoball Cl LE3 . . . . 153 E8
Hobart St LE2 . . . . 155 B5
Hobbs Wick LE12 . . . . 77 C3
Hobby Cl LE9 . . . . 218 F7
Hobill Cl
  Huncote LE9 . . . . 200 E8
  Leicester Forest East
  LE3 . . . . 153 B2
Hobrook Rd LE8 . . . . 223 A6
Hobson Rd LE4 . . . . 128 F3
HOBY 79 D7
Hoby Rd
  Asfordby LE14 . . . . 57 C2
  Ragdale LE14 . . . . 56 C4
  Thrussington LE7 . . . . 79 A5
Hoby St LE3 . . . . 154 D6
Hockey Cl LE11 . . . . 52 A6
Hockley Farm Rd LE3 . . 153 D4
Hockley The LE67 . . . . 71 F5
Hodgson Cl LE3 . . . . 128 A1
Hodson Cl LE8 . . . . 201 F6
Hodson Ct LE11 . . . . 52 B2
Hogarth Cl LE10 . . . . . . 197 A3
Hogarth Rd LE10 . . . . . . 197 A3
Hogarth Rd
  Birstall LE4 . . . . 101 C1
  Whitwick LE67 . . . . 71 F5
Hog La
  Foxton LE16 . . . . 224 E1
  Hallaton LE16 . . . . 209 D6
Hoke Ct LE17 . . . . 218 E1
Holbeck Dr LE19 . . . . . . 219 A6
Holbein Cl LE11 . . . . 52 C4
Holbourne Cl LE12 . . . . . 76 C7
Holbrook LE2 . . . . 181 E4
Holbrook Rd LE2 . . . . . . 180 E8
Holcombe Cl LE67 . . . . . . 71 E6
Holden Ave DE72 . . . . 16 A8
Holdenby Cl LE16 . . . . . 241 B3
Holden Cl LE18 . . . . 202 A5
Holden St LE4 . . . . 129 A2
Holderness Rd LE4 . . . . 128 D5
Holdings The DE11 . . . . . . 44 A1
Holgate Cl LE7 . . . . 127 E7
Holkham Ave LE4 . . . . . . 129 D1
Holland Cl LE67 . . . . 71 E5
Holland Mdw NG10 . . . . . 10 D5
Holland Rd
  Leicester LE2 . . . . 155 B6
  Stamford PE9 . . . . 143 E4
Hollands La LE14 . . . . . . 106 E1
Hollands Way DE74 . . . . . 18 D2
Holland Way LE19 . . . . . 201 B8
Holliers Walk Prim Sch
  LE10 . . . . 197 D1
Holliers Way LE10 . . . . . 200 C4
Hollier's Wlk LE10 . . . . . 197 D1
Hollies Cl
  Houghton on t H LE7 . . . 158 A4
  Thurlaston LE9 . . . . 177 A3
Hollies The CV23 . . . . . . 252 F1
Hollies Way LE7 . . . . 156 F4
Hollington Rd LE5 . . . . . 155 D4
Hollins Rd LE3 . . . . 153 E4
Hollinwell Cl LE3 . . . . . . 153 C5
Hollow La
  Burton Lazars LE14 . . . . . 83 A7
  Frisby on t W LE14 . . . . . 80 C8
Hollow Rd
  Anstey LE7 . . . . 127 D6
  Breedon on t H DE73 . . . 26 E2
Hollow The
  Castle Donington DE74 . . 17 B3
  Earl Shilton LE9 . . . . 198 F8
  Knossington LE15 . . . . . 136 A6
  Leicester LE5 . . . . 156 B2
  Normanton Le H LE67 . . . 94 F6
  Thornton LE67 . . . . 124 D5
Hollowtree Rd LE5 . . . . . 130 C2
Holly Ave DE72 . . . . 9 F8
Holly Bank LE67 . . . . 96 D6
Hollybank Cl LE11 . . . . . . 44 A7
Hollybank Cl LE12 . . . . . . 50 C3
Hollybank Ct LE2 . . . . . . 155 C3
Holly Bank Est CV9 . . . . 119 A2
Hollybrook Cl LE4 . . . . . 130 A6
Hollybush Cl
  Leicester LE5 . . . . 156 F2
  Syston LE7 . . . . 102 F4

Holly Bush Cl DE12 . . . . .91 F7
Holly Cl
  Draycott DE72 . . . . .9 A7
  Hinckley LE10 . . . . .215 E5
  Market Harborough
    LE16 . . . . .240 E4
  Moira DE12 . . . . .68 C6
HOLLYCROFT 197 A1
Hollycroft LE10 . . . . .197 C1
Hollycroft Cres LE10 . . . . .197 C1
Holly Ct
  Aston-on-T DE72 . . . . .16 A7
  Leicester, Oadby LE2 . . . . .181 A7
  Woodville DE11 . . . . .44 F2
Hollydene Cres LE9 . . . . . .198 D7
Holly Dr LE17 . . . . .244 B6
Hollygate Cl LE13 . . . . .59 E1
Holly Gr LE8 . . . . .202 B8
Holly Hayes Rd LE67 . . . . . .71 F4
Holly La
  Atherstone CV9 . . . . .170 D2
  Atherstone, Whittington
    CV9 . . . . .170 C2
  Barwell LE9 . . . . .198 B7
Holly Lane Ind Est
  CV9 . . . . .170 C2
Holly Rd LE12 . . . . .93 C5
Holly Tree Ave LE4 . . . . . . .129 A8
Hollytree Cl
  Hoton LE12 . . . . .32 D2
  Loughborough LE11 . . . . . . .75 A7
Hollytree La LE4 . . . . .20 C3
Holly Tree Wlk LE17 . . . . . .232 E6
Holly Wlk CV11 . . . . .214 A2
Holman Row LE4 . . . . .156 A6
Holmdale Rd LE4 . . . . .103 A3
Holmden Ave LE18 . . . . . . .180 B3
Holme Cl PE9 . . . . .142 F1
Holme Dr LE2 . . . . .181 B7
Holme Farm Cl LE12 . . . . . .34 E7
Holmes Cl LE6 . . . . .126 E3
Holmes Ct DE11 . . . . .44 B5
Holmes Dr PE9 . . . . .168 B5
Holmewood Dr LE9 . . . . . .152 F5
Holmfield LE14 . . . . .79 D7
Holmfield Ave
  Leicester LE2 . . . . .155 D2
  Loughborough LE11 . . . . . . .51 F6
Holmfield Ave E LE3 . . . . . .153 C3
Holmfield Ave W LE3 . . . . .153 C3
Holmfield Cl LE17 . . . . .244 A6
Holmfield Prim Sch
  LE3 . . . . .153 B3
Holmfield Rd
  Dadlington LE9 . . . . .151 B3
  Leicester LE2 . . . . .155 D2
Holmleigh Gdns LE7 . . . . . .156 F4
Holmwood Ct LE2 . . . . .127 E1
Holmwood Dr LE3 . . . . .127 E1
Holt Cl LE9 . . . . .199 D2
Holt Cres LE9 . . . . .177 A3
Holt Dr
  Kirby Fields LE9 . . . . .152 F4
  Loughborough LE11 . . . . . . .51 F1
Holte Rd CV9 . . . . .170 D1
Holt La LE17 . . . . .219 F4
HOLWELL 37 F4
Holy Bones LE1 . . . . .259 A4
Holy Cross RC Prim Sch
  Leicester LE2 . . . . .179 F4
  Whitwick LE67 . . . . .71 F5
Holygate Rd LE15 . . . . . . .163 C1
Holyoak Dr LE10 . . . . .217 B5
Holyoake Cres LE67 . . . . . . .95 C2
Holyoake Dr
  Heather LE67 . . . . .95 C2
  Long Eaton NG10 . . . . .10 F7
Holyoake St LE19 . . . . .178 B2
Holyrood Cl LE15 . . . . .137 F5
Holyrood Dr LE8 . . . . .202 D4
HOLYWELL 90 E5
Holywell Ave LE65 . . . . .69 B7
Holywell Cotts LE65 . . . . . . .69 A6
Holywell Dr LE11 . . . . .51 D1
Holywell Prim Sch
  LE11 . . . . .74 C8
Holywell Rd
  Castle Bytham NG33 . . . . . .90 D7
  Clipsham LE15 . . . . .89 F4
  Leicester LE2 . . . . .179 C6
Holywell Way LE11 . . . . .51 C1
Home Ave LE3 . . . . .153 C1
Home Cl
  Blaby LE8 . . . . .202 B8
  Kibworth Beauchamp
    LE8 . . . . .224 A8
  South Croxton LE7 . . . . . .105 C1
Home Close Rd LE7 . . . . . .158 A4
Home Croft Dr LE65 . . . . . . .69 C2
Home Ct LE15 . . . . .140 F6
Home Farm Barns
  LE67 . . . . .94 D1
Home Farm Cl
  Burley LE15 . . . . .111 F2
  East Farndon LE16 . . . . . .250 B7
  Gilmorton LE17 . . . . .235 C5
  Great Casterton PE9 . . . . .142 E6
  Leicester LE4 . . . . .128 C3

Home Farm *continued*
  Witherley CV9 . . . . .194 B8
  Woodhouse LE12 . . . . .75 B3
Home Farm Ct LE4 . . . . . . .128 C3
Home Farm Mews
  CV13 . . . . .148 F3
Home Farm Sq LE4 . . . . . .128 C3
Home Farm Wlk LE4 . . . . .128 C3
Homefield La LE7 . . . . .101 F7
Homefield Rd LE12 . . . . . . .77 C4
Homemead Ave LE4 . . . . . .128 D2
Home Pastures LE14 . . . . . .20 F7
Home Rd LE67 . . . . .71 D5
Homer Dr LE13 . . . . .201 A8
Homestead Cl LE7 . . . . . . .102 D8
Homestead Dr LE18 . . . . . .180 D1
Homestead Rd LE67 . . . . . .71 D8
Homestead The
  Earl Shilton LE9 . . . . .198 D8
  Mountsorrel LE12 . . . . .76 E3
Homestone Gdns LE16 . . . .156 E6
Homestone Rise LE16 . . . . .156 C6
Homeway Cl LE12 . . . . .50 C3
Homeway Rd LE15 . . . . . . .155 E3
Homewelland Ho
  LE16 . . . . .240 D4
Honeybourne Cl LE2 . . . . . .181 A4
Honeycomb Cl LE19 . . . . . .201 A8
Honeypot La LE17 . . . . . . .247 E5
Honey Pot La NG33 . . . . . . .65 E8
Honeysuckle Cl
  Coalville LE67 . . . . .97 A8
  East Goscote LE7 . . . . . . .103 F7
  Lutterworth LE17 . . . . . . .244 A6
  Swadlincote DE11 . . . . .44 A6
Honeysuckle Rd LE5 . . . . . .130 C2
Honeysuckle Way
  Loughborough LE11 . . . . . . .75 A6
  Melton Mowbray LE13 . . . . .82 A8
Honeywell Cl LE2 . . . . .181 A5
Honiton Cl LE18 . . . . .180 C1
Hooby La LE15 . . . . .88 C6
Hood Ct LE65 . . . . .69 B6
Hoods Cl LE4 . . . . .128 D6
Hooley Cl NG10 . . . . .10 B6
Hoopers Cl NG13 . . . . .3 A2
Hopefield Rd LE4 . . . . .154 C2
Hope Hamilton CE Prim
  Sch LE5 . . . . .130 C3
Hope St DE73 . . . . .26 A7
Hope's Yd LE15 . . . . .189 B4
Hoppner Cl LE4 . . . . .101 D1
Hopton Fields LE16 . . . . . .250 D8
Hopwell Rd DE72 . . . . .9 A8
Hopwood Cl LE4 . . . . .128 B3
Hopyard Cl LE12 . . . . .76 B7
Horeston Grange Sh Ctr
  CV11 . . . . .214 A5
Hornbeam Cl
  Leicester, Oadby LE2 . . . . .181 A7
  Loughborough LE11 . . . . . . .75 A7
  Narborough LE19 . . . . . . .201 A8
Hornbeam Rd LE9 . . . . . . .150 B4
Hornby Rd LE3 . . . . .130 C3
Horn Cl LE15 . . . . .147 E8
Horndean Ave LE18 . . . . . .180 D3
Horncroft LE67 . . . . .101 E6
HORNINGHOLD 210 B7
Horninghold La LE16 . . . . .210 A5
Horninghold Rd LE16 . . . . .209 F6
Horn La LE16 . . . . .209 D6
Horsefair Cl LE16 . . . . .240 D4
Horsefair St LE1 . . . . .259 B3
Horsefair The [5]
  LE16 . . . . .215 D8
Horse Field View LE15 . . . . .59 A5
Horseguards Way LE13 . . . .59 A6
Horse Hill LE7 . . . . .185 C1
Horsepool LE10 . . . . .216 A5
Horsepool The CV23 . . . . . .258 A7
Horseshoe Cl
  Cosby LE9 . . . . .201 D4
  Market Bosworth CV13 . . . .148 C3
Horseshoe La [5] PE9 . . . . .143 D3
Horse Shoe La LE16 . . . . . .241 B6
Horse Shoes The DE74 . . . .17 D4
Horses La DE12 . . . . .93 D4
Horsewell La LE18 . . . . . . .180 D1
HORSTON HILL 155 F3
Horston Rd LE15 . . . . .155 E3
Horton Ct LE8 . . . . .202 A8
Horton's Cl LE12 . . . . .179 B3
Hortons La LE15 . . . . .85 A1
Horwood Cl LE18 . . . . .180 E4
HOSE 20 F8
Hose CE Prim Sch
  LE14 . . . . .20 F7
Hose La
  Colston Bassett LE14 . . . . . .11 B3
  Harby LE14 . . . . .12 A1
  Hose LE14 . . . . .21 A8
  Long Clawson LE14 . . . . . . .20 F5
Hoselett Field Rd
  NG10 . . . . .10 E5
Huskins Cl LE10 . . . . .202 E9
Hospital La LE16 . . . . .156 A4
Hospital La
  Blaby LE8 . . . . .202 D6
  Ravenstone LE67 . . . . .95 E8
  Swannington LE67 . . . . . . .71 B7
Hospital of Christ The
  LE15 . . . . .189 A4
Hospital Way LE11 . . . . .51 E4
Hotel St
  Coalville LE67 . . . . .71 D1
  Leicester LE1 . . . . .259 B3
Hothorpe Rd LE17 . . . . . . .248 D8
Hotoft Rd LE5 . . . . .156 B8

HOTON 32 C1
Hoton Rd LE12 . . . . .33 B3
Hough Hill LE67 . . . . .71 A3
Houghton La
  Gaulby LE7 . . . . .183 D7
  Houghton on t H LE2,
    LE7 . . . . .157 B1
HOUGHTON ON THE HILL
  . . . . .157 E3
Houghton-on-the-Hill CE
  Prim Sch LE7 . . . . .157 F3
Houghton St LE5 . . . . .155 D7
Houlditch Rd LE2 . . . . .180 B8
Housman Wlk LE4 . . . . . . .155 B8
Howard Cl
  Barwell LE9 . . . . .198 A7
  Loughborough LE11 . . . . . . .51 C5
Howard Rd
  Glen Parva LE2 . . . . .179 B3
  Leicester LE2 . . . . .155 B2
Howard St LE11 . . . . .52 B5
Howard Way LE16 . . . . . . .240 D1
Howarth Cl NG10 . . . . .10 A7
Howden Cl
  Loughborough LE11 . . . . . . .51 B3
  Swadlincote DE11 . . . . .44 A5
Howden Rd LE2 . . . . .179 C4
Howdon Rd LE2 . . . . .181 B3
Howe Cl LE9 . . . . .199 C1
Howe Ct LE67 . . . . .71 D5
Howe La LE7 . . . . .101 E6
Howe Rd
  Loughborough LE11 . . . . . . .52 B1
  Whitwick LE67 . . . . .71 D5
Howitts Rd NG13 . . . . .3 A1
Howitt St NG10 . . . . .10 E7
Hoylake Cl
  Leicester LE5 . . . . .155 E2
  Nuneaton CV11 . . . . .214 B1
Hoy Wlk NN17 . . . . .230 C1
Hubbard Cl LE8 . . . . .202 A5
Hubbard Rd LE2 . . . . .54 A7
Hubbards Cl LE17 . . . . .220 A2
Hubble Rd NN17 . . . . .230 F1
Hudson Cl
  Leicester LE3 . . . . .154 A8
  Oakham LE15 . . . . .137 D6
Hudson Rd LE2 . . . . .77 C4
Hudson St LE11 . . . . .52 C4
Huggett Cl LE4 . . . . .129 E4
HUGGLESCOTE 96 C6
Hugglescote Com Prim
  Sch LE67 . . . . .96 C6
Hughenden Dr LE2 . . . . . . .154 E1
Hugh Lupus Ct LE12 . . . . . .76 D3
Humber Cl LE5 . . . . .130 B1
Humberstone LE5 . . . . .91 B1
HUMBERSTONE 156 A8
Humberstone Ct LE5 . . . . . .156 B8
Humberstone Dr LE5 . . . . . .156 A8
HUMBERSTONE GARDEN
  . . . . .130 C1
Humberstone Gate
  LE1 . . . . .259 B4
Humberstone Inf Sch
  LE5 . . . . .130 B1
Humberstone Jun Sch
  LE5 . . . . .130 B1
Humberstone La LE4 . . . . .129 F5
Humberstone Mall [1]
  LE1 . . . . .259 B4
Humberstone Rd
  Leicester LE5 . . . . .155 C7
  Leicester LE5 . . . . .259 C4
Humber Wlk NN17 . . . . . . .230 D2
Humble La LE7 . . . . .102 E8
Humes Cl LE8 . . . . .201 F4
Hume St LE11 . . . . .52 C4
Humphrey Cl LE11 . . . . .52 C2
Humphrey Perkins High
  Sch LE12 . . . . .76 C8
Humphries Cl LE5 . . . . . . .156 A5
HUNCOTE 200 D8
Huncote Com Prim Sch
  LE9 . . . . .200 D8
Huncote Rd
  Croft LE9 . . . . .200 B5
  Narborough LE9, LE19 . . . .200 F7
  Stoney Stanton LE9 . . . . . .199 E4
HUNGARTON 132 B3
Hungarton Bvd LE5 . . . . . .156 B8
Hungarton Dr LE7 . . . . . . .103 C3
Hungarton La LE7 . . . . . . .131 E4
Hungarton Rd LE7 . . . . . . .132 F3
Hungary La LE12 . . . . .30 C7
HUNGERTON 25 D8
Hunt Cotts NG32 . . . . .8 B2
Hunt Dr LE13 . . . . .59 E6
Hunter Bvd LE17 . . . . .243 C7
Hunter Rd LE4 . . . . .129 A1
Hunters Ave LE7 . . . . .160 A2
Hunters Cl LE17 . . . . .247 E6
Hunters Dr LE17 . . . . .244 B5
Hunters La CV13 . . . . .195 A6
Hunters Rd LE13 . . . . .59 D1
Hunters Rise LE14 . . . . .80 B7
Hunters Row LE9 . . . . .201 D3
Hunters Way
  Leicester Forest East
    LE3 . . . . .152 F2
  Leicester, Oadby LE2 . . . . .181 D5
Hunters Wlk CV9 . . . . .194 B7
Huntingdon Cl LE12 . . . . . . .54 A7
Huntingdon Ct
  [5] Ashby-de-la-Z LE65 . . .69 B6
  Measham DE12 . . . . .93 A5
  Melbourne DE73 . . . . .26 B8
Huntingdon Dr DE74 . . . . . .17 A4

Huntingdon Gdns
  LE16 . . . . .240 E1
Huntingdon Rd
  Ashby-de-la-Z LE65 . . . . . . .68 F5
  Leicester LE4 . . . . .129 E2
Huntingdon Way DE12 . . . . .93 A4
Huntings The LE9 . . . . .152 C6
Hunt La CV9 . . . . .194 B7
Hunts Cl LE9 . . . . .151 C8
Hunts La
  Desford LE9 . . . . .150 F4
  Nethersal DE12 . . . . .91 E7
Hunt's La
  Hallaton LE16 . . . . .209 D6
  Ketton PE9 . . . . .167 F6
Huntsmans Cl LE67 . . . . . .125 E8
Huntsman's Cl LE12 . . . . . .76 B6
Huntsman's Dale LE7 . . . . .103 D8
Huntsmans Dr LE15 . . . . . .137 E7
Huntsmans Way LE4 . . . . .129 E3
Hunts Orch LE12 . . . . .53 A8
Hunt St LE15 . . . . .87 E2
Hunt Way DE11 . . . . .44 E4
Hurds Cl LE7 . . . . .127 D6
Hurlingham Rd LE16 . . . . .240 F1
Hursley Cl LE2 . . . . .181 C5
Hurst Cl DE12 . . . . .91 E8
Hurst Rd
  Earl Shilton LE9 . . . . .198 E7
  Hinckley LE10 . . . . .215 D8
Hurst Rise LE5 . . . . .156 A5
Hurstwood Rd LE11 . . . . . . .51 B3
HUSBANDS BOSWORTH
  . . . . .247 D5
Husbands Bosworth CE
  Prim Sch LE17 . . . . .247 E5
Huss's La NG10 . . . . .10 F7
Huston Cl LE12 . . . . .76 F5
Huston Ct LE11 . . . . .52 B3
Hutchinson St LE2 . . . . . . .155 B5
Hyacinth Way LE10 . . . . . .215 D5
Hyam's La DE74 . . . . .28 D6
Hyde Cl
  Leicester LE3 . . . . .128 B1
  Leicester, Oadby LE2 . . . . .181 C3
  Narborough LE19 . . . . . . .201 B8
Hyde Lodge Rd LE7,
  LE15 . . . . .134 E3
Hydes La LE10 . . . . .214 E4
Hydra Wlk [4] LE2 . . . . . . .155 B5
Hylion Rd LE2 . . . . .180 A6

I

Ibbetson Ave LE3 . . . . .153 C7
Ibsley Way LE2 . . . . .179 D3
IBSTOCK 95 F2
Ibstock Com Coll LE67 . . . . .95 F1
Ibstock Jun Sch LE67 . . . . .95 F1
Ibstock Rd
  Ellistown LE67 . . . . .96 D3
  Nailstone CV13 . . . . .123 A4
  Ravenstone LE67 . . . . .95 F8
Ickworth Cl LE5 . . . . .155 E8
Iffley Cl LE5 . . . . .156 A8
Iffley Ct LE5 . . . . .156 A5
Iliffe Ave LE4 . . . . .180 F5
Iliffe Ho
  Hinckley LE10 . . . . .215 B7
  Leicester, Oadby LE2 . . . . .180 F5
Iliffe Rd LE4 . . . . .129 E1
Iliffes Cl LE12 . . . . .76 E8
Iliffe's Rd LE4 . . . . .156 B5
Illston Cross Roads
  LE7 . . . . .184 C2
Illston Gdns LE12 . . . . .76 E7
Illston La LE7 . . . . .183 F4
ILLSTON ON THE HILL
  . . . . .183 F3
Illston Rd
  Gaulby LE7 . . . . .183 E5
  Tilston on t H LE7 . . . . . .184 D3
Ilmington Cl LE3 . . . . .127 C1
Ilminster Cl LE10 . . . . .216 B7
Imperial Ave LE3 . . . . .154 B3
Imperial Avenue Inf Sch
  LE3 . . . . .154 B3
Imperial Rd LE8 . . . . .223 F8
Impey Cl LE13 . . . . .82 A8
Industrial Heritage Mus*
  .71 B1
Infirmary Cl LE1 . . . . .259 B2
Infirmary Rd LE1, LE2 . . . .259 B2
Infirmary Sq LE1 . . . . .259 B2
Ingarsby Cl LE7 . . . . .158 A4
Ingarsby Dr LE5 . . . . .156 C3
Ingarsby La LE7 . . . . .158 A6
Ingarsby Old Hall Cott
  LE5 . . . . .158 B7
Ingarsby Rd LE12 . . . . . . .131 E2
Ingleberry Rd LE12 . . . . . . .73 D6
Ingleborough Gdns [6]
  NG10 . . . . .10 A8
Ingleby Cl DE11 . . . . .44 A3
Ingleby Rd
  Long Eaton NG10 . . . . .9 F4
  Whitwick LE8 . . . . .180 C3
Ingle Dr
  Ashby-de-la-Z LE65 . . . . . . .68 F7
  Ratby LE6 . . . . .126 B1
Inglehurst Jun & Inf Schs
  LE3 . . . . .154 B4
Inglenook Mobile Home
  Pk LE4 . . . . .102 F1
Ingles Hill LE65 . . . . .68 F7
Ingle St LE3 . . . . .154 B7
Ingleton Cl CV11 . . . . .214 A2

Ingold Ave LE4 . . . . .128 D3
Ingrams Way LE18 . . . . . . .203 E8
INGTHORPE 142 C6
Inhams The LE15 . . . . .189 E4
Inleys The LE12 . . . . .50 D3
Innage Park Small Ind
  Units CV9 . . . . .170 C1
Insley's La CV13 . . . . .121 E2
Interlink Ind Pk LE67 . . . . . .97 B3
Invergarry Cl LE4 . . . . .129 D4
Iona Cl LE4 . . . . .128 B3
Iona Rd LE4 . . . . .102 F4
Iona Way LE8 . . . . .202 F3
Ipswich Cl LE4 . . . . .128 A6
Irene Pollard Ho LE4 . . . . .129 B3
Ireton Ave LE4 . . . . .129 F2
Ireton Rd
  Leicester LE4 . . . . .129 E2
  Market Harborough
    LE16 . . . . .240 D2
Iris Ave
  Birstall LE4 . . . . .129 B8
  Glen Parva LE2 . . . . .179 B3
Iris Cl
  Hinckley LE10 . . . . .215 E5
  Mountsorrel LE12 . . . . .76 F2
Irlam St LE18 . . . . .202 F8
Irnham Rd PE9 . . . . .143 E5
Ironmonger St [6]
  PE9 . . . . .143 E3
Ironworks Rd LE4 . . . . . . .155 C8
Irwell Cl
  Melton Mowbray LE13 . . . . .59 B1
  Oakham LE15 . . . . .137 C5
Irwin Ave LE11 . . . . .51 C6
Isabel La LE8 . . . . .224 A8
Isis Cl LE2 . . . . .181 D6
Island Cl
  Hinckley LE10 . . . . .197 E2
  Swadlincote DE11 . . . . .67 C8
ISLEY WALTON 27 D7
Islington St LE2 . . . . .154 F2
Isobella Rd LE8 . . . . .153 C1
Ivanhoe Cl LE3 . . . . .153 C7
Ivanhoe Dr LE65 . . . . .69 B7
Ivanhoe Ind Est LE65 . . . . . .69 A8
Ivanhoe Rd LE18 . . . . .179 F2
Ivanhoe St LE3 . . . . .154 C7
Ivatt Cl LE7 . . . . .157 A5
Iveagh Cl DE12 . . . . .93 D5
Ivens Cl LE9 . . . . .198 A5
Iveshead La LE12 . . . . .73 B8
Iveshead Rd LE12 . . . . .73 A7
Ivychurch Cres LE15 . . . . .130 E1
Ivy Cl
  Donisthorpe DE12 . . . . .67 C2
  Stoke Golding CV13 . . . . . .196 D7
Ivydale Rd LE4 . . . . .129 F6
Ivydene Cl LE17 . . . . .198 F8
Ivy House Cl LE12 . . . . .78 A8
Ivy Rd LE3 . . . . .154 C3

J

Jack Hardy Cl LE7 . . . . . . .103 C4
Jacklin Dr LE4 . . . . .129 D5
Jacknell Rd LE10 . . . . .214 D8
Jackson Cl
  Leicester, Oadby LE2 . . . . .181 D5
  Market Harborough
    LE16 . . . . .250 D8
  Overseal DE12 . . . . .67 B3
Jackson Rd
  Bagworth LE67 . . . . .124 A7
  Rugby CV21 . . . . .257 A1
Jackson St
  Coalville LE67 . . . . .71 C1
  Leicester LE4 . . . . .129 B2
Jacks Wlk LE67 . . . . .96 B7
Jacob Cl LE3 . . . . .178 A3
Jacqueline Rd LE67 . . . . . .125 F8
Jacquemart Cl LE67 . . . . . .72 D1
Jacques Cl LE3 . . . . .178 A3
Jacques St LE2 . . . . .95 F2
James Ave LE11 . . . . .51 C6
James Bond Cvn Pk
  LE2 . . . . .244 B4
James Gavin Way
  LE2 . . . . .181 E4
James Lambert Dr
  LE13 . . . . .58 F5
James St
  Anstey LE7 . . . . .127 C7
  Blaby LE8 . . . . .202 A8
  Coalville LE67 . . . . .96 C8
  Earl Shilton LE9 . . . . .198 E7
  Stoney Stanton LE9 . . . . . .199 D3
  Swadlincote DE11 . . . . .44 D5
Jamesway LE9 . . . . .201 D4
Jamia Islamia (Islamic
  Studies Ctr) CV11 . . . . . .196 C2
Janes Way LE67 . . . . .125 E8
Japonica Cl LE17 . . . . .244 A5
Jardine Ct DE72 . . . . .9 B7
Jarrett Cl LE19 . . . . .178 A3
Jarrom St LE2 . . . . .259 A2
Jarrow St LE2 . . . . .259 A2
Jarvis Cl LE10 . . . . .197 D4
Jarvis Dr LE13 . . . . .59 B4
Jarvis St LE4 . . . . .259 A4
Jarvis Way LE67 . . . . .71 E5
Jasmine Cl
  Hamilton LE5 . . . . .130 B3

Jasmine Cl continued
Loughborough LE11. . . . . .75 A7
Lutterworth LE17. . . . . .244 A6
Jasmine Ct
Narborough LE19. . . . . .177 F1
Wigston LE18. . . . . .179 F1
Jasper Rd LE15. . . . . .138 B6
Jawbone La DE73. . . . . .26 C8
Jay Cl LE15. . . . . .138 B8
Jay's Cl NG13. . . . . .3 A1
Jean Dr LE4. . . . . .128 D1
Jeffares Cl DE74. . . . . .18 C3
Jeffcoats La LE47. . . . . .71 B7
Jefferies Cl LE10. . . . . .197 E2
Jellicoe Rd LE6. . . . . .155 E6
Jellicoe Way LE10. . . . . .197 D3
Jenkins Rd
Coalville LE67. . . . . .71 E1
Rugby CV21. . . . . .257 A1
Jennett Cl LE5. . . . . .156 C6
Jenny's La LE67. . . . . .95 F8
Jeremy Cl LE4. . . . . .129 B2
Jericho La NG13. . . . . .6 B2
Jermyn St LE4. . . . . .129 B2
Jersey Rd LE4. . . . . .128 E5
Jersey Way LE9. . . . . .198 A6
Jerwood Way LE16. . . . . .240 F2
Jessons Cl LE14. . . . . .129 D3
Jessop Cl LE13. . . . . .154 A8
Jetcott Ave LE11. . . . . .75 A7
Jetties The LE15. . . . . .166 C3
Jetty The LE15. . . . . .165 A3
Jewry Wall Mus & Site★
LE1. . . . . .259 A3
Jewsbury Ave DE12. . . . . .93 D5
Jewsbury Way LE3. . . . . .153 D2
Joe Moore's La LE12. . . . . .99 E6
John Bold Ave LE9. . . . . .199 E3
John Cleveland Coll
LE10. . . . . .197 F1
John Ferneley High Sch
LE13. . . . . .59 C7
John Minto Ho LE4. . . . . .155 B8
John Nichols St LE10. . . . . . . .215 B7
Johnnie Johnson Dr
LE17. . . . . .244 C8
JOHN O' GAUNT 133 F8
John O' Gaunt Rural Ind
Est LE14. . . . . .134 A8
John Phillips Cl LE11. . . . . . . .51 E4
Johns Ave LE12. . . . . .101 E8
Johnscliffe Cl LE6. . . . . .215 D5
Johnscliffe Ct LE6. . . . . .99 D1
John's Cl LE18. . . . . .202 B8
John's Lee Cl LE11. . . . . .51 F1
Johnson Cl
Barrow-u-S LE12. . . . . .76 D7
Broughton Astley LE9. . . . . . .219 A5
Melton Mowbray LE13. . . . . . .59 C4
North Luffenham LE15. . . . . .166 D3
Whetstone LE8. . . . . .202 A7
Johnson Rd
Birstall LE4. . . . . .128 F7
Uppingham LE15. . . . . .189 A4
Johnson Rise LE9. . . . . .199 E1
Johnson St LE1. . . . . .259 A5
John St
Enderby LE19. . . . . .178 B3
Hinckley LE10. . . . . .197 E1
Oakham LE15. . . . . .137 F6
Swadlincote DE11. . . . . .44 C2
Swadlincote, Lower Midway
DE11. . . . . .44 C5
Thringstone LE67. . . . . .71 D7
John Taylor Bellfoundry
Mus★ LE11. . . . . .52 C4
John Wesley Cl LE12. . . . . .76 D1
John Wycliffe Prim Sch
LE17. . . . . .244 B5
Jolly Farmers La LE12. . . . . . . .73 A8
Jonathan Cl LE6. . . . . .127 A3
Jon Baker Ct LE10. . . . . .215 E8
Jordan Ave LE18. . . . . .180 A1
Jordan Cl
Glenfield LE3. . . . . .153 C8
Market Harborough
LE16. . . . . .241 A3
Jordan Ct LE6. . . . . .152 D8
Jordean Ct 6 LE12. . . . . .77 C3
Joseph Cl
Cropston LE7. . . . . .100 E2
Hoton LE12. . . . . .32 C2
Journeyman's Gn LE6. . . . . . .152 D8
Jovian Dr LE10. . . . . .197 A1
Jowett Cl LE3. . . . . .153 A3
Joyce Rd LE3. . . . . .154 B8
Jubilee Ave
Asfordby LE14. . . . . .58 A3
Sileby LE12. . . . . .77 D5
Jubilee Cl
Melbourne DE73. . . . . .26 B7
Syston LE7. . . . . .103 B5
Jubilee Cres LE19. . . . . .201 C7
Jubilee Croft LE67. . . . . .94 D2
Jubilee Ct
Newbold Verdon LE9. . . . . . . .150 B4
Oakham LE15. . . . . .137 F6
Jubilee Dr
Earl Shilton LE9. . . . . .198 E7
Glenfield LE3. . . . . .153 C7
Langham LE15. . . . . .110 C2
Loughborough LE11. . . . . .52 A6
Jubilee Gdns
Leicester LE4. . . . . .155 D8

Jubilee Gdns continued
Market Harborough
LE16. . . . . .240 F4
Jubilee Ho 5 LE10. . . . . .197 D1
Jubilee Pk DE11. . . . . .44 F4
Jubilee Rd
Broughton Astley LE9. . . . . . .218 E6
Leicester LE1. . . . . .259 B5
Newbold Verdon LE9. . . . . . . .150 B4
Jubilee St LE13. . . . . .59 C3
Jubilee Terr DE12. . . . . .67 E1
Judgemeadow Com Coll
LE5. . . . . .156 C3
Judges St LE11. . . . . .52 D3
Judith Dr
Countesthorpe LE8. . . . . .202 F4
Leicester LE5. . . . . .156 B4
Julian Rd LE2. . . . . .179 C2
Juliet Cl CV11. . . . . .214 A1
Junction Rd
7 Leicester LE1. . . . . .155 A7
Long Eaton NG10. . . . . .10 F6
Wigston LE18. . . . . .180 D3
June Ave LE4. . . . . .130 A5
Junior St LE1. . . . . .259 A4
Juniper Cl
Leicester Forest East
LE3. . . . . .152 F2
Lutterworth LE17. . . . . .244 B7
Juniper Way LE11. . . . . .75 A7
Juno Cl LE3. . . . . .153 C7
Jupiter Cl LE2. . . . . .155 B6
Jurist Ho 3 LE10. . . . . .197 D1
Justin Park Cvn Site
LE16. . . . . .250 F7

K

Kamloops Cres LE1. . . . . .259 C5
Kane Cl LE67. . . . . .71 C1
Kapelle Cl LE13. . . . . .59 E6
Kashmir Rd LE1. . . . . .155 B7
Kate St LE3. . . . . .154 D5
Katrine Cl NN17. . . . . .230 B1
Kay Cl LE67. . . . . .97 B8
Kayes Garden Nursery
LE7. .78 F1
Kay Rd LE3. . . . . .153 F8
Keats Cl
Earl Shilton LE9. . . . . .175 F1
Long Eaton NG10. . . . . .10 B5
Melton Mowbray LE13. . . . . . .59 B6
Narborough LE19. . . . . .178 A3
Keats Dr DE11. . . . . .44 C6
Keats Gr PE9. . . . . .143 A3
Keats La LE9. . . . . .175 F1
Keats Wlk LE4. . . . . .155 B8
Keays Way LE7. . . . . .156 F8
Keble Cl PE9. . . . . .143 C5
Keble Ct PE9. . . . . .143 C5
Keble Dr LE7. . . . . .103 C3
Keble Rd LE2. . . . . .155 A1
Kedleston Ave LE4. . . . . .129 A5
Kedleston Cl NG10. . . . . .10 A5
Kedleston Rd LE5. . . . . .155 D4
Keel Dr NG13. . . . . .3 A2
Keenan Cl LE2. . . . . .179 B5
Keepers Cl
Moira DE12. . . . . .68 A4
Swithland LE12. . . . . .100 E6
Keepers' Croft LE7. . . . . .103 E7
Keepers Wlk LE4. . . . . .128 B3
Keep The
East Leake LE12. . . . . .31 F8
Kirby Muxloe LE19. . . . . .152 D5
KEGWORTH. 18 D3
Kegworth Ave LE5. . . . . .155 F5
Kegworth La LE12,
DE74. . . . . .29 C5
Kegworth Mus★ DE74. . . . . . .18 C2
Kegworth Prim Sch
DE74. . . . . .18 D2
Kegworth Rd NG11. . . . . .18 F5
Keightley Rd LE3. . . . . .153 E8
Keightley Wlk LE4. . . . . .129 F6
Kelbrook Cl LE4. . . . . .128 C4
Kelcey Rd LE12. . . . . .75 F7
Kelham Cl LE11. . . . . .75 A6
Kelham Gr LE67. . . . . .95 E8
Kelmarsh Ave LE18. . . . . .180 E2
Kelso Cl
Ashby-de-la-Z LE65. . . . . .69 C6
Measham DE12. . . . . .93 C6
Kelso Ct LE67. . . . . .71 E8
Kelso Gn LE2. . . . . .179 D3
Kelthorpe Cl PE9. . . . . .168 A4
Kelvon Cl LE3. . . . . .127 D1
Kemble Sq 10 LE1. . . . . .259 B4
Kemp Ho NN17. . . . . .230 F3
Kemp La LE14. . . . . .22 C1
Kemp Rd
Coalville LE67. . . . . .96 C7
Leicester LE5. . . . . .127 F1
Kempson Rd LE2. . . . . .179 E8
Kendal Cl CV11. . . . . .214 A6
Kendall's Ave LE9. . . . . .200 C4
Kendal Rd LE67. . . . . .96 D4
Kendal Rd
Ellistown LE67. . . . . .96 D4
Leicester LE4. . . . . .129 D3
Sileby LE12. . . . . .77 D2
Kendrick Cl LE67. . . . . .71 B2
Kendrick Dr LE67. . . . . .181 B5
Kendricks Cl DE11. . . . . .45 A7
Kenilworth Ave LE11. . . . . .51 C4
Kenilworth Cl
Broughton Astley LE9. . . . . . .218 E8

Kenilworth Cl continued
Mountsorrel LE12. . . . . .76 C1
Kenilworth Ct LE18. . . . . .179 F3
Kenilworth Dr
4 Ashby-de-la-Z LE65. . . . . .69 C5
Leicester, Oadby LE2. . . . . . . .180 F5
Kenilworth Rd LE18. . . . . .179 F2
Ken Mackenzie Cl
LE17. . . . . .244 C8
Kenmore Cres LE67. . . . . .97 D8
Kenmore Dr LE10. . . . . .197 B2
Kennedy Ave NG10. . . . . .10 C5
Kennedy Cl LE15. . . . . .137 E6
Kennedy Way LE13. . . . . .153 B2
Kennel La CV9. . . . . .194 B7
Kenneth Gamble Ct
LE18. . . . . .180 B4
Kennet Way LE13. . . . . .59 A1
Kenny Cl LE8. . . . . .202 A6
Kensington Ave LE11. . . . . . . .51 C5
Kensington Cl
Glen Parva LE2. . . . . .179 D1
Leicester, Oadby LE2. . . . . . . .181 C3
Kensington Dr LE18. . . . . .180 D5
Kensington Rd LE67. . . . . .97 A8
Kensington St LE4. . . . . .129 A1
Kent Cres LE18. . . . . .179 F3
Kent Dr
Hinckley LE10. . . . . .197 A4
Leicester, Oadby LE2. . . . . . . .181 C5
Kenton Ave LE18. . . . . .180 C1
Kent St LE1. . . . . .155 B6
Kent The CV21. . . . . .257 A2
Kentworth Terr 1
LE65. . . . . .69 B6
Kenwood Rd LE2. . . . . .180 C7
Kepston Cl LE2. . . . . .179 D4
Kernan Dr LE11. . . . . .51 F6
Kerrial Gdns LE3. . . . . .153 E7
Kerrial Rd LE3. . . . . .153 E7
Kerry Cl LE9. . . . . .197 F7
Kerrysdale Ave LE4. . . . . .129 D2
Kertley LE8. . . . . .222 F8
Kesteven Rd PE9. . . . . .143 E5
Kestian Cl LE16. . . . . .240 D5
Kestrel Ave DE11. . . . . .44 F3
Kestrel Cl
Broughton Astley LE9. . . . . . .218 E7
Fleckney LE8. . . . . .223 A6
Hinckley LE10. . . . . .215 F6
Leicester Forest East
LE3. . . . . .152 E2
Leicester LE5. . . . . .155 C7
Syston LE7. . . . . .102 F4
Kestrel La
Hamilton LE5. . . . . .130 C2
Mountsorrel LE12. . . . . .76 F2
Kestrel Rd
Melton Mowbray LE13. . . . . . .82 B8
Oakham LE15. . . . . .138 B8
Kestrels' Field Prim Sch
LE5. . . . . .130 D2
Keswick Ave LE11. . . . . .51 D1
Keswick Cl
Birstall LE4. . . . . .128 B8
Leicester LE2. . . . . .179 C3
Nuneaton CV11. . . . . .214 A6
Keswick Ho LE1. . . . . .259 A3
Keswick Rd LE8. . . . . .202 A7
Ketco Ave PE9. . . . . .168 B7
Kettering Rd
Market Harborough
LE16. . . . . .241 B2
Wothorpe PE9. . . . . .169 C8
KETTON. 167 F6
Ketton CE Prim Sch
PE9. . . . . .168 A5
Ketton Rd
Collyweston PE9. . . . . .168 C3
Ketton PE9, LE15. . . . . .167 B3
Upper Hambleton LE15. . . . . .139 C4
Kevern Cl LE18. . . . . .180 C1
Kew Dr
Leicester, Oadby LE2. . . . . . . .181 C3
Wigston LE18. . . . . .180 B5
KEYHAM. 131 D1
Keyham Cl LE5. . . . . .130 B1
Keyham Ct LE5. . . . . .156 A8
Keyham La
Keyham LE7. . . . . .131 C3
Leicester LE5. . . . . .130 D1
Keyham La E LE7. . . . . .131 C2
Keyham La W LE5. . . . . .130 E1
Keyham Lodge Sch
LE5. . . . . .130 D1
Keythorpe St LE2. . . . . .155 B6
KIBWORTH BEAUCHAMP
. . . . .206 B1
Kibworth CE Prim Sch
LE8. . . . . .206 A1
KIBWORTH HARCOURT
. . . . .206 B2
Kibworth High Sch
LE8. . . . . .224 A7
Kibworth High Sch
(Annexe) LE8. . . . . .224 A8
Kibworth Rd
Carlton Curlieu LE8. . . . . .206 E7
Fleckney LE8. . . . . .223 A7
Great Glen LE8. . . . . .205 A3
Saddington LE8. . . . . .223 C6
Tur Langton LE8. . . . . .206 E2
Wistow LE8. . . . . .204 E4
Kidger Cl LE12. . . . . .50 C4
Kielder Cl LE19. . . . . .177 F2
Kilberry Cl LE10. . . . . .197 A1
Kilbourne Cl LE7. . . . . .77 C2
Kilburn Ave LE2. . . . . .180 F6

Kilburn End LE15. . . . . .137 F8
Kilburn Rd LE15. . . . . .137 F7
KILBY. 204 A3
Kilby Ave LE4. . . . . .129 A5
KILBY BRIDGE. 203 D6
Kilby Dr LE18. . . . . .180 E1
Kilby Gn LE10. . . . . .215 F6
Kilby Ho NG10. . . . . .10 E7
Kilby Rd
Fleckney LE8, LE18. . . . . .222 D8
Wistow LE8. . . . . .204 C4
Kilby St Mary's CE Prim
Sch LE18. . . . . .203 F3
Kildare St LE1. . . . . .259 B4
Kildare Wlk 12 LE1. . . . . .259 B4
Kilmarie Cl LE10. . . . . .197 A1
Kilmelford Cl LE4. . . . . .129 D4
Kiln Ave LE4. . . . . .129 E6
Kiln Cl LE9. . . . . .219 A5
Kiln Garth LE7. . . . . .76 F1
Kiln Way DE11. . . . . .44 D3
Kilverstone Ave LE5. . . . . .156 D3
Kilwardby St LE65. . . . . .69 A6
Kilworth Dr LE5. . . . . .155 E3
Kilworth Rd
Husbands Bosworth
LE17. . . . . .247 D4
North Kilworth LE17. . . . . . . .246 C6
Swinford LE17. . . . . .254 C4
Kimball Cl LE15. . . . . .111 B4
Kimberley Rd LE2. . . . . .155 C3
Kimberley St LE8. . . . . .223 F8
KIMCOTE. 235 E1
Kimcote Rd LE17. . . . . .236 A2
Kincaple Rd LE4. . . . . .129 D4
Kinchley Cl LE3. . . . . .127 F3
Kinchley La LE7. . . . . .76 B1
Kincraig Rd LE4. . . . . .129 D4
Kinder Ave DE11. . . . . .44 A5
Kinder Cl LE8. . . . . .202 A5
Kingcup Cl LE13. . . . . .152 F2
King Edward Ave
LE19. . . . . .201 B8
King Edward Rd
Leicester LE5. . . . . .155 F7
Loughborough LE11. . . . . .52 C3
King Edward's Way
LE15. . . . . .166 B7
King Edward VII Com Coll
LE67. . . . . .72 D2
King Edward VII Sch
LE13. . . . . .82 D8
Kingfisher Ave
Leicester LE5. . . . . .155 C7
Woodville DE11. . . . . .44 F3
Kingfisher Ct
Barrow-u-S LE12. . . . . .76 E8
Coalville LE67. . . . . .72 B2
Desford LE9. . . . . .151 B2
Great Glen LE8. . . . . .182 B1
Leicester Forest East
LE3. . . . . .152 E2
Oakham LE15. . . . . .138 B8
Syston LE7. . . . . .102 F4
Twyford LE14. . . . . .106 D1
Kingfisher Dr
Hinckley LE10. . . . . .214 F6
Loughborough LE11. . . . . .52 A2
Melton Mowbray LE13. . . . . . .59 B3
Kingfisher Rd LE12. . . . . .76 F2
Kingfisher Way
Loughborough LE11. . . . . .52 A2
Sheepy Magna CV9. . . . . .171 C7
Kingfisher Wlk LE5. . . . . .155 C7
King George Ave
Ashby-de-la-Z LE65. . . . . .69 B7
Loughborough LE11. . . . . .52 D2
King George Rd LE11. . . . . .52 D2
King George's Way
LE10. . . . . .215 B7
King John's Rd LE67. . . . . .72 C1
King Richard Inf Sch
LE3. . . . . .154 D5
King Richard Rd LE10. . . . . . .197 C2
King Richard's Hill
Earl Shilton LE9. . . . . .176 B1
Whitwick LE67. . . . . .71 F5
King Richards Rd LE3. . . . . . .154 C5
King Richard Way
LE5. .69 D7
Kings Ave LE11. . . . . .51 F6
Kingsbridge Cl LE19. . . . . .201 A8
Kingsbridge Cres LE4. . . . . . .128 B7
Kings Brook Cl LE12. . . . . .32 D6
Kingsbrook Ct LE12. . . . . .31 E4
Kingsbury Ave LE5. . . . . .156 C4
Kings Cl
Market Overton LE15. . . . . . . .86 F5
Thringstone LE67. . . . . .71 D8
King's Cl LE14. . . . . .38 C5
Kingscliffe Cres LE5. . . . . . . .156 D4
King's Ct 2 LE10. . . . . .240 E4
Kingsdale Cl NG10. . . . . .10 A5
Kings Dr
Leicester Forest East
LE3. . . . . .153 A3
Wigston LE18. . . . . .180 D3
Kingsfield Rd
Barwell LE9. . . . . .198 B7
Cosby LE9. . . . . .201 C2
Kings Gate LE4. . . . . .17 F4
Kingsgate Ave LE4. . . . . .128 F8
King's Head Pl LE16. . . . . .240 E3
Kings La
Barrowden LE15. . . . . .191 F5
Keyham LE7. . . . . .131 E2
South Croxton LE7. . . . . .105 B1

King's La continued
Burrough on t H LE14. . . . . . .107 D2
Newton Regis B79. . . . . .118 D5
Kingsley Cl LE19. . . . . .178 A1
Kingsley Cres NG10. . . . . .10 A8
Kingsley St LE2. . . . . .180 A8
Kings Lock Cl LE2. . . . . .179 B4
Kingsmead Cl LE2. . . . . .180 C6
Kingsmead Rd LE2. . . . . .180 C6
Kings Mill La 4 PE9. . . . . .143 D2
KING'S MILLS. 16 B4
Kings Newton St LE2. . . . . . . .155 C4
KING'S NORTON. 183 B5
Kings Rd
Long Clawson LE14. . . . . .20 C2
North Luffenham LE15. . . . . .166 D3
Stamford PE9. . . . . .143 D4
Swadlincote DE11. . . . . .44 B6
King's Rd
Market Harborough
LE16. . . . . .240 E3
Melton Mowbray LE13. . . . . . .59 D4
Oakham LE15. . . . . .137 E6
Shepshed LE12. . . . . .50 B2
Kings Row LE9. . . . . .198 E8
King St
Barkby LE7. . . . . .130 D7
Barwell LE9. . . . . .198 B6
Coalville LE67. . . . . .96 D8
Enderby LE19. . . . . .178 B3
Leicester LE1. . . . . .259 B2
Leicester, Oadby LE2. . . . . . . .181 B5
Long Eaton NG10. . . . . .10 D8
Loughborough LE11. . . . . .52 C3
Melton Mowbray LE13. . . . . . .59 C3
Nether Broughton LE14. . . . . . .36 D8
Scalford LE14. . . . . .38 E5
Seagrave LE12. . . . . .77 F8
Sileby LE12. . . . . .77 C3
Twyford LE14. . . . . .133 D8
Whetstone LE8. . . . . .201 F7
Kingsthorpe Cl LE4. . . . . .128 F3
Kingston Ave LE18. . . . . .180 C4
Kingston Dr LE10. . . . . .197 E4
Kingston La DE74, NG11. . . . . .18 F4
KINGSTON ON SOAR. 18 E4
Kingston Rd LE2. . . . . .155 C3
Kingston Way LE16. . . . . .240 E6
King Street La LE14. . . . . .41 C3
Kingsway
Braunstone Town LE3. . . . . . .178 F8
Leicester LE3. . . . . .179 A7
Kings Way LE6. . . . . .126 F2
Kings Way N LE3. . . . . .153 C2
Kingsway Prim Sch
LE3. . . . . .153 E2
Kingsway Rd LE5. . . . . .153 D8
Kings Wlk LE3. . . . . .153 A3
King's Wlk LE9. . . . . .198 E8
Kingswood Ave
Leicester LE3. . . . . .154 B5
Loughborough LE11. . . . . .51 A5
Kingswood Ct LE18. . . . . .180 C2
King Williams Way
LE7. . . . . .127 E7
Kinley Rd LE4. . . . . .128 E4
Kinross Ave LE5. . . . . .156 E6
Kinross Cres LE11. . . . . .51 D5
Kinross Way LE10. . . . . .196 F1
Kinsdale Dr LE5. . . . . .156 F7
Kintyre Cl LE10. . . . . .197 B1
Kintyre Dr LE4. . . . . .129 C4
Kiplin Dr LE19. . . . . .178 A2
Kipling Cl PE9. . . . . .143 A3
Kipling Dr LE13. . . . . .59 B5
Kipling Gr LE2. . . . . .128 A2
KIRBY BELLARS. 81 B8
Kirby Cl
Swannington LE12. . . . . .101 D8
Sapcote LE9. . . . . .217 D8
Kirby Dr DE74. . . . . .18 C1
KIRBY FIELDS. 152 F4
KIRBY GRANGE. 151 D7
Kirby Hall LE14. . . . . .81 B7
Kirby Ho LE14. . . . . .240 F3
Kirby La
Eye Kettleby LE13,
LE14. . . . . .81 E8
Leicester Forest East
LE3. . . . . .152 F3
Melton Mowbray LE13. . . . . . .82 D7
KIRBY MUXLOE. 152 E5
Kirby Muxloe Castle★
LE9. . . . . .152 E6
Kirby Muxloe Prim Sch
LE9. . . . . .152 E6
Kirby Rd
Glenfield LE3. . . . . .153 A8
Gretton NN17. . . . . .213 C1
Leicester LE3. . . . . .154 C5
Kirfield Dr LE10. . . . . .197 F3
Kirk Ave DE74. . . . . .18 D2
Kirkby La
Newbold Verdon LE9. . . . . . . .150 C3
Peckleton LE9. . . . . .175 E6
KIRKBY MALLORY. 175 D6
Kirkby Rd
Barwell LE9. . . . . .175 B2
Desford LE9. . . . . .151 A3
Kirkdale Gdns NG10. . . . . .10 B6
Kirkdale Rd
Long Eaton NG10. . . . . .10 B6
Wigston LE18. . . . . .180 D7
Kirkewhite Ave NG10. . . . . . . .10 D7
Kirkewhite Ho NG10. . . . . .10 D7
Kirke Wlk LE3. . . . . .153 D6

Kirkfield Dr DE72 . . . . 9 D8
Kirkfield Rd LE8 . . . . 202 F4
Kirkhill LE12 . . . . 50 C3
Kirkhill Cl LE67 . . . . 72 D1
Kirk La LE19 . . . . 178 C3
Kirkland Cl
  Ashby-de-la-Z LE65 . . . . . . 69 B6
  Castle Donington DE74 . . . . . 17 A3
Kirkland Rd LE3 . . . . . . 178 F8
Kirkland Way DE11 . . . . . . 44 B1
Kirk Ley Rd LE12 . . . . 31 D8
Kirkman Cl CV13 . . . . . 149 C7
Kirk's Cl LE15 . . . . 88 B1
Kirkscroft Wlk LE4 . . . . 128 F3
Kirkstead Wlk 🔲 LE4 . . . 128 F3
Kirkstone Cl LE3 . . . . . . 127 D1
Kirkstone Dr LE11 . . . . . . 51 D1
Kirkstone Wlk CV11 . . . . 214 A4
Kirkwall NN17 . . . . 230 C1
Kirkwall Cres LE5 . . . . . 156 E7
Kirloe Ave LE3 . . . . 152 F3
Kirminton Gdns LE5 . . . . 136 C6
Kirtland Cl CV9 . . . . 119 B1
Kirtley Way LE7 . . . . 219 A6
Kirton Ave NG10 . . . . 10 D7
Kirton Dr LE13 . . . . 59 A6
Kirton Rd LE67 . . . . 72 D1
Kitchener Rd
  Anstey LE7 . . . . 127 E7
  Leicester LE5 . . . . 155 E6
Kite Cl LE9 . . . . 218 E8
Klevedon Cl CV11 . . . . . 214 A1
Klondyke La LE14 . . . . . 106 F5
Klondyke Way LE14 . . . . . 57 E2
Knapton Cl LE10 . . . . . . 197 A3
Knight Cl LE4 . . . . 129 E7
KNIGHTON 180 B7
Knighton Church Rd
  LE2 . . . . 180 D7
Knighton Cl LE9 . . . . . . 219 A4
Knighton Ct LE2 . . . . . . 155 C2
Knighton Dr LE2 . . . . . . 155 D1
KNIGHTON FIELDS 180 A8
Knighton Fields Prim Sch
  LE2 . . . . 179 F8
Knighton Fields Rd E
  LE2 . . . . 180 A8
Knighton Fields Rd W
  LE2 . . . . 179 F8
Knighton Grange Rd
  LE2 . . . . 180 E8
Knighton Hayes LE2 . . . . 180 E8
Knighton Junction La
  LE2 . . . . 155 A1
Knighton La LE2 . . . . . . 179 E8
Knighton La E LE2 . . . . . 180 A7
Knighton Park Rd
  LE2 . . . . 155 C2
Knighton Rd LE2 . . . . . . 155 D1
Knighton Rise LE2 . . . . . 155 E1
Knighton St LE2 . . . . . . 259 B2
Knighton Yd LE17 . . . . . 246 F4
Knightsbridge Rd
  LE2 . . . . 179 D1
Knights Cl
  🔲 Ashby-de-la-Z LE65 . . . 69 A7
  Billesdon LE7 . . . . 159 B2
  Hinckley LE10 . . . . 215 D4
  Stoney Stanton LE9 . . . . 199 D3
Knight's Cres LE7 . . . . . 101 E6
Knight's End LE12 . . . . . 214 E8
Knight's End Rd LE12 . . . 261 B6
Knight's Garth LE67 . . . . 71 F5
Knights Link LE9 . . . . . . 176 B1
Knights Rd LE4 . . . . 128 C6
Knightsyard Ct NG10 . . . . 10 C5
Knightthorpe Ct LE11 . . . . 51 D4
Knightthorpe Lo LE11 . . . . 51 B3
Knightthorpe Rd LE11 . . . . 51 E5
KNIPTON 14 F3
Knipton Dr LE11 . . . . 51 C1
Knipton La NG32 . . . . 15 A4
Knipton Rd NG32 . . . . 23 C7
Knob Hill Rd LE15 . . . . . 210 C8
Knollgate Cl LE4 . . . . . . 128 E8
Knoll St LE16 . . . . 240 C3
Knoll The DE11 . . . . 44 B6
KNOSSINGTON 108 B6
Knossington Rd
  Braunston-in-R LE15 . . . 137 A2
  Owston LE15 . . . . 135 D8
  Somerby LE14, LE15 . . . . 135 D8
Knowles Rd LE3 . . . . 153 E7
Knowles View DE11 . . . . . 44 D4
Konfidence Wks The
  LE9 . . . . 198 B7
Koppe Cl DE12 . . . . 68 B6
Krefeld Way LE4 . . . . . . 128 B4

L

Labrador Cl LE1 . . . . . . 259 C5
Laburnum Ave
  Lutterworth LE17 . . . . . 244 B6
  Newbold Verdon LE9 . . . . 150 A3
Laburnum Cl LE12 . . . . . . 30 A1
Laburnum Dr LE9 . . . . . . 198 D7
Laburnum Rd
  Leicester LE5 . . . . 130 C1
  Swadlincote DE11 . . . . . . 44 A6
Laburnum Way LE11 . . . . . 75 A6
Lacey Cl LE17 . . . . 244 C8
Lacey Ct LE12 . . . . 50 B3
Ladbroke Gr LE8 . . . . . . 202 F4
Ladybower Rd DE11 . . . . . 44 A2
Ladybower Rd LE11 . . . . . 51 B3
Ladyfields DE11 . . . . 44 D6

Lady Gate DE74 . . . . 28 C5
Lady Hay Rd LE3 . . . . . . 127 F3
Lady Jane Grey Prim Sch
  LE6 . . . . 126 E2
Lady Jane Mobile Home
  Pk LE6 . . . . 126 E8
Lady Jane Wlk LE7 . . . . . 156 F8
Ladylea Rd NG10 . . . . 10 A4
Lady Leys LE9 . . . . 201 C3
Lady Romayne Cl PE9 . . . 143 E2
Ladysmith Rd
  Kirby Muxloe LE9 . . . . . 152 D5
  Wigston LE18 . . . . 179 E3
Ladywell LE15 . . . . 138 B7
Ladywood Ct LE17 . . . . . 244 C7
Lag La LE13, LE14 . . . . . . 60 A4
Lagoona Cvn Pk DE12 . . . . 67 C3
Laithwaite Ct LE4 . . . . . 128 B6
Lakeside * LE12 . . . . 34 C4
Lakeside Bsns Pk
  LE4 . . . . 129 D6
Lakeside Cres
  Long Eaton NG10 . . . . . . 10 D5
  Whitwick LE67 . . . . 71 E4
Lakeside Ct LE7 . . . . . . 156 F4
Lakeside Inf Sch NG10 . . . 10 C5
Lakeside View LE7 . . . . . 71 E3
Lake Terr LE13 . . . . 59 A2
Lakeview Chase LE5 . . . . 130 C3
Lakeview Ct 🔲 LE5 . . . . 130 C3
Lakin Dr LE3 . . . . 153 C2
Lakins The DE12 . . . . 93 D5
Lambert Ave LE12 . . . . . . 50 B3
Lambert Cl LE13 . . . . 59 C6
Lambert Ct LE5 . . . . 156 A7
Lambert Mews PE9 . . . . . 143 E2
Lambert Rd
  Allington NG32 . . . . 4 F5
  Leicester LE3 . . . . 154 C2
Lambert's Cl LE15 . . . . . 191 A6
Lambeth Wlk PE9 . . . . . . 143 C4
Lambley Lodge La
  LE15 . . . . 187 D8
Lamborne Rd LE2 . . . . . . 180 A6
Lambourne Rd LE4 . . . . . 129 B8
Lamen Rd LE3 . . . . 127 E1
Lamford Cl LE10 . . . . . . 197 B1
Lammas Cl
  Ashby Parva LE17 . . . . . 233 F5
  Braunston-in-R LE15 . . . 137 B2
  Husbands Bosworth
    LE17 . . . . 247 E5
Lammas Cotts LE15 . . . . . 84 F1
Lampad Cl 🔲 DE73 . . . . . 26 A8
Lamplighters LE8 . . . . . 222 F7
Lamport Cl
  Loughborough LE11 . . . . . 51 C4
  Wigston LE18 . . . . 180 F2
Lancashire St LE4 . . . . . 129 C3
Lancaster Ave CV13 . . . . 148 E2
Lancaster Cl
  Atherstone CV9 . . . . . . 170 E1
  Coalville LE67 . . . . 72 D1
  Desford LE9 . . . . 151 B3
  🔲 Lutterworth LE17 . . . 244 C5
Lancaster Pl LE1 . . . . . . 259 C1
Lancaster Rd
  Hinckley LE10 . . . . 215 D8
  Leicester LE1 . . . . 259 B2
  Leicester, South Fields
    LE1 . . . . 259 C1
  Stamford PE9 . . . . 143 D4
Lancaster Sch The
  LE2 . . . . 180 A7
Lancaster St LE5 . . . . . . 155 E6
Lancaster Way LE2 . . . . . 179 D1
Lance Cl LE10 . . . . 215 D5
Lancelot Ct LE3 . . . . . . 153 A2
Lancers Dr LE13 . . . . 59 A6
Lancing Ave LE3 . . . . . . 154 A6
Lancut Hill CV23 . . . . . . 252 D1
Landcroft La LE2 . . . . . . 30 B8
Landor Cl NN17 . . . . 230 D1
Landscape Dr LE5 . . . . . 156 C4
Landsdowne Rd LE2 . . . . 179 E8
Landseer Cl CV21 . . . . . 257 B1
Landseer Dr LE2 . . . . . . 179 E7
Landseer Rd LE2 . . . . . . 155 B1
Lands End Way LE15 . . . . 137 A8
Land Society La LE9 . . . . 198 E8
Landyke La LE14 . . . . 38 B7
Lane Cl LE3 . . . . 153 C8
Lanesborough Ct LE11 . . . 50 F2
Lanesborough Dr LE7 . . . 101 B3
Lanesborough Rd
  LE4 . . . . 129 B3
Lanes Cl LE12 . . . . 77 D4
Laneshaw Ave LE11 . . . . . 51 B2
Lanes Hill Gr LE19 . . . . 199 E1
Laneside Dr LE10 . . . . . 197 F3
Lane The
  Barsby LE7 . . . . 105 D3
  Easton o t H PE9 . . . . . 169 A5
  Rotherby LE14 . . . . 79 F6
  Weston by W LE16 . . . . . 227 B4
Lanfear Ct LE10 . . . . . . 215 C7
LANGAR 11 D8
Langar Airfield NG13 . . . . 11 F7
Langar La
  Colston Bassett NG12 . . . 11 A8
  Harby LE14 . . . . 12 A4
  Langdale LE8 . . . . 222 F8
Langdale Ave LE11 . . . . . 51 D1
Langdale Dr
  Long Eaton NG10 . . . . . . 10 A6
  Nuneaton CV11 . . . . . . 214 A6

Langdale Rd
  Hinckley LE10 . . . . 215 A8
  Thurmaston LE4 . . . . . . 129 F7
Langdale Wlk LE16 . . . . . 240 E1
Langen Ct NG10 . . . . 10 E6
LANGHAM 110 D2
Langham CE Prim Sch
  LE15 . . . . 110 C2
Langham Dr LE18 . . . . . . 201 B8
Langham La LE15 . . . . . . 111 C2
Langham Rd
  Ashwell LE15 . . . . 110 F7
  Leicester LE4 . . . . 129 F3
Langhill The LE5 . . . . . . 155 F6
Langholm Rd LE16 . . . . . 156 E6
Langley Ave LE4 . . . . . . 128 F3
Langley Cl LE9 . . . . 200 E8
Langley Dr DE74 . . . . 18 C2
Langley Wlk 🔲 LE4 . . . . 128 F3
Langmoor Prim Sch
  LE2 . . . . 180 F5
Langton Cl LE67 . . . . 71 E6
Langton La LE16 . . . . . . 240 E3
Langton Rd
  Foxton LE16 . . . . 225 A2
  Great Bowden LE16 . . . . 241 A7
  Kibworth Beauchamp
    LE8 . . . . 206 B1
  Slawston LE16 . . . . 209 B4
  Wigston LE18 . . . . 180 D1
Lank's La LE15 . . . . 87 E8
Lansbury Ho 🔲 PE9 . . . . 143 E3
Lansdowne Ave LE12 . . . . 50 C5
Lansdowne Gr LE18 . . . . 180 A1
Lansdowne Rd
  Shepshed LE12 . . . . 50 B5
  Swadlincote DE11 . . . . . . 44 A3
Lant The LE12 . . . . 50 C4
Lapwing Cl LE4 . . . . 128 B6
Lapwing Ct LE19 . . . . . . 201 A7
Larch Dr LE7 . . . . 244 B6
Larchfield LE15 . . . . . . 138 A8
Larch Gr LE3 . . . . 153 C3
Larchmont Rd LE4 . . . . . 154 D8
Larch Rd NN17 . . . . 230 D1
Larch St LE5 . . . . 155 C7
Larchwood LE2 . . . . 202 E4
Larchwood Ave LE6 . . . . 126 F2
Larchwood Cl LE2 . . . . . 180 A7
Larchwood Rise LE5 . . . . 136 A6
Larcot Garden Cl
  LE12 . . . . 101 E8
Lark Cl LE3 . . . . 152 F2
Larkin La LE11 . . . . 51 D4
Lark Rise LE11 . . . . 75 A6
Larkspur Cl LE13 . . . . . . 130 B3
Larkswood LE8 . . . . 224 B8
Lastingham Cl LE2 . . . . . 180 A6
Lathkilldale Cres NG10 . . 10 A5
Latham Ho LE16 . . . . . . 240 F1
Latimer Cl
  Blaby LE8 . . . . 202 A6
  Gretton NN17 . . . . 213 C1
Latimer Cres LE16 . . . . . 240 F2
Latimer Ct LE7 . . . . 127 D5
Latimer Prim Sch The
  LE7 . . . . 237 E5
Latimer Rd LE7 . . . . 100 F3
Latimer St
  Anstey LE7 . . . . 127 E6
  Leicester LE3 . . . . 154 D4
Latymer Cl LE16 . . . . . . 251 E5
Laud Cl LE15 . . . . 95 E1
LAUGHTON 238 C7
Laughton Cl LE2 . . . . . . 155 D1
Laughton La LE17 . . . . . 238 A6
Laughton Rd
  Laughton LE17 . . . . . . 238 F5
  Lubenham LE16 . . . . . . 239 C4
Launceston Ct LE67 . . . . . 96 C7
Launceston Ho LE18 . . . . 203 C8
Launceston Rd LE18 . . . . 180 C1
Launde Cross Rds
  LE7 . . . . 161 C6
Launde Gdns LE9 . . . . . . 143 A2
Launde Pk LE16 . . . . . . 241 A2
Launde Prim Sch LE2 . . . 181 B6
Launde Rd
  Leicester, Oadby LE2 . . . 181 C6
  Markfield LE67 . . . . . . 125 E8
  Tilton on t H LE7 . . . . . 161 B6
Laundon Cl LE16 . . . . . . 126 F7
Laundon Way
  Groby LE6 . . . . 126 E2
  Whetstone LE8 . . . . . . 202 A5
Laundry La LE4 . . . . 129 B3
Launds Gn NG33 . . . . 65 A4
Laura Davies Cl LE3 . . . . 59 C6
Laural Bank Cl LE17 . . . . 103 E6
Laurel Cl
  Glenfield LE3 . . . . 153 E8
  Mountsorrel LE12 . . . . . . 76 E2
Laurel Cres LE9 . . . . 10 C6
Laurel Dr
  Aston-on-T DE72 . . . . . . 16 A7
  Countesthorpe LE8 . . . . 202 E4
  Leicester, Oadby LE2 . . . 181 D3
Laurel Fields LE17 . . . . . 232 E6
Laurel Rd
  Blaby LE8 . . . . 202 B7
  Great Bowden LE16 . . . . 240 F6
  Narborough LE19 . . . . . 178 C4
  Swithland LE12 . . . . . . 100 F8
Laurel Way NG13 . . . . 2 F3
Laureston Dr LE2 . . . . . 155 D2

Lavender Cl
  Blaby LE8 . . . . 202 B8
  Loughborough LE11 . . . . . 75 A6
  Lutterworth LE17 . . . . . 244 A6
Lavender Ho LE13 . . . . . . 59 D3
Lavender Rd LE3 . . . . . . 154 C3
Lavender Way PE9 . . . . . 142 F5
Lavender Wlk LE70 . . . . . 70 B7
Laverstock Rd LE18 . . . . 203 C8
Lawford Rd LE7 . . . . 179 D4
Lawn Ave LE4 . . . . 129 B7
Lawn Cl LE4 . . . . 129 F6
Lawn La LE14 . . . . 35 E2
Lawns Bsns Ctr The 🔲
  LE10 . . . . 215 E8
Lawns Dr DE11 . . . . 44 A7
Lawns The
  Aston-on-T DE72 . . . . . . 16 B8
  Hinckley LE10 . . . . 215 E8
Lawnswood LE10 . . . . . . 215 A8
Lawnwood Rd LE16 . . . . 126 D3
Lawrence Ave LE72 . . . . . . 9 D8
Lawrence Cl
  Birstall LE4 . . . . 101 C1
  Ellistown LE67 . . . . 96 C4
  Market Overton LE15 . . . . 86 F5
Lawrence Rd 🔲 LE10 . . . 197 D1
Lawrence St NG10 . . . . . . 10 D8
Lawrence Way LE11 . . . . . 51 C7
Lawson Ave NG10 . . . . . . 10 C7
Lawson Cl LE19 . . . . 178 A2
Law St LE4 . . . . 129 A1
Lawton Cl LE10 . . . . 214 F8
Lawyers La LE7 . . . . 181 A5
Laxford Cl
  Hinckley LE10 . . . . 196 F1
  Leicester LE4 . . . . 128 C2
Laxton Cl
  Birstall LE4 . . . . 129 B8
  Wigston LE18 . . . . 180 F2
Laycock Ave LE13 . . . . . . 59 C4
Layton Cl LE4 . . . . 129 B8
Layton Rd LE5 . . . . 155 C7
Lea Cl
  Broughton Astley LE9 . . . 219 A5
  Thurmaston LE4 . . . . . . 129 F7
Leacrofts The LE67 . . . . . 95 E8
Lea Dr LE11 . . . . 75 B7
Leake La LE12 . . . . 31 D3
Lea La LE67 . . . . 98 F4
Lealand The LE16 . . . . . . 250 B8
Leamington Dr LE9 . . . . . 219 A5
Leamington Terr
  LE15 . . . . 189 B4
Leas Cl LE15 . . . . 156 F6
Leas The LE15 . . . . 112 C8
Lea The LE8 . . . . 206 B1
Leatherlands DE74 . . . . . . 18 D3
Leather Mill La CV10 . . . 194 D4
Lea View PE9 . . . . 116 C2
Leawood Rd DE11 . . . . . . 44 F2
Leckhampton Rd LE1 . . . . 51 C4
Leconfield Rd LE11 . . . . . 74 C8
Ledbury Cl LE2 . . . . 181 D4
Ledbury Gn LE4 . . . . . . 128 D5
Ledbury Rd LE11 . . . . 74 F7
Ledbury Wlk LE15 . . . . . . 87 E2
Ledwell Dr LE3 . . . . 127 C1
Lee Cl LE9 . . . . 199 E3
Leecrofts The LE9 . . . . . 198 F8
Lee Rise LE6 . . . . 152 D8
Lees Cres LE67 . . . . 72 A5
Leeside LE9 . . . . 150 B4
Leeson St LE2 . . . . 179 E7
Lee St LE1 . . . . 259 C4
LEESTHORPE 108 D7
Leesthorpe Rd LE14 . . . . 108 D6
Legion Dr LE67 . . . . 122 F8
Legion Way LE19 . . . . . . 178 D8
LEICESTER 259 C1
Leicester Airport LE2 . . . 182 B8
Leicester Coll (Abbey Park
  Campus) LE1 . . . . 155 A8
Leicester Coll (Bede
  Island Campus) LE3 . . . 154 D3
Leicester Coll (Freeman's
  Park Campus) LE2 . . . . 154 F3
Leicester Coll (St
  Margarets Campus)
    LE1 . . . . 259 B5
Leicester Commercial Coll
  LE1 . . . . 259 A3
Leicester Cres LE9 . . . . . 170 E1
LEICESTER FOREST EAST
  . . . . 152 D2
LEICESTER FOREST WEST
  . . . . 177 A8
Leicester General Hospl
  LE5 . . . . 156 A4
Leicester Gram Jun Sch
  LE5 . . . . 156 C4
Leicester Gram Sch
  LE1 . . . . 259 A3
Leicester High Sch for
  Girls LE2 . . . . 180 F8
Leicester Hospl (BUPA)
  LE2 . . . . 156 A1
Leicester Islamic Acad
  LE5 . . . . 155 C2
Leicester La
  Desford LE9 . . . . 151 D2
  Great Bowden LE16 . . . . 240 D7
  Narborough LE19 . . . . . 178 C4
  Swithland LE12 . . . . . . 100 F8
Leicester Mus of Science,
  Ind & Tech* LE2 . . . . . 128 F2

Leicester North Sta*
  LE4 . . . . 128 F5
Leicester Pl LE13 . . . . . . 59 C3
Leicester Rd
  Anstey LE7 . . . . 127 E5
  Ashby-de-la-Z LE65 . . . . . 69 D5
  Barwell LE9 . . . . 198 C5
  Belton-in-R LE15 . . . . . 187 C6
  Billesdon LE7 . . . . 158 E3
  Blaby LE8 . . . . 202 B8
  Broughton Astley LE9 . . . 218 E7
  Countesthorpe LE8 . . . . 202 F5
  Croft LE9 . . . . 200 D1
  Earl Shilton LE9 . . . . . 175 F2
  Fleckney LE8 . . . . 222 F8
  Frisby on t W LE14 . . . . . 80 D7
  Glenfield LE3 . . . . 127 D2
  Glen Parva LE2, LE8 . . . 179 B3
  Groby LE6 . . . . 127 A3
  Hinckley LE9, LE10 . . . . 197 F2
  Husbands Bosworth
    LE17 . . . . 247 D7
  Ibstock LE67 . . . . 96 A3
  Kibworth Beauchamp
    LE8 . . . . 205 F3
  Leicester, Oadby LE2 . . . 180 F7
  Loughborough LE11,
    LE12 . . . . 52 C2
  Lutterworth LE17 . . . . . 234 C2
  Market Harborough
    LE16 . . . . 240 D5
  Markfield LE67 . . . . 98 D1
  Markfield LE67 . . . . . . 125 F8
  Measham DE12 . . . . 93 D5
  Melton Mowbray LE13 . . . 59 B2
  Mountsorrel LE7, LE12 . . . 76 F1
  Mowsley LE17 . . . . 237 E6
  Narborough LE19 . . . . . 178 D1
  Narborough LE19 . . . . . 201 C8
  Quorn (Quorndon) LE12 . . 76 B5
  Ravenstone LE67 . . . . . . 96 A7
  Sapcote LE9 . . . . 217 C2
  Sharnford LE10 . . . . . . 217 C4
  Shepshed LE12 . . . . 50 C2
  South Croxton LE7 . . . . 133 B7
  Thurcaston LE4, LE7 . . . 101 B2
  Tilton on t H LE7 . . . . . 159 F8
  Uppingham LE15 . . . . . . 188 F5
  Uppingham, Wardley
    LE15 . . . . 188 C6
  Whitwick LE67 . . . . 72 B4
  Wigston LE18 . . . . 180 C4
Leicester Royal Infmy LE1,
  LE2 . . . . 259 B2
Leicester Royal Infmy
  Mus* LE2 . . . . 259 B2
Leicester St Martins
  Cathedral Church*
    LE1 . . . . 259 B3
Leicestershire Cty Crkt
  Gd* LE2 . . . . 179 E8
Leicestershire Hospice
  The LE3 . . . . 128 A1
Leicester St
  Leicester LE5 . . . . 155 D6
  Long Eaton NG10 . . . . . . 10 E6
  Melton Mowbray LE13 . . . 59 C3
Leicester Sta LE2 . . . . . . 259 C3
Leicester Tigers (Rugby
  Football Gd) LE2 . . . . . 259 B1
Leighfield Prim Sch
  LE15 . . . . 189 A3
Leighton Ave LE11 . . . . . 51 B3
Leighton Cres LE9 . . . . . 198 F5
LEIRE 218 F1
Leire La
  Ashby Parva LE17 . . . . . 233 F7
  Broughton Astley LE9 . . . 218 E4
  Dunton Bassett LE17 . . . 219 C1
Leire Rd LE17 . . . . 218 D1
Leire St LE4 . . . . 129 B2
Leith Cl LE65 . . . . 69 D5
Lema Cl LE4 . . . . 129 E5
Lemon Gr DE11 . . . . 44 B7
Lemontree La LE11 . . . . . 75 A7
Lemyngton St LE11 . . . . . 52 B4
Lena Dr LE6 . . . . 126 C5
Len Hollis Ct 🔲 LE2 . . . 155 A5
Lenthall Sq LE16 . . . . . . 240 E1
Leopold Cl LE8 . . . . 202 D4
Leopold Rd LE2 . . . . 155 A1
Leopold St
  Long Eaton NG10 . . . . . . 10 D8
  Loughborough LE11 . . . . . 51 F4
  Wigston LE18 . . . . 179 F1
Leslie Cl LE11 . . . . 51 D7
Leslie Holes Ct LE1 . . . . 259 B2
Lester Ct LE12 . . . . 29 A4
Letchworth Rd LE3 . . . . . 154 A5
Lethbridge Cl
  Leicester LE1 . . . . 259 C5
  Oakham LE15 . . . . 138 B6
Leven Cl LE10 . . . . 215 B8
Leven Way NN17 . . . . . . 230 B1
Leveret Dr LE3 . . . . 201 F6
Leveric Rd LE5 . . . . 155 E8
Lever Rd CV21 . . . . 257 A1
Lewell Cl LE4 . . . . 128 D4
Lewes Cl LE4 . . . . 128 B2
Lewisher Rd LE4 . . . . . . 129 F3
Lewis Rd LE10 . . . . 215 D5
Lewis Way LE19 . . . . . . 202 F3
Lexham St LE4 . . . . 129 B2
Leyburn Cl
  Nuneaton CV11 . . . . . . 214 A2

Leyburn Cl continued
Swadlincote DE11 . . . . 44 B1
Leybury Way LE7 . . . . .156 F7
Leycroft Rd LE4 . . . . 128 C5
Leyland Rd LE3 . . . . .178 F7
Leys Cl LE2 . . . . 181 C6
Leys Cres LE17 . . . . 246 D1
Leysdale Cl LE4 . . . . 128 B3
Leys Dr LE2 . . . . 181 B4
Leysland Ave LE8 . . . . . . 202 C4
Leysland High Sch
  LE8 . . . . 202 C4
Leysmill Cl LE10 . . . . . . .196 F1
Leys The
  Countesthorpe LE8 . . . . . 202 C3
  East Goscote LE7 . . . . . . 103 E8
  Hathern LE12 . . . . 51 A8
  Hinckley LE10 . . . . 216 A6
  Kibworth Beauchamp
    LE8 . . . . 206 A1
  Leicester LE4 . . . . 128 B3
  Newton CV23 . . . . 253 A1
  Welford NN6 . . . . 256 E5
Leyton Cl LE17 . . . . .244 D5
Liberty Pk LE2 . . . . 259 A1
Liberty Rd LE3 . . . . 153 D7
Libra Par LE4 . . . . 129 B7
Library Cl LE10 . . . . 216 A5
Lichfield Ave
  Broughton Astley LE9 . . . 218 D8
  Swadlincote DE11 . . . . 44 E5
Lichfield Cl CV11 . . . . . . 214 A7
Lichfield Dr LE8 . . . . 202 B6
Lichfield St LE1 . . . . 259 B5
Lidster Cl LE5 . . . . 156 B8
Lightfoot La LE16 . . . . . . 229 B1
Lilac Ave LE5 . . . . 130 C1
Lilac Cl
  Hinckley LE10 . . . . .215 E6
  Loughborough LE11 . . . . . .75 A7
Lilac Dr LE17 . . . . 244 A6
Lilac Way
  East Goscote LE7 . . . . . . .103 F7
  Melton Mowbray LE13 . . . . 59 B5
LILBOURNE 258 A6
Lilbourne Rd CV23 . . . . . 257 C5
Lilleshall Way LE11 . . . . . .51 B5
Lillingstone Cl LE67 . . . . . 98 E1
Lily Bank LE67 . . . . 71 C8
Lily Cotts LE67 . . . . 71 A8
Lily Marriott Ho LE2 . . . . 179 B4
LILYPOOL 26 B7
Lilypools The DE73 . . . . . 26 B7
Limber Cres LE3 . . . . . . .153 E3
Limby Hall La LE67 . . . . . . 71 A6
Lime Ave
  Groby LE6 . . . . .126 F1
  Loughborough LE11 . . . . . .52 C3
  Measham DE12 . . . . 93 C6
Lime Cl LE7 . . . . 103 C3
Lime Dr LE7 . . . . 103 B2
Limefield LE15 . . . . 138 A8
Lime Gr
  Bagworth LE67 . . . . .124 B5
  Blaby LE8 . . . . 202 B8
  Bottesford NG13 . . . . 3 A2
  Earl Shilton LE9 . . . . . . .198 E7
  Kirby Muxloe LE9 . . . . . . 152 D5
  Long Eaton NG10 . . . . 10 D8
Lime Grove Cl LE4 . . . . . 128 C4
Limehurst Ave LE11 . . . . . .52 A5
Limehurst High Sch
  LE11 . . . . .52 B5
Limehurst Rd LE5 . . . . . 130 D1
Lime Kilns LE18 . . . . 203 E8
Limekilns The DE73 . . . . . .26 F2
Lime Kilns The LE12 . . . . .93 C6
Limekiln The* PE9 . . . . . . .115 B8
Limes Ave LE13 . . . . .59 D4
Lime St LE14 . . . . .82 F6
Limes The
  Market Overton LE15 . . . . .86 F5
  Ravenstone LE67 . . . . .71 A2
  Thorpe Langton LE8 . . . . 226 A5
Limestone Cl DE11 . . . . . . 45 A4
Lime Terr NG10 . . . . .10 D8
Limetree Ave DE11 . . . . . . 44 B7
Lime Tree Ave
  Birstall LE4 . . . . 129 A8
  Uppingham LE15 . . . . . . 189 A5
Limetree Gr 🟦 LE11 . . . . 52 C3
Lime Tree Rd LE19 . . . . . 178 D2
Linacres Rd LE3 . . . . 153 E3
Lincoln Cl LE16 . . . . .240 F5
Lincoln Dr
  Blaby LE8 . . . . 202 B6
  Melton Mowbray LE13 . . . .82 D8
  Syston LE7 . . . . 103 C2
  Wigston LE18 . . . . .179 F2
Lincoln Rd
  Barwell LE9 . . . . 198 A6
  Stamford PE9 . . . . .143 E5
Lincoln St LE2 . . . . 155 B5
Lincoln Way DE11 . . . . . . .44 E5
Linden Ave LE8 . . . . 202 C4
Linden Cl LE67 . . . . .95 E2
Linden Dr
  Leicester LE5 . . . . 156 A3
  Lutterworth LE17 . . . . . . 244 B6
Linden Farm Dr LE8 . . . . 202 E4
Linden La LE12 . . . . .76 E1
Linden La LE12 . . . . 152 F4
Linden Prim Sch LE5 . . . 156 A3
Linden Rd
  Hinckley LE10 . . . . 197 C1

Linden Rd continued
  Loughborough LE11 . . . . . .52 A5
Linden St LE5 . . . . 155 E5
Linden Way LE67 . . . . . . .71 C2
Lindfield Rd LE3 . . . . . . .153 B1
Lindisfarne Dr LE11 . . . . .51 B5
Lindisfarne Rd
  Corby NN17 . . . . 230 C1
  Syston LE7 . . . . 102 F3
Lindrick Dr LE5 . . . . 155 E2
Lindridge La LE9 . . . . . . 151 A6
Lindsay Ct DE11 . . . . 44 B3
Lindsay Rd LE3 . . . . 154 B1
Lindsey Gdns LE16 . . . . 250 D8
Lindsey Rd
  Stamford PE9. . . . . 143 E4
  Uffington PE9. . . . . 144 E4
Lindum Cl LE7 . . . . 102 F2
Lineker Rd LE2 . . . . 154 E3
Linford Cl LE18 . . . . 180 E3
Linford Cres
  Coalville LE67 . . . . .72 B1
  Markfield LE67 . . . . 125 E8
Linford Rd LE11 . . . . .51 E1
Linford St LE4 . . . . 129 A3
Ling Dale LE7 . . . . .103 E8
Lingdale Cl LE11 . . . . . . .52 B1
Lingdale Ho LE11 . . . . . . .52 B1
Ling Rd LE11 . . . . .52 B1
Lings Cl NG32 . . . . .22 F7
Linkfield Ave LE12 . . . . . .76 E1
Linkfield Rd LE12 . . . . . . .76 E1
Link Rd
  Anstey LE7. . . . . 127 D7
  Leicester LE7. . . . . 180 E7
  Queniborough LE7 . . . . . 103 D5
Link Rise LE67 . . . . 125 F8
Links Cl LE67 . . . . .96 D6
Links Rd
  Kibworth Beauchamp
    LE8 . . . . 224 B8
  Kirby Muxloe LE9 . . . . . . 152 C5
Linkway Gdns LE3 . . . . . 154 C5
Linley Ave LE12 . . . . .50 C2
Linley La LE9 . . . . 201 D3
Linnet Cl
  Melton Mowbray LE13 . . . .82 B8
  Rugby CV23 . . . . 252 C1
Linnet Ct LE15 . . . . 189 A5
Linnett Cl LE11 . . . . 201 A7
Linney Rd LE4 . . . . 128 C3
Linthwaite Ct DE74 . . . . . 28 B5
Lintlaw Cl LE4 . . . . 129 D4
Linton St LE5 . . . . 155 C4
Linval Ave LE7 . . . . 157 F4
Linwood Cl LE10 . . . . . . 197 B2
Linwood La LE2 . . . . 179 F5
Lionville Cotts LE14. . . . . .38 D8
Lipton Rd LE4 . . . . 128 B6
Liskeard Cl CV11. . . . . . . 214 A5
Lisle St LE11 . . . . .52 A5
Lismore Dr LE10 . . . . . . 197 C1
Lismore Wlk NN17 . . . . . 230 C1
Lister Cl NN17 . . . . 230 F1
Lister Rd CV9 . . . . 170 E1
Litelmede LE15 . . . . 155 E7
Little Ave LE4 . . . . 129 B3
Little Barley Cl LE4 . . . . 128 B3
LITTLE BOWDEN 241 A2
Little Bowden Manor
  LE16. . . . . 240 F3
Little Bowden Sch
  LE16. . . . . 240 F2
LITTLE CASTERTON . . . 143 C8
Little Casterton Rd
  PE9. . . . . 143 B6
Little Church La LE12 . . . .77 C3
Little Cl DE11. . . . . 44 B5
Little Connery Leys
  LE4. . . . . 102 A1
LITTLE DALBY 83 A1
Little Dalby Rd
  Great Dalby LE14. . . . . . . .82 B1
  Little Dalby LE14. . . . . . . .83 A1
Little Dale LE18 . . . . 180 A2
Little Dunmow Rd
  LE9. . . . . 155 F8
Little End LE12 . . . . 236 C8
Littlefare The LE3 . . . . . 153 D2
Littlefield La LE9 . . . . . . 151 B3
Littlegarth LE2 . . . . 179 F4
Little Glen Rd LE2 . . . . . 179 D1
Little Haw La LE12 . . . . . . .50 A3
Little Hill Prim Sch
  LE18. . . . . 180 C1
Little Holme St LE3 . . . . 154 D5
Littlejohn Rd LE2 . . . . . . 179 E4
Little La
  Desford LE9 . . . . 151 B4
  Greetham LE15 . . . . 88 B1
  Leire LE17 . . . . 233 F8
  Mountsorrel LE12 . . . . . . .76 E2
Little London La
  CV23. . . . . 253 A1
Little Lunnon LE17. . . . . . 219 C1
Little Masons Cl LE3 . . . 153 D1
Littlemeer Cl LE3 . . . . . . 153 D1
Little Mill Cl CV13 . . . . . 149 C8
Little Moor La LE11 . . . . . .52 D4
Little Moorside DE72 . . . . 16 B8
Littlemore Cl LE5 . . . . . 155 F6
LITTLE ORTON 145 F8
Little Shaw La LE67 . . . . . .98 A3
LITTLE STRETTON 182 E5
Little Thorn Ind Est
  DE11 . . . . .44 F2
LITTLETHORPE 201 C6

Littleton St LE4 . . . . 154 D7
LITTLE TWYCROSS 146 E7
LITTLE WALTON 242 E3
Littleway The LE5 . . . . . . 155 F6
Little Wood Cl LE4 . . . . . 128 C4
LITTLEWORTH 67 D8
Littleworth La LE15 . . . . 187 D6
Livesey Dr LE9 . . . . 217 C7
Livia Cl LE10 . . . . 196 F1
Livingstone Cl LE15 . . . . NG18
Livingstone St LE3 . . . . . 154 C4
Llewellyn Ct LE2 . . . . . . 155 D1
Loake Cl 🟦 DE73 . . . . . . .26 A8
Lobbs Wood Cl LE5 . . . . 156 B8
Lobbs Wood Ct LE5 . . . . 156 B8
Lobelia Cl
  Hinckley LE10 . . . . .215 E5
  Narborough LE19. . . . . . 200 F8
LOBTHORPE 66 A6
Lochmore Cl LE10 . . . . . 215 A8
Lochmore Dr LE10 . . . . . 215 A8
Lochmore Way LE10 . . . . 215 A8
Locke Ave LE4 . . . . 129 D5
Lockerbie Ave LE4 . . . . . 129 C4
Lockerbie Wlk LE4 . . . . . 129 D4
Lock Gate Cl LE18 . . . . . 203 A8
Lockhouse Cl LE2 . . . . . .179 B4
LOCKINGTON 17 F5
Lockington Rd DE74. . . . . 17 D5
Lock Keeper Cl LE18 . . . 203 A8
Lock La NG10 . . . . .10 C4
Lockley Cl LE6 . . . . 152 D8
Lock's Cl LE15 . . . . 88 A1
Lockside Cl LE2 . . . . 179 A2
Locksley Cl 🟦 LE65 . . . . .69 A7
Locks The
  Loughborough LE11. . . . . .51 F6
  Rugby CV23 . . . . 257 B1
Lockton Cl LE65 . . . . .69 C7
LODDINGTON 161 E1
Loddington La
  Belton-in-R LE15 . . . . . . 187 B8
  East Norton LE7. . . . . . . 186 D7
Loddington Rd LE7 . . . . . 160 C6
Loddon Cl LE13. . . . . .59 B1
Lodge Cl
  Ashby-de-la-Z LE65 . . . . . .69 A5
  Atherstone CV9 . . . . 194 A6
  Barrow-u-S LE12 . . . . .76 D7
  Hinckley LE10 . . . . 216 A5
  Huncote LE9 . . . . 200 D8
  Kibworth Beauchamp
    LE8 . . . . 205 F2
  Melton Mowbray LE13 . . . .59 B2
  Syston LE7 . . . . 103 C4
  Thurmaston LE4 . . . . . . 129 F6
Lodge Est DE72 . . . . .16 B7
Lodge Farm Rd LE5 . . . . 156 C6
Lodge Gdns LE15 . . . . . . 138 A6
Lodge La LE7 . . . . 100 D3
Lodge Mews
  Aston-on-T DE72 . . . . 16 B7
  Thornby LE7 . . . . 156 E4
Lodge Park Tech Coll
  NN17 . . . . 230 B1
Lodge Pk LE15 . . . . 110 B2
Lodge Rd
  Fleckney LE8 . . . . 222 F6
  Long Eaton NG10. . . . . . . 10 D5
  Nethersea DE12 . . . . 91 F8
  Quorn (Quorndon) LE12 . . . .9 A7
Lodge Stables 🟦
  LE15. . . . . 138 A6
Lodge The LE15 . . . . 138 A6
Lodgewood Ave LE4 . . . . 128 F7
Logan Ave LE2. . . . . 179 C6
Logan Cres LE15 . . . . . . 240 C4
Logan Cl LE16 . . . . 240 D4
Logan St LE16 . . . . 240 D3
Loire Cl LE65 . . . . .69 A7
Lombard St NG13 . . . . .2 A6
Lombardy Rise LE5 . . . . 155 C7
Lomond Cl
  Corby NN17 . . . . 230 C1
  Hinckley LE10 . . . . .215 B8
Lomond Cres LE4. . . . . . 128 C2
London La
  Willoughby-on-t-W
    LE12. . . . . .34 D7
  Wymeswold LE12. . . . . . . 33 B3
London Rd
  Castle Donington DE72 . . . 17 B8
  Coalville LE67 . . . . .96 E8
  Great Glen LE8 . . . . 205 D6
  Hinckley LE10 . . . . .215 E8
  Kegworth DE74. . . . . .29 F6
  Leicester LE2 . . . . 155 B3
  Leicester, Oadby LE2. . . . 181 B5
  Leicester, Oadby LE2 . . . 181 E2
  Leicester, South Knighton
    LE2 . . . . 180 E8
  Markfield LE67 . . . . 125 E8
  Shardlow DE72 . . . . 9 A1
  Uppingham LE15 . . . . . . 189 B3
  Wothorpe PE9 . . . . 169 F7
London St LE5 . . . . 155 D6
Longate Rd LE13 . . . . 59 C3
Long Brimley Cl LE16 . . . 241 B3
Long Cl
  Anstey LE7. . . . . 127 C7
  Barrow-u-S LE12 . . . . .76 C8
  Quorn (Quorndon) LE12. . . .75 F7
LONG CLAWSON 20 D3
Long Clawson CE Prim
  Sch LE14. . . . . 20 D3
Longcliff Cl LE14. . . . . . . .35 E4
Longcliffe Gdns LE11 . . . .74 A7

Longcliffe Rd
  Leicester LE5. . . . . 155 C7
  Shepshed LE12 . . . . .50 A3
Longcliff Hill LE14. . . . . . .35 E4
Longcliff Rd LE67. . . . . . . .97 B8
Long Croft DE72 . . . . .16 A8
LONG EATON 10 C7
Long Eaton Sch The
  NG10 . . . . .10 C6
Long Eaton Sta NG10 . . . .10 C5
Long Eaton Trade Ctr
  NG10 . . . . .10 F8
Longfellow Rd LE2 . . . . . 180 A8
Long Field High Sch The
  LE13. . . . . .59 A2
Longfield Rd LE13 . . . . . . 59 D6
Longford Cl LE18 . . . . . . 203 C8
Long Furlong LE12. . . . . . 101 D8
Long Furrow LE7 . . . . . . 103 E8
Longgrey LE8 . . . . 204 E1
Longhade Furlong
  LE7. . . . . 127 F7
Long Hassocks CV23. . . . 252 E1
Longhedge La
  Bottesford NG13 . . . . 2 F3
  Orston NG13 . . . . 2 E7
Long Hedge La LE65 . . . . .47 E6
Longhedge Lane Ind Est
  NG13 . . . . .2 F3
Long Holden DE74. . . . . . .28 E5
Longhurst Cl LE4 . . . . . . 129 E5
Long La
  Billesdon LE7 . . . . .159 B2
  Bottesford NG13 . . . . 2 F4
  Coalville LE67 . . . . .71 E1
  Hickling LE14 . . . . 19 C6
  Kegworth DE74 . . . . 18 D5
  Leicester LE1 . . . . 259 A4
  Owston LE15 . . . . .135 B4
  Redmile NG13 . . . . 6 F1
  Stathern LE14 . . . . .12 F4
Longlands Rd DE11 . . . . . .44 D7
Longlands The LE16. . . . . 241 B3
Longleat Cl
  Leicester LE5 . . . . 155 D8
  Market Harborough
    LE16. . . . . 241 B3
Long Mdw LE18 . . . . 203 E8
Long Meadow Dr
  LE10. . . . . 214 F7
Long Meadow Way
  LE15. . . . . 112 D8
Long Mere La LE12,
  DE74. . . . . 28 C3
Long Row
  Newton Harcourt LE8 . . . 204 D6
  Oakham LE15 . . . . .137 F6
  Shardlow DE72 . . . . 9 B2
  Sibson CV13. . . . . 172 A6
Long Shoot The CV11 . . . 214 C6
Longslade Com Coll
  LE4. . . . . 102 B1
Long St
  Belton LE12 . . . . .49 B6
  Stoney Stanton LE9 . . . . 199 E2
  Wigston LE18 . . . . 180 D2
Longstock Rd CV23 . . . . 252 D1
Longstone Gn LE15 . . . . 156 E7
LONG WHATTON 29 B3
Long Whatton CE Prim
  Sch LE12. . . . . 29 C3
Longwill Ave LE13 . . . . . . 59 D4
Lonsborough Gdns
  LE15. . . . . 110 B2
Lonsdale Ct LE4 . . . . 129 E6
Lonsdale Rd
  Stamford PE9. . . . . 143 A3
  Thurmaston LE4 . . . . . . 129 E6
Lonsdale St LE2 . . . . 155 C4
Lonsdale Way LE15 . . . . 137 E6
Lord Burghley's Hospl
  PE9. . . . . 143 E2
Lord Byron St LE2 . . . . . 180 A8
Lord Cl LE19. . . . . 201 B7
Lord Crewe Cl LE9 . . . . . 150 B4
Lord Morton's Covert
  (Nature Reserve)*
  LE7. . . . . 159 C7
Lords Ave LE4 . . . . 128 C7
Lords Cl LE67. . . . . .97 A7
Lordship La NG13. . . . . 2 A6
Lord's La NG33 . . . . .43 B8
Lorne Rd LE2 . . . . 155 B1
Lorraine Rd LE2 . . . . 179 E7
Lorrimer Rd LE2 . . . . . . 179 E8
Lorrimer Way LE11 . . . . . .51 D5
Loseby La LE1 . . . . 259 B3
Losecoat Cl PE9 . . . . 143 F5
Lossiemouth Rd LE10 . . . 196 F1
Lothair Rd LE2 . . . . 154 E1
Lothian Pl DE74 . . . . .17 A3
Loudon Ct 🟦 LE65. . . . . . .69 B6
Loudon Pl DE74 . . . . .17 A4
Loudoun Way LE65 . . . . . .68 F5
Loughbon NG13 . . . . 2 A4
LOUGHBOROUGH 52 D1
Loughborough CE Prim
  Sch LE11. . . . . 51 F3
Loughborough Coll
  LE11. . . . . .52 A3
Loughborough Cotts
  LE4. . . . . 129 A2
Loughborough Gram Sch
  LE11. . . . . .52 B2
Loughborough High Sch
  LE11. . . . . .52 B3

Loughborough Hospl
  LE11. . . . . .51 E4
Loughborough Pk
  LE11. . . . . .51 B1
Loughborough Rd
  Asfordby LE14 . . . . .57 D3
  Birstall LE4 . . . . 129 A7
  Burton o t W LE12 . . . . . . 53 E7
  Cotes LE11. . . . . .52 F6
  Cotes LE12. . . . . .53 B6
  East Leake LE12 . . . . .31 F7
  Hathern LE12 . . . . .51 A8
  Hoton LE12 . . . . .53 B8
  Loughborough LE12. . . . . .75 C8
  North End LE12 . . . . .76 D3
  Peggs Green LE67 . . . . . .71 A7
  Quorn (Quorndon) LE12. . .75 E6
  Rempstone LE12 . . . . . . .32 D6
  Rothley LE7 . . . . 102 A5
  Shepshed LE12 . . . . .50 C4
  Thringstone LE67 . . . . . . .71 D8
  Walton on t W LE12 . . . . . 53 F4
  Whitwick LE67 . . . . .71 F6
Loughborough Sta
  LE11. . . . . .52 C5
Loughborough Tech Ctr
  LE11. . . . . .51 F3
Loughborough Univ
  LE11. . . . . .51 E3
Loughborough Univ Sch of
  Art & Design
  Loughborough LE11. . . . . .51 F3
  Loughborough LE11. . . . . .52 A4
Loughland Cl LE8 . . . . . . 202 A8
Louise Ave LE6 . . . . 126 F2
Lount La LE65 . . . . 217 D8
LOUNT 47 B3
Lount Rd CV13 . . . . 148 F8
Lounts Cres LE16 . . . . . . 229 D7
Loveday Cl CV9. . . . . 170 D2
Love La LE10 . . . . 216 A6
Lovelace Cl CV13 . . . . . . 172 A6
Lovelace Cres LE9 . . . . . 198 F5
Lovelace Way LE8 . . . . . . 223 A7
Loves La
  Dunton Bassett LE17 . . . 219 D1
  Empingham LE15 . . . . . . 141 A8
Lovett Cl LE12 . . . . .77 C3
Lovetts Cl LE10 . . . . 214 F8
Loveys Croft DE73 . . . . . . 26 E2
Lowcroft Dr LE2 . . . . 181 C4
Lower Bond St LE10 . . . . 197 D1
Lower Brand LE67 . . . . . . .44 A4
Lower Brook St NG10 . . . .10 F8
Lower Brown St LE1 . . . . 259 B2
Lower Cambridge St
  LE11. . . . . .52 B5
Lower Church St
  Ashby-de-la-Z LE65 . . . . . .69 B6
  Syston LE7 . . . . 103 B4
Lower Farm Cl LE15 . . . . 141 B6
Lower Free La LE1 . . . . . 259 B4
Lower Gladstone St
  LE11. . . . . 259 C2
Lower Gn LE11 . . . . .74 D8
Lower Hastings St
  LE1. . . . . 259 C2
Lower Hill St LE1 . . . . . . 259 B4
Lower Hilmorton Rd 🟥
  CV21 . . . . 257 A1
Lower Holme LE12 . . . . . . .30 B3
Lower Keyham La
  LE5. . . . . 130 B1
Lower Lee St LE1 . . . . . . 259 B4
Lower Leicester Rd
  LE17. . . . . 244 D6
LOWER MIDWAY 44 E6
Lower Moor Rd LE67. . . . . .70 E8
Lower Packington Rd
  LE65. . . . . .69 B4
Lower St CV21 . . . . 257 B1
Lower Willow St LE15 . . . 138 C4
LOWESBY 133 D3
Lowesby Cl LE13. . . . . . . .59 E2
Lowesby La
  Tilton on t H LE7 . . . . . . 133 D4
  Twyford LE14 . . . . 133 E8
Loweswater Cl
  Barrow-u-S LE12 . . . . .53 D1
  Nuneaton CV11 . . . . 214 A6
Loweswater Dr LE11 . . . . .51 D1
Loweswater Gr LE65 . . . . .69 C4
Lowfields La NG32 . . . . . . 4 E6
Lowick Dr LE18. . . . . 180 C2
Lowland Ave LE3 . . . . . . 153 A2
Lowther Cl LE15. . . . . . . 110 C2
Lowther Way LE11 . . . . . .52 B1
Low Woods La LE12. . . . . .49 B3
Loxley Dr LE13 . . . . .59 B1
Loxley Rd LE3 . . . . 127 C1
Lubbesthorpe Bridle Rd
  Braunstone Town LE3 . . . 153 E1
  Enderby LE19 . . . . 177 F8
Lubbesthorpe Rd LE3 . . . 178 E6
Lubbesthorpe Way
  LE19. . . . . 178 E7
LUBENHAM 239 E3
Lubenham All Saints CE
  Prim Sch LE16 . . . . . . 239 D3
Lubenham Hill LE16 . . . . 240 C2
Lubenham Rd
  East Farndon LE16. . . . . . 240 B1
  Marston Trussell LE16 . . . 239 C6
Lucas Rd LE10 . . . . 215 D6
Lucas Way LE9 . . . . 198 E7
Ludford Cl NG10 . . . . .10 E4
Ludgate Cl LE4 . . . . 128 E8
Ludlam Cl LE8. . . . . 202 C4

Ludlow Cl
Leicester, Oadby LE2 181 C4
Loughborough LE11 74 C8
Ludlow Dr LE13 59 C5
Ludlow Pl LE12 50 A2
Luffenham Cl PE9 143 A3
Luffenham Rd
Barrowden LE15 191 F6
Ketton PE9 167 E4
Lyndon LE15 165 E5
Lullington Mews DE12 67 A3
Lullington Rd DE12 67 A3
Lulworth Cl
Leicester LE5 156 A4
Wigston LE18 203 D7
Lumby's Terr PE9 143 E2
Lundy Cl LE10 197 B1
Lunsford Rd LE5 155 D8
Lupin Cl LE10 215 D5
Luther St LE3 154 C4
LUTTERWORTH 244 A7
Lutterworth Gram Sch & Com Coll LE17 244 B6
Lutterworth High Sch LE17 244 B5
Lutterworth Mus* LE17 244 D6
Lutterworth Rd
Arnesby LE8, LE17 221 D4
Bitteswell LE17 244 B8
Blaby LE8 202 B7
Churchover CV23, LE17 252 D5
Dunton Bassett LE17 219 E2
Gilmorton LE17 235 B2
Hinckley LE10 216 C3
Kimcote LE17 235 E2
Leicester LE2 179 C6
Lutterworth LE17 244 D4
Nuneaton CV11 214 A1
Pailton CV23, LE17 242 D2
Shawell LE17 253 D6
Swinford LE17 254 B6
Ullesthorpe LE17 233 C3
Walcote LE17 245 C4
Whetstone LE8 202 A3
Lyall Cl LE11 51 D6
Lychgate Cl
Cropston LE7 100 E2
Hinckley LE10 216 A5
Lychgate La LE10 216 C5
Lydall Rd LE2 179 E4
LYDDINGTON 212 C7
Lyddington Rd
Caldecott LE15, L16 212 D2
Gretton NN17 213 A1
Lydford Rd LE4 129 E2
Lyle Cl
Leicester LE4 129 E5
Melton Mowbray LE13 59 C6
Lyme Rd LE2 155 C3
Lymington Rd LE5 156 D8
Lyn Cl LE3, LE7 127 F3
Lyncote Rd LE3 179 B8
Lyncroft Leys LE7 156 F7
Lyndale Cl LE4 129 E6
Lyndale Rd LE3 178 F8
Lynden Ave NG10 10 D5
Lyndene Cl LE9 198 F7
Lyndhurst Cl LE10 216 A7
Lyndhurst Ct LE2 155 C2
Lyndhurst Rd LE2 181 A6
LYNDON 165 D5
Lyndon Dr LE2 180 F6
Lyndon Hill Nature Reserve Visitor Ctr* LE15 165 A8
Lyndon Rd
Manton LE15 164 F6
North Luffenham LE15 166 B4
Lyndon Way PE9 143 A3
Lyndwood Ct LE2 155 D1
Lyneham Cl LE10 197 A1
Lyngate Ave LE4 129 A8
Lynholme Rd LE2 180 B6
Lynmouth Cl LE3 153 C7
Lynmouth Dr
Gilmorton LE17 235 C4
Wigston LE18 180 A5
Lynmouth Rd LE5 156 D8
Lynton Cl
Gilmorton LE17 235 C4
Sileby LE12 77 C1
Lynton Ct LE9 198 B6
Lynton Rd LE13 59 A6
Lynwood Cl LE9 151 B3
Lyon Cl LE18 180 A4
Lysander Cl LE10 215 E4
Lytham Rd LE2 155 A1
Lytton Rd LE2 155 B1

M

Mablowe Field LE19 203 F8
Macaulay Rd
Lutterworth LE17 244 C8
Rothley LE7 101 E6
Macaulay St LE2 179 F8
McCarthy Cl LE67 71 E5
McCarthy Rd LE12 50 A3
Macdonald Rd LE4 129 A1
McDowell Way LE19 201 B7
Machin Dr LE9 219 A4
Mackaness Cl LE17 235 C4
Mackenzie Way LE1 259 C5
McKenzie Wlk LE5 156 A5
Mackworth Cl DE11 44 B7
Maclean Ave LE11 51 C6
McNeil Gr DE72 9 A7
McVicker Cl LE5 156 A6
Madeline Cl LE16 241 A5
Madeline Rd LE4 128 C6
Madras Rd LE1 155 B6
Magee Cl LE10 197 C2
Magna Pk LE17 243 C6
Magna Rd LE18 180 A1
Magnolia Ave LE11 75 A7
Magnolia Cl
Leicester Forest East LE3 152 E2
Leicester LE2 179 C5
Magnolia Dr LE17 244 B7
Magnus Rd LE4 129 C2
Mahatma Gandhi Ho LE4 155 B8
Maidenhair Cl LE11 75 A6
Maidenhead Ave LE5 130 D3
Maiden La PE9 143 E3
Maiden St LE7 102 F3
Maidenwell Ave LE5 130 C2
Maidstone Ho 12 LE2 155 B5
Maidstone Rd LE2 155 B5
Maidwell Cl LE18 180 F2
Maino Cres LE17 244 B5
Main Rd
Allexton LE15 187 D5
Asfordby Valley LE14 58 B3
Austrey CV9 119 B1
Barleythorpe LE15 137 E8
Bilstone CV13 147 C8
Brentingby LE14 60 D2
Claybrooke Magna LE17 232 E5
Collyweston PE9 168 D2
Dingley LE16 241 F3
Glaston LE15 190 B5
Granby NG13 5 A4
Kirby Bellars LE14 81 B8
Nether Broughton LE14 36 C7
Newton Regis B79 118 C2
Old Dalby LE14 35 E4
Ratcliffe Culey CV9 171 B4
Redmile NG13 6 E4
Sheepy Magna CV9 171 A6
Stainby NG33 43 D2
Twycross CV9 146 D7
Twyford LE14 106 D1
Uffington PE9 144 E3
Upton CV13 172 C4
Whitwell LE15 140 A6
Wycomb LE14 39 A6
Main St
Allington NG32 4 F5
Asfordby LE14 57 F3
Ashby Parva LE17 233 F5
Ashley LE16 227 F2
Bagworth LE67 124 B5
Barkby LE7 130 C8
Barlestone CV13 149 D8
Barrowden LE15 191 F5
Barsby LE7 105 D3
Barton in t B CV13 122 D1
Beeby LE7 131 C5
Belmesthorpe PE9 117 A1
Belton-in-R LE15 187 D7
Bisbrooke LE15 189 E4
Blackfordby DE11 68 B8
Botcheston LE9 151 C6
Branston NG32 23 C8
Breaston DE72 9 D8
Breedon on t H DE73 26 F2
Broughton Astley LE9 218 E7
Bruntingthorpe LE17 221 C1
Buckminster NG33 42 D2
Burrough on t H LE14 107 D2
Burton Overy LE8 182 F1
Cadeby CV13 149 C1
Caldecott LE16 230 B8
Carlton CV13 148 D7
Clifton u D CV23 257 A5
Clipsham LE15 89 E5
Congerstone CV13 147 D7
Cosby LE9 201 D2
Cossington LE7 102 D8
Cotesbach LE17 244 B1
Cottesmore LE15 112 C8
Countesthorpe LE8 202 F3
Croxton Kerrial LE14 24 B7
Dadlington CV13 173 E1
Drayton LE16 229 A5
Dunton Bassett LE17 219 D2
East Farndon LE16 250 B7
East Langton LE16 225 D6
Eastwell LE14 22 B6
Eaton NG32 22 F7
Egleton LE15 138 D3
Empingham LE15 141 A6
Fleckney LE8 222 F7
Foxton LE16 224 E1
Frisby on t W LE14 80 D8
Frolesworth LE17 218 B2
Gaddesby LE7 105 B7
Gaulby LE7 103 D6
Gilmorton LE17 235 C4
Glenfield LE3 127 B1
Glooston LE16 208 C4
Goadby Marwood LE14 22 C1
Granby NG13 5 C5
Great Bowden LE16 241 A6
Great Dalby LE14 82 A1
Great Glen LE8 205 B8
Great Oxendon LE16 250 E3
Greetham LE15 88 B1
Grimston LE14 57 B8
Gumley LE16 239 A8
Gunby NG33 64 E8
Main St *continued*
Harby LE14 12 A2
Hartshorne DE11 45 B6
Heather LE67 95 C2
Hemington DE74 17 D5
Hickling LE14 19 C6
Higham on t H CV13 196 A3
Hoby LE7 79 E8
Holwell LE14 37 F4
Houghton on t H LE7 157 F3
Huncote LE9 200 D7
Hungarton LE7 132 C3
Illston on t H LE7 183 F3
Keyham LE7 131 D1
Kibworth Beauchamp LE8 206 A2
Kilby LE18 204 A3
Kirby Bellars LE14 81 B8
Kirby Muxloe LE9 152 E6
Kirkby Mallory LE9 175 C6
Knossington LE15 136 A6
Laughton LE17 238 C7
Leicester, Evington LE5 156 B3
Leicester, Humberstone LE5 156 B8
Leicester LE3 153 F2
Leire LE17 218 F1
Lockington DE74 17 F5
Loddington LE7 161 D1
Long Eaton NG10 10 E7
Long Whatton LE12 29 B4
Lubenham LE16 239 F3
Lyddington LE15 212 C7
Market Bosworth CV13 148 F3
Market Overton LE15 86 F5
Markfield LE67 98 D1
Medbourne LE16 228 A7
Moira DE11 44 C1
Mowsley LE17 237 F7
Muston NG13 3 F1
Nailstone CV13 123 B3
Netherseal DE12 91 F7
Newbold Verdon LE9 150 B4
Newton Burgoland LE67 121 E7
Newton CV23 253 A1
Newtown Linford LE6 126 D8
Normanton Le H LE67 94 F6
Normanton on S LE12 30 D3
Norton-J-T CV9 120 A2
Oakthorpe DE12 93 A7
Old Dalby LE14 36 A5
Orton-on-t-H CV9 145 D4
Osgathorpe LE12 48 D3
Overseal DE12 67 B3
Owston LE15 135 B4
Peatling Magna LE8 221 A6
Peatling Parva LE17 235 F8
Peckleton LE9 175 F7
Pickwell LE14 108 D3
Preston LE15 164 C2
Queniborough LE7 103 F5
Ragdale LE14 56 C4
Ratby LE6 152 C8
Ratcliffe on t W LE7 78 C2
Ravenstone LE67 95 E8
Redmile NG13 6 F3
Rempstone LE12 32 D5
Ridlington LE15 163 D2
Rockingham LE16 230 B4
Rotherby LE14 79 F6
Saddington LE8 223 B4
Saltby LE14 24 E1
Saxelbye LE14 57 E7
Scraptoft LE7 156 F8
Seaton LE15 190 C1
Sewstern NG33 63 F8
Shackerstone CV13 121 E2
Shangton LE8 207 B5
Shawell LE17 253 C5
Shearsby LE17 222 A2
Shenton CV13 173 B5
Skeffington LE7 160 A2
Slawston LE16 209 B1
Smeeton Westerby LE8 223 F6
Smisby LE65 45 F3
Snarestone DE12 121 A8
South Croxton LE7 105 B1
Sproxton LE14 41 F5
Stanford on S LE12 31 C1
Stanton u B LE67 97 F1
Stapleton LE9 174 F1
Stathern LE14 13 A3
Stoke Dry LE15 211 F6
Stoke Golding CV13 196 D7
Stonesby LE14 40 E6
Sutton Bassett LE16 227 A1
Sutton Bonington LE12 30 B7
Sutton Cheney CV13 174 B6
Swannington LE67 71 B5
Swepstone LE67 94 D2
Swithland LE12 100 E7
Theddingworth LE17 248 D8
Thistleton LE15 87 E8
Thornton LE67 124 E4
Thorpe by Water LE15 213 A5
Thorpe Satchville LE14 106 E4
Thringstone LE67 71 D8
Thurlaston LE9 177 A3
Thurmaston LE4 103 C1
Thurnby LE7 157 A4
Tilton on t H, Cold Newton LE7 133 B1
Tilton on t H LE7 160 A8
Tugby LE7 185 E6
Tur Langton LE16 207 A2
Twyford LE14 106 D1
Ullesthorpe LE17 233 B4
Main St *continued*
Wakerley LE15 192 A4
Wardley LE15 188 A5
Whissendine LE15 84 F1
Willey CV23 242 F6
Willoughby-on-t-W LE12 34 D7
Willoughby Waterleys LE8 220 C5
Wilson DE73 26 E6
Woodhouse Eaves LE12 75 A2
Woodthorpe LE12 75 C7
Worthington LE65 47 F5
Wymondham LE14 62 E2
Zouch LE12 30 B3
Maitland Ave LE12 76 E1
Maizefield LE10 197 C4
Majolica Mews DE11 44 F2
Makey's Cl LE15 166 A7
Malabar Rd LE1 155 B7
Malcolm Arc 2 LE1 259 B4
Malcolm Sargent Prim Sch The PE9 143 A3
Malham Cl
Leicester LE4 128 C3
Nuneaton CV11 214 A2
Malham Way LE2 181 D5
Mallard Ave LE6 126 E3
Mallard Cl
Essendine PE9 117 B6
Measham DE12 93 B4
Mallard Ct
Oakham LE15 137 F7
Stamford PE9 143 D2
Mallard Dr
Hinckley LE10 215 A7
Syston LE7 102 F4
Mallard Rd
Barrow-u-S LE12 76 E8
Mountsorrel LE12 76 F2
Mallard Way LE3 152 E2
Malling Ave LE9 218 E7
Malling Cl LE4 102 B1
Mallory Cl LE9 150 B3
Mallory Ho LE10 215 D7
Mallory La 11 PE9 143 D3
Mallory Pl LE5 155 E8
Mallory St LE9 198 C8
Mallow Cl LE5 130 C3
Malmesbury Ave DE11 44 D6
Malthouse Cl CV13 123 B3
Maltings Cl NN17 213 B1
Maltings Rd NN17 213 B1
Maltings The
Ashley LE16 227 F3
Glenfield LE3 127 B1
Hamilton LE5 130 D3
10 Market Harborough LE16 240 E3
3 Oakham LE15 138 A6
Shardlow DE72 9 B1
Sileby LE12 77 C3
Stamford PE9 143 E2
Wothorpe PE9 169 E8
Maltings Yd LE15 113 A3
Malting Yd PE9 143 E2
Malt Mill Bank 6 LE9 198 A6
Malton Dr LE2 181 C6
Malvern Ave LE12 50 C2
Malvern Cres
Ashby-de-la-Z LE65 69 A8
Cosby LE9 201 D3
Malvern Gdns 3 NG10 10 A8
Malvern Rd LE2 155 D2
Malvern Wlk LE15 137 D6
Mammoth St LE67 71 D1
MANCETTER 194 A6
Mancetter Rd CV9 194 A6
Manchester La DE11 45 C5
Manchester St NG10 10 D6
Mandarin Cl LE10 215 A6
Mandarin Way LE8 201 F4
Mandervell Rd LE2 180 F5
Mandora La 6 LE2 155 B4
Manitoba Rd LE1 259 C5
Mann Cl LE3 153 D2
Manners Cl PE9 144 F4
Manners Dr LE13 59 D6
Manners Rd LE2 179 E7
Mannion Cres NG10 10 B5
Manor Brook Cl
Coalville LE67 96 C5
Stoney Stanton LE9 199 E3
Manor Cl
1 Ashby-de-la-Z LE65 69 C5
Hinckley LE10 215 C5
Leicester, Oadby LE2 181 B8
Long Whatton LE12 29 B4
Melton Mowbray LE13 59 E5
Ryhall PE9 116 F3
Manor Cres LE9 174 E2
Manor Ct
Blaby LE8 179 C1
Breaston DE72 9 E8
Breedon on t H DE73 26 F3
Cottingham LE16 229 C1
Leicester LE3 128 A1
Little Stretton LE2 182 D5
Waltham on t W LE14 40 A6
Willoughby-on-t-W LE12 34 C7
Wymeswold LE12 33 D4
Manor Dr
Leicester LE4 128 A5
Loughborough LE11 75 B8
Netherseal DE12 91 F6
Sileby LE12 77 C2
Worthington LE65 47 F6
Manor Farm Animal Ctr* LE12 31 F8
Manor Farm Cl LE9 218 F6
Manor Farm Ct LE7 160 A8
Manor Farm La PE9 117 B6
Manor Farm Mews DE72 16 B8
Manor Farm Rd DE72 16 B8
Manor Farm Way LE3 153 C7
Manor Farm Wlk LE7 160 A8
Manor Farm Yd LE7 160 A8
Manorfield CE Prim Sch LE9 199 D2
Manor Gdns
Desford LE9 151 B3
Glenfield LE3 153 C8
Shepshed LE12 50 B4
Manor Gn PE9 167 F5
Manor High Sch LE2 181 D7
Manor House Cl LE10 216 E6
Manor House Gdns LE5 156 B8
Manor House Prep Sch LE65 69 C6
Manor House Rd NG10 10 F6
Manor La
Barleythorpe LE15 137 D8
Clifton u D CV23 257 A5
Glaston LE15 190 B6
Granby NG13 5 A8
Langham LE15 110 C3
Peckleton LE9 175 F6
Somerby LE14 108 B1
Manorleigh DE72 9 E8
Manor Leigh DE72 9 E8
Manor Paddock NG32 4 F5
Manor Pl 5 LE10 197 D1
Manor Rd
Barlestone CV13 149 C8
Bitteswell LE17 244 B8
Carlby PE9 117 C8
Claybrooke Magna LE17 232 D6
Coalville LE67 96 C6
Cosby LE9 201 D4
Desford LE9 151 B3
Easthorpe NG13 3 C2
Fleckney LE8 223 A7
Great Bowden LE16 241 A6
Heather LE67 95 B2
Leicester, Oadby LE2 181 A8
Loughborough LE11 75 B8
Medbourne LE16 228 A7
Sapcote LE9 217 D8
Stretton LE15 88 F4
Thurmaston LE4 129 D6
Ullesthorpe LE17 233 A4
Manor Road Extension LE2 181 B7
Manor St
Hinckley LE10 197 C1
Wigston LE18 180 B2
Manor View
Hartshorne DE11 45 B6
Ketton PE9 168 A6
Sibson CV13 172 A6
Manor Way LE10 215 D5
Manor Wlk LE16 240 E3
Mansfield Ave LE12 76 A6
Mansfield Cl DE11 44 D4
Mansfield St
Leicester LE1 259 B4
Quorn (Quorndon) LE12 76 A6
Mansion House Gdns LE13 59 C6
Mansion House Hospl LE3 127 F2
Mansion St 1 LE10 215 D8
Mansion The DE72 16 B7
Manston Cl LE4 130 A5
Mantle La LE67 71 C2
Mantle Rd LE3 154 D6
MANTON 164 E6
Manton Cl LE9 219 B6
Manton Grange LE15 164 E5
Manton Rd
Corby NN17 230 F2
Edith Weston LE15 166 A7
Maple Ave
Blaby LE8 202 B7
Braunstone Town LE3 153 C3
Countesthorpe LE8 202 F4
Maple Cl
East Leake LE12 31 D8
Hinckley LE10 215 E5
Leicester LE4 128 E2
Melton Mowbray LE13 59 B5
Maple Ct NN17 230 E1
Maple Dr
Aston-on-T DE72 16 A7
Ibstock LE67 95 E2
Lutterworth LE17 244 B6
Maple Gr DE72 9 F8
Maple Rd
Castle Donington DE74 17 A5
Loughborough LE11 75 B8
Swadlincote DE11 44 B6
Thurmaston LE4 129 D6
Maple Rd N LE11 75 B8
Maple Rd S LE11 75 B7
Maple St LE2 155 B5
Mapleton Rd
Draycott DE72 9 A8
Wigston LE18 180 C3
Maple Tree Wlk LE19 201 C7

Maple Way
Desford LE9 . . . . **151** A3
Earl Shilton LE9 . . . . **198** A6
Maplewell LE67 . . . . **72** B1
Maplewell Dr LE4 . . . . **128** A6
Maplewell Hall Sch
LE12 . . . . **99** E7
Maplewell Rd LE12 . . . . **99** F7
Maplin Rd LE5 . . . . **130** E1
Mapperley Ho LE13 . . . . **59** D3
Marble St LE1 . . . . **259** B3
Marchant Rd LE10 . . . . **215** C8
Marchfont Cl CV11 . . . . . . **214** A1
Marcian Cl LE10 . . . . **196** F1
Marcus Cl LE7 . . . . **102** E2
Mardale Way LE11 . . . . **74** D8
MAREFIELD **134** B5
Marefield Cl LE7 . . . . **157** A5
Marefield La
Burrough on t H LE14 . . . **134** C8
Lowesby LE7 . . . . **133** E5
Tilton on t H LE7 . . . . **134** B1
Twyford LE14 . . . . **133** F8
Marfitt St LE3 . . . . **129** B2
Margam Cl LE3 . . . . **128** B2
Margaret Anne Rd
LE2 . . . . **181** B4
Margaret Cl LE4 . . . . **129** E8
Margaret Cres LE18 . . . . . **180** B3
Margaret Keay Rd
LE11 . . . . **51** C2
Margaret Rd LE5 . . . . **155** E5
Margaret St LE67 . . . . **71** C1
Marie Cl CV9 . . . . **194** A7
Marigold Cl PE9 . . . . **142** E4
Marigold Cres LE13 . . . . **82** B8
Marigold Dr LE10 . . . . **215** E5
Marigold La LE12 . . . . **76** F2
Marigold Pl DE11 . . . . **44** F4
Marigold Way LE19 . . . . . **200** F8
Marina Dr LE6 . . . . **127** A3
Marina Rd LE5 . . . . **155** D4
Marion Cl LE3 . . . . **127** F2
Marion's Way LE9 . . . . **200** D4
Marjorie St LE14 . . . . **155** A8
MARKET BOSWORTH
. . . . **148** E3
Market Bosworth Ctry
Pk* CV13 . . . . **149** A3
Market Bosworth High
Sch & Com Coll
CV13 . . . . **148** E3
Market Bosworth Sta*
CV13 . . . . **148** C3
Market Ct NG33 . . . . **65** B3
MARKET HARBOROUGH
. . . . **240** C2
Market Harborough CE
Prim Sch LE16 . . . . **240** D3
Market Harborough
District Hospl LE16 . . . . **240** D3
Market Harborough Mus*
LE16 . . . . **240** D2
Market Harborough Sta
LE16 . . . . **241** A3
Market Mews CV13 . . . . . . **148** F3
MARKET OVERTON **86** F6
Market Pl
Belton LE12 . . . . **49** B6
Billesdon LE7 . . . . **159** B2
Hinckley LE10 . . . . **215** D8
Kegworth DE74 . . . . **18** D2
Leicester LE1 . . . . **259** B3
Long Eaton NG10 . . . . **10** E8
Loughborough LE11 . . . . . **52** B4
Market Bosworth CV13 . . **148** F3
Melbourne DE73 . . . . **26** B7
Melton Mowbray LE13 . . . . **59** C3
Mountsorrel LE12 . . . . **76** E3
Oakham LE15 . . . . **138** A6
Shepshed LE12 . . . . **50** B4
Uppingham LE15 . . . . **189** B4
Whitwick LE67 . . . . **71** F5
Market Place App
LE1 . . . . **259** B3
Market Pl S LE1 . . . . **259** B3
Market St
Ashby-de-la-Z LE65 . . . . . . **69** B6
Bottesford NG13 . . . . **3** B2
Castle Donington DE74 . . . **17** B3
Coalville LE67 . . . . **71** C1
Draycott DE72 . . . . **9** A7
Leicester LE1 . . . . **259** B3
Loughborough LE11 . . . . . **52** A4
Lutterworth LE17 . . . . **244** C6
Oakham LE15 . . . . **138** A6
Swadlincote DE11 . . . . **44** B4
MARKFIELD **125** E7
Markfield Equestrian Ctr*
LE67 . . . . **98** A3
Markfield La
Botcheston LE9 . . . . **151** C8
Markfield LE67 . . . . **98** F1
Thornton LE67 . . . . **124** F6
Markfield Rd
Groby LE6 . . . . **126** D4
Ratby LE6 . . . . **126** B2
Markham Ret Pk PE9 . . . **143** F5
Markland LE2 . . . . **179** C4
Marlborough Cl LE10 . . . . **216** B7
Marlborough Dr LE28 . . . . **223** A6
Marlborough Ho LE3 . . . . **152** F3
Marlborough Pl LE17 . . . . **244** C5
Marlborough Rd
Breaston DE72 . . . . **9** D7

Marlborough Rd *continued*
Long Eaton NG10 . . . . **10** F8
Marlborough Sq LE67 . . . . **71** C1
Marlborough St LE1 . . . . . **259** B3
Marlborough Way
Ashby-de-la-Z LE65 . . . . . . **69** A7
Market Harborough
LE16 . . . . **240** E5
Marle Pit Hill LE12 . . . . **30** A8
Marl Fields LE7 . . . . **76** F1
Marlow Ct LE16 . . . . **228** A8
Marlow Rd LE3 . . . . **154** D2
Marlsbury Ave LE7 . . . . . . **157** A8
Marmion Cl LE8 . . . . **202** D3
Maromme Sq LE18 . . . . . . **180** D3
Marquis Ct DE12 . . . . **67** E5
Marquis Dr DE12 . . . . **67** E5
Marquis Rd LE14 . . . . **36** B6
Marquis St LE1 . . . . **259** B2
Marriott Cl
Asfordby LE14 . . . . **58** A3
Leicester Forest East
LE3 . . . . **153** B3
Marriott Dr LE8 . . . . **224** B8
Marriott Ho LE2 . . . . **181** A5
Marriott Prim Sch
LE2 . . . . **179** E6
Marriott Rd LE2 . . . . **179** E6
Marsden Ave LE7 . . . . **103** D5
Marsden Cl LE67 . . . . **70** F2
Marsden La LE2 . . . . **179** B6
Marshall Ave LE12 . . . . **77** D4
Marshall Cl LE16 . . . . **240** F2
Marshall Farm CM NG13 . . **6** B2
Marshall St LE3 . . . . **154** D7
Marsham Cl LE5 . . . . **130** B2
Marsh Ave LE8 . . . . **206** B1
Marsh Cl LE4 . . . . **129** E5
Marsh Ct NG13 . . . . **3** B3
Marsh Dr LE8 . . . . **206** A1
Marsh Rd LE12 . . . . **76** F1
Marsh's Paddock LE14 . . . **19** C6
Marston Cl
Leicester, Oadby LE2 . . . . **181** A3
Moira DE12 . . . . **68** A5
Marston Cres LE8 . . . . **202** E3
Marston Dr LE16 . . . . **126** F3
Marston La
Allington NG32 . . . . **4** F5
East Farndon LE16 . . . . . . **250** A7
Marston Rd
Croft LE9 . . . . **200** B5
Leicester LE4 . . . . **129** E2
Lubenham LE16 . . . . **239** D2
MARSTON TRUSSELL
. . . . **249** C8
Marston Trussell Rd
LE16 . . . . **249** F7
Marston Way LE67 . . . . **95** B2
Marstown Ave LE18 . . . . . **179** F2
Marteg Cl LE13 . . . . **59** B1
Martin Ave
Barrow-u-S LE12 . . . . **76** D7
Leicester Forest East
LE9 . . . . **152** F3
Leicester, Oadby LE2 . . . . **181** B5
Mountsorrel LE12 . . . . **76** D1
Martin Cl
Leicester LE4 . . . . **155** B8
Oakham LE15 . . . . **138** B8
Syston LE7 . . . . **199** D1
Whitwick LE67 . . . . **71** D6
Martin Ct LE7 . . . . **127** D5
Martindale Cl
Leicester LE2 . . . . **259** B1
Loughborough LE11 . . . . . **51** D1
Martin Dr LE7 . . . . **102** E4
Martin High Sch LE7 . . . . **127** D7
Martins Dr CV9 . . . . **170** E2
Martinshaw La LE6 . . . . . **126** E3
Martinshaw Prim Sch
LE6 . . . . **126** D4
Martinshaw Wood Nature
Trail* LE6 . . . . **126** C3
Martin Sq LE6 . . . . **152** D8
Martin St LE4 . . . . **155** C8
Martival LE5 . . . . **155** E7
Marvin Cl LE3 . . . . **154** B7
Marwell Cl LE4 . . . . **128** F4
Marwell Wlk LE4 . . . . **128** F4
Marwood Rd LE4 . . . . **128** D4
Mary Gee Hos LE2 . . . . . . **180** D8
Mary La LE14, NG32 . . . . . . **40** C8
Maryland Cl LE9 . . . . **197** F6
Maryland Ct DE11 . . . . **44** A7
Marylebone Dr LE17 . . . . **244** D6
Mary Rd LE3 . . . . **154** B8
Mary's Cl LE12 . . . . **33** C3
Marys Ct LE7 . . . . **127** D6
Marys St LE9 . . . . **198** F8
Mary St LE9 . . . . **198** F8
Marywell Cl LE10 . . . . **196** F1
Masefield Ave
Loughborough LE19 . . . . . **178** A2
Swadlincote DE11 . . . . **44** C6
Masefield Cl
Barwell LE9 . . . . **198** C8
Measham DE12 . . . . **93** B3
Mason Cres DE11 . . . . **44** E4
Mason Ct LE10 . . . . **215** B8
Mason Row LE5 . . . . **130** D3
Masons Cl LE19 . . . . **201** B7
Masterton Dr PE9 . . . . . . **143** F5
Masterton Rd PE9 . . . . . . **143** E5
Matlock Ave LE18 . . . . **180** A1

Matlock Ct NG10 . . . . **9** F5
Matlock St LE2 . . . . **155** C6
Matthew Arnold Ct
LE11 . . . . **51** D5
Matthew Clarke Ho 4
LE16 . . . . **240** E4
Matthew Ct LE11 . . . . **52** D4
Matthews Ct LE65 . . . . **68** F7
Matts Cl LE2 . . . . **179** D5
Maughan St LE9 . . . . **175** F1
Maura Cl LE8 . . . . **201** F5
Maurice Dr LE8 . . . . **202** D3
Maurice Rd LE16 . . . . **250** D8
Mavis Ave LE3 . . . . **154** C2
Mawby Cl LE8 . . . . **202** A5
Mawby's La DE12 . . . . **119** F8
Maxfield Ho LE2 . . . . **155** B5
Maxwell Dr LE11 . . . . **51** C5
Maxwell St DE72 . . . . **9** F8
Maxwell Way LE17 . . . . . . **244** C8
May Cl LE3 . . . . **154** A4
Mayfield LE15 . . . . **138** A8
Mayfield Dr
Loughborough LE11 . . . . . **52** B2
Wigston LE18 . . . . **180** D4
Mayfield Rd LE2 . . . . **155** C3
Mayfield St LE13 . . . . **59** B5
Mayfield Way LE9 . . . . **198** C2
Mayflower Cl LE67 . . . . . . **125** E8
Mayflower Dr LE8 . . . . **125** E8
Mayflower Mews
LE15 . . . . **189** B4
Mayflower Prim Sch
LE5 . . . . **155** F4
Mayflower Rd LE5 . . . . . . **155** E3
Mayflower Wlk LE67 . . . . **125** E8
Maylands Ave DE72 . . . . **9** E8
Maylan Rd NN17 . . . . **230** F3
May Meadow Cl CV13 . . . . **149** D8
Maynard Cl LE7 . . . . **124** A6
Maynard Pk* LE67 . . . . . . **123** F8
Maynard Rd LE2 . . . . **155** B6
Maynard Wlk LE67 . . . . . . **124** A6
Mayns La LE8 . . . . **205** E7
Mayo Cl LE11 . . . . **74** F7
Mayor's Wlk LE1 . . . . **155** A3
Maypole Hill DE11 . . . . **44** A6
Mayre Cl LE9 . . . . **219** B5
Mays Farm Dr LE9 . . . . . . **199** D3
Maytree Cl LE9 . . . . **152** E3
Maytree Ct LE9 . . . . **152** E3
Maytree Dr LE9 . . . . **152** E2
May Tree La LE3 . . . . **75** B4
Meadhurst Gdns LE15 . . . **189** B4
Meadhurst Rd LE3 . . . . . . **154** A5
Meadow Ave LE11 . . . . **52** B6
Meadowbrook Ct
DE12 . . . . **119** F8
Meadowbrook Rd LE8 . . . **223** F8
Meadow Cl
Bagworth LE67 . . . . **124** B5
Barrow-u-S LE12 . . . . **76** E8
Draycott DE72 . . . . **9** A7
Market Harborough
LE16 . . . . **240** F4
Ratby LE6 . . . . **152** D8
Sheepy Magna CV9 . . . . . **171** B7
Stoney Stanton LE9 . . . . . **199** D3
Meadow Com Prim Sch
The LE18 . . . . **180** A3
Meadowcourt Rd LE2 . . . . **180** F7
Meadow Court Rd
Earl Shilton LE9 . . . . **198** F7
Groby LE6 . . . . **126** F3
Meadow Cres LE8 . . . . **17** B2
Meadowcroft Cl LE3 . . . . . **153** B7
Meadow Ct LE19 . . . . **178** A1
Meadowdale Prim Sch
LE16 . . . . **241** B4
Meadowdale Rd LE16 . . . . **241** B4
Meadow Dr LE10 . . . . **216** A7
Meadow Edge LE19 . . . . . **178** A2
Meadowfield LE15 . . . . **138** A8
Meadow Furlong
CV23 . . . . **252** D1
Meadow Gdns
Leicester LE2 . . . . **180** A5
Measham DE12 . . . . **93** C3
Meadow Hill LE8 . . . . **182** A1
Meadow La
Birstall LE4 . . . . **129** C8
Coalville LE67 . . . . **72** B2
Long Eaton NG10 . . . . **10** F7
Loughborough LE11,
LE12 . . . . **52** B7
Markfield LE67 . . . . **98** E1
Ryhall PE9 . . . . **116** E1
Stanton u B LE67 . . . . **97** F1
Swadlincote DE11 . . . . **44** A6
Syston LE7 . . . . **102** E4
Thringstone LE67 . . . . **48** D2
Meadow Lane Ind Est
LE11 . . . . **52** B6
Meadow Park Ind Est
PE9 . . . . **117** B5
Meadow Rd
Barlestone CV13 . . . . **149** D7
Barwell LE9 . . . . **198** C7
Mountsorrel LE12 . . . . **101** D8
Woodhouse Eaves LE12 . . **75** A1
Meadowside CV11 . . . . . . **214** B1
Meadows La LE14 . . . . **11** D1
Meadows Rise LE14 . . . . . . **62** D2
Meadow St LE16 . . . . **240** E4
Meadows The
East Goscote LE7 . . . . . . **103** E8
Hinckley LE10 . . . . **216** A7
Littlethorpe LE19 . . . . **201** D7

Meadows The *continued*
Shepshed LE12 . . . . **50** A3
Meadowsweet PE9 . . . . . . **142** E5
Meadowsweet Cl LE13 . . . . **82** A8
Meadowsweet Rd
LE5 . . . . **130** C1
Meadow The LE9 . . . . **219** A5
Meadow View
Botcheston LE9 . . . . **151** C8
Coalville LE67 . . . . **96** C5
East Goscote LE7 . . . . . . **103** F7
Leicester, Oadby LE2 . . . . **181** B5
Stamford PE9 . . . . **144** A4
Meadow Way
Desford LE9 . . . . **151** C2
Egleton LE15 . . . . **138** D3
Groby LE6 . . . . **126** F3
Melton Mowbray LE13 . . . . **59** D1
Swadlincote DE11 . . . . **44** A6
Wigston LE18 . . . . **180** F2
Meadow Wlk LE67 . . . . **95** F2
Meads The LE3 . . . . **153** E5
Meadvale Rd LE2 . . . . **180** C7
Meadway LE3 . . . . **154** A6
Meadway The
Birstall LE4 . . . . **129** A8
Hinckley LE10 . . . . **215** F7
Syston LE7 . . . . **102** F2
Meadwell Rd LE3 . . . . **153** D3
Mease Cl DE12 . . . . **93** C4
MEASHAM **93** B5
Measham CE Prim Sch
DE12 . . . . **93** D5
Measham Rd
Appleby Magna DE12. . . . . **92** F1
Ashby-de-la-Z LE65 . . . . . . **68** F3
Donisthorpe DE12 . . . . **92** D6
Moira DE12 . . . . **67** F3
Oakthorpe DE12 . . . . **93** A2
Packington LE65 . . . . **69** B1
Snarestone DE12 . . . . **120** E8
MEDBOURNE **227** F6
Medbourne Rd
Ashley LE16 . . . . **227** E4
Drayton LE16 . . . . **228** E4
Hallaton LE16 . . . . **209** E5
Slawston LE16 . . . . **209** C1
Medhurst Cl LE8 . . . . **202** A5
Medina Rd
Corby NN17 . . . . **230** C1
Leicester LE3 . . . . **154** D8
Medway Cl LE16 . . . . **241** A3
Medway Com Prim Sch
LE2 . . . . **155** C4
Medway Dr LE13 . . . . **59** B1
Medway St LE2 . . . . **155** C4
Meer The LE8 . . . . **223** A6
Meeting House Cl LE12 . . . **31** F8
Meeting St LE12 . . . . **75** F5
Melba Way LE4 . . . . **102** B1
Melbourn Brothers
Brewery Mus* PE9. . . . . **143** D3
MELBOURNE **26** B8
Melbourne Cl LE18 . . . . . . **223** F8
Melbourne Ct NG10 . . . . **9** F4
Melbourne Dr LE13 . . . . . . **59** A3
Melbourne Hall & Gdns*
DE73 . . . . **26** C7
Melbourne Ho LE13 . . . . . . **59** D3
Melbourne Inf Sch
DE73 . . . . **26** B8
Melbourne Jun Sch
DE73 . . . . **26** B8
Melbourne La DE73 . . . . . . **26** E2
Melbourne Rd
Ibstock LE67 . . . . **122** E8
Leicester LE2 . . . . **155** C5
Newbold LE67 . . . . **47** D2
Ravenstone LE67 . . . . **71** A8
Stamford PE9 . . . . **143** F4
Melbourne St
Coalville LE67 . . . . **71** D1
Leicester LE2 . . . . **155** B6
Melbray Dr LE13 . . . . **59** C6
Melbreak Ave LE11 . . . . . . **74** E8
Melcombe Wlk 5
LE4 . . . . **128** F3
Melcroft Ave LE3 . . . . **154** B5
Melford St LE5 . . . . **155** F7
Melland Pl LE2 . . . . **179** D5
Mellerstain Wlk LE5 . . . . . **155** E7
Mellier Cl LE19 . . . . **178** A2
Mellor Com Prim Sch
LE4 . . . . **129** B3
Mellor Rd LE3 . . . . **154** A5
Melody Ave LE7 . . . . **127** E6
Melody Dr LE12 . . . . **77** C2
Melrose Cl
Ashby-de-la-Z LE65 . . . . . . **69** D6
Hinckley LE10 . . . . **215** B8
Stamford PE9 . . . . **143** A4
Melrose Rd LE13 . . . . **71** E8
Melrose St LE5 . . . . **129** B1
Melton Ave
Leicester LE4 . . . . **129** C5
Melbourne DE73 . . . . **26** B8
Melton Carnegie Mus*
LE13 . . . . **59** D3
Melton Ctry Pk & Visitor
Ctr* LE13 . . . . **59** D6
Melton & District War
Meml Hospl LE13 . . . . . . **59** C2
Melton Dr LE19 . . . . **218** E8
Melton La LE14 . . . . **107** C5
MELTON MOWBRAY **59** F4
Melton Mowbray Sta
LE13 . . . . **59** C2

Melton Rd
Asfordby Hill LE14 . . . . **58** C3
Barrow-u-S LE12 . . . . **76** E8
Burton Lazars LE14 . . . . . . **83** B4
Burton o t W LE12 . . . . **54** C6
East Goscote LE7 . . . . . . **103** F8
East Langton LE16 . . . . . . **225** C5
East Leake LE12 . . . . **31** E5
Langham LE15 . . . . **110** C2
Leicester LE4 . . . . **129** C3
Long Clawson LE14 . . . . . . **20** B1
Oakham LE15 . . . . **137** F6
Rearsby LE7 . . . . **79** C2
Scalford LE14 . . . . **38** C3
Shangton LE8 . . . . **207** B6
Syston LE7 . . . . **103** C4
Thurmaston LE4 . . . . **129** D7
Tilton on t H LE7 . . . . **159** E5
Twyford LE7 . . . . **133** D4
Upper Broughton LE14 . . . . **19** A1
Waltham on t W LE14 . . . . . **40** A6
Whissendine LE15 . . . . **84** C2
Wymondham LE14 . . . . **62** C2
Melton Spinney Rd LE14,
LE13. . . . . **59** F7
Melton St
Earl Shilton LE9 . . . . **198** E8
Leicester LE1 . . . . **155** A7
Melville Cl LE11 . . . . **51** B6
Memorial Sq LE67 . . . . **71** C1
Memory La LE1 . . . . **155** A7
Mendip Ave LE4 . . . . **128** D1
Mendip Cl
Ashby-de-la-Z LE65 . . . . . . **69** B5
Shepshed LE12 . . . . **50** C3
Mendip Rd
Edith Weston LE15. . . . . . . **166** C7
Oakham LE15. . . . . **137** D6
Mennecy Cl LE8 . . . . **202** D3
Mensa Cl LE2 . . . . **155** C6
Menzies Rd LE4 . . . . **128** E2
Meon Cl NN17 . . . . **230** C1
Mercenfeld Prim Sch
LE67 . . . . **125** D8
Mercer's Way LE7 . . . . **103** E7
Merchant's Comm
LE7 . . . . **103** E7
Mercia Dr LE2 . . . . **180** F6
Mercury Cl LE2 . . . . **155** B5
Mere Cl
Leicester LE5 . . . . **155** C6
Mountsorrel LE12 . . . . **101** E8
Meredith Rd LE3 . . . . **154** B1
Mere La
Copston Magna LE10. . . . . **231** C3
Leicester, Oadby LE2 . . . . **181** D2
Queniborough LE7 . . . . . . **103** F5
Mere Rd
Great Stretton LE2 . . . . . . **182** C6
Leicester LE5 . . . . **155** C5
Shangton LE8 . . . . **206** F4
Upper Bruntingthorpe
LE17 . . . . **236** D5
Waltham on t W LE14 . . . . . **40** A7
Meres La LE18 . . . . **180** E3
Mere The LE8 . . . . **205** A8
Merevale Ave LE10 . . . . . . **215** C7
Merevale Cl LE10 . . . . **215** C7
Merevale La CV9 . . . . **170** B1
Merevale Rd CV9 . . . . **170** C1
Mereworth Cl LE5 . . . . . . **155** D8
Merganster Way LE67 . . . . **97** A8
Meridian Bsns Pk
LE19 . . . . **178** D6
Meridian E LE19 . . . . **178** D7
Meridian N LE19 . . . . **178** D8
Meridian S LE19 . . . . **178** C6
Meridian W LE19 . . . . **178** D7
Meridian Way LE3 . . . . . . **153** D1
Meriton Rd LE17 . . . . **244** B5
Merlin Cl
Broughton Astley LE9 . . . **218** E7
Leicester Forest East
LE3 . . . . **153** A2
Mountsorrel LE7 . . . . **76** F1
Merlin Way DE11 . . . . **44** F3
Merrick Ct LE10 . . . . **215** F5
Merrifield Gdns LE10 . . . . **215** E5
Merrin Ct LE11 . . . . **52** B4
Merrydale Inf Sch
LE5 . . . . **155** E8
Merrydale Jun Sch
LE5 . . . . **155** E8
Merry Husrt Pl LE10 . . . . **214** E7
MERRY LEES **151** A8
Merry Lees Ind Est
LE9 . . . . **150** F8
Merrylees Rd
Desford LE9 . . . . **125** A2
Newbold Verdon LE9 . . . . **150** D8
Mersey Gn NN17 . . . . **230** C1
Merton Ave
Leicester LE5 . . . . **154** C5
Syston LE7 . . . . **103** B3
Merton Cl LE18 . . . . **218** D7
Merton Prim Sch The
LE7. . . . . **103** B2
Mervyn Rd LE5 . . . . **155** D4
Messenger Cl LE11 . . . . **51** E7
Metcalf Cl LE2 . . . . **199** D2
Metcalfe St LE9 . . . . **198** E7
Methuen Ave LE4 . . . . **129** E8
Metropolitan Apartments
LE1 . . . . **259** C4

Mews Cotts
Arnesby LE8 . . . . 221 F5
Great Oxendon LE16 . . . . . . 250 E3
Mews The
Great Bowden LE16 . . . . . . 240 E7
Melbourne DE73 . . . . 26 B7
Queniborough LE7 . . . . 104 A5
4 Rugby CV21 . . . . 257 A1
Meynell Cl
Leicester, Oadby LE2 . . . . . 181 C4
Melton Mowbray LE13 . . . . . 82 C8
Meynell Rd
Leicester LE5 . . . . 155 D7
Long Eaton NG10 . . . . 10 D5
Quorn (Quorndon) LE12 . . . . 76 A7
Meynell St DE11 . . . . 44 A1
Michael Cl LE7 . . . . 103 E6
Michael Lewis Ho
LE3 . . . . 154 B6
Michael Ramsey Ct
LE2 . . . . 179 C3
Michael's Wlk LE16 . . . . . . 230 B4
Mickleborough Cl
LE16 . . . . 227 B3
Mickleden Gn LE67 . . . . 72 A2
Mickledon Cl **1** NG10 . . . . 10 B8
Mickleton Cl DE11 . . . . 44 B1
Mickleton Dr LE5 . . . . 156 B3
Middelburg Cl CV11 . . . . . . 214 A1
Middle Ave LE11 . . . . 51 F6
Middlebrook Cl LE6 . . . . . . 152 D8
Middlebrook Gn LE16 . . . . . 241 A4
Middle Cl DE11 . . . . 44 B4
Middledale Rd LE16 . . . . . . 241 A3
Middlefield Cl LE10 . . . . . . 197 D2
Middlefield Ct LE10 . . . . . . 197 D2
Middlefield La LE10 . . . . . . 197 D3
Middlefield Pl LE10 . . . . . . 197 D3
Middlefield Rd LE7 . . . . 102 D7
MIDDLE HAMBLETON
. . . . 139 B3
Middle La LE14 . . . . 36 D8
Middle Orch LE12 . . . . 77 C1
Middle Rd LE67 . . . . 48 A1
Middlesex Rd LE2 . . . . 179 D7
Middle St
Barkestone-le-V NG13 . . . . . 6 C2
Croxton Kerrial NG32 . . . . . 24 B7
Foxton LE16 . . . . 224 E1
Hose LE14 . . . . 20 F7
Owston LE15 . . . . 135 B4
Skillington NG33 . . . . 43 B8
Stainby NG33 . . . . 43 D2
Wing LE15 . . . . 165 A3
MIDDLETON 229 B1
Middleton Cl
Stoney Stanton LE9 . . . . . . 199 E2
Wigston LE18 . . . . 180 F3
Middleton Pl LE11 . . . . 52 B2
Middleton Rd
Ashley LE16 . . . . 228 B3
Bringhurst LE16 . . . . 229 C4
Middletons Cl LE8 . . . . 222 F8
Middleton St LE2 . . . . 179 C6
Midhurst Ave LE13 . . . . 178 F8
Midland Cotts LE18 . . . . . . 180 B2
Midland Ct
Lutterworth LE17 . . . . 244 D8
Oakham LE15 . . . . 137 F7
Midland Rd
Ellistown LE67 . . . . 96 D4
Swadlincote DE11 . . . . 44 B4
Midland Road Ind Est
DE11 . . . . 44 B4
Midland St
Leicester LE1 . . . . 259 C4
Long Eaton NG10 . . . . 10 E8
Midway La LE17 . . . . 236 B3
Midway Rd
Leicester LE5 . . . . 155 D2
Swadlincote DE11 . . . . 44 C5
Mikado Rd NG10 . . . . 10 C5
Milby Dr CV11 . . . . 214 A7
Mildenhall Rd LE11 . . . . 51 C4
Mildmay Cl LE16 . . . . 59 C6
Milestone Cl LE8 . . . . 224 C8
Milestone Mews LE16 . . . . . 229 C1
Milford Cl LE10 . . . . 214 A7
Milford Ct LE19 . . . . 201 A8
Milford Rd LE2 . . . . 180 B8
Mill DE72 . . . . 9 A1
Millais Rd LE10 . . . . 197 A3
Mill Bank LE65 . . . . 69 B6
Millbrook Cl LE4 . . . . 128 F3
Millbrook Dr LE18 . . . . 218 F5
Millbrook Wlk **1** LE4 . . . . 128 F3
Mill Cl
Birstall LE4 . . . . 129 B6
Sapcote LE9 . . . . 217 E8
Shepshed LE12 . . . . 50 C5
Smeeton Westerby LE8 . . . . 223 F6
Stapleton LE9 . . . . 174 E2
Swadlincote DE11 . . . . 44 C5
Wigston LE18 . . . . 202 F8
Wing LE15 . . . . 165 B2
Milldale Rd NG10 . . . . 10 B6
Mill Dam LE67 . . . . 96 D6
Mill Dr LE6 . . . . 152 D7
Millenium Ave DE12 . . . . . . 67 E5
Millennium Cl LE17 . . . . . . 246 F4
Miller Cl LE4 . . . . 129 E5
Millers Cl
Glenfield LE3 . . . . 153 B8
Huncote LE9 . . . . 200 D7
Millersdale Ave LE5 . . . . . . 156 D5
Millers Gdns LE16 . . . . 240 B2
Millers Gn LE10 . . . . 215 F6

Millers Grange LE9 . . . . . . 218 F5
Millers Wlk LE67 . . . . 95 E7
Miller's Yd **5** LE12 . . . . . . 240 E3
Millfield DE72 . . . . 9 B2
Millfield Ave LE16 . . . . 229 D1
Millfield Cl
Anstey LE7 . . . . 127 D5
Ashby-de-la-Z LE65 . . . . . . 69 A8
Millfield Com Sch
LE3 . . . . 178 E7
Millfield Cres LE18 . . . . . . 178 F6
Millfield Croft **1** DE11 . . . 44 B7
Millfield St **1** 45 A2
Mill Furlong CV23 . . . . 252 D1
Millgate Sch LE2 . . . . 180 A8
Mill Gdns CV13 . . . . 196 A3
Mill Gn DE72 . . . . 9 A1
Mill Gr
Lutterworth LE17 . . . . 244 D5
Whissendine LE15 . . . . 84 E1
Mill Hill
Enderby LE19 . . . . 178 A4
Laughton LE17 . . . . 238 C4
Leicester LE4 . . . . 129 A2
Lubenham LE16 . . . . 239 E3
Stathern LE14 . . . . 13 B2
Mill Hill Cl LE8 . . . . 202 A7
Mill Hill Ind Est LE19 . . . . . 178 A4
Mill Hill La
Leicester LE2 . . . . 155 B4
Markfield LE67 . . . . 98 D1
Mill Hill Rd
Arnesby LE8 . . . . 221 F5
Hinckley LE10 . . . . 197 C1
Market Harborough
LE16 . . . . 240 F3
Mill Ho
1 Hinckley LE10 . . . . 197 C1
Melton Mowbray LE13 . . . . 59 D3
Millhouse Ct DE72 . . . . 9 B7
Millhouse Est LE67 . . . . 71 C8
Milligan Rd LE2 . . . . 179 E7
Mill La
Asfordby LE14 . . . . 57 F2
5 Ashby-de-la-Z LE65 . . . . 69 B6
Atherstone CV9 . . . . 194 A6
Barrowden LE15 . . . . 192 A5
Barrow-u-S LE12 . . . . 76 D6
Belton LE12 . . . . 49 B7
Bilstone CV13 . . . . 147 C7
Blaby LE8 . . . . 202 E8
Caldecott LE16 . . . . 230 B8
Copston Magna LE10 . . . . . 231 A5
Cottesmore LE15 . . . . 112 C8
Croxton Kerrial NG32 . . . . . 24 B7
Earl Shilton LE9 . . . . 199 C8
East Leake LE12 . . . . 31 F8
Empingham LE15 . . . . 141 B6
Enderby LE19 . . . . 178 B2
Frisby on t W LE14 . . . . . . 80 D8
Gilmorton LE17 . . . . 235 D5
Heather LE67 . . . . 95 C2
Hickling LE14 . . . . 19 B7
Kegworth DE74 . . . . 18 D2
Ketton PE9 . . . . 168 A5
Leicester LE2 . . . . 259 A2
Long Clawson LE14 . . . . . . 20 D3
Long Whatton LE12 . . . . . . 29 D4
Loughborough LE11 . . . . . . 52 C5
Melton Mowbray LE13 . . . . 59 D2
Newbold Verdon LE9 . . . . . 150 B4
Orston NG13 . . . . 2 A8
Peggs Green LE67 . . . . 71 A7
Stamford LE15 . . . . 217 C5
Shearsby LE17 . . . . 222 A2
Sheepy Magna CV9 . . . . . . 171 B7
Shenton CV13 . . . . 173 B3
Smeeton Westerby LE8 . . . . 223 F7
Somerby LE14 . . . . 108 B2
South Witham NG33 . . . . . . 64 E2
Thornton LE67 . . . . 124 E4
Thurmaston LE4 . . . . 129 D8
Tinwell PE9 . . . . 142 F1
Waltham on t W LE14 . . . . . 40 A4
Willoughby-on-t-W LE12 . . . 34 D8
Witherley CV9 . . . . 194 A8
Mill Lane Ind Est LE13 . . . . 127 A1
Mill La The LE3 . . . . 153 A8
Mill Pond LE67 . . . . 96 D6
Millpool Cl DE11 . . . . 45 A7
Mill Race View CV9 . . . . . . 170 D2
Mill Rd
Cottingham LE16 . . . . 229 C2
Gretton LE15, NN17 . . . . . . 212 F2
Rearsby LE7 . . . . 78 F1
Thurcaston LE7 . . . . 101 B3
Ullesthorpe LE17 . . . . 233 B4
Woodhouse Eaves LE12 . . . 74 F1
Mills Cl DE72 . . . . 9 A1
Mill St
Barwell LE9 . . . . 198 A5
Duddington PE9 . . . . 193 B6
Leicester LE2 . . . . 259 B2
Melton Mowbray LE13 . . . . 59 C2
Oakham LE15 . . . . 138 A6
Packington LE65 . . . . 69 B8
Ryhall PE9 . . . . 116 F3
Mills The LE12 . . . . 76 A5
Millstone La
Leicester LE1 . . . . 259 B3
Syston LE7 . . . . 103 C4
Mills Yd LE11 . . . . 52 B3
Mill View
Hinckley LE10 . . . . 197 E1
Huncote LE9 . . . . 200 D7
Millwood Cl LE4 . . . . 128 E5
Milner Ave DE72 . . . . 9 A7
Milner Cl LE12 . . . . 77 C2

Milner Rd NG10 . . . . 10 D8
Milners Row **6** PE9 . . . . . . 143 E3
Milnroy Rd LE5 . . . . 156 E7
Milton Ave DE11 . . . . 44 C6
Milton Cl
Hinckley LE10 . . . . 197 C1
Measham DE12 . . . . 93 C3
Melton Mowbray LE13 . . . . 59 B5
Wigston LE18 . . . . 180 E2
Milton Cres LE4 . . . . 128 B2
Milton Ct LE11 . . . . 51 D5
Milton Gdns LE2 . . . . 181 A5
Milton Ho LE4 . . . . 128 B3
Milton St
Long Eaton NG10 . . . . 10 D7
Loughborough LE11 . . . . . . 51 E5
Narborough LE19 . . . . 178 A1
Milton Terr NG10 . . . . 10 D7
Milverton Ave LE4 . . . . 128 D1
Milverton Cl LE18 . . . . 180 E2
Milverton Dr LE18 . . . . 180 C4
Mimosa Cl LE11 . . . . 75 A6
Minehead St LE3 . . . . 154 B5
Minster Cres LE4 . . . . 128 D1
Minster Ct LE2 . . . . 259 B2
Minstrel's Wlk LE7 . . . . 103 D7
Mint Gr NG10 . . . . 10 A7
Minton Rd DE74 . . . . 17 B4
Mint Rd LE2 . . . . 154 D4
Mira Dr CV10 . . . . 195 D3
MISTERTON 244 F4
Misterton Way LE17 . . . . . . 244 D5
Mistletoe Dr DE11 . . . . 44 F2
Mistral Cl LE14 . . . . 215 F8
Mitchell Ct CV23 . . . . 252 C2
Mitchell Dr LE11 . . . . 51 B6
Mitchell Ct LE4 . . . . 157 A8
Mitchell Rd LE19 . . . . 178 A3
Mitchell St LE10 . . . . 10 E7
Moat Cl LE9 . . . . 176 F3
Moat Com Coll LE2 . . . . . . 155 B5
Moat Ct LE5 . . . . 156 C8
Moat Gdns LE9 . . . . 217 D7
Moat Rd
Leicester LE5 . . . . 155 D5
Loughborough LE11 . . . . . . 74 E8
Moat St
Swadlincote DE11 . . . . 44 B1
Wigston LE18 . . . . 180 D2
Moat The DE74 . . . . 17 B4
Moat Way LE9 . . . . 197 F6
Modbury Ave LE4 . . . . 128 E4
Model Farm Cl LE11 . . . . . . 51 E1
MOIRA 67 E3
Moira Dale DE74 . . . . 17 C3
Moira Furnace Mus*
DE12 . . . . 67 E3
Moira Inf Sch DE12 . . . . . . 68 B6
Moira Rd
Donisthorpe DE12 . . . . 67 F1
Overseal DE12 . . . . 67 B3
Shellbrook LE65 . . . . 68 E6
Swadlincote DE11 . . . . 67 E8
Woodville DE11 . . . . 44 E2
Moira St
Leicester LE4 . . . . 129 B1
Loughborough LE11 . . . . . . 52 B3
Melbourne DE73 . . . . 26 A7
Moir Cl LE12 . . . . 77 C3
Moles La LE15 . . . . 190 C1
Molesworth Bglws
PE9 . . . . 168 A6
Molyneux Dr LE17 . . . . 77 D1
Monal Cl LE8 . . . . 201 F4
Monarch Cl LE4 . . . . 129 C8
Monarch Way LE11 . . . . 52 A6
Monar Cl LE4 . . . . 129 D4
Mona St LE9 . . . . 198 E7
Monckton Cl LE7 . . . . 259 C5
Moneyhill LE65 . . . . 68 B7
Monica Rd LE13 . . . . 178 F7
Monks Cres LE4 . . . . 128 C8
Monks Kirby La CV23 . . . . . 231 F1
Monmouth Dr LE2 . . . . 179 D2
Monroe Cl LE16 . . . . 240 D5
Monsaldale Cl NG10 . . . . . . 10 B6
Monsarrat Way LE11 . . . . . . 51 D6
Monsell Dr LE2 . . . . 179 C5
Montague Ave LE7 . . . . 163 B2
Montague Rd LE7 . . . . 150 B5
Montague Dr LE11 . . . . 74 C8
Montague Rd
Broughton Astley LE9 . . . . . 218 F7
Leicester LE2 . . . . 155 B2
Monteith Pl DE11 . . . . 44 B4
Montford Mews DE74 . . . . . 17 B4
Montgomery Cl LE7 . . . . . . 244 A5
Montgomery Rd LE9 . . . . . . 199 A8
Montilo La CV23 . . . . 242 D2
Montral Rd LE1 . . . . 155 A7
Montrose Cl
Market Harborough
LE16 . . . . 240 D1
Stamford PE9 . . . . 143 A4
Montrose Ct LE16 . . . . 156 A8
Montrose Rd LE2 . . . . 179 D5
Montrose Rd S LE2 . . . . 179 D5
Montrose Sch LE2 . . . . 179 D6
Montsoreau Way
LE12 . . . . 101 D8
Montvale Gdns LE16 . . . . . 154 D8
Moon Cl LE2 . . . . 155 B5
Moorbarns La LE17 . . . . . . 244 B4
Moorcroft Cl CV11 . . . . 214 B1
Moore Rd
Barwell LE9 . . . . 198 C7

Moore Rd continued
Ellistown LE67 . . . . 96 E4
Moores Cl LE18 . . . . 179 E2
Moores La LE9 . . . . 178 B4
Moores Rd LE4 . . . . 129 B2
Moorfield Pl LE12 . . . . 50 B4
Moorfields LE5 . . . . 156 D8
Moorgate Ave LE4 . . . . 128 F8
Moorgate St LE4 . . . . 155 A8
Moorhen Way LE11 . . . . 51 F3
Moor Hill LE7 . . . . 186 C2
Moorings The LE12 . . . . 76 E6
Moor La
Aston-on-T DE72 . . . . 16 B8
Coleorton LE67 . . . . 70 F6
East Norton LE7 . . . . 186 C4
East Norton LE7 . . . . 186 D5
Loughborough LE11 . . . . . . 52 E3
Normanton on S LE12 . . . . . 30 C4
North Luffenham LE15 . . . . 166 D2
South Witham NG33 . . . . . . 64 D4
Stathern LE14 . . . . 13 A4
Staunton in t V NG23 . . . . . 1 E6
Tonge DE73, DE74 . . . . 27 B4
Moorland Cl CV13 . . . . 148 F3
Moorland Rd LE7 . . . . 102 E3
Moorlands Mobile Home
Pk The LE67 . . . . 70 E3
Moorlands The LE67 . . . . . . 70 E4
Moorleas La LE14 . . . . 39 F5
Moor The LE67 . . . . 70 E6
Moray Cl
Hinckley LE10 . . . . 215 A8
Stamford PE9 . . . . 142 F4
Morban Rd LE2 . . . . 179 B6
Morcote Rd LE3 . . . . 153 E3
MORCOTT 191 A5
Morcott Rd
Barrowden LE15 . . . . 191 D5
Glaston LE15 . . . . 190 D5
Wing LE15 . . . . 165 A2
Moreton Ct LE67 . . . . 96 D7
Moreton Dale LE2 . . . . 177 D6
Moreton Wlk LE65 . . . . 69 F5
Morgans Orch LE12 . . . . . . 76 D8
Moriston Cl NN17 . . . . 230 C1
Morkery La NG33 . . . . 66 C5
Morkery Wood Nature
Trail* LE15 . . . . 66 A3
Morland Ave LE2 . . . . 180 E8
Morland Dr LE10 . . . . 197 B3
Morledge St LE1 . . . . 259 C4
Morley Arc **5** LE1 . . . . . . 259 B4
Morley Cl LE13 . . . . 59 A4
Morley La LE12 . . . . 50 B1
Morley Rd
Leicester LE5 . . . . 155 C6
Sapcote LE9 . . . . 217 E7
Morley St
Loughborough LE11 . . . . . . 52 C5
Market Harborough
LE16 . . . . 240 D3
Mornington St LE5 . . . . 155 D7
Morpeth Ave LE4 . . . . 128 D4
Morpeth Dr LE2 . . . . 181 D4
Morris Cam Wlk LE14 . . . . . 57 E3
Morris Cl
Braunstone Town
LE3 . . . . 153 D2
Morris Ct LE17 . . . . 252 C4
Morrison Cl LE8 . . . . 224 A8
Morris Rd LE2 . . . . 155 A1
Mortiboys Way LE9 . . . . . . 199 D2
Mortimer Pl LE3 . . . . 154 B1
Mortimer Rd
Melton Mowbray LE13 . . . . 59 C4
Narborough LE19 . . . . 201 A7
Mortimer Way
Leicester LE3 . . . . 154 B1
Loughborough LE11 . . . . . . 51 B6
Mortoft Rd LE4 . . . . 128 D4
Morton Wlk LE4 . . . . 155 E8
Morwoods The LE2 . . . . 181 B5
Moscow La
Great Dalby LE14 . . . . 107 D8
Shepshed LE12 . . . . 50 A1
Moseley Cl LE16 . . . . 71 E6
Mossdale Rd LE3 . . . . 178 E8
Mosse Way LE2 . . . . 181 C6
Mossgate LE3 . . . . 154 A7
Mosswood Cres LE4 . . . . . . 222 F6
Mostyn Ave LE7 . . . . 103 C4
Mostyn St LE3 . . . . 154 B5
Mottisford Rd LE4 . . . . 128 F4
Mottisford Wlk LE4 . . . . . . 128 F4
Mottram Rd LE16 . . . . 229 D7
Mountain Rd LE4 . . . . 130 A4
Mount Ave
Barwell LE9 . . . . 198 C2
Leicester LE5 . . . . 155 D6
Mountbatten Ave PE9 . . . . . 143 C4
Mountbatten Rd LE15 . . . . . 137 C6
Mountbatten Way
LE17 . . . . 244 B5
Mountcastle Rd LE4 . . . . . . 154 F7
Mountfield Rd LE9 . . . . 198 E8
Mountfields Dr LE11 . . . . . . 51 E2
Mountfields Lodge Sch
LE11 . . . . 51 F2
Mount Grace High Sch
LE10 . . . . 197 E1
Mount Grace Rd LE11 . . . . . 51 B5
Mount Pleasant
Castle Donington DE74 . . . . 17 B3
Kegworth DE74 . . . . 18 D3
Leicester, Oadby LE2 . . . . . 181 E3
Morcott LE15 . . . . 191 A6

Mount Pleasant continued
Uppingham LE15 . . . . 189 B4
Mount Pleasant La
DE12 . . . . 92 A8
Mount Pleasant Rd
Morcott LE15 . . . . 191 A6
Swadlincote DE11 . . . . 44 A1
Mount Rd
Cosby LE9 . . . . 201 D3
Hartshorne DE11 . . . . 45 A4
Hinckley LE10 . . . . 215 D8
Leicester LE5 . . . . 155 C6
Leicester, Oadby LE2 . . . . . 181 B5
Mount St Bernard Abbey
(Monastery)* LE67 . . . . 72 C5
MOUNTSORREL 76 D2
Mountsorrel Cotts
LE9 . . . . 199 D2
Mountsorrel La
Rothley LE7 . . . . 101 E7
Sileby LE12 . . . . 77 A3
Mount St DE72 . . . . 9 F7
Mount The
Dunton Bassett LE17 . . . . . 219 D2
Scraptoft LE7 . . . . 156 F8
Mount View LE8 . . . . 182 B1
Mowbray Ct LE13 . . . . 59 B2
Mowbray Dr LE7 . . . . 103 C4
MOWMACRE HILL 128 D5
Mowmacre Hill LE4 . . . . . . 128 E5
Mowmacre Hill Prim Sch
LE4 . . . . 128 D5
MOWSLEY 237 F6
Mowsley Ct LE17 . . . . 247 E6
Mowsley End LE18 . . . . 180 D2
Mowsley La LE17 . . . . 236 D4
Mowsley Rd
Husbands Bosworth
LE17 . . . . 247 E6
Saddington LE8 . . . . 223 B2
Theddingworth LE17 . . . . . 238 B2
Mowsley St Nicholas CE
Prim Sch LE17 . . . . 237 F7
Muckle Gate La LE12 . . . . . 54 F1
Muirfield Cl LE3 . . . . 153 C6
Mulberry Ave LE5 . . . . 153 C6
Mulberry Cl LE17 . . . . 244 B7
Mulberry Ct LE16 . . . . 229 A5
Mulberry Gdns DE74 . . . . . 18 D2
Mulberry Way DE72 . . . . . . 16 A6
Mull Way LE8 . . . . 202 F3
Mumford Way LE11 . . . . . . 51 D3
Muncaster Cl LE9 . . . . 219 A4
Mundella St LE2 . . . . 155 C3
Mundy Cl LE2 . . . . 53 F7
Munnings Cl LE4 . . . . 155 B8
Munnings Dr LE10 . . . . 197 A3
Munnmore Cl DE74 . . . . . . 18 C2
Muntjack Rd LE8 . . . . 201 F5
Murby Way LE3 . . . . 153 C1
Murdoch Rise LE11 . . . . 51 D6
Muriel Rd LE3 . . . . 154 C5
Murphy Dr LE67 . . . . 124 A6
Murray Cl LE4 . . . . 218 F4
Murrayfield Rd LE3 . . . . . . 153 C5
Murray St LE2 . . . . 155 B6
Muscovey Rd LE67 . . . . 97 A8
Museum Sq LE1 . . . . 259 C2
Musgrove Cl **3** LE3 . . . . . 154 D5
Mushill La LE12 . . . . 33 D5
Mushroom La DE11 . . . . . . 67 D8
Musk Cl LE4 . . . . 229 D7
Musson Dr LE65 . . . . 69 A5
Musson Rd LE3 . . . . 153 E7
MUSTON 7 F8
Muston Gdns LE2 . . . . 180 B7
Muston La NG13 . . . . 3 D1
Myrtle Ave
Birstall LE4 . . . . 102 B1
Long Eaton NG10 . . . . 10 C5
Myrtle Cl LE9 . . . . 198 A7
Myrtle Rd LE2 . . . . 155 C4
Mythe La CV9 . . . . 194 A8
Mythe View CV9 . . . . 170 E1

N

Nagle Gr LE4 . . . . 129 D5
NAILSTONE 123 B3
Nailstone Rd
Barton in t B CV13 . . . . . . 122 C1
Carlton CV13 . . . . 148 E8
Nairn Rd PE9 . . . . 143 A3
NAMS Tutorial Coll
LE1 . . . . 259 C4
Namur Rd LE18 . . . . 179 E3
Nanhill Dr LE12 . . . . 100 A8
NANPANTAN 74 B7
Nanpantan Rd LE11 . . . . . . 74 B7
Nansen Rd LE5 . . . . 155 E4
NARBOROUGH 201 B8
Narborough Rd
Cosby LE9, LE19 . . . . 201 D4
Huncote LE9 . . . . 200 D7
Leicester LE3 . . . . 154 C3
Narborough Rd N
LE3 . . . . 154 D5
Narborough Rd S
LE19 . . . . 178 E4
Narborough Sta LE19 . . . . . 201 C7
Narrow Boat Cl LE18 . . . . . 203 A8
Narrow La
Donisthorpe DE12 . . . . 92 E8
Hathern LE12 . . . . 30 A1

Narrow La *continued*
Leicester LE2 ... 179 C6
Stathern LE14 ... 13 A3
Wymeswold LE12 ... 34 B2
Narrows The 1 LE10 ... 215 E8
Naseby Cl
Market Harborough
LE16 ... 240 E2
Wigston LE18 ... 180 E2
Naseby Dr
Ashby-de-la-Z LE65 ... 69 D7
Long Eaton NG10 ... 10 E4
Loughborough LE11 ... 51 A2
Naseby Rd
Leicester LE4 ... 129 E2
Sibbertoft LE16 ... 248 F2
Welford NN6 ... 256 F6
Naseby Sq LE16 ... 240 E2
Naseby Way LE8 ... 205 B8
Nathaniel Rd NG10 ... 10 F7
National Space Ctr*
LE4 ... 128 F2
Navigation Cl LE13 ... 59 B2
Navigation Dr LE2 ... 179 A2
Navigation St
Leicester LE1 ... 154 F7
Measham DE12 ... 93 C5
Navigation Way LE11 ... 52 A5
Navins The LE12 ... 76 E2
Naylor Ave LE11 ... 52 D2
Naylor Rd LE7 ... 103 C5
Neal Ave LE3 ... 153 E2
Neale St NG10 ... 10 E7
Near Mdw NG10 ... 10 E5
Near The Church
LE16 ... 226 A5
Necton St LE7 ... 103 A3
Nedham St LE2 ... 155 B6
Ned Ludd Cl LE7 ... 127 E6
Needham Ave LE2 ... 179 A3
Needham Cl
Leicester, Oadby LE2 ... 181 E4
Melton Mowbray LE13 ... 59 C4
Needlegate LE1 ... 259 A5
Needleworks The
Leicester LE1 ... 259 B3
4 Loughborough LE11 ... 52 B4
Needwood Way LE19 ... 177 F2
Nelot Way LE5 ... 156 B5
Nelson Cl LE12 ... 50 D4
Nelson Dr LE10 ... 197 D4
Nelson Fields LE67 ... 72 A2
Nelson Pl LE65 ... 45 F3
Nelson St
Leicester LE1 ... 259 C2
Long Eaton NG10 ... 10 D6
Market Harborough
LE16 ... 240 D3
Swadlincote DE11 ... 44 B5
Syston LE7 ... 103 B3
Nene Cl LE13 ... 59 B1
Nene Cres
Corby NN17 ... 230 C1
Oakham LE15 ... 137 F5
Nene Ct
Leicester, Oadby LE2 ... 181 C5
3 Stamford PE9 ... 143 C3
Nene Dr LE2 ... 181 C5
Nene Way LE67 ... 97 A7
Neptune Cl LE2 ... 155 C5
Neston Gdns LE2 ... 179 F6
Neston Rd LE2 ... 179 F6
NETHER BROUGHTON
... 36 C8
Nether Cl LE15 ... 112 D8
Nethercote LE67 ... 121 D7
Nethercroft Dr LE65 ... 69 C2
Nether End
Gaddesby LE7 ... 105 B6
Great Dalby LE14 ... 82 B2
Nether Farm Cl LE17 ... 235 C4
Netherfield Cl LE9 ... 219 B6
Netherfield La DE72,
DE74 ... 17 F8
Netherfield Rd
Anstey LE7 ... 127 E7
Long Eaton NG10 ... 10 C4
Nether Field Way
LE3 ... 153 D1
NETHER HALL ... 130 F1
Netherhall La LE4 ... 129 B6
Netherhall Rd LE5 ... 130 D1
Nether Hall Sch LE5 ... 130 D1
Netherley Ct LE10 ... 197 D3
Netherley Rd LE10 ... 197 D3
NETHERSEAL ... 91 E7
Netherseal Rd DE12 ... 91 F4
Nether St
Belton-in-R LE15 ... 187 D7
Harby LE14 ... 12 A3
Netherwood Ind Est
CV9 ... 170 F1
Netton Cl LE18 ... 203 C8
Nevada Pk LE13 ... 59 B3
Nevanthon Rd LE3 ... 154 B5
Neville Cl LE12 ... 50 B4
Neville Day Cl PE9 ... 168 F5
Neville Dr
Coalville LE67 ... 72 A1
Markfield LE67 ... 125 D8
Neville Rd LE3 ... 154 B5
Neville Smith Cl LE9 ... 217 D7
NEVILL HOLT ... 228 D8
Nevill Holt Rd LE16 ... 228 F6
Nevis Cl NN17 ... 230 C1
Newall Cl LE17 ... 244 C7
Newark Cl LE12 ... 49 F3
Newarke Cl LE2 ... 259 A2
Newarke Houses Mus*
LE1 ... 259 A3
Newarke Point LE2 ... 259 A2
Newarke St LE1 ... 259 B3
Newarke The LE2 ... 259 A3
Newark Rd LE4 ... 129 E7
New Ashby Ct LE11 ... 51 B2
New Ashby Rd LE11 ... 51 B2
New Ave LE7 ... 79 A1
Newbery Ave NG10 ... 10 F6
New Bldgs LE10 ... 197 D1
NEWBOLD
Ashby-de-la-Zouch ... 47 E3
Somerby ... 134 E7
Newbold CE Prim Sch
LE67 ... 47 E2
Newbold Cl LE12 ... 77 D4
Newbold Ct CV13 ... 149 D8
Newbold Dr DE74 ... 17 B5
NEWBOLD HEATH ... 150 A7
Newbold La LE65 ... 47 E5
Newbold Rd
Barlestone CV13 ... 149 E7
Desford LE9 ... 151 A4
Kirkby Mallory LE9 ... 175 C7
Owston LE14, LE15 ... 134 F7
NEWBOLD VERDON ... 150 A5
Newbold Verdon Prim Sch
LE9 ... 150 A4
Newbon Cl LE11 ... 51 E4
New Bond St LE1 ... 259 B4
Newborough Cl CV9 ... 119 A2
Newboults La PE9 ... 143 C3
New Brickyard La
DE74 ... 18 D1
Newbridge High Sch
LE67 ... 96 D7
New Bridge Rd LE2 ... 179 B2
New Bridge St LE2 ... 154 E3
New Broadway LE67 ... 71 C1
Newbury Ave LE13 ... 59 A5
Newbury Cl LE18 ... 180 C1
Newby Cl LE8 ... 178 F1
Newby Gdns LE2 ... 181 D4
New Causeway NG13 ... 6 C2
New Cl
Leicester LE5 ... 155 D4
Swannington LE67 ... 71 A4
New College Leicester
LE3 ... 153 F7
New Coll Stamford
PE9 ... 143 E4
Newcomb Ct 2 PE9 ... 143 D3
Newcombe Rd LE3 ... 154 B2
Newcombe St LE16 ... 240 E2
New Cotts NG32 ... 15 D5
Newcroft Prim Sch
LE12 ... 50 C2
New Cross Rd PE9 ... 143 D4
New Field Rd LE15 ... 113 B3
Newfields DE12 ... 68 A4
New Fields Ave LE3 ... 154 A2
New Fields Sq LE3 ... 154 B1
New Forest Cl LE18 ... 203 D8
NEW FOUND POOL ... 154 C7
Newgate End LE18 ... 180 C2
Newgates 2 PE9 ... 143 E3
Newhall Rd DE11 ... 44 C5
Newham Cl LE4 ... 130 A5
Newham Rd PE9 ... 143 C5
Newhaven Rd LE5 ... 156 D3
New Henry St LE3 ... 259 A5
Newington St LE4 ... 129 B2
Newington Wlk LE4 ... 129 B2
NEW INN ... 184 C5
New Inn Cl LE9 ... 219 B5
New Inn La LE7 ... 184 C3
New King St LE11 ... 52 C3
New La LE12 ... 54 A4
Newlands Ave LE12 ... 50 C2
Newlands Cl DE11 ... 44 A2
Newlands Rd
Barwell LE9 ... 198 B7
Welford NN6 ... 256 E5
Newland St LE16 ... 251 E5
New Lount (Nature
Trail)* LE67 ... 47 D2
Newlyn Par LE5 ... 130 D1
Newmans Cl LE15 ... 166 D3
Newmarket St LE2 ... 180 B8
New Park Rd LE2 ... 179 E8
NEW PARKS ... 153 F7
New Parks Bvd LE3 ... 153 E7
New Parks Cres LE3 ... 154 A8
New Park St LE3 ... 154 D5
New Parks Way LE3 ... 153 E7
New Pingle St LE3 ... 259 A5
Newpool Bank LE2 ... 181 E4
Newport Ave LE13 ... 59 C4
Newport Lo LE13 ... 59 C4
Newport Pl LE1 ... 259 C3
Newport St LE3 ... 154 C7
Newquay Cl LE10 ... 197 E4
Newquay Dr LE3 ... 127 C1
New Rd
Appleby Magna DE12 ... 119 E7
Belton-in-R LE15 ... 187 C6
Burton Lazars LE14 ... 82 F6
Clipsham LE15 ... 89 D5
Collyweston PE9 ... 168 C2
Easton o t H PE9 ... 169 A5
Hinckley LE10 ... 216 A6
Illston on t H LE7 ... 183 E4
Kibworth Beauchamp
LE8 ... 224 B8
New Rd *continued*
Leicester LE1 ... 259 B4
Peggs Green LE67 ... 71 A8
Ryhall PE9 ... 116 E2
Staunton in t V NG13 ... 1 D3
Stoney Stanton LE9 ... 199 D2
Stretton LE15 ... 88 B7
Woodville DE11 ... 44 E2
New Romney Cl LE5 ... 156 E8
New Romney Cres
LE5 ... 156 E8
New Row
Ibstock LE67 ... 122 F8
Moira DE12 ... 68 A4
Willoughby-on-t-W LE12 ... 34 E7
Woolsthorpe by B NG32 ... 8 B1
Newry The LE2 ... 179 F5
NEW SAWLEY ... 10 B5
New St
Asfordby LE14 ... 57 F3
Barlestone CV13 ... 149 D8
Barrow-u-S LE12 ... 76 D7
Blaby LE8 ... 202 B8
Coalville LE67 ... 96 D8
Countesthorpe LE8 ... 202 F4
Donisthorpe DE12 ... 67 E1
Draycott DE72 ... 9 A7
Earl Shilton LE9 ... 198 E7
Hinckley LE10 ... 197 D1
Kegworth DE74 ... 18 E3
Leicester LE1 ... 259 B3
Leicester, Oadby LE2 ... 181 B6
Long Eaton NG10 ... 10 E8
Loughborough LE11 ... 52 B3
Lutterworth LE17 ... 244 C6
Measham DE12 ... 93 C6
Melton Mowbray LE13 ... 59 C3
Oakham LE15 ... 137 F6
Oakthorpe DE12 ... 93 A7
Queniborough LE7 ... 103 E5
Scalford LE14 ... 38 E5
Stamford PE9 ... 143 E4
Swadlincote DE11 ... 44 B2
New Star Rd LE4 ... 130 A4
NEWSTEAD ... 144 B4
Newstead Ave
Bushby LE7 ... 157 A4
Hinckley LE10 ... 215 D4
Leicester LE3 ... 128 C1
Wigston LE18 ... 180 C4
Newstead Mill PE9 ... 144 B4
Newstead Rd
Belmesthorpe PE9 ... 144 A8
Leicester LE2 ... 180 C8
Newstead Way LE11 ... 75 A6
NEW SWANNINGTON ... 71 D4
New Swannington Prim
Sch LE67 ... 71 C5
NEWTON ... 253 A1
NEWTON BURGOLAND
... 121 E7
Newton Burgoland Prim
Sch LE67 ... 121 E6
Newton Cl
Barrow-u-S LE12 ... 76 E8
Hartshill Green CV10 ... 194 B2
Loughborough LE11 ... 51 D6
Newton Ct CV23 ... 257 A8
Newton Dr LE4 ... 129 B8
NEWTON HARCOURT
... 204 D7
Newton La
Great Glen LE8 ... 205 A7
Newton CV23 ... 253 A3
Newton Regis CV9 ... 118 F2
Odstone CV13 ... 122 B5
Seckington B79 ... 118 B3
Wigston LE18 ... 180 E1
Newton Manor La
CV23 ... 257 A8
NEWTON-NETHERCOTE
... 121 C7
Newton Park Cl 2
DE11 ... 44 A7
Newton Rd
Clifton u D CV23 ... 257 A7
Heather LE67 ... 95 B1
Hinckley LE10 ... 214 E7
Odstone CV13 ... 122 C4
Swepstone LE67 ... 121 D8
NEWTON REGIS ... 118 D4
Newton Regis CE Prim
Sch B79 ... 118 E3
NEWTON UNTHANK ... 151 D6
Newton Way
Braybrooke LE16 ... 251 F6
Broughton Astley LE9 ... 219 A4
NEWTOWN ... 143 F2
New Town PE9 ... 169 A5
Newtown Cl LE8 ... 223 F8
Newtown Cres LE15 ... 189 A3
Newtown Grange Farm
Bsns Pk LE9 ... 151 E5
NEWTOWN LINFORD
... 126 D8
Newtown Linford La
LE6 ... 126 E5
Newtown Linford Prim
Sch LE6 ... 126 D8
Newtown Rd LE15 ... 188 F3
Newtown St LE1 ... 259 B2
New Tythe St NG10 ... 10 F7
New Walk Mus & Art
Gall* LE1 ... 259 C2
New Way Rd LE5 ... 155 D2
New Wharf LE2 ... 259 A3
New Wlk
Leicester LE1 ... 259 C2
New Wlk *continued*
Sapcote LE9 ... 217 D7
Shepshed LE12 ... 50 B4
NEW YORK ... 26 A7
New Zealand La LE7 ... 103 C6
Nicholas Dr LE6 ... 152 D8
Nichols St LE1 ... 259 C4
Nicklaus Rd LE4 ... 129 E5
Nicolson Rd LE11 ... 74 C8
Nidderdale Rd LE18 ... 180 F2
Nightingale Ave LE12 ... 30 B1
Nightingale Cl CV9 ... 170 E1
Nightingale Dr DE11 ... 44 F3
Nightingale Gdns
CV23 ... 252 C1
Nightingale Way
LE15 ... 138 B7
Nine Acres DE74 ... 18 C2
Nithsdale Ave LE16 ... 240 F2
Nithsdale Cres LE16 ... 240 F2
Nob Hill CV9 ... 120 A2
Noble Cl LE17 ... 244 C8
Noble St LE3 ... 154 D6
Nock Verges
Earl Shilton LE9 ... 176 A1
Stoney Stanton LE9 ... 199 D2
Noel Ave LE15 ... 137 E5
Noel St LE3 ... 154 D3
NO MANS HEATH ... 118 F6
No Man's Heath La
CV9 ... 119 A3
No Man's Heath Rd
DE12 ... 91 F3
Nook Cl
Ratby LE6 ... 126 C1
Shepshed LE12 ... 50 C2
Nook La LE15 ... 140 F5
Nooks Country Park The*
LE8 ... 204 D6
Nook St LE3 ... 154 B7
Nook The
Anstey LE7 ... 127 E6
Bitteswell LE17 ... 244 B8
Cosby LE9 ... 201 D2
Cottingham LE16 ... 229 D1
Croxton Kerrial NG32 ... 24 A7
Easton o t H PE9 ... 169 A5
Enderby LE19 ... 178 A3
Great Glen LE8 ... 205 A8
Markfield LE67 ... 98 D1
Sproxton LE14 ... 41 F5
Walcote LE17 ... 245 B4
Whetstone LE8 ... 201 F7
Whissendine LE15 ... 84 F1
Wymeswold LE12 ... 33 C3
Noon Ct LE4 ... 129 A2
Norbury Ave LE4 ... 129 C1
Norbury Cl LE16 ... 240 D3
Norfolk Cl LE10 ... 215 D4
Norfolk Dr LE13 ... 82 D8
Norfolk Ho 4 LE3 ... 154 D5
Norfolk Rd
Desford LE9 ... 151 B2
Long Eaton NG10 ... 10 F8
Wigston LE18 ... 179 F3
Norfolk Sq PE9 ... 143 D4
Norfolk St LE3 ... 154 D5
Norfolk Wlk LE3 ... 154 D5
Norman Ct
Kegworth DE74 ... 18 D1
Leicester, Oadby LE2 ... 181 D4
Norman Dagley Cl
LE9 ... 198 E7
Normandy Cl LE3 ... 153 C7
Normandy Way LE10 ... 197 A3
Norman Rd LE4 ... 129 E8
Norman St LE3 ... 154 D4
NORMANTON
3 C6
140 D1
Normanton Church Mus*
LE15 ... 140 C1
Normanton Dr
Loughborough LE11 ... 52 B6
Oakham LE15 ... 138 B7
Normanton Gdns*
LE15 ... 140 D2
Normanton Gr LE9 ... 177 A3
Normanton La
Bottesford NG13 ... 3 B4
Heather LE67 ... 95 B3
Stanford on S LE12 ... 31 B1
NORMANTON LE HEATH
... 94 E6
NORMANTON ON SOAR
... 30 D3
Normanton on Soar Prim
Sch LE12 ... 30 D3
Normanton Park Rd
Empingham LE15 ... 141 A4
Normanton LE15 ... 140 E2
Normanton Rd
Edith Weston LE15 ... 166 B8
Leicester LE5 ... 155 D4
Packington LE65 ... 69 C1
NORMANTON THURVILLE
... 176 D1
Norman Way LE13 ... 59 C3
Norris Cl LE4 ... 128 A3
NORRIS HILL ... 68 A6
Norris Hill DE12 ... 68 B6
Northage Cl LE12 ... 76 B4
Northampton Rd
Great Oxendon LE16 ... 250 F1
Market Harborough
LE16 ... 240 F3
Welford NN6 ... 256 E4
Northampton Sq LE1 ... 259 C3
Northampton St LE1 ... 259 C3
North Ave
Coalville LE67 ... 96 D7
Leicester LE2 ... 155 C2
Northbank LE16 ... 240 E3
North Bridge Pl LE3 ... 259 A5
North Brook Cl LE15 ... 88 A1
North Cl
Blackfordby DE11 ... 68 B8
Hinckley LE10 ... 215 E6
Northcote Rd LE2 ... 180 B8
Northcote St NG10 ... 10 E7
Northcote Wlk CV9 ... 170 D2
North Cres NG13 ... 3 A2
Northdene Rd LE2 ... 180 B5
Northdown Dr LE4 ... 129 E6
North Dr LE5 ... 156 A8
NORTH END ... 76 D3
North End LE16 ... 209 D6
North End Cl LE2 ... 179 F6
Northern's Cl NG33 ... 65 B8
NORTH EVINGTON ... 155 E6
Northfield LE67 ... 124 A7
Northfield Ave
Birstall LE4 ... 129 B8
Long Eaton NG10 ... 10 B4
Wigston LE18 ... 180 B4
Northfield Cl LE13 ... 59 C4
Northfield Dr LE67 ... 97 B8
Northfield House Prim
Sch LE4 ... 129 E1
Northfield Rd
Blaby LE8 ... 179 B1
Hinckley LE10 ... 215 C7
Leicester LE4 ... 129 E1
Northfields LE65 ... 69 B8
NORTHFIELDS ... 129 E1
Northfields NG10 ... 10 B4
NORTHFIELDS ... 143 E4
Northfields LE7 ... 103 B4
Northfields Ct PE9 ... 143 E4
Northfold Rd LE2 ... 180 C6
Northgate LE15 ... 137 F6
Northgates LE1 ... 259 A4
Northgate St LE3 ... 259 A5
North Hall Dr LE7 ... 105 B7
North Ho LE2 ... 155 B2
Northill Cl LE12 ... 77 E3
NORTH KILWORTH ... 246 F3
North La LE16 ... 224 D1
North Lea LE16 ... 227 B3
Northleigh Gr LE16 ... 240 D4
Northleigh Way LE9 ... 198 F7
NORTH LUFFENHAM
... 166 D4
North Luffenham Rd
North Luffenham
LE15 ... 166 B2
South Luffenham LE15 ... 166 D1
North Meml Homes
LE2 ... 181 B6
North Rd
Clifton u D CV23 ... 257 A6
Long Eaton NG10 ... 10 C6
Loughborough LE11 ... 52 B6
South Kilworth LE17 ... 246 D1
North St E LE15 ... 189 B4
North St W LE15 ... 189 A4
North St
Asfordby Valley LE14 ... 58 B3
Ashby-de-la-Z LE65 ... 69 B6
Barrow-u-S LE12 ... 76 D8
Leicester, Oadby LE2 ... 181 A6
Melbourne DE73 ... 26 A7
Melton Mowbray LE13 ... 59 C4
Rothley LE7 ... 101 E6
Stamford PE9 ... 143 D3
Swadlincote DE11 ... 44 B5
Swinford LE17 ... 254 B4
Syston LE7 ... 103 A4
Whitwick LE67 ... 71 E5
Wigston LE18 ... 180 D3
Northumberland Ave
Leicester LE4 ... 129 C2
Market Bosworth CV13 ... 148 E2
Stamford PE9 ... 143 C4
Northumberland Rd
LE18 ... 179 F3
Northumberland St
LE1 ... 259 A5
North View Cl LE14 ... 58 B3
North Warwickshire &
Hinckley Coll LE10 ... 215 F8
North Way LE7 ... 157 F4
Northwick Rd PE9 ... 167 F5
NORTH WITHAM ... 65 B8
North Witham Rd
NG33 ... 65 B4
North Wlk DE12 ... 93 D7
Northwood Dr LE12 ... 50 C6
NORTON-JUXTA-
TWYCROSS ... 120 B3
Norton La
Austrey CV9 ... 119 D1
Gaulby LE7 ... 183 C6
Orton-on-t-H CV9 ... 145 D6
Norton Rd LE9 ... 198 C8
Norton St
Leicester LE1 ... 259 B2
Uppingham LE15 ... 189 B4
Norwich Cl
Nuneaton CV11 ... 214 A8
Shepshed LE12 ... 50 A2
Norwich Rd LE4 ... 128 E3
Norwood Cl LE10 ... 197 E3
Norwood Rd LE5 ... 155 E3
NOSELEY ... 184 F2
Noseley Rd LE7 ... 184 A3

Notley Ct LE9 . . . . 198 C8
Notley Manor Dr LE9 . . . 198 C8
Nottingham East Midlands
Int Airport DE74 . . . . 28 C8
Nottingham La LE14 . . . . . 35 C5
Nottingham Rd
  Ab Kettleby LE14 . . . . 37 C4
  Ashby-de-la-Z LE65 . . . . . 69 D7
  Ashby-de-la-Z, Lount
    LE65 . . . . 46 F1
  Barrow-u-S LE12 . . . . 53 E3
  Bottesford NG13 . . . . 2 F2
  Breedon on t H DE73 . . . . 26 D1
  Kegworth DE74 . . . . 18 D2
  Leicester LE5 . . . . 155 D6
  Long Eaton NG10 . . . . 10 E8
  Loughborough LE11,
    LE12 . . . . 52 D6
  Melton Mowbray LE13 . . . 59 B5
  Peggs Green LE67 . . . . . . 71 A8
  Worthington LE65 . . . . . . 47 C5
Nottingham Road Ind Est
  LE65 . . . . 69 D8
Nottingham St LE13 . . . . 59 C3
Nowell Cl LE2 . . . . 179 D1
Nuffield Hospi The
  LE5 . . . . 156 B8
Nuffield Rd LE10 . . . . . . 214 E7
Nugent St LE3 . . . . 154 D6
NUNEATON 214 A4
Nuneaton La CV13 . . . . . 195 F2
Nuneaton Rd
  Atherstone CV9,
    CV10 . . . . 194 B4
  Hartshill Green CV10 . . . 194 B2
Nunneley Way LE16 . . . . 240 F5
Nursery Cl
  Empingham LE15 . . . . . . 141 A4
  Queniborough LE7 . . . . . 103 E5
  Shepshed LE12 . . . . 50 C6
  Swadlincote DE11 . . . . . . 44 A6
  Thurlaston LE9 . . . . 177 A2
  Thurmaston LE4 . . . . 129 D6
Nursery End
  Loughborough LE11 . . . . . 74 D8
  Market Harborough
    LE16 . . . . 240 C2
Nursery Gdns
  Coalville LE67 . . . . 71 E1
  Earl Shilton LE9 . . . . . . 198 D7
Nursery Gr LE12 . . . . 76 E8
Nursery Hollow LE2 . . . . 179 A1
Nursery La
  Hanwell LE14 . . . . 37 D4
  Knipton NG32 . . . . 14 E3
  Quorn (Quorndon) LE12 . . 76 A6
Nursery Rd LE5 . . . . 156 D7
Nurses La LE14 . . . . 62 E2
Nutfield Rd LE3 . . . . 154 C3
Nuthall Gr LE2 . . . . 179 B4
Nutkin Cl LE11 . . . . 51 F2
Nutt's La LE10 . . . . 215 A7

O

OADBY 181 C7
Oadby Ct LE2 . . . . 180 F6
Oadby Hill Dr LE2 . . . . . 180 F6
Oadby Ind Est LE2 . . . . . 180 F5
Oadby Rd LE18 . . . . 180 E3
Oak Ave LE17 . . . . 218 E1
Oakberry Rd LE17 . . . . . 244 D8
Oakberry Road Ind Est
  LE17 . . . . 244 D8
Oak Bsns Ctr The LE12 . . 77 D3
Oak Cl
  Coalville LE67 . . . . 97 A8
  Hinckley LE10 . . . . 215 E5
  Loughborough LE11 . . . . . 75 A6
  Market Harborough
    LE16 . . . . 240 F4
  Measham DE12 . . . . 93 C5
  Thurlaston LE9 . . . . 177 A3
  Uppingham LE15 . . . . . . 189 A5
Oak Cres
  Braunstone Town LE3 . . . 153 C2
Oakcroft Ave LE9 . . . . . . 152 E5
Oakdale Cl LE3 . . . . 153 C6
Oakdale Rd LE9 . . . . 198 D7
Oakdene Rd LE2 . . . . 180 A6
Oak Dr
  Ibstock LE67 . . . . 95 E1
  Syston LE7 . . . . 103 B2
Oakenshaw Cl LE4 . . . . . 128 E5
Oakfield LE15 . . . . 138 A8
Oakfield Ave
  Birstall LE4 . . . . 128 F7
  Glenfield LE3 . . . . 127 D2
  Lutterworth LE17 . . . . . . 244 B6
  Markfield LE67 . . . . 125 D8
Oakfield Cl LE8 . . . . 182 B1
Oakfield Cres LE8 . . . . . . 202 C6
Oakfield Rd LE2 . . . . 155 C8
Oak Gn LE8 . . . . 125 E6
OAKHAM 138 B8
Oakham Castle*
  LE15 . . . . 138 A6
Oakham CE Prim Sch
  LE15 . . . . 138 A7
Oakham Cl LE11 . . . . 51 E6
Oakham Dr LE67 . . . . 72 C2
Oakham Gr LE65 . . . . 69 A7
Oakham Rd
  Ashwell LE15 . . . . 111 B7
  Braunston-in-R LE15 . . . . 137 B3

Oakham Rd continued
  Exton LE15 . . . . 113 A2
  Greetham LE15 . . . . 88 A1
  Knossington LE15 . . . . . . 136 A6
  Langham LE15 . . . . 110 D2
  Leesthorpe LE14 . . . . 83 D2
  Oakham LE15 . . . . 138 C8
  Owston LE7, LE15 . . . . . . 161 C8
  Preston LE15 . . . . 164 C3
  Somerby LE14 . . . . 108 D1
  Whissendine LE15 . . . . . . 84 F1
Oakham Sch (Old Sch)
  LE15 . . . . 138 A6
Oakham Sta LE15 . . . . . . 137 F7
Oakhurst Ct LE11 . . . . . . 51 C4
Oak La LE18 . . . . 221 F5
Oakland Ave
  Leicester LE4 . . . . 129 C4
  Long Eaton NG10 . . . . . . 10 C5
Oakland Rd LE2 . . . . 155 A1
Oaklands Ave LE11 . . . . . 51 F2
Oaklands Pk [4] LE6 . . . . 240 F2
Oaklands Sch LE6 . . . . . . 156 B4
Oaklands Way DE73 . . . . . 26 B8
Oakland Terr NG10 . . . . . 10 C5
Oakleigh Ave LE2 . . . . . . 179 E1
Oakley Ave LE12 . . . . 50 B5
Oakley Cl LE12 . . . . 50 B5
Oakley Dr
  Long Whatton LE12 . . . . . 29 D2
  Loughborough LE11 . . . . . 51 F1
Oakley Mews LE16 . . . . . 240 D3
Oakley Rd
  Cottesmore LE15 . . . . 87 E2
  Leicester LE5 . . . . 155 D7
  Shepshed LE12 . . . . 50 B5
Oakley's Rd W NG10 . . . . 10 D6
Oakmeadow LE3 . . . . 153 B7
Oakmeadow Way LE2 . . . 126 E2
Oakpool Gdns LE2 . . . . . 179 D3
Oak Rd
  Desford LE9 . . . . 151 A3
  Littlethorpe LE19 . . . . . . 201 C6
  Melton Mowbray LE13 . . . 59 C3
  Stamford PE9 . . . . 142 F4
Oakridge Cl LE5 . . . . 130 C3
Oakridge Pk DE74 . . . . . . 17 A5
Oaks Ct LE19 . . . . 201 A8
Oaks Dr
  Blaby LE8 . . . . 202 C7
  Newbold Verdon LE9 . . . . 150 C4
Oakside Cl LE5 . . . . 156 C4
Oakside Cres LE5 . . . . . . 156 C5
OAKS IN CHARNWOOD
  . . . . 73 A6
Oaks Ind Est
  Loughborough LE11 . . . . . 52 A6
  Lutterworth LE17 . . . . . . 244 D7
  Ravenstone LE67 . . . . 71 A1
Oaks Ind Est The
  . . . . 201 A7
Oak Spinney Pk LE3 . . . . 153 B4
Oaks Rd
  Great Glen LE8 . . . . 205 C8
  Whitwick LE67 . . . . 72 C5
Oak St
  Leicester LE5 . . . . 155 C7
  Swadlincote DE11 . . . . . . 44 A2
Oaks Way
  Earl Shilton LE9 . . . . . . 198 E8
  Leicester, Oadby LE2 . . . 180 F8
OAKTHORPE 93 B7
Oakthorpe Ave LE3 . . . . . 154 B4
Oakthorpe Prim Sch
  DE12 . . . . 93 A7
Oaktree Cl
  Groby LE6 . . . . 126 E3
  Hamilton LE5 . . . . 130 C2
  Kibworth Beauchamp
    LE8 . . . . 206 B1
Oak Tree Rd LE67 . . . . . . 96 B7
Oak Way LE14 . . . . 80 D8
Oakwood Ave LE18 . . . . . 180 D4
Oakwood Cl
  Leicester Forest East
    LE3 . . . . 152 F2
  Thornton LE67 . . . . 124 F3
Oakwood Dr LE11 . . . . . . 51 B1
Oakwood Rd LE4 . . . . . . 128 D1
Oasis The LE3 . . . . 153 B8
Oban Cl PE9 . . . . 143 A4
Oban Rd LE10 . . . . 215 A7
Oban St LE3 . . . . 154 C7
Oberon Cl CV11 . . . . 214 A1
Occupation La
  Willoughby-on-t-W
    LE12 . . . . 34 E5
  Woodville DE11 . . . . 44 D1
Occupation Rd
  Middleton LE16 . . . . 229 B2
  Nailstone CV13 . . . . 123 B3
  Swadlincote DE11 . . . . . . 67 C8
Ocean Cl LE5 . . . . 156 C7
Ocean Rd LE5 . . . . 156 C7
Octopus Bsns Pk
  LE15 . . . . 166 F2
Odam Cl LE3 . . . . 153 F2
Oddfellows Row DE11 . . . 93 C5
Odeon Arc LE1 . . . . 259 B4
ODSTONE 122 D4
Odstone Dr LE10 . . . . . . 214 F8
Odstone La LE67 . . . . 121 F6
Odstone Rd CV13 . . . . . . 122 D2
Office Village The
  LE4 . . . . 52 B6
Offramville LE14 . . . . . . 129 F6
Ogwen Cl LE5 . . . . 156 D6

Okehampton Ave LE5 . . . 155 F3
Old Ashby Rd LE11 . . . . . 51 B2
Old Barn Pas [8] PE9 . . . 143 D2
Old Barn Wlk LE4 . . . . . 128 C3
Old Braunstone The
  LE3 . . . . 154 C2
Old Bridwell LE13 . . . . . . 59 D6
Old Dairy Rd CV10 . . . . . 194 A1
Oldbury View CV10 . . . . 194 B1
Old Chapel Wlk LE17 . . . 232 E6
Old Charity Farm LE12 . . 156 E1
Old Church St LE2 . . . . . 179 C7
Old City Of Dan LE67 . . . 71 F4
Old Coach Rd The
  LE17 . . . . 219 D2
Old Coffee Mills The [6]
  LE16 . . . . 240 F2
Old Dairy The LE13 . . . . . 59 C4
Old Dairy Yd LE15 . . . . . 113 B3
OLD DALBY 35 E4
Old Dalby CE Prim Sch
  LE14 . . . . 35 E4
Old Dalby La LE14 . . . . . 36 C6
Old Dalby Trad Est
  LE14 . . . . 36 A5
Old End DE12 . . . . 92 F1
Old Engine Yd The
  LE12 . . . . 32 E5
Oldershaw Ave DE74 . . . . 18 C2
Oldershaw Rd LE12 . . . . . 31 F8
Olders Valley DE11 . . . . . 44 E4
Old Field Cl LE8 . . . . 202 C4
Oldfield Dr DE11 . . . . . . 44 C5
Oldfield La LE17 . . . . 101 F8
Old Forge Cl LE12 . . . . . . 30 A1
Old Forge La NG13 . . . . . . 5 C5
Old Forge Rd
  Ashby Magna LE17 . . . . . 220 A2
  Fenny Drayton CV13 . . . . 195 A6
Old Garden Cl LE8 . . . . . 202 B7
Old Gate Rd LE7 . . . . 78 E7
Old Gn LE16 . . . . 227 F6
Old Granary The LE7 . . . . 160 A7
Old Hall Cl
  Groby LE6 . . . . 126 F3
  Thurmaston LE4 . . . . 129 E8
Old Hall La LE17 . . . . 118 D3
Old Hall Gdns DE11 . . . . 44 A2
Old Hall La LE16 . . . . 239 F3
Old Hill The NG32 . . . . . . 14 F3
Old Holly La CV9 . . . . . . 170 C3
Old Holt Rd LE16 . . . . . . 227 C1
OLD INGARSBY
  . . . . 158 B7
Old La The NG13 . . . . 6 C2
Old Manor Farm LE8 . . . . 20 C3
Old Mill Cl LE9 . . . . 218 F5
Old Mill La LE1 . . . . 259 A5
Old Mill Prim Sch
  LE9 . . . . 218 F6
Old Mill Rd LE9 . . . . 218 F5
Old Mill The LE12 . . . . . . 30 B3
Old Milton St LE1 . . . . . 259 C4
Old Nurseries The
  LE67 . . . . 95 F8
Old Park Cl NG11 . . . . . . 18 F6
Old Parsonage La
  LE12 . . . . 32 C1
Old Post La NG33 . . . . . . 65 B8
Old Rectory Camping &
  Cvn Pk The LE15 . . . . . 187 C7
Old Rectory Cl
  Broughton Astley LE9 . . . 218 F6
  Churchover CV23 . . . . . . 252 C6
Old Rectory Mus*
  LE11 . . . . 52 B4
Old School Cl
  Ellistown LE67 . . . . 96 E2
  North Luffenham LE15 . . . 166 D3
  Walton LE17 . . . . 236 A2
Old School Ct [6] LE9 . . . 198 F8
Old School La LE67 . . . . . 124 B4
Old School Mews
  Aston-on-T DE72 . . . . . . 16 B8
  Market Harborough
    LE16 . . . . 240 E3
  Uppingham LE15 . . . . . . 189 B3
Old School Wlk LE16 . . . 225 D7
Old School Yd LE9 . . . . . 217 D7
Old Stableyard The
  LE16 . . . . 225 D6
Old Station Cl
  Coalville LE67 . . . . 71 D1
  Shepshed LE12 . . . . 50 B2
Old Station Dr LE14 . . . . 61 C3
Old Station Rd LE7 . . . . . 103 A3
Old Station Yd NG13 . . . . 3 C3
Old Surgery The LE7 . . . . 96 D6
Old Tannery Dr [1]
  LE14 . . . . 77 C3
Old Vicarage Gdns
  LE14 . . . . 37 D3
Old Way LE12 . . . . 30 A1
Old Woodyard The
  LE12 . . . . 30 A1
Oliver Cl LE7 . . . . 102 F2
Oliver Ct LE2 . . . . 155 D2
Oliver Rd
  Leicester LE4 . . . . 129 D2
  Loughborough LE11 . . . . . 52 B2
Oliver St LE2 . . . . 179 E8
Olphin St LE4 . . . . 155 A8
Olympic Cl LE4 . . . . 128 A3
One Barrow La LE12 . . . . 72 E7
Onslow St [3] LE2 . . . . . . 155 C4
Ontario Cl LE1 . . . . 259 C5

Orange Hill LE17 . . . . . . 244 D5
Orange St
  Uppingham LE15 . . . . . . 189 B4
  Wigston LE18 . . . . 202 F8
Orchard Ave
  Castle Donington DE74 . . 17 A3
  Glen Parva LE2 . . . . 179 B3
Orchard Bank LE67 . . . . . 235 F8
Orchard CE Prim Sch
  LE9 . . . . 218 D7
Orchard Cl
  Austrey CV9 . . . . 119 A2
  Barkestone-le-V NG13 . . . 6 B2
  Barlestone CV13 . . . . 149 D8
  Breaston DE72 . . . . 9 F8
  Cosby LE9 . . . . 201 D3
  Diseworth DE74 . . . . 28 C5
  East Leake LE12 . . . . 31 D8
  Egleton LE15 . . . . 138 C3
  Gilmorton LE17 . . . . 235 C4
  Glaston LE15 . . . . 190 B5
  Hinckley LE10 . . . . 216 A5
  Leicester, Oadby LE2 . . . 181 A4
  Melbourne DE73 . . . . 26 A7
  Osgathorpe LE12 . . . . . . 48 C4
  Ravenstone LE67 . . . . 70 F2
  Shepshed LE12 . . . . 50 B3
  Stamford PE9 . . . . 143 D3
  Sutton Bonington LE12 . . 30 C5
  Uppingham LE15 . . . . . . 190 B5
  Witherley CV9 . . . . 194 B8
Orchard Com Prim Sch
  DE74 . . . . 17 A3
Orchard Est LE2 . . . . 75 F6
Orchard Gdns LE4 . . . . . 129 F6
Orchard Ho LE1 . . . . 259 B5
Orchard La
  Countesthorpe LE8 . . . . . 202 F3
  Great Glen LE8 . . . . 205 B7
  Gretton NN17 . . . . 213 C1
Orchard Pk Mobile Home
  Pk LE3 . . . . 103 B4
Orchard Rd
  Birstall LE4 . . . . 129 B7
  Broughton Astley LE9 . . . 218 E7
  Langham LE15 . . . . 110 C3
  Lutterworth LE17 . . . . . . 244 B5
  Stamford PE9 . . . . 143 D3
  Willoughby Waterleys
    LE8 . . . . 220 C5
Orchards Dr LE18 . . . . . . 180 B2
Orchardson Ave LE4 . . . . 155 B8
Orchard St
  Fleckney LE8 . . . . 222 F7
  Hinckley LE10 . . . . 215 E8
  Ibstock LE67 . . . . 95 F1
  Leicester LE1 . . . . 259 B5
  Long Eaton NG10 . . . . . . 10 E7
  Loughborough LE11 . . . . . 52 A4
  Market Harborough
    LE16 . . . . 240 E4
Orchards The
  Leicester LE5 . . . . 156 E8
  Newton CV23 . . . . 252 F1
  Thornton LE67 . . . . 124 F4
Orchard Terr NN6 . . . . . . 256 E6
Orchard The
  Groby LE6 . . . . 126 E3
  Lyndon LE15 . . . . 165 D5
  Seagrave LE12 . . . . 77 F8
  Sibbertoft LE16 . . . . 249 A2
  Swadlincote DE11 . . . . . . 44 D4
Orchard View LE19 . . . . . 199 E2
Orchard View LE12 . . . . . 101 E3
Orchard Way
  Easton o t H PE9 . . . . . . 168 F6
  Measham DE12 . . . . 93 C5
  Syston LE7 . . . . 103 C3
  Wymeswold LE12 . . . . . . 33 D4
Orchard Wlk LE17 . . . . . 233 B4
Orchid Cl
  Hamilton LE5 . . . . 130 C2
  Melton Mowbray LE13 . . . 82 A8
  Mountsorrel LE12 . . . . . . 76 F2
  Narborough LE19 . . . . . . 178 A1
Orchid Pl LE9 . . . . 219 B4
Oriel Dr LE7 . . . . 103 C3
Orkney Cl LE10 . . . . 197 C1
Orkney Way LE8 . . . . 202 F3
Orlando Rd LE2 . . . . 155 B2
Orly Ave DE74 . . . . 17 A2
Orme Cl LE4 . . . . 128 A3
Ormen Gn LE3 . . . . 153 D6
Ormes La CV9 . . . . 171 B4
Ormond Cl LE2 . . . . 198 A4
Oronsay Ho LE4 . . . . 128 B3
Oronsay Rd LE4 . . . . 128 B3
Orpine Rd LE5 . . . . 130 B3
Orsett Cl LE5 . . . . 156 D3
Orson Dr LE18 . . . . 180 B3
Orson St LE5 . . . . 155 D5
ORSTON 2 A6
Orston La NG13 . . . . 2 E4
Orston Prim Sch NG13 . . . 2 A7
Orton Cl LE7 . . . . 78 F1
Orton Hill CV9 . . . . 145 E8
Orton La
  Austrey CV9 . . . . 145 A8
  Norton-J-T CV9 . . . . 120 A2
  Orton-on-t-H CV9 . . . . . 145 C3
  Orton-on-t-H CV9 . . . . . 145 C1
  Sheepy Magna CV9 . . . . . 146 A8
  Twycross CV9 . . . . 146 B6
ORTON-ON-THE-HILL
  . . . . 145 D4
Orton Rd
  Earl Shilton LE9 . . . . . . 198 F8
  Leicester LE4 . . . . 128 F3
Ortons Ind Est LE67 . . . . 71 D1

Orwell Cl
  Clifton u D CV23 . . . . . . 257 A5
  Loughborough LE11 . . . . . 51 D6
Orwell Dr LE4 . . . . 128 A4
OSBASTON 149 D5
Osbaston Cl LE10 . . . . . . 197 F3
OSBASTON HOLLOW
  . . . . 123 B1
Osbaston La CV13 . . . . . . 149 D5
Osborne Rd
  Leicester LE5 . . . . 155 D5
  Loughborough LE11 . . . . . 51 C6
Osbourne Ct LE8 . . . . . . 201 F8
OSGATHORPE 48 D4
Osiers Business Pk The
  LE19 . . . . 178 E6
Osiers The
  Braunstone Town LE3 . . . 178 F7
  Kegworth DE74 . . . . 18 E2
  Loughborough LE11 . . . . . 75 A7
  Mountsorrel LE12 . . . . . . 76 C1
Osmaston Cl NG10 . . . . . . 9 F5
Osmaston Rd LE5 . . . . . . 155 C4
Osprey Cl LE3 . . . . 218 F7
Osprey Rd LE3 . . . . 128 A6
Osterley Cl LE11 . . . . 51 C4
Ostler La LE14 . . . . 57 D7
Oswin Rd LE3 . . . . 153 E5
Ottawa Rd LE1 . . . . 259 C4
Otter La LE2 . . . . 76 F2
Otter Way LE8 . . . . 201 F5
Oundle Cl LE65 . . . . 69 A8
Our Lady's Convent Sch
  LE11 . . . . 52 B2
Outfields Dr LE7 . . . . . . 100 F2
Outlands Dr LE10 . . . . . . 197 A2
Outram Dr DE11 . . . . 44 D4
Outwood Cl LE3 . . . . 153 D5
OUTWOODS 47 E1
Outwoods Ave LE11 . . . . 51 F1
Outwoods Dr LE11 . . . . . 51 F1
Outwoods Edge Prim Sch
  LE11 . . . . 75 A7
Outwoods La LE67 . . . . . 70 E8
Out Woods Nature
  Reserve* LE11 . . . . 74 C5
Outwoods Nature Trail
  The* LE11 . . . . 74 C5
Outwoods Rd LE11 . . . . . 74 F8
Outwoods The LE10 . . . . 215 F8
Oval Cl LE15 . . . . 166 D4
Oval The
  Coalville LE67 . . . . 97 A7
  Leicester LE1 . . . . 259 C2
  Leicester, Oadby LE2 . . . 180 F4
  Market Harborough
    LE16 . . . . 240 E4
  Nailstone CV13 . . . . 123 B3
  Stoney Stanton LE9 . . . . 199 E2
  Wigston LE18 . . . . 75 A3
Overbrook Grange
  CV11 . . . . 196 A1
Overdale Ave LE4 . . . . . . 127 B3
Overdale Cl
  Anstey LE7 . . . . 127 B2
  Long Eaton NG10 . . . . . . 10 A6
  Market Harborough
    LE16 . . . . 241 A3
Overdale Inf Sch LE2 . . . 180 C6
Overdale Jun Sch
  LE2 . . . . 180 C7
Overdale Rd
  Leicester LE2 . . . . 180 C7
  Thurmaston LE4 . . . . 129 F6
Overfield Ave LE16 . . . . . 240 F5
Overfield Cl
  Narborough LE19 . . . . . . 201 A7
  Wigston LE18 . . . . 152 D8
Overfield Wlk LE6 . . . . . 126 D1
Overing Cl LE4 . . . . 129 A3
Overpark Ave LE3 . . . . . . 154 A3
OVERSEAL 67 A3
Overseal Prim Sch
  DE12 . . . . 67 B4
Overseal Rd LE3 . . . . 153 E8
Overton Cl LE67 . . . . 70 C7
Overton Rd
  Ibstock LE67 . . . . 122 F7
  Leicester LE5 . . . . 155 D7
Owen Ave NG10 . . . . 10 F6
Owen Cl
  Braunstone Town
    LE3 . . . . 153 D1
  Leicester LE5 . . . . 129 E5
Owen Cres LE13 . . . . 59 D4
Owen Dr LE13 . . . . 59 D4
Owen St LE67 . . . . 71 C1
OWSTON 135 E4
Owston Dr LE18 . . . . 180 B3
Owston Rd
  Knossington LE15 . . . . . . 135 F5
  Somerby LE14 . . . . 108 C1
Owston Wood Rd
  LE15 . . . . 135 E5
Oxbow Cl LE13 . . . . 59 A2
Oxburgh Cl LE11 . . . . 51 D6
Oxendon Hall LE16 . . . . . 250 E3
Oxendon Rd
  Braybrooke LE16 . . . . . . 251 D5
  Clipston LE16 . . . . 250 B1
  East Farndon LE16 . . . . . 250 B5
  Great Oxendon LE16 . . . . 251 A1
Oxendon St LE2 . . . . 155 B5
Oxendon Wlk [8] LE2 . . . 155 B5
Oxey Cross Rds LE7 . . . . 161 B3

Oxford Ave LE2..........155 B3
Oxford Ct
  Leicester LE1..........259 B2
  Syston LE7..........103 C4
Oxford Dr
  Melton Mowbray LE13....82 D8
  Wigston LE18..........179 F2
Oxford Rd
  Desford LE9..........151 A3
  Leicester LE2..........155 B2
  Stamford PE9..........143 C5
Oxford St
  Barwell LE9..........198 B7
  Coalville LE67..........71 E1
  Earl Shilton LE9..........198 F8
  Leicester LE1..........259 B2
  Long Eaton NG10..........10 D8
  Loughborough LE11..........51 F4
  Shepshed LE12..........50 B2
  Swadlincote DE11..........44 A1
  Syston LE7..........103 C3
Oxley Cl LE2..........50 A3
Oxley Prim Sch LE12......50 A3
Oxon Way LE5..........156 A6
Oxted Rise LE2..........181 A3
Ozier Holt NG10..........10 C6

P

Packer Ave LE3..........153 B4
Packe St LE11..........52 A4
Packe Terr LE8..........205 B8
Packhorse Dr LE9..........178 D2
Packhorse Gn LE2..........179 D3
Pack Horse La LE11..........52 B3
Packhorse Rd LE9..........179 D3
Pack Horse Rd DE73......26 B8
PACKINGTON..........69 C2
Packington CE Prim Sch
  LE65..........69 B2
Packington Hill DE74....18 C2
Packington Nook La
  LE65..........69 A4
Packman Gn LE8..........202 F3
Packwood Rd LE4..........128 E3
Paddock Cl
  Castle Donington DE74....16 F3
  Countesthorpe LE8..........202 E4
  Leicester, Oadby LE2....180 F6
  Melton Mowbray LE13....59 D1
  Quorn (Quorndon) LE12...76 B5
  Rothley LE7..........101 E5
  Whissendine LE15..........85 A1
Paddock Ct LE16..........240 E3
Paddock La LE18..........228 D8
Paddock St LE18..........180 D2
Paddocks The
  Bottesford NG13..........3 A2
  Carlby PE9..........117 C8
  Littlethorpe LE19..........201 D7
  Queniborough LE7..........104 A5
  Sedgebrook NG32..........8 F8
  Sutton Bonington LE12...30 B6
  Tinwell PE9..........142 F1
  Waltham on t W LE14....40 A7
  Willoughby Waterleys
  LE8..........220 C5
Paddocks View NG10......10 B8
Paddock The
  Allington NG32..........4 F5
  Claybrooke Magna
  LE17..........232 E6
  Kibworth Beauchamp
  LE8..........224 A8
  Markfield LE67..........98 E1
  Newbold Verdon LE9.....150 A4
  Newton CV23..........253 A1
  Shepshed LE12..........50 B4
  Stamford PE9..........143 C3
Paddock View
  Skillington NG33..........43 B8
  Syston LE7..........102 F3
Paddock Way LE10.......214 F6
Paddy's La LE14..........35 A1
Padgate Cl LE7..........156 F6
Padstow Rd LE4..........129 E3
Padwell La LE7..........157 A4
Page Cl LE17..........244 C8
Page La DE74..........28 C5
Paget Ave LE4..........129 B7
Paget Ct LE8..........224 A8
Paget Rd
  Heather LE67..........95 F3
  Leicester LE3..........154 D6
  Lubenham LE16..........239 E3
Paget's End LE14..........20 D4
Paget St
  Kibworth Beauchamp
  LE8..........224 A8
  Leicester LE2..........179 C6
  Loughborough LE11..........51 F4
Paigle Rd LE2..........179 C6
PAILTON..........242 A1
Painter St LE1..........155 A8
Palace Hill LE7..........158 C4
Palfreyman La LE2.......181 A4
Palissy Cl DE11..........44 D4
Pall Mall LE13..........59 E5
Palmer Ave LE11..........51 F5
Palmer Dr LE17..........244 C5
Palmer Rd LE7..........197 B2
Palmers La LE17..........185 C3
Palmer St LE4..........129 A3
Palmerston Bvd LE2....180 C6
Palmerston Cl LE8.......223 F8
Palmerston Dr DE73......26 B7
Palmerston Rd LE13....159 A6
Palmerston Way LE2....180 D6
Palms Pk LE11..........51 D5
Pamela Pl LE4..........128 E4
Pankhurst Rd LE4.......128 B6
Pantain Rd LE11..........51 F1
Paper Mill Cl LE7........127 D6
Parade The
  Glen Parva LE2..........179 A2
  D Hinckley LE10........215 D8
  Leicester, Oadby LE2....181 A6
  Shepshed LE12..........50 A2
Paradise Cl DE12..........68 A4
Paradise La LE14..........35 F4
Paramore Cl LE8........202 A5
Pares Cl LE67..........71 E5
Parham Cl LE3..........128 B1
Paris Cl LE65..........69 A7
Park Ave
  Allington NG32..........4 F5
  Castle Donington DE74..16 F3
  Leicester LE2..........179 E8
  Loughborough LE11..........52 B1
  Markfield LE67..........98 E1
  Melton Mowbray LE13....59 B3
  Shepshed LE12..........50 C2
Park Cl
  Ashby-de-la-Z LE65......69 A5
  Cosby LE9..........201 D2
  Earl Shilton LE9..........175 E1
  Foxton LE16..........224 E1
  Shepshed LE12..........50 B4
Park Cotts LE15..........190 A5
Park Cres LE2..........181 C4
Park Ct
  Loughborough LE11..........52 B2
  Swadlincote DE11..........44 C5
Parkdale LE67..........95 E1
Parkdale Rd LE4........129 E6
Park Dr
  Braunstone Town LE3...153 C3
  Glenfield LE3..........153 C8
  Market Harborough
  LE16..........240 E4
Parker Dr LE4..........128 E2
Parkers Cl
  Blackfordby DE11..........45 B1
  Ellistown LE67..........96 D3
Parkers Fields LE12......76 A7
Park Farm LE15..........93 F8
Park Farm Bsns Units
  LE7..........159 E2
Parkfield Cl LE6........152 D8
Parkfield Cres DE12......92 F1
Parkfield Rd
  Oakham LE15..........137 E7
  Ryhall PE9..........116 F1
Park Hill LE7..........105 B7
Park Hill Ave LE8.......179 D7
Park Hill Dr LE2........179 D8
Park Hill La LE12..........78 B6
Park Ho LE16..........240 E4
Park House Cl LE4......129 A5
Park House Ct
  Blaby LE8..........202 B8
  Sapcote LE9..........217 D7
Parkinson Dr CV9......170 E2
Park La
  Bagworth LE67..........124 A7
  Castle Donington DE74..16 E3
  Leicester LE2..........155 D2
  Melton Mowbray LE13....59 C3
  Oakham LE15..........137 F6
  Skillington NG33..........43 B8
  Stamford PE9..........143 E2
  Sutton Bonington LE12...30 C5
  Walton LE17..........236 B3
  Wymondham LE14......50 B4
Parkland Mews NG10...10 D8
Parkland Prim Sch The
  LE18..........179 F1
Parklands Ave LE6.....126 D3
Parklands Dr LE11..........75 A8
Park Mews
  Market Harborough
  LE16..........240 E4
  Wigston LE18..........202 F8
Park Rd
  Allington NG32..........4 F5
  Anstey LE7..........127 D5
  Ashby-de-la-Z LE65......69 B7
  Birstall LE4..........128 F6
  Blaby LE8..........202 B8
  Coalville LE67..........71 D1
  Cosby LE9..........201 D3
  Donisthorpe DE12..........67 E2
  Earl Shilton LE9..........198 E8
  Hinckley LE10..........215 E8
  Ketton PE9..........167 F5
  Loughborough LE11..........52 B2
  Loughborough, Shelthorpe
  LE11..........75 A8
  Melton Mowbray LE13....59 C3
  Narborough LE19..........201 B7
  Overseal LE12..........67 A6
  Ratby LE6..........152 D7
  Sapcote LE9..........217 D7
  Sileby LE12..........77 C4
  Swadlincote, Church Gresley
  DE11..........44 C2
  Tilton on t H LE7......133 B4
  Wigston LE18..........202 F8
Park Rise
  Leicester LE3..........153 C5
  Shepshed LE12..........50 B4

Parkside LE6..........126 F4
Parkside Ave NG10......10 B8
Parkside Cl LE4..........128 A6
Parkside Ct LE10........215 E8
Parkside Dr NG10..........10 B8
Parkside The NG33......65 B4
Parks Prim Sch LE5.....154 A8
Park Specl Sch The
  LE15..........137 F7
Park St
  Breaston DE72..........9 F8
  Fleckney LE8..........222 F8
  Leicester LE1..........259 B3
  Loughborough LE11..........52 B3
  Market Bosworth CV13..148 F3
  Swadlincote DE11..........44 A6
Parkstone Cl LE18......203 C8
Parkstone Rd
  Desford LE9..........151 B2
  Leicester LE5..........156 D8
  Syston LE7..........103 B5
Park The
  Langham LE15..........110 B2
  Leicester LE2..........155 B3
  Market Bosworth CV13..149 A3
  Park Vale Rd LE5.......155 C5
Park View
  Aston-on-T DE72..........16 B7
  Leicester LE3..........153 E5
  Sharnford LE10..........217 B4
  Sheepy Magna CV9.....171 B7
  Stamford PE9..........143 F2
Park View Cl LE9.......218 F6
Park View Riding Sch*
  LE7..........101 A1
Parkway The LE5........156 B7
Park Wlk PE9..........169 A6
Parlour Cl LE12..........180 C2
Parnell Cl LE19..........201 C6
Parnham's Cl LE14......36 C8
Parry St LE5..........155 C7
Parsons Cl
  Swadlincote DE11..........44 A1
  Willey CV23..........242 F6
Parsons Dr
  Glen Parva LE2..........179 A3
  Sileby LE12..........77 E4
Parsons La LE10........217 C4
Parson's La LE10.......215 F8
Parsonwood Hill LE67...71 E5
Partridge Cl
  Mountsorrel LE12..........76 F2
  Syston LE7..........102 F4
Partridge Dr LE13........44 F3
Partridge Rd LE4........129 F6
Partridge Way LE5.....138 B8
Parvian Rd LE2..........180 A4
Paske Ave LE7..........105 C7
Pasley Cl LE2..........179 D4
Pasley Rd LE2..........179 D4
Pass Ctyd 5 LE65......69 B6
Pasture La
  Barleythorpe LE15.....137 D8
  Gaddesby LE7..........105 B8
  Hathern LE12..........30 B2
  Hose LE14..........21 A4
  Knipton NG32..........14 F4
  Leicester LE1..........259 A5
  Newbold Verdon LE9...150 B4
  Stathern LE14..........12 F4
  Sutton Bonington LE12..30 A6
  Thorpe Satchville LE14..106 B7
Pasture La N LE14, LE7...80 E1
Pastures De LE12..........93 C7
Pastures Prim Sch The
  LE19..........177 F2
Pastures The
  Barrow-u-S LE12..........76 E6
  Broughton Astley LE9...218 F5
  Cottesmore LE15..........112 D8
  Leicester, Oadby LE2...181 A4
  Market Harborough
  LE16..........240 C3
  Narborough LE19..........178 A1
  Shepshed LE12..........73 A8
  Sileby LE12..........102 E3
Pate Rd LE13..........81 F8
Paterson Cl LE4........128 B6
Paterson Dr LE12..........74 F1
Paterson Pl LE12........50 B5
Paton St LE3..........154 D4
Patrick St LE16........240 F2
Patterdale Dr LE11......51 C1
Patterdale Rd LE4......129 E6
Paudy Cross Roads
  LE12..........54 D2
Paudy La LE12..........55 C5
Paul Dr LE4..........129 F4
Pauline Ave LE4........129 B4
Paulyn Way LE65..........68 F5
Pavilion Way LE5..........52 A6
Pawley Cl LE8..........202 A6
Pawley Gdns LE2.......179 D4
Pawley Gr LE2..........179 D4
Payne's La LE10........227 F7
Payne St LE4..........129 B3
Peace Hill LE7..........185 C2
Peach La NG32..........4 F4
Peacock Dr LE8........201 F5
Peacock La LE1........259 A3
Peakdale LE18..........180 F1
Peakdale Cl NG10..........10 A6
Peartree Ave LE12.....129 D1
Peartree Cl

Peartree Cl *continued*
  Castle Donington DE74...17 A3
  Glenfield LE3..........153 B7
Pear Tree Cl
  Barwell LE9..........198 B8
  Hartshorne DE11..........45 A7
  Lutterworth LE17.......244 A6
Peartree Ct LE65..........47 F5
Pear Tree La LE11..........51 A6
Pear Tree Way LE11.....51 B6
Peashill Cl LE12..........77 E3
Peatling Grainger
  LE17..........220 A2
PEATLING MAGNA......221 B6
PEATLING PARVA......235 F8
Peatling Rd
  Ashby Magna LE17.....220 B1
  Countesthorpe LE8.....202 F2
  Leicester LE17..........248 D8
Pebble Cotts LE17.....248 D8
PECKLETON..........176 A7
Peckleton Comm LE9...176 B7
Peckleton Gn LE9......198 B8
Peckleton La
  Desford LE9..........151 B2
  Peckleton LE9..........176 E8
Peckleton Lane Bsns Pk
  LE9..........176 C7
Peckleton Rd LE9......175 D6
Peckleton View LE9...151 B2
Pedlars Cl LE4..........128 B3
Peebles Way LE4.......129 D3
Peeble Yd LE14..........82 A1
Peel Cl LE8..........223 F8
Peel Dr LE11..........52 C4
Peel St NG10..........10 E8
Peewit Cl LE2..........179 A3
Peggs Cl LE2..........155 B5
Peggs Cl
  Earl Shilton LE9......198 F8
  Measham DE12..........93 D3
Peggs Grange LE67......96 D6
Peggs La LE7..........103 F5
Peldar Pl LE67..........97 B8
Peldar Cl LE4..........128 D2
Pelham St
  Leicester LE2..........259 B2
  Leicester, Oadby LE2...181 A6
Pelham Way LE1.......259 B2
Pell Cl LE12..........76 E8
Pells Cl LE8..........222 F8
Pembroke Ave
  Syston LE7..........103 C2
  Wigston LE18..........179 F2
Pembroke Rd PE9......143 C5
Pembroke St LE5.......155 C7
Pembury Cl LE3........182 B1
Pen Cl LE2..........179 E4
Penclose Rd LE18......222 E8
Pendene Rd LE2........155 C1
Pendlebury Dr LE2....180 A7
Pendleton CV13..........65 B3
Pendragon Way LE3...153 A2
Penfold Cl
  Hathern LE12..........30 A2
  Sapcote LE9..........217 D8
Penfold Dr LE8........202 D4
Penhale Rd LE18......178 F8
Penistone St LE67......95 F2
Peniston Rise DE73......26 A7
Penkridge Rd DE11......44 A1
Penkridge Wlk LE4....128 E4
Penman Way LE19......178 E5
Pennant Cl LE3..........153 D7
Pennant Rd LE10.......215 D5
Penney Cl LE18..........202 D1
Pennie Cl NG10..........10 D4
Pennine Cl
  Leicester, Oadby LE2...181 D5
  Shepshed LE12..........50 C2
Pennine Dr LE15.......166 C7
Pennine Way
  Ashby-de-la-Z LE65......69 B5
  Swadlincote DE11..........44 A3
Pennine Way Jun Sch
  DE11..........44 A2
Penn La
  Melbourne DE73..........26 B7
  Stathern LE14..........12 F4
  Wibtoft LE17..........232 C2
Penn Moor Cl NG10.....10 A6
Penn St LE15..........138 A6
Pennyfields Bvd NG10..10 B7
Penny La LE9..........198 B8
Penny Long La LE3....152 F3
Penrith Ave LE12..........49 F2
Penrith Rd LE4..........129 C2
Penryn Cl CV11..........214 A4
Penryn Dr LE18..........180 C1
Pensilva Cl LE18........180 C1
Pentland Ave LE12......50 D3
Pentland Cl LE10......197 B1
Pentland Ct LE65..........69 D6
Pentridge Cl LE18......203 C8
Penzance Ave LE18....180 D1
Penzance Cl LE18......180 D1
Penzance Way CV11...197 E4
Penzance Way CV11...214 A5
Peppercorn Cl LE4.....128 D3
Pepper Dr LE12..........75 F7
Pepper's Cl LE12..........76 D4
Peppers Dr DE74..........18 B2
Pepper's La LE14........82 F7
Pera Tech Pk LE19......59 B4
Percival St LE5..........155 D7
Percy Rd
  Cottesmore LE15..........87 E2

Percy Rd *continued*
  Leicester LE2..........179 E7
Percy St LE3..........179 A8
Peregrine Cl DE12..........93 C4
Peregrine Rd LE9......218 E7
Peregrine Rise LE4....128 A6
Perkins Cl LE16........240 F4
Perkin's La LE7..........36 A1
Perkyn Rd LE5..........156 D6
Perran Ave LE67..........72 A2
Perry Cl LE12..........74 F2
Perry St LE11..........52 C1
Perseverance Rd LE4..129 A5
Perth Ave LE3..........154 A7
Perth Dr PE9..........143 A4
Peterborough Ave
  LE15..........138 B6
Peterborough Rd
  LE15..........191 D6
Peterfield Rd LE67......72 A3
Petergate 8 LE17......210 D3
Peterhouse Cl PE9......143 D5
Peterlees The DE12......67 E1
Peters Ave LE12........150 C4
Peter's Cl DE73..........27 B3
Peter's Cl LE9..........199 C2
Peters Dr LE5..........156 B7
Petersfield LE16......200 D4
Petersfield Rd LE13...159 B4
Petersham Rd NG10....10 B8
Peters Way LE15......189 F3
Pettiver Cres 2 CV21..257 A1
Petunia Cl LE3..........152 F2
Petworth Dr
  Leicester LE3..........154 A5
  Loughborough LE11......51 C5
Pevensey Ave LE15....156 D3
Pevensey Rd LE11......51 E5
Peverel Cl LE3..........153 E1
Peverel Rd LE3........154 A2
Peverel Cres LE19......9 F5
Peveril Rd LE17........220 A2
Phillip Dr LE2..........179 E1
Phillips Cres LE4......128 B6
Phillips Ct PE9..........143 E2
Phipps Cl LE8..........202 A6
Phoenix Bsns Pk
  LE10..........214 E8
Phoenix Cl LE3........154 B7
Phoenix Dr LE12..........77 D2
Phoenix Pk LE67..........71 B3
Phyllis Gr NG10..........10 F7
Piccaver Rise LE3.....153 D6
Pickards La LE14..........39 A6
Pick Bldg The LE1......259 B3
Pickering Cl
  Leicester LE4..........129 C1
  Stoney Stanton LE9...199 D2
Pickering Dr LE67......96 C4
Pickering Rd LE19......218 F4
Pickford Cl CV11......214 A1
Pickhill Rd LE5..........130 D3
Picks Cl LE16..........241 B3
Pick St LE12..........30 B4
PICKWELL..........108 C3
Pickwell Cl LE3........153 E8
Pickwell Rd
  Leesthorpe LE14........108 A8
  Somerby LE14..........108 C2
PICKWORTH..........115 C8
Pickworth Ct LE15.....138 B7
Pickworth Rd PE9......115 D3
Pied Bull Cl PE9......168 A6
Piers Rd LE3..........127 C1
Pike Cl LE10..........215 D5
Pilgrim Gdns LE5......156 A3
Pilgrims Gate LE10....216 A6
Pilgrims La CV23......253 A1
Pilkington Rd LE3.....153 C3
Pillings Rd LE15......137 F8
PILTON..........165 F2
Pilton Cl LE15..........138 B6
Pilton Rd LE15..........166 B2
Pimpernel Cl LE19.....177 F1
Pincet La
  Husbands Bosworth
  LE17..........237 B2
  North Kilworth LE17...247 A6
Pindar Rd LE3..........154 A7
Pine Cl
  Ashby-de-la-Z LE65......69 D7
  East Leake LE12..........31 D8
  Loughborough LE11......75 A7
  Lutterworth LE17.......244 A7
  Stamford PE9..........142 F4
  Stoke Golding CV13....196 F7
Pine Ct DE12..........68 B6
Pine Dr LE12..........103 B2
Pine Gr CV21..........257 A1
Pinehurst Cl LE3.......153 C6
Pinel Cl LE9..........219 A4
Pine Rd LE3..........153 C8
Pines The
  Bushby LE7..........157 B4
  Draycott DE72..........9 B7
  Great Bowden LE16....241 A6
Pine Tree Ave
  Groby LE6..........126 F2
  Leicester LE5..........156 A8
Pine Tree Cl
  Leicester, Oadby LE2...181 A4
  Newbold Verdon LE9...150 C4
Pine Tree Gdn LE2.....181 A4
Pine Tree Gr CV13.....196 D7
Pine View LE3..........153 B4
Pine Wlk NN17..........230 E1

Pinewood Ave LE4 129 E6
Pinewood Cl
Countesthorpe LE8 202 E4
Leicester LE4 128 A5
Pinewood Ct LE67 125 E6
Pinewood Dr LE67 125 E6
Pinfold LE3 178 F7
Pinfold Cl
Bottesford NG13 3 A3
Hinckley LE10 214 F7
North Luffenham LE15 166 C4
South Luffenham LE15 191 E8
Pinfold Ct LE14 106 E4
Pinfold Gate
Ketton PE9 167 F5
Loughborough LE11 52 B4
Pinfold Gdns LE11 52 B4
Pinfold Jetty 6 LE11 52 B4
Pinfold La
Bottesford NG13 3 A3
Harby LE14 12 C3
Market Overton LE15 87 A6
North Luffenham LE15 166 C4
South Luffenham LE15 166 E1
Stamford PE9 143 E2
Stamford PE9 143 F3
Pinfold Pl LE14 12 C3
Pinfold Rd LE4 129 D6
Pinfold The
Markfield LE67 125 E8
Newton Burgoland
LE67 121 D7
Ratby LE6 152 C8
Pingle La
Morcott LE15 191 B6
Potters Marston LE9 199 E6
Pingle Sch The DE11 44 A5
Pingle St LE3 259 A5
Pingle The
Barlestone CV13 149 D8
Long Eaton NG10 10 D8
Melbourne DE73 26 A7
Quorn (Quorndon) LE12 75 E5
Pintail Cl LE8 201 F4
Pintail Ct DE12 93 B4
PINWALL 170 D5
Pinwall La CV9 170 E4
Pipe La CV9 145 C4
Piper Cl
Leicester LE3 154 A7
Long Whatton LE12 29 D3
Loughborough LE11 51 F1
Shepshed LE12 50 C6
Piper Dr LE12 29 C2
Piper La LE67 95 F8
Piper Way LE3 154 A7
Pipewell Wlk 2 LE4 128 E3
Pipistrelle Dr CV13 148 C3
Pipistrelle Way LE2 181 E4
Pipit Cl DE12 93 C4
Pipit Wlk CV23 252 C1
Pisca La LE67 95 D2
Pitchens Cl LE4 127 F5
Pitchers La LE16 229 D7
Pit Hill LE8 223 F6
Pithiviers Cl LE65 69 A5
Pit La PE9 168 A7
Pits Ave LE3 178 E7
Pitsford Dr LE11 51 A2
Pitt La LE67 70 E5
Pitton Cl LE18 203 C8
Plackett Cl DE72 9 D8
Plain Gate LE7 101 C8
Plantagenet Way LE65 69 D7
Plantation Ave LE2 179 C6
Plantations The 7
NG10 10 A8
Plantation The LE8 202 E4
Plant La NG10 10 A4
Platts La LE7 102 C7
Player Cl LE4 129 D5
Pleasant Cl
Leicester Forest East
LE3 152 F2
Loughborough LE11 52 A4
Pleasant Pl DE74 18 D2
Pleasant Terr LE15 189 B4
Plough Cl
Broughton Astley LE9 219 A4
Leicester Forest East
LE3 152 F1
Mountsorrel LE12 101 D8
Ploughmans Dr LE12 50 C5
Ploughman's Lea LE7 103 D7
Ploughmans Yd 11
LE16 240 E3
Plover Ave DE11 44 F3
Plover Cl LE15 138 B8
Plover Cres LE4 128 B6
Plover Rd PE9 117 A6
Plowman Cl LE3 127 C1
Plummer La DE74 18 C2
Plummer Rd DE11 44 A5
Plumtree Cl LE11 51 F6
Plumtree Way LE7 103 B3
PLUNGAR 12 F8
Plungar La NG13 6 A1
Plungar Rd NG13 5 C4
Pluto Cl LE2 155 B5
Plymouth Dr LE5 155 F4
Plymstock Cl LE3 154 B6
Poachers Cl LE3 153 B8
Poachers Cnr LE67 72 B8
Poachers Pl LE2 181 D4
Pochin Dr LE16 240 F5
Pochin's Bridge Rd
LE18 203 A8
Pochin Sch The LE7 130 D8
Pochins Cl LE18 180 C1
Pochin St LE9 200 C4
Pochin Way LE12 77 D4
Pocket End LE11 74 E8
Pocklingtons Wlk
LE1 259 B3
Polaris Cl LE2 155 B5
Polden Cl LE12 50 C2
Polebrook Cl LE3 127 E3
Polebrook Mews LE9 151 D8
Police Hos LE15 138 A7
Pollard Cl LE13 59 E5
Pollard Ct LE2 155 D2
Pollard Rd LE3 153 E3
Pollards Cl LE15 191 F5
Pollard Way LE67 71 A2
Polly Bott's Lane Or Lea La
LE67 98 F4
Pomeroy Dr LE2 180 F5
Pond End DE74 17 B6
Pond La LE15 88 B1
Pond St LE12 77 F7
Pool Rd
Leicester LE3 154 C6
Melbourne DE73 26 D6
Pool St DE11 44 D2
Pope Cres LE19 178 A3
Pope St LE2 180 A8
Poplar Ave
Birstall LE4 129 A7
Countesthorpe LE8 202 E4
East Leake LE12 31 D8
Lutterworth LE17 244 B6
Markfield LE67 125 D8
Moira DE12 67 E2
Swadlincote DE11 44 B6
Poplar Cl LE15 189 B5
Poplar Dr DE12 93 C6
Poplar Hill LE12 54 A4
Poplar Rd
Breaston DE72 9 F8
Corby NN17 230 D1
Littlethorpe LE19 201 B6
Loughborough LE11 75 B7
Poplars Cl LE6 126 E3
Poplars Ct LE16 240 D4
Poplars The
Billesdon LE7 159 C2
Earl Shilton LE9 176 A1
Hartshill Green CV10 194 B2
Leicester LE3 179 A7
Ratby LE6 126 B1
Poplar Terr CV13 147 E8
Poppins The LE4 128 B6
Popple Cl LE9 219 A5
Poppy Cl
Coalville LE67 97 A8
Groby LE6 127 A3
Leicester LE2 179 F4
Loughborough LE11 75 A6
Porlock Cl
2 Long Eaton NG10 10 A8
Shepshed LE12 50 C2
Porlock Dr LE17 235 C4
Porlock St LE3 154 B5
Portcullis Rd LE5 130 E1
Porter's La PE9 169 A5
Portgate LE18 180 E1
Portia Cl CV11 214 A1
Portishead Rd LE5 155 E8
Portland Dr LE10 197 E4
Portland Rd
Kirby Fields LE9 152 E4
Leicester LE2 155 C1
Long Eaton NG10 10 B4
Portland St LE9 201 D4
Portland Twrs LE2 180 E8
Portland Wlk LE2 181 C3
Portloc Dr LE18 203 D8
Portman St LE4 129 B2
Portmore Cl LE4 128 C2
Portreath Dr CV11 214 A5
Portsdown Rd LE2 180 D6
Portslade Ho LE3 153 C6
Portsmouth Rd LE4 129 B1
Portwey The LE5 155 F8
Portwood Ind Est DE11 44 A1
Post Office Hill NG33 43 D2
Post Office La
Lyndon LE15 165 D5
Newton Harcourt LE8 204 D6
Plungar NG13 5 F1
Redmile NG13 6 F4
Ryhall PE9 116 F2
Twyford LE14 106 E1
Witherley CV9 194 B7
Post Office Row NG13 7 F8
Post Rd LE4 102 E1
Posy La DE72 16 A7
Pott Acre LE7 76 F1
Potters Croft DE11 44 A5
Potters La LE12 31 F8
POTTERS MARSTON 199 F5
Potter St
Leicester LE1 259 C4
Melbourne DE73 26 B7
Potters Yd DE73 26 B7
Potterton Rd LE4 128 D3
Pougher Cl LE9 217 E7
Poulteney Dr LE12 75 F6
Poultney La LE17 235 F1
Powell Row LE17 244 B8
Powers Rd LE9 197 F5
Powys Ave LE2 155 E1
Powys Gdns LE2 155 E1
Poynings Ave LE3 154 A6
Praetor Ho 2 LE10 197 D1
Prebend St LE2 155 B4
Preceptory The NG33 43 D2
Precinct The LE17 244 B1
Premier Drum Works
LE18 202 F8
Prentice Cl DE12 68 A4
Presents La LE12 49 B6
Prestbury Rd LE11 51 B4
PRESTON 164 B2
Preston Cl
Ratby LE6 152 E8
Sileby LE12 77 C2
Stanton u B LE67 97 F1
Preston Ct LE15 164 C1
Preston Dr LE9 150 B5
Preston Rd
Hinckley LE10 197 B2
Wing LE15 164 E2
Preston Rise LE5 130 C1
Preston's La LE67 70 E6
Prestop Dr LE65 68 F6
PRESTWOLD 53 D8
Prestwold La LE12 53 D7
Prestwold Rd LE5 155 D8
Prestwood Park Dr
DE11 44 D5
Pretoria Cl LE4 128 C7
Pretoria Rd
Ibstock LE67 96 B2
Kirby Muxloe LE9 152 D5
Prevost Gdns LE12 76 A6
Price Way LE4 130 A7
Pride Pl LE16 240 D2
Priesthills Rd LE10 215 D8
Priestley Rd LE3 154 A4
Priestman Rd LE3 153 C1
Priest Mdw LE8 222 F7
Primethorpe Wlk LE9 218 E7
Primrose Cl
Groby LE6 127 A3
Narborough LE19 201 A8
Primrose Dr LE10 215 E5
Primrose Hill LE2 180 F6
Primrose Mdw DE11 44 B7
Primrose Way
Kirby Muxloe LE9 152 F6
Queniborough LE7 103 E6
Stamford PE9 142 E5
Prince Albert Dr LE3 153 C7
Prince Charles St LE14 57 F3
Prince Dr LE2 181 C5
Princes Cl LE7 127 E6
Princes Rd
Old Dalby LE14 36 C6
Stamford PE9 143 E4
Princess Anne Sq LE14 57 F3
Princess Ave
Leicester, Oadby LE2 181 C4
Oakham LE15 137 E6
Princess Cl DE11 44 F2
Princess Ct LE11 52 A6
Princess Dr
Kirby Muxloe LE9 152 D4
Melton Mowbray LE13 82 C7
Princess Rd
Atherstone CV9 170 E1
Hinckley LE10 215 E8
Princess Rd E LE1 259 C2
Princess Rd W LE1 259 C2
Princess Road Backways
LE1 259 B2
Princess St
Long Eaton NG10 10 D8
Loughborough LE11 52 B3
Narborough LE19 201 C8
Swadlincote DE11 67 A8
Prince St
Coalville LE67 96 D8
Long Eaton NG10 10 D8
Prince William Rd
LE11 52 A6
Prince William Way
LE11 52 A6
Princewood Rd NN17 230 E3
Printers Yd LE15 189 B4
Print Room The LE1 259 B3
Priorfields LE65 69 C5
Prior Park Flats 6
LE65 69 C5
Prior Park Ho 7 LE65 69 C5
Prior Park Rd LE65 69 B5
Priory Bsns Pk LE8 205 E2
Priory Cl
Swadlincote DE11 44 A6
Syston LE7 102 F3
Thringstone LE67 71 C8
Priory Cres LE3 153 E5
Priory Ct NG33 65 B3
Priory Gdns PE9 143 F3
Priory La LE67 98 E4
Priory Rd
Loughborough LE11 74 E8
Manton LE15 164 E6
Market Bosworth CV13 148 D2
Stamford PE9 143 F3
Priory View LE14 81 B8
Priory Wlk
4 Hinckley LE10 197 E1
Leicester Forest East
LE3 153 A3
Private Rd LE67 96 B7
Proctor's Park Rd LE12 76 C7
Progress Way LE4 130 A3
Prospect Hill LE5 155 C6
Prospect Rd
Kibworth Beauchamp
LE8 223 F8
Leicester LE5 155 D6
Prospect Way LE9 198 E8
Providence Ct DE11 44 F2
Pryor Rd LE12 77 D4
Pudding Bag La
Exton LE15 113 A3
Shepshed LE12 72 F8
Pudding La LE14 19 C5
Pughe's Cl LE10 216 A6
Pulford Dr LE7 157 A6
Pullman Rd LE18 180 B2
Pullman Trad Est
LE15 189 C3
Pulteney Ave LE11 75 B8
Pulteney Rd LE11 75 B8
Pumping Station Cott
LE16 230 A7
Pump La
Asfordby LE14 57 F2
Shenton CV13 173 B5
Purbeck Ave LE12 50 D3
Purbeck Cl
Long Eaton NG10 10 A8
Wigston LE18 203 D8
Purcell Rd LE4 155 A8
Purdy Ct LE15 137 F6
Purdy Mdw NG10 9 F5
Purley Rd LE4 129 C1
Purley Rise LE12 50 C2
Putney Rd LE2 155 A2
Putney Rd W LE2 154 F2
Pyeharps Rd LE10 215 E5
Pyke The LE7 76 F1
Pym Leys NG10 9 F5
Pymm Ley Cl LE6 126 F3
Pymm Ley Gdns LE6 126 F3
Pymm Ley La LE6 126 F3
Pytchley Cl
Cottesmore LE15 87 F4
Leicester LE4 128 E5
Pytchley Dr LE11 74 F8

Q

Quadrant The
Leicester LE4 128 F2
Uppingham LE15 189 B4
Quaker Cl
Fenny Drayton CV13 195 A6
Melbourne DE73 26 A8
Quaker Rd LE12 77 C1
Quantock Rise LE12 50 C2
Quarry Berry La
Chilcote DE12 91 F1
Newton Regis DE12 118 E8
Quarry La
Atherstone CV9 194 A6
Enderby LE19 178 A4
Snarestone DE12 93 F1
Quarrymans Ct LE67 98 D1
Quarry Mobile Home Pk
LE67 125 D8
Quay The LE12 76 D3
Quebec Rd LE1 259 C4
Queen Eleanor Tech Coll
PE9 143 D5
Queen's Cl LE14 38 E5
Queens Ct DE72 9 A7
Queens Dr
Leicester Forest East
LE3 153 A3
Narborough LE19 178 D2
Wigston LE18 180 B2
Queen's Dr DE11 44 B6
Queensferry Par LE2 179 C3
Queensgate Dr LE4 128 E8
Queensmead Cl LE6 126 E2
Queensmead Com Prim
Sch LE3 153 F4
Queen's Park Ct 3
LE10 215 E8
Queen's Park Flats 2
LE10 215 E8
Queen's Park Terr 4
LE10 215 E8
Queens Park Way
LE2 179 D2
Queens Rd
Kegworth DE74 18 D2
Leicester LE2 155 B1
Queen's Rd
Blaby LE8 202 B7
Hinckley LE10 215 E8
Loughborough LE11 52 C4
Oakham LE15 138 A7
Uppingham LE15 189 A4
Queens St PE9 143 D4
Queen's St DE12 93 C5
Queen St
Barkby LE7 130 C7
Barwell LE9 198 B6
Bottesford NG13 3 B2
Coalville LE67 96 D8
Leicester LE1 259 C3
Leicester, Oadby LE2 181 B5
Long Eaton NG10 10 E7
2 Loughborough LE11 52 C3
Market Harborough
LE16 241 A2
Markfield LE67 125 D8
Shepshed LE12 50 B4
Swadlincote DE11 44 A1
Uppingham LE15 189 B4
Queensway
Barwell LE9 198 C7
Castle Donington DE74 16 F4
Melbourne DE73 26 B8
Melton Mowbray LE13 82 C8
Old Dalby LE14 36 C6
Queensway Ho DE12 93 C5
Queen's Wlk PE9 143 C3
Queen Victoria Ct 10
LE10 197 D1
Queen Victoria Dr
DE11 44 B5
Quelch Cl LE67 96 D6
Quemby Cl LE4 129 A2
Quenby Cres LE7 103 C3
Quenby Hall LE7 132 E2
Quenby St LE5 155 D7
QUENIBOROUGH 103 F5
Queniborough CE Prim
Sch LE7 103 F5
Queniborough Hall
LE7 104 A5
Queniborough Ind Est
LE7 103 D5
Queniborough Rd
Leicester LE4 129 D1
Queniborough LE7 103 E5
Syston LE7 103 D2
Quick Cl DE73 26 A7
Quickthorns LE2 181 B7
Quiney Way LE2 181 C6
Quinton Rise LE2 181 A4
Quorn Ave
Ab Kettleby LE14 37 C2
Leicester, Oadby LE2 181 D4
Melton Mowbray LE13 59 B3
Quorn Cl LE11 52 C2
Quorn Cres
Coalville LE67 97 B8
Cottesmore LE15 87 F3
Quorndon Cres NG10 10 D5
Quorndon Rise LE6 126 E2
Quorndon Terr LE12 75 F6
Quorndon Waters Ct
LE12 75 F6
Quorn Flats LE12 76 A5
Quorn Hunt Kennels The
LE14 81 B4
Quorn Mill LE12 76 A5
Quorn Pk LE12 54 B1
QUORN (QUORNDON)
76 B6
Quorn Rd LE5 155 D7
Quorn & Woodhouse Sta
LE12 75 D5

R

Racecourse La LE14 83 A6
Racecourse Rd PE9 169 D5
Racemeadow Prim Sch
CV9 170 E1
Racemeadow Rd CV9 170 E1
Radar Rd LE3 153 D5
Radcliffe Cl PE9 143 D3
Radcliffe Rd PE9 143 D3
Radcot Lawns LE2 179 D3
Radford Cl CV9 170 E2
Radford Dr LE3 153 C3
Radford Ho LE3 153 C3
Radford Mdw DE74 16 F3
Radiant Rd LE5 156 C7
Radleigh Grange DE11 45 A2
Radley Cl LE65 69 A8
Rad Mdws NG10 10 C6
Radmoor Rd LE11 51 F3
Radmore Rd LE10 197 D3
Radnor Ct LE19 177 F2
Radnor Dr LE12 50 B5
Radnor Rd LE18 180 A3
Radstone Wlk LE5 156 A6
Raeburn Rd LE2 155 B1
RAGDALE 56 D4
Ragdale Rd
Leicester LE4 129 D1
Ragdale LE14 56 D1
Railway Cl NG33 65 B3
Railway Side DE11 44 B1
Railway St LE18 202 F8
Railway Terr LE11 52 C5
Raine Way LE2 181 D3
Rainsborough Gdns
LE16 250 D8
Rainsbrook Dr CV11 214 A1
Rainsford Cres LE4 128 E3
Raleigh Cl LE10 197 D4
Ralph Cl LE11 74 D8
Ralph's Cl LE17 219 D2
Ralph Toon Ct LE14 57 F3
Rambler Cl DE11 44 A5
Ramsbury Rd LE2 180 B5
Ramscliff Ave DE12 92 F8
Ramsdean Ave LE18 180 C3
Ramsden Rd CV9 194 A7
Ramsey Cl
Hinckley LE10 197 B1
Lutterworth LE17 244 D6
Ramsey Gdns LE5 130 E1
Ramsey Way LE5 130 E1
Ramson Cl LE5 130 C2
Rancliffe Cres LE3 154 A4
Randall Cl LE7 105 D3
Randall Dr DE11 44 B4
Randles Cl LE7 157 A4
Range Rd LE65 69 C6
Range The LE15 110 B3
Ranksborough Dr
LE15 110 B3
Ranksborough Hall*
LE15 110 B2

Rannoch Cl
Hinckley LE10 ....215 B8
Leicester LE4 ....128 C2
Rannoch Way NN17 ....230 C1
Ranton Way LE3 ......154 C8
Ranworth Wlk LE4 ....128 E4
RATBY 152 B8
Ratby La
 Braunstone Town LE3 ..153 A5
 Kirby Muxloe LE9 ....152 E7
 Markfield LE67 ......125 E7
Ratby Meadow La
 LE19 ....178 E3
Ratby Prim Sch LE6 ..152 C8
Ratby Rd LE6 ....126 E3
Ratcliff Cl LE65 ....69 A6
Ratcliffe Coll LE7 ..78 A3
Ratcliffe Ct LE2 ...180 D8
RATCLIFFE CULEY 171 B3
Ratcliffe Dr LE9 ...200 D7
Ratcliffe House La
 CV9 ....171 C4
Ratcliffe La
 Atherstone CV9 ......170 F4
 Lockington DE74 .....18 C7
 Sheepy Magna CV9 ...171 A5
RATCLIFFE ON SOAR ..18 F6
RATCLIFFE ON T WREAKE
 ....78 C2
Ratcliffe Rd
 Atherstone CV9 ......170 E1
 Hinckley LE10 ......215 F6
 Leicester LE2 ......180 D8
 Loughborough LE11 ..52 C5
 Sileby LE12 ....77 E3
 Thrussington LE7 ...74 E5
Ratcliffe St LE4 ....129 B2
Ratts La LE15 ....137 A2
Ravel Cl PE9 ....143 B4
Raven Cl LE12 ....93 B4
Ravenhurst Prim Sch
 LE3 ....178 F8
Ravenhurst Rd LE3 ..178 F8
Raven Rd LE3 ....153 E3
Ravensbridge Dr LE4 .154 E8
Ravenslea LE67 .....95 E8
Ravensthorpe Dr LE11 .51 B3
Ravensthorpe Rd
 LE18 ....180 E2
RAVENSTONE 95 F8
Ravenstone Ct LE67 ..95 E8
Ravenstone Rd
 Heather LE67 ....95 C4
 Ibstock LE67 ....95 E3
 Ravenstone LE67 ....71 A2
Ravenwood DE11 .....44 C3
Rawdon Cl DE74 .....17 A4
Rawdon Rd DE12 .....67 E5
Rawdon Side DE11 ...44 D4
Rawdon Terr 11 LE65 .69 B6
Raw Dykes Rd LE2 ...154 E2
Rawlings Cl LE2 ....181 E4
Rawlins Cl LE3 .....75 A1
Rawlins Com Coll LE12 .76 A6
Rawlinson Ct LE3 ...128 A1
Rawson St
 Enderby LE19 ....178 B3
 Leicester LE1 ......259 C2
Rawsthorne Wlk LE4 .155 A8
Rayleigh Gn LE5 ....130 E1
Rayleigh Way LE5 ...130 C1
Raymond Ave LE11 ...51 D6
Raymond Rd LE3 ....154 C3
Rayner Rd LE4 ......129 F3
Raynes Wlk LE13 ....59 D4
Raynham Dr LE11 ...51 C5
REARSBY 79 A1
Rearsby La LE7 .....104 E7
Rearsby Rd
 Leicester LE4 ......129 C1
 Queniborough LE7 ..103 E6
 Thrussington LE7 ...79 A3
Recreation Ground Rd
 PE9 ....143 E3
Recreation St NG10 .10 F7
Rectory Cl
 Breedon on h t DE73 .26 E2
 Swinford LE17 ......254 C4
 Wigston LE18 ......180 D1
Rectory Ct
 Bottesford NG13 ....3 B3
 East Farndon LE16 ..250 B6
Rectory Dr LE14 ...19 A1
Rectory Gdns
 Aston-on-T DE72 ...16 A7
 Leicester LE2 .....156 B2
Rectory La
 Appleby Magna DE12 .92 E1
 Bottesford NG13 ...3 B3
 Burrough on t H LE14 .107 D2
 Cadeby CV13 ......149 D1
 Edith Weston LE15 ..166 B7
 Kibworth Beauchamp
  LE8 ....206 A1
 Market Bosworth CV13 .148 F3
 Market Harborough
  LE16 ....241 A2
 Medbourne LE16 ...228 A7
 Nailstone CV13 ....123 B3
 North Witham NG33 .65 B8
 Thurcaston LE7 ....101 B2
 Woolsthorpe by B NG32 .15 B8
Rectory Pl
 Loughborough LE11 .52 B4
 Wymeswold LE12 ...33 C3

Rectory Rd
 Breaston DE72 ......9 E8
 Loughborough LE11 .52 B5
 Markfield LE67 ....98 E1
 Wanlip LE7 ....102 B2
Redbrook Cres LE13 .59 A1
Redburrow La LE65,
 LE67 ....94 C7
Redcar Rd LE4 .....129 C1
Redcliffe Cl LE3 ...127 F3
Redcot Gdns PE9 ...143 D4
Redcot Mews PE9 ...143 D3
Red Cswy The LE14 .128 B2
Redens The NG10 ...10 B4
REDGATE 189 B3
Red Hall Dr LE9 ...198 B7
Red Hall Rd LE9 ...198 C7
RED HILL 200 F8
Red Hill
 Leicester LE4 .....128 F5
 Uppingham LE15 ...189 B3
 Leicester LE4 .....201 A8
 Redhill Circ LE4 ..128 F4
 Red Hill Cl LE4 ...129 E8
Red Hill Field Prim Sch
 LE19 ....201 A8
Redhill La LE3 ....71 C6
Red Hill La LE4 ...129 F8
Redhill Lodge Rd 6
 DE11 ....44 A7
Red Hill Way LE4 ..128 D4
Red House Cl LE2 ..179 C4
Red House Gdns
 Allington NG32 ....4 F5
 Leicester LE2 .....179 C4
Red House Rd LE2 ..179 C4
Red House Rise LE2 .179 C4
Redland Cl LE15 ...191 F5
Redland Rd LE15 ...137 D7
Redlands Com Prim Sch
 LE2 ....77 C3
Redlands Est LE67 .96 A3
Redliech Cl LE16 ..241 B3
Red Lion La LE9 ...150 C4
Red Lion Sq 12 PE9 .143 D3
Red Lion St
 8 Stamford PE9 ...143 D3
 Stathern LE14 .....13 A3
Red Lodge Rd LE7,
 LE15 ....134 B2
Redmarle Rd LE3 ..154 A3
REDMILE 6 F3
Redmile CE Prim Sch
 NG13 ....6 F3
Redmile's La PE9 ..168 A5
Redmires Cl LE11 ..51 B3
Redmoor Cl CV13 ...148 D2
Redmoor High Sch
 LE10 ....197 B3
Redpath Cl LE4 ....155 B7
Redruth Ave LE18 ..180 C1
Redruth Cl CV11 ...214 A4
Redruth Ct LE18 ...203 C8
Redway Croft 8 DE73 .26 A8
Redwing Cl LE15 ...138 B7
Redwing Wlk LE5 ...154 C2
Redwood Ave LE13 ..59 D5
Redwood Rd LE11 ..75 A7
Redwood Wlk LE5 ..154 C2
Reedman Rd NG10 ..10 B4
Reedpool Cl LE8 ...202 F4
Rees Cl LE15 .....189 A5
Rees Gr LE4 ......129 D5
Reeth Cl LE4 .....128 C3
Reeves Cl LE18 ...201 F5
Reeves La LE15 ...165 A3
Reeves Rd LE10 ...215 F6
Reeve's Yd LE15 ..189 B4
Reform St PE9 ....143 B3
Regal Ct LE19 ....178 D2
Regal Gdns NG33 ..90 C8
Regan Rd DE12 ...68 A4
Regency Ct LE2 ...179 D1
Regency Ct
 Hinckley LE10 ....216 A7
 Leicester LE3 .....154 C5
Regency Rd LE14 ..57 F3
Regent Cl LE18 ...180 B2
Regent Coll LE1 ..259 C1
Regent Ct
 8 Hinckley LE10 ..215 D8
 Loughborough LE11 .52 A5
 6 Lutterworth LE17 .244 C5
 Swadlincote DE11 .44 B2
Regent Pl LE13 ...59 D2
Regent Pl Ret Pk LE11 .52 A4
Regent Rd
 Countesthorpe LE8 .202 F4
 Hoby LE14 ....79 D7
 Leicester LE1 .....259 C2
Regent St
 Barwell LE9 ....198 B7
 Hinckley LE10 ....215 D8
 Leicester LE1 .....259 C2
 Leicester, Oadby LE2 .181 A6
 Long Eaton NG10 ..10 D8
 Loughborough LE11 .52 A4
 Lutterworth LE17 .244 C5
 Melton Mowbray LE13 .59 D2
 Narborough LE19 .178 D2
 Swadlincote DE11 .44 B2
 Thrussington LE7 .78 F5
Regent Street Ind Est
 LE19 ....201 C7
Regents Wlk LE3 ..153 A3
Reg's Way LE67 ...97 B4
Reliant Cl LE4 ...44 E1

REMPSTONE 32 D6
Rempstone Rd
 Belton LE12 ....49 D7
 East Leake LE12 ..31 E7
 Griffydam LE67 ...47 F2
 Hoton LE12 ....32 C2
 Wymeswold LE12 ..33 B4
 Zouch LE12 ....31 B6
Rendell Prim Sch LE11 .52 B5
Rendell Rd LE4 ...129 B1
Rendell St LE11 ..52 B5
Renfrew Rd LE5 ..156 E8
Renishaw Dr LE5 .155 C2
Rennes Cl LE65 ..69 A8
Renning End LE12 ..101 E8
Repington Ave CV9 .170 D2
Repington Row LE2 .179 F5
Repton Cl LE65 ..69 A8
Repton Dr
 Hartshorne DE11 ..44 F8
 Long Eaton NG10 ..9 F4
 Oakthorpe DE12 ..93 A5
 Wigston LE18 ....180 B4
Repton St LE3 ...154 D7
Rescue Way LE65 .69 B5
Reservoir Hill DE12 .67 D6
Reservoir Rd
 Cropston LE7 .....100 C3
 Thornton LE67 ...125 A3
Reservoir View LE8 .223 B4
Reservoir Way DE11 .44 E1
Resolution Way LE65 .69 D7
Resthaven DE11 ..44 B5
Retreat The
 Barrow-u-S LE12 .76 D8
 Easton o t H PE9 .168 F5
 Leicester LE5 ....155 F5
Revell Cl LE12 ..76 B6
Reynolds Chase LE18 .180 E3
Reynolds Cl
 Hinckley LE10 ...197 A3
 Rugby CV21 ......257 B1
Reynolds Pl LE2 .154 A2
Rhodes Cl LE16 ..240 C2
Ribble Ave LE2 ..181 D6
Ribble Dr LE12 ..76 D6
Ribblesdale Ave LE10 .197 E3
Ribblesdale Rd NG10 .10 A5
Ribble Way LE13 .59 B1
Ribble Wlk LE15 .137 E5
Riber Cl NG10 ...10 A5
Richard Cl
 Braunstone Town LE3 .153 C3
 Melton Mowbray LE13 .59 D3
Richard Hill CE Prim Sch
 LE7 ....101 B2
Richard III Rd LE3 .259 A3
Richardson Cl LE9 .199 D1
Richardsons Cl LE9 .219 A5
Richil Ct LE15 ..189 B4
Richil Ho LE15 ..189 B4
Richmond Ave
 Leicester LE2 ....179 E8
 Long Eaton DE72 .10 A8
Richmond Cl
 Cosby LE9 ....201 C2
 Desford LE9 .....151 B2
 Fleckney LE8 ....222 F7
 Leicester LE8 ...179 E8
Richmond Dr
 Glen Parva LE2 ..179 E1
 Melton Mowbray LE13 .82 D8
Richmond Gate LE10 .197 C3
Richmond Ho LE10 .197 C3
Richmond Prim Sch
 LE10 ....197 C3
Richmond Rd
 Coalville LE67 ...96 B4
 Hinckley LE10 ...197 C3
 Leicester LE2 ...179 E8
Richmond St LE2 .259 A2
Richmond Way LE2 .181 C3
Richmore Rd LE5 .130 C1
Rickmans Cnr Cvn Site
 DE12 ....67 A6
Riddington Rd
 Braunstone Town LE3 .178 F7
 Littlethorpe LE19 .201 C6
Riddon Dr LE10 ..215 B8
Ridgemere Cl LE7 .103 D4
Ridgemere La LE7 .104 B2
Ridge View LE16 .240 F5
Ridgeway LE5 ....201 C6
Ridge Way LE2 ..181 B3
Ridgeway Dr LE14 .58 A3
Ridgeway Prim Sch
 LE16 ....240 F5
Ridgeway The
 Hinckley LE10 ...215 D6
 Leicester LE3 ...154 A7
 Market Harborough
  LE16 ....240 F5
 Rothley LE7 .....101 C6
Ridgeway W LE16 .240 E5
Ridgway Rd
 Ashby-de-la-Z LE65 .68 F5
 Leicester LE2 ...180 D8
 Leicester LE3 ...58 A3
Ridings The
 Mountsorrel LE7 .101 C7
 Queniborough LE7 .103 E5
 Riding The LE4 ..128 B6
Ridley Cl
 Blaby LE8 ....202 A6
 Cropston LE7 ...100 E2
Ridley St LE3 ...154 D4
RIDLINGTON 163 D2
Ridlington Rd LE15 .164 B1

Rigsty The LE12 ..75 E6
Riley Cl
 Market Harborough
  LE16 ....240 B2
 Stoney Stanton LE9 .199 D1
Rills The LE10 ..197 E2
Ringers Cl LE2 ..181 A8
Ringer's Spinney LE2 .181 A8
Ring Fence LE12 .50 B2
Ring Rd LE2 ....180 E7
Ringway The LE7 .103 F6
Ringwood Cl
 Desford LE9 .....151 B3
 Wigston LE18 ...180 C1
Ringwood Rd
 Leicester LE5 ...130 E1
 Shepshed LE12 ..50 C5
Rink Dr DE11 ...44 B3
Ripley Cl LE16 ..241 B3
Ripley Rd LE16 ..229 D1
Ripon Dr LE8 ...202 B6
Ripon St LE2 ...155 C3
Risholme Cl LE4 4 .178 F7
Rise The
 Houghton on t H LE7 .157 F4
 Narborough LE19 .178 A2
 Rothley LE7 .....102 A6
Risley La DE72 ..9 E8
Riston Cl LE2 ..181 B3
Ritchie Pk LE16 .250 E8
River Bldg The 2
 LE3 ....154 D4
River Ct PE9 ...143 B8
Riverdale Cl LE7 .103 A4
River Dr CV9 ...170 D2
Riversdale Cl LE4 .129 B6
Riversdale Rd CV9 .194 A8
River Sence Way LE67 .96 D6
Riverside
 Market Harborough
  LE16 ....241 A4
 Witherley CV9 ..194 B7
Riverside Cl
 Bottesford NG13 .3 A3
 Great Glen LE8 ..182 B1
 Sheepy Magna CV9 .171 B8
Riverside Com Coll
 LE8 ....179 B8
Riverside Com Prim Sch
 LE4 ....129 B2
Riverside Ct
 Littlethorpe LE19 .201 C7
 Market Harborough
  LE16 ....240 D2
Riverside Dr LE2 .179 C7
Riverside Ind Est
 LE16 ....241 A3
Riverside Mews LE7 .102 C2
Riverside Pl LE7 .143 E2
Riverside Rd
 Lutterworth LE17 .244 D5
 Melton Mowbray LE13 .59 A3
Riverside Way LE19 .201 C7
Riverside Wlk
 Asfordby LE14 ...57 F2
 Bottesford NG13 .3 A3
River Soar Living 3
 LE3 ....154 D4
Rivers St LE3 ...154 D6
River View
 Barrow-u-S LE12 .76 F6
 Long Eaton NG10 .10 A3
Riverview Ct LE2 .154 E1
Rivets Meadow Cl
 LE3 ....153 D1
Rivington Dr LE11 .51 B2
RNIB Vocational Coll
 LE11 ....51 F3
Robert Bakewell Prim Sch
 LE11 ....51 D6
Robert Hall Rd LE8 .221 F5
Robert Hall St LE4 .128 F3
Robert Hardy Wharf
 LE11 ....52 A4
Robert Hill Cl CV21 .257 A1
Robertsbridge Ave
 LE4 ....128 E3
Robertsbridge Wlk 8
 LE4 ....128 E3
Roberts Cl DE74 ..18 D1
Roberts Dr NG13 .2 F3
Robert Smyth Sch The
 LE16 ....240 E5
Robertson Cl
 Clifton u D CV23 .257 A5
 Stoney Stanton LE9 .199 D2
Roberts Rd LE4 ..129 A1
Robian Way DE11 .44 A4
Robin Cl
 Leicester LE2 ...179 E7
 Oakham LE15 ...138 B8
Robin Cres LE13 .82 B8
Robin Hood Pl DE11 .44 C2
Robinia Cl LE17 .244 A5
Robin Mews LE2 .52 A3
Robin Rd LE67 ..96 F8
Robin Field LE12 .152 D8
Robinson Rd
 Leicester LE5 ...155 E2
 Swadlincote DE11 .44 A6
 Whitwick LE67 ..71 D5
Robinson Way
 Hinckley LE10 ...215 F4
 Markfield LE67 ..125 F8
Roborough Gn LE5 .156 E6
Robotham Cl
 Huncote LE9 .....200 E7

Robotham Cl continued
 Narborough LE19 .201 B7
Roby Lea DE74 ...16 F4
Rochdale Cres LE67 .72 D1
Roche Cl LE2 ....179 C4
Rochester Cl
 Kibworth Beauchamp
  LE8 ....205 F2
 Long Eaton NG10 .10 A7
 Mountsorrel LE12 .101 C8
Rochester Gdns LE16 .240 D1
Rockbridge Rd LE2 .181 D4
Rockcliffe Cl LE11 .44 B1
Rockery Cl LE5 ..156 A7
Rockhill Dr LE2 .76 E1
ROCKINGHAM 230 B4
Rockingham Castle &
 Gdns* LE16 ...230 B3
Rockingham Cl
 3 Ashby-de-la-Z LE65 .69 C5
 Blaby LE8 ....202 B6
 Leicester LE5 ...156 B6
 Shepshed LE12 ..50 A2
Rockingham Dr LE13 .59 C4
Rockingham Ind Est
 LE16 ....241 B3
Rockingham Rd
 Caldecott LE16 ..230 B6
 Corby NN17 .....230 E2
 Cottingham LE16 .209 A2
 Gretton LE16, NN17 .230 E7
 Gretton NN17 ...213 A1
 Loughborough LE11 .51 E6
 Market Harborough
  LE16 ....241 B4
 Mountsorrel LE12 .101 C8
 Stamford PE9 ...143 A4
Rockland Rise LE67 .71 F6
Rockleigh Gdns LE65 .69 A6
Rockley Rd LE4 ..128 C1
Rock Rd PE9 ....143 C3
Rock Terr LE67 ..143 D3
Rock The NG32 ..23 C7
Rodney Cl LE10 ..197 D4
Roebuck Cl LE8 ..201 F5
Roecliff Cl LE67 .98 E1
Roecliffe Rd LE7 .100 B4
Roedean Cl LE65 .69 A7
Roehampton Dr LE18 .180 B5
Roe House La CV9,
 DE12 ....119 D4
Roesta Cl LE12 ..49 B6
Rogerstone Rd LE5 .156 D4
Rogue's La
 Cottesmore LE15 .87 D1
 Hinckley LE10 ...197 C6
ROLLESTON 184 E6
Rolleston Cl LE2 .241 A3
Rolleston Prim Sch
 LE2 ....179 D2
Rolleston Rd
 Billesdon LE7 ...184 C8
 Wigston LE18 ...180 B3
Rolleston St LE5 .155 D6
Roman Cl
 Claybrooke Magna
  LE17 ....232 E6
 Desford LE9 ....151 C3
 Earl Shilton LE9 .176 A1
Roman Hill LE18 .203 E8
Roman Rd LE4 ...129 A5
Romans Cres LE67 .72 D1
Roman St LE3 ...154 D4
Romans The LE2 .76 C1
Roman Way
 Market Harborough
  LE16 ....240 E4
 Syston LE7 ......102 E2
Romney Cl LE10 .197 A3
Romorantin Pl NG10 .10 E7
Romulus Ct LE19 .178 D5
Romway Ave LE5 .155 C2
Romway Cl LE12 .50 C3
Romway Rd LE5 .155 E2
Rona Gdns LE5 ..156 E7
Ronald Ct LE2 ..155 C1
Ronald Toon Rd LE9 .199 A8
Ronald West Ct LE11 .51 D1
Roods The LE7 ..101 E6
Rookery Cl LE3 ..126 F3
Rookery Cl
 Fenny Drayton CV13 .195 A4
 Kibworth Beauchamp
  LE8 ....224 B8
Rookery La
 Groby LE6 ....126 F3
 Stretton LE15 ...88 F4
 Wymondham LE14 .129 D6
 Wymondham LE14 .62 D2
Rookery The
 Barrow-u-S LE12 .76 C8
 Heather LE67 ...95 B2
 Langham LE15 ..110 C3
 Woodville DE11 .44 F2
Rookwell Dr LE4 .240 F1
Roosevelt Ave NG10 .10 C5
Rosamund Ave LE3 .179 A8
Rose Acre Cl LE7 .156 F7
Rosebank Rd LE8 .202 F4
Rosebank View DE12 .9 F5
Rosebarn Way LE5 .130 C1
Roseberry Ave LE4 .58 B3
Rosebery Ave
 Kibworth Beauchamp
  LE8 ....223 F8
 Melton Mowbray LE13 .59 D3

Rosebery Rd LE7...127 E7
Rosebery St
  Leicester LE5...155 D6
  Loughborough LE11...51 F4
Rose Cl LE15...166 D3
Rose Cres LE3...152 F2
Rosecroft Gdns DE11...44 C3
Rosedale LE67...71 E7
Rose Dale LE17...247 A4
Rosedale Ave LE4...129 D2
Rosedale Cl NG10...10 B6
Rosedale Rd LE18...180 F2
Rosedene Cl LE4...129 E6
Rosedene Cl LE9...152 F4
Rosedene View DE12...67 C4
Rose Farm Cl LE3...153 F4
Rosehill LE11...51 C4
Rose Hill DE11...44 E3
Rosemary Cres LE67...72 A4
Rosemary Way LE10...215 B7
Rosemead Dr LE2...181 A4
Rosemoor Cl LE16...241 B3
Roseneath Ave LE4...129 E3
Rose St LE4...128 F2
Rose Tree Ave LE4...129 A8
Rose Valley DE11...44 A5
Roseway
  Leicester LE4...129 D3
  Stoke Golding CV13...196 D7
Rosewood Cl LE18...215 F6
Rosewood Way LE15...75 A6
Roslyn St LE2...155 C4
Rosminian Way LE7...78 A2
Rossal Dr LE65...69 A7
Ross Cl LE13...59 E5
Rossendale Rd LE9...198 E7
Rossett Dr LE4...128 D2
Rossetti Rd LE19...178 A3
Rosslyn Cres LE5...156 E7
Rosslyn Ave LE12...76 C1
Rosslyn Rd LE67...71 F4
Ross Wlk LE4...129 A1
Ross' Wlk LE4...155 A8
Roston Dr LE10...215 A8
ROTHERBY...79 F6
Rotherby Ave LE4...129 D1
Rotherby Rd LE7...80 B7
Rotherby Rd LE7...80 B1
Rotherwood Dr LE9...69 B7
ROTHLEY...101 E6
Rothley CE Prim Sch
  LE7...101 E7
ROTHLEY PLAIN...101 B8
Rothley Rd LE12...76 B3
Rothley St LE4...129 A1
Rothley Sta* LE7...101 B5
Rouen Way LE65...69 A6
Roughton St LE4...129 B2
Roundhay Rd LE3...154 C2
Roundhill LE9...152 E5
Roundhill Cl
  Market Harborough
  LE16...241 B2
  Syston LE7...102 F2
Roundhill Com Coll
  LE4...102 E1
Roundhill Rd LE5...155 C3
Roundhills The LE9...198 F5
Roundhill Way LE11...51 B3
Roundway The LE4...129 F5
Routh Ave DE74...17 B2
Rowan Ave
  Coalville LE67...97 B8
  Hathern LE12...30 A2
  Market Harborough
  LE16...240 D1
Rowanberry Ave LE3...153 C6
Rowan Cl
  Measham DE12...93 C5
  Moira DE12...68 B6
Rowan Ct NN17...230 E1
Rowan Dr
  Ibstock LE67...95 E1
  Lutterworth LE17...244 B6
Rowan St LE3...154 C7
Rowans The LE8...202 E4
Rowan Way LE9...151 B3
Rowbank Way LE11...51 B3
Rowe Leyes Furlong
  LE7...76 F1
Rowena Ct LE12...101 E8
Rowena Dr LE65...69 B7
Rowlandson Cl LE4...101 D1
Rowlands The LE67...70 F6
Rowlands Way LE2...179 B2
Rowland Way CV9...170 C2
Rowlatts Hill Prim Sch
  LE5...156 A6
Rowlatts Hill Rd LE5...156 A6
Rowlett Rd NN17...230 E1
Rowley Cl
  Fleckney LE8...223 A6
  Swadlincote DE11...44 D5
Rowley Ct DE74...44 B4
ROWLEY FIELDS...154 D1
Rowley Fields Ave
  LE3...179 B8
Rowsley Ave
  Leicester LE5...155 D4
  Long Eaton NG10...10 A5
Rowsley St LE5...155 D4
Row The
  Garthorpe LE14...62 A6
  Rotherby LE14...79 F5
  Slawston LE16...209 B1
Roxburgh Rd PE9...143 B4
Royal Arc ◆ LE1...259 B4
Royal Ct LE15...215 D7

Royal East St LE1...259 B5
Royal Kent St LE1...259 A5
Royal La DE12...67 B4
Royal Meadow Dr
  CV9...170 E2
Royal Oak Cl LE12...122 E8
Royal Rd LE4...129 B2
Royal Way LE11...52 A6
Royce Cl
  Braunstone Town LE3...153 C2
  Corby NN17...230 F1
Roy Cl LE19...201 C8
Roydale Cl LE11...51 E6
Roydene Cres LE4...128 C2
Royland Rd LE2...52 B3
Royston Cl LE2...179 D2
Rubicon Cl LE12...76 F1
Ruby St LE3...154 C7
Rudbeck Ave LE13...59 A4
Ruddington Wlk LE4...128 E4
Ruddle Way LE15...110 D3
Ruding Rd LE3...154 D4
Ruding St LE3...259 A4
Rudyard Cl LE11...51 B2
Rufford Cl
  Hinckley LE10...215 D3
  Loughborough LE11...51 B5
Rufford Rd NG10...10 B4
Rufford St LE5...155 E6
RUGBY...257 B2
Rugby Cl
  Ashby-de-la-Z LE65...69 A8
  Market Harborough
  LE16...240 D2
Rugby Rd
  Cotesbach LE17...244 B1
  Hinckley LE10...215 D5
  Lilbourne CV23...257 F6
  South Kilworth LE17...254 E6
  Swinford LE17...254 B3
Rugby St LE3...154 D7
Rugeley Ave NG10...10 F7
Rumsey Cl
  Quorn (Quorndon) LE12...75 E6
  Thringstone LE67...71 C8
Rumsey Dr LE8...202 A8
Runcorn Cl LE2...179 D3
Runcorn Rd LE2...179 D3
Runnymede Gdns
  LE3...153 D7
Rupert Brooke Rd
  LE11...51 D4
Rupert Cres LE7...103 E6
Rupert Ho LE2...179 C2
Rupert Law Cl LE12...75 F7
Rupert Rd LE16...240 E3
Rupert St LE1...259 B3
Ruperts Way LE8...205 B8
Rushby Rd LE67...96 E3
Rush Cl LE9...150 B3
Rushden Ho LE3...153 C6
Rushes La LE16...239 F3
Rushes The LE11...52 A4
Rushes The LE11...52 A4
Rushes The LE11...98 E1
Rushey Cl
  Barlestone CV13...149 D7
  Leicester LE4...129 C4
Rushey La LE17...76 B2
RUSHEY MEAD...129 C4
Rushey Mead Prim Sch
  LE4...129 C2
Rushey Mead Sec Sch
  LE4...129 C4
Rushford Cl LE4...129 D1
Rushford Dr LE4...129 D1
Rush Leys NG10...10 D5
Rushmere Wlk LE3...153 A2
Rushton Dr LE2...179 B4
Rushton Yd ◆ LE65...69 B6
Ruskin Ave
  Long Eaton NG10...10 B5
  Syston LE7...103 C2
Ruskin Field LE7...127 C7
Ruskington Dr LE18...180 D5
Russ Cl LE19...75 F7
Russell Ct LE2...179 C6
Russell Sq ◆ LE1...155 A7
Russell St
  Loughborough LE11...52 C4
  Swadlincote DE11...44 C3
Russett Cl
  Barwell LE9...198 A7
  Market Harborough
  LE16...240 F5
Russet Way LE4...102 C1
Ruston Cl DE11...44 B4
Rutherford Rd LE4...128 A4
Rutland Ave
  Hinckley LE10...215 C7
  Leicester LE4...154 E1
  Wigston LE18...180 B3
Rutland Belle Cruise*
  LE15...140 B4
Rutland Cl
  Leicester Forest East
  LE3...153 A3
  South Witham NG33...65 B3
  Uppingham LE15...189 A5
Rutland Coll The
  LE15...137 F7
Rutland Ctr LE1...259 C4
Rutland Cty Mus*
  LE15...138 A6
Rutland Dr LE4...129 E7

Rutland Falconry & Owl
  Ctr* LE15...112 C1
Rutland Farm Pk*
  LE15...138 A5
Rutland Ho LE13...59 D3
Rutland La NG13...3 B2
Rutland Meml Hospl
  LE15...137 E6
Rutland Open Air
  Theatre* PE9...116 C2
Rutland Railway Line*
  LE15...111 F8
Rutland Railway Mus*
  LE15...111 F8
Rutland Rd PE9...143 F5
Rutland Sq NG13...6 C2
Rutland St
  Leicester LE1...259 C3
  Loughborough LE11...52 C3
  Melton Mowbray LE13...59 D3
Rutland Terr PE9...143 C2
Rutland Water* LE15...139 E1
Rutland Water Nature
  Reserve* LE15...138 F6
Rutland Water
  Watersports Ctr*
  LE15...140 B5
Rutland Way
  Loughborough LE11...51 E3
  Ryhall PE9...116 F1
Rutland Wlk LE16...240 F5
Rycroft Rd DE74...17 D6
Rydal Ave
  Loughborough LE11...51 D1
  Nuneaton CV11...214 A6
Rydal Cl LE16...214 F7
Rydal Gdns LE65...69 C4
Rydal St LE2...259 A2
Ryde Ave LE2...180 D7
Ryder Rd LE3...153 C6
Rydermay LE17...244 B5
Rye Cl LE2...179 E4
Ryefield LE15...138 A8
Ryegate Cres LE4...128 F8
Rye Hill Ave LE17...244 D5
RYHALL...116 F1
Ryhall CE Prim Sch
  PE9...116 F2
Ryhall Rd
  Great Casterton PE9...115 F1
  Stamford PE9...143 F5
Ryhall Rd Ind Est PE9...143 F5
Rylands LE16...241 B3

S

Sabaramati Ho LE1...155 B7
Sacheverell Way LE6...126 E1
Sacheverel Rd LE3...153 D6
Sackville Gdns LE2...180 C8
Sacred Heart RC Prim Sch
  Leicester LE5...155 C6
  Loughborough LE11...52 A1
SADDINGTON...223 C4
Saddington Rd
  Fleckney LE8...223 A7
  Mowsley LE17...237 F7
  Shearsby LE8, LE17...222 C3
  Smeeton Westerby LE8...223 B6
Saddle Cl LE13...59 A5
Saddler Rd LE13...130 C3
Saddlers Cl
  Glenfield LE3...153 B8
  Hinckley LE10...215 F6
  Loughborough LE11...51 F6
Saddlers' Cl LE7...103 D7
Sadlers Wells LE12...49 B6
Saffron Ct
  ◆ Barwell LE9...198 A6
  Leicester LE2...179 F5
Saffron Hill Rd LE2...179 E8
Saffron La LE2...179 E7
Saffron Rd LE18...180 D2
Saffron Way LE2...179 E6
Sage Cross St LE13...59 C3
Sage Dr DE11...44 F4
Sage Rd LE2...154 D4
St Aidan's Ave LE7...102 F3
St Albans Cl
  Long Eaton NG10...10 E5
  Oakham LE15...138 B6
St Albans Rd ◆ LE2...155 B4
St Andrew's CE Prim Sch
  LE17...246 E3
St Andrews Cl
  Burton o t W LE12...54 A7
  Great Easton LE16...229 D7
  Whissendine LE15...84 F1
St Andrew's Cl LE67...71 D8
St Andrews Ct LE5...156 A2
St Andrew's Dr CV11...214 B1
St Andrews Dr LE17...155 F1
St Andrews Rd LE2...179 E2
St Andrew's Rise DE74...18 C1
St Annes Cl
  Coalville LE67...137 F6
  Syston LE7...103 C2
St Annes Dr LE2...179 D7
St Anne's La
  Castle Donington DE74...17 B3
  Sutton Bonington LE12...30 B6
St Augustine Rd LE3...154 D5
St Augustine's RC Prim
  Sch The PE9...143 E5
St Austell Cl CV11...214 A5
St Austell Rd LE5...156 E7

St Barnabas CE Prim Sch
  LE5...155 F2
St Barnard's Rd LE67...72 A4
St Bartholomew CE Prim
  Sch LE12...75 C5
St Bartholomews Way LE13,
  LE14...58 F6
St Bernards Ave LE3...129 B3
St Bernard's Cl LE12...50 A3
St Bernard St LE4...129 B2
St Botolph Rd LE2...50 B3
St Botolph's CE Prim Sch
  LE12...50 C4
St Buryan Cl CV11...214 A5
St Catharine St LE13...127 D2
St Catharines Terr
  LE7...157 F4
St Catharines Way
  LE7...157 F4
St Catherines Ave
  CV13...148 E3
St Catherine's Cl LE10...215 F7
St Chad's Cl DE72...9 A7
St Charles's RC Prim Sch
  DE12...93 D5
St Christophers Pk Cvn
  Site LE7...96 F3
St Christopher's Rd
  LE67...96 E8
St Clares Ct LE67...96 E8
St Clement's PE9...143 C3
St Clements Cl LE3...154 B7
St Columba Way LE7...102 F4
St Crispin's Sch LE2...155 B2
St Crispin's Way LE4...102 E1
St Cuthbert's Ave LE8...205 B8
St Cuthbert's CE Prim Sch
  LE8...182 C1
St Davids Cl LE3...152 F3
St David's Cl LE2...155 E1
St David's Cres LE3...72 C1
St Davids Ct LE67...72 C1
St Davids Rd LE3...153 C6
St Denys CE Inf Sch
  LE67...95 E1
St Denys' Cres LE67...95 E1
St Dunstan Rd LE3...154 C6
St Edwards Ce Prim Sch
  DE74...17 B3
St Edward's RC Prim Sch
  DE11...44 B5
St Edward's Rd DE74...17 D7
St Faiths Dr LE67...96 C8
St Francis Cl LE10...197 C3
St Francis RC Prim Sch
  LE13...59 B2
St Georges Ave PE9...143 F4
St George's Ave LE11...197 C1
St George's CE Prim Sch
  Stamford PE9...143 E5
  Swadlincote DE11...44 B1
St Georges Cl LE9...150 B5
St George's Hill LE7...71 A7
St George's Rd CV9...170 E1
St George's Ret Pk
  LE1...155 B6
St George's Sq ◆
  PE9...143 E3
St George's St LE1...259 C3
St George's St PE9...143 E3
St Giles Cl CV13...149 D8
St Gregory's Dr LE12...77 D3
St Helens Cl LE4...128 C1
St Helen's Cl LE10...217 C4
St Helens Dr LE4...128 D1
St Hildas Cl LE7...103 C2
St Ives LE67...97 B8
St Ives Rd
  Leicester LE4...129 E2
  Wigston LE18...180 D1
St James Cl
  Huncote LE9...200 D7
  Leicester, Oadby LE2...181 C3
  Shepshed LE12...50 B2
  Twycross CV9...146 D6
St James Ct LE4...129 B7
St James' Ct LE2...155 C3
St James Rd
  Leicester LE2...155 C3
  Shepshed LE12...50 B3
St James's Cl LE10...215 D5
St James St LE1...259 C4
St James Terr LE2...155 C3
St John Fisher RC Prim
  Sch LE18...180 E4
St Johns
  Hinckley LE10...197 E1
  Narborough LE19...178 E3
St John's Ave LE7...103 C3
St John's Bsns Pk
  LE17...244 D4
St John's CE
  Coalville LE67...96 D6
  Heather LE67...95 B2
  Lutterworth LE17...244 B5
  Ryhall PE9...116 F2
St Johns Cl LE13...59 C5
St John's Dr LE13...59 C5
St Johns Rd
  Asfordby Hill LE14...58 D4
  Leicester LE2...155 C2
St John's St
  Long Eaton NG10...10 D7
  Stamford PE9...143 D3

St John St LE1...259 B5
St John's Terr ◆ PE9...143 C3
St John the Baptist CE
  Prim Sch LE2...155 C2
St Joseph's RC Prim Sch
  Leicester LE5...156 D8
  Market Harborough
  LE16...240 D3
St Laurence CE Prim Sch
  NG10...10 E6
St Laurence Ct NG10...10 E6
St Leonards Cl LE12...54 A7
St Leonards Ct LE2...155 B2
St Leonards Rd
  Leicester LE2...155 B1
  Leicester LE2...155 B2
St Leonard's St PE9...143 E3
St Luke's CE Prim Sch
  LE7...156 F4
St Luke's Cl LE7...156 F4
St Luke's Hospl LE16...240 D5
St Margaret Rd LE3...196 E7
St Margaret's CE Prim Sch
  CV13...196 F7
St Margarets Dr LE17...233 E8
St Margaret's St LE1...259 B3
St Margaret's Way LE4,
  LE1...154 E8
St Marks
  Leicester LE1...259 B3
  Stapleton LE9...174 C2
St Martin's LE1...215 E6
St Martin's Cl PE9...143 E2
St Martins Dr LE9...151 A3
St Martins E LE1...259 B3
St Martin's RC Sch
  CV13...196 F7
St Martins Sq LE1...259 B3
St Martins Wlk LE1...259 B3
St Martins Yd ◆ LE1...240 E3
St Mary & St John CE
  Prim Sch LE15...166 C3
St Marys Ave LE5...156 C8
St Mary's Ave
  Barwell LE9...197 F5
  Braunstone Town LE3...153 C3
  Coalville LE67...96 B6
  Draycott DE72...9 A7
St Mary's CE Prim Sch
  Bitteswell LE17...244 B8
  Hinckley LE10...215 D8
  Melton Mowbray LE13...59 A6
St Marys Cl
  Broughton Astley LE9...218 E6
  Burton o t W LE12...54 A7
  Cosgerstone CV13...147 D7
  Osgathorpe LE12...48 E4
St Mary's Cl
  Bottesford NG13...3 B3
  Edith Weston LE15...166 B7
  Loughborough LE11...51 F4
St Marys Ct
  Barwell LE9...198 A5
  Braunstone Town LE3...153 C3
  Market Harborough
  LE16...241 A4
St Mary's Fields Inf Sch
  LE1...154 C2
St Marys Gr LE9...118 D3
St Mary's Ho LE17...244 C4
St Mary's Hospl LE3...59 D3
St Mary's La
  Bottesford NG13...3 B2
  Ravenstone LE67...96 A7
St Mary's Mews LE9...198 A5
St Mary's Pl
  Market Harborough
  LE16...240 F3
  Stamford PE9...143 D3
St Mary's RC Prim Sch
  LE11...52 A4
St Mary's Rd
  Hinckley LE10...215 D8
  Market Harborough
  LE16...244 B5
  Manton LE15...164 D6
  Market Harborough
  LE16...240 D3
  Sileby LE12...77 C4
St Mary's St PE9...143 D3
St Mary's Way LE15...155 B2
St Matthew's Ave LE65...47 F6
St Matthews Bsns Ctr
  LE1...259 C5
St Matthews Way LE1...259 C4
St Maxime Ho LE2...155 C1
St Mellion Cl LE4...128 B7
St Michael & All Angels
  CE Prim Sch LE7...79 A1
St Michaels Ave LE4...129 C3
St Michaels Cl CV9...170 F1
St Michael's Cl
  Ashby-de-la-Z LE65...69 C5
  Markfield LE67...98 D1
St Michael's Ct LE4...129 E7
St Michaels Dr LE67...95 E8
St Michael's Dr DE12...119 F8
St Michaels Ho LE2...30 B8
St Michaels Wlk LE7...183 F3

St Nicholas CE Prim Sch
  LE15 . . . . 112 C8
St Nicholas Circ LE1 . . . . 259 A3
St Nicholas Cl
  Austrey CV9 . . . . 119 B2
  Market Harborough
  LE16 . . . . 240 F2
St Nicholas Ct LE15 . . . . . 112 C8
St Nicholas Pl LE1 . . . . . . 259 A3
St Nicholas Way LE16 . . . 240 F2
ST NICOLAS PARK 214 A7
St Nicolas Park Dr
  CV11 . . . . 214 A6
St Olaves Cl LE1 . . . . 51 B5
St Oswalds Rd LE3 . . . . . . 153 F8
St Patrick's RC Prim Sch
  LE4 . . . . 129 B2
St Paul's CE Prim Sch
  LE12 . . . . 75 A1
St Pauls Cl LE2 . . . . 181 D6
St Pauls Ct LE7 . . . . 103 B4
St Paul's Dr LE7 . . . . 103 A2
St Pauls Gdns LE18 . . . . . 197 E1
St Pauls RC Sch LE15 . . . . 156 C4
St Pauls Rd LE3 . . . . 154 C6
St Paul's St PE9 . . . . 143 E3
St Peter & St Paul CE
  Prim Sch LE7 . . . . 103 B5
St Peters Ave LE12 . . . . 30 A1
St Peter's Ave LE9 . . . . . . 194 B7
St Peter CE Prim Sch
  Market Bosworth
  CV13 . . . . 148 D3
  Netherseal DE12 . . . . 91 F6
  Whetstone LE8 . . . . 201 F7
  Wymondham LE14 . . . . 62 D2
St Peter's Cl
  Glenfield LE3 . . . . 153 B8
  Leire LE17 . . . . 218 F1
  Market Bosworth CV13 . . . 148 D3
  Oakham LE15 . . . . 138 A6
  Witherley CV9 . . . . 194 B7
St Peters Ct
  2 Hinckley LE10 . . . . . . 197 E1
  Leicester LE2 . . . . 155 B4
  Market Bosworth CV13 . . . 148 F3
  Mountsorrel LE12 . . . . 76 E3
St Peter's Ct
  3 Stamford PE9 . . . . . . 143 D2
  Syston LE7 . . . . 103 B4
St Peters Dr LE8 . . . . 201 F8
St Peter's Dr LE67 . . . . . . 124 F3
St Peter's Hill **13** PE9 . . 143 D3
St Peters La LE1 . . . . 259 A4
St Peter's Path LE2 . . . . . 181 A5
St Peters Pl CV13 . . . . 121 E2
St Peter's RC Prim Sch
  LE9 . . . . 176 A1
St Peter's RC Sch
  LE10 . . . . 197 E1
St Peters Rd
  Atherstone CV9 . . . . 194 A7
  Leicester LE2 . . . . 155 C4
St Peter's Rd LE8 . . . . 221 F5
St Peter's St
  Stamford PE9 . . . . 143 D3
  Syston LE7 . . . . 103 A3
St Peters Terr LE7 . . . . . . 160 A8
St Peter's Vale PE9 . . . . . 143 D2
St Philip's Ct LE5 . . . . 155 D3
St Philips Rd
  Burton o t W LE12 . . . . 54 A7
  Leicester LE5 . . . . 155 D3
St Saviour's Hill LE5 . . . . 155 C6
St Saviours Rd
  Coalville LE67 . . . . 96 C8
  Leicester LE5 . . . . 155 C6
St Saviour's Rd LE5 . . . . . 155 E5
St Stephen's Ct DE11 . . . . . 44 E3
St Stephens Rd LE2 . . . . . 155 C4
St Swithin's Rd LE5 . . . . . 156 D5
St Thomas More RC Prim
  Sch LE2 . . . . 180 C8
St Thomas Rd LE2,
  LE18 . . . . 179 E1
St Thomas' Rd LE8 . . . . . . 182 C1
St Tibba Way PE9 . . . . 116 E1
St Vincent Cl NG10 . . . . 10 E7
St Vincents Cl LE67 . . . . . . 96 C7
St Wilfrid's Ct LE8 . . . . . . 206 A1
St Winefride Rd LE12 . . . . . 50 B3
St Winefride's RC Prim
  Sch LE12 . . . . 50 B4
St Winifreds Ct NG10 . . . . . 18 F4
St Wolstan's Ct LE18 . . . . 180 E3
Salcombe Cl LE18 . . . . 180 C1
Salcombe Dr LE3 . . . . 153 C8
Salem Rd LE10 . . . . 215 F5
Salford Cl NN6 . . . . 256 E6
Salisbury Ave
  Croft LE9 . . . . 200 C4
  5 Leicester LE2 . . . . . . 155 B4
  Melton Mowbray LE13 . . . . . 59 D4
Salisbury Cl
  Blaby LE8 . . . . 202 B6
  Desford LE9 . . . . 151 A2
Salisbury Ct **10** LE2 . . . 155 B4
Salisbury Dr DE11 . . . . 44 A5
Salisbury Ho LE10 . . . . . . 197 C4
Salisbury La DE73 . . . . 26 B7
Salisbury Rd
  Hinckley LE10 . . . . 216 B7
  Leicester LE1 . . . . 155 B4
Salisbury St
  Long Eaton NG10 . . . . 10 E7

Salisbury St continued
  Loughborough LE11 . . . . 52 C4
Salkeld Rd LE2 . . . . 179 C2
Salmon Mews LE12 . . . . 50 B4
Saltash Cl LE18 . . . . 180 C1
SALTBY 24 E1
Saltby Rd
  Croxton Kerrial NG32 . . . . . 24 B7
  Sproxton LE14 . . . . 41 F6
Saltcoates Ave LE4 . . . . . 129 C4
Salter Cl DE74 . . . . 16 F4
Saltersford Rd LE5 . . . . . 155 F7
Saltersgate Dr LE4 . . . . . 129 A8
Salter's Hill Dr LE14 . . . . 106 E4
Salt's Cl LE19 . . . . 178 B2
Salt St B79, CV9 . . . . 119 B5
Sam Brown Ind Est
  LE8 . . . . 201 F5
Samphire Cl LE5 . . . . 130 D2
Samson Rd
  Coalville LE67 . . . . 71 D3
  Leicester LE5 . . . . 154 B7
Samual Ct LE15 . . . . 189 A5
Samuel St LE1 . . . . 155 B6
Sanara Cl LE14 . . . . 129 B3
Sandacre St LE1 . . . . 259 B4
Sandalwood Rd LE11 . . . . . 51 F1
Sandcliffe Pk DE11 . . . . . . 44 D7
Sandcliffe Rd DE11 . . . . . . 44 D6
Sandcroft Cl DE11 . . . . 44 D5
Sanderman Ho DE11 . . . . . 44 E3
Sanders Cl CV9 . . . . 170 E1
Sanderson Cl LE18 . . . . . . 202 A6
Sanders Rd LE12 . . . . 75 F5
Sandfield Cl LE4 . . . . 129 E5
Sandfield Close Prim Sch
  LE4 . . . . 129 E5
Sandford Ave NG10 . . . . . . 10 E7
Sandford Cl
  Hinckley LE10 . . . . 197 F1
  Leicester LE5 . . . . 156 A6
Sandford Rd LE5 . . . . 156 A6
Sandford Rd LE17 . . . . . . 103 A3
Sand Furrows PE9 . . . . . . 167 F5
Sandgate Ave LE4 . . . . . . 128 F6
Sandham Bridge Rd
  LE7 . . . . 100 F3
Sandhill Dr LE19 . . . . 178 D1
Sandhills Ave LE5 . . . . . . 130 C3
Sandhills Cl
  Belton LE12 . . . . 49 B6
  Measham DE12 . . . . 93 C4
Sandhills The LE12 . . . . 75 E6
Sandhole La LE12 . . . . 49 D1
Sandhurst Cl LE3 . . . . 154 B6
Sandhurst Gdns LE3 . . . . 154 B6
Sandhurst Rd LE3 . . . . . . 154 B6
Sandhurst St LE2 . . . . 181 A6
Sandiacre Dr LE4 . . . . 129 F8
Sandlands The DE11 . . . . . 44 D6
Sandown Rd
  Glenfield LE3 . . . . 127 C1
  Leicester LE2 . . . . 155 D1
  Wigston LE18 . . . . 180 D4
Sandpiper Cl
  Leicester LE5 . . . . 155 C7
  Rugby CV23 . . . . 252 C1
Sand Pit La LE14 . . . . 20 C2
Sandringham Ave
  Earl Shilton LE9 . . . . 198 D7
  Leicester LE4 . . . . 129 B3
Sandringham Cl
  Oakham LE15 . . . . 137 E5
  Stamford PE9 . . . . 143 D5
  Swadlincote DE11 . . . . 44 B5
Sandringham Rd
  Coalville LE67 . . . . 96 F8
  Glen Parva LE2 . . . . 179 E1
Sandringham Rise
  LE12 . . . . 49 F2
Sandringham Way
  LE16 . . . . 241 B3
Sands The LE14 . . . . 20 D3
Sandstone Cl DE11 . . . . . . 68 B8
Sandtop La DE11 . . . . 68 C8
Sandwell Cl NG10 . . . . 10 A6
Sandy Cres LE10 . . . . 197 C1
Sandyhurst LE3 . . . . 153 E4
Sandy La
  Melton Mowbray LE13,
  LE14 . . . . 82 D5
  Newton Regis B79 . . . . 118 D6
  Scalford LE14 . . . . 38 E5
Sandy Rise LE18 . . . . 180 F4
Sankey Dr DE11 . . . . 44 C1
Sanvey Cl LE2 . . . . 179 C6
Sanvey Gate LE1 . . . . 259 A5
Sanvey La LE2 . . . . 179 C6
Sanvey Mill LE1 . . . . 259 A5
SAPCOTE 217 D7
Sapcote Dr LE13 . . . . 59 E1
Sapcote Rd
  Hinckley LE10 . . . . 216 B7
  Stoney Stanton LE9 . . . . . . 199 E1
Sargent's Ct PE9 . . . . 143 C4
Sarson Cl LE14 . . . . 58 A2
Sarson St LE12 . . . . 75 F6
Saunderson Rd LE4 . . . . . 128 C4
Savernake Rd LE4 . . . . . . 128 C1
Saville Cl LE10 . . . . 197 E2
Saville Dr LE12 . . . . 77 C2
Saville Rd LE8 . . . . 202 C6
Saville St LE5 . . . . 155 E6
Sawbridge Cl LE67 . . . . 96 E8
Sawbrook LE8 . . . . 223 A7
Sawday St LE2 . . . . 154 E3
Sawgate Rd LE14 . . . . 83 D7

SAWLEY 10 A4
Sawley Inch Sch NG10 . . . 10 A5
Sawley Jun Sch NG10 . . . . 10 A5
Sawley Rd
  Breaston DE72 . . . . 9 E6
  Draycott DE72 . . . . 9 B7
Sawley St LE5 . . . . 155 D3
Sawmand Cl NG10 . . . . 10 C6
SAXBY 61 E4
Saxby Rd LE13 . . . . 59 E3
Saxby Road Ind Est
  LE13 . . . . 59 E3
Saxby St LE2 . . . . 155 B4
SAXELBYE 57 E7
Saxelbye La LE14 . . . . 57 B8
Saxelby Rd LE14 . . . . 57 E4
Saxon Cl
  Breedon on t H DE73 . . . . . 26 F2
  Market Harborough
  LE16 . . . . 240 F4
Saxon Ct PE9 . . . . 143 E2
Saxon Dale LE2 . . . . 179 C2
Saxondale Rd LE18 . . . . . 203 E8
Saxons Lea LE14 . . . . 108 D3
Saxons Rise LE16 . . . . . . 126 C1
Saxon St LE3 . . . . 154 D4
Saxon Way LE65 . . . . 69 A7
Saxthorpe Rd LE5 . . . . . . 130 B2
Scalborough Cl LE8 . . . . . 202 C4
SCALFORD 38 E5
Scalford CE Prim Sch
  LE14 . . . . 38 E5
Scalford Rd
  Eastwell LE14 . . . . 22 A5
  Melton Mowbray LE13 . . . . . 59 C6
Scalpay Cl LE4 . . . . 128 B3
Scarborough Ct LE5 . . . . . 155 D4
Scarborough Rd LE4 . . . . 129 C2
Schofield Rd
  Loughborough LE11 . . . . 51 C3
  Oakham LE15 . . . . 138 A8
Scholars Wlk LE15 . . . . . . 155 C2
School Cl
  Croft LE9 . . . . 200 C3
  Hinckley LE10 . . . . 216 A6
  Moira DE11 . . . . 44 C1
School Cotts LE14 . . . . . . 108 B2
School Cres LE9 . . . . 218 F7
School Farm Yd LE16 . . . . 227 B3
Schoolgate LE2 . . . . 179 F5
School Gdns CV21 . . . . . . 257 A1
School Hill
  Sproxton LE14 . . . . 41 F5
  Walton on t V LE12 . . . . 54 A4
School House Cl LE7 . . . . 127 D5
School La
  Barkby LE7 . . . . 130 D8
  Barrowden LE15 . . . . 191 F5
  Belton LE12 . . . . 49 B6
  Birstall LE4 . . . . 129 A6
  Braybrooke LE16 . . . . 251 F5
  Castle Donington DE74 . . . . 17 A4
  Cottingham LE16 . . . . 229 C1
  Cranoe LE16 . . . . 208 E3
  Croxton Kerrial NG32 . . . . . 24 A7
  Empingham LE15 . . . . 141 B6
  Gaulby LE7 . . . . 183 D6
  Harby LE14 . . . . 142 B8
  Houghton on t H LE7 . . . . . 157 F3
  Huncote LE9 . . . . 200 D7
  Husbands Bosworth
  LE17 . . . . 247 E5
  Leicester LE5 . . . . 156 B2
  Long Clawson LE14 . . . . 20 C3
  Lubenham LE16 . . . . 239 F3
  Market Harborough
  LE16 . . . . 240 E3
  Morcott LE15 . . . . 191 A6
  Narborough LE19 . . . . 201 B7
  Newbold LE67 . . . . 47 E2
  Newton Burgoland
  LE67 . . . . 121 C6
  Normanton le H LE67 . . . . . 94 F6
  Peatling Magna LE8 . . . . . 221 B6
  Peggs Green LE67 . . . . 48 A1
  Queniborough LE7 . . . . 103 F5
  Quorn (Quorndon) LE12 . . . 76 A6
  Rempstone LE12 . . . . 32 D5
  Scalford LE14 . . . . 38 E5
  Sedgebrook NG32 . . . . 8 F8
  Sewstern NG33 . . . . 42 E1
  Sharnford LE10 . . . . 217 C4
  South Croxton LE7 . . . . . . 105 B3
  Staple Hill LE16 . . . . 174 E2
  Stathern LE14 . . . . 13 A2
  Swinford LE17 . . . . 254 B4
  Thistleton LE15 . . . . 64 E1
  Uffington PE9 . . . . 144 E4
  Uppingham LE15 . . . . 189 B4
  Whitwick LE67 . . . . 71 D6
  Woodhouse LE12 . . . . 75 B3
School Rd
  Gretton NN17 . . . . 213 B1
  Kibworth Beauchamp
  LE8 . . . . 224 A8
  Oakham LE15 . . . . 138 A7
School St
  Churchover CV23 . . . . 252 C6
  Fleckney LE8 . . . . 222 F7
  Loughborough LE11 . . . . 52 B4
  Moira DE12 . . . . 67 F2
  Oakthorpe DE12 . . . . 93 A7
  Rothley LE7 . . . . 101 F6
  Rugby CV21 . . . . 257 A1
  Swadlincote DE11 . . . . 44 B2
  Syston LE7 . . . . 103 B4
School View NG13 . . . . 3 A2
School Wlk LE8 . . . . 224 A8

Scoborough Rd LE16,
  LE17 . . . . 239 A1
Scotgate
  Harringworth NN17 . . . . . . 213 F7
  Stamford PE9 . . . . 143 D3
SCOTLAND 182 F1
Scotland End LE16 . . . . . . 240 F1
Scotland La
  Burton Overy LE8 . . . . 182 F1
  Houghton on t H LE7 . . . . . 157 F4
Scotland Rd LE16 . . . . 241 A2
Scotlands Dr LE67 . . . . 96 D8
Scotlands Ind Est LE67 . . 96 E8
Scotlands Rd LE67 . . . . 96 D8
Scotland Way LE8 . . . . . . 202 F3
Scotswood Cres LE2 . . . . 179 D3
Scott Cl
  Market Harborough
  LE16 . . . . 240 E5
  Uppingham LE15 . . . . 189 B4
Scott Ct LE2 . . . . 180 A8
Scotts Cl LE65 . . . . 69 B7
Scott St LE2 . . . . 180 A8
SCRAPTOFT 156 F8
Scraptoft La
  Beeby LE7 . . . . 131 C4
  Leicester LE7 . . . . 156 C7
Scraptoft Mews LE5 . . . . 156 A7
Scraptoft Rise LE7 . . . . . . 156 F8
Scraptoft Valley Prim Sch
  LE5 . . . . 156 E8
Scrivener Cl LE7 . . . . 157 B5
Scudamore Rd LE3 . . . . . 153 C5
Sculthorpe Cl LE15 . . . . . 138 B6
Seacole Cl LE3 . . . . 153 D2
Seaford Rd LE2 . . . . 179 D5
Seaforth Dr LE10 . . . . 197 A1
SEAGRAVE 77 F8
Seagrave Dr LE2 . . . . 72 D1
Seagrave Dr LE2 . . . . 180 F6
Seagrave Rd
  Sileby LE12 . . . . 77 D5
  Thrussington LE7 . . . . 78 E5
Seagrave Village Prim Sch
  LE12 . . . . 77 F8
SEAGRAVE WOLDS 55 C4
Seals Cl LE15 . . . . 54 A7
Seals Rd DE12 . . . . 67 E1
SEATON 190 C1
Seaton Cl LE10 . . . . 216 B7
Seaton Dr LE15 . . . . 189 C4
Seaton Rd
  Barrowden LE15 . . . . 191 C4
  Braunstone Town LE3 . . . . 153 C1
  Glaston LE15 . . . . 190 B4
  Harringworth NN17 . . . . . . 213 E8
  Stamford PE9 . . . . 143 D2
  Uppingham LE15 . . . . 189 C4
  Wigston LE18 . . . . 180 C2
Seaton Rise LE5 . . . . 130 E1
SECKINGTON 118 A3
Seckington La B79 . . . . . . 118 C3
Second Drift PE9 . . . . 169 D8
Seddons Cl LE4 . . . . 128 D4
SEDGEBROOK 8 E8
Sedgebrook Rd
  Allington NG32 . . . . 4 F4
  Leicester LE5 . . . . 156 E4
Sedgefield Dr
  Leicester LE7 . . . . 156 F6
  Syston LE7 . . . . 102 E3
Sedgemoor Rd NG10 . . . . . 10 E5
Segrave Rd LE3 . . . . 154 B2
Seine La LE19 . . . . 177 F4
Selbourne Ct LE11 . . . . 52 C4
Selbourne St LE11 . . . . . . 52 C4
Selbury Dr LE2 . . . . 180 F5
Selby Ave LE5 . . . . 130 D1
Selby Cl LE16 . . . . 250 E8
Selina Cl DE74 . . . . 17 A4
Selina St DE73 . . . . 26 A7
Selkirk Rd LE4 . . . . 129 D4
Sellars Way LE8 . . . . 76 B5
Selwyn Rd PE9 . . . . 143 C5
Senator Cl LE7 . . . . 102 F2
Sence Cres LE8 . . . . 205 A8
Sence Valley Forest Pk*
  LE67 . . . . 95 E3
Sennen Cl CV11 . . . . 214 A5
Seton Cl LE11 . . . . 51 C7
Severn Ave LE10 . . . . 215 A8
Severn Cl
  Cosby LE9 . . . . 201 D3
  Oakham LE15 . . . . 137 E5
Severn Cres LE15 . . . . 166 D7
Severn Hill LE9 . . . . 59 B1
Severn Rd LE2 . . . . 181 D6
Severn St LE2 . . . . 155 B4
Severn Wlk NN17 . . . . 230 C1
Seward St LE11 . . . . 52 A3
SEWSTERN 63 F8
Sewstern La
  Allington NG23 . . . . 4 B8
  Harston NG32 . . . . 15 D6
  Muston NG32 . . . . 8 B8
Sewstern Rd NG33 . . . . . . 64 D8
Sextant Rd LE3 . . . . 156 C7
Seymour Cl LE11 . . . . 51 B5
Seymour Rd
  Burton o t W LE12 . . . . 53 F7
  Leicester LE2 . . . . 155 B1
Seymour St LE2 . . . . 155 B4
Seymour Way LE3 . . . . . . 152 F3
Shackelton Way LE17 . . . 243 D5
Shackerdale Rd LE2,
  LE18 . . . . 180 B5

SHACKERSTONE 121 E2
Shackerstone Rd
  CV13 . . . . 147 D8
Shackerstone Sta*
  CV13 . . . . 121 F2
Shackerstone Wlk
  CV13 . . . . 148 C6
Shackland Dr LE3 . . . . 93 D5
Shackleton Dr LE11 . . . . . 215 E4
Shackleton **4** LE1 . . . . . 155 A7
Shades Cl LE9 . . . . 200 C4
Shadows La CV13 . . . . . . 147 D7
Shadrack Cl LE9 . . . . 199 D1
Shady La LE2 . . . . 156 B1
Shaeffer Ct LE4 . . . . 128 B2
Shaftesbury Ave
  Leicester LE4 . . . . 129 B2
  Long Eaton NG10 . . . . 10 B4
Shaftesbury Jun Sch
  LE3 . . . . 154 D4
Shaftesbury Rd LE3 . . . . . 154 D4
Shakespear CI DE74 . . . . . 28 C5
Shakespeare Cl
  Braunstone Town LE3 . . . . 153 E1
  Coalville LE67 . . . . 44 C6
Shakespeare Dr
  Diseworth DE74 . . . . 28 C5
  Hinckley LE10 . . . . 197 C1
  Leicester LE3 . . . . 153 F1
  Nuneaton CV11 . . . . 214 A1
Shakespeare St
  Leicester LE2 . . . . 179 F8
  Loughborough LE11 . . . . 52 B4
Shakespeare Way
  NN17 . . . . 230 D1
Shambles Ct LE17 . . . . . . 244 D6
SHANGTON 207 A5
Shangton Rd LE8 . . . . 207 B3
Shanklin Ave LE2 . . . . . . 180 D7
Shanklin Dr LE2 . . . . 180 D7
Shanklin Gdns
  Leicester Forest East
  LE3 . . . . 153 B3
  Leicester LE2 . . . . 180 D7
Shannon Way LE15 . . . . . 137 E5
Shanti Margh LE4 . . . . . . 129 C2
SHARDLOW 9 B1
Shardlow Rd
  Aston-on-T DE72 . . . . 16 B7
  Wigston LE18 . . . . 180 C3
Sharmon Cres LE3 . . . . . 153 D6
Sharnbrook Gdns
  LE10 . . . . 217 C4
SHARNFORD 217 C6
Sharnford CE Prim Sch
  LE10 . . . . 217 C6
Sharnford Rd
  Aston Flamville LE10 . . . . 216 F6
  Sapcote LE9 . . . . 217 E6
Sharp Cl NG10 . . . . 10 C6
Sharpe's Plain PE9 . . . . . 167 F5
Sharpe Way LE19 . . . . 201 B7
Sharpland LE2 . . . . 179 C5
Sharpless Rd LE10 . . . . . . 215 F7
Sharpley Ave LE67 . . . . . . 72 A2
Sharpley Dr LE4 . . . . 128 A6
Sharpley Rd LE11 . . . . 51 C2
Sharply Hill LE6 . . . . 99 E3
Sharp's Cl LE12 . . . . 50 A4
Sharpswood Manor
  DE11 . . . . 44 E4
Sharrads Way LE15 . . . . . 110 D3
Shaw Cl LE18 . . . . 201 F6
SHAWELL 253 D5
Shawell Rd
  Cotesbach LE17 . . . . 244 D1
  Swinford LE17 . . . . 254 A4
Shaw La LE67 . . . . 97 E4
Shaw Wood Cl LE6 . . . . . 126 E3
Shearer Cl LE4 . . . . 129 E4
Shearers Ct LE11 . . . . 52 C5
SHEARSBY 222 A2
Shearsby Cl LE18 . . . . . . 180 D2
Shearsby Rd LE3 . . . . 204 C3
Sheene Cl LE4 . . . . 252 C1
Sheene Rd LE14 . . . . 128 A4
Sheepcote LE7 . . . . 101 E7
Sheepdyke LE15 . . . . 112 C8
Sheep Market **14** PE9 . . 143 D3
Sheepy Cl LE10 . . . . 197 F1
Sheepy La CV9 . . . . 145 E3
SHEEPY MAGNA 146 A3
Sheepy Magna CE Prim
  Sch CV9 . . . . 171 B8
SHEEPY PARVA 171 C7
Sheepy Rd
  Atherstone CV9 . . . . 170 D6
  Atherstone, Pinwall
  CV9 . . . . 170 C6
  Sibson CV13 . . . . 172 A6
  Twycross CV9 . . . . 146 C5
Sheet Hedges Wood Ctry
  Pk* LE6 . . . . 126 C4
Sheets Stores Ind Est
  NG10 . . . . 10 C5
Sheffield St LE3 . . . . 154 D3
Shelbourne St LE5 . . . . . . 155 C6
Sheldon Cl LE11 . . . . 51 B6
Sheldon St LE1 . . . . 155 B6
Sheldon's La LE67 . . . . . . 124 F4
Shelford Wlk **7** LE2 . . . 181 D5
Shelland Cl LE16 . . . . 241 C2
SHELLBROOK 68 E6
Shellbrook Cl LE65 . . . . . . 68 E5
Shellduck Cl LE8 . . . . 201 F4
Shelley Ave LE13 . . . . 59 B5
Shelley Cl
  Measham DE12 . . . . 93 C3

Shelley Cl continued
Stamford PE9 . . . . 143 A4
Shelley Dr
Corby NN17 . . . . 230 D1
Lutterworth LE17 . . . . . . 244 C7
Shelley Gdns LE10 . . . . 197 E3
Shelley Rd
Narborough LE19 . . . . . . 178 A2
Swadlincote DE11 . . . . . . 44 C5
Shelley St
Leicester LE2 . . . . 180 A8
Loughborough LE11 . . . . . 51 D5
SHELTHORPE 75 C8
Shelthorpe Com Sch
LE11 . . . . 52 C1
Shelthorpe Rd LE11 . . . . . 52 B1
Shelthorpe Rd LE8 . . . . . 180 E4
SHENTON 173 B5
Shenton Cl
Stoke Golding CV13 . . . . . 196 E7
Thurmaston LE4 . . . . 130 A6
Whetstone LE8 . . . . 201 F7
Wigston LE18 . . . . 180 C3
Shenton La
Market Bosworth
CV13 . . . . 148 E2
Shenton CV13 . . . . 173 C4
Sibson CV13 . . . . 172 C5
Upton CV13 . . . . 172 E4
Shenton Prim Sch
LE5 . . . . 155 C7
Shenton Rd LE9 . . . . 198 B4
Shenton Sta* CV13 . . . . 173 D5
Shepeard Cl LE15 . . . . . . 130 C3
Shepeard Cl LE9 . . . . 152 E3
Shepherds Cl
Loughborough LE11 . . . . . 51 D1
Shepshed LE12 . . . . 50 C5
Shepherds Croft LE15 . . . . 59 B5
Shepherds La LE15 . . . . . . 88 B2
Shepherd's Way LE15 . . . 188 F5
Shepherd's Wlk PE9 . . . 117 A1
Shepherd's Wlk LE7 . . . 103 D7
Shepherd Wlk DE74 . . . . . 18 C1
Sheppards Ct NG13 . . . . . . 3 A2
Sheppards Orch LE12 . . . . 33 C4
SHEPSHED 50 A4
Shepshed High Sch
LE12 . . . . 50 C4
Shepshed Rd LE12 . . . . . . 50 C4
Sherard Prim Sch
LE13 . . . . 59 E1
Sherborne Ave LE18 . . . 203 D8
Sherborne Rd LE10 . . . . 216 B7
Sherbourne Dr LE65 . . . . . 69 A7
Sherford Cl LE18 . . . . . . 180 C2
Sheridan Cl LE17 . . . . . . 178 A2
Sheridan St LE2 . . . . . . 179 F8
Sheringham Rd LE4 . . . . 128 D2
Sherioyd Cl LE4 . . . . 129 F4
Sherrard Cl LE15 . . . . 84 F2
Sherrard Dr LE12 . . . . 77 C1
Sherrard Rd
Leicester LE5 . . . . 155 C6
Market Harborough
LE16 . . . . 240 E5
Sherrard St LE13 . . . . 59 C3
Sherrard Way LE3 . . . . . 153 D1
Sherrier CE Prim Sch
LE17 . . . . 244 C7
Sherrier Way LE17 . . . . . 244 C8
Sherwood Cl
Ellistown LE67 . . . . 96 D4
Stamford PE9 . . . . 143 B3
Sherwood Dr LE13 . . . . . . 59 A4
Sherwood Rd CV13 . . . . 196 F4
Sherwood St LE5 . . . . . . 155 E6
Shetland Rd LE4 . . . . . . 129 C1
Shetland Way
Corby NN17 . . . . 230 C1
Countesthorpe LE8 . . . . . 202 F4
Shield Cres LE2 . . . . 179 C2
Shields Cl LE15 . . . . 189 A4
Shields Cres DE74 . . . . . . 16 F3
Shilling Way NG10 . . . . . . 10 A7
Shilton Rd
Barwell LE9 . . . . 198 B6
Kirkby Mallory LE9 . . . . . 175 E4
Shipley Rd LE5 . . . . 155 D4
Shipman Rd LE3 . . . . . . 178 F7
Shipston Hill LE2 . . . . . . 181 A4
Shipton Cl LE18 . . . . . . 180 F2
Shipton Rd LE5 . . . . 130 C3
Shire Cl LE3 . . . . 153 E5
Shire Rd NN17 . . . . 230 C1
Shires La LE1 . . . . 259 A4
Shires Orch NG32 . . . . . . 24 B7
Shires The LE1 . . . . 259 B4
Shirley Ave LE4 . . . . 180 D8
Shirley Cl DE74 . . . . 17 A4
Shirley Cres DE72 . . . . 9 D8
Shirley Dr LE7 . . . . 103 B5
Shirley Pk fP7? 16 B7
Shirley Rd LE2 . . . . 180 D8
Shirley St
Leicester LE4 . . . . 129 A2
Long Eaton NG10 . . . . 10 A4
Shirreffs Cl LE12 . . . . 76 E8
SHOBY 57 A5
Shoby La LE14 . . . . 57 A8
Shoe Makers The
LE12 . . . . 76 D7
Shoesmith Cl ■ LE9 . . . 198 A6
Shooting Close La
LE12 . . . . 76 D7
Short Cl LE8 . . . . 222 F7

Shortheath DE12 . . . . 67 C3
SHORT HEATH 67 D2
Shortheath Rd DE12 . . . . 67 E3
Short Hill DE73 . . . . 26 E6
Short La DE74 . . . . 16 F4
Shortridge La LE19 . . . . 178 B2
Short Row LE8 . . . . 204 D6
Short St LE1 . . . . 259 B4
Shortwheat Hill CV23 . . 252 D1
Shottens Cl LE4 . . . . 128 B2
Shottery Ave LE3 . . . . . 153 F1
Shoulbard LE8 . . . . 222 E8
Shrewsbury Ave
Leicester LE2 . . . . 180 A6
Market Harborough
LE16 . . . . 241 B2
Shrewsbury Cl LE9 . . . . . 198 A7
Shrewsbury Wlk LE67 . . . . 71 F2
Shropshire Cl LE16 . . . . 240 E4
Shropshire Pl LE16 . . . . 240 E4
Shropshire Rd LE2 . . . . 179 D7
Shrubbery The DE11 . . . . . 45 A2
Shuttleworth La LE19 . . 219 D7
SIBBERTOFT 248 F2
Sibbertoft Rd
Clipston LE16 . . . . 249 E1
Husbands Bosworth
LE17 . . . . 247 F2
Marston Trussell LE16 . . . 249 B6
SIBSON 172 A7
Sibson Dr DE74 . . . . 18 B2
Sibson La CV13 . . . . 172 E6
Sibson Rd
Birstall LE4 . . . . 129 A7
Ratcliffe Culey CV9 . . . . 171 E4
Sheepy Magna CV9 . . . . 171 D7
Sibton La LE2 . . . . 181 A4
Sickleholm Dr LE5 . . . . . 155 E2
Side La DE74 . . . . 18 C3
Side St NG32 . . . . 4 F5
Sidings The
Bottesford NG13 . . . . 2 F3
Oakham LE15 . . . . 137 F6
Swannington LE67 . . . . . 71 B7
Sidmouth Ave LE5 . . . . . 156 A4
Sidney Ho LE13 . . . . 59 D3
Sidney Rd LE2 . . . . 180 D7
Sidney St NG10 . . . . 10 D6
Sidwell St LE5 . . . . 155 E5
Signal Rd LE14 . . . . 36 A5
Silbury Rd LE4 . . . . 128 C1
SILEBY 77 C4
Sileby Rd
Barrow-u-S LE12 . . . . . . 76 E6
Mountsorrel LE12 . . . . . . 76 E3
Sileby Sta LE12 . . . . 77 C3
Silkstone Cl DE11 . . . . . . 44 B1
Silsden Rise LE9 . . . . . . 179 D3
Silver Arc ◼ LE1 . . . . . 259 B4
Silver Birches LE2 . . . . . 75 F6
Silver Birch Way LE7 . . . 103 E8
Silverdale Dr LE4 . . . . . 129 F6
Silver La ⑩ PE9 . . . . . . 143 D3
Silver St
Leicester LE1 . . . . 259 B4
Newton CV23 . . . . 253 A1
Oakthorpe DE12 . . . . 93 A6
Whitwick LE67 . . . . 71 F4
Silverstone Dr LE4 . . . . . 129 D5
Silverton Rd
Leicester, Oadby LE2 . . . . 181 C6
Loughborough LE11 . . . . . 74 F8
Silver Wlk LE1 . . . . 259 B4
Silverwood Cl LE15 . . . . 156 C6
Silverwood Rd NG13 . . . . . 3 A2
Simborough Way
LE16 . . . . 241 B3
Simmins Cl LE2 . . . . 179 D4
Simmins Cres LE2 . . . . . 179 D4
Simmonds Way CV9 . . . 170 D2
Simons Cl LE18 . . . . 203 E8
Simon's Orch LE17 . . . . . 233 F5
Simons Wlk ◻ LE12 . . . . 77 C3
Simpson Cl
Blaby LE8 . . . . 202 A6
Syston LE7 . . . . 102 E2
Sir Henry's La DE73 . . . . . 26 A6
Sir Herbert Wragg Way
DE11 . . . . 44 C3
Sir John Moore CE Prim
Sch DE12 . . . . 119 E7
Sir Jonathan North Com
Coll LE2 . . . . 180 A7
Sir Robert Martin Ct
LE11 . . . . 51 D5
Siskin Cl LE10 . . . . 93 B4
Siskin Hill LE4 . . . . 181 A4
Siskin Rd LE15 . . . . 189 A5
Sisley Way LE10 . . . . . . 197 A3
Sitch Cl LE9 . . . . 219 A5
Sitwell Wlk LE5 . . . . 155 F2
Six Acre Cl LE18 . . . . . . 152 D8
Six Acre Cl LE15 . . . . . . 218 E6
SIX HILLS 55 F6
Six Hills La LE14 . . . . 56 C0
Six Hills Rd
Ragdale LE14 . . . . 56 C4
Walton on t W LE12 . . . . . 54 D4
Skampton Gn LE5 . . . . . 156 B5
Skampton Rd LE5 . . . . . 156 B5
SKEFFINGTON 160 A2
Skeffington Glebe Rd
LE7 . . . . 160 A6
Skeffington Rd LE7 . . . . 184 E6
Skeffington Wood Rd
LE7 . . . . 160 C3
Skeg Hill LE7 . . . . 133 C2

Skeg Hill Rd LE7 . . . . . . 133 B2
Skelton Dr LE2 . . . . 180 A6
Skelwith Rise CV11 . . . . 214 A6
Skerry La NG13 . . . . 4 A2
SKETCHLEY 215 C6
Sketchley Cl LE5 . . . . . . 156 D6
Sketchley Hall Gdns
LE10 . . . . 215 C5
SKETCHLEY HILL 215 E7
Sketchley Hill Prim Sch
LE10 . . . . 215 C5
Sketchley La
Hinckley LE10 . . . . 215 C5
Ratcliffe Culey CV9 . . . . 171 B4
Sketchley La Ind Est
LE10 . . . . 215 B5
Sketchley Manor La
LE10 . . . . 215 D5
Sketchley Mdws LE10 . . 215 C5
Sketchley Meadows Bsns
Pk LE10 . . . . 215 C4
Sketchley Old Village
LE10 . . . . 215 C5
Sketchley Rd LE10 . . . . 215 E5
Skevington Ave LE11 . . . . 51 E4
SKILLINGTON 43 B8
Skillington Rd NG33 . . . . 43 D3
Skinner's La LE67 . . . . . . 71 F5
Skinners Way DE11 . . . . . 44 D5
Skippon Cl LE10 . . . . . . 240 D2
Skipworth St LE2 . . . . . . 155 C4
Skye Rd NN17 . . . . 230 B1
Skye Way LE8 . . . . 202 F3
Skylark Ave LE2 . . . . 76 F1
Skylark Cl DE12 . . . . 93 B4
Slackey La DE72 . . . . 9 C8
Slack La DE11 . . . . 45 B6
Slade Cl LE3 . . . . 153 C2
Slade Gns The LE2 . . . . 179 C4
Slade La DE73, DE74 . . . . 26 F6
Slade Pl LE2 . . . . 179 C4
Slash La LE12 . . . . 76 F4
Slate Brook Cl LE6 . . . . . 126 F3
Slate Cl LE3 . . . . 153 B8
Slate Drift LE9 . . . . 168 E3
Slate Pit La LE6 . . . . 126 B4
Slater Prim Sch LE3 . . . 259 A5
Slater St LE4 . . . . 154 E7
Slater St LE2 . . . . 259 C3
SLAWSTON 209 B1
Slawston Rd
Medbourne LE16 . . . . . . 227 E7
Slawston LE16 . . . . 209 A2
Welham LE16 . . . . 226 F6
Slaybarns Way LE67 . . . . 95 F2
Sloane Cl LE19 . . . . 178 A3
Sludge Hall Hill LE7 . . . 159 C7
Small Thorn Pl DE11 . . . . 44 E1
Smart Cl LE3 . . . . 153 D2
Smedley Cl LE65 . . . . 68 F5
Smedmore Rd LE5 . . . . . 155 D8
Smeeton Rd LE8 . . . . . . 224 A7
SMEETON WESTERBY
LE8 . . . . 223 F6
SMISBY 45 F3
Smisby Rd LE65 . . . . 69 B8
Smith Ave
Melbourne DE73 . . . . 26 B8
Thurmaston LE4 . . . . 129 F6
Smith Cres LE67 . . . . 97 C8
Smith Cl LE67 . . . . 71 D5
Smith Dorrien Rd LE5 . . . 155 C7
Smith Way LE19 . . . . . . 178 E4
Smithy Cl CV13 . . . . 149 D8
Smithy Farm Dr LE9 . . . 199 D2
Smithy La
Burbage LE9, LE10 . . . . . 198 C1
Long Whatton LE12 . . . . . 29 A2
Odstone CV13 . . . . 122 C4
Sapcote LE9 . . . . 216 D8
Smithy Rd LE65 . . . . 69 E7
Smithy Way LE12 . . . . . . 50 C4
SMOCKINGTON 231 D8
Smockington La LE10 . . . 231 B7
Smore Slade Hills
LE2 . . . . 181 E4
Smyth Cl LE10 . . . . 240 E5
Snarestone Rd
DE12 . . . . 120 F7
Snarestone CE Prim Sch
DE12 . . . . 120 E7
Snarestone Rd
Appleby Magna LE12 . . . 120 B8
Newton Burgoland
LE67 . . . . 121 C7
Snarrow's Rd LE67 . . . . . . 48 E2
Snell's Nook La LE11 . . . . 74 A8
Snelston Cl LE15 . . . . . . 138 B7
SNIBSTON 96 A7
Snibston Ct LE67 . . . . . . 71 B2
Snibston Discovery Pk*
LE67 . . . . 71 B1
Snibston Dr LE67 . . . . . . 71 A1
Snipe Cl LE67 . . . . 96 B7
Snowdens End LE18 . . . . 180 C1
Snowdon Ave LE15 . . . . 137 E6
Snowdon Cl LE7? 50 C2
Snowdrop Cl LE19 . . . . . 200 F8
Snow Hill
Leicester LE4 . . . . 128 C1
Melton Mowbray LE13 . . . . 59 D4
Snows La LE7 . . . . 131 D1
Soarbank Way LE11 . . . . . 51 E7
Soar Cl LE13 . . . . 59 B1
Soar Gn NN17 . . . . 230 C1
Soar La
Leicester LE3 . . . . 259 A4
Normanton on S LE12 . . . . 30 D3

Soar La continued
Sutton Bonington LE12,
DE74 . . . . 30 A8
Soar Mill La LE9 . . . . . . 218 D8
Soar Rd
Quorn (Quorndon) LE12 . . 76 B6
Thurmaston LE4 . . . . 102 E1
Soar Valley Coll LE4 . . . 129 D3
Soar Valley Way LE2,
LE19 . . . . 179 A5
Soar Way LE10 . . . . 215 A8
Soho St LE13 . . . . 59 C3
Solway Cl LE13 . . . . 59 B1
SOMERBY 108 B1
Somerby Cl PE9 . . . . 143 D5
Somerby Dr LE2 . . . . . . 181 C5
Somerby Prim Sch
LE14 . . . . 108 B2
Somerby Rd
Burrough on t H LE14 . . . 107 E3
Cold Overton LE14,
LE16 . . . . 136 A8
Knossington LE15 . . . . . 135 C6
Owston LE15 . . . . 135 F7
Pickwell LE14 . . . . 108 C2
Somerfield Way LE3 . . . 153 A8
Somerfield Wlk LE4 . . . . 155 B7
Somerset Ave LE4 . . . . . 128 D2
Somerset Cl
Burton o t W LE12 . . . . . . 53 F7
Melton Mowbray LE13 . . . . 82 D8
Somerset Dr LE3 . . . . . . 153 C7
Somerset Rd LE15 . . . . . . 87 E2
Somerset St LE4 . . . . . . 155 C6
Somerville Rd
Leicester LE3 . . . . 154 C1
Stamford PE9 . . . . 143 C4
Somes Cl PE9 . . . . 144 E4
Sonning Way LE2 . . . . . 179 C2
Sopers Rd LE9 . . . . 200 C3
Sorrel Cl PE9 . . . . 142 F4
Sorrel Cl LE13 . . . . 59 B1
Sorrel Dr LE2 . . . . 76 E2
Sorrel Rd LE5 . . . . 44 E4
Sorrel Rd LE5 . . . . 130 C2
Sorrel Way LE19 . . . . . . 177 F1
South Albion St LE1 . . . . 259 C3
Southampton St LE1 . . . . 259 C4
South Ave
Leicester Forest East
LE3 . . . . 153 B3
Ullesthorpe LE17 . . . . . . 233 B4
Wigston LE18 . . . . 180 C2
South Charnwood High
Sch LE12 . . . . 125 A7
South Church Gate
LE1 . . . . 259 A5
South Cl
Arnesby LE8 . . . . 221 F5
Blackfordby DE11 . . . . . . 68 B8
Scalford LE14 . . . . 38 E5
South Cres NG13 . . . . 3 A2
SOUTH CROXTON 105 C1
South Croxton Rd
Queniborough LE7 . . . . . 104 C4
South Croxton LE7 . . . . . 132 E4
Southdown Dr LE4 . . . . 129 E5
Southdown Rd
Leicester LE5 . . . . 155 D6
Loughborough LE11 . . . . . 75 A8
Southdown Wlk LE15 . . . 87 E2
South Dr
Leicester LE5 . . . . 156 A8
Stoney Stanton LE9 . . . . 199 E2
SOUTH END 76 E2
Southernhay Ave LE2 . . . 155 C1
Southernhay Cl LE2 . . . . 155 C1
Southernhay Rd LE2 . . . 155 C1
Southey Cl
Enderby LE19 . . . . 178 A2
Leicester LE4 . . . . 155 B8
Southfield Ave LE3 . . . . . 103 B3
Southfield Cl
Glen Parva LE2 . . . . 179 A3
Scraptoft LE7 . . . . 156 F7
Southfield Prim Sch
LE15 . . . . 137 C5
Southfield Rd
Gretton NN17 . . . . 213 C1
Hinckley LE10 . . . . 215 D8
Loughborough LE11 . . . . . 52 B3
Southfields NG10 . . . . 10 E7
SOUTH FIELDS 259 C2
Southfields Ave LE2 . . . 155 B8
Southfields Dr LE2 . . . . . 179 F5
Southfield Way CV13 . . . 148 E2
Southgates LE1 . . . . 259 A3
Southgates Underpass
LE1 . . . . 259 A3
SOUTH KILWORTH 255 D8
South Kilworth CE Prim
Sch LE17 . . . . 255 C8
South Kilworth Rd
North Kilworth LE17 . . . . 246 E2
Walcote LE17 . . . . 245 D3
Welford NN6 . . . . 256 B5
South Kingsmead Rd
LE2 . . . . 180 C6
SOUTH KNIGHTON 180 D7
South Knighton Rd
LE2 . . . . 180 C7
South La LE67 . . . . 97 D4
Southland Rd LE2 . . . . . . 180 D6
South Leicester Ind Est
LE67 . . . . 96 E4
South Leicestershire Coll
LE18 . . . . 180 B2

Southleigh Gr LE16 . . . . 240 D4
SOUTH LUFFENHAM
. . . . 191 D8
Southmeade LE2 . . . . . 180 F8
Southmeads Ct LE2 . . . . 181 A7
Southmeads Rd LE2 . . . 181 A7
South Par LE13 . . . . 59 C3
South Rd
Clifton u D CV23 . . . . . 257 A5
Ibstock LE67 . . . . 122 F8
Southside Rd LE3 . . . . . 178 F6
South St
Asfordby Hill LE14 . . . . . . 58 D3
Ashby-de-la-Z LE65 . . . . 69 B6
Draycott DE72 . . . . 9 A7
Ellistown LE67 . . . . 96 D4
Leicester, Oadby LE2 . . . 181 A6
Long Eaton NG10 . . . . 10 E7
Loughborough LE11 . . . . . 52 B3
Melbourne DE73 . . . . 26 A7
Oakham LE15 . . . . 137 F6
Oakham LE15 . . . . 138 A6
Leicester LE4 . . . . 38 E4
Swadlincote DE11 . . . . . . 45 A1
South View
Asfordby LE14 . . . . 57 E2
Burrough on t H LE14 . . . 107 E2
Preston LE15 . . . . 164 C1
Uppingham LE15 . . . . . . 189 B4
South View Bsns Pk
LE15 . . . . 163 B1
South View Cl LE15 . . . . 164 E5
Southview Ct LE67 . . . . . 152 F3
Southview Dr LE5 . . . . . 155 F2
Southway LE8 . . . . 202 B6
South Way LE8 . . . . 206 B1
Southwell Cl LE13 . . . . . 59 A7
South Wigston High Sch
LE2, LE18 . . . . 179 E1
South Wigston Sta
LE18 . . . . 179 F2
SOUTH WITHAM 65 C4
South Witham Com Prim
Sch NG33 . . . . 65 B3
South Witham Nature
Res* NG33 . . . . 65 E3
South Wlk LE6 . . . . 126 C1
SOUTHWOOD 62 E2
Southworth Rd DE73 . . . . 26 E2
Sovereign Ct LE11 . . . . . 52 B3
Sovereign Gn NG10 . . . . . 10 B7
Sovereign Pk LE16 . . . . 240 F1
Sowters La LE12 . . . . 54 B6
Spa Cl LE10 . . . . 197 E1
Spa Dr LE9 . . . . 217 D8
Spa La
Hinckley LE10 . . . . 197 E1
Orston NG13 . . . . 3 A3
Wigston LE18 . . . . 180 D2
Spalding St LE5 . . . . 155 E6
Sparkenhoe
Croft LE9 . . . . 200 C3
Newbold Verdon LE9 . . . 150 C4
Sparkenhoe Com Sch
LE2 . . . . 155 B4
Sparkenhoe Com Prim
Sch (Gopsall Annexe)
LE2 . . . . 155 B5
Sparkenhoe Est LE67 . . . 95 B2
Sparkenhoe St LE2 . . . . 155 B5
Sparrow Hill LE11 . . . . . . 52 B4
Sparsis Gdns LE19 . . . . . 178 D1
Speeds Pingle LE11 . . . . . 52 A4
Speedwell Cl
Coalville LE67 . . . . 71 E1
Narborough LE19 . . . . . . 177 F1
Woodville DE11 . . . . 44 F4
Speedwell Dr
Broughton Astley LE9 . . . 219 A4
Hamilton LE5 . . . . 130 B3
Speedwell Rd LE12 . . . . . 76 F2
Speers Rd LE3 . . . . 153 E8
Spellow Cl CV23 . . . . 252 D1
Spencefield Dr LE5 . . . . 156 B3
Spencefield La LE5 . . . . . 156 C4
Spencer Ave LE4 . . . . . . 129 C7
Spencer Rd LE17 . . . . . . 244 C6
Spencers Rd PE9 . . . . . . 167 F5
Spencer St
Hinckley LE10 . . . . 197 D1
Leicester, Oadby LE2 . . . 181 A6
Market Harborough
LE16 . . . . 240 D3
Spencer View LE67 . . . . . . 96 E3
Spence St LE5 . . . . 155 D7
Spendlove Dr NN17 . . . . . 213 C1
Spendlow Gdns LE8 . . . . 179 E4
Spendlow Gn LE8 . . . . . . 179 E4
Sperry Ct LE17 . . . . 95 F1
Spey Dr LE15 . . . . 137 E6
Spiers Cl LE19 . . . . 201 B7
Spindle Rd LE11 . . . . 75 A6
Spindles The LE10 . . . . . 215 E5
Spinner Cl LE9 . . . . 219 B6
Spinners Way LE12 . . . . . 50 B3
Spinney Ave LE8 . . . . . . 202 F4
Spinney Cl
Ashby-de-la-Z LE65 . . . . 69 B5
Broughton Town LE13 . . . 153 C2
Gilmorton LE17 . . . . 235 C4
Glen Parva LE2 . . . . 179 A3
Groby LE6 . . . . 126 E2
Market Harborough
LE16 . . . . 240 C3

Spinney Cl continued
Melton Mowbray LE13 . . . . . . **59** E5
Ryhall PE9 . . . . **116** A2
Syston LE7 . . . . **102** E3
Spinney Ct LE9 . . . . **200** C4
Spinney Dr
Barlestone CV13 . . . . **149** D7
Botcheston LE9 . . . . **151** C8
Kibworth Beauchamp
LE8 . . . . **206** A1
Quorn (Quorndon) LE12 . . . . **75** F5
Spinney Farm Cotts
LE14 . . . . **79** F4
Spinney Halt LE8 . . . . **201** F7
Spinney Hill
Market Bosworth
CV13 . . . . **148** D3
Melbourne DE73 . . . . **26** A7
Spinney Hill Dr LE11 . . . . . . **51** D2
Spinney Hill Prim Sch
LE5 . . . . **155** D5
Spinney Hill Rd LE5 . . . . . . **155** C7
SPINNEY HILLS **155** C5
Spinney La
Ryhall PE9 . . . . **116** E2
Stretton LE15 . . . . **88** F4
Spinney Mdw LE7 . . . . **159** C1
Spinney Mobile Home Pk
The LE7 . . . . **70** E3
Spinney Nook LE7 . . . . **185** E6
Spinney Rd
Hinckley LE10 . . . . **215** C6
Ketton PE9 . . . . **167** F5
Spinney Rise LE4 . . . . **129** A7
Spinneyside LE6 . . . . **126** E2
Spinney The
Atherstone CV9 . . . . **194** A7
Castle Donington DE74 . . . . . **17** A4
Coalville LE67 . . . . **96** C6
Cottesmore LE15 . . . . **112** B7
Leicester, Oadby LE2 . . . . . . **182** A4
Thurnby LE7 . . . . **156** E4
Spinney View LE8 . . . . **182** C1
Spion Kopje LE2 . . . . **181** E1
Spires The LE17 . . . . **235** C4
Spire View NG13 . . . . **3** B3
Spittal DE74 . . . . **17** A4
Spittal Hill DE74 . . . . **17** A4
Sponne Rise LE2 . . . . **179** E4
Sports Field La LE9 . . . . . . **200** D8
Sports Rd LE3 . . . . **153** D8
Spring Back Way
LE15 . . . . **189** A4
Spring Bank LE16 . . . . **227** F7
Springbrook Dr LE7 . . . . . . **156** F6
Spring Cl
Breaston DE72 . . . . **9** C8
Leicester LE2 . . . . **179** D5
Lutterworth LE17 . . . . **244** C5
Market Overton LE15 . . . . . . **86** F5
Ratby LE6 . . . . **152** D8
Shepshed LE12 . . . . **50** C2
Swadlincote DE11 . . . . **44** A4
SPRING COTTAGE **67** D5
Spring Cottage Rd
DE12 . . . . **67** D5
Springdale Rd LE4 . . . . . . **129** E6
Springfield
Kegworth DE74 . . . . **18** B2
Thringstone LE67 . . . . **71** E8
Springfield Ave
Long Eaton NG10 . . . . **10** F8
Market Bosworth CV13 . . . . **148** D3
Springfield Cl
Broughton Astley LE9 . . . . . **218** F5
Burton o t W LE12 . . . . **53** F7
Ibstock LE67 . . . . **95** F1
Kibworth Beauchamp
LE8 . . . . **224** B7
Loughborough LE11 . . . . **74** E8
Rothley LE7 . . . . **101** E7
Swadlincote DE11 . . . . **44** B6
Spring Field Cl LE3 . . . . . . **153** B7
Springfield Cres LE8 . . . . . **224** B8
Springfield Ct 1
LE16 . . . . **240** F2
Springfield Jun Sch
DE11 . . . . **44** A5
Springfield La LE8 . . . . . . **224** A6
Springfield Pk LE10 . . . . . **197** A3
Springfield Rd
Hinckley LE10 . . . . **215** D7
Leicester LE2 . . . . **155** C2
Shepshed LE12 . . . . **50** B3
Sileby LE12 . . . . **77** D4
Swadlincote DE11 . . . . **44** B6
Springfield St
Market Harborough
LE16 . . . . **240** F2
Melton Mowbray LE13 . . . . . **59** B5
Springfield Way LE15 . . . . **138** A8
Spring Gdns
Littlethorpe LE19 . . . . **201** C6
Sapcote LE9 . . . . **217** E8
Springhill DE11 . . . . **45** A8
Springhill Gdns LE16 . . . . **240** C2
Spring La
Ab Kettleby LE14 . . . . **37** A3
Glaston LE15 . . . . **190** B5
Long Whatton LE12 . . . . **29** D2
Packington LE65 . . . . **69** F1
Shepshed LE12 . . . . **50** B2
Swannington LE67 . . . . **71** B4
3 Wigston LE18 . . . . **180** D3
Wymondham LE14 . . . . **62** D2

Spring Rd LE67 . . . . **96** A2
Spring St DE11 . . . . **67** A8
Springs The
Broughton Astley LE9 . . . . . **218** E6
Swinford LE17 . . . . **254** C4
Spring Terr LE16 . . . . **228** A6
Spring The NG10 . . . . **10** D5
Springway LE15 . . . . **156** E5
Springwell Cl LE8 . . . . **202** E4
Springwell Dr LE8 . . . . **202** D4
Springwell La LE8 . . . . **201** F4
Springwood Farm Rd
DE11 . . . . **44** B7
SPROXTON **41** E5
Sproxton Rd
Buckminster NG33 . . . . **42** D2
Skillington NG33 . . . . **43** A8
Spruce Ave LE11 . . . . **75** A7
Spruce Way LE17 . . . . **244** B7
Square Ct LE4 . . . . **129** B7
Square The
Bagworth LE67 . . . . **124** B5
Bottesford NG13 . . . . **3** A3
Countesthorpe LE8 . . . . **202** F3
Earl Shilton LE9 . . . . **198** E8
Frolesworth LE17 . . . . **218** B1
Glenfield LE3 . . . . **127** B1
Littlethorpe LE19 . . . . **201** C6
Long Whatton LE12 . . . . **29** B4
Market Harborough
LE16 . . . . **240** E3
Newton Harcourt LE8 . . . . . **204** D6
Oakthorpe DE12 . . . . **93** A7
Ryhall PE9 . . . . **116** F2
Shearsby LE17 . . . . **222** A2
Skillington NG33 . . . . **43** B8
South Luffenham LE15 . . . . . **191** D8
Sutton Cheney CV13 . . . . . **174** B6
Wetford NN6 . . . . **256** E6
Squires Cl LE15 . . . . **110** C3
Squires Gn LE10 . . . . **215** F6
Squire's Ride LE7 . . . . **103** D8
Squirrel Cl LE19 . . . . **201** A7
Squirrel La DE73 . . . . **26** C3
Squirrel's Cnr LE7 . . . . . . **103** E8
Squirrel Way LE11 . . . . **51** F2
Squirrel Wlk DE12 . . . . **67** B3
Stable Cl LE19 . . . . **201** C7
Stablegate Way LE4 . . . . . **241** A3
Stable Mews DE11 . . . . **44** F2
Stables Ct LE15 . . . . **137** F6
Stables The
Burley LE15 . . . . **111** A1
Hinckley LE10 . . . . **215** D5
Stable Yd The
Coleorton LE67 . . . . **70** C7
Stoke Golding CV13 . . . . . . **196** D7
Stablford Cl LE12 . . . . **50** B4
Stackley Rd LE8 . . . . **182** B1
Stackyard The NG32 . . . . . . **24** A7
Stadium Cl LE67 . . . . **124** A6
Stadium Ind Pk NG10 . . . . . **10** F8
Stadium Pl LE4 . . . . **128** E2
Stadon Rd LE7 . . . . **127** D6
Stafford Ave LE13 . . . . **59** D4
Stafford Dr LE18 . . . . **179** F2
Stafford Leys LE3 . . . . . . **152** F3
Stafford Leys Com Prim
Sch LE3 . . . . **152** F2
Staffords Acre DE74 . . . . . . **18** C2
Stafford St
Barwell LE9 . . . . **198** A6
Leicester LE4 . . . . **129** C3
Long Eaton NG10 . . . . **10** F8
STAINBY **43** E2
Stainby Rd
Buckminster NG33 . . . . **42** E2
Gunby NG33 . . . . **64** B8
Staindale LE18 . . . . **180** F2
Stainforth Cl CV11 . . . . . . **214** A2
Stainmore Ave LE19 . . . . . **178** A2
Stainsdale Gn LE67 . . . . . . **72** A2
Staley Ave LE65 . . . . **68** F5
STAMFORD **143** E1
Stamford Bsns Pk
PE9 . . . . **143** F4
Stamford Cl
Glenfield LE3 . . . . **153** C8
Long Eaton NG10 . . . . **10** E4
Market Harborough
LE16 . . . . **240** E2
Ratby LE6 . . . . **126** C1
Stamford Dr
Coalville LE67 . . . . **72** D1
Cropston LE7 . . . . **100** F2
Groby LE6 . . . . **126** F2
Stamford End LE15 . . . . . . **113** B3
Stamford Hall LE2 . . . . . . **180** F8
Stamford High Sch
PE9 . . . . **143** E2
Stamford Jun Sch
PE9 . . . . **143** D2
Stamford Mus* PE9 . . . . . **143** E3
Stamford Rd
Carlby PE9 . . . . **117** C8
Duddington PE9 . . . . **193** C7
Easton o t H PE9 . . . . **169** B5
Empingham LE15, PE9 . . . . **141** C4
Essendine PE9 . . . . **117** A5
Exton LE15 . . . . **113** B3
Ketton PE9 . . . . **168** C8
Kirby Fields LE9 . . . . **152** E4
Oakham LE15 . . . . **138** B5
Sewstern NG33 . . . . **64** A8
South Luffenham LE15 . . . . . **191** D7
Stamford Ret Pk PE9 . . . . . **143** F4
Stamford Rise LE6 . . . . . . **126** E8

Stamford & Rutland Hospl
PE9 . . . . **143** F4
Stamford St Gilbert CE
Prim Sch PE9 . . . . **143** C3
Stamford Sch (Welland
Ho) PE9 . . . . **143** D2
Stamford St
Glenfield LE3 . . . . **153** B8
Leicester LE1 . . . . **259** B3
Ratby LE6 . . . . **126** C1
Stamford Sta PE9 . . . . **143** D2
Stamford Wlk 7 PE9 . . . . **143** E3
Stanage Rd LE12 . . . . **77** E4
Stanbrig LE18 . . . . **203** E8
Stancliff Rd LE4 . . . . **129** F5
Standard Hill LE67 . . . . **96** B7
Stanfell Rd LE2 . . . . **180** B8
Stanford Hall* LE17 . . . . . **254** F3
Stanford Hill LE11 . . . . **52** B6
STANFORD HILLS **31** D4
Stanford La LE12 . . . . **52** D7
STANFORD ON AVON
. . . . **254** F2
STANFORD ON SOAR **31** C1
Stanford Rd
Normanton on S LE12 . . . . . . **30** F2
Swinford LE17 . . . . **254** D3
Stanhope Glade DE15 . . . . **44** A8
Stanhope Rd
Swadlincote DE11 . . . . **44** B3
Wigston LE18 . . . . **180** E1
Stanhope St
Leicester LE5 . . . . **155** D5
Long Eaton NG10 . . . . **10** D8
Stanier Dr LE4 . . . . **130** A4
Stanier Rd
Broughton Astley LE9 . . . . . **219** A6
Corby NN17 . . . . **230** F1
Staniforth Ct 8 LE9 . . . . . **198** A6
Stanilands LE15 . . . . **84** E1
Stanleigh Gdns DE12 . . . . . **92** E8
Stanleigh Ho DE12 . . . . **92** E8
Stanleigh Rd DE12 . . . . **67** B4
Stanley Burroughs
Almshouses LE16 . . . . . . **217** D7
Stanley Cl
Nethersea l DE12 . . . . **91** F7
Woodville DE11 . . . . **44** F3
Stanley Ct LE2 . . . . **155** C3
Stanley Dr LE5 . . . . **156** A8
Stanley Rd
Hinckley LE10 . . . . **197** C2
Leicester LE2 . . . . **155** C3
Market Bosworth CV13 . . . . **148** E2
Stanleys La LE14 . . . . **22** A6
Stanley St
4 Barwell LE9 . . . . **198** A6
Long Eaton NG10 . . . . **10** E7
Loughborough LE11 . . . . **52** B2
Melton Mowbray LE13 . . . . . **59** D3
Stamford PE9 . . . . **143** D3
Swadlincote DE11 . . . . **44** C4
Stanton La
Croft LE9 . . . . **200** A5
Sapcote LE9 . . . . **217** B8
Stanton u B LE67 . . . . **97** F3
Thornton LE67 . . . . **124** E6
Stanton Rd
Asfordby Hill LE14 . . . . **58** D3
Elmesthorpe LE9 . . . . **199** B3
Sapcote LE9 . . . . **217** D8
STANTON UNDER
BARDON **97** E2
Stanton under Bardon
Prim Sch LE67 . . . . **97** F1
Stanton Vale Sch
NG10 . . . . **10** C7
Stanway Cl LE4 . . . . **241** A3
Stanyon Cl LE8 . . . . **202** F4
STAPLEFORD **61** B1
Stapleford Rd
Leicester LE4 . . . . **128** D4
Whissendine LE15 . . . . **84** E3
Staplehurst Ave LE3 . . . . . **178** E8
Staples Dr LE67 . . . . **97** B7
STAPLETON **174** F2
Stapleton La
Barwell LE9 . . . . **197** F8
Dadlington CV13 . . . . **174** A1
Kirkby Mallory LE9 . . . . . . **175** B5
Starkie Ave DE74 . . . . **16** F3
Star La 3 PE9 . . . . **143** E3
Star Lane Mews 18
PE9 . . . . **143** E3
Starmer Cl LE19 . . . . **201** E3
Statham St LE19 . . . . **150** B5
STATHERN **13** A3
Stathern Prim Sch
LE14 . . . . **13** A2
Stathern Rd
Eastwell LE14 . . . . **22** B6
Harby LE14 . . . . **12** C3
Station App LE18 . . . . **137** F7
Station App The LE17 . . . . **133** F3
Station Ave
Loughborough LE11 . . . . **51** F5
South Witham NG33 . . . . **65** B3
Station Cl LE9 . . . . **152** E4
Station Cotts LE14 . . . . **21** B2
Station Dr
Kirby Fields LE9 . . . . **152** E4
Moira DE12 . . . . **67** F4
Station Hill
Swannington LE67 . . . . **71** A4
Twyford LE14 . . . . **133** F8
Station Hollow LE8 . . . . . . **224** A8

Station La
Asfordby LE14 . . . . **57** F2
Leire LE17 . . . . **218** E1
Scraptoft LE7 . . . . **156** F7
Station Mews LE65 . . . . . . **69** B5
Station Rd
Ashby-de-la-Z LE65 . . . . . . **69** B5
Bagworth LE67 . . . . **124** A6
Birstall LE4 . . . . **128** F5
Bottesford NG13 . . . . **3** B3
Broughton Astley LE9 . . . . . **219** A5
Castle Bytham NG33 . . . . . . **90** C8
Castle Donington DE74 . . . . . **17** B5
Coalville LE67 . . . . **96** D6
Countesthorpe LE8 . . . . **202** E3
Croft LE9 . . . . **200** C4
Cropston LE7 . . . . **101** A4
Desford LE9 . . . . **151** C3
Draycott DE72 . . . . **9** B7
Dunton Bassett LE17 . . . . . . **219** E2
Earl Shilton LE9 . . . . **198** E7
Ellistown LE67 . . . . **96** F1
Elmesthorpe LE9 . . . . **198** F5
Essendine PE9 . . . . **117** B6
Glenfield LE3 . . . . **127** C1
Great Bowden LE16 . . . . . . **241** A6
Great Glen LE8 . . . . **205** A6
Gretton NN17 . . . . **213** B1
Hemington DE74 . . . . **17** C5
Higham on t H CV13 . . . . . . **195** F4
Hinckley LE10 . . . . **215** D8
Husbands Bosworth
LE17 . . . . **247** D3
Ibstock LE67 . . . . **95** D1
Kegworth DE74, LE12 . . . . . **18** E3
Ketton PE9 . . . . **168** A5
Kirby Fields LE9 . . . . **152** E4
Leicester LE5, LE2 . . . . . . **156** F6
Libourne CV23 . . . . **258** A7
Littlethorpe LE19 . . . . **201** C7
Long Eaton NG10 . . . . **10** F8
Lutterworth LE17 . . . . **244** D5
Market Bosworth CV13 . . . . **148** D3
Melbourne DE73 . . . . **26** C8
Morcott LE15 . . . . **191** B6
North Kilworth LE17 . . . . . **247** A4
Oakham LE15 . . . . **137** F7
Old Dalby LE14 . . . . **35** F5
Quorn (Quorndon) LE12 . . . . **76** A6
Ratby LE6 . . . . **152** D7
Rearsby LE7 . . . . **79** A2
Shackerstone CV13 . . . . . . **121** E2
South Luffenham LE15 . . . . **166** E2
Stamford PE9 . . . . **143** D2
Stamford PE9 . . . . **143** E2
Stoke Golding CV13 . . . . . . **196** C7
Stoney Stanton LE9 . . . . . . **199** E3
Theddingworth LE17 . . . . . **248** D8
Ullesthorpe LE17 . . . . **233** B4
Upper Broughton LE14 . . . . **35** C8
Uppingham LE15 . . . . **189** B4
Waltham on t W LE14 . . . . . . **22** F3
Whissendine LE15 . . . . **85** A4
Wigston LE18 . . . . **180** B2
Wing LE15 . . . . **164** E3
Woodville DE11 . . . . **44** F2
Station Road Ind Est
CV13 . . . . **148** C3
Station St
Kibworth Beauchamp
LE8 . . . . **224** A8
Leicester LE2 . . . . **259** C3
Long Eaton NG10 . . . . **10** E7
Loughborough LE11 . . . . **51** F5
Swadlincote DE11 . . . . **67** A8
Whetstone LE8 . . . . **201** F8
Wigston LE18 . . . . **180** A1
Station Terr
Bagworth LE67 . . . . **124** A7
Heather LE67 . . . . **95** D2
Station Yd DE73 . . . . **26** C8
Staunton Cl DE74 . . . . **17** A4
STAUNTON IN THE VALE
. . . . **1** B4
Staveley Cl
Sileby LE12 . . . . **77** D2
Wigston LE18 . . . . **180** E2
Staveley Ct LE11 . . . . **51** D2
Staveley Rd
Leicester LE5 . . . . **155** D4
Melton Mowbray LE13 . . . . . **59** A4
Staythorpe Rd LE4 . . . . . . **130** A3
Steadfold La PE9 . . . . **168** C8
Steadman Ave LE9 . . . . . . **201** E3
Stebbings Rd LE2 . . . . **179** D5
Steele Cl LE15 . . . . **156** A5
Steeple Cl LE18 . . . . **180** E4
Steeple Ct LE11 . . . . **52** B4
Steeple Row LE11 . . . . **52** B4
Steins La LE5 . . . . **156** B8
Stelle Way LE7 . . . . **127** D3
Stemborough La
LE17 . . . . **219** A2
Stenor Cl LE18 . . . . **222** E8
Stenson Rd
Coalville LE67 . . . . **71** E2
Leicester LE5 . . . . **128** A1
Stephens Ct LE7 . . . . **102** F3
Stephenson Cl
Broughton Astley LE9 . . . . . **219** A5
Groby LE6 . . . . **126** E3
Stephenson Coll
Ashby-de-la-Z LE65 . . . . . . **69** C6
Coalville LE67 . . . . **71** C3
Stephenson Ct
Glenfield LE3 . . . . **127** C2
Ravenstone LE67 . . . . **71** A3
Stephenson Dr LE3 . . . . . . **154** C7

Stephenson Ind Est
LE67 . . . . **71** B2
Stephenson Pl LE67 . . . . . . **96** D8
Stephenson Rd LE10 . . . . . **214** E7
Stephenson Way
Coalville LE67 . . . . **71** D3
Groby LE6 . . . . **126** E3
Sterling Pk LE10 . . . . **214** D8
Sterndale Rd NG10 . . . . **10** B6
Stevens Cl
Stoney Stanton LE9 . . . . . . **199** E2
Ullesthorpe LE17 . . . . **233** B4
Stevens La DE72 . . . . **9** D8
Stevenson Ave DE72 . . . . **9** B8
Stevenson Gdns LE9 . . . . . **201** D4
Stevens St LE16 . . . . **240** D3
Stevenstone Cl LE2 . . . . . . **181** D5
Stewards Ct LE19 . . . . **151** B3
Stewart Ave LE19 . . . . **178** A2
Stewart Dr LE11 . . . . **51** C6
Steyning Cres LE3 . . . . . . **127** D1
Stiles Cl LE9 . . . . **218** F5
Stiles The LE7 . . . . **103** B4
Stimpson Rd LE67 . . . . **71** E1
Stinford Leys LE16 . . . . . . **241** B3
Stinson Way LE67 . . . . **71** E5
Stirling Ave
Hinckley LE10 . . . . **197** A1
Loughborough LE11 . . . . **51** D5
Stirling Cl
Mountsorrel LE12 . . . . **101** C8
Quorn (Quorndon) LE12 . . . . **75** F7
Stirling Dr LE7 . . . . **156** F6
Stirling Rd
Melton Mowbray LE13 . . . . . **59** B4
Stamford PE9 . . . . **143** B2
Stocken Hall Farm Cotts
LE15 . . . . **66** B1
Stocken Hall Mews
LE15 . . . . **66** B1
STOCKERSTON **211** B8
Stockerston Cres
LE15 . . . . **188** F3
Stockerston Cross Rds
LE16 . . . . **210** F5
Stockerston La LE16 . . . . . **211** B3
Stockerston Rd
Allexton LE15 . . . . **187** E4
Uppingham LE15 . . . . **188** D2
Stockingers Ct LE11 . . . . . . **52** C5
STOCKING FARM **128** E3
Stocking La DE73 . . . . **48** B8
Stockland Rd LE2 . . . . **179** E4
Stocks Hill LE15 . . . . **166** F4
Stock's Hill PE9 . . . . **168** A5
Stocks Rd LE7 . . . . **156** F8
Stockton Ho LE3 . . . . **153** C6
Stockton Rd LE4 . . . . **129** E1
Stockwell Cl LE16 . . . . . . **241** B3
Stockwell Head LE10 . . . . **197** D1
Stockwell Rd LE2 . . . . **180** D7
Stockwood Dr NN17 . . . . . **230** F1
Stoke Albany Rd LE16 . . . . **227** E1
STOKE DRY **211** E6
STOKE GOLDING **196** E7
Stoke La
Higham on t H CV13 . . . . . . **196** A4
Stoke Golding CV13 . . . . . . **196** E8
Stoke Rd
Hinckley LE10, CV13 . . . . . **197** A4
Lyddington LE15 . . . . **212** C7
Upton CV13 . . . . **172** D2
Stokes Cl LE8 . . . . **202** A8
Stokes Paddock LE14 . . . . . **20** B3
Stokes Wood Prim Sch
LE3 . . . . **154** B8
Stonebow Cl LE11 . . . . **51** B6
Stonebow La LE15 . . . . **51** B6
Stonebridge St LE15 . . . . . **155** D6
Stonechat Rd CV23 . . . . . . **252** D1
Stonechat Wlk LE15 . . . . . **155** C6
Stone Cl LE4 . . . . **128** A6
Stonecroft LE8 . . . . **202** C3
Stonecrop Rd LE5 . . . . **130** C2
Stone Dr NG33, LE15 . . . . . . **66** A2
Stonehaven Rd LE67 . . . . . . **72** D1
Stonehaven Rd LE4 . . . . . . **129** D4
Stonehill DE74 . . . . **17** B2
Stonehill Ave LE4 . . . . **129** A8
Stonehill Ct LE8 . . . . **182** C1
Stonehill Dr LE8 . . . . **182** C1
Stonehill High Sch The
LE4 . . . . **102** B1
Stonehills DE74 . . . . **17** B2
Stonehouse Ct CV23 . . . . . **258** A6
Stonehurst Family Farm &
Mus* LE12 . . . . **76** D3
Stonehurst La LE12 . . . . **30** D3
Stonehurst Rd LE3 . . . . . . **178** F8
Stoneleigh LE2 . . . . **155** B2
Stoneleigh Cl CV10 . . . . . . **194** B2
Stoneleigh Manor 1
LE2 . . . . **155** B2
Stoneleigh Way LE14 . . . . **154** C8
Stoneley Rd CV13 . . . . **196** D6
Stone Mdws NG10 . . . . **10** E5
Stonepit Dr LE16 . . . . **229** D1
Stonepit La NG33 . . . . **43** B8
Stonepit Terr LE14 . . . . . . **108** D3
Stone Row LE67 . . . . **71** D1
STONESBY **40** E6
Stonesby Ave LE2 . . . . . . **179** F4
Stonesby Rd
Saltby LE14 . . . . **24** D1

Stonesby Rd continued
Sproxton LE14.............41 E5
Waltham on t W LE14.......40 B6
Stonestyle Gdns LE14....38 E5
Stoney CI LE17..........246 F3
Stoney Cove Diving Ctr *
LE9..................199 E1
Stoneycroft 2 LE2.......155 D2
Stoneycroft Rd LE9......198 E7
STONEYGATE.............155 C1
Stoneygate Ave LE2......155 C1
Stoneygate Coll LE2.....155 C2
Stoneygate Ct LE2.......155 C1
Stoneygate Dr LE10......197 F3
Stoneygate Sch LE8......205 C6
Stoney Hollow LE17......244 C5
Stoney La
Appleby Magna DE12.......92 F1
Coleorton LE67...........70 F8
Stanton u B LE67.........98 B1
STONEY STANTON..........199 D3
Stoneywell Rd LE4.......127 F5
Stonton Rd LE16.........225 D8
STONTON WYVILLE.........207 F3
Stoop La LE12...........76 A6
Stordon La LE67.........68 B2
Storer CI LE12..........77 D3
Storer Rd LE11..........51 F4
Stores La LE8...........222 F7
Storey St LE3...........154 D7
Stornaway Rd LE5........156 D6
Stornoway Rd NN17.......230 C1
STOUGHTON..............155 D1
Stoughton Ave LE2.......155 D1
Stoughton CI LE2........181 B6
Stoughton Dr LE5........155 F2
Stoughton Dr N LE5......155 D3
Stoughton Dr S LE2......180 F8
Stoughton Farm Pk *
LE2..................156 C2
Stoughton La LE2........156 C2
Stoughton Rd
Gaulby LE7...............183 C6
Leicester LE2............155 D1
Leicester, Oadby LE2.....181 B7
Thurnby LE5, LE7.........156 F3
Stoughton St S LE2......155 B5
Stoughton St LE2........155 B5
Stour CI LE2............181 D6
Stourdale CI NG10.......10 A6
Stour Rd NN17...........230 D1
Stove Ct LE15...........89 A7
Stove CI
Ashby-de-la-Z LE65.......69 A7
Leicester LE3............128 A1
Stow Hill LE14..........41 F5
Strachan CI LE12........76 F1
Strancliffe La LE12.....53 C1
Strand The 1 LE2........155 A1
Strasbourg Dr LE4.......128 E3
Stratford Rd LE3........153 F1
Strathaven Rd LE4.......129 D4
Strathay Wlk NN17.......230 C1
Strathern Rd LE3, LE7...127 F3
Strathmore Ave LE4......129 D3
Strathmore CI LE67......97 C8
Strathmore Rd LE10......215 A7
Stratton CI LE16........240 D1
Strawberry Ct LE14......108 D3
Strawberry Gdns
LE19.................177 F4
Strawberry La DE11......45 B1
Streamside CI LE18......218 F5
Street The
Goadby LE7...............185 B2
South Luffenham LE15.....191 E8
Strensall Rd LE2........179 D3
STRETTON................88 F4
Stretton CI LE10........215 D6
Stretton Ct
Great Glen LE8...........205 B8
Hinckley LE10............215 D3
Stretton Dr LE67........72 C1
STRETTON EN LE FIELD
....................92 D4
Stretton Hall Dr LE2....181 F3
Stretton La LE7.........157 E2
Stretton Rd
Clipsham LE15............89 C4
Great Glen LE8...........182 C3
Greetham LE15............88 D2
Leicester LE3............154 C5
Stretton View DE12......93 A6
Stroller's Way LE7......103 F7
Stroma Way LE8..........202 F3
Stroud Ct NG13..........3 B3
Stroud Rd LE5...........155 D7
Stroud's CI LE14........20 F8
Strudwick Way LE8.......179 A1
Strutt Rd LE10..........216 A5
Stuart Cres LE16........239 F7
Stuart Ct LE8...........224 A8
Stuart Rd
Glen Parva LE2...........179 C2
Market Harborough
LE16.................240 E2
Stuart St
Kibworth Beauchamp
LE8..................224 A8
Stuart Way LE65.........69 B5
Stubbs Rd LE4...........155 B8
Studbrook CI DE74.......16 F3
Studfall Ave NN17.......230 F1
Studfarm CI DE73........26 F2
Sturdee CI LE2..........179 D4
Sturdee Gn LE2..........179 C4

Sturdee Rd LE2..........179 D4
Sturrock CI LE7.........156 F6
Stygate La LE14.........108 E5
Styon Rd LE3............127 E1
Sudbury Ct NG10.........9 F4
Sudeley Ave LE4.........128 E2
Suffolk CI
Melton Mowbray LE13.....82 E8
Wigston LE18.............180 A3
Suffolk St LE5..........155 E5
Suffolk Way LE9.........151 B2
Sulby Hall Old Dr
NN6..................248 B1
Sulby Rd
Welford NN6..............248 B1
Welford NN6..............256 F7
Sulgrave Rd LE5.........155 D7
Sullington Rd LE12......50 C3
Sullivan Way LE11.......51 F6
Sulthorpe Rd LE5........130 C3
Sulthorpe Rd PE9........167 F5
Summerfield LE15........138 A8
Summerlea Rd LE5........156 C6
Summerpool Rd LE11......51 F7
Summers Ct LE9.........175 D6
Summers Way LE16........240 D2
Sunbury Gn LE5.........156 E7
Sunbury Rise LE8.......202 C4
Sundew Rd LE5..........130 C3
Sundial Rd LE5.........130 C3
Sunningdale CI CV11....214 A1
Sunningdale Ind Pk
LE3..................153 B4
Sunningdale Rd
Coalville LE67...........96 F8
Leicester LE3............153 B4
Sunnybank PE9..........143 E3
Sunnycroft Rd LE3......154 A5
Sunnydale Cres LE10....215 A7
Sunnydale Rd LE10......214 F7
Sunnyfield LE15........138 A8
Sunnyfield CI LE5......156 C5
Sunnyhill LE10.........215 F7
Sunnyhill Rd LE11......51 F1
Sunnyhill S LE10.......215 F6
Sunnyside
Hinckley LE10............197 D3
Ibstock LE67.............122 E8
Sunny Side LE2.........181 C4
Sunnyside CI LE8.......178 F1
Sunnyside Hospl
LE10.................197 D5
Sunnyside Ind Est
LE10.................197 D4
Sun Ct LE11............44 F2
Sun Way LE3............153 D3
Surrey CI LE10.........215 E4
Surrey St LE4..........155 B8
Susan Ave LE5..........156 B4
Sussex Ave LE13........82 D8
Sussex Rd
Stamford PE9.............143 D4
Wigston LE18.............179 F3
Sussex St LE1..........155 B6
Sutherington Way
LE7..................127 E7
Sutherland St 1 LE1....155 B5
Sutherland Way PE9.....143 B3
Suthern CI LE15........138 A8
Suthers Rd DE74........18 C2
Sutton Ave LE4.........129 C2
SUTTON BASSETT.........227 A1
SUTTON BONINGTON.......30 B8
Sutton Bonington Prim
Sch LE12.............30 B6
SUTTON CHENEY..........174 B6
Sutton CI
Hinckley LE10............197 F3
Leicester, Oadby LE2.....181 B3
Quorn (Quorndon) LE12....75 F5
Sutton Bonington LE12....30 C5
Sutton CI LE16.........240 E1
SUTTON IN THE ELMS
....................218 E8
Sutton La
Dadlington CV13..........173 F1
Granby NG13..............5 D1
Market Bosworth CV13.....148 F1
Sutton Cheney CV13.......174 D8
Sutton PI
Leicester LE2............129 C2
Swadlincote DE11.........44 F3
Sutton Rd
Great Bowden LE16........241 B6
Kegworth DE74............18 C1
Leicester LE2............148 A8
Sutton Bassett LE16......241 E7
Weston by W LE16.........227 B3
Suttons Ave DE11.......44 E1
Suttons Bsns Pk DE11...44 E3
SWADLINCOTE............44 D4
Swadlincote Rd DE11....44 E3
Swadlincote Ski Ctr
DE11.................44 C3
Swains Gn LE10.........215 F6
Swainson Rd LE4........155 E8
SWAINSPARK.............67 B7
Swainspark Ind Est
DE12.................67 B6
Swain St LE1...........259 C3
Swale CI
Corby NN17...............230 D1
Leicester, Oadby LE2.....181 D6
Melton Mowbray LE13......59 B1
Swallow CI LE12........76 F2
Swallow Ct LE10........214 F7
Swallow Dale LE67......71 D7
Swallowdale Dr LE4.....128 B6

Swallowdale Prim Sch
LE13.................82 B8
Swallowdale Rd LE13....82 B8
Swallow Dr LE7.........102 F4
Swallow Rd DE11........44 F3
Swallows CI LE3........152 E1
Swallow's Dale LE7.....103 E8
Swallows Dr LE14.......12 F3
Swallow Wlk LE12.......30 A1
Swan CI
Barrow-u-S LE12..........76 E8
Glen Parva LE2...........179 A2
Melton Mowbray LE13......82 B8
Mountsorrel LE12.........76 F2
Swan Ct LE12...........30 B6
Swann CI LE15..........166 D3
SWANNINGTON............71 A5
Swannington CE Prim Sch
LE67.................71 A5
SWANNINGTON COMMON
....................71 B7
Swannington Rd
Broughton Astley LE9.....219 A6
Leicester LE3............154 C7
Ravenstone LE67.........70 F2
Swannymote Rd LE67,
LE12.................72 B7
Swanscombe Rd LE2......154 D1
Swanson Ho PE9.........143 F4
Swan St
Leicester LE3............259 A4
Loughborough LE11........52 B4
Seagrave LE12............77 F8
Sileby LE12..............77 C3
Swan Way
Coalville LE67...........96 F8
Syston LE7...............102 E4
Swedish CI LE16........224 E1
Sweetbriar PE9.........142 E5
Sweetbriar Rd LE3......154 C3
Sweethill LE67.........68 A5
SWEPSTONE..............94 D2
Swepstone Rd
Heather LE67.............95 A2
Measham DE12.............94 B4
Snarestone DE12, LE67....94 C1
Swift CI
Melton Mowbray LE13......82 B8
Syston LE7...............102 F4
Woodville DE11...........44 F3
Swifts CI LE67.........95 F2
Swift's CI LE12........33 C3
Swift Valley Ind Est
CV21.................252 A1
Swift Way LE7..........244 C7
Swinburne Rd LE9.......197 C1
Swindale CI LE2........259 A2
Swinfen CI LE67........96 C3
Swinfield Rd LE13......76 A6
SWINFORD...............254 C3
Swinford Ave LE2.......179 D2
Swinford CE Prim Sch
LE17.................254 B4
Swinford Cnr LE17......254 A8
Swinford Ct LE17.......179 D2
Swinford Rd
Cotesbach LE17...........244 E2
Shawell LE17.............253 D5
Walcote LE17.............245 B2
Swingbridge Rd LE17....253 A7
Swingbridge St LE16....239 E8
Swinstead Rd LE5.......156 D4
SWITHLAND..............100 D7
Swithland Ave LE4......128 F1
Swithland CI
Loughborough LE11........51 C5
Markfield LE67...........125 E8
Swithland Ct
8 Braunstone Town
LE3..................178 F7
Swithland LE12...........100 A8
Swithland La LE7.......101 B7
Swithland Rd
Coalville LE67...........97 C8
Swithland LE67...........100 E4
Swithland Resr Nature
Reserve *
Mountsorrel LE7..........75 F1
Swithland LE7............100 B5
Swithland St Leonard's CE
Prim Sch LE12........100 E7
Swithland Woods Nature
Reserve * LE12........100 B5
Sword CI LE3...........153 C7
Sword Dr LE10..........197 B3
Sybil Rd LE3...........154 B1
Sycamore Ave DE11......44 A7
Sycamore CI
Barton in t B CV13.......122 D1
Corby NN17...............230 E1
Hinckley LE10............215 E5
Ibstock LE67.............95 E1
Leicester LE2............155 F1
Leicester, Oadby LE2.....182 A3
Sapcote LE9..............199 A8
Newbold Verdon LE9......150 A6
Syston LE7...............103 B2
Sycamore Dr
Ashby-de-la-Z LE65.......69 D7
Groby LE6................126 F2
Lutterworth LE17.........244 A6
Moira DE12...............68 B6
Sycamore Gr LE6........126 F3
Sycamore La LE14.......62 D2
Sycamore Rd
Birstall LE4.............129 A8
Castle Donington DE74....17 B5
Coalville LE67...........97 A8

Sycamore Rd continued
East Leake LE12..........31 D8
Long Eaton NG10..........10 C5
North Luffenham LE15.....166 D3
Sycamore St LE8........202 B8
Sycamores The
South Kilworth LE17......255 D8
Swadlincote DE11.........44 E4
Sycamore Way
Littlethorpe LE19........201 B6
Loughborough LE11........75 A7
Market Bosworth CV13.....148 F2
Sydney Rd DE72.........9 A7
Sykefield Ave LE3......154 C4
Sykes La LE15..........140 E5
Sylvan Ave LE5.........155 D6
Sylvan St LE3..........154 C7
Sylvan Way LE3.........153 B4
Symington Way LE16.....240 E3
SYSONBY................58 E2
Sysonby Grange La
LE13.................58 F2
Sysonby St LE13........59 A4
SYSTON.................103 D3
Syston Rd
Cossington LE7...........102 C7
Queenborough LE7.........103 E6
South Croxton LE7........104 F1
Syston St E LE1........155 B7
Syston St W LE1........155 A8
Syston Sta LE7.........103 A3
Sywell Ave LE11........51 C3
Sywell Dr LE18.........180 F2

T

Tabberer CI LE15.......138 A8
Tadcaster Ave LE2......179 D3
Tadcaster Gn LE2.......179 D3
Tailby Ave LE5.........155 E8
Tailor's Link LE7......103 D7
Talbot La
Leicester LE1............259 A3
Whitwick LE67............71 C7
Talbot PI DE12.........92 E8
Talbot St
Leicester LE4............129 A3
Swadlincote DE11.........44 A1
Whitwick LE67............71 D6
Talbott CI LE9.........219 A4
Talbot Yd LE16.........240 E3
Tamar Gn NN17..........230 D1
Tamar Rd
Leicester LE4............129 D1
Melton Mowbray LE13......59 B1
Tamerton Rd LE2........179 C5
Tame Way LE10..........215 A8
Tamworth CI LE12.......49 F2
Tamworth Rd
Appleby Magna DE12.......92 E2
Ashby-de-la-Z LE65.......69 A5
Castle Donington DE72,
NG10.................9 E1
Long Eaton NG10..........10 C5
Measham DE12.............93 B4
Tandy Ave DE12.........68 B5
Tanner's La LE12.......30 A1
Tannery The LE15.......192 A5
Tanni Gray Ho 6 LE11...52 E4
Tanser Cott LE12.......55 C8
Tansey Cres LE9........199 C2
Tansley Ave LE18.......180 A1
Tanyard Ct DE74........17 B4
Tan Yd LE67............71 B5
Tara St LE67...........97 B4
Tarbat Rd LE5..........156 D4
Tarragon Rd LE2........154 D7
Tatlow Rd LE3..........153 D6
Tatlow Rd LE3..........153 C6
Tatmarsh LE11..........52 A5
Tatton CI LE3..........128 A1
Tatwin Ct DE73.........26 F2
Taunton CI LE18........180 C1
Taunton Rd LE3.........154 B5
Taurus CI LE2..........155 A4
Taverner Dr LE6........152 D7
Taverners Rd LE4.......128 C2
Tavistock CI LE67......96 C6
Tavistock Dr LE5.......155 F3
Tay CI
Corby NN17...............230 D1
Oakham LE15..............137 E4
Tayleur CI LE67........96 E8
Taylor CI
Moira DE12...............68 A4
Syston LE7...............103 A3
Taylor Ho
Loughborough LE11........52 C4
Uppingham LE15...........189 A4
Taylor Rd LE1..........155 A7
Taylor Road Prim Sch
LE1..................155 B7
Taylor's Bridge Rd
LE18.................180 A1
Taylors CI LE9.........199 D2
Teal Bsns Ctr LE10.....214 D7
Tealby CI LE17.........235 C4
Teal CI
Coalville LE67...........96 F8
Leicester Forest East
LE3..................152 F2
Teal Dr LE10...........215 A8
Teal Way LE67..........102 E4
Teasel CI LE19.........201 B8
Teasel Dr
Melton Mowbray LE13......82 A8

Teasel Dr continued
Woodville DE11...........44 F4
Tebbs CI LE8...........202 C4
Tedder CI LE17.........244 A5
Tedworth Gn LE4........128 D5
Tees CI LE15...........137 F5
Teesdale Rd NG10.......10 A6
TEIGH..................86 A5
Teigh Rd
Ashwell LE15.............86 A1
Market Overton LE15......86 D5
Teign Bank CI LE10.....197 D2
Teign Bank Rd LE10.....197 D2
Teignmouth CI LE15.....155 F3
Telford Way
Coalville LE67...........71 B2
Leicester LE5............156 E5
Tellis PI DE12.........93 D5
Tempest Rd LE4.........128 F6
Templars Way
South Witham NG33........65 A4
Whitwick LE67............71 F5
Templar Way LE7........101 E6
Temple Bldgs LE5.......155 F3
Temple CI LE12.........50 C1
Temple Hill LE7........71 F6
Temple Rd LE5..........155 E5
Tendring Dr LE18.......180 F3
Tennis Ave LE13........59 C1
Tennis Court Dr LE5....156 A8
Tennyson Ave LE16......44 C6
Tennyson CI DE12.......93 B4
Tennyson Rd
Hinckley LE10............197 C1
Loughborough LE11........51 D4
Lutterworth LE17.........244 C7
Tennyson St
Leicester LE2............155 C3
Narborough LE19.........178 A1
Tennyson Way
Melton Mowbray LE13......59 B6
Stamford PE9.............143 A4
Tentas The LE67........48 A2
Tenter CI NG10.........10 C5
Tentercroft Ave LE17...103 C4
Tenter Ct PE9..........143 E2
Tenterfield DE74.......28 B5
Tenter La 1 PE9........143 E3
Tern Ave DE11..........44 F3
Terrace Cotts LE7......200 C4
Terrace The
Copt Oak LE67............98 C8
1 Lutterworth LE17.......244 C5
Test Gn NN17...........230 D1
Tetbury Dr LE2.........49 F2
Tetuan Rd LE3..........154 C6
Teviot CI NN17.........230 D1
Tewkesbury Rd NG10.....10 E4
Tewkesbury St LE3......154 D6
Thackeray St LE2.......179 F8
Thames Dr LE13.........59 B1
Thames St LE1..........259 B5
Thames Wlk NN17........230 D1
Thatcher CI LE4........128 B4
Thatchers' Cnr LE7.....103 D7
Thatch Meadow Dr
LE16.................241 B3
Theatre Mall 8 LE1.....259 B4
THEDDINGWORTH..........248 C8
Theddingworth Rd
Husbands Bosworth
LE17.................248 A6
Lubenham LE16...........239 C2
Marston Trussell LE16....249 B8
Mowsley LE17............237 F5
THE FORTIES............45 F4
Thimble Hall Rd LE7,
LE14.................133 C8
Thirlmere CI LE67......72 C1
Thirlmere Ct LE2.......76 D8
Thirlmere Dr LE11......74 D8
Thirlmere Gdns LE65....69 C4
Thirlmere Rd
Barrow-u-S LE12..........76 D8
Barwell LE9..............215 A7
Wigston LE18.............180 E3
Thirlmere St LE2.......259 A1
Thistle CI
Cropston LE7.............100 F2
Narborough LE19.........201 A8
Woodville DE11...........44 F4
THISTLETON.............87 F8
Thistleton La NG33.....65 C5
Thistleton Rd LE15.....87 A6
Thistley CI LE3........153 C2
Thistly Meadow Prim Sch
LE8..................202 C7
Thomas CI
Houghton on t H LE7......157 F4
Leicester LE3............179 A8
Thomas Cook CI LE67....
LE9..................218 F6
Thomas Estley Com Coll
LE9..................218 F6
Thomas Firr CI LE17....76 A7
Thomas Fryer's
Almshouses LE15........164 E6
Thomas Rd
Kegworth DE74............18 C1
Whitwick LE67............71 D5
Thomas Rd LE15.........59 C6
Thomas St
Ibstock LE67.............122 F8
Loughborough LE11........52 D3
Thompson Ave LE12......49 B6

Thompson Cl
Quorn (Quorndon) LE12......75 F6
Swadlincote DE11..........44 E4
Thompsons La LE15....190 C1
Thomson Cl LE4........129 D6
Thomson Ct LE67......125 F8
Thoresby Rd NG10......10 C6
Thoresby St LE5......155 E6
THORNBOROUGH..........71 D3
Thornborough Cl
Market Harborough
LE16................241 A2
Narborough LE19..........200 F7
Thornborough Rd
LE67..................71 C3
Thornby Gdns LE18....180 E2
Thorndale LE67........95 E1
Thorndale Rd LE4......129 D7
Thorneycroft Cl LE9...219 B4
Thorneywood Rd NG10...10 F8
Thornfield Ave CV13..196 E7
Thornfield Sq NG10....10 E8
Thornfield Way LE10..215 C8
Thornhills LE19.......178 A2
Thornhills Gr LE19....178 A2
Thornholme Cl LE4....128 C4
Thorn St DE11.........44 F2
Thorn Street Mews
DE11.................44 F2
THORNTON.............124 E4
Thornton Cl
Braunstone Town
LE3.................153 D3
Broughton Astley LE9...219 A4
Coalville LE67..........72 C1
Thornton Com Prim Sch
LE67.................124 E4
Thornton Cres LE16...225 D7
Thornton Dr LE19.....201 C8
Thornton La
Bagworth LE67.........124 C4
Markfield LE67.........125 C5
Stanton u B LE67.......124 E7
Thorntop Cl DE11......68 B8
Thorntree Cl
Leicester LE3.........127 F2
Ravenstone LE67.........70 F2
Thornville Cl LE4.....129 E1
Thorny Cl LE11.........51 D6
Thornycroft Rd LE10..215 E8
THORPE ACRE..........51 C4
Thorpe Acre Inf Sch
LE11..................51 D4
Thorpe Acre Jun Sch
LE11..................51 D4
Thorpe Acre Rd LE11...51 D5
THORPE ARNOLD.........60 A5
THORPE ASTLEY........153 C1
THORPE BY WATER......213 A6
Thorpe Downs Rd
DE11..................44 B1
Thorpe Dr LE18.......180 D4
Thorpe End LE13.......59 D3
Thorpe Field Dr LE4..129 F8
Thorpe Gdns LE15......84 E1
Thorpe Hill LE11......51 C4
THORPE IN THE GLEBE
.....................33 D8
Thorpe La LE7........130 D8
THORPE LANGTON.......226 A5
Thorpe Langton Rd
East Langton LE16......225 D6
Welham LE16...........226 D6
Thorpe Leys NG10.....10 D5
Thorpe Rd
Lyddington LE15........212 D6
Melton Mowbray LE13....59 E4
Shepshed LE12..........50 A3
THORPE SATCHVILLE
....................106 E4
Thorpe Satchville Rd
Great Dalby LE14.......82 A1
Kirby Bellars LE14......81 C5
Thorpe Satchville LE14..106 F7
Twyford LE14...........106 E2
Thorpe Side LE4.......38 F4
Thorpes La NG32.......24 B7
Thorpe St LE3.......154 D5
Thorpe's Terr LE15...189 A4
Thorpe Way LE19.....178 D4
Thorpewell LE5.......155 F6
Threadcutters Way
LE12..................50 B3
Threadgold Cl LE4....128 B6
Three Gates Rd LE7...184 C2
Three Pots Rd LE10...215 E4
Three Turns La LE7...105 C2
Threshers Wlk LE7....103 E7
THRINGSTONE...........71 D8
Thringstone Prim Sch
LE67..................71 D8
Thrumpton Ave NG10....10 F7
Thrush Cl LE13.........82 B8
THRUSSINGTON..........78 F4
Thrussington CE Prim Sch
LE7..................78 F5
Thrussington Rd
Hoby LE14.............79 C6
Thrussington LE7........79 D3
THURCASTON...........101 C2
Thurcaston La LE7....101 B4
Thurcaston Rd
Leicester, Mowmacre Hill
LE4.................128 D6

Thurcaston Rd continued
Leicester, Stocking Farm
LE4.................128 F4
Thurcroft Cl LE27....179 D3
THURLASTON...........177 B3
Thurlaston CE Prim Sch
LE9.................177 A3
Thurlaston La
Croft LE9.............200 B7
Enderby LE9, LE19.....177 D4
Thurlaston LE9........176 B1
Thurlby Rd LE5.......155 D7
Thurlington Rd LE3...154 A3
Thurlow Cl
Atherstone CV9........170 D2
Leicester, Oadby LE2..181 D4
Thurlow Rd LE2.......155 A1
THURMASTON...........129 E7
Thurmaston Bvd LE4..129 F3
Thurmaston Footpath
LE4.................129 F4
Thurmaston La LE4....130 A3
THURNBY.............156 F5
Thurnby Hill LE5, LE7.156 E5
Thurnby La LE5, LE2..156 E2
THURNBY LODGE.......156 E7
Thurnby Lodge Prim Sch
LE5.................156 D6
Thurncourt Cl LE5....156 C7
Thurncourt Gdns LE5..156 D6
Thurncourt Rd LE5....156 D6
Thurnview Rd LE5.....156 C3
Thurso Wlk NN17.....230 D1
Thyme Cl LE2.........259 A2
Thythorn Field Com Prim
Sch LE18............203 D7
Tiber Way LE19.......178 D8
Tichborne Ct LE2.....155 B4
Tichborne St LE2.....155 B4
TICKENCOTE..........142 B8
Ticknall Rd DE11......45 B7
Tickow La LE12........49 E3
Tiffany Ct LE2.......155 D2
Tigers Cl LE18.......179 E2
Tigers Rd LE18.......179 F2
Tigers Way LE1, LE2..259 C1
Tilbury Cres LE4.....130 A5
Tilford Cres LE2.....179 D2
Tillett Rd LE3.......153 D2
Tilley Cl LE3........153 D1
Tillingham Rd LE5....155 F8
Tilling Rd LE4.......128 C4
Tilton Cutting Nature
Reserve* LE7.........160 E7
Tilton Dr LE2........181 A3
Tilton La LE7........159 C7
TILTON ON THE HILL
....................160 B8
Tilton Rd
Hinckley LE10........215 E6
Twyford LE14..........106 D1
Timbergate Rd PE9...167 E5
Timber Hill NG33.....64 A8
Timber St LE18.......179 F1
Timberwood Dr LE6...126 E2
Timson Cl LE14.......240 D5
Tindall Sq LE15.......87 D2
Tinker's Dell LE7....103 D8
Tinsel La CV13.......172 D8
Tintagel Way CV11....214 A5
TINWELL.............142 E1
Tinwell Rd PE9.......143 B2
Tinwell Road La PE9..143 B2
Tipnall Rd DE74.......17 A3
Tippings La LE15.....191 F5
Tiptree Cl LE4.......128 D2
Tithe Barn Row LE15...88 B2
Tithe Cl
Stoke Golding CV13....196 D6
Thringstone LE67.......71 C8
Tithe St LE5.........155 E6
Tithings The LE8.....206 A1
Tiverton Ave
Coalville LE67..........72 A2
Leicester LE4.........129 C2
Tiverton Cl
Leicester, Oadby LE2..181 C5
Narborough LE19.......200 F8
Tiverton Mews LE4....129 C2
Tiverton Rd
Cottesmore LE15........87 E2
Loughborough LE11......74 F7
TIXOVER.............192 E5
Tixover Grange PE9...192 F8
Tobias Gr PE9........142 E5
Todd's Hill PE9......193 B6
Tod's Terr LE15......129 C2
Tod's Hill LE14......189 A3
Tofts The LE18.......180 D1
Toft The LE12.........49 B6
Tokye's Cl LE15......187 D7
Tolcarne Rd LE5......156 C8
Tolchard Cl LE5......156 A5
Tolethorpe Cl LE15...138 B6
Tolethorpe Sq PE9....143 D4
TOLL BAR............142 F6
Toll Bar LE15........112 D8
Toll Bar Ave NG13.....3 A3
Tollemache Ave LE4...128 C2
Tollemache Fields
NG33.................65 B3
Toller Rd
Leicester LE2.........155 C1
Quorn (Quorndon) LE12..75 E5
Tolton Rd LE4........128 D4
Tolwell Rd LE4.......128 C5
Tom Eatough Ct LE9...199 A8
Tomlin Rd LE4........129 E1

Tomlinson Ct LE2.....181 A6
Tom Paine Cl LE3.....153 D2
Toms Cl LE17.........248 D8
Toms Ct DE74..........18 D2
TONGE................27 B3
Tonge La
Breedon on t h DE73....26 F3
Tonge DE73.............27 A3
Toon Cl LE2..........50 A1
Toothill Rd LE11......52 B5
Tooth St DE11.........44 E1
Top Cl LE3...........153 D1
Topcliffe Wlk LE4....128 E3
Top End LE14..........82 A1
Top Gn LE14...........19 A1
Tophall Dr LE8.......202 E3
Top La LE15..........189 E4
Top Lo NN17..........193 A1
Top Mdw DE11..........44 B7
Top Rd
Croxton Kerrial NG32...24 B7
Griffydam LE67.........48 A2
Ridlington LE15.......163 E2
Top St
Appleby Magna DE12....119 F7
Exton LE15............113 B3
Wing LE15.............165 A2
Top Yard Farm LE16...240 F6
Torch Cl LE16.......209 E6
Torch Way LE16.......250 F8
Torcross Cl LE3......153 E8
Torkington Gdns 4
.....................143 D3
Torkington St PE9....143 C3
Toronto Cl LE1.......259 C5
Torrance Dr LE13......59 C6
Torridon Cl
Corby NN17............230 C1
Leicester LE4.........128 D3
Torridon Way LE10....197 B1
Torrington Ave LE67...72 A2
Torrington Cl LE18...203 D8
Totland Rd LE3.......154 C8
Totnes Cl LE67........96 C7
Toulmin Dr LE11.......44 B4
Toulouse Pl LE65......69 A7
Tournament Rd LE3....153 D7
Tovey Cres LE2.......179 D4
Tower Ct LE16........239 F3
Tower Furlong CV23...252 D1
Tower Gdns LE16.......69 A6
Tower Rd
Earl Shilton LE9......198 F8
Hartshorne DE11........45 A6
Towers Cl LE9........152 E4
Towers Dr LE9........152 E4
Towers Hospl The
LE5.................129 F1
Tower St LE1.........259 B2
Towers The LE1........51 E3
Towers Way LE1........51 E3
Towle Rd LE3.........153 E8
Towles Fields LE12....53 F6
Towles Mill LE11......52 C5
Towles Pastures DE74..17 A3
Towle St NG10.........10 A4
TOWN END.............28 C5
Town End
Barkestone-le-V NG13....6 C2
Hungarton LE7.........132 B3
Somerby LE14..........108 C1
Townend Cl LE14.......57 E2
Townend Rd LE9.......198 A2
Town End Rd DE72......9 B7
TOWN GREEN...........101 E5
Town Green St LE7....101 E5
Town Hall Mews 8
.....................69 B6
Townlands CE Prim Sch
LE9.................198 F7
Townsend Cl
Broughton Astley LE9...219 B5
Leicester LE4.........129 D5
Newton Regis B79......118 D4
Townsend La LE67......96 B5
Townsend Rd
Enderby LE19..........178 B3
Stoney Stanton LE9....199 D1
Townsends Cl CV11....215 A1
Townside Cl NG10......10 B4
Towns La LE14.........22 C1
Town Sq LE7..........103 B4
Town St LE8..........205 F8
Towpath Cl LE11.......52 C5
Towpath Link LE18....203 A8
Trackside Cl LE11.....51 D4
Trafalgar Cl LE7......103 A3
Trafalgar Rd NG10.....10 D6
Trafalgar Sq NG10.....10 E7
Trafalgar Terr
Long Eaton NG10........10 F7
Stamford PE9.........143 E4
Trafalgar Way LE7....179 D1
Trafford Cl CV9......170 D2
Trafford Rd
Hinckley LE10.........197 F2
Leicester LE5.........155 F7
Tranter Pl LE4.......129 D2
Travell's Hill LE12...31 A7
Treasure Cl LE3......153 C7
Treaty Rd LE3........153 D7
Tredington Rd LE3....127 D1
Treetops Cl LE5......156 B7
Trefoil Cl
Broughton Astley LE9...219 B4
Hamilton LE5.........130 C2
Melton Mowbray LE13....82 B8
Trelissick Cl LE11...51 B5

Tremaine Dr LE18.....179 C1
Trenant Rd LE2.......179 F4
Trent Ave LE4........128 D7
Trent Bank LE13.......59 A1
Trent Bridge LE67.....97 A7
Trent Cl
Broughton Astley LE9...219 A6
Leicester, Oadby LE2..181 D5
Trent Coll NG10.......10 C8
Trent Cotts NG10......10 F6
Trentham Rd CV10....194 B2
Trent Ho NG10.........10 A4
Trent La
Castle Donington DE74..17 A5
Long Eaton NG10........10 F5
Trent Lane Ind Est
DE74.................17 B5
TRENTLOCK............10 E3
Trent Rd
Corby NN17............230 D1
Hinckley LE10.........215 A8
Oakham LE15..........137 E4
Trent St NG10.........10 E8
Trescoe Rise LE3.....153 E5
Tressall Rd LE67......72 A3
Tressell Way LE3.....153 D2
Trevanth Rd LE4......129 F3
Trevino Dr LE4.......129 E5
Trevor Rd LE10.......197 F1
Trevose Gdns LE5.....156 E7
Tribune Ho 1 LE10...197 D1
Trigo Cl LE4.........128 A4
Trillium Cl LE5......130 C3
Trinity Cl
Allington NG32..........4 F5
Ashby-de-la-Z LE65.....69 A5
Syston LE7...........103 B3
Trinity Crest LE12....33 B3
Trinity Ct
Ashby-de-la-Z LE65.....69 B6
Hinckley LE10........215 C8
Leicester LE1........259 B2
Trinity Gr DE11.......44 B3
Trinity Hospl LE2....259 A3
Trinity La
Hinckley LE10........215 C8
Leicester LE1........259 B2
Trinity Rd
Narborough LE19......178 E2
Stamford PE9.........143 C4
Whetstone LE8........201 F8
Trinity St LE11.......52 C3
Trinity Vicarage Rd
LE10................215 C8
Trinity View NG10.....10 E8
Tripontium Bsns Ctr
CV23................253 A4
Tristram Cl LE3......153 A2
Triumph Rd LE3.......153 D7
Trojan Way LE7.......102 E2
Troon Cl PE9.........143 A4
Troon Ind Area LE4....30 A8
Troon Ind Est LE4....129 F3
Troon Way
Hinckley LE10........215 D4
Leicester LE4.........129 C4
Troon Way Bsns Ctr
LE4.................129 F4
Troughton Wlk NG33....65 A4
Trowell La LE12.......30 E7
Truesdale's 5 PE9...143 D3
Trueway Dr LE12.......50 C2
Trueway Dr S LE12.....50 C2
Trueway Rd LE5.......155 E2
Truro Cl
Hinckley LE10........197 E4
Swadlincote DE11.......44 E5
Truro Dr LE18........180 D1
Trusteel Hos CV23....252 C5
Tuckers Cl LE11.......52 D2
Tuckers Rd LE11.......52 D2
Tuckett Rd LE12.......74 F2
Tuckey Cl LE9........217 E7
Tudor Cl
Ashby-de-la-Z LE65.....69 B5
Leicester LE3.........154 D5
Market Bosworth CV13..148 E2
Tudor Cres CV9.......170 D1
Tudor Dr
Cosby LE9............201 D2
Leicester, Oadby LE2..181 B6
Tudor Gdns LE6.......126 F1
Tudor Hill LE13.......82 C8
Tudor House Cl DE11...44 A7
Tudor Rd
Hinckley LE10.........197 C3
Leicester LE3.........154 D6
Tudor Way DE11.........44 A6
Tuffleys Way LE3.....153 C1
TUGBY...............185 E7
Tugby CE Prim Sch
LE7.................185 E6
Tugby Rd
Goadby LE7...........185 C3
Tilton on t h LE7.....160 F6
Tugwell La LE16......209 D6
Tumbledown Farm Pk★
LE14.................60 A7
Tungstone Way LE16...240 E1
Tunicliffe Ct DE11...44 D4
Tunstall Cres LE4....155 E8
TUR LANGTON.........207 A2
Turnbull Cl LE17.....159 B2
Turnbull Dr LE3......153 F8
Turnbury Way LE5.....155 E1
Turner Ave LE11.......52 A2
Turner Cl LE12........75 F7
Turner Dr LE10.......197 A3

Turner Rd
Leicester LE5.........155 F7
Long Eaton NG10........10 C4
Turner Rise LE2......181 B4
Turner St LE1........259 B2
Turnpike Cl
Lutterworth LE17......244 D8
Market Harborough
LE16................240 D5
Turnpike Way LE67....96 C5
Turnpike Way LE67...125 E8
Turnpole Cl PE9......143 F5
Turn St LE7..........103 A4
Turnstone Wlk LE5....155 C7
Turolough Rd LE67.....71 E7
Turvey La LE12........29 D2
Turville Cl
Hinckley LE10.........215 F5
Wigston LE18.........203 E8
Turville Rd
Gilmorton LE17........235 C5
Leicester LE3.........154 B3
Tuskar Rd LE15......156 D7
Tutbury Cl 5 LE65....69 C5
Tuthill Furlong CV23..252 D1
Tuxford Rd LE4.......130 A3
Tweed Dr LE13........59 B1
Tweedside Cl LE10....197 F3
Tweentown LE67.......96 C5
Twells Rd LE14.......40 B6
Twenty Acre La LE13..174 B5
Twickenham Rd LE2....179 C2
Twin Lakes Pk★ LE14...60 A7
Twitchbed La LE15....189 B5
Twitchell La CV9.....171 B7
TWYCROSS............146 D7
Twycross House Prep Sch
CV9.................146 D6
Twycross La
Bilstone CV9, CV13....147 A7
Orton-on-t-H CV9.....145 F6
Twycross Rd
Bilstone CV13.........147 C7
Hinckley LE10.........215 F6
Sheepy Magna CV9......146 C2
Sibson CV13..........172 B7
Twycross St LE2......155 C5
Twycross Zoo* CV9...119 F1
Twycross Zoo Staff
Apartments CV9.......120 B1
TWYFORD.............106 E1
Twyford Cl LE67.......72 C1
Twyford Ct LE2.......198 B7
Twyford Rd
Burrough on t H LE14..107 C1
Long Eaton NG10........10 E8
South Croxton LE7.....105 E1
Thorpe Satchville LE14..106 E3
Twyford LE7..........133 F5
Tyburn Cl LE3, LE7....127 F3
Tyers Cl LE19........177 A3
Tyes End LE4.........128 A3
Tyler Ave LE11........51 F5
Tyler Ct LE65........166 B7
Tyler Rd LE16........152 D8
Tylers Rd LE12........49 B6
Tymecrosse Gdns
LE16................240 D5
Tyndale St LE3.......154 D4
Tyndale Cl
Leicester, Oadby LE2..181 D5
Long Eaton NG10........10 A6
Tynedale Rd LE11......74 C8
Tyne Rd
Corby NN17............230 D1
Oakham LE15..........137 F5
Tyringham Rd LE18....180 E2
Tyrrell St LE3.......154 D6
Tysoe Hill LE3.......127 D1
Tythe The DE11........44 B7
Tythorn Dr LE18......180 A5

U

UFFINGTON...........144 F4
Uffington CE Prim Sch
LE9.................144 F4
Uffington Rd LE9.....144 A4
Uist Wlk NN17.......230 C1
Uldale Gr LE11........44 C1
ULLESTHORPE.........233 C4
Ullesthorpe CE Prim Sch
LE17................233 B4
Ullesthorpe Ho LE17..233 A4
Ullesthorpe Rd
Ashby Parva LE17......233 E5
Bittesvell LE17......233 E2
Gilmorton LE17........234 C2
Ulleswater Cres LE65..69 C4
Ullswater Ave
Barrow-u-S LE12........53 D1
Edith Weston LE15.....165 F7
Nuneaton CV11........214 A6
Ullswater Dr LE2.....181 E6
Ullswater Rd LE13.....59 A2
Ullswater St LE2.....259 A2
Ullswater Wlk LE2....181 C5
Ulverscroft Dr LE6...126 F2
Ulverscroft La LE6.....99 B3
Ulverscroft Rd
Leicester LE4.........155 C8
Loughborough LE11.....74 E8
Ulvers Croft Way LE67..99 A3
Una Ave LE3..........179 A8
Underwood Cres LE9...217 C8

Underwood Ct LE3......153 B8
Underwood Dr LE9......199 D1
Unicorn St LE4..........129 E8
Union Pas **14** LE65.....69 B6
Union Rd DE11..........44 B5
Union St
  Long Eaton NG10........10 E8
  Loughborough LE11......52 A4
  Melbourne DE73.........26 A7
  Swadlincote DE11.......51 E3
Unitt Rd LE12...........76 B4
Unity Cl DE11...........44 A1
Unity Rd LE3...........153 C8
University Cl LE7.......103 B3
University Rd
  Leicester LE1..........259 C1
  Loughborough LE11......51 D2
Univ of Leicester
  Leicester LE1..........155 A3
  Leicester LE1..........155 B4
Univ of Leicester Botanic
  Gdn* LE2.............180 F7
Univ of Nottingham Dept
  of Ag Economics
  LE12.................30 B8
Univ of Nottingham Sutton
  Bonington Campus
  LE12.................30 B8
Unwin Gn NG33.........65 A4
Upex Cl LE18..........201 F4
Upland Cl LE67.........98 D1
Upland Dr LE67.........98 D1
Uplands Farm The
  LE12.................29 A4
Uplands Inf & Jun Sch
  LE12................155 C5
Uplands Pl LE12.........29 A4
Uplands Rd
  Leicester LE2.........179 F5
  Leicester, Oadby LE2...181 C6
  Measham DE12..........93 C4
Uplands The LE13........59 B2
Upper Bond St LE10....197 D1
Upper Brown St LE1....259 B3
UPPER BRUNTINGTHORPE
  ....236 D5
Upper Charnwood St
  LE2................155 B6
Upper Church St
  Ashby-de-la-Z LE65.....69 C6
  Syston LE7...........103 B4
Upper George St LE1...259 C5
Upper Gn LE11..........74 D8
Upper Green Pl LE16...241 A6
Upper Hall Cl LE5......156 C8
Upper Hall Gn LE5......156 C8
UPPER HAMBLETON
  ....139 C4
Upper Holme LE12.......30 B3
Upper King St LE1.....259 B3
UPPER MIDWAY..........44 C7
Upper Nelson St LE1...259 C2
Upper New Wlk LE1....155 B4
Upper Packington Rd
  LE65.................69 C5
Upper Temple Wlk
  LE4.................128 A3
Upper Tichborne St
  LE2.................155 B4
Upperton Rd LE2.......259 A1
Upperton Rise LE3.....154 C4
UPPINGHAM............189 A3
Uppingham CE Prim Sch
  LE15................189 A5
Uppingham Cl LE15.....156 C5
Uppingham Com Coll
  LE15................189 B2
Uppingham Dr
  Ashby-de-la-Z LE65.....69 A7
  Broughton Astley LE9..218 D8
Uppingham Rd
  Billesdon LE7........159 C2
  Bisbrooke LE15.......189 F5
  Blaston LE16.........210 D3
  Caldecott LE16.......212 B2
  Corby NN17...........230 B1
  East Norton LE7......186 C5
  Houghton on t H LE7..157 E5
  Houghton on t H LE7..158 D3
  Leicester LE5........156 C6
  Oakham LE15.........138 A5
  Preston LE15.........189 B8
  Stockerston LE15.....211 B8
  Thurnby LE7.........157 A5
Uppingham Sch
  Uppingham LE15......189 A4
  Uppingham LE15......189 B4
UPTON................172 C4
Upton Cl DE74..........17 B4
Upton Dr LE18.........180 F2
Upton La
  Shenton CV13........173 A5
  Sibson CV13..........172 D2
  Stoke Golding CV13...196 D7
  Upton CV13..........172 B2
Utah Cl LE3...........153 C7
Uttoxeter Cl LE4......129 D5
Uxbridge Rd LE4......129 C4

V

Valebrook Rd LE14......12 F3
Vale Cl
  Leicester LE5........156 C2
  Loughborough LE11.....75 B7
Vale End LE7..........156 F5

Valence Rd LE3........154 B4
Valentine Dr LE2......180 F6
Valentine Rd LE5......156 D5
Vale of Catmose Coll
  LE15................137 E7
Vale Rd
  Hartshorne DE11.......45 A3
  Swadlincote DE11......44 B6
Valerie Rd DE72........16 A7
Vale The LE15.........138 A5
Valiant Cl
  Glenfield LE3........153 D7
  Hinckley LE10........215 E4
Valjean Cres LE9......152 E3
Valley Ct LE15........189 B4
Valley Dr
  Braunstone Town LE3..153 C2
  Rugby CV21..........252 A1
Valley House Mews
  LE8.................205 B7
Valley La
  Bitteswell LE17......244 B8
  Staunton in t V NG23...1 D8
Valley Rd
  Ibstock LE67..........95 E1
  Leicester LE5........130 B4
  Loughborough LE11.....74 E8
  Markfield LE67.......125 E8
  Melton Mowbray LE13...82 B8
  Overseal LE12.........67 A3
  Weston by W LE16....227 B3
Valley Rise DE11........44 B5
Valley View LE67........47 E3
Valley Way
  Market Harborough
  LE16................241 B4
  Whitwick LE67.........71 D5
Val Wilson Ct LE11......51 B2
Vancouver Rd LE1.....155 A7
Vandyke Rd LE2.......181 B4
Vanguard Rd
  Diseworth DE74.........28 A8
  Long Eaton NG10.......10 D5
Vann Wlk LE4..........129 A2
Vaughan Ave NG13.......3 C2
Vaughan Cl LE16......250 E8
Vaughan Coll LE1.....259 A3
Vaughan Rd LE2.......179 E7
Vaughan St
  Coalville LE67.........96 C8
  Leicester LE3........154 D6
Vaughan Way LE1.....259 A3
Velbert Ho NN17.......230 E1
Vence Cl PE9..........143 C3
Ventnor Rd LE2.......180 D7
Ventnor Rd S LE2.....180 D6
Ventnor St LE5........155 D5
Venture Ct LE10......214 E8
Vercor Cl LE67.........72 D1
Verdale Ave LE4.......130 A5
Verdon Cres LE67......72 B1
Vernon Rd LE2........179 E7
Vernon Row NG13........6 F3
Vernon St LE3........154 D6
Verona Cl CV11.......214 A1
Vero's La CV13........123 B3
Vestry St LE1.........259 C4
Vetch Cl LE19........200 F8
Viadevana DE12.........67 E3
Vicarage Cl
  Billesdon LE7........159 C1
  Blackfordby DE11......68 C8
  Kirby Muxloe LE9.....152 E7
  Newbold LE67..........47 E3
  Syston LE7...........103 B4
Vicarage Ct LE9......198 F8
Vicarage Dr LE16.....224 E1
Vicarage Gdns DE11....44 C4
Vicarage La
  Barkby LE7...........130 D8
  Belton LE12...........49 B6
  Eaton NG32...........22 F7
  Leicester, Humberstone
  LE5.................156 B8
  Whetstone LE8.......178 F1
Vicarage Rd
  Oakham LE15.........138 A6
  Swadlincote DE11......44 C4
  Woodville DE11........44 E2
Vicarage St
  5 Earl Shilton LE9..198 F8
  Whitwick LE67.........71 F5
Vicars Cl LE15.........113 B2
Vicary La LE72..........75 C3
Victoria Ave
  Draycott DE72..........9 A7
  Leicester LE2........155 B4
  Market Harborough
  LE16................240 D5
Victoria Cl LE67........71 D5
Victoria Ct
  Leicester LE1........155 C2
  Leicester, Oadby LE2..180 F7
  Long Eaton NG10.......10 D7
Victoria Dr
  Groby LE6............126 F2
  Woodville DE11........44 E1
Victoria Gdns LE2.....155 C3
Victoria Par **6** LE4.259 C2
Victoria Park Rd LE2..155 B2
Victoria Pl LE11........52 B3
Victoria Rd
  Coalville LE67.........71 D1
  Draycott DE72..........9 A7
  Heather LE67..........95 F3
  Hinckley LE10.......215 F5

Victoria Rd continued
  Ibstock LE67..........97 A1
  Stamford PE9.........143 D4
  Whetstone LE8.......201 F8
  Woodhouse Eaves LE12..99 F4
Victoria Rd E LE5.....129 E1
Victoria Rd N LE4.....129 B3
Victoria St
  Castle Donington DE74..17 B5
  Fleckney LE8.........222 F7
  Hinckley LE10.......197 D1
  Long Eaton NG10......10 B5
  Loughborough LE11.....52 B3
  Melbourne DE73........26 A7
  Melton Mowbray LE13...59 C1
  Narborough LE19.....201 C8
  Quorn (Quorndon) LE12..76 B6
  Syston LE7...........103 B3
  Thurmaston LE4......129 E8
  Wigston LE18........180 D3
Victoria Terr LE2......155 B3
Victor Rd LE3.........153 D8
Victory Cl LE12........179 C4
Victory Cl NG10........10 E5
Viking Bsns Ctr DE11...44 F3
Viking Rd LE18.......180 A4
Vilia Cl LE10.........215 F4
Village Rd LE12.........30 D2
Village St
  Sedgebrook NG32.......8 F8
  Woolsthorpe by B NG32..15 A8
Villa St DE72...........9 B7
Villas The LE8........206 A1
Villers Ct LE8........202 B8
Vincent Cl LE3........154 B6
Vine Cl NG13............3 A1
Vinehouse Cl LE7......101 B3
Vineries The LE8......202 D3
Vine St
  Leicester LE1........259 A4
  Stamford PE9.........143 E3
Vine Tree Terr LE2.....32 C1
Vineyard The LE17....232 E6
Violet Cl DE12..........67 E1
Viscount Beaumont's CE
  Prim Sch LE67........70 D6
Viscount Rd DE74......28 C7
Vislok Cl LE16........240 E1
Vitruvius Way LE19...178 C8
Vostock Cl LE2........155 B5
Vulcan Ct LE67........71 D2
Vulcan Ho LE5........156 C6
Vulcan Rd LE5........156 C6
Vulcan Way
  Coalville LE67.........71 D2
  Willey LE17..........243 C7
Vyner Cl LE3.........153 C2
Vyse Dr NG10..........10 C6

W

Waddesdon Wlk LE4...155 D8
Wade St LE4..........128 F3
Wade's Terr LE15.....189 B4
Wadkins Way LE7.....157 B5
Wagtail Cl LE8........223 A6
Wain Bri LE11..........51 C6
Waingroves Wlk **2**
  LE4.................128 F3
Wainwright Ave LE5...130 C3
Wainwright Rd LE67....96 D6
Waistrell Dr LE11......51 B6
Wakefield Ct DE74......17 C4
Wakefield Dr
  Welford NN6.........256 D5
  Whitwick LE67.........71 E5
Wakefield Pl LE4......129 C5
Wakefield Way LE67....96 D7
Wakeling Cl LE8......201 F5
WAKERLEY.............192 A3
Wakerley Ct LE5......155 D6
Wakerley Great Wood
  Forest Trail* LE15..192 C2
Wakerley Great Wood
  Orienteering Course*
  LE15................192 B2
Wakerley Rd
  Barrowden LE15......192 A4
  Harringworth NN17...213 F7
  Leicester LE5........155 F3
Wakes Cl LE17........219 D2
Wakes Rd LE18.......180 D3
Walcote Cl LE4........245 C4
Walcote Cl LE10......214 F8
Walcote Rd
  Leicester LE4........129 E2
  South Kilworth LE17..246 B2
Walcot Rd LE16.......240 E2
Walcot Way PE9.......143 A4
Waldale Dr LE2........155 D2
Waldron Ct LE11.......52 A6
Waldron Dr LE2.......181 C5
Wales Orch LE12.....218 E1
Walford Cl LE9.......198 D7
Walk Cl DE72...........9 A7
Walker Cl LE2........219 A4
Walker Manor Ct
  LE17................244 B6
Walker Rd
  Bardon LE67..........97 C4
  Birstall LE4.........128 F6
  Thurmaston LE4......129 C6
Walkers Cl NG13........3 D2
Walkers La LE7.......101 E5
Walkers Stad (Leicester
  City FC) LE2.........154 E2

Walkers Way LE7......103 B4
Walks The PE9........168 D2
Wallace Dr
  Groby LE6............126 D5
  Sileby LE12...........77 C1
Wallace Rd LE11........52 A2
Walled Gdn The
  Hallaton LE16........209 E6
  West Langton LE16....225 A7
Wallingford Ave
  CV11................214 A7
Wallingford Rd LE4...128 F2
Wallis Cl
  Draycott DE72..........9 A7
  Thurcaston LE7......101 B3
Wallis Ho DE11.........44 E3
Walney Cl LE10.......197 B1
Walney Rd LE4........128 F7
Walnut Cl
  Aston-on-T DE72.......16 B8
  Bisbrooke LE15......189 E3
  Broughton Astley LE9.219 A6
  Empingham LE15.....141 A6
  Leicester, Oadby LE2..181 A5
  Markfield LE67.......125 D8
  Stathern LE14.........13 A2
  Stretton LE15..........2 A1
  Swadlincote DE11......44 A5
Walnut Gr LE2........179 B4
Walnut Leys LE2.....201 D2
Walnut Paddock LE14..12 B3
Walnut Rd
  Bottesford NG13........3 A2
  Loughborough LE11.....75 A8
Walnut St LE2........259 A1
Walnut Way
  Blaby LE8............202 B6
  Countesthorpe LE8...202 E4
  Leicester, Oadby LE2..181 A5
Walpole Cl LE3.......153 F5
Walsgrave Ave LE5...156 D5
Walshe Rd LE5........156 B6
Walsingham Cres LE3.153 B3
Walter Hull Ct LE12....52 C2
Waltham Ave LE3......152 B4
Waltham Cl NN17.....230 D1
Waltham Ho LE15.....137 F5
Waltham La
  Eaton NG32...........22 F5
  Harby LE14...........12 B1
  Long Clawson LE14....20 E2
WALTHAM ON THE
  WOLDS...............40 B7
Waltham on the Wolds CE
  Prim Sch LE14.........40 A6
Waltham Rd
  Branston NG32.........23 C7
  Eastwell LE14.........40 A6
  Stonesby LE14.........40 D6
Waltham Rise LE13.....59 E2
WALTON...............236 B3
Walton Cl
  Kirby Fields LE9.....152 F4
  Swadlincote DE11......44 A3
  Whissendine LE15.....84 E1
Walton Ct DE74.........18 C2
Walton Hill
  Castle Donington DE74..17 A4
  Isley Walton DE74.....27 D7
Walton La LE12.........53 C4
Walton New Road Ind Est
  LE17................236 C5
WALTON ON T W.......54 B4
Walton Rd LE17.......235 F2
Walton St
  Leicester LE5........154 D3
  Long Eaton NG10......10 D8
Walton Way LE17.....101 D8
Wand St LE4..........129 A1
WANLIP..............102 C2
Wanlip Ave LE4.......129 B7
Wanlip La LE4........129 B8
Wanlip Rd LE7........102 E3
Wanlip St LE1........155 A7
Wansbeck Gdns LE5...156 C8
Wanstead Ind Pk LE3.153 A5
Wanstead Rd LE3.....153 A5
Ward Cl LE2..........179 C7
Wardens Wlk LE3.....153 C3
Wardley La LE15.....187 E8
WARDLEY.............188 A5
Wards Closes LE18...203 E8
Ward's Cres LE12......77 D3
Ward's End LE11.......52 A3
Ward's La DE72.........9 B8
Wareham Rd LE8.....202 B6
Warehouse The LE16..240 D4
Warning Cl LE3.......127 E1
Warke Flatt DE74......17 B6
War Meml Homes
  LE7.................156 E8
Warmsley Ave LE18...180 C4
Warn Cres LE15......137 D5
Warner Cl
  Markfield LE67........98 D1
  Whetstone LE8.......202 A8
Warner Pl LE11........52 C4
Warner's La **14** LE1.52 B4
Warner St LE12........76 D7
Warren Ave LE4......130 A5
Warren Cl
  Leicester LE5........156 A8
  Markfield LE67.......125 E8
Warren Ct LE19......178 B5
Warren Dr LE4........130 A5
Warren Hills Com Prim
  Sch LE67.............72 D2
Warren Hills Rd LE67..72 D2

Warren La
  Castle Donington DE74,
  NG10.................10 B2
  Leicester Forest East
  LE3.................152 E2
  Whitwick LE67.........71 F7
Warrenne Keep PE9...143 D2
Warren Park Way
  LE19................178 A5
Warren Rd
  Narborough LE19.....178 D1
  Wothorpe PE9........169 E7
Warren St LE3........154 D6
Warren The LE7......103 C7
Warren View LE4.....130 A5
Warrington Dr LE6...126 E2
Warsaw Cl LE1.......259 A1
WARTNABY.............37 A3
Wartnaby Rd LE14.....37 C3
Wartnaby St LE16....240 D3
Warton La
  Austrey CV9.........119 A1
  Orton-on-t-H CV9....145 C4
Warwick Ave LE12......75 E6
Warwick Cl
  Bagworth LE67......124 B6
  Desford LE9.........151 A2
  Market Bosworth CV13.148 F3
  Market Harborough
  LE16................240 F5
  Swadlincote DE11......44 E5
  Thornton LE67.......124 F3
Warwick Ct LE11.......51 D5
Warwick Dr CV9......170 D2
Warwick Flats NG13....3 A2
Warwick Gdns LE10..197 E3
Warwick La CV13.....148 E3
Warwick Rd
  Broughton Astley LE9.218 E8
  Kibworth Beauchamp
  LE8.................205 E1
  Littlethorpe LE8, LE19.201 E6
  Long Eaton NG10.....10 F7
  Melton Mowbray LE13...59 C1
  Wigston LE18........180 B3
Warwick St LE3.......154 D6
Warwick Way
  Ashby-de-la-Z LE65....69 C5
  Loughborough LE11.....51 E6
Washbrook La
  Burton Overy LE8...182 E1
  Wigston LE2.........180 F4
Washdyke La LE14.....58 B1
Washdyke Rd LE15...134 F4
Washington Cl
  Barwell LE9.........198 A6
  Melbourne DE73.......26 A7
Wash La LE67..........70 F1
Wash Pit La LE17....246 F4
Washstones La LE14...80 B8
Waste La CV9.........170 A1
Watchcrete Ave LE9..103 D5
Watchorn Cl DE11......44 D5
Watchorn Ct LE15.....137 C7
Waterfall Way
  Barwell LE9.........198 A5
  Melbourne DE73......227 F6
Waterfield Cl LE5....156 B5
Waterfield Pl LE16...240 E5
Waterfield Rd LE7....100 F2
Waterfield Way LE10.215 C5
Waterfront The LE3...259 A3
Waterfurlong PE9....143 C2
Watergate
  East Goscote LE7....103 E7
  8 Stamford PE9...143 E3
Watergate Ct **1** LE3.178 F6
Watergate La LE3,
  LE19................178 E7
Water La
  Ashwell LE15........111 B8
  Eastwell LE14.........22 B6
  Frisby on t W LE14....80 C8
  Long Clawson LE14....20 E4
  Seagrave LE12.........77 F8
  South Witham NG33....65 B3
  Stainby NG33..........43 D2
  Stathern LE14.........13 A2
Water Leys Prim Sch
  LE18................180 B4
Waterloo Cres
  Countesthorpe LE8...202 D3
  Wigston LE18........180 E4
Waterloo Pl DE11......44 B4
Waterloo Rd LE10....215 D8
Waterloo Spinney La
  LE12.................75 B4
Waterloo Way LE2....259 C2
Watermead Ctry Pk*
  LE4.................129 D8
Watermead Ctry Pk
  (North)* LE7.........129 D8
Watermead La LE7.....74 D8
Watermeadows The
  NG10.................10 B8
Water Meadow Way
  LE67................122 F8
Watermead Visitor Ctr*
  LE7.................129 D8
Waters End LE9......198 A5
Waterside PE9........116 F2
Waterside Cl
  Loughborough LE11.....52 B5
  Melton Mowbray LE13...59 D6
Waterside Ct LE10...214 F7
Waterside Rd LE5....130 A4

Waterside The LE12 . . . . 76 D3
Water St PE9 . . . . 143 E2
Waterville Cl LE3 . . . . 153 C6
Waterworks Rd LE67 . . . . 97 A7
Waterworks Way
LE17 . . . . 247 F5
Watery Gate La LE9 . . . . . . 199 F8
Watkin Rd LE2 . . . . 154 D3
Watling Cl LE10 . . . . 215 C4
Watling Cres CV23 . . . . 253 C1
Watling Dr LE10 . . . . 215 C4
Watling St
Atherstone CV9 . . . . 170 A1
Mountsorrel LE12 . . . . 76 E2
Nuneaton CV11, LE10 . . . . . 214 C8
Watson Ave LE16 . . . . 250 D8
Watson Cl NN17 . . . . 230 E2
Watson Rd LE4 . . . . 129 C2
Watson's La LE14 . . . . 12 B2
Watt La LE8 . . . . 221 A6
Watts Cl LE4 . . . . 128 A3
Waudby Cl LE19 . . . . 201 C6
Waughs Dr LE10 . . . . 101 D8
Waveney Cl LE10 . . . . 215 A8
Waveney Rise LE4 . . . . 181 D6
Waverley Cl LE11 . . . . 51 B5
Waverley Ct LE13 . . . . 59 D1
Waverley Gdns PE9 . . . . 143 B4
Waverley Pl PE9 . . . . 143 B4
Waverley Rd
Blaby LE8 . . . . 202 C6
Rugby CV21 . . . . 257 A1
Wigston LE18 . . . . 179 F2
Waverley St NG10 . . . . 10 E8
Wavertree Cl LE9 . . . . 201 D4
Wavertree Dr LE4 . . . . 129 B3
Wayfarer Dr LE7 . . . . 103 E8
Wayne Way The
Birstall LE4 . . . . 129 A7
Leicester LE5 . . . . 155 F6
Wayside Dr
Leicester, Oadby LE2 . . . . . . 181 C5
Thurmaston LE4 . . . . 129 C6
Weare Cl LE7 . . . . 159 C1
Weares Cl LE15 . . . . 191 B5
Weaver Cl
Loughborough LE11 . . . . 52 C1
Whitwick LE67 . . . . 71 E3
Weaver Gn LE13 . . . . 59 B4
Weaver Rd
Earl Shilton LE9 . . . . 199 A8
Leicester LE5 . . . . 156 F7
Weavers Ave LE12 . . . . 50 B3
Weavers Cl LE12 . . . . 76 A5
Weavers Close CE Prim
Sch LE9 . . . . 198 F8
Weavers Ct
8 Hinckley LE10 . . . . 197 D1
Narborough LE19 . . . . 201 B3
Weaver's Wynd LE7 . . . . 103 E7
Webb Cl LE3 . . . . 153 B2
Webbs Way LE19 . . . . 199 D2
Webster Rd LE3 . . . . 153 E4
Websters Cl LE10 . . . . 50 A1
Weddington Country
Wlk * CV10 . . . . 195 C1
Weddington La CV10 . . . . . . 195 B1
Weddington Rd CV10 . . . . . . 195 B3
Weir Cl LE18 . . . . 203 B8
Weir La LE7 . . . . 158 A3
Weir Rd
Kibworth Beauchamp
LE8 . . . . 224 A7
Saddington LE8 . . . . 223 B4
Welbeck Ave
Hinckley LE10 . . . . 215 D4
Leicester LE4 . . . . 128 C2
Welbeck Cl LE18 . . . . 202 C6
Welbeck The Defence
Sixth Form Coll LE12 . . . . 75 B3
Welby La LE13 . . . . 58 E6
Welby Rd LE14 . . . . 58 A6
Welcombe Ave LE3 . . . . 153 F1
Weldon Ave LE12 . . . . 77 D4
Weldon Rd
Loughborough LE11 . . . . 51 E7
Wigston LE18 . . . . 180 D4
WELFORD 256 E5
Welford Ct LE2 . . . . 180 B7
Welford Pl LE1 . . . . 259 B3
Welford Rd
Blaby LE8 . . . . 202 B8
Husbands Bosworth
LE17 . . . . 247 E3
Kilby LE8, LE18 . . . . 203 C6
Leicester, Knighton LE2 . . . . 180 B7
Leicester LE1 . . . . 259 B2
Shearsby LE8, LE17 . . . . 222 A2
Sibbertoft LE16 . . . . 248 D2
South Kilworth LE17 . . . . 255 D7
Welford NN6 . . . . 256 E7
Welford Sibbertoft &
Sulby Endowed Sch
NN6 . . . . 256 E5
WELHAM 226 E5
Welham La
Cranoe LE16 . . . . 208 D2
Great Bowden LE16 . . . . 241 C8
Welham Rd
Great Bowden LE16 . . . . 241 B8
Slawston LE16 . . . . 209 B1
Thorpe Langton LE16 . . . . . . 226 B5
Weston by W LE16 . . . . 227 A4
Welham Wlk LE4 . . . . 129 F4

Welland Ave LE16 . . . . 239 E7
Welland Bsns Pk
LE16 . . . . 241 B4
Welland Cl
Caldecott LE16 . . . . 230 C8
Coalville LE67 . . . . 97 A8
Welland Ct
3 Market Harborough
LE16 . . . . 240 F2
Market Harborough, Little
Bowden LE16 . . . . 241 A4
Welland Mdws PE9 . . . . 192 F8
Welland Mews PE9 . . . . 143 F2
Welland Park Com Coll
LE16 . . . . 240 D2
Welland Park Rd
LE16 . . . . 240 D2
Welland Rd
Barrow-u-S LE12 . . . . 76 D6
Edith Weston LE15 . . . . 166 D7
Welland Rise
Melton Mowbray LE13 . . . . . . 59 C1
Sibbertoft LE16 . . . . 248 F2
Welland St LE2 . . . . 155 B4
Welland Vale Rd
Corby NN17 . . . . 230 E1
Leicester LE5 . . . . 156 D4
Welland View PE9 . . . . 142 F1
Welland View Rd
LE16 . . . . 229 D1
Welland Way LE15 . . . . 137 E5
Wellbrook Ave LE12 . . . . 77 D3
Well Cross LE15 . . . . 166 B7
Well Ct LE15 . . . . 140 F6
Wellesbourne Dr LE3 . . . . . . 127 D1
Welles St LE1 . . . . 259 A4
Wellfield Cl
South Witham NG33 . . . . 65 B4
Tugby LE7 . . . . 185 C6
Well Field La LE14 . . . . 80 C8
Wellgate Ave LE14 . . . . 129 A8
Wellhouse Cl LE18 . . . . 203 C8
Wellingar Cl LE3 . . . . 153 C2
Wellingar Way LE15 . . . . 153 C4
Wellington Cl LE10 . . . . 215 E4
Wellington La **9** PE9 . . . . . 143 D3
Wellington Parkway
LE17 . . . . 243 D6
Wellington St
Leicester LE1 . . . . 259 B3
Loughborough LE11 . . . . 52 C3
Syston LE7 . . . . 103 B3
Wellington Way LE13 . . . . 59 A5
Well La
Ab Kettleby LE14 . . . . 37 D2
Blackfordby DE11 . . . . 45 B1
4 Hinckley LE10 . . . . 197 D1
Upper Broughton LE14 . . . . . . 19 A1
Wells Ave LE18 . . . . 203 F3
WELLSBOROUGH 147 C1
Wellsborough Rd
Sheepy Parva CV9,
CV13 . . . . 146 E1
Wellsborough CV13 . . . . 147 D2
Wells Cl LE17 . . . . 247 E5
Wellsic La LE7 . . . . 101 E6
Well Spring Hill LE8 . . . . . . 203 E8
Well St LE65 . . . . 68 F4
Well St LE15 . . . . 110 C3
Wells Yard Ct LE12 . . . . 44 A6
Ward Ct LE12 . . . . ar7 . . 50 C3
Welton Cl LE8 . . . . 223 F8
Welwyn Rd LE10 . . . . 197 F1
Wembley Rd LE3 . . . . 153 B5
Wembrook Coppice
CV9 . . . . 171 B8
Wembury Gdns LE4 . . . . 128 E4
Wendover Dr LE10 . . . . 197 E4
Wendys Cl LE5 . . . . 156 D7
Wendock Way LE4 . . . . 130 A3
Wensleydale Ave LE4 . . . . . . 198 A5
Wensleydale Cl LE9 . . . . 198 A5
Wensum Cl
Hinckley LE10 . . . . 215 B8
Oakham LE15 . . . . 138 B7
Wentbridge Rd LE4 . . . . 129 D3
Wenton Cl LE15 . . . . 112 B7
Went Rd LE4 . . . . 129 A6
Wentworth Cl
Hinckley LE10 . . . . 197 E3
Kibworth Beauchamp
LE8 . . . . 224 B7
Wentworth Ct LE15 . . . . 156 A2
Wentworth Dr CV11 . . . . 214 A1
Wentworth Gn LE9 . . . . 152 D4
Wentworth Rd
Coalville LE67 . . . . 96 C8
Fleckney LE8 . . . . 223 A7
Leicester LE3 . . . . 154 C6
Wesley Cl
Hathern LE12 . . . . 30 A1
Loughborough LE11 . . . . 51 B6
Ratby LE6 . . . . 152 C8
Sapcote LE9 . . . . 217 E7
West Ave
Leicester LE2 . . . . 155 B2
Melton Mowbray LE13 . . . . . . 59 C3
Wigston LE18 . . . . 180 B3
West Bank Mews DE74 . . . . . 18 C2

Westbourne Ho LE13 . . . . 59 B3
Westbourne St LE4 . . . . 155 A8
Westbridge Cl LE3 . . . . 259 A3
Westbridge Ind Est
LE3 . . . . 259 A3
Westbury Rd LE2 . . . . 155 A1
West Cl LE10 . . . . 215 D7
WESTCOTES 154 C4
Westcotes Dr LE3 . . . . 154 C4
West Cross La LE12 . . . . 101 C7
West Ct LE1 . . . . 259 C2
Westdale Ave LE2 . . . . 179 A2
Westdale Cl NG10 . . . . 10 A5
Westdown Dr LE4 . . . . 129 E6
West Dr LE5 . . . . 156 A8
WEST END 48 C4
West End
Barlestone CV13 . . . . 149 D8
Barton in E CV13 . . . . 122 C1
Exton LE15 . . . . 113 A3
Long Clawson LE14 . . . . 20 C3
Long Whatton LE12 . . . . 29 A4
Welford NN6 . . . . 256 D4
Wymondham LE14 . . . . 62 D2
West End Cl NG13 . . . . 3 A3
West End Cotts LE14 . . . . . . 108 C3
West End Villas **5**
PE9 . . . . 143 C3
Westerby Cl LE18 . . . . 180 D4
Westerby Ct LE17 . . . . 244 B5
Westerby La LE8 . . . . 223 F6
Westerdale Rd LE18 . . . . 180 F2
Western Ave
Easton o t H PE9 . . . . 168 F5
Fleckney LE8 . . . . 222 F6
Market Harborough
LE16 . . . . 240 D1
Ravenstone LE67 . . . . 71 A2
Western Bvd LE2 . . . . 259 A2
Western Cl LE65 . . . . 69 B4
Western Cotts LE17 . . . . 246 F4
Western Dr
Blaby LE8 . . . . 202 B7
Claybrooke Parva LE17 . . . . . 232 E5
Westernhay Rd LE2 . . . . 155 C1
WESTERN PARK 154 A6
Western Park Rd LE3 . . . . . . 154 A5
Western Rd
Asfordby LE14 . . . . 57 F3
Leicester LE3 . . . . 154 D4
Old Dalby LE14 . . . . 36 A5
West Farm Dr LE15 . . . . 191 E5
Westfield Ave
Countesthorpe LE8 . . . . 202 D4
Oakham LE15 . . . . 137 E6
Wigston LE18 . . . . 180 B4
Westfield Cl
Market Harborough
LE16 . . . . 240 C3
Rearsby LE7 . . . . 103 F8
Westfield Cres NN6 . . . . 256 E6
Westfield Dr LE10 . . . . 215 C7
Westfield Dr LE11 . . . . 51 F4
Westfield Inf Sch
LE10 . . . . 215 B7
Westfield Jun Sch
LE10 . . . . 215 B7
Westfield La LE7 . . . . 101 D5
Westfield Rd
Leicester LE3 . . . . 154 A6
Swadlincote DE11 . . . . 44 B6
Westfields LE15 . . . . 149 D8
West Fields PE9 . . . . 168 F5
Westfields Ave LE65 . . . . 68 F6
Westfields Terr LE65 . . . . 68 F7
Westgate
Market Harborough
LE16 . . . . 122 D8
West Gate NG10 . . . . 10 E7
Westgate Ave LE14 . . . . 128 C6
Westgate La LE16 . . . . 239 E3
Westgate Rd LE2 . . . . 180 B6
Westgate St LE15 . . . . 137 F6
Westhaven PE9 . . . . 169 A5
Westhaven Ct CV13 . . . . 148 E3
Westhill Rd LE3 . . . . 154 A6
West Holme St LE3 . . . . 154 D5
Westhorpe
Ashley LE16 . . . . 227 E2
Sibbertoft LE16 . . . . 248 F2
Westhorpe Dr NG10 . . . . 10 C8
West Hyde LE10 . . . . 214 F7
WEST KNIGHTON 180 B6
West La
Bardon LE67 . . . . 97 C3
Billesdon LE7 . . . . 159 B2
Ridlington LE15 . . . . 163 D2
Westland Cl LE16 . . . . 239 E3
Westland Rd LE15 . . . . 112 D8
WEST LANGTON 225 B6
West Langton Rd LE8,
LE16 . . . . 224 E7
Westleigh Ave LE3 . . . . 154 C3
Westleigh Bsns Pk
LE8 . . . . 179 B1
Westleigh Rd
Glen Parva LE2 . . . . 179 C1
Leicester LE3 . . . . 154 C3
Westley Grange LE18 . . . . . . 180 B3
West Mdws NG32 . . . . 4 F1
West Meadow Rise
DE74 . . . . 16 E5
Westmeadow La LE14 . . . . . . 28 F3
West Mill PE9 . . . . 168 F4
Westminster Cl LE13 . . . . 59 A6

Westminster Dr
Glen Parva LE2 . . . . 179 D1
Hinckley LE10 . . . . 215 F4
Westminster Ind Est
DE12 . . . . 93 B4
Westminster Rd LE2 . . . . . . 155 E1
Westminster Way LE65 . . . . . 69 A8
Westmorland Ave
Leicester LE4 . . . . 129 C2
Loughborough LE11 . . . . 51 D1
Wigston LE18 . . . . 179 F2
Westoby CI LE12 . . . . 50 D4
WESTON BY WELLAND
. . . . 227 A3
Weston Cl
Hinckley LE10 . . . . 197 A1
Leicester, Oadby LE2 . . . . . . 181 E4
Rearsby LE7 . . . . 78 F1
Weston Cres NG10 . . . . 9 F4
Weston Dr CV13 . . . . 148 E2
Weston Rd
Ashley LE16 . . . . 227 D3
Aston-on-T DE72 . . . . 16 A7
Edith Weston LE15 . . . . 166 A7
Sutton Bassett LE16 . . . . 227 A2
Welham LE16 . . . . 226 F5
Weston's La LE15 . . . . 110 C3
Weston St DE11 . . . . 44 B8
Westonville Rd LE2 . . . . 168 D2
West Orch LE12 . . . . 77 C1
Westover Rd LE3 . . . . 153 D3
West Park Ct NG10 . . . . 10 D7
Westray Dr LE10 . . . . 197 C1
West Rd LE15 . . . . 137 F6
West St Open **1** LE3 . . . . . 154 D4
West Side LE14 . . . . 58 D3
Westside Ct **4** LE9 . . . . . . 198 F8
West St
Blaby LE8 . . . . 179 A1
Clipsham LE15 . . . . 89 D5
Earl Shilton LE9 . . . . 175 F1
Easton o t H PE9 . . . . 169 A5
Enderby LE19 . . . . 178 B2
Glenfield LE3 . . . . 127 C1
Leicester LE1 . . . . 259 C2
Stamford PE9 . . . . 143 D3
Swadlincote DE11 . . . . 44 B4
Syston LE7 . . . . 103 A4
Welford NN6 . . . . 256 E6
West Street Gdns
PE9 . . . . 143 C2
West Thorpe LE12 . . . . 34 C7
West View
Somerby LE14 . . . . 108 B1
Stamford PE9 . . . . 142 D7
West View Ave LE3 . . . . 179 B3
West Way NG32 . . . . 4 F4
West Wlk
Ibstock LE67 . . . . 95 F1
Leicester LE1 . . . . 259 C2
Wetherby Cl LE7 . . . . 103 E6
Wetherby Rd LE4 . . . . 129 D3
Wexford Ct LE2 . . . . 179 D8
Weymouth Cl LE18 . . . . 203 D8
Weymouth St LE4 . . . . 155 B8
Whaddon Chase LE15 . . . . . . 87 E2
Whaddon Dr LE11 . . . . 52 C1
Whall Cl LE12 . . . . 76 A5
Wharfedale Rd
Corby NN17 . . . . 230 E1
Long Eaton NG10 . . . . 10 A6
Wharf La PE9 . . . . 143 E3
Wharf Rd PE9 . . . . 143 E3
Wharf St N LE1 . . . . 259 C5
Wharf St S LE1 . . . . 259 C4
Wharfe La LE15 . . . . 137 E8
Wharf The DE72 . . . . 9 A2
Wharf View DE12 . . . . 93 C5
Wharf Way LE2 . . . . 179 B2
Wharf Yd LE10 . . . . 215 A7
Wharncliffe Rd LE11 . . . . 52 C4
Whatborough Rd LE7,
LE15 . . . . 135 B2
Whatoff Lodge Farm*
LE12 . . . . 75 D5
Whatton Oaks LE7 . . . . 101 E8
Whatton Rd
Hathern LE12 . . . . 29 E2
Kegworth DE74, LE12 . . . . . . 29 C7
Whatton's Cl NG32 . . . . 4 F1
Wheat Cl LE12 . . . . 76 D3
Wheatfield Cl LE3 . . . . 153 C7
Wheatfield Way LE10 . . . . . . 197 C4
Wheatland Cl LE2 . . . . 181 D5
Wheatland Dr LE11 . . . . 52 C2
Wheatlands DE11 . . . . 44 B7
Wheatlands Cl PE9 . . . . 167 F5
Wheatlands Dr LE8 . . . . 202 D4
Wheatley Ave LE15 . . . . 189 B5
Wheatley Rd LE12 . . . . 76 E2
Wheatley's Rd LE14 . . . . 129 D7
Wheatsheaf Ctyd
CV13 . . . . 148 F3
Wheatsheaf La LE15 . . . . 88 B1
Wheat St LE1 . . . . 259 C4
Wheeldale LE18 . . . . 180 F2
Wheeldale Cl LE4 . . . . 128 D3
Wheeler Cl LE17 . . . . 244 C5
Wheel La LE15 . . . . 191 F5
Wheel Tappers Way
LE11 . . . . 51 F4
Wheightel Cl LE7 . . . . 246 F4
Whetstone Ct LE8 . . . . 201 E7
Whetstone Dr LE67 . . . . 71 E1

Whetstone Gorse La
LE8 . . . . 202 A1
Whiles La LE4 . . . . 129 B7
Whinchat Ct DE12 . . . . 93 B4
Whinchat Rd LE5 . . . . 155 C6
Whincups Yd PE9 . . . . 143 E2
Whinham Ave LE4 . . . . 218 D7
WHISSENDINE 84 E1
Whissendine CE Prim Sch
LE15 . . . . 84 F1
Whissendine Dr LE4
Ashwell LE15 . . . . 110 E8
Leesthorpe LE14 . . . . 83 E3
Whissendine Windmill*
LE15 . . . . 84 E1
Whiston Cl LE15 . . . . 156 D7
Whitby Cl
Broughton Astley LE9 . . . . . . 218 E8
Loughborough LE11 . . . . 51 B5
Whitcroft Ct LE2 . . . . 125 E8
Whitcroft's La LE67 . . . . 98 D6
Whiteacres LE8 . . . . 201 E5
White Barn Dr LE9 . . . . 201 D3
Whitebeam Cl LE19 . . . . 201 A8
Whitebeam Rd LE2 . . . . 181 A7
White Gate LE4 . . . . 219 A6
Whitefield Rd LE4 . . . . 128 F3
Whitehall La LE15 . . . . 52 C5
Whitegates Field
LE18 . . . . 180 E1
Whitehall Cl CV10 . . . . 194 A2
Whitehall Prim Sch
LE5 . . . . 156 A4
Whitehall Rd LE5 . . . . 156 A4
White Hart Cl LE7 . . . . 159 B2
Whitehead Cres LE18 . . . . . . 180 B3
Whitehill Rd LE67 . . . . 96 E3
White Horse Ct LE12 . . . . 33 C4
White Horse La LE4 . . . . 129 B6
White Hos CV13 . . . . 172 A7
Whitehouse Ave LE11 . . . . 52 C2
White House Cl
Bagworth LE67 . . . . 124 B5
Groby LE6 . . . . 126 E3
Leire LE12 . . . . 218 E1
Whitehouse Way DE12 . . . . . . 93 C6
Whitelake Cl LE13 . . . . 59 A1
White Leys Ct LE67 . . . . 71 C1
White Lion Gdns LE15 . . . . . 137 F6
Whitemoors Cl CV13 . . . . . . 196 E7
Whitemoors Rd CV13 . . . . . 196 E7
Whiteoaks Rd LE2 . . . . 181 C3
White Post Ct NN17 . . . . 230 E2
Whites Cl LE13 . . . . 127 D1
White St
Kibworth Beauchamp
LE8 . . . . 223 F8
Quorn (Quorndon) LE12 . . . . . 75 F3
Whitethorns Cl LE17 . . . . . . 254 B3
Whitley Cl LE3 . . . . 154 B8
Whitlock Way LE14 . . . . 57 F3
Whitman Cl LE3 . . . . 153 D6
Whitmore Dr LE3 . . . . 153 D6
Whittier Rd LE2 . . . . 179 F7
WHITTINGTON 170 B3
Whittington Ct LE6 . . . . 126 C1
Whittington Dr LE6 . . . . 126 C1
Whittington La CV9 . . . . 170 B2
Whittington Rd LE3 . . . . 127 F3
Whittle Cl LE8 . . . . 201 F6
Whittle Rd
Hinckley LE10 . . . . 214 F7
Lutterworth LE17 . . . . 244 B5
WHITWELL 140 B6
Whitwell Nature Trail*
LE15 . . . . 140 A5
Whitwell Rd LE15 . . . . 140 D5
Whitwell Row LE15 . . . . 179 C5
WHITWICK 71 F5
Whitwick Bsns Pk
LE67 . . . . 71 D2
Whitwick Moor LE67 . . . . 71 D7
Whitwick Rd
Coalville LE67 . . . . 71 D2
Copt Oak LE67 . . . . 98 C4
Whitwick St John the
Baptist CE Prim Sch
LE67 . . . . 71 E6
Whitwick Way LE3 . . . . 154 C8
Whitworth Ave LE10 . . . . . . 214 F9
Whitworth Cl DE12 . . . . 67 E4
Whysall Rd NG10 . . . . 10 B7
WIBTOFT 232 B4
Wicken Rise LE18 . . . . 180 E1
Wickham Rd LE2 . . . . 181 B4
Wicklow Ave LE13 . . . . 59 D1
Wicklow Cl LE12 . . . . 50 D2
Wicklow Dr LE5 . . . . 156 A6
Wicklow Lo LE3 . . . . 59 D1
Wiclif Way LE17 . . . . 244 C7
Widdowson Rd NG10 . . . . . . 10 B5
Wide La
Hathern LE12 . . . . 30 A1
Wymeswold LE12 . . . . 34 C3
Wideshaft DE11 . . . . 44 B3
Widley La LE18 . . . . 51 A8
Widford Cl LE15 . . . . 156 A8
Widmerpool La LE14 . . . . 34 D8
Widon The LE11 . . . . 74 E8
Wigeon Dr DE12 . . . . 93 B4
Wightman Cl
Shepshed LE12 . . . . 50 B3
Stoney Stanton LE9 . . . . 199 D3
Wightman Rd LE9 . . . . 198 C2
Wigley Rd LE5 . . . . 156 A5
WIGSTON 179 E2
Wigston Framework
Knitters Mus* LE18 . . . . . 180 C2

WIGSTON HARCOURT
.....................203 F8
Wigston La LE2.........179 D6
WIGSTON MAGNA 180 D2
WIGSTON PARVA . 231 F8
Wigston Rd
Blaby LE8...............202 C8
Leicester, Oadby LE2...180 F4
3 Rugby CV21........257 A1
Wigston St
Countesthorpe LE8.....202 F4
Leicester LE1............259 C3
Wilberforce Rd LE3....154 D3
Wildgoose Cl LE67......95 F2
Wild Rose Wlk LE4.....103 E8
Wileman's Cl LE9......198 E6
Wilf Brown Cl LE9.....176 B1
Wilfred Rd LE8.........202 A8
Wilfred Gdns LE65......69 A5
Wilfred Pl LE65.........69 B5
Wilkes Ave DE12........93 C4
Wilkes Gdns LE15......189 B4
Wilkes Way LE7........102 F2
Willars Way LE67........95 F8
Willcox Dr LE13.........59 E1
Willday Dr CV9.........170 D2
Willersley Ho NG10....10 A5
WILLESLEY...........68 E2
Willesley Cl LE65.......68 F4
Willesley Gdns LE65....68 F4
Willesley La
Moira DE12.............68 B4
Willesley LE65..........68 D3
Willesley Prim Sch
LE65...................69 A4
Willesley Woodside
LE65...................68 D2
Willet Cl **4** LE12......77 C3
WILLEY...............242 E6
William Bradford Com
Coll LE9................198 C8
William Cl LE7.........103 E6
William Ct
Enderby LE19...........178 A3
Stamford PE9............143 C5
William Dalby Ho
LE15...................138 A5
William Dalby Wlk
LE15...................137 F6
William Iliffe St LE10..215 B7
William Lyon Ct LE11...52 B5
William Peardon Ct
LE18...................180 C3
Williams Cl LE19.......201 B6
William St
Leicester LE1...........259 C4
Loughborough LE11......52 A3
Narborough LE19........201 B7
Willn Cl LE67............97 B8
Willoughby Cl
Breaston DE72............9 F8
Melton Mowbray LE13....59 E2
Willoughby Ct LE15....189 A4
Willoughby Dr LE15....141 A6
Willoughby Gdns
Leicester Forest East
LE3....................153 A3
Oakham LE15...........137 F6
Willoughby Ho DE11....44 C4
WILLOUGHBY-ON-THE-
WOLDS 34 C8
Willoughby Prim Sch
LE12...................34 C7
Willoughby Rd
Ashby Magna LE17......220 B4
Countesthorpe LE8.....202 C2
Morcott LE15...........191 A6
Stamford PE9............143 E5
WILLOUGHBY WATERLEYS
.......................220 D6
Willowbank Rd LE10...215 C7
Willowbrook Cl
Ashby-de-la-Z LE65......69 B8
Broughton Astley LE9...218 F7
Queniborough LE7......103 E6
Sharnford LE10.........217 C4
Willow Brook Cl LE4....127 C2
Willowbrook Pk LE11....51 E6
Willowbrook Prim Sch
LE5....................156 A6
Willow Brook Rd
Corby NN17.............230 D1
Leicester LE5...........155 D7
Willowbrook View
LE5....................156 E6
Willowbrook Way
LE7....................103 E7
Willow Cl
Aston-on-T DE72........16 B7
East Leake LE12.........31 D8
Hinckley LE10..........215 E5
Littlethorpe LE19......201 C6
Measham DE12...........93 C6
Moira DE12..............68 B6
Newbold Verdon LE9....150 B3
Uppingham LE15........189 B5
Whissendine LE15.......84 F2
Willow Cres
Market Harborough
LE16...................240 C2
Oakham LE15...........138 B7
Willowcroft LE12........75 E5
Willow Ct
1 Braunstone Town
LE3....................178 F7
10 Leicester LE2.......155 B5
Swadlincote DE11.......44 C4
Willowdale LE10........215 A7

Willowdene Way LE9....198 B6
Willow Dr
Countesthorpe LE8.....202 E4
Groby LE6...............126 E1
Melton Mowbray LE13...59 D4
Willow Farm Bsns Pk
DE74....................17 B6
Willowfields Rd CV11...214 A1
Willow Gn LE67..........72 C2
Willow Gr LE12..........76 C1
Willow Herb Cl LE2.....181 E4
Willow Park Dr LE18....180 C3
Willow Park Ind Est
CV13...................196 C7
Willow Park Way LE7....16 A7
Willow Pl LE18...........180 D2
Willow Poole La LE12....30 C5
Willow Rd
Barrow-u-S LE12.........53 D1
Blaby LE8...............202 B7
Castle Donington DE74...17 B5
Loughborough LE11......75 A8
Stamford PE9...........142 F5
Willow St
Desford LE9.............151 A3
Leicester LE1...........155 A4
Willows The
Atherstone CV9.........170 E2
Burton o t W LE12.......53 F6
Willowtree Cl LE5......130 C2
Willow Tree Cl LE9.....198 B8
Willow Tree Cres
LE17...................244 A6
Willow Way LE67........95 E1
Willow Wlk LE67........102 F3
Willwer Cl LE19.........219 A5
Wilson Cl LE16..........241 A3
Wilmington Ct
Leicester, Oadby LE2...180 F8
Loughborough LE11......52 C2
Wilmington Rd LE3.....154 C3
Wilmore Cres LE3......153 D3
Wilmot Rd DE11..........44 B3
Wilmot St NG10..........10 A5
Wilne Ave NG10.........10 A4
Wilne Cl NG10...........9 F4
Wilne La
Breaston DE72............9 D4
Shardlow DE72...........9 B2
Wilne Rd
Draycott DE72............9 B5
Long Eaton NG10.........9 F4
Wilne St LE2............155 C4
Wilnicott Rd LE3.......153 F1
Wilsford Cl LE18.......203 C8
Wilshere Cl LE9........152 D5
WILSON..................26 F6
Wilson Cl LE3..........153 D2
Wilson Ct LE15..........89 A7
Wilson Rd LE18.........179 E1
Wilson Rise DE73........26 E6
Wilson St LE12..........155 C6
WILSTHORPE..............10 B7
Wilsthorpe Rd
Breaston DE72............9 F8
Long Eaton, New Sawley
NG10....................10 B7
Wilstone Cl LE11........51 C3
Wilton Ave LE11.........52 C2
Wilton Cl LE13.........181 C5
Wilton Ct LE13..........59 B2
Wilton Pl LE13..........59 C3
Wilton Rd LE13..........59 D3
Wilton St LE1...........259 B5
Wilton Terr LE13........59 C3
Wiltshire Ho LE4.......128 D2
Wiltshire Rd
Leicester LE4...........128 D2
Wigston LE18...........180 B3
Wimberley Way NG33....65 A4
Wimbishthorpe Cl NG13...3 A3
Wimbledon St LE1......259 C4
Wimborne Cl LE18......180 C1
Wimborne Rd LE2......180 D6
Winchendon Cl LE5....155 E8
Winchester Ave
Blaby LE8...............179 A1
Leicester LE3...........154 C3
Winchester Cl LE67.....95 F2
Winchester Dr
Hinckley LE10..........216 B7
Melton Mowbray LE13....59 A6
Swadlincote DE11.......44 D6
Winchester Rd LE8.....202 C6
Winchester Way LE65...69 A7
Winchilsea Dr NN17....213 B1
Winckley Cl LE7........157 F4
Windermere Ave
Ashby-de-la-Z LE65......69 C5
Nuneaton CV11.........214 A6
Windermere Cl LE19....198 F8
Windermere Dr LE9....200 D4
Windermere Rd
Barrow-u-S LE12........76 D8
Edith Weston LE15.....166 A7
Wigston LE18...........180 F3
Windermere St LE2.....259 A1
Winders Ct LE2.........179 D5
Winder's Way LE2......179 D5
Windleden Rd LE11.....51 B3
Windley Rd LE2.........180 A5
Windmill Ave LE4......129 B8
Windmill Bank LE18...180 E1
Windmill Cl
Ashby-de-la-Z LE65......69 C5
Castle Donington DE74...17 B2
Cottingham LE16........229 D1
Mountsorrel LE12.......76 D3

Windmill Cl continued
Ratby LE6..............152 D8
Ravenstone LE67........95 E7
Thurmaston LE4........129 F8
Windmill End LE67.....101 E7
Windmill Gdns LE8.....206 A1
Windmill La CV9........119 C3
Windmill Rd
Atherstone CV9.........170 D1
Loughborough LE11......52 D3
Windmill Rd Ind Est
LE11....................52 D3
Windmill Rise
Cottingham LE16........229 D1
Groby LE6...............126 E3
Woodhouse Eaves LE12...74 F2
Windmill St DE11........44 A1
Windmill View LE67.....71 A6
Windmill Way
Kegworth DE74..........18 B2
Lyddington LE15........212 D6
Windrush Dr
Hinckley LE10..........215 A8
Leicester, Oadby LE2...181 D6
Windsor Ave
Glen Parva LE2.........179 E1
Groby LE6...............126 F2
Leicester LE4...........129 B2
Melbourne DE73.........26 A8
Windsor Cl
Coalville LE67...........72 B1
Leicester, Oadby LE2...181 C3
Mountsorrel LE12.......101 D8
Quorn (Quorndon) LE12..76 B6
Stamford PE9...........143 D5
Swadlincote DE11.......44 A6
Windsor Ct
Hinckley LE10..........216 A5
Long Eaton NG10........10 E7
Market Harborough
LE16...................240 D4
Stoney Stanton LE9....199 D2
Windsor Dr
Oakham LE15...........137 E5
Shepshed LE12..........50 A2
Windsor Rd
Ashby-de-la-Z LE65......69 B5
Loughborough LE11......51 D5
Waltham on t W LE14....40 B7
Windsor St
Hinckley LE10..........216 A5
Melton Mowbray LE13....59 C3
Windyridge PE9.........142 D7
Winfield Cres LE15....153 D4
WING...................165 A2
Wingfield St LE4.......129 B2
Wing Hall LE15.........165 A2
Wing Maze* LE15......165 B2
Wing Rd
Glaston LE15...........190 B6
Manton LE15...........164 A5
Morcott LE15...........190 F7
Winifred St LE2........259 A2
Winkadale Hill LE7....157 C4
Winser Ct DE74..........18 D2
Winslow Dr LE18.......180 E4
Winslow Gn LE15......156 C8
Winstanley Com Coll
LE3....................153 E1
Winstanley Dr LE3.....154 A4
Winster Cres LE13......59 B1
Winster Dr LE4.........129 E8
Winster Way NG10.......9 F5
Winstone Ave LE9......200 D4
Winston Cl LE9.........167 F5
Winterbeck Ind Est
NG13.....................2 F3
Winterbeck Ind NG13....3 A3
Winterburn Gdns LE8..201 F7
Winterburn Way LE11...51 B3
Winterfield Cl LE3.....153 B7
Wintergreen Cl LE15...130 C3
Wintersdale Rd LE5....156 D5
Winterton Cl LE4......129 F8
Winton Ave LE3.........154 C2
Wire La LE16...........228 D2
Wisp The LE15..........136 D1
WISTOW................204 E4
Wistow Cl LE18.........204 A3
Wistow Rd
Kibworth Beauchamp
LE8....................205 D2
Kilby LE18.............204 B3
Newton Harcourt LE8...204 D6
Wigston LE18...........180 E1
Wistow Way LE5........155 C5
Witham Ave LE15.......137 E5
Witham Cl
Melton Mowbray LE13....59 B1
Stamford PE9...........143 E4
Witham Rd
Gunby NG33.............64 F8
Thistleton LE15.........65 A1
Witham Way LE2........180 A6
Withens Cl LE3.........154 A7
Withens Cl LE13........153 D2
Witherdell LE4.........178 A3
WITHERLEY.............194 B7
Witherley CE Prim Sch
CV9....................194 B7
Witherley Rd CV9......194 B6
Withers Cl LE15........138 A8
Withers Way LE9, LE3..153 D1
Withington Cl LE3.....153 D2
Wittering Cl NG10......10 E5
Woburn Cl
Hinckley LE10..........197 E3
Leicester LE2...........179 C4
Loughborough LE11......51 C4

Woburn Cl continued
Market Harborough
LE16...................241 A3
Wigston LE18...........180 E2
Wodehouse Rd LE3.....154 A4
Wokingham Ave LE2...179 D2
Wolds Cl LE12...........32 E5
Wolds La LE10..........231 B3
Wolds The LE7..........103 E8
Wollaton Ave LE11......51 C4
Wollaton Cl LE3........153 B8
Wolsey Cl
Fleckney LE8...........222 F8
Groby LE6..............126 E2
Leicester Forest East
LE3....................152 F2
Wolsey Dr LE6..........126 B1
Wolsey House Prim Sch
LE4....................128 C3
Wolsey La LE8..........222 F8
Wolsey Rd LE8..........126 E2
Wolsey St LE4..........71 C2
Wolsey St LE4.........154 E8
Wolsey Way
Loughborough LE11......52 C4
Syston LE7.............102 F3
Wolverton Rd LE3......154 C2
Wolvey Rd LE10........215 E4
Woodbank
Glen Parva LE2.........179 B2
Hinckley LE10..........216 A7
Woodbank Rd
Groby LE6..............126 D3
Leicester LE2...........180 C6
Woodbine Ave **7** LE2..155 B4
Woodbine Cres LE17...244 C5
Woodborough Rd
LE5....................156 B4
Woodboy St LE1.........155 A7
Woodbreach Dr LE16..241 B3
Woodbridge Rd LE4....129 B3
Woodbrook Rd LE11.....51 E1
Woodbrook Vale High Sch
LE11....................74 F7
Woodbury Rise LE8....182 C1
Woodby La LE17.........243 E8
Wood Cl LE12............50 D3
Woodcock Cl LE17.....235 C4
Woodcock Dr LE13......82 B8
Woodcock Way LE65....69 C7
Woodcote LE65..........69 B8
Woodcote Prim Sch
LE65....................69 B7
Woodcote Rd LE3......178 E7
Woodcroft Ave LE2....180 A6
Woodcroft The DE74....28 C5
Wood End LE3..........154 A7
Wood Farm La DE11.....44 E4
Woodfield PE9..........168 D1
Woodfield Cl LE19.....201 B8
Woodfield Cotts DE12...93 D5
Woodfield Dr DE11......44 C5
Woodfield Rd
Hinckley LE10..........215 C6
Leicester, Oadby LE2...181 B7
Rothley LE7............101 E6
Woodfold La LE14.......60 D5
Woodford Cl LE18.....203 C8
Woodford Glebe NN6...256 E5
Woodford La CV10.....194 C4
Woodford Rd LE2......154 D3
Woodgate
Leicester LE3...........239 E8
Leicester LE3...........154 D7
Rothley LE7............101 E6
Wood Gate LE11.........52 B3
Woodgate Cl LE16.....241 B2
Woodgate Dr LE4......128 F8
Woodgate Hill LE14....82 B1
Woodgate Rd
East Leake LE12........31 C8
Hinckley LE10..........216 A8
Woodgon Rd LE7......127 D6
Woodgreen Rd LE4.....129 D1
Woodgreen Wlk LE4...129 D1
Woodhall Cl
Leicester LE3...........153 D5
Loughborough LE11......52 B1
Woodhead Cl
Market Overton LE15....86 F5
Stamford PE9...........143 F5
Wood Hill
Leicester LE5...........155 D6
Old Dalby LE14..........35 E3
Woodhill Ind Est LE14...35 D3
WOODHOUSE.............75 A2
Woodhouse Cl LE67.....98 E1
WOODHOUSE EAVES.....75 A1
Woodhouse La LE11.....74 C5
Woodhouse Rd
Asfordby LE14...........57 F3
Coalville LE67...........97 B8
Narborough LE19.......201 A8
Quorn (Quorndon) LE12..75 E6
WOODHOUSES............26 A5
Woodhouses St DE11....44 D3
Wood La
Barkestone-le-V NG13,
LE14....................13 E6
Braunston-in-R LE15...137 A1
Cadeby CV13...........149 C1
Higham on t H CV13....195 E3
Norton-J-T CV9.........120 C2
Quorn (Quorndon) LE12..76 B5
Stathern LE14...........13 B4
Swadlincote DE11.......44 A7
Tugby LE7..............185 F8
Woodland Ave
Breaston DE72...........9 F8

Woodland Ave continued
Claybrooke Magna
LE17...................232 E6
Hinckley LE10..........216 A7
Leicester LE2...........155 C1
Melton Mowbray LE13....59 D1
Narborough LE19.......178 B1
Woodland Cl LE67.....125 E8
Woodland Dr LE3......153 D3
Woodland Grange Prim
Sch LE2...............181 D4
Woodland Rd
Cottesmore LE15........87 E2
Hinckley LE10..........197 F1
Leicester LE5...........155 D7
Woodlands Ave
Breaston DE72............9 F8
Corby NN17............230 F1
Woodlands Cl
Leicester, Oadby LE2...182 A4
Melbourne DE73.........26 A8
Wymeswold LE12........33 C3
Woodlands Cres DE12...67 B4
Woodlands Ct LE2......181 E4
Woodlands Dr
Groby LE6..............126 D3
Loughborough LE11......52 A2
Shepshed LE12..........50 C5
Woodlands La LE9......152 E6
Woodlands Rd DE12.....67 B4
Woodlands The
Countesthorpe LE8.....202 D4
Hartshill CV10.........194 A1
Leicester LE2...........155 C1
Market Harborough
LE16...................240 C4
Melbourne DE73.........26 B8
Wigston LE18...........180 F4
Woodlands Way
Melbourne DE73.........26 B8
Moira DE12..............68 B6
Woodland View
Chilcote DE12...........91 F3
Oakham LE15...........138 B7
Woodlawn LE2..........180 D8
Woodlea Ave LE17.....244 A6
Woodley Rd LE6........152 C8
Woodman's Chase
LE7....................103 D7
Woodmans Way LE12....50 C5
Woodmarket LE17.....244 C5
Woodnewton Dr LE5...156 D4
Woodpecker Cl LE3....152 E2
Wood Rd LE67..........123 E6
Woods Cl
Coalville LE67...........96 C6
Leicester, Oadby LE2...181 C7
Woodshawe Rise LE3...153 C2
Woodside
Ashby-de-la-Z LE65......68 F5
Barrow-u-S LE12........76 C8
Woodside
Leicester LE5...........129 D1
Narborough LE19.......200 F8
Woodside Cres NG10...10 B8
Woodside Rd LE2......181 D3
Woods Mews LE12......30 B4
Wood St
Ashby-de-la-Z LE65......69 C5
Earl Shilton LE9.......198 E8
Hinckley LE10..........197 D1
Leicester LE1...........259 B5
Swadlincote DE11.......44 B2
Woodstock Cl
Hinckley LE10..........216 A5
Leicester LE4...........128 C4
Woodstock Prim Sch
LE4....................128 C4
Woodstock Rd LE4.....128 C4
Woodstone Com Prim Sch
LE67....................95 E7
Wood Street Cl LE1....197 E1
WOODTHORPE.............75 C7
Woodthorpe Ave LE11...52 B1
Woodthorpe Rd LE11....52 B1
WOODVILLE.............44 E3
Woodville CE Jun Sch
DE11...................44 F2
Woodville Gdns LE3...180 C5
Woodville Inf Sch
DE11....................44 F2
Woodville Rd
Hartshorne DE11.......45 A5
Leicester LE3...........154 B5
Overseal DE12..........67 B4
Woodward Ave LE12....75 E6
Woodward's Pl DE11....44 D3
Woodward Way DE11....44 D4
Woodway La LE17......232 D4
Woodway Rd LE17.....244 B5
Woodwell Head La....86 A8
Woodyard La LE18......78 F1
Woodgate Cl LE7.......127 E7
Wooldon Hill Com Prim
Sch LE7...............127 E7
Woolley's La NG33......66 B7
Woolrooms The LE67...70 F8
WOOLSTHORPE BY
BELVOIR.................8 B1
Woolsthorpe La
Harston NG32...........15 B5
Muston NG32.............8 C5
Woolsthorpe Rd NG33...43 F3
Woolstitch Pk DE12....91 F7
Woolston Ct NN17.....213 C1

Wootton Cl LE8.........201 F6
Wootton Rise LE2......179 D5
Worcester Ave LE4.....129 C8
Worcester Cl LE9.......198 A7
Worcester Cres PE9 ....143 D4
Worcester Dr
  Market Harborough
  LE16 ....240 E5
  Melton Mowbray LE13....82 D8
  Wigston LE18..........179 F2
Worcester Rd LE2 .... 179 D7
Wordsworth Ave
  Corby NN17 ....230 D1
  Swadlincote DE11 ......44 C6
Wordsworth Cl LE67 ....70 E7
Wordsworth Cres
  LE19 ....178 A1
Wordsworth Rd
  Leicester LE2 ....180 A8
  Loughborough LE11......51 D4
Wordsworth Way DE12...93 C3
Workhouse La LE10.....216 A4
Workspace 17 LE67.....96 C7
Worrall Cl LE3.........153 D4
Worrall Rd LE3 ....153 D4
Worsh Cl LE8...........201 F5
Worsley Way LE8 ......202 A6
WORTHINGTON 47 F5
Worthington La
  Breedon on t H DE73......26 F1
  Newbold LE65, LE67.......47 E4
  Woolsthorpe by B NG32 ....8 B1
Worthington Sch LE65 ....47 F6
Worthington St LE2.... 155 C5
Wortley Cl
  Coalville LE67 ....71 E1
  Shepshed LE12 ....50 C6
Wortley Cotts LE9 .....198 F5
Wortley Ct LE11 ....52 B4
WOTHORPE 169 D8
Wothorpe Hill PE9.....169 C7
Wothorpe Mews PE9...143 D2
Wothorpe Rd PE9......143 E2
Wothorpe Villas PE9 ...169 D8

Woulds Ct DE12 ....68 B6
Wranglands The LE8... 223 A7
Wreake Cl LE7..........103 B4
Wreake Cres LE14 ......57 E2
Wreake Dr LE7 ....79 A3
Wreake Rd LE4 ....129 E8
Wreake Valley Com Coll
  LE7..................103 C5
Wreake Wlk LE15......137 E5
Wreford Cres LE5......156 E7
Wrekin Cl LE65 ....69 C4
Wren Cl
  Appleby Magna DE12....119 E8
  Leicester LE2..........179 E7
  Loughborough LE11......51 F3
  Melton Mowbray LE13.....82 B8
  Oakham LE15..........138 A8
  Syston LE7............102 E4
  Woodville DE11.........44 F3
Wren Ct NG10..........10 A3
Wrendyke Cl LE15 .....191 A6
Wright Cl LE8 ....202 A4
Wright La LE2..........181 E4
Wrights Acre LE12......77 B4
Wrights Cl LE12 ....75 F5
Wrights La LE14 ....62 E2
Wroxall Way LE3......154 C8
Wyatt Cl LE3 ....153 C4
Wyatt Rd LE67.........71 E2
Wych Elm Cl LE8......182 B1
Wych Elm Rd LE2......181 A7
Wychwood Rd LE8.....202 A5
Wycliffe Ave
  Barrow-u-S LE12 ....76 D8
  Melton Mowbray LE13.....59 C4
Wycliffe Ind Est LE17 ..244 D7
Wycliffe St LE1.........259 B3
Wycliffe Terr LE17.....244 D6
WYCOMB 39 A6
Wycombe Gr LE13......59 E2
Wycombe Rd LE5......155 F8
Wycomb La LE14 ....22 B1
Wye Cl LE10...........215 A8
Wye Dean Dr LE18.....180 D2
WYFORDBY 60 E3
Wyfordby Cl LE13......59 E1
Wyggeston Ave NG13 .....3 B2

Wyggeston & Queen
  Elizabeth I Coll LE1 ... 155 A2
Wyggeston Rd
  Bottesford NG13 ....3 B3
  Coalville LE67 ....96 D8
Wyggeston's Hospl
  LE3 ....154 C4
Wyggeston Terr NG13 ....3 B2
Wygston's House Mus*
  LE1.................259 A3
Wykeham Cl LE8.......202 B6
WYKIN 196 F4
Wykin La CV13, LE10....196 E5
Wylam Cl LE3 ....154 A8
Wymar Cl LE4 ....128 C3
WYMESWOLD 33 C4
Wymeswold CE Prim Sch
  LE12.................33 C3
Wymeswold Ind Est
  LE12.................33 A1
Wymeswold La LE12.....54 A8
Wymeswold Rd
  Hoton LE12............32 F2
  Rempstone LE12 ....32 F5
  Thorpe in t G NG12......33 C8
WYMONDHAM 62 D1
Wymondham Drift
  LE14.................62 F2
Wymondham Rd LE14...62 A6
Wymondham Way
  LE13.................59 C6
Wymondham Windmill &
  Craft Ctr* LE14 ....62 D3
Wyndale Dr LE7 ....103 B5
Wyndale Rd LE2........180 B7
Wyndham Ave LE13.....59 C1
Wyndham Cl LE2 .....181 C7
Wyndham Rd LE11.....51 B6
Wynfield Rd LE3.......154 B5
Wyngate Dr LE3 ......154 B4
Wynthorpe Rise LE3 ... 154 A4
Wynton Cl LE8.........202 C6
Wysall La
  Rempstone LE12 ....32 F6
  Wymeswold LE12.......33 D5
Wytchley Rd PE9.......167 E5
Wythburn Cl LE11......51 D1

Wyvelle Cres DE74......18 C3
Wyvenhoe Dr LE12......75 E5
Wyvern Ave
  Leicester LE4..........129 D2
  Long Eaton NG10.......10 D5
Wyvern Cl
  Broughton Astley LE9 ....219 A5
  Hinckley LE10 ....215 E4
Wyvern Prim Sch LE4... 129 D2
Wyvern Terr LE13.......59 D3
WYVILLE 25 E7
Wyville Row LE3........154 A1

Y

Yard Cl DE11 ....44 B4
Yardley Cl NN17 ....230 D1
Yardley Dr LE2.........180 B5
Yarmouth St LE1.......259 B5
Yarrow Cl LE5 ....130 C1
Yarwell Dr LE18 ....180 E2
Yates Ave DE72.........16 A7
Yates Cl DE12..........68 A5
Yaxley Cl LE7 ....157 A5
Yeats Cl LE3...........153 D2
Yelvertoft Rd CV23.....258 D6
Yelverton Ave LE5 ....156 C3
Yeoman La LE1........259 C4
Yeomanry Ct LE16 .....240 E3
Yeoman's Dale LE7 ....103 D8
Yeoman's Keep LE17...244 B8
Yeoman St LE1........259 C4
Yew Cl
  Corby NN17 ....230 E1
  East Leake LE12 ....31 D8
Leicester Forest East
  LE3 ....152 F1
Yews The
  Great Dalby LE14........82 B2
  Leicester, Oadby LE2...181 B6
Yew Tree Cl
  Barwell LE9 ....198 C8
  Lutterworth LE17......244 A6
  Willoughby Waterleys
  LE8 ....220 D6
Yew Tree Cres LE13.....59 C5

Yew Tree Ct CV9 ......119 A2
Yew Tree Dr LE3 ......153 C6
York Ave CV9..........170 E1
York Cl
  Glen Parva LE2 ....179 E1
  Market Bosworth CV13....148 E2
  Measham DE12 ....93 C5
  Mountsorrel LE12 ......101 D8
  Swadlincote DE11 ......44 D6
York Pl
  Coalville LE67 ....72 D1
  Leicester LE1..........259 C3
York Rd
  Hinckley LE10 ....197 D3
  Leicester LE1..........259 B3
  Loughborough LE11......52 A4
  Stamford PE9..........143 D4
  Swadlincote DE11 ......44 B2
Yorkshire Rd LE4 ......129 C2
York St
  Leicester LE1..........259 C3
  Market Harborough
  LE16 ....240 F3
Yukon Way LE1 ....259 C5

Z

Zara Ct PE9 ....143 D4
Zealand Cl LE10 ....197 F3
Zebra Cotts PE9........143 B4
Zenith Bldg LE1 ....259 C3
Zetland Cl LE67.........96 C8
Zetland Sq LE15 ....87 F4
Zetland Wlk LE4.......128 E5
Zion Hill LE67 ....71 A8
Zion Ho DE11..........44 C1
ZOUCH 30 B3
Zouch Rd LE12 ....30 A3

Addresses

Name and Address	Telephone	Page	Grid reference

NG NH NJ NK
NM NN NO NP
NR NS NT NU
NX NY NZ
SC SD SE TA
SH SJ SK TF TG
SM SN SO SP TL TM
SR SS ST SU TQ TR
SW SX SY SZ TV

Any feature in this atlas can be given a unique reference to help you find the same feature on other Ordnance Survey maps of the area, or to help someone else locate you if they do not have a Street Atlas.

The grid squares in this atlas match the Ordnance Survey National Grid and are at 500 metre intervals. The small figures at the bottom and sides of every other grid line are the National Grid kilometre values (**00°** to **99°** km) and are repeated across the country every 100° km (see left).

To give a unique National Grid reference you need to locate where in the country you are. The country is divided into 100 km squares with each square given a unique two-letter reference. Use the administrative map to determine in which 100 km square a particular page of this atlas falls.

The bold letters and numbers between each grid line (**A** to **F**, **1** to **8**) are for use within a specific Street Atlas only, and when used with the page number, are a convenient way of referencing these grid squares.

Example *The railway bridge over DARLEY GREEN RD in grid square B1*

Step 1: Identify the two-letter reference, in this example the page is in **SP**

Step 2: Identify the 1 km square in which the railway bridge falls. Use the figures in the southwest corner of this square: Eastings **17**, Northings **74**. This gives a unique reference: **SP 17 74**, accurate to 1° km.

Step 3: To give a more precise reference accurate to 100 m you need to estimate how many tenths along and how many tenths up this 1 km square the feature is (to help with this the 1 km square is divided into four 500 m squares). This makes the bridge about **8** tenths along and about **1** tenth up from the southwest corner.

This gives a unique reference: **SP 178 741**, accurate to 100° m.

Eastings (read from left to right along the bottom) come before Northings (read from bottom to top). If you have trouble remembering say to yourself Along the hall, THEN up the stairs !

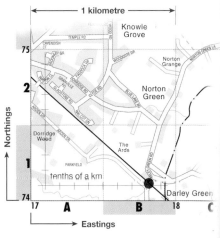

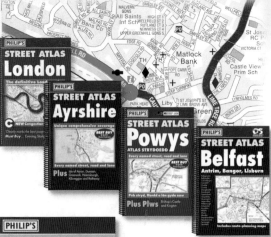